ISBN 978-0-428-59773-3
PIBN 11211506

For support please visit www.forgottenbooks.com

1 MONTH OF
FREE
READING

at

www.ForgottenBooks.com

By purchasing this book you are eligible for one month membership to ForgottenBooks.com, giving you unlimited access to our entire collection of over 1,000,000 titles via our web site and mobile apps.

To claim your free month visit:

www.forgottenbooks.com/free1211506

English
Français
Deutsche
Italiano
Español
Português

www.forgottenbooks.com

Mythology Photography **Fiction**
Fishing Christianity **Art** Cooking
Essays Buddhism Freemasonry
Medicine **Biology** Music **Ancient**
Egypt Evolution Carpentry Physics
Dance Geology **Mathematics** Fitness
Shakespeare **Folklore** Yoga Marketing
Confidence Immortality Biographies
Poetry **Psychology** Witchcraft
Electronics Chemistry History **Law**
Accounting **Philosophy** Anthropology
Alchemy Drama Quantum Mechanics
Atheism Sexual Health **Ancient History**
Entrepreneurship Languages Sport
Paleontology Needlework Islam
Metaphysics Investment Archaeology
Parenting Statistics Criminology
Motivational

DOCUMENTS

PRINTED BY ORDER OF

THE LEGISLATURE

OF THE

STATE OF MAINE,

DURING ITS SESSION

A. D. 1846.

~~~~~~~~~~~~~~~~~~~~

AUGUSTA:
Wm. T. JOHNSON, PRINTER TO THE STATE.

1847.

CONTENTS.

MISCELLANEOUS DOCUMENTS

Rules and Orders of the House of Representatives.
Senate.
Inaugural Message of the Governor.
Annual Report of the Treasurer of State.
Bank Commissioners.
Trustees of the Insane Hospital.
List of Stockholders in the Banks of Maine.
Abstract of the Returns of Corporations
from the Returns of the Cashiers of the several incorporated Banks in
Maine.

DOCUMENTS—HOUSE AND SENATE.

No. 1. Annual Report of the Adjutant General.
    2. Land Agent.
    3. Report of the Committee on Elections in the case of Messrs. Colburn and Hersey.
    4. An act to repeal chapter one hundred twenty-six of the Revised Statutes.
    5. An act in addition to the sixteenth chapter of the Revised Statutes
    6. Message of the Governor with a Communication from the Secretary of War calling for Volunteers.
    7. Abstract of the proceedings of the Courts since August, 1841, under the thirty-sixth chapter of the Revised Statutes.
    8. An act providing for the prosecution of the existing War between the United States and the Republic of Mexico.
    9. Annual Report of the Warden of the State Prison.
  10. Memorial of Amos Brown and others.
  11. An act in relation to fugitives from justice.
  12. Annual Report of the Inspectors of Maine State Prison.
  13. An act to incorporate the Georges Canal Company.
  14. Statement of facts relative to the amount expended on roads by the State during the last ten years.
  15. Resolve providing for an amendment to the Constitution, in relation to the choice of Representatives to the Legislature.

CONTENTS.

No. 16. Petition of Lydia Merrill and James Merrill.

17. Report of the Committee on Education.

18.

19. An act relating to Hawkers and Pedlers.

20. An additional act relating to the Kennebec Log Driving Company.

21. An act to promote the improvement of the Navigation of the Penobscot river.

22. An act to incorporate the Mousam Navigation Company.

23. An act to incorporate the St. Croix River Canal Company

24. An act to authorize School Districts to borrow money for certain purposes.

25. An act to incorporate the Telos Canal Company.

26. An act granting appeals from the decision of County Commissioners.

27. An act to restrict the sale of Intoxicating Drinks.

28. Amendment to a bill entitled "an act to repeal chapter 126 of the Revised Statutes."

29. Resolves providing for amendments to the Constitution in relation to the meeting of the Legislature, and the term of office of the Governor and other officers.

30. Report of the Committee on Banks and Banking.

31. Report of the Committee on the Insane Hospital.

32. An act to incorporate the Lake Telos and Webster Pond Dam and Sluiceway Company.

33. An act for the appointment of District Attorneys.

34. Report of Committee on the "Aroostook Fund."

RULES AND ORDERS

OF THE

HOUSE OF REPRESENTATIVES,

OF THE

STATE OF MAINE,

1846.

AUGUSTA:
WILLIAM T. JOHNSON, PRINTER.

1846.

STATE OF MAINE.

HOUSE OF REPRESENTATIVES, May 15, 1846.

ORDERED, That six hundred copies of the Rules and Orders, hereafter to be adopted for the government of the House, during the present session, together with the Valuation of 1845, and the documents accompanying the Rules and Orders of last year, be printed for the use of the House.

SAMUEL BELCHER, *Clerk*

CONSTITUTION

OF THE

UNITED STATES.

WE, the people of the United States, in order to form a more perfect union, establish justice, insure domestic tranquility, provide for the common defence, promote the general welfare, and secure the blessings of liberty to ourselves and our posterity, do ordain and establish this constitution for the United States of America.

ARTICLE I.

SECTION I.

All legislative powers herein granted shall be vested in a congress of the United States, which shall consist of a senate and house of representatives.

SECTION II.

1. The house of representatives shall be composed of members chosen every second year by the people of the several states; and the electors in each state shall have the qualifications requisite for electors of the most numerous branch of the state legislature.

2. No person shall be a representative, who shall not

have attained to the age of twenty five years and been seven years a citizen of the United States; and who shall not, when elected, be an inhabitant of that state in which he shall be chosen.

3. Representatives and direct taxes shall be apportioned among the several states, which may be included within this Union, according to their respective members, which shall be determined by adding to the whole number of free persons, including those bound to service for a term of years, and including Indians not taxed, three fifths of all other persons. The actual enumeration shall be made within three years after the first meeting of the congress of the United States, and within every subsequent term of ten years, in such manner as they shall by law direct. The number of representatives shall not exceed one for every thirty thousand; but each state shall have at least one representative: and until such enumeration shall be made, the state of *New Hampshire* shall be entitled to choose three, *Massachusetts* eight, *Rhode Island* and *Providence plantations* one, *Connecticut* five, *New York* six, *New Jersey* four, *Pennsylvania* eight, *Delaware* one, *Maryland* six, *Virginia* ten, *North Carolina* five, *South Carolina* five, *Georgia* three.

4. When vacancies happen in the representation from any state, the executive authority thereof shall issue writs of election to fill such vacancies.

5. The house of representatives shall choose their speaker and other officers, and shall have the sole power of impeachment.

SECTION III.

1. The senate of the United States shall be composed of two senators from each state, chosen by the legislature thereof, for six years; and each senator shall have one vote.

2. Immediately after they shall be assembled in consequence of the first election, they shall be divided as

equally as may be into three classes. The seats of the senators of the first class shall be vacated at the expiration of the second year; of the second class, at the expiration of the fourth year; and of the third class, at the expiration of the sixth year so that one third may be chosen every second year; and if vacancies happen by resignation or otherwise, during the recess of the legislature of any state, the executive thereof may make temporary appointments, until the next meeting of the legislature, which shall then fill such vacancies.

3. No person shall be a senator, who shall not have attained to the age of thirty years, and been nine years a citizen of the United States, and who shall not, when elected, be an inhabitant of that state for which he shall be chosen.

4. The vice president of the United States shall be president of the senate, but shall have no vote, unless they be equally divided

5. The senate shall choose their other officers, and also a president pro-tempore, in the absence of the vice president, or when he shall exercise the office of president of the United States

6 The senate shall have the sole power to try all impeachments. When sitting for that purpose, they shall be on oath or affirmation. When the president of the United States is tried, the chief justice shall preside, and no person shall be convicted without the concurrence of two thirds of the members present.

7 Judgment in cases of impeachment shall not extend further than to removal from office, and disqualification to hold and enjoy any office of honor, trust or profit under the United States; but the party convicted shall nevertheless be liable and subject to indictment, trial, judgment and punishment, according to law.

SECTION IV.

1. The times, places, and manner of holding elections

1*

for senators and representatives, shall be prescribed in
each state by the legislature thereof; but the congress
may at any time by law make or alter such regulations,
except as to the places of choosing senators.

2. The congress shall assemble at least once in every
year, and such meeting shall be on the first Monday in
December, unless they shall by law appoint a different
day.

SECTION V

1 Each house shall be the judge of the elections,
returns and qualifications of its own members, and a
majority of each shall constitute a quorum to do business; but a smaller number may adjourn from day to
day, and may be authorized to compel the attendance of
absent members, in such manner and under such penalties as each house may provide

2. Each house may determine the rules of its proceedings, punish its members for disorderly behaviour, and
with the concurrence of two thirds expel a member.

3. Each house shall keep a journal of its proceedings,
and from time to time publish the same, excepting such
parts as may in their judgment require secrecy; and the
yeas and nays of the members of either house, on any
question, shall, at the desire of one fifth of those present,
be entered on the journal.

4. Neither house, during the session of congress, shall,
without the consent of the other, adjourn for more than
three days, nor to any other place than that in which the
two houses shall be sitting.

SECTION VI.

1. The senators and representatives shall receive a
compensation for their services, to be ascertained by law,
and paid out of the treasury of the United States. They
shall in all cases, except treason, felony and breach of

the peace, be privileged from arrest during their attendance at the session of their respective houses, and in going to, or returning from the same; and for any speech or debate in either house, they shall not be questioned in any other place.

2. No senator or representative shall, during the time for which he was elected, be appointed to any civil office under the authority of the United States, which shall have been created, or the emoluments whereof shall have been increased during such time, and no person holding any office under the United States, shall be a member of either house during his continuance in office.

SECTION VII.

1. All bills for raising revenue shall originate in the house of representatives; but the senate may propose or concur with amendments, as on other bills

2. Every *bill*, which shall have passed the house of *representatives* and the senate, shall, before it become a *law*, *be presented* to the president of the United States. If he approve, he shall sign it; but if not, he shall return it, with his objections, to that house in which it shall have originated, who shall enter the objections at large on their journal, and proceed to re-consider it. If, after such re-consideration, two thirds of the house shall agree to pass the bill, it shall be sent, together with the objections, to the other house, by which it shall likewise be re-considered; and if approved by two thirds of that house, it shall become a law. But in all such cases, the votes of both houses shall be determined by yeas and nays; and the names of the persons voting for and against the bill, shall be entered on the journal of each house respectively. If any bill shall not be returned by the president, within ten days (Sundays excepted) after it shall have been presented to him, the same shall be a law in like manner as if he had signed it, unless the congress, by their adjournment, prevent its return; in which case it shall not be a law.

3. Every order, resolution or vote, to which the concurrence of the senate and house of representatives may be necessary (except on a question of adjournment) shall be presented to the president of the United States; and, before the same shall take effect, shall be approved by him, or being disapproved by him, shall be re-passed by two thirds of the senate and house of representatives, according to the rules and limitations prescribed in the case of a bill.

SECTION VIII.

The congress shall have power,

1 To lay and collect taxes, duties, imposts and excises; to pay the debts and provide for the common defense and general welfare of the United States, but all duties, imposts and excises shall be uniform throughout the United States

2. To borrow money on the credit of the United States.

3. To regulate commerce with foreign nations, and among the several states, and with the Indian tribes.

4. To establish an uniform rule of naturalization and uniform laws on the subject of bankruptcies throughout the United States·

5 To coin money; regulate the value thereof and of foreign coin, and fix the standard of weights and measures

6. To provide for the punishment of counterfeiting the securities and current coin of the United States

7 To establish post offices and post roads

8 To promote the progress of science and useful arts, by securing for limited times to authors and inventors, the exclusive right to their respective writings and discoveries

9 To constitute tribunals inferior to the supreme court· To define and punish piracies and felonies committed on the high seas, and offenses against the law of nations.

10. To declare war; grant letters of marque and reprisal; and make rules concerning captures on land and water:

11 To raise and support armies, but no appropriation of money to that use shall be for a longer term than two years:

12. To provide and maintain a navy ·

13. To make rules for the government and regulation of the land and naval forces ·

14. To provide for calling forth the militia to execute the laws of the union, suppress insurrections and repel invasions:

15. To provide for organizing, arming and disciplining the militia, and for governing such part of them as may be employed in the service of the United States, reserving to the states respectively, the appointment of the officers and the authority of training the militia, according to the discipline prescribed by congress

16. To exercise exclusive legislation, in all cases whatsoever, over such district (not exceeding ten miles square) as may, by cession of particular states, and the acceptance of congress, become the seat of the government of the United States, and to exercise like authority over all places purchased by the consent of the legislature of the state in which the same shall be, for the erection of forts, magazines, arsenals, dock-yards and other needful buildings and

17. To make all laws, which shall be necessary and proper for carrying into execution the foregoing powers, and all other powers vested by this constitution in the government of the United States, or in any department or officer thereof

SECTION IX.

1. The migration or importation of such persons, as any of the states now existing shall think proper to admit,

shall not be prohibited by the congress, prior to the year one thousand eight hundred and eight, but a tax or duty may be imposed on such importation, not exceeding ten dollars for each person.

2. The privilege of the writ of habeas corpus shall not be suspended, unless when, in cases of rebellion or invasion, the public safety may require it.

3. No bill of attainder, or ex post facto law shall be passed.

4. No capitation or other direct tax shall be laid, unless in proportion to the census or enumeration, herein before directed to be taken

5. No tax or duty shall be laid on articles exported from any state. No preference shall be given, by any regulation of commerce or revenue, to the ports of one state over those of another, nor shall vessels bound to or from one state, be obliged to enter, clear, or pay duties in another.

6 No money shall be drawn from the treasury, but in consequence of appropriations made by law ; and a regular statement and account of the receipts and expenditures of all public money shall be published from time to time.

7. No title of nobility shall be granted by the United States; and no person holding any office of profit or trust under them, shall, without the consent of the congress, accept of any present, emolument, office or title, of any kind whatever, from any king, prince or foreign state

SECTION X.

1. No state shall enter into any treaty, alliance, or confederation, grant letters of marque and reprisal ; coin money; emit bills of credit, make any thing but gold and silver coin a tender in payment of debts, pass any bill of attainder, ex post facto law, or law impairing the obligation of contracts; or grant any title of nobility.

2. No state shall, without the consent of the congress, lay any imposts or duties on imports or exports, except what may be absolutely necessary for executing its inspection laws; and the net produce of all duties and imposts, laid by any state on imports or exports, shall be for the use of the treasury of the United States; and all such laws shall be subject to the revision and control of the congress. No state shall, without the consent of congress, lay any duty of tonnage, keep troops or ships of war in time of peace, enter into any agreement or compact with another state or with a foreign power, or engage in war, unless actually invaded or in such imminent danger as will not admit of delay.

ARTICLE II.

SECTION I.

1. The executive power shall be vested in a president of the United States of America He shall hold his office during the term of four years, and together with the vice president, chosen for the same term, be elected as follows :

2. Each state shall appoint, in such manner as the legislature thereof may direct, a number of electors, equal to the whole number of senators and representatives to which the state may be entitled in the congress; but no senator or representative, or person holding an office of trust or profit under the United States, shall be appointed an elector.

3. *The electors shall meet in their respective states, and vote by ballot for two persons, of whom one at least shall not be an inhabitant of the same state with themselves : and they shall make a list of all the persons voted for, and of the number of votes for each; which list they shall sign and certify, and transmit, sealed, to the seat of the government of the United States, directed to the president of the senate. The president of the senate shall,*

*in the presence of the senate and house of representatives,
open all the certificates, and the votes shall then be counted.
The person having the greatest number of votes shall be
the president, if such number be a majority of the whole
number of electors appointed ; and if there be more than
one who have such majority, and have an equal number of
votes, then the house of representatives shall immediately
choose by ballot one of them for president : and if no
person have a majority, then from the five highest on the
list, the said house shall in like manner choose the president : but in choosing the president, the votes shall be
taken by states, the representation from each state having
one vote ; a quorum for this purpose shall consist of a
member or members from two thirds of the states, and a
majority of all the states shall be necessary to a choice.
In every case, after the choice of the president, the person
having the greatest number of votes of the electors, shall
be the vice president. But if there should remain two or
more who have equal votes, the senate shall choose from
them by ballot, the vice president.*

4 The congress may determine the time of choosing
the electors, and the day on which they shall give their
votes; which day shall be the same throughout the United
States

5. No person, except a natural born citizen, or a citizen of the United States at the time of the adoption of
this constitution, shall be eligible to the office of president ; neither shall any person be eligible to that office,
who shall not have attained to the age of thirty five years,
and been fourteen years a resident within the United
States

6 In case of the removal of the president from office,
or of his death, resignation, or inability to dischage the
powers and duties of the said office, the same shall devolve on the vice president; and the congress may by
law provide for the case of removal, death, resignation
or inability, both of the president and vice president,

declaring what officer shall then act as president, and such officer shall act accordingly, until the disability be removed, or a president shall be elected.

7. The president shall, at stated times, receive for his services a compensation, which shall neither be increased nor diminished during the period for which he shall have been elected; and he shall not receive, within that period, any other emolument from the United States, or any of them.

8. Before he enter on the execution of his office, he shall take the following oath or affirmation:

9. "I do solemnly swear (or affirm) that I will faithfully execute the office of president of the United States, and will, to the best of my ability, preserve, protect and defend the constitution of the United States."

SECTION II.

1. The president shall be commander in chief of the army and navy of the United States, and of the militia of the several states, when called into the actual service of the United States. He may require the opinion, in writing, of the principal officer in each of the executive departments upon any subject, relating to the duties of their respective offices; and he shall have power to grant reprieves and pardons for offenses against the United States, except in cases of impeachment.

2. He shall have power, by and with the advice and consent of the senate, to make treaties, provided two thirds of the senators present concur; and he shall nominate, and by and with the advice and consent of the senate, shall appoint ambassadors, other public ministers and consuls, judges of the supreme court and all other officers of the United States, whose appointments are not herein otherwise provided for, and which shall be established by law: but the congress may by law vest the appointment of such inferior officers, as they think proper,

2

in the president alone, in the courts of law, or in the heads of departments.

3. The president shall have power to fill up all vacancies, that may happen during the recess of the senate, by granting commissions, which shall expire at the end of their next session.

SECTION III.

He shall from time to time give to the congress information of the state of the union, and recommend to their consideration such measures as he shall judge necessary and expedient; he may on extraordinary occasions, convene both houses, or either of them, and in case of disagreement between them with respect to the time of adjournment, he may adjourn them to such time as he shall think proper; he shall receive ambassadors and other public ministers; he shall take care that the laws be faithfully executed; and shall commission all the officers of the United States.

SECTION IV.

The president, vice president and all civil officers of the United States shall be removed from office on impeachment for, and conviction of, treason, bribery, or other high crimes and misdemeanors.

ARTICLE III.

SECTION I.

The judicial power of the United States shall be vested in one supreme court, and in such inferior courts as the congress may, from time to time, ordain and establish. The judges, both of the supreme and inferior courts, shall hold their offices during good behavior, and shall, at stated times, receive for their services a compensation, which shall not be diminished during their continuance in office.

SECTION II.

1. The judicial power shall extend to all cases, in law and equity, arising under this constitution, the laws of the United States, and treaties made, or which shall be made, under their authority; to all cases affecting ambassadors, other public ministers and consuls; to all cases of admiralty and maratime jurisdiction; to controversies to which the United States shall be a party; to controversies between two or more states, *between a state and citizens of another state*, between citizens of different states, between citizens of the same state claiming lands under grants of different states, and between a state, or the citizens thereof and foreign states, citizens or subjects.

2. In all cases affecting ambassadors, other public ministers and consuls, and those in which a state shall be a party, *the* supreme court shall have original jurisdiction. *In all* the other cases before mentioned, the *supreme court* shall have appellate jurisdiction, both as to law and fact, with such exceptions and under such regulations, as the congress shall make.

3. The trial of all crimes, except in cases of impeachment, shall be by jury, and such trials shall be held in the state where the said crimes shall have been committed; but when not committed within any state, the trial shall be at such place or places as the congress may by law have directed.

SECTION III.

1. Treason against the United States shall consist only in levying war against them, or in adhering to their enemies, giving them aid and comfort. No person shall be convicted of treason, unless on the testimony of two witnesses to the same overt act, or on confession in open court.

2. The congress shall have power to declare the pun-

ishment of treason, but no attainder of treason shall
work corruption of blood, or forfeiture, except during
the life of the person attainted.

ARTICLE IV.

SECTION I.

Full faith and credit shall be given in each state to
the public acts, records and judicial proceedings of every
other state. And the congress may by general laws prescribe the manner in which such acts, records and proceedings shall be proved, and the effect thereof.

SECTION II.

1. The citizens of each state shall be entitled to all
privileges and immunities of citizens in the several states.
2. A person charged in any state with treason, felony
or other crime, who shall flee from justice and be found
in another state, shall, on demand of the executive
authority of the state from which he fled, be delivered
up, to be removed to the state having jurisdiction of the
crime
3. No person held to service or labor in one state,
under the laws thereof, escaping into another, shall, in
consequence of any law or regulation therein, be discharged from such service or labor; but shall be delivered up on claim of the party, to which such service or
labor may be due.

SECTION III.

1. New states may be admitted by the congress into
this Union; but no new state shall be formed or erected
within the jurisdiction of any other state; nor any state
be formed by the junction of two or more states, or parts
of states, without the consent of the legislatures of the
states concerned, as well as of the congress.

2. The congress shall have power to dispose of, and make all needful rules and regulations, respecting the territory or other property belonging to the United States; and nothing in this constitution shall be so construed, as to prejudice any claims of the United States, or of any particular state.

SECTION IV.

The United States shall guarantee to every state in the Union a republican form of government; and shall protect each of them against invasion; and on application of the legislature, or of the executive (when the legislature cannot be convened,) against domestic violence.

ARTICLE V.

The congress, whenever two thirds of both houses shall deem it necessary, shall propose amendments to this constitution; or, on the application of the legislatures of two thirds of the several states, shall call a convention for proposing amendments, which, in either case, shall be valid to all intents and purposes as a part of this constitution, when ratified by the legislatures of three fourths of the several states, or by conventions in three fourths thereof, as the one or the other mode of ratification may be proposed by the congress · *provided*, that no amendment, which may be made prior to the year one thousand eight hundred and eight, shall in any manner affect the first and fourth clauses in the ninth section of the first article; and that no state, without its consent, shall be deprived of its equal suffrage in the senate.

ARTICLE VI.

1. All debts contracted, and engagements entered into, before the adoption of this constitution, shall be as valid against the United States under this constitution, as under the confederation.

2*

2. This constitution and the laws of the United States which shall be made in pursuance thereof, and all treaties made, or which shall be made, under the authority of the United States, shall be the supreme law of the land: and the judges in every state shall be bound thereby, any thing in the constitution or laws of any state to the contrary notwithstanding.

3. The senators and representatives before mentioned, and the members of the several state legislatures, and all executive and judicial officers, both of the United States and of the several states, shall be bound, by oath or affirmation, to support this constitution; but no religious test shall ever be required as a qualification to any office or public trust under the United States.

ARTICLE VII.

The ratification of the conventions of nine states shall be sufficient for the establishment of this constitution, between the states so ratifying the same.

AMENDMENTS TO THE CONSTITUTION.

Art. 1. Congress shall make no law respecting an establishment of religion, or prohibiting the free exercise thereof; or abridging the freedom of speech, or of the press, or the right of the people peaceably to assemble, and to petition the government for a redress of grievances.

Art. 2. A well regulated militia being necessary to the security of a free state, the right of the people to keep and bear arms shall not be infringed.

Art. 3. No soldier shall in time of peace, be quartered in any house, without the consent of the owner; nor in time of war, but in a manner to be prescribed by law.

Art. 4. The right of the people to be secure in their persons, houses, papers and effects, against unreasonable searches and seizures, shall not be violated; and no warrants shall issue, but upon probable cause, supported by oath or affirmation, and particularly describing the place to be searched, and the persons or things to be seized.

Art. 5. No person shall be held to answer for a capital or otherwise infamous crime, unless on a presentment or indictment of a grand jury, except in cases arising in the land or naval forces, or in the militia, when in actual service, in time of war or public danger; nor shall any person be subject for the same offense to be twice put in jeopardy of life or limb; nor shall be compelled, in any criminal case, to be a witness against himself, nor be deprived of life, liberty or property, without due process of law; nor shall private property be taken for public use without just compensation.

Art 6. In all criminal prosecutions, the accused shall enjoy the right to a speedy and public trial, by an impartial jury of the state and district, wherein the crime shall have been committed, which district shall have been previously ascertained by law, and to be informed of the nature and cause of the accusation; to be confronted with the witnesses against him; to have compulsory process for obtaining witnesses in his favor; and to have the assistance of counsel for his defence.

Art 7. In suits at common law, where the value in controversy shall exceed twenty dollars, the right of trial by jury shall be preserved; and no fact tried by jury shall be otherwise re-examined in any court of the United States, than according to the rules of the common law.

Art. 8. Excessive bail shall not be required, nor excessive fines imposed, nor cruel and unusual punishments inflicted.

Art. 9. The enumeration in the constitution of certain rights, shall not be construed to deny or disparage others retained by the people.

Art. 10. The powers not delegated to the United States by the constitution, nor prohibited by it to the states, are reserved to the states respectively, or to the people.

Art. 11. The judicial power of the United States shall not be construed to extend to any suit in law or equity, commenced or prosecuted against one of the United States by citizens of another state, or by citizens or subjects of any foreign state.

Art. 12. The electors shall meet in their respective states, and vote by ballot for president and vice president, one of whom, at least, shall not be an inhabitant of the same state with themselves; they shall name in their ballots the person voted for as president, and in distinct ballots the person voted for as vice president; and they shall make distinct lists of all persons voted for as president, and of all persons voted for as vice president, and

of the number of votes for each; which lists they shall sign and certify, and transmit sealed to the seat of the government of the United States, directed to the president of the senate ; the president of the senate shall, in the presence of the senate and house of representatives, open all the certificates, and the votes shall then be counted ; the person having the greatest number of votes for president shall be the president, if such number be a majority of the whole number of electors appointed ; and if no person have such majority, then from the persons, having the highest numbers, not exceeding three, on the list of those voted for as president, the house of representatives shall choose, immediately, by ballot, the president. But, in choosing the president, the votes shall be taken by states, the representation from each state having one vote; a quorum for this purpose shall consist of a member or members from two thirds of the states, and a majority of all the states shall be necessary to a choice : and if the house of representatives shall not choose a president, whenever the right of choice shall devolve upon them, before the fourth day of March next following, then the vice president shall act as president, as in the case of the death or other constitutional disability of the president.

The person having the greatest number of votes as vice president, shall be the vice president, if such number be a majority of the whole number of electors appointed ; and if no person have a majority, then from the two highest numbers on the list, the senate shall choose the vice president; a quorum for the purpose shall consist of two thirds of the whole number of senators, and a majority of the whole number shall be necessary to a choice.

But no person constitutionally ineligible to the office of president, shall be eligible to that of vice president of the United States.

CONSTITUTION OF MAINE.

WE the people of Maine, in order to establish justice, insure tranquility, provide for our mutual defense, promote our common welfare, and secure to ourselves and our posterity the blessings of liberty, acknowledging with grateful hearts the goodness of the Sovereign Ruler of the Universe in affording us an opportunity so favorable to the design; and, imploring His aid and direction in its accomplishment, do agree to form ourselves into a free and independent state, by the style and title of the STATE OF MAINE, and do ordain and establish the following constitution for the government of the same.

ARTICLE I.

DECLARATION OF RIGHTS.

SECTION 1. All men are born equally free and independent, and have certain natural, inherent and unalienable rights, among which are those of enjoying and defending life and liberty, acquiring, possessing and protecting property, and of pursuing and obtaining safety and happiness.

SEC 2. All power is inherent in the people; all free governments are founded in their authority and instituted for their benefit; they have therefore an unalienable and indefeasible right to institute government, and to alter, reform, or totally change the same, when their safety and happiness require it.

SEC. 3. All men have a natural and unalienable right to worship Almighty God according to the dictates of their own consciences, and no one shall be hurt, molested or restrained in his person, liberty or estate for worshipping God in the manner and season most agreeable to the dictates of his own conscience, nor for his religious professions or sentiments, provided he does not disturb the public peace, nor obstruct others in their religious worship:—and all persons demeaning themselves peaceably, as good members of the state, shall be equally under the protection of the laws, and no subordination or preference of any one sect or denomination to another shall ever be established by law, nor shall any religious test be required as a qualification for any office or trust, under this state; and all religious societies in this state, whether incorporate or unincorporate, shall at all times have the exclusive right of electing their public teachers and contracting with them for their support and maintenance.

SEC. 4. Every citizen may freely speak, write and publish his sentiments on any subject, being responsible for the abuse of this liberty; no laws shall be passed regulating or restraining the freedom of the press; and in prosecutions for any publications respecting the official conduct of men in public capacity, or the qualifications of those who are candidates for the suffrages of the people, or where the matter published is proper for public information, the truth thereof may be given in evidence, and in all indictments for libels, the jury, after having received the direction of the court, shall have a right to determine, at their discretion, the law and the fact.

SEC. 5. The people shall be secure in their persons, houses, papers and possessions from all unreasonable searches and seizures; and no warrant to seach any place, or seize any person or thing, shall issue without a special designation of the place to be searched, and the person or thing to be seized, nor without probable cause —supported by oath or affirmation.

Sec. 6. In all criminal prosecutions, the accused shall have a right to be heard by himself and his counsel, or either, at his election;

To demand the nature and cause of the accusation, and have a copy thereof;

To be confronted by the witnesses against him;

To have compulsory process for obtaining witnesses in his favor;

To have a speedy, public and impartial trial, and, except in trials by martial law or impeachment, by a jury of the vicinity. He shall not be compelled to furnish or give evidence against himself, nor be deprived of his life, liberty, property or privileges, but by judgment of his peers or the law of the land.

Sec. 7. No person shall be held to answer for a capital or infamous crime, unless on a presentment or indictment of a grand jury, except in cases of impeachment, or in such cases of offenses, as are usually cognizable by a justice of the peace, or in cases arising in the army or navy, or in the militia when in actual service in time of war or public danger. The legislature shall provide by law a suitable and impartial mode of selecting juries, and their usual number and unanimity, in indictments and convictions shall be held indispensable.

Sec. 8. No person, for the same offense, shall be twice put in jeopardy of life or limb.

Sec. 9. Sanguinary laws shall not be passed; all penalties and punishments shall be proportioned to the offense · excessive bail shall not be required, nor excessive fines imposed, nor cruel nor unusual punishments inflicted.

Sect. 10. *All persons, before conviction, shall be bailable, except for capital offense, where the proof is evident or the presumption great.* And the privilege of the writ of *habeas corpus* shall not be suspended, unless when in cases of rebellion or invasion the public safety may require it.

SEC. 11. The legislature shall pass no bill of attainder, *ex post facto* law, nor law impairing the obligation of contracts, and no attainder shall work corruption of blood nor forfeiture of estate.

SEC. 12. Treason against this state shall consist only in levying war against it, adhering to its enemies, giving them aid and comfort. No person shall be convicted of treason unless on the testimony of two witnesses to the same overt act, or confession in open court.

SEC. 13. The laws shall not be suspended but by the legislature or its authority.

SEC. 14. No person shall be subject to corporal punishment under military law, except such as are employed in the army or navy, or in the militia when in actual service in time of war or public danger.

SEC. 15. The people have a right at all times in an orderly and peaceable manner to assemble to consult upon the common good, to give instructions to their representatives, and to request, of either department of the government by petition or remonstrance, redress of their wrongs and grievances.

SEC. 16. Every citizen has a right to keep and bear arms for the common defense, and this right shall never be questioned.

SEC. 17. No standing army shall be kept up in time of peace without the consent of the legislature, and the military shall, in all cases, and at all times, be in strict subordination to the civil power.

SEC. 18 No soldier shall in time of peace be quartered in any house without the consent of the owner or occupant, nor in time of war, but in a manner to be prescribed by law.

SEC 19 Every person, for an injury done him in his person, reputation, property or immunities, shall have remedy by due course of law · and right and justice shall be administered freely and without sale, completely and without denial, promptly and without delay.

3

Sec. 20. In all civil suits, and in all controversies concerning property, the parties shall have a right to a trial by jury, except in cases where it has heretofore been otherwise practiced; the party claiming the right may be heard by himself or his counsel, or either, at his election.

Sec. 21. Private property shall not be taken for public uses without just compensation; nor unless the public exigencies require it.

Sec. 22. No tax or duty shall be imposed without the consent of the people or of their representatives in the legislature.

Sec. 23. No title of nobility or hereditary distinction, privilege, honor or emolument, shall ever be granted or confirmed, nor shall any office be created, the appointment to which shall be for a longer time than during good behavior.

Sec. 24. The enumeration of certain rights shall not impair nor deny others retained by the people.

ARTICLE II.

ELECTORS.

Sec. 1. Every male citizen of the United States of the age of twenty one years and upwards, excepting paupers, persons under guardianship, and Indians not taxed, having his residence established in this state for the term of three months next preceding any election, shall be an elector for governor, senators and representatives, in the town or plantation where his residence is so established; and the election shall be by written ballot. But persons in the military, naval or marine service of the United States, or this state, shall not be considered as having obtained such established residence by being stationed in any garrison, barrack or military place in any town or plantation; nor shall the residence of a student at any seminary of learning entitle him to the right of suffrage in the town or plantation where such seminary is established.

Sec 2. Electors shall, in all cases, except treason, felony or breach of the peace, be privileged from arrest on the days of election, during their attendance at, going to, and returning therefrom.

Sec. 3. No elector shall be obliged to do duty in the militia on any day of election, except in time of war or public danger.

Sec. 4. The election of governor, senators and representatives, shall be on the second Monday of September annually forever.

ARTICLE III.

DISTRIBUTION OF POWERS.

Sec. 1. The powers of this government shall be divided into three distinct departments, the *legislative*, *executive* and *judicial*.

Sec. 2. No person or persons, belonging to one of these departments, shall exercise any of the powers properly belonging to either of the others, except in cases herein expressly directed or permitted.

ARTICLE IV.—Part First.

LEGISLATIVE POWER—HOUSE OF REPRESENTATIVES.

Sec. 1. The legislative power shall be vested in two distinct branches, a house of representatives, and a senate, each to have a negative on the other, and both to be styled the *Legislature of Maine*, and the style of their acts and laws, shall be, " *Be it enacted by the senate and house of representatives in legislature assembled.*"

Sec. 2. The house of representatives shall consist of [not less than one hundred nor more than two hundred] members, to be elected by the qualified electors for one

year from the day next preceding the annual meeting of
the legislature. The legislature, which shall first be
convened under this constitution, shall, on or before the
fifteenth day of August, in the year of our Lord one
thousand eight hundred and twenty one, and the legislature, within every subsequent period of at most ten years
and at least five, cause the number of the inhabitants of
the state to be ascertained, exclusive of foreigners not
naturalized, and Indians not taxed. The number of
representatives shall, at the several periods of making
such enumeration, be fixed and apportioned among the
several counties, as near as may be, according to the
number of inhabitants, having regard to the relative increase of population. The number of representatives
shall, on said first apportionment, be not less than one
hundred nor more than one hundred and fifty; [and,
whenever the number of representatives shall be two
hundred, at the next annual meetings of elections, which
shall thereafter be had, and at every subsequent period
of ten years, the people shall give in their votes, whether
the number of representatives shall be increased or diminished; and if a majority of votes are in favor thereof,
it shall be the duty of the next legislature thereafter to
increase or diminish the number by the rule hereinafter
prescribed.]

SECT. 3. Each town having fifteen hundred inhabitants
may elect one representative; each town having three
thousand seven hundred and fifty may elect two; each
town having six thousand seven hundred and fifty may
elect three; each town having ten thousand five hundred
may elect four; each town having fifteen thousand may
elect five; each town having twenty thousand two hundred and fifty may elect six; each town having twenty
six thousand two hundred and fifty inhabitants may elect
seven; but no town shall ever be entitled to more than
seven representatives: and towns and plantations duly

organized, not having fifteen hundred inhabitants, shall be classed, as conveniently as may be, into districts containing that number, and so as not to divide towns; and each such district may elect one representative; and, when on this apportionment the number of representatives shall be two hundred, a different apportionment shall take place upon the above principle; and, in case the fifteen hundred shall be too large or too small to apportion all the representatives to any county, it shall be so increased or diminished as to give the number of representatives according to the above rule and proportion; and whenever any town or towns, plantation or plantations not entitled to elect a representative shall determine against a classification with any other town or plantation, the legislature may, at each apportionment of representatives, on the application of such town or plantation, authorize it to elect a representative for such portion of time and such periods, as shall be equal to its portion of representation, and the right of representation, so established, shall not be altered until the next general apportionment.

Sec. 4. No person shall be a member of the house of representatives, unless he shall, at the commencement of the period for which he is elected, have been five years a citizen of the United States, have arrived at the age of twenty one years, have been a resident in this state one year, or from the adoption of this constitution; and for the three months next preceding the time of his election shall have been, and, during the period for which he is elected, shall continue to be a resident in the town or district which he represents.

Sec. 5. The meetings for the choice of representatives shall be warned in due course of law by the selectmen of the several towns seven days at least before the election, and the selectmen thereof shall preside impartially at such meetings, receive the votes of all the qualified electors present, sort, count and declare them in

3*

open town meeting, and in the presence of the t
clerk, who shall form a list of the persons voted for,
the number of votes for each person against his n:
shall make a fair record thereof in the presence of
selectmen, and in open town meeting; and a fair (
of this list shall be attested by the selectmen and t
clerk, and delivered by said selectmen to each repre:
ative within ten days next after such election. Anc
towns and plantations organized by law, belongin
any class herein provided, shall hold their meetin;
the same time in the respective towns and plantati
and the town and plantation meetings in such towns
plantations shall be notified, held and regulated,
votes received, sorted, counted and declared in
same manner. And the assessors and clerks of pli
tions shall have all the powers, and be subject to all
duties, which selectmen and town clerks have, anc
subject to by this constitution. And the selectme:
such towns, and the assessors of such plantations
classed, shall, within four days next after such meet
meet at some place to be prescribed and notified by
selectmen or assessors of the eldest town or planta:
in such class, and the copies of said lists shall be
examined and compared; and in case any person :
be elected by a majority of all the votes, the select
or assessors shall deliver the certified copies of such
to the person so elected, within ten days next after
election; and the clerks of towns and plantation:
spectively shall seal up copies of all such lists and c
them to be delivered into the secretary's office tw
days at least before the [first Wednesday of January
nually; but in case no person shall have a majority of v
the selectmen and assessors shall, as soon as ma:
notify another meeting, and the same proceedings sh:
had at every future meeting until an election shall
been effected : *provided*, that the legislature may bj
prescribe a different mode of returning, examining

ascertaining the election of the representatives in such
classes.

Sec. 6 Whenever the seat of a member shall be vacant by death, resignation, or otherwise, the vacancy
may be filled by a new election

Sec. 7. The house of representatives shall choose
their speaker, clerk, and other officers.

Sec. 8. The house of representatives shall have the
sole power of impeachment.

ARTICLE IV.—Part Second.

SENATE.

Sec. 1. The senate shall consist of not less than
twenty, nor more than thirty one members, elected at the
same time, and for the same term as the representatives,
by the qualified electors of the districts, into which the
state shall, from time to time be divided.

Sec. 2. The legislature, which shall be first convened
under this constitution, shall on or before the fifteenth
day of August in the year of our Lord one thousand
eight hundred and twenty one, and the legislature at every
subsequent period of ten years, cause the state to be
divided into districts for the choice of senators.   The
districts shall conform, as near as may be, to county
lines, and be apportioned according to the number of
inhabitants.   The number of senators shall not exceed
twenty at the first apportionment, and shall at each apportionment be increased, until they shall amount to thirty
one, according to the increase in the house of representatives.

Sec. 3. The meetings for the election of senators
shall be notified, held and regulated, and the votes received, sorted, counted, declared and recorded, in the
same manner as those for representatives.   And fair
copies of the list of votes shall be attested by the selectmen and town clerks of towns, and the assessors and

clerks of plantations, and sealed up in open town and
plantation meetings; and the town and plantation clerks
respectively shall cause the same to be delivered into the
secretary's office thirty days at least before the [first
Wednesday of January.] All other qualified electors, living in places unincorporated, who shall be assessed to the
support of the government by the assessors of an adjacent
town, shall have the privilege of voting for senators, representatives and governor in such town, and shall be
notified by the selectmen thereof for that purpose accordingly.

SEC 4. The governor and council shall, as soon as
may be, examine the returned copies of such lists, and,
twenty days before the said [first Wednesday of January,]
issue a summons to such persons, as shall appear to be
elected by a majority of the votes in each district, to
attend that day and take their seats.

SEC. 5. The senate shall, on the said [first Wednesday
of January,] annually, determine who are elected by a
majority of votes to be senators in each district; and in
case the full number of senators to be elected from each
district shall not have been so elected, the members of
the house of representatives and such senators as shall
have been elected, shall, from the highest numbers of the
persons voted for, on said lists, equal to twice the number
of senators deficient, in every district, if there be so
many voted for, elect by joint ballot the number of senators required; and in this manner all vacancies in the
senate shall be supplied as soon as may be, after such
vacancies happen.

SEC. 6 The senators shall be twenty five years of age
at the commencement of the term, for which they are
elected, and in all other respects their qualifications shall
be the same, as those of the representatives.

SEC. 7. The senate shall have full power to try all
impeachments, and when sitting for that purpose shall
be on oath or affirmation, and no person shall be con-

victed without the concurrence of two thirds of the members present. Their judgment, however, shall not extend father than to removal from office, and disqualification to hold and enjoy any office of honor, trust or profit under this state. But the party, whether convicted or acquitted, shall nevertheless be liable to indictment, trial, judgment and punishment according to law.

SEC. 8. The senate shall choose their president, secretary and other officers.

ARTICLE IV.—Part Third.

LEGISLATIVE POWER.

SEC. 1. The legislature shall convene on the [first Wednesday of January] annually, and shall have full power to make and establish all reasonable laws and regulations for the defense and benefit of the people of this state, not repugnant to this constitution, nor to that of the United States.

SEC. 2. Every bill or resolution, having the force of law, to which the concurrence of both houses may be necessary, except on a question of adjournment, which shall have passed both houses, shall be presented to the governor, and if he approve, he shall sign it; if not, he shall return it with his objections to the house, in which it shall have originated, which shall enter the objections at large on its journals, and proceed to reconsider it. If after such reconsideration, two thirds of that house shall agree to pass it, it shall be sent together with the objections, to the other house, by which it shall be reconsidered, and if approved by two thirds of that house, it shall have the same effect, as if it had been signed by the governor: but in all such cases, the votes of both houses shall be taken by yeas and nays, and the names of the persons, voting for and against the bill or resolution, shall be entered on the journals of both houses respectively. If the bill or resolution shall not be returned by the gov-

ernor, within five days, (Sundays excepted) after it shall
have been presented to him, it shall have the same force
and effect as if he had signed it, unless the legislature
by their adjournment prevent its return, in which case it
shall have such force and effect, unless returned within
three days after their next meeting.

SEC. 3. Each house shall be the judge of the elections
and qualifications of its own members, and a majority
shall constitute a quorum to do business; but a smaller
number may adjourn from day to day, and may compel
the attendance of absent members in such manner and
under such penalties as each house shall provide.

SEC. 4. Each house may determine the rules of its
proceedings, punish its members for disorderly behavior,
and, with the concurrence of two thirds, expel a member,
but not a second time for the same cause.

SEC. 5. Each house shall keep a journal, and from
time to time publish its proceedings, except such parts
as in their judgment may require secrecy; and the yeas
and nays of the members of either house on any question, shall, at the desire of one fifth of those present, be
entered on the journals.

SEC. 6. Each house, during its session, may punish by
imprisonment, any person not a member, for disrespectful
or disorderly behavior, in its presence, for obstructing
any of its proceedings, threatening, assaulting or abusing
any of its members, for any thing said, done, or doing in
either house. *provided*, that no imprisonment shall extend beyond the period of the same session.

SEC. 7. The senators and representatives shall receive
such compensation, as shall be established by law; but
no law increasing their compensation shall take effect
during the existence of the legislature which enacted it.
The expenses of the members of the house of representatives in traveling to the legislature, and returning therefrom, once in each session and no more, shall be paid
by the state out of the public treasury to every member

who shall seasonably attend, in the judgment of the house, and does not depart therefrom without leave.

Sec. 8. The senators and representatives shall, in all cases except treason, felony or breach of the peace, be privileged from arrest during their attendance at, going to and returning from each session of the legislature, and no member shall be liable to answer for any thing spoken in debate in either house, in any court or place elsewhere.

Sec. 9. Bills, orders or resolutions, may originate in either house, and may be altered, amended or rejected in the other; but all bills for raising a revenue shall originate in the house of representatives, but the senate may propose amendments as in other cases. *provided*, that they shall not, under color of amendment, introduce any new matter, which does not relate to raising a revenue.

Sec. 10. No senator or representative shall, during the term for which he shall have been elected, be appointed to any civil office of profit under this state, which shall have been created, or the emoluments of which increased during such term, except such offices as may be filled by elections by the people: *provided* that this prohibition shall not extend to the members of the first legislature.

Sec. 11. No member of congress, nor person holding any office under the United States (post offices excepted) nor office of profit under this state, justices of the peace, notaries public, coroners and officers of the militia excepted, shall have a seat in either house during his being such member of congress, or his continuing in such office.

Sec. 12. Neither house shall during the session, without the consent of the other, adjourn for more than two days, nor to any other place than that in which the houses shall be sitting.

ARTICLE V.—Part First.

EXECUTIVE POWER.

SEC. 1. The supreme executive power of this ↑
shall be vested in a governor.

SEC. 2. The governor shall be elected by the qual
electors, and shall hold his office one year from the [
Wednesday of January] in each year.

SEC. 3. The meetings for election of governor ↑
be notified, held and regulated, and votes shall be re
ed, sorted, counted, declared and recorded, in the ↑
manner as those for senators and representatives. ↑
shall be sealed and returned into the secretary's offi
the same manner, and at the same time, as those
senators. And the secretary of state for the time be
shall, on the [first Wednesday of January] then next
the lists before the senate and house of representat
to be by them examined, and, in case of a choice
majority of all the votes returned, they shall declare
publish the same. But, if no person shall have a m
ity of votes, the house of representatives shall by ba
from the persons having the four highest numbers of v
on the lists, if so many there be, elect two persons,
make return of their names to the senate, of whom
senate shall, by ballot, elect one, who shall be decl
the governor.

SEC. 4. The governor shall, at the commencemen
his term, be not less than thirty years of age; a nat
born citizen of the United States, have been five y
or from the adoption of this constitution, a reside
the state; and at the time of his election and during
term for which he is elected, be a resident of said st

SEC. 5. No person holding any office or place u
the United States, this state, or any other power, ↑
exercise the office of governor.

SEC. 6. The governor shall, at stated times, receiv
his services a compensation, which shall not be incre
or diminished during his continuance in office.

Sec. 7. He shall be commander in chief of the army and navy of the state, and of the militia, except when called into the actual service of the United States; but he shall not march nor convey any of the citizens out of the state without their consent or that of the legislature, unless it shall become necessary, in order to march or transport them from one part of the state to another for the defense thereof.

Sec. 8. He shall nominate, and, with the advice and consent of the council, appoint all judicial officers, the attorney general, the sheriffs, coroners, registers of probate, and notaries public; and he shall also nominate, and with the advice and consent of the council appoint all other civil and military officers, whose appointment is not by this constitution, or shall not by law be otherwise provided for; and every such nomination shall be made seven days, at least, prior to such appointment.

Sec. 9. He shall from time to time give the legislature information of the condition of the state, and recommend to their consideration such measures as he may judge expedient.

Sec. 10. He may require information from any military officer, or any officer in the executive department, upon any subject relating to the duties of their respective offices.

Sec. 11. He shall have power, with the advice and consent of the council, to remit, after conviction, all forfeitures and penalties, and to grant reprieves and pardons, except in cases of impeachment.

Sec. 12. He shall take care that the laws be faithfully executed.

Sec. 13. He may, on extraordinary occasions, convene the legislature; and in case of disagreement between the two houses with respect to the time of adjournment, adjourn them to such time, as he shall think proper, not beyond the day of the next annual meeting, and if, since the last adjournment, the place where the legislature

4

were next to convene shall have become dangerous from
an enemy or contagious sickness, may direct the session
to be held at some other convenient place within the
state.

SEC. 14. Whenever the office of governor shall become vacant by death, resignation, removal from office
or otherwise, the president of the senate shall exercise
the office of governor until another governor shall be
duly qualified; and in case of the death, resignation, removal from office or other disqualification of the president
of the senate, so exercising the office of governor, the
speaker of the house of representatives shall exercise the
office, until a president of the senate shall have been
chosen; and when the office of governor, president of
the senate, and speaker of the house shall become vacant,
in the recess of the senate, the person, acting as secretary
of state for the time being, shall by proclamation convene
the senate, that a president may be chosen to exercise
the office of governor. And whenever either the president of the senate or speaker of the house shall so exercise said office, he shall receive only the compensation of
governor but his duties as president or speaker shall be
suspended; and the senate or house shall fill the vacancy,
until his duties as governor shall cease.

ARTICLE V.—Part Second.

COUNCIL.

SEC. 1. There shall be a council, to consist of seven
persons, citizens of the United States, and residents of
this state, to advise the governor in the executive part of
government, whom the governor shall have full power, at
his discretion, to assemble; and he with the councilors,
or a majority of them, may from time to time, hold and
keep a council, for ordering and directing the affairs of
state according to law.

SEC. 2. The councilors shall be chosen annually, on

the [first Wednesday of January,] by joint ballot of the senators and representatives in convention; and vacancies, which shall afterwards happen, shall be filled in the same manner; but not more than one councilor shall be elected from any district, prescribed for the election of senators; and they shall be privileged from arrest in the same manner as senators and representatives.

Sec. 3. The resolutions and advice of council shall be recorded in a register, and signed by the members agreeing thereto, which may be called for by either house of the legislature; and any councilor may enter his dissent to the resolution of the majority.

Sec. 4. No member of congress, or of the legislature of this state, nor any person holding any office under the United States, (post officers excepted) nor any civil officers under this state, (justices of the peace and notaries public excepted) shall be councilors. And no councilor shall be appointed to any office during the time for which he shall have been elected.

ARTICLE V.—Part Third.
SECRETARY.

Sec. 1. The secretary of state shall be chosen annually at the first session of the legislature, by joint ballot of the senators and representatives in convention.

Sec. 2. The records of the state shall be kept in the office of the secretary, who may appoint his deputies, for whose conduct he shall be accountable.

Sec. 3. He shall attend the governor and council, senate and house of representatives, in person or by his deputies as they shall respectively require.

Sec. 4. He shall carefully keep and preserve the records of all the official acts and proceedings of the governor and council, senate and house of representatives, and, when required, lay the same before either branch of the legislature, and perform such other duties as are enjoined by this constitution, or shall be required by law.

ARTICLE V.—Part Fourth.

TREASURER.

SEC. 1. The treasurer shall be chosen annually, at the first session of the legislature, by joint ballot of the senators and representatives in convention, but shall not be eligible more than five years successively.

SEC. 2. The treasurer shall, before entering on the duties of his office, give bond to the state with sureties, to the satisfaction of the legislature, for the faithful discharge of his trust.

SEC. 3. The treasurer shall not, during his continuance in office, engage in any business or trade or commerce, or as a broker, nor as an agent or factor for any merchant or trader.

SEC. 4 No money shall be drawn from the treasury, but by warrant from the governor and council and in consequence of appropriations made by law ; and a regular statement and account of the receipts and expenditures of all public money, shall be published at the commencement of the annual session of the legislature.

ARTICLE VI.

JUDICIAL POWER.

SEC. 1. The judicial power of this state shall be vested in a supreme judicial court, and such other courts as the legislature shall from time to time establish.

SEC. 2. The justices of the supreme judicial court shall, at stated times, receive a compensation, which shall not be diminished during their continuance in office, but they shall receive no other fee or reward.

SEC. 3. They shall be obliged to give their opinions upon important questions of law, and upon solemn occasions, when required by the governor, council, senate or house of representatives.

SEC. 4. [All judicial officers, except justices of the

peace, shall hold their offices during good behavior, but not beyond the age of seventy years.]

Sec. 5. Justices of the peace and notaries public, shall hold their offices during seven years, if they so long behave themselves well, at the expiration of which term, they may be reappointed or others appointed, as the public interest may require.

Sec. 6. The justices of the supreme judicial court shall hold no office under the United States, nor any state, nor any other office under this state, except that of justice of the peace.

ARTICLE VII.

MILITARY.

Sec. 1. The captains and subalterns of the militia shall be elected by the written votes of the members of their respective companies. The field officers of regiments by the written votes of the captains and subalterns of their respective regiments. The brigadier generals in like manner, by the field officers of their respective brigades.

Sec. 2. The legislature shall, by law, direct the manner of notifying the electors, conducting the elections, and making the returns to the governor of the officers elected; and, if the electors shall neglect or refuse to make such elections, after being duly notified according to law, the governor shall appoint suitable persons to fill such offices.

Sec. 3. The major generals shall be elected by the senate and house of representatives, each having a negative on the other. The adjutant general and quartermaster general shall be appointed by the governor and council; but the adjutant general shall perform the duties of quarter-master general, until otherwise directed by law. The major generals and brigadier generals, and the commanding officers of regiments and battalions shall

4*

appoint their respective staff officers; and all militar
officers shall be commissioned by the governor.

Sec. 4 The militia, as divided into divisions, bri
ades, regiments, battalions and companies pursuant
the laws now in force, shall remain so organized, unt
the same shall be altered by the legislature.

Sec. 5. Persons of the denominations of quakers ar
shakers, justices of the supreme judicial court and mi
isters of the gospel, may be exempted from military dut
but no other person of the age of eighteen and under tl
age of forty five years, excepting officers of the milit
who have been honorably discharged, shall be so exem
ed, unless he shall pay an equivalent to be fixed by la

ARTICLE VIII.

LITERATURE.

A general diffusion of the advantages of education
ing essential to the preservation of the rights and liberl
of the people , to promote this important object, the le
lature are authorized, and it shall be their duty to requ
the several towns to make suitable provisions, at tl
own expense, for the support and maintenance of pul
schools; and it shall further be their duty to encour
and suitably endow, from time to time, as the circ
stances of the people may authorize, all academies,
leges and seminaries of learning within the state :
vided, that no donation, grant or endowment shall at
time be made by the legislature to any literary institu
now established, or which may hereafter be establis
unless, at the time of making such endowment, the l
lature of the state shall have the right to grant any fui
powers to, alter, limit or restrain any of the po
vested in, any such literary institutions as shall be ju
necessary to promote the best interests thereof.

ARTICLE IX.

GENERAL PROVISIONS.

Sec. 1. Every person elected or appointed to either of the places or offices provided in this constitution, and every person elected, appointed, or commissioned to any judicial, executive, military or other office under this state, shall, before he enter on the discharge of the duties of his place or office, take and subscribe the following oath or affirmation . " I   do swear, that I will support the constitution of the United States and of this state, so long as I shall continue a citizen thereof. So help me God."

" I   do swear, that I will faithfully discharge, to the best of my abilities, the duties incumbent on me as   according to the constitution and the laws of the state. So help me God." *Provided*, that an affirmation in the above forms may be substituted, when the person shall be conscientiously scrupulous of taking and subscribing an oath.

The oaths or affirmations shall be taken and subscribed by the governor and councilors before the presiding officer of the senate, in the presence of both houses of the legislature, and by the senators and representatives before the governor and council, and by the residue of said officers before such persons as shall be prescribed by the legislature; and whenever the governor or any councilor shall not be able to attend during the session of the legislature to take and subscribe said oaths or affirmations, such oaths or affirmations may be taken and subscribed in the recess of the legislature before any justice of the supreme judicial court · *provided*, that the senators and representatives, first elected under this constitution, shall take and subscribe such oaths and affirmations before the president of the convention.

Sec. 2. No person holding the office of justice of the supreme judicial court, or of any inferior court, attorney

general, county attorney, treasurer of the state, adjutant general, judge of probate, register of probate, register of deeds, sheriffs or their deputies, clerks of the judicial courts, shall be a member of the legislature; and any person holding either of the foregoing offices, elected to, and accepting a seat in the congress of the United States, shall thereby vacate said office; and no person shall be capable of holding or exercising at the same time within this state, more than one of the offices before mentioned.

Sec. 3. All commissions shall be in the name of the state, signed by the governor, attested by the secretary or his deputy, and have the seal of the state thereunto affixed.

Sec. 4. And in case the elections, required by this constitution on the [first Wednesday of January] annually, by the two houses of the legislature, shall not be completed on that day, the same may be adjourned from day to day, until completed, in the following order. the vacancies in the senate shall first be filled; the governor shall then be elected, if there be no choice by the people; and afterwards the two houses shall elect the council.

Sec. 5. Every person holding any civil office under this state may be removed by impeachment, for misdemeanor in office; and every person holding any office, may be removed by the governor, with the advice of the council, on the address of both branches of the legislature. But before such address shall pass either house, the causes of removal shall be stated and entered on the journal of the house in which it originated, and a copy thereof served on the person in office, that he may be admitted to a hearing in his defense.

Sec. 6 The tenure of all offices, which are not or shall not be otherwise provided for, shall be during the pleasure of the governor and council.

Sec 7. While the public expenses shall be assessed on polls and estates, a general valuation shall be taken at least once in ten years.

Sec 8. All taxes upon real estate, assessed by authority of this state, shall be apportioned and assessed equally, according to the just value thereof.

ARTICLE X.

SCHEDULE.

Sec. 1. The first legislature shall meet on the last Wednesday in May next. The elections on the second Monday in September annually shall not commence until the year one thousand eight hundred and twenty one, and in the mean time the election for governor, senators and representatives shall be on the first Monday in April, in the year of our Lord one thousand eight hundred and twenty, and at this election the same proceedings shall be had as are required at the elections, provided for in this constitution, on *the* second Monday in September annually, and the *list of the* votes for the governor and senators shall *be transmitted,* by the town and plantation clerks respectively, to the secretary of state *pro tempore,* seventeen days at least before the last Wednesday in May next, and the president of the convention shall, in presence of the secretary of state *pro tempore,* open and examine the attested copies of said lists so returned for senators, and shall have all the powers, and be subject to all the duties, in ascertaining, notifying, and summoning the senators, who appear to be elected, as the governor and council have, and are subject to, by this constitution · *provided,* he shall notify said senators fourteen days at least before the last Wednesday in May, and vacancies shall be ascertained and filled in the manner herein provided . and the senators to be elected on the said first Monday of April, shall be appointed as follows

The county of York shall elect three.
The county of Cumberland shall elect three.
The county of Lincoln shall elect three.
The county of Hancock shall elect two.

The county of Washington shall elect one.

The county of Kennebec shall elect three.

The county of Oxford shall elect two.

The county of Somerset shall elect two.

The county of Penobscot shall elect one.

And the members of the house of representatives shall be elected, ascertained and returned in the same manner as herein provided at elections on the second Monday of September, and the first house of representatives shall consist of the following number, to be elected as follows :

County of York. The towns of York and Wells may each elect two representatives ; and each of the remaining towns may elect one.

County of Cumberland. The town of Portland may elect three representatives ; North Yarmouth, two ; Brunswick, two ; Gorham, two ; Freeport and Pownal, two ; Raymond and Otisfield, one ; Bridgton, Baldwin and Harrison, one ; Poland and Danville, one , and each remaining town one.

County of Lincoln. The towns of Georgetown and Phipsburg, may elect one representative , Lewiston and Wales, one ; St. George, Cushing and Friendship, one ; Hope and Appleton Ridge, one ; Jefferson, Putnam and Patricktown plantation, one ; Alna and Whitefield, one ; Montville, Palermo and Montville plantation, one ; Woolwich and Dresden, one ; and each remaining town, one.

County of Hancock The town of Bucksport may elect one representative ; Deer Island, one ; Castine and Brooksville, one ; Orland and Penobscot, one ; Mt. Desert and Eden, one , Vinalhaven and Islesborough, one ; Sedgwick and Bluehill, one ; Gouldsborough, Sullivan and plantations No. 8 and 9 north of Sullivan, one ; Surry, Ellsworth, Trenton and plantation of Mariaville, one ; Lincolnville, Searsmont and Belmont, one ; Belfast and Northport, one ; Prospect and Swanville, one ; Frankfort and Monroe, one ; Knox, Brooks, Jackson and Thorndike, one.

County of Washington. The towns of Steuben, Cherryfield and Harrington, may elect one representative; Addison, Columbia and Jonesborough, one; Machias, one; Lubec, Dennysville, plantations No. 9, No. 10, No. 11, No. 12, one; Eastport, one; Perry, Robbinston, Calais, plantations No. 3, No. 6, No. 7, No. 15, and No. 16, one.

County of Kennebec. The towns of Belgrade and Dearborn may elect one representative; Chesterville, Vienna and Rome, one; Wayne and Fayette, one; Temple and Wilton, one; Winslow and China, one; Fairfax and Freedom, one; Unity, Joy and twenty five mile pond plantation, one; Harlem and Malta, one; and each remaining town one.

County of Oxford The towns of Dixfield, Mexico, Weld and plantations No 1 and 4, may elect one representative; Jay and Hartford, one; Livermore, one; Rumford, East Andover and plantations Nos. 7 and 8, one; Turner, one; Woodstock, Paris and Greenwood, one; Hebron and Norway, one, Gilead, Bethel, Newry, Albany and Howard's Gore, one; Porter, Hiram and Brownfield, one; Waterford, Sweden and Lovell, one; Denmark, Fryeburg, and Fryeburg add ition, one; Buck-

may elect one representative, Norridgewock and Bloomfield, one; and New

1, one; Canaan, Warsaw, Palmyra, St. Albans and Corinna, one; Madison, Solon, Bingham, Moscow and Northhill, one; Cornville, Athens, Harmony, Ripley, and Warrenston, one.

County of Penobscot. The towns of Hampden and Newburg, may elect one representative; Orrington, Brewer and Eddington and plantations adjacent on the east side of Penobscot river, one; Bangor, Orono, and Sunk-

baze plantation, one; Dixmont, Newport, Carmel, Hermon, Stetson, and plantation No. 4, in the 6th range, one, Levant, Cornith, Exeter, New Charleston, Blakesburg, plantation No. 1 in 3d range, and plantation No. 1 in 4th range, one, Dexter, Garland, Guilford, Sangerville, and plantation No. 3, in 6th range, one; Atkinson, Sebec, Foxcroft, Brownville, Williamsburg, plantation No. 1, in 7th range, and plantation No. 3, in 7th range, one.

And the secretary of state *pro tempore*, shall have the same powers, and be subject to the same duties, in relation to the votes for governor, as the secretary of state has, and is subject to, by this constitution, and the election of governor shall, on the said last Wednesday in May, be determined and declared, in the same manner, as other elections of governor are by this constitution; and in case of vacancy in said office, the president of the senate and speaker of the house of representatives, shall exercise the office, as herein otherwise provided, and the councilors, secretary and treasurer, shall also be elected on said day, and have the same powers, and be subject to the same duties, as is provided in this constitution; and in case of the death or other disqualification of the president of this convention, or of the secretary of state *pro tempore*, before the election and qualification of the governor or secretary of state under this constitution, the persons to be designated by this convention at their session in January next, shall have all the powers and perform all the duties, which the president of this convention, or the secretary *pro tempore*, to be by them appointed, shall have and perform.

SEC. 2. The period for which the governor, senators and representatives, councilors, secretary and treasurer, first elected or appointed, are to serve in their respective offices and places, shall commence on the last Wednesday in May, in the year of our Lord one thousand eight hundred and twenty, and continue until the first Wednesday of January, in the year of our Lord one thousand eight hundred and twenty two.

Sec. 3. All laws now in force in this state, and not repugnant to this constitution, shall remain, and be in force until altered or repealed by the legislature, or shall expire by their own limitation.

Sec. 4. The legislature, whenever two thirds of both houses shall deem it necessary, may propose amendments to this constitution; and when any amendments shall be

the several plantations, empowering and directing them to notify the inhabitants of their respective towns and plantations, in the manner prescribed by law, at their

the inhabitants voting on the question are in favor of such amendment, it shall become a part of this constitution.

Sec. 5. All officers provided for in the sixth section

from Massachusetts proper, and forming the same into a separate and independent state," shall continue in office as therein provided; and the following provisions of said act shall be a part of this constitution, subject however to be modified or annulled as therein is prescribed, and not otherwise, to wit:

" *Sec.* 1. Whereas it has been represented to this legislature, that a majority of the people of the district of Maine are desirous of establishing a separate and independent government within said district: therefore,

" *Be it enacted by the senate and house of representatives in general court assembled, and by the authority of the same,* That the consent of this commonwealth be, and

5

the same is hereby given, that the district of Maine may
be formed and erected into a separate and independent
state, if the people of the said district shall in the manner, and by the majority hereinafter mentioned, express
their consent and agreement thereto, upon the following
terms and conditions. and provided the congress of the
United States shall give its consent thereto, before the
fourth day of March next: which terms and conditions
are as follows, viz.

"*First.* All the lands and buildings belonging to the
commonwealth, within Massachusetts proper, shall continue to belong to said commonwealth, and all the lands
belonging to the commonwealth, within the district of
Maine, shall belong, the one half thereof to the said
commonwealth, and the other half thereof, to the state to
be formed within the said district, to be divided as is
hereinafter mentioned; and the lands within the said
district, which shall belong to the said commonwealth,
shall be free from taxation, while the title to the said
lands remains in the commonwealth; and the rights of
the commonwealth to their lands, within said district,
and the remedies for the recovery thereof, shall continue
the same, within the proposed state, and in the courts
thereof, as they now are within the said commonwealth,
and in the courts thereof; for which purposes, and for
the maintenance of its rights, and recovery of its lands,
the said commonwealth shall be entitled to all other
proper and legal remedies, and may appear in the courts
of the proposed state and in the courts of the United
States, holden therein; and all rights of action for, or
entry into lands, and of actions upon bonds, for the breach
of the performance of the condition of settling duties, so
called, which have accrued or may accrue, shall remain
in this commonwealth, to be enforced, commuted, released, or otherwise disposed of, in such manner as this commonwealth may hereafter determine: *provided however,*
that whatever this commonwealth may hereafter receive

or obtain on account thereof, if any thing, shall, after deducting all reasonable charges relating thereto, be divided, one third part thereof to the new state, and two third parts thereof to this commonwealth.

"*Second.* All the arms which have been received by the commonwealth, from the United States, under the law of congress, entitled, " an act making provisions for arming and equipping the whole body of militia of the United States," passed April the twenty third, one thousand eight hundred and eight, shall, as soon as the said district shall become a separate state, be divided between the two states, in proportion to the returns of the militia, according to which, the said arms have been received from the United States, as aforesaid.

"*Third.* All money, stock or other proceeds, hereafter derived from the United States, on account of the claim of this commonwealth, for disbursements made, and expenses incurred, for the defense of the state, during the late war with Great Britain, shall be received by this commonwealth, and when received, shall be divided between the two states, in the proportion of two thirds to this commonwealth, and one third to the new state.

"*Fourth.* All other property of every description, belonging to the commonwealth, shall be holden and receivable by the same as a fund and security, for all debts, annuities, and Indian subsidies, or claims due by said commonwealth; and within two years after the said district shall have become a separate state, the commissioners to be appointed, as hereinafter provided, if the said states cannot otherwise agree, shall assign a just portion of the productive property, so held by said commonwealth, as an equivalent and indemnification to said commonwealth, for all such debts, annuities or Indian subsidies or claims, which may then remain due, or unsatisfied: and all the surplus of the said property, so holden as aforesaid, shall be divided between the said commonwealth and the said district of Maine, in the

proportion of two thirds to the said commonwealth, and
one third to the said district—and if, in the judgment of
the said commissioners, the whole of said property, so
held, as a fund and security, shall not be sufficient indemnification for the purpose, the said district shall be
liable for and shall pay to said commonwealth, one third
of the deficiency.

"*Fifth.* The new state shall, as soon as the necessary
arrangements can be made for that purpose, assume and
perform all the duties and obligations of this commonwealth, towards the Indians within said district of Maine,
whether the same arise from treaties or otherwise; and
for this purpose shall obtain the assent of said Indians,
and their release to this commonwealth of claims and
stipulations arising under the treaty at present existing
between the said commonwealth and said Indians; and
as an indemnification to such new state, therefor, this
commonwealth, when such arrangements shall be completed, and the said duties and obligations assumed, shall
pay to said new state, the value of thirty thousand dollars, in manner following, viz: the said commissioners
shall set off by metes and bounds, so much of any part
of the land within the said district, falling to this commonwealth, in the division of the public lands, hereinafter
provided for, as in their estimation shall be of the value
of thirty thousand dollars; and this commonwealth shall
thereupon assign the same to the said new state, or in
lieu thereof, may pay the sum of thirty thousand dollars
at its election; which election of the said commonwealth,
shall be made within one year from the time that notice
of the doings of the commissioners, on this subject, shall
be made known to the governor and council; and if not
made within that time, the election shall be with the new
state.

"*Sixth.* Commissioners with the powers and for the
purposes mentioned in this act, shall be appointed in
manner following: the executive authority of each state

shall appoint two; and the four so appointed or the major part of them, shall appoint two more: but if they cannot agree in the appointment, the executive of each state shall appoint one in addition; not however in that case, to be a citizen of its own state. And any vacancy happening with respect to the commissioners, shall be supplied in the manner provided for their original appointment; and in addition to the powers herein before given to said commissioners, they shall have full power and authority to divide all the public lands within the district, between the respective states, in equal shares, or moieties, in severalty, having regard to quantity, situation and quality; they shall determine what lands shall be surveyed and divided from time to time, the expense of which surveys, and of the commissioners, shall be borne equally by the two states. They shall keep fair records of their doings, and of the surveys made by their direction, copies of which records, authenticated by them, shall be deposited from time to time in the archives of the respective states; transcripts of which, properly certified, may be admitted in evidence, in all questions touching the subject to which they relate. The executive authority of each state may revoke the power of either or both its commissioners · having, however, first appointed a substitute, or substitutes, and may fill any vacancy happening with respect to its own commissioners; four of said commissioners shall constitute a quorum for the transaction of business; their decision shall be final upon all subjects within their cognizance. In case said commission shall expire, the same not having been completed, and either state shall request the renewal or filling up of the same, it shall be renewed or filled up in the same manner as herein provided for filling the same, in the first instance, and with the like powers; and if either state shall, after six months' notice, neglect or refuse to appoint its commissioners, the other may fill up the whole commission.

5*

"*Seventh.* All grants of land, franchises, immunities, corporate or other rights, and all contracts for, or grants of land not yet located, which have been or may be made by the said commonwealth, before the separation of said district shall take place, and having or to have effect within the said district, shall continue in full force, after the said district shall become a separate state. But the grant which has been made to the president and trustees of Bowdoin College, out of the tax laid upon the banks within this commonwealth, shall be charged upon the tax upon the banks within the said district of Maine, and paid according to the terms of said grant; and the president and trustees, and the overseers of said college, shall have, hold and enjoy their powers and privileges in all respects; so that the same shall not be subject to be altered, limited, annulled or restrained except by judicial process, according to the principles of law; and in all grants hereafter to be made, by either state, of unlocated land within the said district, the same reservations shall be made for the benefit of schools and of the ministry, as have heretofore been usual, in grants made by this commonwealth. And all lands heretofore granted by this commonwealth, to any religious, literary, or eleemosynary corporation, or society, shall be free from taxation, while the same continues to be owned by such corporation or society.

"*Eighth.* No laws shall be passed in the proposed state with regard to taxes, actions, or remedies at law, or bars or limitations thereof, or otherwise making any distinction between the lands and rights of property of proprietors, not resident in, or not citizens of said proposed state, and the lands and rights of property of the citizens of the proposed state resident therein; and the rights and liabilities of all persons, shall after the said separation, continue the same as if the said district was still a part of this commonwealth, in all suits pending, or judgments remaining unsatisfied on the fifteenth day of March next, where the suits have been commenced in Massachusetts proper, and process has been served within the district of Maine; or commenced in the district of Maine, and process has been served in Massachusetts proper, either by taking bail, making attachments, arresting and detaining persons, or otherwise, where execution remains to be done; and in such suits the courts within Massachusetts proper, and within the proposed state, shall continue to have the same jurisdiction as if the said district had still remained a part of the commonwealth. And this commonwealth shall have the same remedies within the proposed state, as it now has, for the collection of all taxes, bonds or debts, which may be assessed, due, made, or contracted, by, to, or with the commonwealth, on or before the said fifteenth day of March, within the said district of Maine; and all officers within Massachusetts proper and the district of Maine, shall conduct themselves accordingly.

"*Ninth.* These terms and conditions, as here set forth, when the said district shall become a separate and independent state, shall, *ipso facto* be incorporated into, and become and be a part of any constitution, provisional or other, under which the government of the said proposed state, shall, at any time hereafter, be administered; subject however, to be modified, or annulled, by the agreement of the legislature of both the said states; but by no other power or body whatsoever."

Sec. 6. This constitution shall be enrolled on parchment, deposited in the secretary's office, and be the supreme law of the state, and printed copies thereof shall be prefixed to the books containing the laws of this state.

AMENDMENTS

TO THE

CONSTITUTION OF MAINE,

Adopted in pursuance of the fourth section of the
tenth article of the original constitution.

ARTICLE I.

The electors resident in any city may, at any meeting duly notified for the choice of representatives, vote for such representatives in their respective ward meetings, and the wardens in said wards shall preside impartially at such meetings, receive the votes of all qualified electors present, sort, count and declare them in open ward meetings, and in the presence of the ward clerk, who shall form a list of the persons voted for, with the number of votes for each person against his name, shall make a fair record thereof in the presence of the warden, and in open ward meeting; and a fair copy of this list shall be attested by the warden and ward clerk, sealed up in open ward meeting, and delivered to the city clerk within twenty four hours after the close of the polls. And the aldermen of any city shall be in session at their usual place of meeting, within twenty four hours after any election, and in the presence of the city clerk shall examine and compare the copies of said lists, and in case any person shall have received a majority of all the votes, he shall be declared elected by the aldermen, and the city clerk of any city shall make a record thereof, and the aldermen and city clerk shall deliver certified copies of such lists to the person or persons so elected, within ten days after the election. And the electors resident in any city may at any meetings duly notified and holden for the choice of any other civil officers, for whom they have been required heretofore to vote in town meeting, vote for such officers in their respective wards, and the same proceedings shall be had by the warden and ward clerk in each ward, as in the case of votes for representatives. And the aldermen of any city shall be in session within twenty four hours after the close of the polls in such meetings, and in the presence of the city clerk shall open, examine and compare the copies from the lists of votes given in the several wards, of which the city clerk shall make a record, and return thereof shall be made into the secretary of state's office in the same manner as selectmen of towns are required to do.

ARTICLE II.

No person before conviction shall be bailable for any of the crimes, which now are, or have been denominated capital offenses since the adoption of the constitution, where the proof is evident or the presumption great, whatever the punishment of the crimes may be.

ARTICLE III.

All judicial officers now in office or who may be hereafter appointed shall, from and after the first day of March in the year eighteen hundred and forty, hold their offices for the term of seven years from the time of their respective appointments (unless sooner removed by impeachment or by address of both branches of the legislature to the executive) and no longer, unless reappointed thereto.

ARTICLE IV.

The second section, article fourth, part first, of the constitution, is amended by substituting the words *one hundred and fifty one* for "not less than one hundred nor more than two hundred," before the word "members' in said section, so as to establish the number of representatives for the state at the number of one hundred and fifty one; and the latter part of said section, being the words and sentences following; "and whenever the number of representatives shall be two hundred, at the next annual meetings of elections which shall thereafter be had, and at every subsequent period of ten years, the people shall give in their votes, whether the number of representatives shall be increased or diminished, and if a majority of votes are in favor thereof, it shall be the duty of the next legislature thereafter to increase or diminish the number by the rule hereinafter prescribed," shall not be a part of the constitution; but one hundred and fifty one representatives shall be apportioned according to the rule in this constitution.

ARTICLE V.

The annual meeting of the legislature shall be on the second Wednesday of May in each year; and the governor and other state officers elected for the political year commencing on the first Wednesday of January, in the year of our Lord one thousand eight hundred and forty five, shall hold their offices till the second Wednesday of May, in the year of our Lord one thousand eight hundred and forty six.

RULES AND ORDERS

OF THE

HOUSE OF REPRESENTATIVES,

1846.

RULES AND ORDERS.

DUTIES AND POWERS OF THE SPEAKER.

1. The speaker shall take the chair at the hour to which the house shall have adjourned; shall call the members to order; and on the appearance of a quorum, shall cause the journal of the preceding day to be read.

2. He shall preserve decorum and order; may speak to points of order in preference to other members; shall decide all questions of order, subject to an appeal to the house, on motion regularly seconded; and may vote in all cases.

3. *He shall* declare all votes; but if any member doubt the vote, the speaker shall order a return of the house, with the number voting for and against the question and declare the result.

4. He shall rise to put a question, or to address the house, but may read sitting.

5. When the house shall determine to go into a committee of the whole house, the speaker shall appoint the member who shall take the chair.

6. He shall propound all questions in the order they were moved, unless the subsequent motion be previous in its nature; except that in filling blanks, and in assigning times for the consideration of business, the largest sum and longest time shall be put first.

7. He shall consider a motion to adjourn as always first in order, and it shall be decided without debate.

8. He shall put the previous question in the following form: "shall the main question be now put?" and all

6

amendment or further debate of the main question shall
be suspended until the previous question shall be decided ; and the previous question shall not be put unless
one third of the members present are in favor of it. And
a call for the yeas and nays, or for a division of the question, shall be in order after the main question has been
ordered to be put. While a motion for the previous
question is pending, a motion to lay on the table shall be
decided without debate. After the adoption of the previous question, the vote shall forthwith be taken upon
amendments reported by a committee, upon pending
amendments, and then upon the main question.

9. When two or more members rise at the same time,
the speaker shall name the person to speak ; but in all
cases the member who shall first rise and address the
chair shall speak first.

10. All committees, except such as the house shall
from time to time determine to select by ballot, shall be
nominated by the speaker, unless a majority of members
shall be in favor of a nomination by the house, in which
case the nomination shall be made by the house.

11. Every question of order, which shall be decided
on appeal, shall be entered on the journal of the house,
with the decision thereon.

12. The speaker shall have a right to name a member
to perform the duties of the chair during his absence, but
such substitution shall not extend beyond an adjournment

DUTIES OF THE CLERK.

13. All messages from the house to the senate, and to
the governor, or governor and council, shall be carried by
the clerk, unless when the house shall otherwise decide.

14. All papers shall be transmitted to the governor and
council, and to the senate, by the clerk, or the assistant
clerk.

15. In case the speaker shall be absent at the hour to which the house was adjourned, the clerk shall preside until a speaker pro tem. be chosen.

OF THE CHAPLAIN.

16 A chaplain or chaplains, shall be appointed at the commencement of the session, in such manner as the house may direct, who shall perform religious services every morning immediately after the reading of the journal. They may exchange with the chaplain or chaplains of the senate, when it may be convenient to themselves.

DUTIES, RIGHTS AND DECORUM OF MEMBERS.

seat *during that* session,
speaker to change it.

19. No member shall speak out of his place without leave from the chair, nor without first rising and addressing the speaker; and he shall sit down as soon as he has done speaking.

20. No member shall interrupt another while speaking, except to call to order, or to correct a mistake.

21. No member shall speak more than twice to the same question, without first obtaining leave of the house, unless he be the mover, proposer, or introducer, of the matter pending; in which case he shall be permitted to speak in reply, but not until every member choosing to speak shall have spoken.

22. When a motion is made and seconded, it shall be received and considered by the house, and not otherwise; and no member shall be permitted to lay a motion in

writing on the table, until he shall have read the same in
his place, and the same shall have been seconded; and
no new bill or resolve of a public nature shall be re
ceived, except it be reported by a committee, unless the
house otherwise order; and all bills and resolves, not re
ported by a committee, shall be referred to the appro
priate committees, or shall be laid upon the table for one
day, before further action thereon.

23. No member shall nominate more than one person
for one committee, provided the person nominated by
him be chosen.

24. When a motion has been once made and carried
in the affirmative, or negative, it shall not be in order for
any member who voted in the minority, to move for a
reconsideration thereof; but any member who voted with
the majority, may move to reconsider on the same or the
succeeding day. A motion to reconsider shall not be
postponed nor laid on the table without a time certain
assigned for its further consideration. When a motion
for reconsideration has been decided, that vote shall not
be reconsidered. A motion to reconsider shall not be
in order, more than once on the same question.

25. Bills, resolves, and other papers, in reference to
which, any member having a right to move a reconsidera
tion, shall give notice of a motion to that effect, to be
made within the time allowed for that purpose, shall re
main in the possession of the clerk, until the question of
reconsideration is determined, or the right to move that
question is lost; but the operation of this rule shall be
suspended during the last week of the session.

26. No member shall be obliged to be on more than
two committees at the same time, nor chairman of more
than one. No member of this house shall act as counse
for any party, before a joint committee of the legislati
or a committee of this house.

27. No member shall be permitted to stand up, to the interruption of another, while any member is speaking, or pass unnecessarily between the speaker of the house and the person speaking. Nor shall any member or other person be permitted to stand in the alleys during the session of the house.

28. Every member shall keep an account of his own attendance and travel, and deliver the same to the clerk, or to the committee appointed to make up the pay roll; and on failure thereof, shall not be made up in the roll.

29. When the galleries shall be ordered to be cleared or shut, the matter which may occasion such order, shall be kept secret by each member, until the house shall order such injunction of secrecy to be taken off.

30. Every member who shall neglect to give his attendance in the house for more than six days after the session commences, shall, on making his appearance therein, be held to render the reason of such neglect; and in case the reason assigned shall be deemed by the house sufficient, such member shall be entitled to receive pay for his travel and not otherwise; and no member shall be absent more than two days without leave of the house, and no member shall have such leave, unless it be reported by the committee on leave of absence; and no leave of absence shall avail any member who retains his seat, more than five days from the time the same was obtained.

31. When any member shall be guilty of a breach of any of the rules and orders of the house, and the house has determined he has so transgressed, he shall not be allowed to vote or speak, unless by way of excuse for the same, until he has made satisfaction.

32. No member shall be permitted to vote on any question where his private right distinct from public interest, is immediately concerned.

6*

33. Every member who shall be in the house when a question is put, where he is not excluded by interest, shall give his vote unless the house, for special reason, shall excuse him, and when the yeas and nays are ordered, no member shall leave his seat until the vote is declared. In all elections by the house, or in joint ballot of the two houses, no member shall leave his seat, after voting, before a return of the house is had.

ORDER IN PROCEEDINGS AND DEBATES.

34. Every motion shall be reduced to writing, if required by the speaker or by any member.

35. On the previous question, no member shall speak more than once, without leave.

36. A motion to amend a report shall not be in order; but a report may be recommitted, and all orders and motions may be amended, committed or recommitted, at the pleasure of the house.

37. A motion to non-concur, except upon verbal messages, shall not be in order; but in all other cases of concurrent action, the chair shall state the question affirmatively, " Will the house concur?"

38. No new motions or propositions shall be admitted under color of amendment, as a substitute for the motion or question under debate.

39. Propositions to amend by striking out and inserting dates, numbers and sums are not divisible; but all propositions, otherwise divisible, shall be divided at the request of any ten members. A motion to strike out being lost, shall neither preclude amendments, nor a motion to strike out and insert.

40. When the reading of a paper is called for, which has been before read to the house, and the same is ob-

jected to by any member, it shall be determined by a vote of the house.

41 After a motion or order is stated or read by the speaker, and seconded, it shall be deemed to be in the possession of the house and shall be disposed of by vote of the house. Any motion or order may be withdrawn by the mover at any time before a decision or amendment, except a motion to reconsider, which shall not be withdrawn except by consent of the house.

42. When a question is under debate, no motion shall be received, but

1st—To adjourn ;
2d—To lay on the table ;
3d—For the previous question ;
4th—To commit ;
5th—To amend ;
6th—To postpone to a day certain ;
7th—To postpone indefinitely ;

Which several motions shall have precedence in the order in which they are arranged.

43. The unfinished business in which the house was engaged at the time of the last adjournment, shall have preference in the orders of the day, and no motion or other business shall be received, without special leave of the house, until the former is disposed of.

44. A proposition to require the opinions of the judges of the supreme court, as provided by the constitution, shall not be acted upon, until the next day after such proposition is made.

45 When a bill or resolve shall be returned by the Governor with his objections, the question shall be stated by the chair, *Shall this bill become a law notwithstanding the objections of the governor?* and the same in substance, in case of a resolve; which question may be postponed to a day within the session, not exceeding one week, or may be committed. But no other question

shall be taken upon such bill or resolve; and this rule shall apply to bills and resolves originating in either branch.

46. No rule or order of the house shall be dispensed with, unless two thirds of the members present shall consent thereto.

47. No rule or order of the house shall be altered nor repealed, nor shall any new standing rule or order be adopted, unless one day's previous notice thereof be given in each case; and such notice shall be entered on the journal.

48. When a vote having been declared by the speaker, is doubted, the members for and against the question, when called on by the speaker, shall rise and stand uncovered till they are counted, and the vote made certain without any further debate. But a call for the yeas and nays shall be in order at any time before such vote is made certain and declared.

49. A member who is absent from his seat when a vote is taken upon any question, shall not afterwards be allowed to vote on that question except by consent of the house.

50. One monitor shall be appointed by the speaker, for each division of the house, whose duty shall be, to see to the observance of the orders of the house, and on demand of the speaker, to return the number of votes and members in his division.

51. If any member shall transgress any of the rules and orders of the house, and persist therein, after being notified thereof by any monitor, it shall be the duty of such monitor to give information thereof to the house.

52. The rules of parliamentary practice comprised in Jefferson's Manual shall govern the house in all cases to which they are applicable, and in which they are not inconsistent with the standing rules and orders of the

house, and the joint rules of the senate and house of representatives.

PETITIONS, MEMORIALS, &c.

53. All petitions, memorials, and other papers, addressed to the house, shall be presented by the speaker, or by a member in his place, and shall be indorsed with the name of the person presenting it, and the subject matter of the same. They shall be read by the speaker, clerk, or such other person as the speaker may request, and shall be taken up in the order they were first presented, unless when the house shall otherwise direct.

BILLS, RESOLVES AND GRANTS.

54. Every bill or resolve providing for the grant of money, land, or other public property, which may be laid on the table by leave, shall be referred to a committee, and the report of a committee upon any bill or resolve providing for such grant, shall be accompanied by a written statement of facts in each case; and no such bill or resolve shall pass, without being read on two several days.

55. No engrossed bill or resolve shall be sent to the senate, without notice thereof being given to the house by the speaker.

56. No bill shall pass to be engrossed, until it shall have had three several readings; the times for the second and third readings shall be assigned by the house, but, if no objection is made, the second reading may be by title, and at the time of the first. Every resolve, which shall require the approval of the. Governor, shall have two several readings; the second reading shall be subject to the provision for the second reading of bills.

57. No act or resolve shall be passed, affecting the

rights of individuals or corporations, without previous notice to such individuals or corporations.

58. All bills in their third reading, and resolves in their second reading, shall be committed to the standing committee on bills in the third reading, to be by them examined, corrected, and so reported to the house.

59. All engrossed bills and resolves shall be committed to the standing committee on engrossed bills, to be strictly examined ; and if found by them to be truly and strictly engrossed, they shall so report to the house, and the same shall pass to be enacted without any further reading, unless on motion of any member, a majority of the house shall be in favor of reading the same as engrossed.

COMMITTEES.

60. The following standing committees shall be appointed at the commencement of the session, with leave to report by bill or otherwise, viz :

> On elections,
> On engrossed bills,
> On finance,
> On county estimates,
> On bills in the third reading,
> On leave of absence,
> On the pay roll,

T oconsist of seven members each.

> On change of names,

To consist of three members.

61. In all elections by ballot, of committees of the house, the person having the highest number of votes, shall act as chairman.

62. Any member having obtained leave of absence, and having in his possession any papers relative to the

business before the house, shall leave the same with the clerk.

63. The chairman of every committee, other than of the standing committees, that shall have business referred to it, shall make a report of its doings therein, within four days after its appointment.

ELECTIONS.

64. In all elections by ballot of the house, a time shall be assigned for such election, at least one day previous thereto.

OF THE REPRESENTATIVES' HALL.

65. No person, not a member or officer of the house, except members of the senate, its secretary and assistants, the governor and council, state treasurer, secretary of state, land agent, adjutant general, judges of the supreme judicial court, and district court, chaplains of the house and senate, and reporters of the proceedings and debates of the house, shall be admitted within the representatives' hall, unless invited by the speaker, or some member of the house.

MEMORANDA.

1. Orders, motions in writing, and reports of committee should never be presented on less than a half sheet of paper.
2. When a *report* of a committee is made to the house it should be accompanied by the *order*, appointing said committee.
3. Petitions, memorials and remonstrances from towns in their *corporate capacity*, should be indorsed thus " *Petition of the town of* —," [stating concisely the subject matter thereof]
4. Petitions, memorials and remonstrances from individuals, should be indorsed thus, " *Petition of* —, *and others of the town of* —," [stating concisely the subject matter thereof.]
5. Petitions, memorials and remonstrances from corporations, should be indorsed thus, " *Petition of* —,' [naming the corporation, and stating concisely the subject matter thereof]
6. The name of the member presenting petitions, memorials and remonstrances, should be indorsed on the back thereof, *near the bottom.*
7 The member presenting an *order* should put his name thereto, on the inside, at the bottom of the page, on the left.
8. Petitions, memorials and remonstrances on which *leave to withdraw* was ordered by a former legislature cannot be recalled from the files with a view of being again referred. The *original*, however, may be taken from the files, and the subject presented *de novo.*

9. Bills and resolves *refused a passage, rejected or postponed indefinitely* by a former legislature, cannot be called from the files with a view of being considered by the present legislature.

10. The heading or caption of BILLS, should be as follows:

STATE OF MAINE.

In the year of our Lord one thousand eight hundred and forty-six.

An act ——

Be it enacted by the senate and house of representatives in legislature assembled, as follows :—

11. The caption of RESOLVES, as follows:

STATE OF MAINE.

[*omitting* the year required in bills.]

Resolve ——

CIVIL GOVERNMENT

OF THE

STATE OF MAINE

FOR THE POLITICAL YEAR

1846.

GOVERNOR,

HUGH J. ANDERSON, Belfast.

COUNCIL.

CHARLES STETSON, Bangor.

WILLIAM DUNN, Poland.

SAMUEL MILDRAM, Wells.

FRANKLIN SMITH, North Anson.

STILLMAN HOWARD, Leeds.

THOMAS SIMMONS, Waldoborough.

SAMUEL H. TALBOT, East Machias.

EZRA B. FRENCH, Nobleboro', *Secretary of State.*

JAMES WHITE, Belfast, *Treasurer of State.*

ALFRED REDINGTON, Augusta, *Adjutant General*

LEVI BRADLEY, Charleston, *Land Agent.*

S. HENRY CHASE, of FRYEBURG,
PRESIDENT.

		BOARDING-PLACES
1st Sen. Dist.,	WILLIAM C. ALLEN, of Alfred,	Augusta House.
	CHARLES G. BELLAMY, of Kittery,	do.
	BENJAMIN F. MASON, of Kennebunkport,	Gage House.
2d " "	DAVID DUNN, of Poland,	Mansion House.
	RANDAL SKILLIN, of Cape Elizabeth,	J. H. Arnold.
	ALPHEUS S. HOLDEN, of Casco,	Mr. Ballard.
	RUFUS PORTER, of North Yarmouth,	Augusta House.
3d " "	JOSEPH BERRY, of Georgetown,	do.
	HENRY BARNES, of Bowdoinham,	do.
	SAMUEL W. JACKSON, of Jefferson,	Mansion House.
	THOMAS GORE, of Cushing,	Gilman Turner.
4th " "	DAVID BRONSON, of Augusta,	His house.
	LEAVITT LOTHROP, of Leeds,	Central House.
	ISAAC REDINGTON, of Waterville,	Mansion House.
5th " "	CHARLES SARGENT, of Monroe,	Central House.
	JOHN C. KNOWLTON, of Liberty,	do.
	JAMES H. HAINES, of Burnham,	J. K. Kilns.
6th " "	HENRY PARTRIDGE, of Orland,	Central House.
7th " "	WILLIAM GODFREY, of Gouldsborough,	Mansion House.
8th " "	MATHEW HASTINGS, of Calais,	do.
9th " "	JOHN HODGDON, of Houlton,	Augusta House.
10th " "	JOHN H. PILLSBURY, of Bangor,	Mansion House.
	ASA SMITH, of Mattawamkeag,	do.
	ELISHA M. THURSTON, of Charleston,	J. W. Smith.
11th " "	JOSEPH S. MONROE, of Abbot,	Mansion House.
12th " "	RUFUS K. J. PORTER, of New Portland,	Franklin House.
	JOSEPH BARRETT, of Canaan,	U. L. Pettengill.
13th " "	LEMUEL BURSLEY, Jr., of Farmington,	Cushnoc House.
14th " "	S. HENRY CHASE, PRESIDENT,	Augusta House.
	WILLIAM THOMPSON, of Canton,	Gage House.
	JOHN J. PERRY, of Oxford,	do.
DANIEL T. PIKE, of Augusta, SECRETARY,		His house.
CHARLES C. HARMON, of Portland, ASSISTANT SEC'Y,		Gage House.
BENJAMIN F. CUTTER, of Westbrook, MESSENGER,		Gilman Turner.
SMITH LIBBY, of Exeter, ASSISTANT MESSENGER,		G. Turner.
Rev. JOHN H. INGRAHAM, of Augusta, CHAPLAIN,		His house.

SENATE.

ARRANGEMENT
OF THE MEMBERS AT THE SENATE BOARD.

S. HENRY CHASE, President.

NO. OF SEAT.	LEFT.	NO. OF SEAT.	RIGHT.
1. Charles Sargent.		2. John J. Perry.	
3. James H. Haines.		4. William Thompson	
5. Benjamin F. Mason.		6. Thomas Gore.	
7. Henry Partridge.		8. Alpheus S. Holden	
9 Randal Skillin.		10. Lemuel Bursley, Jr.	
11. John Hodgdon.		12. David Bronson.	
13. Joseph Berry.		14. Leavitt Lothrop.	
15. Asa Smith.		16. Samuel W. Jackson	
17 William C. Allen.		18. John C. Knowlton.	
19 Isaac Redington		20. John H. Pillsbury.	
21 Joseph S Monroe.		22 Mathew Hastings.	
23. Elisha M. Thurston.		24 Rufus Porter	
25 Henry Barnes		26 Wilson Godfrey.	
27. Charles G. Bellamy		28. Joseph Barrett.	
29. David Dunn		30. Rufus K. J. Porter.	

On Bills in the Second Reading

Messrs. Porter,
Dunn,
Allen,
Thompson,
Lothrop,
Jackson,
Knowlton,
Barrett,
Smith,
Partridge,·
Godfrey,
Hastings.

On Engrossed Bills.

Messrs. Bursley, jr.,
Hodgdon,
Pillsbury,
Monroe,
Barnes,
Haines,
Sargent,
Porter,
Redington,
Holden,
Bellamy,
Perry.

7*

EBENEZER KNOWLTON, Esq., Speaker.

COUNTY OF YORK.

Seats.	Names.	Residences.	Boarding-places.
131	William Berry,	Biddeford,	J. H. Arnold.
21	Joseph Burnham,	Kennebunkport,	do.
129	Edmund Currier,	Lyman,	do.
135	Alvah Doe,	Parsonsfield,	do.
146	Samuel Fox,	Berwick,	Cushnoc House.
111	John Hubbard,	South Berwick,	Augusta House.
30	John Lary, jr.,	Acton,	J. K. Killsa.
134	John Milliken,	Buxton,	J. H. Arnold.
46	John Moore,	Newfield,	do.
17	Joseph Perkins,	Wells,	J. K. Killsa.
151	Richard Rogers,	Kittery,	Augusta House.
43	Miles W. Stuart,	Hollis,	Cushnoc House.
104	Samuel Tripp,	Sanford,	do.
88	Gideon Tucker,	Saco,	Augusta House.
148	Tobias Walker,	Kennebunk,	J. H. Arnold.
147	Samuel Webber,	York,	do.

COUNTY OF CUMBERLAND.

Seats.	Names.	Residences.	Boarding-places.
15	Phinehas Barnes,	Portland,	Augusta House.
145	Jeremiah Beedle,	Westbrook,	Central House.
26	John Burnell, jr.,	Baldwin,	John Verney.
7	Thomas Chadwick,	Portland,	Augusta House.
100	Wm. P. Fessenden,	Portland,	Augusta House.
108	Thomas J. Howard,	Auburn,	Cushnoc House,
39	Nathaniel L. Ingersoll,	Danville,	J. H. Arnold.
62	Adam Lemont,	Brunswick,	Central House.
57	Abner Libbey,	Harrison,	J. Verney.
28	Freeland Marble,	Poland,	Mansion House.

Seats.	Names.	Residences.	Boarding-places.
149	Hugh D. McLellan,	Gorham,	Augusta House.
95	Ebenezer Moulton,	Standish,	J. Varney.
84	Frederic Nutting,	Casco,	Ephraim Ballard.
10	Cushing Prince,	N. Yarmouth,	Mr. Marshall.
72	Benjamin Small,	Pownal,	J. H. Arnold.
31	Samuel Soule,	Freeport,	do.
92	Ephraim Sturdivant,	Cumberland,	G. Powers.
96	Levi L. Totman,	Harpswell,	J. H. Arnold.
119	James Trickey,	Cape Elizabeth,	do.
70	Enoch White,	Windham,	Augusta House.

COUNTY OF LINCOLN.

49	James Ayer,	Alna,	J. Young.
101	Joseph B. Bridge,	Dresden,	Augusta House.
76	Oliver B Brown,	Thomaston,	Cushnoc House.
91	Moses Choate, jr.,	Whitefield,	Central House.
69	Joseph Cotter,	Nobleboro',	J. K. Killea.
37	Joseph Day,	Bristol,	do.
152	James Elliot,	Bowdoin,	Central House.
107	George Gilchrest,	St. George,	Cushnoc House.
103	Asa F. Hall,	Wiscasset,	U. L. Pettingill.
34	Reuben Hall,	Warren,	Cushnoc House.
90	Jacob Hill,	Webster,	Mansion House.
71	Atwood Levensaler,	Thomaston,	Cushnoc House.
72	David C. Magoun,	Bath,	Augusta House.
55	Joseph Merry,	Edgecomb,	J H. Arnold.
89	Joseph Moore,	Lisbon,	Mansion House.
132	Edward Rand,	Townsend,	Alvin Fogg.
65	Isaac Reed,	Waldoboro',	Mansion House.
25	William Wildes,	Phipsburg,	Augusta House.
94	William Young,	Washington,	Cushnoc House.

COUNTY OF HANCOCK.

137	Wm. Babbidge,	Deer Isle,	G. Powers.
83	Richard Currier,	Sedgwick,	J. Varney.

SEATS.	NAMES.	RESIDENCES.	BOARDING PLACES.
150	Harvey F. Deming,	Mt. Desert,	J. Verney.
110	Moses McFarland,	Trenton,	John Young.
105	Daniel Harriman,	Orland,	G. Turner.
65	Jonathan Hatch, jr.,	Penobscot,	do.
19	Sylvanus T. Hinks,	Bucksport,	do.
74	Donald Lord,	Surry,	J. H. Arnold.
42	Samuel Stratton,	Hancock,	John Young.

COUNTY OF WASHINGTON.

69	Hiram A. Balch,	Lubec,	Mansion House.
116	John N. Farrar,	Baileyville,	J. K. Killse.
33	Joel Hanscom,	Crawford,	J. Young.
6	Aaron Hayden,	Eastport,	Augusta House.
117	Joseph A. Lee,	Calais,	do
89	Otis Look,	Addison,	Mr. Pinkham.
142	Thomas Milliken,	• Cherryfield,	John Young.
94	Robinson Palmer,	Perry,	Mansion House.
52	Samuel Small,	Machiasport,	do.

COUNTY OF KENNEBEC.

16	Daniel H. Brown,	Sebasticook,	Kennebec House.
126	Jason Chadwick,	China,	John Young.
124	Joseph Edgecomb,	Vienna,	Central House.
92	Isaac Fairfield,	Vassalboro',	Franklin House.
13	Ebenezer Freeman,	Monmouth,	U. L. Pettengill.
77	Moses Frost,	Sidney,	Gage House.
12	William O. Grant,	Litchfield,	U. L. Pettengill.
56	Frederic P Haviland,	Waterville,	Kennebec House.
80	Thomas J. Hayden,	Winslow.	Central House.
36	Charles Keene,	Augusta,	His house.
54	Daniel Marston,	Mt. Vernon,	Central House.
47	John Otis,	Hallowell,	His house.
2	Benjamin Ridley,	Wayne,	Cushnoc House.
141	Simeon Skillin,	Albion,	Franklin House.

Seats.	Names.	Residences.	Boarding-places.
97	Jonathan Tuck,	Fayette,	Mr. Tuck, Hallowell.
128	Noah Woods,	Gardiner,	J. Baker.

COUNTY OF OXFORD.

57	Joseph Child,	Hartford,	Cushnoc House.
55	Almer Davis,	Stow,	G. Powers.
9	Phinehas Frost,	Bethel,	Cushnoc House.
122	John Hill,	Sweden,	J. Varney.
14	John J. Holman,	Dixfield,	Cushnoc House.
150	John F. Holt,	Turner,	do.
52	Alexander Libby,	Sumner,	J. Varney.
64	Philip Munger,	Livermore,	G. Powers.
51	John Reed,	Roxbury,	Cushnoc House.
112	Horatio G. Russ,	Paris,	Gage House.
149	Wm. T. Taylor,	Porter,	J. Varney.
53	Isaac A. Thayer,	Oxford,	Cushnoc House.

COUNTY OF SOMERSET.

11	James Adams,	Norridgewock,	Augusta House.
136	Robert Crosby,	Embden,	Albert Pinkham.
32	Patten Currier,	Cornville,	do.
79	Warren Fuller,	Hartland,	J. H. Arnold.
3	George C. Getchell,	North Anson,	Augusta House.
5	Jabez D. Hill,	Moscow,	J. J. Fuller.
92	Saul Holbrook,	Starks,	Franklin House.
12	Eldridge G. Morrison,	Canaan,	N. Ellis.
123	Wm. F. Pitts,	Bloomfield,	Albert Pinkham.
35	Thomas Smith,	St. Albans,	J. H. Arnold.

COUNTY OF PENOBSCOT.

40	Elisha H. Allen,	Bangor,	Augusta House.
	Ebenezer Briggs,	Kirkland,	
42	George Crane,	Eddington,	Mr. Wade.
75	Andrew Drury,	Enfield,	Mansion House.
1	John C. Friend,	Etna,	Alvin Fogg.

Seats.	Names.	Residences.	Boarding-places.
109	John Gardiner,	Patten,	J. Verney.
90	William Head,	Lagrange,	Central House.
81	Thomas H. Norcross,	Charleston,	Mansion House.
4	Lyndon Oak,	Garland,	W. K. Weston.
8	William Paine,	Bangor,	Augusta House.
149	Thomas P. Rowe,	Brewer,	Gage House.
59	Hiram Ruggles,	Carmel,	G. Turner.
45	Amos Storer,	Dexter,	Dr. Smith.
66	Benjamin B. Thomas,	Newburg,	G. Turner.

COUNTY OF WALDO.

102	Sherburne Bachelder,	Belmont,	G. Turner.
130	Seth Bartlett,	Hope,	Kennebec House.
144	Maurice C. Blake,	Camden,	Mansion House.
87	Henry Colburn,*	Belfast,	do.
113	Jacob Cunningham,	Swanville,	G. Turner.
56	Samuel S. Hersey,*	Belfast,	Central House.
47	Ebenezer Knowlton, (Speaker,)	Montville,	do.
48	Daniel Lampson,	Troy,	W. R. Prescott, Hall.
99	Amos Pitcher,	Northport,	G. Turner.
114	Lot Rust,	Palermo,	Cushnoc House.
67	Seth Thompson,	Unity,	J. Verney.
23	Arthur Treat,	Frankfort,	Central House.
63	Allison Tyler,	Prospect,	G. Turner.
115	David Vinal,	Vinalhaven,	Cushnoc House.

COUNTY OF FRANKLIN.

78	Joseph Dunham,	Madrid,	Cushnoc House.
44	Eliab Eaton,	Farmington,	do.
136	John F. W. Gould,	Wilton,	Gage House.
139	Truman A. Merrill,	Industry,	J. Piper.
123	Stillman Noyes,	Jay,	Cushnoc House.
112	Nathaniel Potter,	Kingfield,	Franklin House.

* Claimants of one seat.

COUNTY OF PISCATAQUIS.

Seats.	Names.	Residences.	Boarding-places.
20	Abijah B. Chase,	Sebec,	Mansion House.
9	George H. Kingsbery,	Kingsbery,	Augusta House.
166	Ebenezer Lambert,	Dover,	Central House.

COUNTY OF AROOSTOOK.

85	Joseph Cyr,	Van Buren Pl.	J. K. Killen.
86	Leander S. Morton,	Bridgewater Pl.	do.
35	Edwin Parker,	Golden Ridge Pl.	G. Turner.

SAMUEL BELCHER, of Farmington, CLERK, — Mansion House.
NATHANIEL PATTERSON, of Belfast, ASSISTANT CLERK, — Augusta House.
PHILIP PHILLIPS, of Turner, MESSENGER, — Augusta House.
WILLIAM SANBORN, of Liberty, ASSISTANT MESSENGER, — J. Verney.
HENRY D. FISK, of Augusta, do. do. — J Fisk.
WILLIAM O. GRANT, Jr., of Litchfield, PAGE. — U. L. Pettengill.

The Clergymen of Augusta and Hallowell, and the ordained ministers of the gospel who are members of the House, officiate as CHAPLAINS, in rotation.

MONITORS.

1st Division, Mr. PARKER, of Golden Ridge.
2d   "   " THOMPSON, of Unity.
3d   "   " MOULTON, of Standish.
4th   "   " TRICKEY, of Cape Elizabeth.
5th   "   " ROGERS, of Kittery.
6th   "   " GRANT, of Litchfield.

Standing Committees of the House.

On Elections.

Messrs. Rogers of Kittery,
Tucker of Saco,
Russ of Paris,
Oak of Garland,
Hill of Moscow,
Chadwick of China,
Pitcher of Northport.

On Engrossed Bills.

Messrs. Magoun of Bath,
Moulton of Standish,
Deming of Mt. Desert,
Blake of Camden,
Beedle of Westbrook,
Merrill of Industry,
Brown of Clinton.

On Finance.

Messrs. Chadwick of Portland,
Hinks of Bucksport,
Lee of Calais,
Stuart of Hollis,
Ingersoll, of Danville,
Marble of Poland,
Bachelder of Belmont.

On County Estimates.

Messrs. Stuart of Hollis,
Frost of Sidney,
Sturdivant of Cumberland,
Hall of Warren,
Hill of Moscow,
Munger of Livermore,
Tyler of Prospect,

On Bills in the Third Reading.

Messrs. Barnes of Portland,
Doe of Parsonsfield,
Oak of Garland,
Getchell of North Anson,
Rowe of Brewer,
Hayden of Eastport,
Parker of Hodgdon,

On Leave of Absence.

Messrs. Edgecomb of Vienna,
Webber of York,
Cunningham of Swanville,
Adams of Norridgewock,
Friend of Etna,
Frost of Sidney,
Lary of Acton.

On Pay Roll.

Messrs. Frost of Bethel,
Choate of Whitefield,
Babbidge of Deer Isle,
Skillin of Albion,
Trickey of Cape Elizabeth,
Burnham of Kennebunkport,
Ruggles of Carmel.

8

On Change of Names.

Messrs. Gardiner of Patten,
   Pitts of Bloomfield,
   Libbey of Sumner.

Joint Rules and Orders of the two Houses.

1 The following joint standing committees shall be appointed at the commencement of the session, viz :

        On the judiciary,
        On education,
        On banks and banking,
        On incorporation of towns,
        On division of towns,
        On division of counties,
        On state lands and state roads,
        On indian affairs,
        On agriculture,
        On fisheries,
        On manufactures,
        On rail roads and bridges,
        On interior waters,
        On accounts,
        On claims,
        On the militia,
        On military pensions,
        On the insane hospital,
        On the state prison,
        On public buildings,
        On the library.

And each of the said committees shall consist of three on the part of the senate, and seven on the part of the house.

2. Whenever a select committee shall be appointed by either house, and be joined by the other, it shall be the duty of the secretary of the senate, or clerk of the house, respectively, as the case may be, to transmit, one to the other, the names of the members so joined, in

order that they may be entered on the journal of both houses.

3. The enacting clause of every bill shall follow its title in these words, namely:

" *Be it enacted by the Senate and House of Representatives in Legislature assembled,* as follows :—"

And if any bill shall contain more than one section, the words "Section 1," shall be inserted immediately after the enacting clause, and before the first part of the bill, and to each subsequent section shall be prefixed the words "Section 2," or otherwise, as the case may be, in conformity with the style of the Revised Statutes. And if any bill shall be found not to conform to the requisitions of this rule, it shall be the duty of the committee on bills in the second reading, or of the secretary of the senate, or of the committee on bills in the third reading or of the clerk of the house, to correct the same, without a proposition to either branch to amend.

4. All indorsements on papers, while on their passage between the two houses, shall be under the signature of the secretary of the senate, or clerk of the house, respectively; but bills and resolves on their final passage shall be signed by the presiding officer of each branch.

5. Every bill that shall have passed both houses to be enacted, and all resolutions, or resolves having the force of law, that shall have finally passed both houses, shall be presented by the secretary of the senate to the governor, for his approval; and the secretary of the senate shall enter on the journal of the senate, the day on which such bills or resolutions are so presented to the governor

6. No business shall be entered on in convention of both branches, except by unanimous consent, other than that which may be agreed on before the convention is formed.

7. When a bill or resolve shall be printed by order of either house, the name of the committee by whom such

bill or resolve was reported, or of the member by whom it was introduced, shall be stated on the printed copies.

8. Whenever the house shall order the printing of any document *for the use of the legislature*, the number of copies so ordered shall be not less than three hundred and fifty, and such order shall be immediately communicated to the senate. If the senate shall desire an additional number of copies, for the use of the senate, its order for that purpose shall be communicated to the house, and the clerk of the house shall without further order, or vote, procure such additional copies to be printed without any change of form, and delivered to the messenger of the senate.

The same course of proceedings shall be observed whenever an order to print for the use of the legislature shall be passed by the senate.

The copies printed for the use of the legislature shall be delivered to the messengers of the two houses, in the proportion of one fourth for the use of the senate, and three fourths for the use of the house, after reserving the usual number of copies for the departments and for binding.

8*

JOINT STANDING COMMITTEES.

On the Judiciary.

Messrs. Allen,
    Bronson, } *Of the Senate*
    Knowlton,

Messrs. Allen of Bangor,
    Levensaler of Thomaston,
    Hayden of Eastport,
    Fox of Berwick, } *Of the House.*
    Getchell of North Anson,
    Frost of Bethel,
    Oak of Garland,

On Education

Messrs Thurston,
    Redington, } *Of the Senate*
    Jackson,

Messrs. Barnes of Portland,
    Hill of Moscow,
    Grant of Litchfield,
    Treat of Frankfort, } *Of the House*
    Edgecomb of Vienna,
    Davis of Stow,
    Chase of Sebec,

On Banks and Banking.

Messrs. Hodgdon,
    Thompson, } *Of the Senate.*
    R. K. J. Porter,

Messrs. Levensaler of Thomaston,
    Lee of Calais,
    Totman of Harpswell,
    Reed of Waldoboro', } *Of the House*
    Palmer of Perry,
    Burnham of Kennebunkport,
    Reed of Roxbury,

On Incorporation of Towns.

Messrs Sargent,
Bursley, } *Of the Senate.*
Monroe,

Messrs. Fox of Berwick,
Soule of Freeport,
Young of Washington,
McFarland of Trenton, } *Of the House*
Look of Addison,
Freeman of Monmouth,
Libby of Sumner,

On Division of Towns.

Messrs. Holden,
Monroe, } *Of the Senate.*
Bursley,

Messrs. Holman of Dixfield,
Eaton of Farmington,
Currier of Sedgwick,
Tripp of Sanford, } *Of the House*
Crosby of Embden,
Treat of Frankfort,
Moore of Lisbon,

On Division of Counties.

Messrs. Pillsbury,
Skillin, } *Of the Senate.*
Barnes,

Messrs. Merry of Edgecomb,
Perkins of Wells,
Ingersoll of Danville,
Hanscom of Crawford, } *Of the House.*
Marston of Mt. Vernon,
Berry of Biddeford,
Webber of York,

On State Lands and State Roads.

Messrs. Hastings,
    Bronson,   } *Of the Senate.*
    Pillsbury,

Messrs. Otis of Hallowell,
    Parker of Golden Ridge,
    Prince of North Yarmouth,
    Brown of Thomaston,   } *Of the House.*
    Norcross of Charleston,
    Smith of St. Albans,
    Moore of Newfield,

On Indian Affairs.

Messrs. Haines,
    Smith,   } *Of the Senate.*
    Barrett,

Messrs. Palmer of Perry,
    Day of Bristol,
    Crane of Eddington,
    Libby of Harrison,   } *Of the House.*
    Skillin of Albion,
    Lary of Acton,
    Taylor of Porter,

On Agriculture.

Messrs. Skillin,
    Lothrop,   } *Of the Senate.*
    R. K. J. Porter,

Messrs. Thomas of Newburg,
    Stuart of Hollis,
    Currier of Cornville,
    Noyes of Jay,   } *Of the House.*
    Hayden of Winslow,
    Trickey of Cape Elizabeth,
    Farrar of Baileyville,

On Fisheries.

Messrs. Partridge,
Godfrey, } Of the Senate.
Barnes,

Messrs. Hall of Warren,
Woods of Gardiner,
Stratton of Hancock,
Bridge of Dresden, } Of the House.
Vinal of Vinalhaven,
Balch of Lubec,
Ruggles of Carmel,

On Manufactures.

Messrs. Bronson,
Barrett, } Of the Senate.
R. Porter,

Messrs. Tucker of Saco,
Brown of Clinton,
Lemont of Brunswick,
Hinks of Bucksport, } Of the House.
Hall of Wiscasset,
Thayer of Oxford,
Morrison of Canaan,

On Rail Roads and Bridges.

Messrs. Smith,
Redington, } Of the Senate.
Bellamy,

Messrs. Paine of Bangor,
Small of Machiasport,
Magoun of Bath,
Pitcher of Northport, } Of the House.
Otis of Hallowell,
White of Windham,
Wildes of Phipsburg,

On Interior Waters.

Messrs. Gore,
       Perry,   } *Of the Senate.*
       Hodgdon,

Messrs. Hill of Webster,
       Russ, of Paris,
       Keene of Augusta,
       Haviland of Waterville,   } *Of the House.*
       Drury of Enfield,
       Holt of Turner,
       Rust of Palermo,

On Accounts.

Messrs. Thompson,
       Knowlton,   } *Of the Senate.*
       Monroe,

Messrs. McLellan of Gorham,
       Adams of Norridgewock,
       Sturdivant of Cumberland,
       Rand of Townsend,   } *Of the House.*
       Gardiner of Patten,
       Gould of Wilton,
       Ridley of Wayne,

On Claims.

Messrs. R. K. J. Porter,
       R. Porter,   } *Of the Senate.*
       Pillsbury,

Messrs. Blake of Camden,
       Gilchrest of St. George,
       Fuller of Hartland,
       Dunham of Madrid,   } *Of the House.*
       Currier of Lyman,
       Milliken of Steuben,
       Bartlett of Hope,

On the Militia.

Messrs. Perry,
Hastings, } *Of the Senate.*
Thurston,

Messrs. Thompson of Unity,
Kingsbery of Kingsbery,
Doe of Parsonsfield,
Frost of Sidney, } *Of the House.*
Marble of Poland,
Cotter of Nobleboro',
Potter of Kingfield,

On Military Pensions.

Messrs. Monroe,
Holden, } *Of the Senate.*
Bellamy,

Messrs. Beedle of Westbrook,
Ayer of Alna,
Cyr of Van Buren Plan.,
Fairfield of Vassalboro', } *Of the House.*
Small of Pownal,
Choate of Whitefield,
Morton of Bridgwater Plan.,

On the Insane Hospital.

Messrs. Barrett,
Thurston, } *Of the Senate.*
Sargent,

Messrs. Reed of Waldoboro',
Moulton of Standish,
Friend of Etna,
Deming of Mt. Desert, } *Of the House.*
Elliot of Bowdoin,
Lamson of Troy,
Tuck of Fayette,

On the State Prison.

Messrs. Knowlton,
　　　　Allen,　　　} Of the Senate.
　　　　Jackson,

Messrs. Magoun of Bath,
　　　　Brown of Thomaston,
　　　　Harriman of Orland,
　　　　Lambert of Dover,　　　} Of the House
　　　　Babbidge of Deer Isle,
　　　　Burnell of Baldwin,
　　　　Pitts of Bloomfield,

On Public Buildings.

Messrs. Bellamy,
　　　　R. Porter,　} Of the Senate.
　　　　Smith,

Messrs. Lemont of Brunswick,
　　　　Howard of Auburn,
　　　　Child of Hartford,
　　　　Holbrook of Starks,　　} Of the House
　　　　Milliken of Buxton,
　　　　Head of Lagrange,
　　　　Rowe of Brewer,

On the Library.

Messrs. Jackson,
　　　　Dunn,　　} Of the Senate.
　　　　Allen,

Messrs. Getchell of North Anson,
　　　　Barnes of Portland,
　　　　Nutting of Casco,
　　　　Paine of Bangor,　　} Of the House
　　　　Briggs of Kirkland,
　　　　Walker of Kennebunk,
　　　　Munger of Livermore,

JOINT SELECT COMMITTEES.

On the Treasurer's Report.

Messrs. Allen,
Hastings,
Hodgdon,
} Of the Senate.

Messrs. Chadwick of Portland,
Hinks of Bucksport,
Lee of Calais,
Stuart of Hollis,
Ingersoll of Danville,
Marble of Poland,
Levensaler of Thomaston,
} Of the House.

To prepare Joint Rules.

Messrs. Perry,
Redington,
Monroe,
} Of the Senate.

Messrs. Barnes of Portland,
Getchell of North Anson,
Levensaler of Thomaston,
Russ of Paris,
Brown of Clinton,
} Of the House

To contract for State Printing and Binding.

Messrs. Perry,
Hastings,
R. K. J. Porter.
} Of the Senate.

Messrs. Russ of Paris,
Keene of Augusta,
Eaton of Farmington,
Hall of Warren,
Rogers of Kittery,
} Of the House.

9

On returns of Votes for Governor.

Messrs. Hodgdon,
  Hastings,
  Bellamy,
  Sargent,
  Haines, } *Of the Senate.*
  Lothrop,
  Thurston,
  Smith,
  Godfrey,

Messrs. Levensaler of Thomaston,
  Stuart of Hollis,
  Fessenden of Portland,
  Hinks of Bucksport,
  Hayden of Eastport,
  Keene of Augusta,
  Getchell of North Anson, } *Of the House*
  Child of Hartford,
  Ruggles of Carmel,
  Thompson of Unity,
  Eaton of Farmington,
  Parker of Golden Ridge,

On reduction of State Valuation in certain towns

Messrs. Bellamy,
  Skillin, }
  Mason,

Messrs. Barnes of Portland,
  Getchell of North Anson,
  . Levensaler of Thomaston,
  Russ of Paris,
  Brown of Clinton,

On the License Laws.

Messrs. Redington,
 Haines,
 Gore,   } *Of the Senate.*
 Mason,
 Barrett,

Messrs Davis of Stow,
 Milliken of Buxton,
 Chadwick of Portland,
 Magoun of Bath,
 Hatch of Penobscot,
 Small of Machiasport,
 Grant of Litchfield, } *Of the House*
 Adams of Norridgewock,
 Gardiner of Patten,
 Bartlett of Hope,
 Gould of Wilton,
 Chase of Sebec,
 Parker of Golden Ridge,

Third Senatorial Apportionment.

Resolve for dividing the state into districts, for the choice of senators.

Resolved, That from and after the passing of this resolve, the state be, and hereby is divided into fourteen districts for the choice of senators, and each district shall be entitled to elect the number of senators herein provided for the term of ten years, in the manner prescribed by the constitution, to wit :—The several towns composing the county of York, except the towns of Parsonsfield, Cornish and Limington, shall form the first district, and be entitled to elect three senators.

The several towns composing the county of Cumberland, except the towns of Standish and Baldwin, shall form the second district, and be entitled to four senators.

The several towns and plantations composing the county of Lincoln, together with the island of Matinicus and islands contiguous thereto, shall form the third district, and be entitled to four senators

*The several towns in the county of Kennebec, with the exception of China, Albion, Clinton, the territory north of Albion, and the Clinton Gore, shall constitute the fourth senatorial district, and be entitled to three senators.

, *The several towns in the county of Waldo, with the the towns and plantations excepted in the fourth district, shall constitute the fifth senatorial district, and be entitled to three senators.

The towns of Bucksport, Orland, Dedham, Penobscot,

[* Vide Resolves of April 2, 1841, and March 16, 1842.]

Bluehill, Castine, Brooksville, Sedgwick, Deer Isle, the plantations of Wetmore Isle, Swan Island, Long Island and the islands west of Long Island, in the county of Hancock, except Matinicus and the islands contiguous thereto, shall form the sixth district, and be entitled to one senator.

The remainder of Hancock county, together with the towns of Steuben, Cherryfield, Annsburg, Beddington, Devereaux, Columbia, Harrington, Addison, Jonesborough, Jonesport, Machias, Northfield, Wesley, and the townships number thirty, thirty-one, twenty-four, twenty-five, eighteen and nineteen, in the middle division, and number twenty-three, in the eastern division, in the county of Washington shall form the seventh district, and be entitled to one senator.

The eighth senatorial district shall consist of the towns of Calais, Cutler, Marion, Dennysville, Eastport, Edmunds, Lubec, Machiasport, East Machias, Pembroke, Perry, Robbinston, Trescott, Whiting and number fourteen and eighteen, in the eastern division, in the county of Washington, and shall be entitled to one senator.

The remainder of the county of Washington, together with the county of Aroostook, shall form the ninth district and be entitled to one senator.

The several towns and plantations in the county of Penobscot shall form the tenth district, and be entitled to three senators.

The several towns and plantations in the county of Piscataquis shall form the eleventh district, and be entitled to one senator.

The several towns and plantations in the county of Somerset shall form the twelfth district, and be entitled to two senators.

The several towns and plantations in the county of Franklin except Carthage, Weld, Berlin, No. two, first range, No. three, first range, No. two and three, second range, and letters D and E, shall form the thirteenth district, and be entitled to one senator.

The remainder of the county of Franklin, together with the several towns and plantations in the county of Oxford, also the towns of Parsonsfield, Cornish, Limington, Baldwin and Standish, shall form the fourteenth district, and be entitled to three senators.

[*Approved April* 2, 1841.]

Fourth Representative Apportionment.

Resolve for apportioning one hundred and fifty-one representatives among the several counties, cities, towns, plantations and classes in the State of Maine, at the fourth apportionment.

Resolved, That the county of York shall choose sixteen representatives, to be apportioned as follows · Saco, one; York, one, Wells, one; Kennebunkport, one; Biddeford, one; Buxton, one; Kittery, one; Parsonsfield, one; South Berwick and Elliot, one; Sanford and Lebanon, one; Waterborough and Lyman, one; Alfred and Kennebunk, one, Limington and Hollis, one; Berwick and North Berwick, one; Shapleigh and Acton, one; Cornish, Limerick and Newfield, one.

That the county of Cumberland shall choose twenty representatives, to be apportioned as follows: city of Portland, three; Westbrook, one; Brunswick, one; Gorham, one; North Yarmouth, one; Freeport, one; Poland, one; Standish, one; Windham, one; Baldwin, Sebago and Naples, one; Casco, Raymond and Otisfield, one; Durham and Pownal, one, Gray and Harpswell, one; Scarborough one for the years eighteen hundred and forty three, eighteen hundred and forty five, eighteen hundred and forty seven, eighteen hundred and forty nine, and eighteen hundred and fifty one, Cape Elizabeth, one for the years eighteen hundred and forty four, eighteen hundred and forty six, eighteen hundred and forty eight, and eighteen hundred and fifty; Auburn, one for the years eighteen hundred and forty three, eighteen hundred and forty five, eighteen hundred and forty six, eighteen hundred and forty nine, and eighteen hundred and fifty one; Minot one for the years eighteen hundred and forty four, eighteen hundred and forty seven, eight.

een hundred and forty eight, and eighteen hundred and fifty; Bridgton and Harrison, one; New Gloucester and Danville, one; Falmouth, one for the years eighteen hundred and forty three, eighteen hundred and forty four, eighteen hundred and forty seven, eighteen hundred and forty nine, and eighteen hundred and fifty one; Cumberland, one for the years eighteen hundred and forty five, eighteen hundred and forty six, eighteen hundred and forty eight, and eighteen hundred and fifty.

That the county of Lincoln shall choose nineteen representatives, to be apportioned as follows: Thomaston, two; Bath, one; Waldoborough, one; Warren and Friendship, one; St. George, Cushing and Muscle Ridge, plantation, one; Union and Washington, one; Whitefield and Patricktown plantation, one; Jefferson and Alna, one; Wiscasset and Woolwich, one, Newcastle and Edgecomb, one; Nobleborough and Bremen, one; Boothbay, Townsend, and Westport, one; Phipsburg, Georgetown and Arrowsic, one; Bristol, Monhegan, Muscongus and Harbor Islands, one; Lewiston and Lisbon, one; Bowdoin and Topsham, one; Richmond, one for the years eighteen hundred and forty three, eighteen hundred and forty five, eighteen hundred and forty seven, eighteen hundred and forty nine, and eighteen hundred and fifty one, Dresden, one for the years eighteen hundred and forty four, eighteen hundred and forty six, eighteen hundred and forty eight, and eighteen hundred and fifty; Webster, one for the years eighteen hundred and forty three, eighteen hundred and forty six, and eighteen hundred and forty nine; Bowdoinham, one for the years eighteen hundred and forty four, eighteen hundred and forty five, eighteen hundred and forty seven, eighteen hundred and forty eight, eighteen hundred and fifty, and eighteen hundred and fifty one.

That the county of Hancock shall choose nine representatives, to be apportioned as follows: Bucksport and Wetmore Isle, one; Penobscot, Castine, Holbrook Island

and Matinicus plantation, one; Brooksville, Sedgwick, Swan's Island plantation, Hog Island plantation, and Long Island plantation, one; Deer Isle, Bear Island, Beach Island, Pickering's Island, Great Sprucehead Island, Little Sprucehead Island, Butter Island, Eagle Island and Hacketash Island, one; Bluehill and Surry, one, Mount Desert, Eden, Cranberry Isles, Mount Desert Rock, and Seaville, one; Orland, Dedham, Otis,

two, twenty eight, thirty two, thirty three, thirty four, thirty five, thirty nine, forty and forty one, one; Ellsworth, Trenton and Waltham, one; Gouldsborough,

seven, and east half of thirty five, one; East Machias, Machiasport, Whiting, Marion, Edmunds, Dennysville and township numbered fourteen, one; Columbia, Harrington and Addison, one; Jonesport, Jonesborough, Machias, townships numbered twenty three, eighteen, nineteen, twenty six, Northfield, Wesley and Crawford, one; Lubec, Trescott and Cutler, one; Pembroke, Perry, Robbinston, Charlotte and Medybemps, one; Baring, Baileyville, Alexander, Princeton, Topsfield and Cooper, together with all the townships and plantations in the county of Washington, not included in any other district, one.

That the county of Kennebec shall choose sixteen representatives, to be apportioned as follows: Augusta, one; Hallowell, one; Gardiner, one; Vassalborough, one; Waterville and Dearborn, one; Winthrop and Mount Vernon, one; Monmouth and Greene, one; Leeds

and Wayne, one; Readfield and Fayette, one; Clinton and Clinton gore, one; China and Albion gore, one Sidney and Rome, one; Pittston, one for the years eighteen hundred and forty three, eighteen hundred and forty four, eighteen hundred and forty five, eighteen hundred and forty seven, eighteen hundred and forty eight, eighteen hundred and forty nine, and eighteen hundred and fifty Vienna, one for the years eighteen hundred and forty six and eighteen hundred and fifty one; Albion, one for the years eighteen hundred and forty four, eighteen hundred and forty six, eighteen hundred and forty eight, and eighteen hundred and fifty; Windsor, one for the years eighteen hundred and forty three, eighteen hundred and forty five, eighteen hundred and forty seven, eighteen hundred and forty nine, and eighteen hundred and fifty one; Litchfield, one for the years eighteen hundred and forty three, eighteen hundred and forty four, eighteen hundred and forty six, eighteen hundred and forty seven, eighteen hundred and forty nine, and eighteen hundred and fifty; Wales, one for the years eighteen hundred and forty five, eighteen hundred and forty eight, and eighteen hundred and fifty one; Belgrade, one for the years eighteen hundred and forty three, eighteen hundred and forty five, eighteen hundred and forty seven, eighteen hundred and forty nine, eighteen hundred and fifty one, Winslow, one for the years eighteen hundred and forty four, eighteen hundred and forty six, eighteen hundred and forty eight, eighteen hundred and fifty.

That the county of Oxford shall choose twelve representatives, to be apportioned as follows. Livermore, one, Turner and Hebron, one; Oxford and Norway, one; Hartford, Canton and Peru, one; Buckfield, Sumner, and township numbered two, one; Paris and Woodstock, one; Dixfield, Mexico and Rumford, one; Bethel, Greenwood and Albany, one; Porter, Hiram and Brownfield, one; Fryeburg, Lovel, Stow and Stoneham, one; Waterford, Sweden and Denmark, one; Andover, Newry,

Gilead, Roxbury, Byron, Fryeburg Academy grant, Batchelder's grant, Riley, Howard's gore, Hamlin's grant, township A, number two, township B, township C, Andover north surplus, townships number five, second range, number five, first range and number four, first range, together with all the remaining territory in Oxford county not included in any other district, one.

That the county of Somerset shall choose ten representatives, to be apportioned as follows: Hartland, Palmyra and Detroit, one; Pittsfield, Canaan and Skowhegan, one; St. Albans, Harmony, Cambridge and Ripley, one; Norridgewock and Madison, one; Athens, Corn-

Smithfield, one; Bingham, Brighton, Moscow, Mayfield, townships number one, third range, number one, fourth range, and number one, fifth range, east of Kennebec river, Holden plantation, township

gether with all the territory in Somerset county not included in any other district, one; Concord, Embden, Lexington, township number one, second range, west of Kennebec river, number one, second range, Pleasant ridge, number one, third range, west of Kennebec river, number one, fourth range, Enchanted stream township, Spencer stream township, number two, second range, number four, fourth range or Flagstaff, number three, third range and Canada road, one; Anson, one for the years eighteen hundred and forty three, eighteen hundred and forty four, eighteen hundred and forty six, eighteen hundred and forty eight, and eighteen hundred and fifty; New Portland, one for the years eighteen hundred and forty five, eighteen hundred and forty seven, eighteen hundred and forty nine, and eighteen hundred and fifty one.

That the county of Penobscot shall choose fourteen

representatives, to be apportioned as follows: Bangor two; Hampden and Carmel, one; Newburg, Dixmon and Plymouth, one; Corinna and Dexter, one; Etna Newport and Stetson, one; Corinth, Charleston and Bradford, one; Exeter and Garland, one; Oldtown, Argyle, Argyle plantation and Lagrange, one; Hermon Levant, Kirkland and Glenburn, one; Orrington and Brewer, one; Orono, Bradley, Eddington and Jarvis gore, one; Burlington, Lowell, Enfield, Passadumkeag Edinburgh, Howland, Matamiscontis, Chester, Maxfield number three, number four, Greenbush and Milford, one Lincoln, Lee, Springfield, west half number six, range second, west half number seven, range third, unincorporated places north of Lincoln, number two Indian purchase, number one Indian purchase, Hopkins' academy grant, Letter A and Patten, together with all the remaining territory in the county of Penobscot not included in any other district, one.

That the county of Waldo shall choose thirteen representatives, to be apportioned as follows: Belfast, one, Camden, one; Frankfort, one; Prospect, one; Appleton, Liberty and Palermo, one; Hope and Searsmont, one; Montville and Freedom, one; Unity, Burnham and Knox, one; Troy, Thorndike and Jackson, one; Belmont, Waldo plantation and Brooks, one; Lincolnville and Northport, one; Monroe and Swanville, one; Islesborough and Vinalhaven, one.

That the county of Piscataquis shall choose four representatives, to be apportioned as follows · Sangerville, Parkman, Wellington and Kingsbery, one; Guilford, Abbot, Greenville, Monson, Blanchard, Eliotsville, Shirley, Wilson, plantation number eight, and township number three, range three, together with the townships north of Greenville and Eliotsville, one; Dover, Foxcroft, Atkinson and Bowerbank, together with the range of townships north of Bowerbank, one; Kilmarnock, Brownville, Barnard, Williamsburg, Milo, Sebec, Milton, township B, in the tenth range, together with all the unsettled townships north of Brownville, Barnard and Kilmarnock, one.

That the county of Franklin shall choose six representatives, to be apportioned as follows: New Sharon, Industry and New Vineyard, one; Farmington and Temple, one; Wilton and Chesterville, one; Jay, Carthage and Weld, one; Avon, Phillips, Berlin, Madrid, townships number three, second range, number two, second range and Letter E, one; Strong, Freeman, Salem, Kingfield, townships numbered three and four, second range, number four, first range, Bigelow township, number one, fourth range, number one, third range, number three, first range, number two, first range, together with all the territory in Franklin county, not included in any other district, one.

That the county of Aroostook shall choose three representatives, to be apportioned as follows: Hodgdon, New Limerick, number five, range three, number five, range four, number five, range five, and all towns, plantations and townships, south of the before mentioned towns and townships in the county, one; Houlton, Belfast Academy grant, Smyrna, number six, range four, number six, range five, and all towns, plantations and townships north to the south line of the following town, and townships, to wit: Masardis, number ten, range four, number ten, range three, Westfield Academy grant, Deerfield Academy grant, and Marshill township, one: all towns, plantations, townships and territory, north of the south line of Masardis, number ten, range four, number ten, range three, Westfield Academy grant, Deerfield Academy grant, and Marshill township, to the north line of the county, one.

[*Approved March* 17, 1842.]

10

CONGRESSIONAL APPORTIONMENT.

EXTRACT from an act entitled " an act providing for the choice of Representatives to Congress."

SEC. 1. The county of York, together with the towns of Hiram, Porter, Brownfield, Denmark, Fryeburg, Lovell, Stow, Stoneham, Sweden, Waterford, Albany, Mason, Gilead, Bethel, Newry, Bachelder's Grant, Riley plantation, Greenwood, Norway, Oxford and Hebron, from Oxford county, shall compose the first district, and be entitled to one representative.

The county of Cumberland shall constitute the second district, and be entitled to one representative.

The counties of Kennebec and Franklin, except the town of Greene, shall compose the third district, and be entitled to one representative.

The county of Lincoln, together with that part of Oxford not annexed to the first congressional district, with the town of Greene from Kennebec county, shall constitute the fourth district, and be entitled to one representative.

The counties of Waldo and Somerset, except Vinalhaven, shall compose the fifth district, and be entitled to one representative.

The counties of Penobscot and Piscataquis, shall compose the sixth district, and be entitled to one representative.

The counties of Hancock, Washington and Aroostook, together with the town of Vinalhaven, in Waldo county, to compose the seventh district, and be entitled to one representative.

[*Approved March 22, 1843.*]

CENSUS OF 1840.

COUNTY OF YORK.

Towns.	Population.	Towns.	Population.
Acton,	1,401	Lyman,	1,478
Alfred,	1,408	Newfield,	1,354
Berwick,	1,698	North Berwick,	1,447
Biddeford,	2,574	Parsonsfield,	2,442
Buxton,	2,687	Saco,	4,408
Cornish,	1,263	Shapleigh,	1,510
Elliot,	1,889	Sanford,	2,233
Hollis,	2,368	South Berwick,	2,314
Kennebunk,	2,323	Waterborough,	1,944
Kennebunkport,	2,770	Wells,	2,978
Kittery,	2,435	York,	3,111
Lebanon,	2,273		
Limerick,	1,509		54,023
Limington,	2,211		

COUNTY OF CUMBERLAND.

Towns.	Population.	Towns.	Population.
Baldwin,	1,134	Otisfield,	1,307
Bridgton,	1,987	Poland,	2,360
Brunswick,	4,259	Portland, city,	15,218
Cumberland,	1,616	Pownal,	1,210
Danville,	1,294	Raymond,	2,032
Durham,	1,836	Scarborough,	2,173
Falmouth,	2,071	Sebago,	707
Freeport,	2,662	Standish,	2,198
Gorham,	3,002	Westbrook,	4,116
Gray,	1,740	Windham,	2,308
Harpswell,	1,448	New Gloucester,	1,946
Harrison,	1,243	Cape Elizabeth,	1,666
Minot,	3,550		
Naples.	758		68,660
North Yarmouth,	2,824		

COUNTY OF LINCOLN.

Towns.	Population.	Towns.	Population.
Alna,	989	Topsham,	1,883
Bath,	5,143	Union,	1,784
Boothbay,	2,631	Waldoborough,	3,661
Bowdoin,	2,073	Webster,	1,133
Bowdoinham,	2,402	Warren,	2,228
Bremen,	837	Washington,	1,600
Bristol,	2,991	Westport,	655
Cushing,	746	Whitefield,	2,142
Dresden,	1,647	Wiscasset,	2,314
Edgecomb,	1,238	Woolwich,	1,416
Friendship,	725	Patricktown plantation,	506
Georgetown,	1,357	Matinicus Island,	177
Jefferson,	2,214	Monhegan Island,	77
Lewiston,	1,801	Matinicus Rock,	10
Lisbon,	1,531	Matinic Island,	19
Newcastle,	1,713	Muscle Ridge Island,	51
Nobleborough,	2,210	Ragged Island,	17
Phipsburg,	1,657	Wooden Ball Island,	9
Richmond,	1,604		
St. George,	2,094		63,512
Thomaston,	6,227		

COUNTY OF HANCOCK

Aurora,	149	Hancock,	760
Amherst,	196	Mariaville,	275
Bluehill,	1,891	Mount Desert,	1,889
Brooksville,	1,246	Orland,	1,418
Bucksport,	3,015	Otis,	88
Castine,	1,188	Penobscot,	1,474
Cranberry Isles,	238	Sedgwick,	1,922
Dedham,	455	Sullivan,	650
Deer Isle,	2,841	Surry,	857
Eastbrook,	155	Waltham,	232
Eden,	1,054	Swan Island,	284
Ellsworth,	2,267	Township No. 33,	34
Franklin,	502	Township No. 21,	37
Gouldsborough,	1,196	Township No. 2,	27
Greenfield,	223	Plantation No. 1,	88

COUNTY OF HANCOCK, (CONTINUED.)

Towns.	Population.	Towns.	Population.
Stmp North No. 1,	23	Black Island,	90
Wetmore Isle,	139	Placentia Island,	32
Seaville,	129	Conway's Island,	8
Plantation No. 7,	61	Calf Island,	18
Plantation No. 10,	19	John's Island,	4
Trenton,	1,061	Pond Island,	11
Bear Island,	11	Harbor Island,	9
Beach Island,	8	Hog Island,	12
Pickering's Island,	14	Conway's Island,	10
Sprucehead Island,	12	Hacketash Island,	18
Little Sprucehead Island,	6	Wooden Ball Island,	7
Butter Island,	8	Matinicus Rock,	10
Eagle Island,	18	Matinicus Island,	182
Harbor Island,	4	Holbrook Island,	8
Marshall's Island,	8		
Duck Island,	6		28,646
Long Island,	114		

COUNTY OF WASHINGTON.

Town	Population	Town	Population
Addison,	1,052	Lubec,	2,307
Alexander,	513	Machias,	1,351
Beddington,	164	Machiasport,	834
Baileyville,	329	Marion,	281
Baring,	376	East Machias,	1,395
Calais,	2,934	Northfield,	232
Columbia,	843	Pembroke,	1,050
Cooper,	657	Perry,	1,008
Cutler,	657	Princeton,	157
Charlotte,	666	Robbinston,	822
Cherryfield,	1,003	Stouben,	884
Crawford,	300	Trescott,	793
Dennysville,	378	Topsfield,	188
Eastport,	2,876	Wesley,	255
Edmonds,	259	Whiting,	460
Harrington,	1,525	Plantation No. 23,	122
Jonesborough,	392	E. half Town'p No. 6, 2d R.	73
Jonesport,	576	Hill's Gore, 4th Range,	30

10*

COUNTY OF WASHINGTON, (CONTINUED.)

Towns.	Population.	Towns.	Population.
No. 9, 2d Range,	12	Township No. 1, 2d Range,	12
Fowler and Ely, 1st Range		Township No. 21, Eastern	
Township No. 1,	13	Division,	26
Township No 9, 4th Range,	49	Annsburg,	23
Danforth half Township, 4th		Devereaux,	30
Range,	45	Township No. 14,	153
Township No. 9, 3d Range,	48	Township No. 18,	35
Township No. 2, 2d Range,	53	Township No. 19,	62
No. 3, 2d Range,	47		
Hinkley Township No. 3, 1st			28,309
Range,	9		

COUNTY OF KENNEBEC

Albion,	1,624	Readfield,	2,037
Augusta,	5,314	Rome,	987
Belgrade,	1,748	Sidney,	2,190
China,	2,675	Vassalborough,	2,951
Clinton,	2,818	Vienna,	891
Dearborn,	168	Waterville,	2,939
Fayette,	1,016	Wayne,	1,201
Greene,	1,406	Windsor,	1,789
Gardiner,	5,044	Winthrop,	1,915
Hallowell,	4,668	Winslow,	1,722
Leeds,	1,736	Clinton Gore,	110
Litchfield,	2,293	Wales,	656
Monmouth,	1,882	Territory North of Albion,	89
Mount Vernon,	1,475		
Pittston,	2,460		55,804

COUNTY OF OXFORD.

Albany,	691	Dixfield,	1,166
Andover,	551	Fryeburg,	1,536
Bethel,	1,994	Greenwood,	836
Brownfield,	1,360	Gilead,	313
Buckfield,	1,629	Hartford,	1,472
Byron,	219	Hebron,	945
Canton,	919	Hiram,	1,232
Denmark,	1,143	Howard's Gore,	131

COUNTY OF OXFORD, (CONTINUED.)

Towns.	Population.	Towns.	Population.
Hamlin's Grant,	80	Turner,	2,479
Lovel,	941	Waterford,	1,381
Livermore,	2,745	Woodstock,	819
Mexico,	447	Township B.,	111
Newry,	463	No. 5, 1st Range,	49
Norway,	1,786	No. 5, 2d Range,	42
Oxford,	1,246	Township C.,	29
Paris,	2,454	Andover North Surplus,	45
Peru,	1,002	Riley Township,	51
Porter,	1,133	Letter A, No. 2,	54
Roxbury,	227	No. 4, 1st Range,	4
Rumford,	1,444	Fryeburg Academy Grant,	153
Stoneham,	313	Number two,	386
Stow,	376	Batchelder's Grant.	3
Sumner,	1,269		
Sweden,	670		38,389

COUNTY OF SOMERSET

Anson,	1,941	Norridgewock,	1,865
Athens,	1,427	Palmyra,	1,500
Bingham,	751	Pittsfield,	951
Bloomfield,	1,093	Ripley,	591
Brighton,	803	Solon,	1,139
Canaan,	1,379	St. Albans,	1,564
Cambridge,	461	Starks,	1,559
Concord,	577	Skowhegan,	1,584
Cornville,	1,140	Smithfield,	789
Chandlerville,	372	No. 1, 2d Range West	
Embden,	993	Kennebec river,	63
Fairfield,	2,198	No. 1, 2d Range, Pleasant	
Hartland,	1,028	Ridge,	167
Harmony,	1,096	No. 1, 3d Range, West	
Lexington,	564	Kennebec River,	85
Madison,	1,701	No. 1, 4th Range,	10
Maxfield,	149	No. 1, 5th Range, Forks	
Mercer,	1,432	Township,	80
Moscow,	562	Enchanted Stream,	5
New Portland,	1,620	Parlin Pond,	9

COUNTY OF SOMERSET, (Continued.)

Towns.	Population.	Towns.	Population.
Jackman's Township,	10	Spencer Stream,	
Holden Plantation, Moose		Long Pond,	1
River,	65	No. 5, 2d Range, Canada	
Canada Road,	6	Road,	1
Canada Line, No. 5, 3d		No. 1, 3d Range, East	
Range,	10	Kennebec River,	16
No. 2, 2d Range,	139	No. 1, 4th Range, East	
No. 3, 3d Range,	106	Kennebec River,	100
Flag Staff Township, No.			
4, 4th Range,	64		33,912

COUNTY OF PENOBSCOT.

Argyle,	527	Lagrange,	386
Bangor, city,	8,634	Lee,	724
Bradford,	1,001	Levant,	1,060
Bradley,	395	Lincoln,	1,121
Brewer,	1,736	Lowell,	255
Burlington,	350	Maxfield,	185
Carmel,	521	Mattamiscontis,	97
Corinna,	1,702	Milford,	474
Corinth,	1,318	Newburg,	963
Charleston,	1,269	Newport,	1,138
Chester,	277	Orono,	1,520
Dexter,	1,464	Orrington,	1,580
Dixmont,	1,498	Oldtown,	2,345
Etna,	745	Passadumkeag,	394
Eddington,	595	Plymouth,	843
Edinburg,	52	Springfield,	546
Enfield,	346	Stetson,	616
Exeter,	2,052	Jarvis' Gore,	185
Garland,	1,065	Township No. 3,	22
Glenburn,	664	Township No. 4,	41
Greenbush,	260	Township, No. 3, Range	
Hampden,	2,665	8th,	29
Hermon,	1,045	Lower Indian Township,	
Howland,	312	West Penobscot River,	32
Kirkland,	351	Indian Township No. 2,	6

COUNTY OF PENOBSCOT, (CONTINUED.)

Towns.	Population.	Towns.	Population.
Hopkins' Academy Grant,	3	W. half of Town'p No. 6,	187
Letter A,	29	Township No. 7,	30
Unincorporated Township,			
North of Lincoln,	147		
			45,705

COUNTY OF WALDO.

Town	Population	Town	Population
Appleton,	891	Monroe,	1,602
Belfast,	4,194	Montville,	2,153
Belmont,	1,578	Northport,	1,207
Brooks,	910	Palermo,	1,594
Burnham,	609	Prospect,	3,492
Camden,	3,005	Searsmont,	1,374
Frankfort,	3,603	Swanville,	919
Freedom,	1,153	Thorndike,	897
Hope,	1,770	Troy,	1,376
Islesborough,	778	Unity,	1,467
Jackson,	652	Vinalhaven,	1,950
Knox,	897	Waldo Plantation,	721
Liberty,	895		
Lincolnville,	2,048		41,535

COUNTY OF PISCATAQUIS.

Town	Population	Town	Population
Abbot,	661	Milton,	469
Atkinson,	704	Milo,	756
Barnard,	153	Parkman,	1,205
Bowerbank,	165	Sangerville,	1,197
Blanchard,	270	Sebec,	1,116
Brownville,	568	Shirley,	190
Dover,	1,597	Wellington,	722
Eliotsville,	60	Wilson,	70
Foxcroft,	926	Williamsburg,	131
Guilford,	892	Township No. 3, 3d Range,	28
Greenville,	128	Plantation No. 8,	31
Kilmarnock,	319	Letter B, 10th Range,	5
Kingsbery,	227		
Monson,	548		13,138

COUNTY OF FRANKLIN

Towns.	Population.	Towns.	Population.
Avon,	827	Weld,	1,04
Berlin,	442	Wilton,	2,19
Carthage,	522	No. 3, 2d Range,	4
Chesterville,	1,098	No. 4, 2d Range,	
Farmington,	2,613	No. 4, 1st Range,	
Freeman,	838	Bigelow Township,	3
Industry,	1,035	Township Letter E.,	7
Jay,	1,750	Township No. 2, 2d Range,	8
Kingfield,	671	Township No.1, 4th Range,	16
Madrid,	368	Township No. 1, 3d Range,	5
New Sharon,	1,829	Township No. 3, 1st Range,	
New Vineyard,	927	Township No. 2, 1st Range,	
Phillips,	1,312	Township No.2, 3d Range,	21
Salem,	561		
Strong,	1,109		20,80
Temple,	955		

COUNTY OF AROOSTOOK.

Amity,	169	Letter A, 1st Range,	17
Belfast Academy Grant,	141	Williams College Grant,	8
Hodgdon,	665	Bridgewater Acad. Grant,	5
Houlton,	1,597	Framingham Acad. Grant.	1
Township No. 5, 3d Range,	9	Westfield Acad. Grant,	
Township A, 2d Range,	6	Letter A, 5th Range,	1
Weston,	249	Benedicta, or No. 2, 5th R.	22
Township No. 2, 2d Range,	43	No 3, 5th Range,	10
Linneus,	311	No. 4, 5th Range,	29
Township No. 11, 1st Range,	66	No. 6, 5th Range,	4
Township No. 1, 4th Range,	69	Nos. 7 and 9, 5th Range,	4
Township No. 2, 3d Range,	14	No. 10, 5th R. or Masardis	14
Township No. 1, 2d Range,	104	No. 11, 5th Range,	4
Township No. 1 3d Range,	24	No. 13, 3d Range,	6
Orient Gore,	68	Letter G, 2d Range,	5
Township No. 9,	50	Letter K, 2d Range,	9
Township No. 3, 2d Range,	20	Plymouth and Eaton Grant,	6
Smyrna,	184	Letters H, and J, 1st and	
New Limerick,	123	2d Ranges,	19

COUNTY OF AROOSTOOK, (CONTINUED.)

Towns.	Population.	Towns.	Population.
Plymouth Grant,	200	Madawaska South of the	
Letter G,	27	St. John river,	1,584
Fort Fairfield, or Letter D,	26	Madawaska North of the	
Number 3, 6th and 7th		St. John river,	1,876
Ranges,	50		
No. 1, 5th Range,	22		9,413

RECAPITULATION.

Counties.	Population.
York,	54,023
Cumberland,	68,660
Lincoln,	63,512
Hancock,	28,646
Washington,	28,309
Kennebec,	55,804
Oxford,	38,539
Somerset,	33,912
Penobscot,	45,705
Waldo,	41,535
Piscataquis,	13,138
Franklin,	20,800
Aroostook,	9,413
Total,	501,796

STATE VALUATION OF 1845.

COUNTY OF YORK.

Towns.	Polls.	Estate.
Acton,	294	173,962
Alfred,	246	184,399
Berwick,	274	199,258
Biddeford,	484	421,117
Buxton,	482	289,740
Cornish,	224	130,765
Eliot,	324	254,048
Hollis,	391	265,597
Kennebunk,	429	581,890
Kennebunkport,	381	400,924
Kittery,	409	242,915
Lebanon,	387	257,996
Limerick,	296	166,080
Limington,	398	265,063
Lyman,	241	159,892
Newfield,	218	156,691
North Berwick,	245	265,838
Parsonsfield,	444	337,517
Saco,	589	1,072,728
Sanford,	381	264,632
Shapleigh,	251	156,352
South Berwick,	402	454,890
Waterborough,	311	188,683
Wells,	475	385,062
York,	579	366,874
	8,874	$7,642,778

COUNTY OF CUMBERLAND.

Towns.	Polls.	Estate
Auburn,		
Baldwin,	339	259,165
Bridgton,	213	125,396
Brunswick,	354	300,200
Cumberland,	840	835,786
Cape Elizabeth,	248	231,426
Casco,	305	152,342
Danville,	163	89,779
Durham,	221	159,336
Falmouth,	335	280,756
Freeport,	369	234,133
Gorham,	508	381,593
Gray,	477	514,348
Harpswell,	290	193,428
Harrison,	281	211,966
Minot,	240	161,529
Naples.	263	228,491
North Yarmouth,	170	85,500
New Gloucester,	532	599,159
Otisfield,	809	287,777
Poland,	188	167,882
Portland,	372	202,500
Pownal,	2,445	4,076,303
Raymond,	221	181,134
Scarborough,	191	103,018
Sebago,	360	308,725
Standish,	150	56,012
Westbrook,	380	292,131
Windham,	738	652,236
	402	304,719
	11,883	$11,627,770

COUNTY OF LINCOLN.

Towns.	Polls.	Estate
Alna,	198	181,895
Arrowsic,	73	44,426
Bath,	736	1,388,175
Boothbay,	395	181,005

COUNTY OF LINCOLN, (CONTINUED.)

Towns.	Polls.	Estate.
Bowdoinham,	349	302,276
Bowdoin,	285	223,629
Bremen,	145	90,273
Bristol,	544	301,266
Cushing,	161	78,902
Dresden,	305	273,080
Edgecomb,	237	124,835
Friendship,	147	69,447
Georgetown,	180	95,433
Jefferson,	381	248,085
Lewiston,	289	272,692
Lisbon,	250	187,282
Newcastle,	291	331,957
Nobleborough,	382	325,060
Phipsburg,	326	213,427
Richmond,	263	212,409
St. George,	370	155,881
Thomaston,	1,226	1,181,229
Topsham,	339	428,931
Union,	345	307,265
Waldoborough,	698	685,557
Webster,	189	162,713
Warren,	431	464,677
Washington,	283	148,828
Westport,	123	66,504
Whitefield,	371	268,936
Wiscasset,	474	474,282
Woolwich,	291	260,733
Patricktown plantation,	97	24,904
Monhegan plantation,	15	3,506
Townsend, •	92	31,242
West Bath,	99	49,129
	11,390	$9,859,871

COUNTY OF HANCOCK.

Towns.	Polls.	Estate.
Aurora,	36	24,016
Amherst,	65	27,549
Bluehill,	392	·274,161
Brooksville,	200	89,526
Bucksport,	636	447,094
Castine,	212	361,878
Cranberry Isles,	55	34,931
Deer Isle,	481	162,699
Dedham,	90	45,853
Ellsworth,	495	366,711
Eden,	208	90,136
Eastbrook,	32	20,373
Franklin,	122	67,865
Gouldsborough,	237	85,864
Greenfield,	53	20,270
Hancock,	145	73,252
Mariaville,	56	27,877
Mount Desert,	328	134,274
Orland,	290	172,465
Otis,	26	14,703
Penobscot,	279	156,640
Seaville,	30	42,214
Sedgwick,	405	179,994
Sullivan,	157	75,690
Surry,	191	108,795
Swan Island,	63	13,147
Trenton,	202	103,659
Waltham,	49	29,744
Wetmore Isle,	37	22,519
	5,572	3,276,902
Wild Lands,		200,400
		$3,477,302

Wild Lands in the County of Hancock.

No. and Range.	Description.	Acres.	Value.
No. 1,	North Division,	23,040	7,000
No. 2,	do	23,040	8,000
No. 3, ·	do.	23,040	16,000
No. 4,	do.	23,040	16,000
	Strip N. of No. 3, N. Divis.,	7,844	2,000
	do. do. 4, do.	7,844	2,000
No. 7,	South Division,	20,475	5,000
No. 8,	do.	9,600	2,400
No. 9,	do.	5,760	2,000
No. 10,	Adjoining Steuben,	23,936	8,300
No. 16,	Middle Division,	23,040	8,000
No. 21,	do.	23,040	8,000
No. 22,	do.	23,040	8,000
No. 28,	do.	23,040	8,000
No. 32,	do.	23,040	8,000
No. 33,	do.	23,040	16,000
No. 34,	do.	23,040	16,000
No. 35,	do.	23,040	16,000
No. 39,	do.	23,040	8,000
No. 40,	do.	23,040	12,300
No. 41,	do.	23,040	16,000
	Butter Island,	240	750
	Eagle Island,	240	1,000
	Spruce-head and Bear Isl ,	172	500
	Beech Island,	96	500
	Hog Island,	75	400
	Bradbury Island,	140	500
	Pond and Western Island,	65	200
	Little Spruce-head Island,	60	200
	Pond Island,	207	1,000
	Calf Island,	256	500
	West Black Island,	150	100
	East Black Island,	300	100
	Placentia Island,	500	200
	Old Harbor Island,	150	300
	Long Island,	500	3,000
	Marshall's Island,	375	500
	Great Duck Island,	100	250
	Pickering's Island,	150	1,000
	Holbrook Island,		400
		424,835	$200,400

COUNTY OF WASHINGTON.

Towns.	Polls.	Estate.
Addison,	200	104,049
Alexander,	103	33,996
Beddington,	34	14,111
Baileyville,	50	23,439
Baring,	64	42,148
Calais,	664	341,312
Centerville,	29	16,012
Columbia,	191	112,888
Cooper,	105	33,390
Cutler,	147	52,552
Charlotte,	108	39,827
Cherryfield,	233	132,045
Crawford,	58	16,800
Dennysville,	69	54,364
East Machias,	233	188,449
Eastport,	511	340,725
Edmunds,	57	38,248
Harrington,	306	115,508
Jonesborough,	97	30,385
Jonesport,	133	34,773
Lubec,	471	161,779
Machias,	256	191,973
Machiasport,	214	80,050
Marion,	37	14,300
Medybemps,	61	15,991
Northfield,	41	16,411
Pembroke,	150	88,333
Perry,	283	85,250
Princeton,	53	18,339
Robbinston,	162	96,372
Steuben,	179	67,328
Trescott,	102	42,515
Topsfield,	46	20,456
Wesley,	52	19,832
Whiting,	88	40,717
Whitneyville,	107	54,850
	5,694	2,778,514
Wild Land,		388,000
		$3,166,514

11*

Wild Lands in the County of Washington.

No and Range	Description.	Acres	Value
No. 14,	East Division,	26,240	5,000
No 18,	do	23,040	4,000
No. 19, .	do.	23,040	4,000
No 21,	do	23,040	8,000
No. 26,	do.	19,000	8,000
No. 27,	do.	17,328	8,000
No. 17,	Middle Division,	23,040	4,000
No. 18,	do.	23,040	4,000
No. 19,	do.	23,040	7,000
No. 24,	do.	23,040	14,000
No. 25,	do.	20,500	11,000
No. 29,	do.	23,040	24,000
No. 30,	do	23,040	21,000
No. 31,	do.	23,040	9,000
No. 36,	do.	23,040	30,000
No. 37,	do.	23,040	16,000
No. 42,	do	23,040	27,000
No. 43,	do	23,040	15,000
No. 5,	North Division,	30,720	10,000
No. 6,	do	30,720	12,000
	Two mile strip N. of No. 5,	7,680	1,500
	do. do. 6,	7,680	1,500
No 1, R 1,	Titcomb's survey,	24,050	9,000
No 3, R 1,	do. do. Hinkley's,	30,770	11,000
No. 1, R, 2,	do. do. Dyer's,	22,990	10,000
No 2, R 2,	do. do. Waite's,	23,040	10,000
No 3, R 2,	do. do. Tallmadge,	23,040	10,000
N ¼ No 1, R 3,		11,850	3,000
S ¼ No 1, R. 3,		11,850	3,000
No 1, R 4,	Vanceboro',	24,000	8,000
W ½ No. 6 R 1,	Lennox,	11,520	4,000
E ½ No 6, R 1,	Vanceboro',	11,520	4,000
N E ¼ No 7, R 2,		7,190	2,000
¼ No 7, R 2,		22,500	7,000
S. ¼ No 9, R. 2,		15,440	6,000
N ¼ No 9, R. 2,		15,440	6,000
No 8, R 3,		23,040	10,000
No. 9, R 3,		23,040	10,000
No. 10, R. 3,		25,811	8,000
No 11, R 3,		8,374	3,000

Wild Lands in the County of Washington—(Contin'd)

No. and Range.	Description.	Acres.	Value.
	Danforth tract,	11,520	4,000
No. 9, R 4,	N. of Bingham Purchase,	23,583	8,000
No. 8, R. 4,	do. do.	23,040	8,000
		876,036	$388,000

COUNTY OF KENNEBEC.

Towns.	Polls.	Estate.
Augusta,	984	1,143,885
Albion,	286	228,475
Belgrade,	311	206,291
China,	501	391,248
Clinton,	251	160,934
Clinton Gore,	25	6,722
Fayette,	205	165,921
Gardiner,	600	878,821
Greene,	208	177,803
Hallowell,	750	851,229
Leeds,	252	219,340
Litchfield,	391	256,133
Monmouth,	432	291,898
Mount Vernon,	275	177,752
Pittston,	446	469,483
Readfield,	311	368,795
Rome,	144	63,493
Sidney,	405	338,603
Sebasticook,	175	103,990
Vassalborough,	491	503,498
Vienna,	150	95,951
Waterville,	571	677,800
Wales,	111	99,654
Wayne,	165	149,549
Windsor,	274	196,348
Winthrop,	396	355,150

COUNTY OF KENNEBEC, (CONTINUED.)

Towns.	Polls.	Estate.
Winslow,	296	221,96
East Livermore,	158	116,92
	9,563	8,912,66
Wind Land,		5,00
		$8,917,66

Wild Land.

Territory North of Albion,	$5,00

COUNTY OF OXFORD.

	Polls.	Estate.
Albany,	142	70,94
Andover,	139	61,49
Bethel,	357	205,55
Buckfield,	286	190,60
Brownfield,	244	125,25
Byron,	56	14,45
Canton,	166	101,75
Denmark,	208	110,12
Dixfield,	186	120,93
Fryeburg,	274	207,93
Gilead,	65	29,44
Greenwood,	154	41,95
Hartford,	255	166,87
Hebron,	147	86,97
Hiram,	216	103,60
Hanover,	48	29,36
Lovel,	210	118,90
Livermore,	282	208,45
Mexico,	94	28,66
Mason,	28	14,10
Newry,	92	28,10
Norway,	333	216,35
Oxford,	174	137,00
Porter,	238	99,95
Paris,	393	306,67
Peru,	185	72,54
Rumford,	258	172,49

COUNTY OF OXFORD, (CONTINUED)

Towns.	Polls.	Estate.
Roxbury,	39	13,251
Sumner,	245	156,213
Sweden,	146	83,578
Stow,	80	27 888
Stoneham,	62	12,380
Turner,	458	305,995
Woodstock,	117	53,314
Waterford,	284	200,209
Hamlin's Grant,	13	2,379
Franklin plantation,	57	3,948
Milton plantation,	30	7,080
	6,756	3,935,536
Wild Lands,		86,250
		$4,021,786

Wild Lands in the County of Oxford.

No. and Range.	Description.	Acres.	Value
	Andover North Surplus,	15,960	
No. 2,	South of Rumford,	26,165	2,500
A, No. 1,		26,880	6,250
B,		25,600	10,000
A, No. 2,		28,507	6,250
C,		21,074	6,250
C,	Surplus,	12,206	6,250
No. 4, R. 1,	West of Bingham Purchase,	24,448	6,250
No. 5, R 1,		31,780	6,250
No. 4, R. 2,		23,040	6,250
No. 5, R 2,		20,904	6,250
No. 4, R. 3,		21,000	3,750
No. 5, R. 3,		22,717	4,375
No. 4, R. 4,		23,040	4,375
No 5, R. 4,		24,436	4,375
S. ½ No. 5, R. 5,		10,404	1,875
N ½ No 5, R. 5,		5,202	1,250
		362,363	$86,250

COUNTY OF SOMERSET.

Towns.	Polls.	Estate.
Anson,	145	86,251
Athens,	222	189,736
Brighton,	123	45,865
Bloomfield,	194	180,814
Bingham,	129	54,505
Cornville,	211	160,645
Canaan,	219	132,075
Concord,	96	27,754
Cambridge,	92	26,150
Detroit,	81	29,896
Embden,	179	105,355
Fairfield,	353	301,690
Hartland,	210	68,255
Harmony,	194	107,339
Lexington,	97	33,122
Mercer,	182	131,608
Madison,	306	230,423
Moscow,	124	44,173
Mayfield,	30	13,508
New Portland,	265	188,311
Norridgewock,	386	306,776
North Anson,	188	163,349
Palmyra,	312	123,511
Pittsfield,	218	77,993
Ripley,	132	44,615
Starks,	242	134,538
Skowhegan,	285	196,403
Solon,	247	128,126
Smithfield,	141	51,091
St. Albans,	334	134,143
	5,917	3,520,488
Wild Lands,		405,115
		$3,925,603

Wild Lands in the County of Somerset.

No. and Range.	Description.	Acres.	Value.
No 1, R. 2,	Bing Pur. W of Ken. riv,	13,116	3,090
No. 2, R. 2,	do. do. do.	23,040	6,180
No. 1, R. 3,	do do. do.	8,883	2,060
No. 2, R. 3,	do. do. do.	24,162	10,300
No 3, R. 3,	do do. do.	24,792	8,240
No. 4, R. 3,	do do. do N ½	11,144	5,050
No. 1, R. 4,	do. do do	17,800	5,050
No. 2, R. 4,	do. do do	25,200	10,300
No. 3, R. 4,	do do do	24,040	9,270
No. 4, R. 4,	do. do do	21,143	10,300
No. 1, R. 5,	do. do do	29,950	10,300
No. 2, R. 5,	do. do. do	22,320	12,360
No. 3, R. 5,	do. do do	23,980	8,240
No. 4, R. 5,	do. do. do.	23,915	8,240
No. 1, R. 6,	do. do. do	24,175	14,420
No. 2, R. 6,	do. Crocker's pt E pt	13,040	6,180
No. 2, R. 6,	do. W.K Riv., W. pt	10,000	2,060
No. 3, R. 6,	do. do do.	23,040	6,180
No. 4, R. 6,	do do. do	23,040	8,240
No. 5, R. 6,	do. do do	23,040	8,240
No. 1, R. 7,	do. do. do.	17,600	8,240
No. 2, R. 7,	do. do. do.	22,9-5	9,270
No. 3, R. 7,	do do. do	14,600	6,180
No. 4, R. 7,	do do do	15,144	7,210
No. 5, R. 7,	do. do. do	15,744	8,240
No. 6, R. 7,	do. do. do.	16,350	4,120
No. 1, R. 3,	do. E. Ken. River,	29,541	7,210
No. 2, R. 3,	do. do.	23,040	14,240
No. 1, R. 4,	do. do.	23,040	14,240
No. 2, R. 4,	do. do.	24,250	12,360
No. 1, R. 5,	do. do.	12,240	4,120
No. 2, R. 5,	do. do.	23,040	8,240
No. 1, R. 6,	do. do.	10,750	5,150
No. 1, R. 1,	S pt , N. of Bing Pur.	11,520	7,210
No. 1, R. 1,	N pt N of B.P , strip north,	4,469	2,060
No. 2, R. 1,	N.B P.,S pt Sandwich acad	11,520	6,180
No. 2, R. 1,	" N pt ,sip N the above,	2,066	1,030
No. 3, R. 1,	" Long Pond,	20,065	10,300
No. 4, R. 1,	" Moose River,	23,040	7,210
No. 5, R. 1,	"	23,040	7,210

Wild Lands in the County of Somerset—(Continued.)

No. and Range.	Description.	Acres.	Value.
No. 1, R. 2,	N. B. P , Tomhegan,	18,224	10,300
No. 2, R. 2,	" Brassua,	21,960	10,300
No. 3, R. 2,	" Thorndike,	23,040	12,360
No. 4, R 2,	" pt. of, granted sold's,	17,000	7,210
No. 5, R 2,	" Dennis,	23,040	8,240
No. 1, R 3,	" W. Middlesex,	23,040	8,240
No. 2, R. 3,	" pt. of, granted sold's,	17,000	6,180
No. 5, R. 3,	" Sandy Bay,	23,040	4,120
No. 1, R. 4,	" Plymouth,	23,040	8,240
No. 2, R. 4,	" ½ of, Pittston,	7,680	5,150
No. 2, R. 4,	" ¾ of,	15,369	8,240
No. 3, R. 3,	" ¼ of East half,	5,480	3,090
No. 3, R. 4,	" ½ of,	11,040	6,180
	Seboomook,	23,040	13,055
		1,012,789	$405,115

COUNTY OF PENOBSCOT.

Towns.	Polls.	Estate.
Alton,	33	9,782
Argyle,	73	19,006
Bangor,	1,549	2,016,914
Bradford,	220	59,342
Bradley,	110	57,338
Brewer,	382	257,560
Burlington,	73	14,596
Carmel,	165	71,546
Carroll,	50	13,500
Corinna,	280	112,819
Corinth,	266	137,357
Charleston,	269	104,410
Chester,	45	11,698
Dexter,	312	174,058
Dixmont,	249	142,528
Eddington,	135	75,545

COUNTY OF PENOBSCOT, (Continued.)

Towns.	Polls.	Estate.
Edinburg,	14	10,147
Enfield,	66	19,137
Etna,	144	33,700
Exeter,	366	169,833
Glenburn,	155	60,124
Garland,	221	100,324
Greenbush,	80	16,322
Hampden,	450	294,967
Hermon,	183	75,525
Howland,	42	22,067
Kirkland,	77	26,422
Lagrange,	73	27,055
Lee,	156	37,738
Levant,	259	100,010
Lincoln,	249	86,901
Lowell,	74	15,988
Mattamiscontis,	9	4,523
Maxfield,	34	5,340
Milford,	104	67,696
Newburg,	170	81,614
Newport,	282	149,568
Orono,	379	176,346
Orrington,	345	188,682
Oldtown,	480	195,705
Passadumkeag,	53	16,838
Plymouth,	152	56,126
Patten,	91	24,319
Springfield,	96	22,209
Stetson,	129	57,220
	9,144	5,421,045
Wild Lands,		330,525
		$5,751,570

12

Wild Lands in the County of Penobscot.

No. and Range.	Description.	Acres.	Value
No 3, R. 1,	North of Bingham Purch ,	26,010	11,250
No 4, R. 1,	do. do. do.	38,424	9,000
No. 5, R. 1,	do. Amherst Acad.,	11,520	5,625
No 6, R 3,	do. Bingham Purch.,	23,040	10,125
No. 7, R. 3,	do. do. do.	23,040	5,625
S. W¼ No 6,R.4,	do. do. do.	5,760	4,500
½ No. 6, R. 4,	do. do. do.	17,280	9,000
No. 7, R 4,	do. do. do.	23,040	12,375
No 4,	River Township,	23,040	45,000
No 2, R 8,	North of Waldo Patent,	23,040	9,000
E ½ No. 3, R. 8,	do. do. do.	11,520	2,250
No. 2, R. 9,	do. do do	23,040	11,250
No. 3, R. 9,	do. do do	23,040	9,000
S. ½ A, R 6,	W. from E. line of State,	12,000	2,700
N. ½ A, R. 6,	do. do. do.	12,000	2,700
S. ½ No. 1, R. 6,	do. do. do.	11,520	2,250
N. ½ No. 1, R. 6,	do. do. do.	11,520	2,250
No. 2, R. 6,	do. do. do.	28,040	7,875
S. ½ No. 3, R 6,	do. do. do	11,520	4,500
Pt.N ½ No 3,R 6	do. do. do.	9,520	4,500
A, R. 7,	do. do do.	24,000	6,750
No. 1, R. 7,	do. do. do	23,040	16,875
No. 2, R. 7,	do. do do.	23,040	4,500
No. 3, R. 7,	do. do. do.	23,040	13,500
No. 6, R. 7,	do. do. do.	23,040	11,250
No. 7, R. 7,	do. do. do.	23,040	11,250
No. 1, R 8,	do. do. do.	11,520	9,000
S. ½ No. 2, R. 8,	do. do. do.	11,520	11,250
N ½ No. 2, R. 8,	do. do. do.	11,520	5,625
E. ½ No. 3, R. 8,	do. do. do.	11,520	5,625
No. 4, R. 8,	do. do. do.	23,040	11,250
No 5, R. 8,	do. do. do.	23,040	11,250
E. ½ No. 6, R. 8,	do. do. do.	11,520	6,750
Part No. 2,	Indian Purchase,	17,040	6,750
No. 3,	do. do.	23,040	13,500
No. 4,	do. do.	15,040	2,250
Z, N. No. 2,	do. do.	2,100	2,250
R. 8,	Hopkins Academy Grant,	11,520	5,625
	Jarvis' Gore,	15,050	4,500
		689,584	$330,595

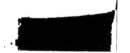

COUNTY OF WALDO.

Towns.	Polls.	Estate.
Appleton,	311	150,000
Belfast,	755	664,474
Belmont,	206	108,000
Brooks,	172	91,000
Burnham,	112	47,000
Camden,	574	367,450
Frankfort,	633	447,000
Freedom,	188	127,200
Hope,	212	122,000
Islesborough,	171	71,000
Jackson,	135	95,000
Knox,	201	102,000
Liberty,	154	74,000
Lincolnville,	326	200,000
Monroe,	287	141,000
Montville,	295	220,000
Northport,	231	107,000
Palermo,	221	138,000
Prospect,	410	260,207
Searsmont,	318	154,000
Searsport,	388	293,648
Swanville,	178	83,000
Thorndike,	172	123,000
Troy,	242	138,000
Unity,	283	190,000
Vinalhaven,	324	124,000
Waldo,	160	65,000
	7,658	$4,702,959

COUNTY OF FRANKLIN.

Avon,	118	53,280
Carthage,	89	30,687
Chesterville,	197	121,158
Farmington,	457	468,386
Freeman,	147	71,062
Industry,	195	137,623
Jay,	281	201,596

COUNTY OF FRANKLIN, (CONTINUED.)

Towns.	Polls.	Estate.
Kingfield,	125	52,798
Madrid,	76	18,242
New Sharon,	327	257,333
New Vineyard,	108	55,624
Phillips,	285	159,897
Salem,	95	31,709
Strong,	197	138,590
Temple,	129	69,726
Weld,	188	83,479
Wilton,	362	272,231
	3,576	2,223,351
Wild Lands,		138,800
		$2,362,151

Wild Lands in the County of Franklin.

No. and Range.	Description.			Acres.	Value
E. part No. 6,	Near Phillips,			10,000	2,400
W. part No. 6,	Walker,			10,000	2,400
N.pt. No 4, R.1,	Bingham Purchase,			18,300	3,200
No 3, R. 2,	do.	do.		26,792	4,800
No 4, R. 2,	do.	do		21,288	4,000
S. ½ No. 4, R. 3,	do	do.		10,644	2,000
D,				20,500	4,800
F,				20,600	5,600
No. 2, R. 1,	West of Bingham Purchase,			22,080	4,800
No 3, R. 1,	do	do.	do.	29,440	6,400
No. 1, R. 2,	do.	do.	do.	23,040	4,000
No. 2, R. 2,	do.	do.	do	23,040	9,600
No 3, R. 2,	do.	do.	do.	30,720	12,000
N. ½ No. 1, R. 3,	do	do	do.	11,520	3,200
S. ½ No. 1, R. 3,	do.	do.	do.	11,520	1,600
No. 2, R 3,	do.	do.	do.	21,000	6,400
No. 3, R. 3,	do	do.	do.	21,000	4,800
N. ½ No. 1, R. 4,	do	do.	do.	11,520	6,400
S. ½ No. 1, R. 4,	do.	do.	do.	11,520	6,400

Wild Lands in the County of Franklin—(Continued.)

No. and Range.	Description.			Acres.	Value.
N. ½ No 2, R. 4,	West of Bingham Purchase,			11,520	5,600
No. 1, R. 5,	do.	do	do.	22,080	11,200
No. 2, R 5,	do.	do	do.	23,040	8,000
S. ½ No 1, R. 6,	do	do	do.	14,694	4,000
W. ½ No. 2, R.7,	do.	do.	do.	10,100	4,000
Gore N. of Nos 2 & 3, R. 6,	Dead River,			20,000	11,200
				455,966	$138,800

COUNTY OF PISCATAQUIS.

Towns.	Polls.	Estate.
Abbot,	138	46,844
Atkinson,	177	68,475
Barnard,	30	12,952
Bowerbank,	32	14,598
Blanchard,	49	12,846
Brownville,	132	48,466
Dover,	275	101,321
Eliotsville,	18	8,944
Foxcroft,	166	68,340
Greenville,	37	17,480
Guilford,	177	72,172
Kilmarnock,	67	22,237
Kingsbery,	43	20,496
Milo,	156	42,245
Monson,	120	54,111
Orneville,	80	21,470
Parkman,	251	88,956
Sangerville,	245	108,952
Sebec,	208	85,455
Shirley,	43	13,890
Wellington,	121	29,825
Williamsburg,	26	11,787

12*

COUNTY OF PISCATAQUIS, (CONTINUED.)

Towns.	Polls.	Estate.
Wilson,	27	10,097
	2,618	981,961
Wild Land,		344,952
		$1,326,913

Wild Lands in the County of Piscataquis.

No. and Range.	Description.	Acres.	Value.
No 4, R. 8,	North of Waldo Patent,	23,040	2,000
No. 8, R 8,	do do	23,040	6,000
No. 5, R. 9,	do do	23,040	4,000
N ½ No 6, R 9	do. do	11,520	2,000
S ½ No 6, R 9,	do do	11,520	2,000
No 3, R. 5,	Bingham Pur E. K R,	23,040	4,500
No. 2, R 6,	do do.	22,640	9,000
No 1, R. 9,	W. from E line of State,	22,104	5,000
No. 2, R. 9,	do do	23,040	7,000
No. 4, R 9,	do do	22,040	5,500
No. 6, R 9,	do do.	23,063	5,500
E. ½ A, R 10,	do. do	11,520	11,000
W ½ A, R 10,	do. do	11,520	9,000
No 1, R, 10,	do. do.	23,040	5,000
No 2, R 10,	do do.	23,040	9,000
No 3, R 10,	do do	23,040	4,500
E. ½ No 5, R.10,	do do	11,040	3,000
W ½ No 5, R 10,	do do	5,732	3,000
No 6, R 10,	do. do.	23,729	10,000
S E ½ No 7, R 10	do. do.	15,785	7,000
A, R 11,	do. do.	23,040	6,000
B, R 11,	do do.	28,736	7,000
No 1, R 11,	do. do	23,040	12,000
S. ½ A, R.12,	do do.	13,638	9,000
N. ½ A, R. 12,	do do.	11,520	11,000
S ½ No 1, R. 12,	do do.	7,680	6,000
N ½ No 1, R 12,	do. do.	15,360	7,000
No 2, R 12,	do do.	23,040	10,000

Wild Lands in the County of Piscataquis—(Continued)

No. and Range.	Description.		Acres.	Value.
E. ½ No.3, R. 12,	W. from E line of State,		11,520	5,000
W.½ No.3, R.12,	do.	do.	11,520	5,000
½ No. 4, R. 12,	do.	do.	11,377	4,000
A, No. 2, R. 13 and 14,	do.	do.	17,925	7,000
A, R. 13,	do.	do.	23,040	11,000
½ No 1, R 13,	do.	do.	15,360	7,000
No 3, R 13,	do.	do.	19,825	15,000
S.pt No.4, R 13,	do.	do.	10,126	7,000
A, R. 14,	do.	do.	19,164	11,000
No. 1, R. 14,	do.	do.	23,941	9,000
E. ½ No 3, R 14 and 15,	do.	do.	19,787	11,000
W ½ No. 3, R 14 and 15,	do.	do.	23,236	9,000
S. E ¼ No. 4, R 14,	do.	do.	6.462	4,000
No 6, R. 10,	do.	do.	23,040	9,216
No. 6, R. 11,	do.	do.	23,040	9,216
No. 6, R 15,	do.	do.	23,040	9,216
N W ¼ No. 5, R. 15,	do	do	5,760	2,304
	Middlesex Canal,		23,040	11,000
	Day's Academy Grant,		11,520	5,000
	Sugar Island,		4,950	5,000
	Deer Island,		2,000	7,000
			854,240	$344,952

COUNTY OF AROOSTOOK.

Towns.	Polls.	Estate
Amity,	34	12,141
Hodgdon,	116	47,377
Houlton,	257	113,517
Linneus,	95	15,901
New Limerick,	29	7,493

COUNTY OF AROOSTOOK, (Continued)

Towns.	Polls.	Estate
Masardis,	25	8,500
Smyrna,	52	9,842
Weston,	51	14,950
	659	229,230
Wild Lands.		207,237
		$436,467

Wild Lands in the County of Aroostook.

No. and Range	Description.	Acres.	Value
No. 1, R, 1,	Gore East of Weston,	6,132	2,000
No. 9,	Greenwood's Survey,	23,040	7,680
No. 1, R. 2,	Fowler and others,	27,576	9,192
No. 2, R. 2,	Pickering,	10,785	3,595
No. 3, R. 2,	Morrill & Pickering,	22,000	7,333
R. 1,	Williams College Grant,	11,520	3,840
R. 1,	Framingham Acad. Grant,	11,520	3,456
A, R. 1,	Monticello,	23,040	7,680
R. 1,	Portland Academy Grant,	11,520	3,456
R. 1,	Bridgewater Academy Gt,	11,520	3,840
R. 1,	Mars Hill Township,	23,040	6,912
R. 1,	Town of Plymouth Grant,	23,040	7,680
R 2,	Belfast Academy Grant,	11,520	3,810
B, R. 2,	W from E line of State,	23,040	7,680
D, R. 2,	do do. do	22,477	7,680
R. 2,	Deerfield Academy Grant,	11,520	3,456
R. 2,	Westfield Academy Grant	11,520	2,771
R. 2,	General Eaton Grant,	10,000	3,000
E, R 2,	W E L. S.,	12,622	3,786
Part No.1, R. 3,	do Nichols Acad.,	7,680	2,393
No. 1, R. 3,	do	23,040	7,680
S. ½ No. 2, R. 3,	do.	11,520	3,840
N. ½ No. 2, R. 3,	do.	11,520	3,840
No. 3, R. 3,	do.	23,040	6,912
¾ S. part No. 4, R. 3,	do.	12,480	3,744

Wild Lands in the County of Aroostook—(Continued.)

No. and Range.	Description.		Acres.	Value.
½ N. part No. 4, R. 3,	W. E. L. S ,		9,600	2,880
No. 7, R. 3,	do.		23,040	4,500
No. 8, R. 3,	do		23,040	4,500
S pt. No.1, R.4,	do		16,520	4,956
No. 1, R. 4,	do.	N. Yarmouth Acd	11,520	4,000
N pt. No.1, R.4,	do.		11,520	4,000
No 2, R. 4,	do		23,040	6,912
No 5, R. 4,	do		23,040	5,000
E ½ No. 6, R 4,	do.		11,520	3,456
N. W. ¼ No 6, R 4,	do.		5,260	'
S. pt. A, R. 5,	do.	Camberlain,	7,680	
N. pt. A, R. 5,	do.	Fisk & Bridge,	11,520	'
S ½ No 1, R. 5,	do.	do.	11,520	
N. ½ No. 1, R. 5,	do.	Harvey Reed,	11,520	1
W ½ No.2, R. 5,	do.	Benedicta,	11,520	3,728
No 3, R. 5,	do.		22,188	6,656
No. 5, R. 5,	do.		23,040	'
No. 7, R. 5,	do.		23,040	5,000
Pt No. 6, R. 5,	do.		13,452	8,000
			690,7⁹₂	$207,237

AGGREGATE

Counties.	Polls	Estates
York,	8,874	7,642,778
Cumberland,	11,883	11,627,770
Lincoln,	11,390	9,859,871
Hancock,	5,572	3,477,302
Washington,	5,694	3,166,514
Kennebec,	9,563	8,917,662
Oxford,	6,756	4,021,786
Somerset,	5,917	3,925,603
Penobscot,	9,094	5,751,570
Waldo,	7,658	4,702,959
Piscataquis,	2,618	1,326,913
Franklin,	3,376	2,362,151
Aroostook,	659	436,467
	89,054	$67,219,356

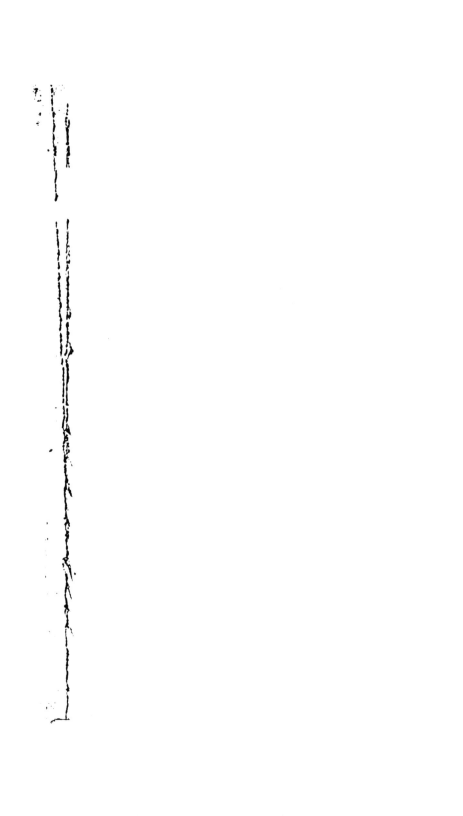

RULES AND ORDERS

OF THE

SENATE OF MAINE,

FOR THE POLITICAL YEAR

1846.

AUGUSTA:
WILLIAM T. JOHNSON, PRINTER.

1846.

STATE OF MAINE.

IN SENATE, May 15, 1846.

ORDERED, That two hundred copies of the Rules and Orders, with the documents ordered by the House of Representatives to accompany its Rules be printed for the use of the Senate

DANIEL T. PIKE, *Secretary.*

RULES AND ORDERS.

1. The president shall take the chair at the time to which the senate stands adjourned; but in case the president shall be absent, the secretary shall preside until a president pro tem. be chosen.

2. When the senate are called together in the morning, on the appearance of a quorum, the journal of the preceding day shall be read.

3. The president shall have the right to name a senator to perform the duties of the chair during his absence; but such substitution shall not extend beyond an adjournment.

4. The president may read sitting, but he shall rise to put a question. He shall declare all votes; but if

6

any senator doubt the vote, all those voting in the affirmative, when called upon by the president, shall rise and stand until they are counted, and also all those in the negative in like manner, to make the vote certain.

5. The president shall consider a motion to adjourn as always first in order, and it shall be decided without debate.

6. A motion when seconded, and not before, shall be received and considered. It shall be reduced to writing and laid on the table, if desired by the president, or any senator, and shall then be deemed to be in possession of the senate, to be disposed of by the senate; but the mover may withdraw it, at any time before a decision or an amendment be made to it.

7. When the president speaks, he shall address the board. When a senator speaks, he shall stand in his place and address the president, and when done speaking shall sit down.

8. The president, when he speaks to any member

of the board, and the members when referring to each other in debate, shall use in their address the title of *senator*, and by way of distinction name the county in which he resides.

9. The president shall name the person to speak, when more than one rise for that purpose at the same time; but in all cases, the senator who shall rise first and address the chair, shall speak first.

10. No member shall speak more than once to the same question, to the prevention of any other who desires to speak and has not spoken, nor more than twice without first obtaining leave of the board, if any senator objects, unless he be the mover in the matter under debate, and then not more than three times without leave as aforesaid.

11. No senator shall interrupt another while speaking, except to call to order, or to correct a mistake in point of fact.

12. No new motion or proposition shall be received

under color of amendment, as a substitute for the motion, or question under debate.

13. When a question is under debate, no motion shall be received, but to adjourn, to lie on the table, to commit, to amend, to postpone to a day certain, or to postpone indefinitely ; which several motions shall have precedence in the order they stand arranged.

14. An amendment proposed may be amended before it is adopted, but not afterwards, except the vote adopting it be first reconsidered.

15. When a motion has been made and carried, it shall be in order for any member of the majority to move for a reconsideration thereof, on the same or succeeding day.

16. Questions of order may be debated, like other questions, and shall be decided by the president, subject to an appeal to the board on motion thereof regularly made and seconded.

17. A question containing two or more propositions

per shall be once read at the table,
r shall be obliged to vote on it, but
g of a paper is called for, that has
to the senate, if any senator object,
I be determined by the senate.

and resolves in the second reading
ed to the committee on bills in the
o be by them examined, corrected,
o the senate.

second reading of a bill or resolve,
all be read through, and before the
pon its passage, it shall be read and
ragraphs, at the request of any mem-
and no bill or resolve shall have a

second reading, unless a time, not less than one hour
be assigned therefor.

22. No bill or resolve shall be passed to be engrossed, without being twice read; and all bills and
resolves, immediately after the same shall have been
passed to be engrossed, shall be committed to the
committee on engrossed bills, whose duty shall be to
examine the same, and to see that the same have been
truly engrossed; and before any bill shall pass to be
enacted, it shall be reported by the committee for the
examination of engrossed bills, to be truly and correctly engrossed, and the title thereof read by the
president.

23. No resolve of any kind, or order making any
grant of money, lands or other public property, shall
be finally passed without being twice read; nor shall
such resolve or order have a second reading, unless a
time, not less than one hour, be assigned therefor; and
before any such resolve or order shall finally pass, it
shall be reported by the committee for the examination
of engrossed bills, to be truly copied from the original
and the title thereof read by the president.

24. Nine o'clock on each day, Mondays and Saturdays excepted, shall be assigned for the consideration of public acts, and business of a general character, which shall have precedence of all business of a private or special nature.

25. When the yeas and nays are taken, the names of the senators shall be called alphabetically.

26. After a question is put to vote, no senator shall speak on it, but every senator who may be at the senate board, shall vote, unless excused by the board, or excluded by interest.

27. The unfinished business, in which the senate was engaged at the time of the last adjournment, shall have preference in the orders of the day.

28. No engrossed bill or resolve shall be sent to the house, without notice thereof being given to the senate by the president.

29. Every member who shall present a petition, shall place his name thereon, and briefly state its subject.

30. All confidential communications made by th
governor to the senate, shall be by the member
thereof kept inviolably secret until the senate sha
by their resolution take off the injunction of secrecy.

31. No rule shall be dispensed with, except by th
consent of two thirds of the members present.

32. Any member of the senate may exchange seat
on consulting the president and obtaining his permis
sion.

33. No member shall absent himself from the senate, without leave, unless there be a quorum left pres
ent at the board.

34. All committees shall be nominated by th
president, (except when it may be determined tha
the election shall be by ballot,) and appointed by th
board.

35. The following standing committees shall b
appointed at the commencement of the session, viz '—

STANDING COMMITTEES OF THE SENATE.

On bills in the second reading,

On engrossed bills,

To consist of twelve members each, any one of the first and any two of the second shall constitute a quorum.

36. No member of the senate shall act as counsel for any party, before any committee of the legislature.

37. All messages from the senate to the house and to the governor, or governor and council, shall be carried by the secretary, and all papers shall be transmitted to the governor and council, and to the house by the secretary or his assistant.

38. No bill or resolve, the subject matter of which has been acted upon by a committee, shall be laid upon the table by leave.

MEMORANDA.

MEMORANDA.

1. Orders, motions in writing, and reports of committees, should never be presented on less than a half sheet of paper.

2. When a *report* of a committee is made to the senate, it should be accompanied by the *order*, appointing said committee.

3. Petitions, memorials and remonstrances from towns, in their *corporate capacity*, should be indorsed thus, "*Petition of the town of* ——," [stating concisely the subject matter thereof.]

4. Petitions, memorials and remonstrances from individuals, should be indorsed thus, "*Petition of* ——, *and others of the town of* ——," [stating concisely the subject matter thereof.]

5. Petitions, memorials and remonstrances from corporations, should be indorsed thus, "*Petition of* ——," [naming the corporation, and stating concisely the subject matter thereof.]

6. The name of the member presenting petitions, memorials and remonstrances, should be indorsed on the back thereof, *near the bottom.*

7. The member presenting an *order* should put his name thereto, on the inside, at the bottom of the page, on the left.

8. Petitions, memorials and remonstrances on which *leave to withdraw* was ordered by a former legislature, cannot be recalled from the files with a view of being again referred. The *original*, however, may be taken from the files, and the subject presented *de novo.*

9 Bills and resolves *refused a passage, rejected or postponed indefinitely* by a former legislature, cannot be called from the files with a view of being considered by the present legislature.

10. The heading or caption of BILLS, should be as follows:

STATE OF MAINE.

In the year of our Lord one thousand eight hundred and forty-six.

An act ——

Be it enacted by the senate and house of representatives in legislature assembled, as follows :—

11. The caption of RESOLVES, as follows.

STATE OF MAINE.

[*omitting* the year required in bills.]

Resolve ——

7

CIVIL GOVERNMENT

OF THE

STATE OF MAINE,

FOR THE POLITICAL YEAR

1846.

GOVERNOR,

HUGH J. ANDERSON, Belfast.

COUNCIL.

CHARLES STETSON, Bangor.
WILLIAM DUNN, Poland.
SAMUEL MILDRAM, Wells.
FRANKLIN SMITH, North Anson.
STILLMAN HOWARD, Leeds.
THOMAS SIMMONS, Waldoborough.
SAMUEL H. TALBOT, East Machias.

EZRA B. FRENCH, Nobleboro', *Secretary of State*.
JAMES WHITE, Belfast, *Treasurer of State*.
ALFRED REDINGTON, Augusta, *Adjutant General*.
LEVI BRADLEY, Charleston, *Land Agent*.

SENATE.

S. HENRY CHASE, of FRYEBURG,
PRESIDENT.

		BOARDING-PLACES.
1st Sen. Dist.,	WILLIAM C. ALLEN, of Alfred,	Augusta House.
	CHARLES G. BELLAMY, of Kittery,	do.
	BENJAMIN F. MASON, of Kennebunkport,	Gage House
2d " "	DAVID DUNN, of Poland,	Mansion House
	RANDAL SKILLIN, of Cape Elizabeth,	J. H. Arnold,
	ALPHEUS S. HOLDEN, of Casco,	Mr. Ballard.
	RUFUS PORTER, of North Yarmouth,	Augusta House.
3d " "	JOSEPH BERRY, of Georgetown,	do.
	HENRY BARNES, of Bowdoinham,	do.
	SAMUEL W. JACKSON, of Jefferson,	Mansion House.
	THOMAS GORE, of Cushing,	Gilman Turner.
4th " "	DAVID BRONSON, of Augusta,	His house.
	LEAVITT LOTHROP, of Leeds,	Central House.
	ISAAC REDINGTON, of Waterville,	Mansion House
5th " "	CHARLES SARGENT, of Monroe,	Central House.
	JOHN C. KNOWLTON, of Liberty,	do.
	JAMES H. HAINES, of Burnham,	J K. Killea.
6th " "	HENRY PARTRIDGE, of Orland,	Central House
7th " "	WILLIAM GODFREY, of Gouldsborough,	Mansion House
8th " "	MATHEW HASTINGS, of Calais,	do.
9th " "	JOHN HODGDON, of Houlton,	Augusta House.
10th " "	JOHN H. PILLSBURY, of Bangor,	Mansion House.
	ASA SMITH, of Mattawamkeag,	do.
	ELISHA M. THURSTON, of Charleston,	J. W. Smith.
11th " "	JOSEPH S. MONROE, of Abbot,	Mansion House.
12th " "	RUFUS K. J. PORTER, of New Portland,	Franklin House
	JOSEPH BARRETT, of Canaan,	U. L. Pettengill.
13th " "	LEMUEL BURSLEY, Jr., of Farmington,	Cushnoc House.
14th " "	S. HENRY CHASE, PRESIDENT,	Augusta House.
	WILLIAM THOMPSON, of Canton,	Gage House.
	JOHN J. PERRY, of Oxford,	do.

DANIEL T. PIKE, of Augusta, SECRETARY,	His house.
CHARLES C. HARMON, of Portland, ASSISTANT SEC'Y,	Gage House.
BENJAMIN P. CUTTER, of Westbrook, MESSENGER,	Gilman Turner
SMITH LIBBY, of Exeter, ASSISTANT MESSENGER,	G. Turner.
Rev. JOHN H. INGRAHAM, of Augusta, CHAPLAIN,	His house.

SENATE.

ARRANGEMENT
OF THE MEMBERS AT THE SENATE BOARD

S. HENRY CHASE, President.

No. of Seat.	Left.	No. of Seat.	Right
1 Charles Sargent.		2. John J. Perry.	
3. James H. Haines.		4. William Thompson.	
5. Benjamin F. Mason.		6. Thomas Gore.	
7. Henry Partridge.		8. Alpheus S. Holden.	
9. Randal Skillin.		10. Lemuel Bursley, jr.	
11. John Hodgdon.		12. David Bronson.	
13. Joseph Berry.		14. Leavitt Lothrop.	
15. Asa Smith.		16. Samuel W. Jackson.	
17. William C. Allen.		18. John C. Knowlton.	
19. Isaac Redington.		20. John H. Pillsbury.	
21. Joseph S. Monroe.		22. Mathew Hastings.	
23. Elisha M. Thurston.		24. Rufus Porter.	
25. Henry Barnes.		26. Wilson Godfrey.	
27. Charles G. Bellamy		28. Joseph Barrett.	
29. David Dunn		30. Rufus K. J. Porter	

Hastings.

On Engrossed Bills.

Messrs. Bursley, jr.,
   Hodgdon,
   Pillsbury,
   Monroe,
   Barnes,
   Haines,
   Sargent,
   Porter,
   Redington,
   Holden,
   Bellamy,
   Perry.

EBENEZER KNOWLTON, Esq., Speaker.

COUNTY OF YORK.

Seats.	Names.	Residences.	Boarding-places.
131	William Berry,	Biddeford,	J. H. Arnold.
21	Joseph Burnham,	Kennebunkport,	do.
129	Edmund Currier,	Lyman,	do.
135	Alvah Doe,	Parsonsfield,	do.
146	Samuel Fox,	Berwick,	Cushnoc House.
111	John Hubbard,	South Berwick,	Augusta House.
30	John Lary, Jr.,	Acton,	J. K. Killea.
134	John Milliken,	Buxton,	J. H. Arnold.
46	John Moore,	Newfield,	do.
17	Joseph Perkins,	Wells,	J. K. Killea.
151	Richard Rogers,	Kittery,	Augusta House.
43	Miles W. Stuart,	Hollis,	Cushnoc House.
104	Samuel Tripp,	Sanford,	do.
88	Gideon Tucker,	Saco,	Augusta House.
148	Tobias Walker,	Kennebunk,	J. H. Arnold.
147	Samuel Webber,	York,	do.

COUNTY OF CUMBERLAND.

Seats.	Names.	Residences.	Boarding-places.
15	Phinehas Barnes,	Portland,	Augusta House.
145	Jeremiah Beedle,	Westbrook,	Central House.
26	John Burnell, Jr.,	Baldwin,	John Varney.
7	Thomas Chadwick,	Portland,	Augusta House.
100	Wm. P. Fessenden,	Portland,	Augusta House.
108	Thomas J. Howard,	Auburn,	Cushnoc House,
39	Nathaniel L. Ingersoll,	Danville,	J. H. Arnold.
62	Adam Lemont,	Brunswick,	Central House.
57	Abner Libbey,	Harrison,	J. Varney.
28	Freeland Marble,	Poland,	Mansion House.

SEATS.	NAMES.	RESIDENCES.	BOARDING PLACES.
140	Hugh D. McLellan,	Gorham,	Augusta House.
95	Ebenezer Moulton,	Standish,	J. Verney.
84	Frederic Nutting,	Casco,	Ephraim Ballard.
10	Cushing Prince,	N. Yarmouth,	Mr. Marshall.
72	Benjamin Small,	Pownal,	J. H. Arnold.
31	Samuel Soule,	Freeport,	do.
22	Ephraim Sturdivant,	Cumberland,	G. Powers.
96	Levi L. Totman,	Harpswell,	J. H. Arnold.
119	James Trickey,	Cape Elizabeth,	do.
70	Enoch White,	Windham,	Augusta House.

COUNTY OF LINCOLN.

SEATS.	NAMES.	RESIDENCES.	BOARDING PLACES.
49	James Ayer,	Alna,	J. Young.
101	Joseph B. Bridge,	Dresden,	Augusta House.
76	Oliver B. Brown,	Thomaston,	Cushnoc House.
91	Moses Choate, jr.,	Whitefield,	Central House.
69	Joseph Cotter,	Nobleboro',	J. K. Kilos.
37	Joseph Day,	Bristol,	do.
152	James Elliot,	Bowdoin,	Central House.
107	George Gilchrest,	St. George,	Cushnoc House.
183	Asa F. Hall,	Wiscasset,	U. L. Pettingill.
34	Reuben Hall,	Warren,	Cushnoc House.
29	Jacob Hill,	Webster,	Mansion House.
71	Atwood Levensaler,	Thomaston,	Cushnoc House.
72	David C. Magoun,	Bath,	Augusta House.
55	Joseph Merry,	Edgecomb,	J. H. Arnold.
89	Joseph Moore,	Lisbon,	Mansion House.
129	Edward Rand,	Townsend,	Alvin Fogg.
68	Isaac Reed,	Waldoboro',	Mansion House.
25	William Wildes,	Phipsburg,	Augusta House.
94	William Young,	Washington,	Cushnoc House.

COUNTY OF HANCOCK.

SEATS.	NAMES.	RESIDENCES.	BOARDING PLACES.
137	Wm. Babbidge,	Deer Isle,	G. Powers.
83	Richard Currier,	Sedgwick,	J. Verney.

SEATS.	NAMES.	RESIDENCES.	BOARDING PLACES.
150	Harvey F. Deming,	Mt. Desert,	J. Varney.
110	Moses McFarland,	Trenton,	John Young.
105	Daniel Harriman,	Orland,	G. Turner.
65	Jonathan Hatch, jr.,	Penobscot,	do.
19	Sylvanus T. Hinks,	Bucksport,	do.
74	Donald Lord,	Surry,	J. H. Arnold.
42	Samuel Stratton,	Hancock,	John Young.

COUNTY OF WASHINGTON.

69	Hiram A. Balch,	Lubec,	Mansion House.
116	John N. Farrar,	Baileyville,	J. K. Killen.
33	Joel Hanscom,	Crawford,	J. Young.
6	Aaron Hayden,	Eastport,	Augusta House.
117	Joseph A. Lee,	Calais,	do.
89	Otis Look,	Addison,	Mr. Pinkham.
142	Thomas Milliken,	Cherryfield,	John Young.
94	Robinson Palmer,	Perry,	Mansion House.
52	Samuel Small,	Machiasport,	do.

COUNTY OF KENNEBEC.

16	Daniel H. Brown,	Sebasticook,	Kennebec House.
126	Jason Chadwick,	China,	John Young.
124	Joseph Edgecomb,	Vienna,	Central House.
92	Isaac Fairfield,	Vassalboro',	Franklin House.
13	Ebenezer Freeman,	Monmouth,	U. L. Pettengill.
77	Moses Frost,	Sidney,	Gage House.
12	William O. Grant,	Litchfield,	U. L. Pettengill.
58	Frederic P Haviland,	Waterville,	Kennebec House.
80	Thomas J. Hayden,	Winslow,	Central House.
36	Charles Keene,	Augusta,	His house.
54	Daniel Marston,	Mt. Vernon,	Central House.
47	John Otis,	Hallowell,	His house.
2	Benjamin Ridley,	Wayne,	Cushnoc House.
141	Simeon Skillin,	Albion,	Franklin House.

Seats.	Names.	Residences.	Boarding-places.
97	Jonathan Tuck,	Fayette,	Mr. Tuck, Hallowell.
126	Noah Woods,	Gardiner,	J. Baker.

COUNTY OF OXFORD.

27	Joseph Child,	Hartford,	Cushnoc House.
125	Abner Davis,	Stow,	G. Powers.
50	Phinehas Frost,	Bethel,	Cushnoc House.
129	John Hill,	Sweden,	J. Varney.
14	John J. Holman,	Dixfield,	Cushnoc House.
130	John F. Holt,	Turner,	do.
93	Alexander Libby,	Sumner,	J. Varney.
64	Philip Manger,	Livermore,	G. Powers.
51	John Reed,	Roxbury,	Cushnoc House.
118	Horatio G. Russ,	Paris,	Gage House.
143	Wm. T. Taylor,	Porter,	J. Varney.
53	Isaac A. Thayer,	Oxford,	Cushnoc House.

COUNTY OF SOMERSET.

11	James Adams,	Norridgewock,	Augusta House.
128	Robert Crosby,	Embden,	Albert Pinkham.
32	Patten Currier,	Cornville,	do.
79	Warren Fuller,	Hartland,	J. H. Arnold.
3	George C. Getchell,	North Anson,	Augusta House.
5	Jabez D. Hill,	Moscow,	J. J. Fuller.
98	Saul Holbrook,	Starks,	Franklin House.
18	Eldridge G. Morrison,	Canaan,	N. Ellis.
123	Wm. F. Pitts,	Bloomfield,	Albert Pinkham.
38	Thomas Smith,	St. Albans,	J. H. Arnold.

COUNTY OF PENOBSCOT.

49	Elisha H. Allen,	Bangor,	Augusta House.
	Ebenezer Briggs,	Kirkland,	
41	George Crane,	Eddington,	Mr. Wade.
75	Andrew Drury,	Enfield,	Mansion House.
1	John C. Friend,	Etna,	Alvin Fogg.

SEATS.	NAMES.	RESIDENCES.	BOARDING-PLACES.
109	John Gardiner,	Patten,	J. Varney.
90	William Head,	Lagrange,	Central House.
81	Thomas H. Norcross,	Charleston,	Mansion House.
4	Lyndon Oak,	Garland,	W. K. Weston.
8	William Paine,	Bangor,	Augusta House.
149	Thomas F. Rowe,	Brewer,	Gage House.
59	Hiram Ruggles,	Carmel,	G. Turner.
45	Amos Storer,	Dexter,	Dr. Smith.
66	Benjamin B. Thomas,	Newburg,	G. Turner.

COUNTY OF WALDO.

102	Sherburne Bachelder,	Belmont,	G. Turner.
130	Seth Bartlett,	Hope,	Kennebec House.
144	Maurice C. Blake,	Camden,	Mansion House.
87	Henry Colburn,*	Belfast,	do.
113	Jacob Cunningham,	Swanville,	G. Turner.
56	Samuel S. Hersey,*	Belfast,	Central House.
	Ebenezer Knowlton, (Speaker,)	Montville,	Gage House.
48	Daniel Lampson,	Troy,	W. R. Prescott, Hall.
99	Amos Pitcher,	Northport,	G. Turner.
114	Lot Rust,	Palermo,	Cushnoc House.
67	Seth Thompson,	Unity,	J. Varney.
23	Arthur Treat,	Frankfort,	Gage House.
63	Allison Tyler,	Prospect,	G. Turner.
115	David Vinal,	Vinalhaven,	Cushnoc House.

COUNTY OF FRANKLIN.

78	Joseph Dunham,	Madrid,	Cushnoc House.
44	Eliab Eaton,	Farmington,	do.
136	John F. W. Gould,	Wilton,	Gage House.
139	Truman A. Merrill,	Industry,	J. Piper.
123	Stillman Noyes,	Jay,	Cushnoc House.
112	Nathaniel Potter,	Kingfield,	Franklin House.

* Claimants of one seat.

COUNTY OF PISCATAQUIS.

Seats.	Names.	Residences.	Boarding-places
20	Abijah B. Chase,	Sebec,	*Mansion House.*
9	George H. Kingsbery,	Kingsbery,	*Augusta House.*
105	Ebenezer Lambert,	Dover,	*Central House.*

COUNTY OF AROOSTOOK.

85	Joseph Cyr,	Van Buren Pl.	*J. K. Killee.*
86	Leander S. Morton,	Bridgewater Pl.	*do.*
35	Edwin Parker,	Golden Ridge Pl.	*G. Turner*

SAMUEL BELCHER, of Farmington, CLERK,   *Mansion House.*

NATHANIEL PATTERSON, of Belfast, ASSISTANT CLERK, *Augusta House*

PHILIP PHILLIPS, of Turner, MESSENGER,   *Augusta House.*

WILLIAM SANBORN, of Liberty, ASSISTANT MESSENGER, *J. Varney.*

HENRY D. FISK, of Augusta,   do.   do.   *J Fisk.*

WILLIAM O. GRANT, Jr., of Litchfield, PAGE.   *U. L. Pettengill.*

The Clergymen of Augusta and Hallowell, and the ordained ministers of the gospel who are members of the House, officiate as CHAPLAINS, in rotation

~~~~~~~~~~~~~~~~

MONITORS.

1st Division, Mr. PARKER, of Golden Ridge.

2d	"	"	THOMPSON, of Unity.
3d	"	"	MOULTON, of Standish.
4th	"	"	TRICKEY, of Cape Elizabeth.
5th	"	"	ROGERS, of Kittery.
6th	"	"	GRANT, of Litchfield.

Standing Committees of the House.

On Elections.

Messrs. Rogers of Kittery,
Tucker of Saco,
Russ of Paris,
Oak of Garland,
Hill of Moscow,
Chadwick of China,
Pitcher of Northport.

On Engrossed Bills.

Messrs. Magoun of Bath,
Moulton of Standish,
Deming of Mt. Desert,
Blake of Camden,
Beedle of Westbrook,
Merrill of Industry,
Brown of Clinton.

On Finance.

Messrs. Chadwick of Portland,
Hinks of Bucksport,
Lee of Calais,
Stuart of Hollis,
Ingersoll, of Danville,
Marble of Poland,
Bachelder of Belmont.

On County Estimates.

Messrs. Stuart of Hollis,
   Frost of Sidney,
   Sturdivant of Cumberland,
   Hall of Warren,
   Hill of Moscow,
   Munger of Livermore,
   Tyler of Prospect,

On Bills in the Third Reading.

Messrs. Barnes of Portland,
   Doe of Parsonsfield,
   Oak of Garland,
   Getchell of North Anson,
   Rowe of Brewer,
   Hayden of Eastport,
   Parker of Hodgdon,

On Leave of Absence.

Messrs. Edgecomb of Vienna,
   Webber of York,
   Cunningham of Swanville,
   Adams of Norridgewock,
   Friend of Etna,
   Frost of Sidney,
   Lary of Acton.

On Pay Roll.

Messrs. Frost of Bethel,
   Choate of Whitefield,
   Babbidge of Deer Isle,
   Skillin of Albion,
   Trickey of Cape Elizabeth,
   Burnham of Kennebunkport,
   Ruggles of Carmel.

8

On Change of Names.

Messrs. Gardiner of Patten,
   Pitts of Bloomfield,
   Libbey of Sumner.

Joint Rules and Orders of the two Houses.

1 The following joint standing committees shall be appointed at the commencement of the session, viz

        On the judiciary,
        On education,
        On banks and banking,
        On incorporation of towns,
        On division of towns,
        On division of counties,
        On state lands and state roads,
        On indian affairs,
        On agriculture,
        On fisheries,
        On manufactures,
        On rail roads and bridges,
        On interior waters,
        On accounts,
        On claims,
        On the militia,
        On military pensions,
        On the insane hospital,
        On the state prison,
        On public buildings,
        On the library.

And each of the said committees shall consist of three on the part of the senate, and seven on the part of the house.

2. Whenever a select committee shall be appointed by either house, and be joined by the other, it shall be the duty of the secretary of the senate, or clerk of the house, respectively, as the case may be, to transmit, one to the other, the names of the members so joined, in

order that they may be entered on the journal of both houses.

3. The enacting clause of every bill shall follow its title in these words, namely :

" *Be it enacted by the Senate and House of Representatives in Legislature assembled,* as follows :—"

And if any bill shall contain more than one section, the words "Section 1," shall be inserted immediately after the enacting clause, and before the first part of the bill, and to each subsequent section shall be prefixed the words "Section 2," or otherwise, as the case may be, in conformity with the style of the Revised Statutes. And if any bill shall be found not to conform to the requisitions of this rule, it shall be the duty of the committee on bills in the second reading, or of the secretary of the senate, or of the committee on bills in the third reading, or of the clerk of the house, to correct the same, without a proposition to either branch to amend.

4. All indorsements on papers, while on their passage between the two houses, shall be under the signature of the secretary of the senate, or clerk of the house, respectively ; but bills and resolves on their final passage shall be signed by the presiding officer of each branch.

5. Every bill that shall have passed both houses to be enacted, and all resolutions, or resolves having the force of law, that shall have finally passed both houses, shall be presented by the secretary of the senate to the governor, for his approval ; and the secretary of the senate, shall enter on the journal of the senate, the day on which such bills or resolutions are so presented to the governor.

6. No business shall be entered on in convention of both branches, except by unanimous consent, other than that which may be agreed on before the convention is formed.

7. When a bill or resolve shall be printed by order of either house, the name of the committee by whom such

bill or resolve was reported, or of the member by whom it was introduced, shall be stated on the printed copies

8. Whenever the house shall order the printing of any document *for the use of the legislature*, the number of copies so ordered shall be not less than three hundred and fifty, and such order shall be immediately communicated to the senate. If the senate shall desire an additional number of copies, for the use of the senate, its order for that purpose shall be communicated to the house, and the clerk of the house shall without further order, or vote, procure such additional copies to be printed without any change of form, and delivered to the messenger of the senate.

The same course of proceedings shall be observed whenever an order to print for the use of the legislature shall be passed by the senate.

The copies printed for the use of the legislature shall be delivered to the messengers of the two houses, in the proportion of one fourth for the use of the senate, and three fourths for the use of the house, after reserving the usual number of copies for the departments and for binding.

8*

JOINT STANDING COMMITTEES.

On the Judiciary.

Messrs. Allen,
Bronson, } *Of the Senate*
Knowlton,

Messrs Allen of Bangor,
Levensaler of Thomaston,
Hayden of Eastport,
Fox of Berwick, } *Of the House*
Getchell of North Anson,
Frost of Bethel,
Oak of Garland,

On Education

Messrs. Thurston,
Redington, } *Of the Senate.*
Jackson,

Messrs. Barnes of Portland,
Hill of Moscow,
Grant of Litchfield,
Treat of Frankfort, } *Of the House.*
Edgecomb of Vienna,
Davis of Stow,
Chase of Sebec,

On Banks and Banking.

Messrs. Hodgdon,
Thompson, } *Of the Senate*
R. K. J. Porter,

Messrs. Levensaler of Thomaston,
Lee of Calais,
Totman of Harpswell,
Reed of Waldoboro', } *Of the House*
Palmer of Perry,
Burnham of Kennebunkport,
Reed of Roxbury,

On Incorporation of Towns.

Messrs Sargent,
Bursley, } Of the Senate.
Monroe,

Messrs. Fox of Berwick,
Soule of Freeport,
Young of Washington,
McFarland of Trenton, } Of the House
Look of Addison,
Freeman of Monmouth,
Libby of Sumner,

On Division of Towns.

Messrs. Holden,
Monroe, } Of the Senate
Bursley,

Messrs. Holman of Dixfield,
Eaton of Farmington,
Currier of Sedgwick,
Tripp of Sanford, } Of the House.
Crosby of Embden,
Treat of Frankfort,
Moore of Lisbon,

On Division of Counties.

Messrs. Pillsbury,
Skillin, } Of the Senate.
Barnes,

Messrs. Merry of Edgecomb,
Perkins of Wells,
Ingersoll of Danville,
Hanscom of Crawford, } Of the House.
Marston of Mt. Vernon,
Berry of Biddeford,
Webber of York,

On State Lands and State Roads.

Messrs. Hastings,
Bronson,   } Of the Senate.
Pillsbury,

Messrs. Otis of Hallowell,
Parker of Golden Ridge,
Prince of North Yarmouth,
Brown of Thomaston,   } Of the House.
Norcross of Charleston,
Smith of St. Albans,
Moore of Newfield,

On Indian Affairs.

Messrs. Haines,
Smith,   } Of the Senate.
Barrett,

Messrs. Palmer of Perry,
Day of Bristol,
Crane of Eddington,
Libby of Harrison,   } Of the House.
Skillin of Albion,
Lary of Acton,
Taylor of Porter,

On Agriculture.

Messrs. Skillin,
Lothrop,   } Of the Senate
R K. J Porter,

Messrs. Thomas of Newburg,
Stuart of Hollis,
Currier of Cornville,
Noyes of Jay,   } Of the House.
Hayden of Winslow,
Trickey of Cape Elizabeth,
Farrar of Baileyville,

On Fisheries.

Messrs. Partridge,
  Godfrey, } *Of the Senate.*
  Barnes,

Messrs. Hall of Warren,
  Woods of Gardiner,
  Stratton of Hancock,
  Bridge of Dresden, } *Of the House.*
  Vinal of Vinalhaven,
  Balch of Lubec,
  Ruggles of Carmel,

On Manufactures.

Messrs. Bronson,
  Barrett, } *Of the Senate.*
  R. Porter,

Messrs. Tucker of Saco,
  Brown of Clinton,
  Lemont of Brunswick,
  Hinks of Bucksport, } *Of the House.*
  Hall of Wiscasset,
  Thayer of Oxford,
  Morrison of Canaan,

On Rail Roads and Bridges.

Messrs. Smith,
  Redington, } *Of the Senate.*
  Bellamy,

Messrs. Paine of Bangor,
  Small of Machiasport,
  Magoun of Bath,
  Pitcher of Northport, } *Of the House.*
  Otis of Hallowell,
  White of Windham,
  Wildes of Phipsburg,

On Interior Waters.

Messrs. Gore,
　　　 Perry,　　} Of the Senate.
　　　 Hodgdon,

Messrs. Hill of Webster,
　　　 Russ, of Paris,
　　　 Keene of Augusta,
　　　 Haviland of Waterville,　} Of the House
　　　 Drury of Enfield,
　　　 Holt of Turner,
　　　 Rust of Palermo,

On Accounts.

Messrs. Thompson,
　　　 Knowlton,　} Of the Senate
　　　 Monroe,

Messrs. McLellan of Gorham,
　　　 Adams of Norridgewock,
　　　 Sturdivant of Cumberland,
　　　 Rand of Townsend,　} Of the House.
　　　 Gardiner of Patten,
　　　 Gould of Wilton,
　　　 Ridley of Wayne,

On Claims.

Messrs. R. K. J. Porter,
　　　 R. Porter,　} Of the Senate.
　　　 Pillsbury,

Messrs. Blake of Camden,
　　　 Gilchrest of St. George,
　　　 Fuller of Hartland,
　　　 Dunham of Madrid,　} Of the House.
　　　 Currier of Lyman,
　　　 Milliken of Steuben,
　　　 Bartlett of Hope,

On the Militia.

Messrs. Perry,
Hastings, } *Of the Senate.*
Thurston,

Messrs. Thompson of Unity,
Kingsbery of Kingsbery,
Doe of Parsonsfield,
Frost of Sidney, } *Of the House*
Marble of Poland,
Cotter of Nobleboro',
Potter of Kingfield,

On Military Pensions.

Messrs. Monroe,
Holden, } *Of the Senate.*
Bellamy,

Messrs. Beedle of Westbrook,
Ayer of Alna,
Cyr of Van Buren Plan.,
Fairfield of Vassalboro', } *Of the House*
Small of Pownal,
Choate of Whitefield,
Morton of Bridgwater Plan.,

On the Insane Hospital.

Messrs. Barrett,
Thurston, } *Of the Senate.*
Sargent,

Messrs. Reed of Waldoboro',
Moulton of Standish,
Friend of Etna,
Deming of Mt. Desert, } *Of the House*
Elliot of Bowdoin,
Lamson of Troy,
Tuck of Fayette,

On the State Prison.

Messrs Knowlton,
Allen, } Of the Senate
Jackson,

Messrs. Magoun of Bath,
Brown of Thomaston,
Harriman of Orland,
Lambert of Dover, } Of
Babbidge of Deer Isle,
Burnell of Baldwin,
Pitts of Bloomfield,

On Public Buildings.

Messrs. Bellamy,
R. Porter, } Of the Senate.
Smith,

Messrs. Lemont of Brunswick,
Howard of Auburn,
Child of Hartford,
Holbrook of Starks, } Of
Milliken of Buxton,
Head of Lagrange,
Rowe of Brewer,

On the Library.

Messrs Jackson,
Dunn, } Of the Senate.
Allen,

Messrs. Getchell of North Anson,
Barnes of Portland,
Nutting of Casco,
Paine of Bangor, } O
Briggs of Kirkland,
Walker of Kennebunk,
Munger of Livermore,

On the Treasurer's Report.

Messrs. Allen,
Hastings, } *Of the Senate.*
Hodgdon,

Messrs. Chadwick of Portland,
Hinks of Bucksport,
Lee of Calais,
Stuart of Hollis, } *Of the House.*
Ingersoll of Danville,
Marble of Poland,
Levensaler of Thomaston,

To prepare Joint Rules.

Messrs. Perry,
Redington, } *Of the Senate.*
Monroe,

Messrs. Barnes of Portland,
Getchell of North Anson,
Levensaler of Thomaston, } *Of the House.*
Russ of Paris,
Brown of Clinton,

To contract for State Printing and Binding.

Messrs. Perry,
Hastings, } *Of the Senate.*
R. K. J. Porter.

Messrs. Russ of Paris,
Keene of Augusta,
Eaton of Farmington, } *Of the House.*
Hall of Warren,
Rogers of Kittery,

9

On returns of Votes for Governor.

Messrs. Hodgdon,
Hastings,
Bellamy,
Sargent,
Haines,   } Of the Senate.
Lothrop,
Thurston,
Smith,
Godfrey,

Messrs. Levensaler of Thomaston,
Stuart of Hollis,
Fessenden of Portland,
Hinks of Bucksport,
Hayden of Eastport,
. Keene of Augusta,
Getchell of North Anson,   } Of the House
Child of Hartford,
Ruggles of Carmel,
Thompson of Unity,
Eaton of Farmington,
Parker of Golden Ridge,

On reduction of State Valuation in certain towns

Messrs. Bellamy,
Skillin,   }
Mason,

Messrs. Barnes of Portland,
Getchell of North Anson,
Levensaler of Thomaston,   }
Russ of Paris,
Brown of Clinton,

On the License Laws.

Messrs. Redington,
      Haines,
      Gore,   } *Of the Senate.*
      Mason,
      Barrett,

Messrs Davis of Stow,
      Milliken of Buxton,
      Chadwick of Portland,
      Magoun of Bath,
      Hatch of Penobscot,
      Small of Machiasport,
      Grant of Litchfield,   } *Of the House.*
      Adams of Norridgewock,
      Gardiner of Patten,
      Bartlett of Hope,
      Gould of Wilton,
      Chase of Sebec,
      Parker of Golden Ridge,

Third Senatorial Apportionment.

Resolve for dividing the state into districts, for the choice of senators.

Resolved, That from and after the passing of this re-solve, the state be, and hereby is divided into fourteen districts for the choice of senators, and each district shall be entitled to elect the number of senators herein provided for the term of ten years, in the manner pre-scribed by the constitution, to wit :—The several towns composing the county of York, except the towns of Par-sonsfield, Cornish and Limington, shall form the first dis-trict, and be entitled to elect three senators.

The several towns composing the county of Cumber-land, except the towns of Standish and Baldwin, shall form the second district, and be entitled to four sen-ators.

The several towns and plantations composing the county of Lincoln, together with the island of Matinicus and islands contiguous thereto, shall form the third dis-trict, and be entitled to four senators.

*The several towns in the county of Kennebec, with the exception of China, Albion, Clinton, the territory north of Albion, and the Clinton Gore, shall constitute the fourth senatorial district, and be entitled to three senators.

*The several towns in the county of Waldo, with the the towns and plantations excepted in the fourth district, shall constitute the fifth senatorial district, and be enti-tled to three senators.

The towns of Bucksport, Orland, Dedham, Penobscot,

[* Vide Resolves of April 2, 1841, and March 16, 1842.]

Bluehill, Castine, Brooksville, Sedgwick, Deer Isle, the plantations of Wetmore Isle, Swan Island, Long Island and the islands west of Long Island, in the county of Hancock, except Matinicus and the islands contiguous thereto, shall form the sixth district, and be entitled to one senator.

The remainder of Hancock county, together with the towns of Steuben, Cherryfield, Annsburg, Beddington, Devereaux, Columbia, Harrington, Addison, Jonesborough, Jonesport, Machias, Northfield, Wesley, and the townships number thirty, thirty-one, twenty-four, twenty-five, eighteen and nineteen, in the middle division, and number twenty-three, in the eastern division, in the county of Washington shall form the seventh district, and be entitled to one senator.

The eighth senatorial district shall consist of the towns of Calais, Cutler, Marion, Dennysville, Eastport, Edmunds, Lubec, Machiasport, East Machias, Pembroke, Perry, Robbinston, Trescott, Whiting and number fourteen and eighteen, in the eastern division, in the county of Washington, and shall be entitled to one senator.

The remainder of the county of Washington, together with the county of Aroostook, shall form the ninth district and be entitled to one senator.

The several towns and plantations in the county of Penobscot shall form the tenth district, and be entitled to three senators.

The several towns and plantations in the county of Piscataquis shall form the eleventh district, and be entitled to one senator.

The several towns and plantations in the county of Somerset shall form the twelfth district, and be entitled to two senators.

The several towns and plantations in the county of Franklin except Carthage, Weld, Berlin, No. two, first range, No. three, first range, No. two and three, second

9*

range, and letters D and E, shall form the t
trict, and be entitled to one senator.

The remainder of the county of Frank
with the several towns and plantations in th
Oxford, also the towns of Parsonsfield, Corn
ton, Baldwin and Standish, shall form the fo
trict, and be entitled to three senators.

[*Approved April* 2, 1841.]

Fourth Representative Apportionment.

RESOLVE for apportioning one hundred and fifty-one representatives among the several counties, cities, towns, plantations and classes in the State of Maine, at the fourth apportionment.

Resolved, That the county of York shall choose sixteen representatives, to be apportioned as follows : Saco, one, York, one; Wells, one; Kennebunkport, one; Biddeford, one; Buxton, one; Kittery, one; Parsonsfield, one; South Berwick and Elliot, one; Sanford and Lebanon, one; Waterborough and Lyman, one; Alfred and Kennebunk, one; Limington and Hollis, one; Berwick and North Berwick, one; Shapleigh and Acton, one; Cornish, Limerick and Newfield, one.

That the county of Cumberland shall choose twenty representatives, to be apportioned as follows: city of Portland, three; Westbrook, one; Brunswick, one; Gorham, one; North Yarmouth, one; Freeport, one; Poland, one; Standish, one; Windham, one; Baldwin, Sebago and Naples, one; Casco, Raymond and Otisfield, one; Durham and Pownal, one; Gray and Harpswell, one; Scarborough one for the years eighteen hundred and forty three, eighteen hundred and forty five, eighteen hundred and forty seven, eighteen hundred and forty nine, and eighteen hundred and fifty one; Cape Elizabeth, one for the years eighteen hundred and forty four, eighteen hundred and forty six, eighteen hundred and forty eight, and eighteen hundred and fifty; Auburn, one for the years eighteen hundred and forty three, eighteen hundred and forty five, eighteen hundred and forty six, eighteen hundred and forty nine, and eighteen hundred and fifty one; Minot one for the years eighteen hundred and forty four, eighteen hundred and forty seven, eight-

een hundred and forty eight, and eighteen hundred and
fifty; Bridgton and Harrison, one; New Gloucester and
Danville, one; Falmouth, one for the years eighteen hundred and forty three, eighteen hundred and forty four,
eighteen hundred and forty seven, eighteen hundred and
forty nine, and eighteen hundred and fifty one; Cumberland, one for the years eighteen hundred and forty five,
eighteen hundred and forty six, eighteen hundred and
forty eight, and eighteen hundred and fifty.

That the county of Lincoln shall choose nineteen representatives, to be apportioned as follows: Thomaston,
two; Bath, one, Waldoborough, one; Warren and
Friendship, one, St. George, Cushing and Muscle Ridge,
plantation, one; Union and Washington, one; Whitefield and Patricktown plantation, one, Jefferson and Alna, one, Wiscasset and Woolwich, one; Newcastle and
Edgecomb, one; Nobleborough and Bremen, one,
Boothbay, Townsend, and Westport, one; Phipsburg,
Georgetown and Arrowsic, one; Bristol, Monhegan,
Muscongus and Harbor Islands, one; Lewiston and Lisbon, one; Bowdoin and Topsham, one; Richmond, one
for the years eighteen hundred and forty three, eighteen
hundred and forty five, eighteen hundred and forty seven,
eighteen hundred and forty nine, and eighteen hundred
and fifty one, Dresden, one for the years eighteen hundred and forty four, eighteen hundred and forty six,
eighteen hundred and forty eight, and eighteen hundred
and fifty, Webster, one for the years eighteen hundred
and forty three, eighteen hundred and forty six, and
eighteen hundred and forty nine; Bowdoinham, one for
the years eighteen hundred and forty four, eighteen hundred and forty five, eighteen hundred and forty seven,
eighteen hundred and forty eight, eighteen hundred and
fifty, and eighteen hundred and fifty one.

That the county of Hancock shall choose nine representatives, to be apportioned as follows · Bucksport and
Wetmore Isle, one; Penobscot, Castine, Holbrook Island

and Matinicus plantation, one; Brooksville, Sedgwick, Swan's Island plantation, Hog Island plantation, and Long Island plantation, one; Deer Isle, Bear Island, Beach Island, Pickering's Island, Great Sprucehead Island, Little Sprucehead Island, Butter Island, Eagle Island and Hacketash Island, one; Bluehill and Surry, one; Mount Desert, Eden, Cranberry Isles, Mount Desert Rock, and Seaville, one; Orland, Dedham, Otis, Mariaville, Aurora, Amherst, Greenfield, townships numbered one, two, three, four, sixteen, twenty one, twenty two, twenty eight, thirty two, thirty three, thirty four, thirty five, thirty nine, forty and forty one, one; Ellsworth, Trenton and Waltham, one; Gouldsborough, Sullivan, Franklin, Eastbrook, Hancock, townships numbered seven, eight, nine and ten, one.

That the county of Washington shall choose nine representatives, to be apportioned as follows: Calais, one; Eastport, one; Steuben, Cherryfield, Annsburg, Beddington, Devereaux, townships numbered eighteen, twenty four, twenty five, thirty, thirty one, thirty six, thirty seven, and east half of thirty five, one; East Machias, Machiasport, Whiting, Marion, Edmunds, Dennysville and township numbered fourteen, one; Columbia, Harrington and Addison, one; Jonesport, Jonesborough, Machias, townships numbered twenty three, eighteen, nineteen, twenty six, Northfield, Wesley and Crawford, one; Lubec, Trescott and Cutler, one; Pembroke, Perry, Robbinston, Charlotte and Medybemps, one; Baring, Baileyville, Alexander, Princeton, Topsfield and Cooper, together with all the townships and plantations in the county of Washington, not included in any other district, one.

That the county of Kennebec shall choose sixteen representatives, to be apportioned as follows: Augusta, one; Hallowell, one; Gardiner, one; Vassalborough, one; Waterville and Dearborn, one; Winthrop and Mount Vernon, one; Monmouth and Greene, one; Leeds and Wayne, one; Readfield and Fayette, one; Clinton and Clinton gore, one; China and Albion gore, one; Sidney and Rome, one; Pittston, one for the years eighteen hundred and forty three, eighteen hundred and forty four, eighteen hundred and forty five, eighteen hundred and forty seven, eighteen hundred and forty eight, eighteen hundred and forty nine, and eighteen hundred and fifty; Vienna, one for the years eighteen hundred and forty six, and eighteen hundred and fifty one, Albion, one for the years eighteen hundred and forty four, eighteen hundred and forty six, eighteen hundred and forty eight, and eighteen hundred and fifty; Windsor, one for the years eighteen hundred and forty three, eighteen hundred and forty five, eighteen hundred and forty seven, eighteen hundred and forty nine, and eighteen hundred and fifty one, Litchfield, one for the years eighteen hundred and forty three, eighteen hundred and forty four, eighteen hundred and forty six, eighteen hundred and forty seven, eighteen hundred and forty nine, and eighteen hundred and fifty; Wales, one for the years eighteen hundred and forty five, eighteen hundred and forty eight, and eighteen hundred and fifty one; Belgrade, one for the years eighteen hundred and forty three, eighteen hundred and forty five, eighteen hundred and forty seven, eighteen hundred and forty nine, eighteen hundred and fifty one; Winslow, one for the years eighteen hundred and forty four, eighteen hundred and forty six, eighteen hundred and forty eight, eighteen hundred and fifty.

That the county of Oxford shall choose twelve representatives, to be apportioned as follows Livermore, one; Turner and Hebron, one; Oxford and Norway, one; Hartford, Canton and Peru, one; Buckfield, Sumner, and township numbered two, one, Paris and Woodstock, one; Dixfield, Mexico and Rumford, one, Bethel, Greenwood and Albany, one; Porter, Hiram and Brownfield, one; Fryeburg, Lovel, Stow and Stoneham, one; Waterford, Sweden and Denmark, one; Andover, Newry,

Gilead, Roxbury, Byron, Fryeburg Academy grant, Batchelder's grant, Riley, Howard's gore, Hamlin's grant, township A, number two, township B, township C, Andover north surplus, townships number five, second range, number five, first range and number four, first range, together with all the remaining territory in Oxford county not included in any other district, one.

That the county of Somerset shall choose ten representatives, to be apportioned as follows: Hartland, Palmyra and Detroit, one; Pittsfield, Canaan and Skowhegan, one, St. Albans, Harmony, Cambridge and Ripley, one; Norridgewock and Madison, one; Athens, Cornville and Solon, one; Fairfield and Bloomfield, one; Starks, Mercer and Smithfield, one, Bingham, Brighton, Moscow, Mayfield, townships number one, third range, number one, fourth range, and number one, fifth range, east of Kennebec river, Holden plantation, township number five, third range, Canada line, Jackman's township, Parlin pond plantation, Long pond plantation, and township number five, second range, Canada road, together with all the territory in Somerset county not included in any other district, one; Concord, Embden, Lexington, township number one, second range, west of Kennebec river, number one, second range, Pleasant ridge, number one, third range, west of Kennebec river, number one, fourth range, Enchanted stream township, Spencer stream township, number two, second range, number four, fourth range or Flagstaff, number three, third range and Canada road, one; Anson, one for the years eighteen hundred and forty three, eighteen hundred and forty four, eighteen hundred and forty six, eighteen hundred and forty eight, and eighteen hundred and fifty; New Portland, one for the years eighteen hundred and forty five, eighteen hundred and forty seven, eighteen hundred and forty nine, and eighteen hundred and fifty one.

That the county of Penobscot shall choose fourteen

representatives, to be apportioned as follows: Bangor,
two; Hampden and Carmel, one; Newburg, Dixmont
and Plymouth, one; Corinna and Dexter, one; Etna,
Newport and Stetson, one; Corinth, Charleston and
Bradford, one; Exeter and Garland, one; Oldtown, Argyle, Argyle plantation and Lagrange, one; Hermon,
Levant, Kirkland and Glenburn, one; Orrington and
Brewer, one; Orono, Bradley, Eddington and Jarvis
gore, one; Burlington, Lowell, Enfield, Passadumkeag,
Edinburgh, Howland, Matamiscontis, Chester, Maxfield,
number three, number four, Greenbush and Milford, one;
Lincoln, Lee, Springfield, west half number six, range
second, west half number seven, range third, unincorporated places north of Lincoln, number two Indian purchase, number one Indian purchase, Hopkins' academy
grant, Letter A and Patten, together with all the remaining territory in the county of Penobscot not included in
any other district, one.

That the county of Waldo shall choose thirteen representatives, to be apportioned as follows: Belfast, one;
Camden, one; Frankfort, one; Prospect, one; Appleton, Liberty and Palermo, one; Hope and Searsmont,
one; Montville and Freedom, one; Unity, Burnham and
Knox, one; Troy, Thorndike and Jackson, one; Belmont, Waldo plantation and Brooks, one; Lincolnville
and Northport, one; Monroe and Swanville, one; Islesborough and Vinalhaven, one.

That the county of Piscataquis shall choose four representatives, to be apportioned as follows: Sangerville,
Parkman, Wellington and Kingsbery, one; Guilford,
Abbot, Greenville, Monson, Blanchard, Eliotsville, Shirley, Wilson, plantation number eight, and township number three, range three, together with the townships north
of Greenville and Eliotsville, one; Dover, Foxcroft,
Atkinson and Bowerbank, together with the range of
townships north of Bowerbank, one; Kilmarnock, Brownville, Barnard, Williamsburg, Milo, Sebec, Milton, town-

ship B, in the tenth range, together with all the unsettled townships north of Brownville, Barnard and Kilmarnock, one.

That the county of Franklin shall choose six representatives, to be apportioned as follows · New Sharon, Industry and New Vineyard, one; Farmington and Temple, one; Wilton and Chesterville, one, Jay, Carthage and Weld, one; Avon, Phillips, Berlin, Madrid, townships number three, second range, number two, second range and Letter E, one; Strong, Freeman, Salem, Kingfield, townships numbered three and four, second range, number four, first range, Bigelow township, number one, fourth range, number one, third range, number three, first range, number two, first range, together with all the territory in Franklin county, not included in any other district, one.

That the county of Aroostook shall choose three representatives, to be apportioned as follows. Hodgdon, New Limerick, number five, range three, number five, range four, number five, range five, and all towns, plantations and townships, south of the before mentioned towns and townships in the county, one; Houlton, Belfast Academy grant, Smyrna, number six, range four, number six, range five, and all towns, plantations and townships north to the south line of the following town, and townships, to wit: Masardis, number ten, range four, number ten, range three, Westfield Academy grant, Deerfield Academy grant, and Marshill township, one: all towns, plantations, townships and territory, north of the south line of Masardis, number ten, range four, number ten, range three, Westfield Academy grant, Deerfield Academy grant, and Marshill township, to the north line of the county, one.

[Approved March 17, 1842.]

10

CONGRESSIONAL APPORTIONMENT.

EXTRACT from an act entitled " an act providing for the choice of Representatives to Congress."

SEC. 1. The county of York, together with the towns of Hiram, Porter, Brownfield, Denmark, Fryeburg, Lovell, Stow, Stoneham, Sweden, Waterford, Albany, Mason, Gilead, Bethel, Newry, Bachelder's Grant, Riley plantation, Greenwood, Norway, Oxford and Hebron, from Oxford county, shall compose the first district, and be entitled to one representative.

The county of Cumberland shall constitute the second district, and be entitled to one representative.

The counties of Kennebec and Franklin, except the town of Greene, shall compose the third district, and be entitled to one representative.

The county of Lincoln, together with that part of Oxford not annexed to the first congressional district, with the town of Greene from Kennebec county, shall constitute the fourth district, and be entitled to one representative.

The counties of Waldo and Somerset, except Vinalhaven, shall compose the fifth district, and be entitled to one representative.

The counties of Penobscot and Piscataquis, shall compose the sixth district, and be entitled to one representative.

The counties of Hancock, Washington and Aroostook, together with the town of Vinalhaven, in Waldo county, to compose the seventh district, and be entitled to one representative.

[*Approved March 22, 1843.*]

m.	Towns.	Population.
101	Lyman,	1,478
408	Newfield,	1,354
598	North Berwick,	1,447
574	Parsonsfield,	2,442
687	Saco,	4,408
	Shapleigh,	1,510
	Sanford,	2,233
363	South Berwick,	2,314
323	Waterborough,	1,944
770	Wells,	2,978
435	York,	3,111
		——
		54,023

F CUMBERLAND.

	Towns.	Population.
134	Otisfield,	1,307
,987	Poland,	2,360
,259	Portland, city,	15,218
616	Pownal,	1,210
,294	Raymond,	2,032
,836	Scarborough,	2,173
	Sebago,	707
,662	Standish,	2,198
,002	Westbrook,	4,116
,740	Windham,	2,303
,448	New Gloucester,	1,946
,243	Cape Elizabeth,	1,666
,550		——
758		68,660
,824		

COUNTY OF LINCOLN.

Towns.	Population.	Towns.	Populati
Alna,	989	Topsham,	1,
Bath,	5,143	Union,	1,
Boothbay,	2,631	Waldoborough,	3,
Bowdoin,	2,073	Webster,	1,
Bowdoinham,	2,402	Warren,	2,
Bremen,	837	Washington,	1,
Bristol,	2,991	Westport,	(
Cushing,	746	Whitefield,	2,
Dresden,	1,647	Wiscasset,	2,
Edgecomb,	1,238	Woolwich,	1,
Friendship,	725	Patricktown plantation,	
Georgetown,	1,357	Matinicus Island,	
Jefferson,	2,214	Monhegan Island,	
Lewiston,	1,801	Matinicus Rock,	
Lisbon,	1,531	Matinic Island,	
Newcastle,	1,713	Muscle Ridge Island,	
Nobleborough,	2,210	Ragged Island,	
Phipsburg,	1,657	Wooden Ball Island,	
Richmond,	1,604		
St. George,	2,094		63,5
Thomaston,	6,227		

COUNTY OF HANCOCK

Towns	Population	Towns	Populati
Aurora,	149	Hancock,	
Amherst,	196	Mariaville,	
Bluehill,	1,891	Mount Desert,	1,
Brooksville,	1,246	Orland,	1,
Bucksport,	3,015	Otis,	
Castine,	1,188	Penobscot,	1
Cranberry Isles,	288	Sedgwick,	1
Dedham,	455	Sullivan,	
Deer Isle,	2,841	Surry,	
Eastbrook,	155	Waltham,	
Eden,	1,054	Swan Island,	
Ellsworth,	2,267	Township No. 33,	
Franklin,	502	Township No. 21,	
Gouldsborough,	1,196	Township No. 2,	
Greenfield,	223	Plantation No. 1,	

COUNTY OF HANCOCK, (CONTINUED.)

Towns.	Population.	Towns.	Population.
Strip North No. 1,	23	Black Island,	30
Wetmore Isle,	139	Placentia Island,	32
Seaville,	129	Conway's Island,	8
Plantation No. 7,	61	Calf Island,	18
Plantation No. 10,	19	John's Island,	4
Trenton,	1,061	Pond Island,	11
Bear Island,	11	Harbor Island,	9
Beach Island,	8	Hog Island,	12
Pickering's Island,	14	Conway's Island,	10
Sprucehead Island,	12	Hacketash Island,	18
Little Sprucehead Island,	6	Wooden Ball Island,	7
Butter Island,	8	Matinicus Rock,	10
Eagle Island,	18	Matinicus Island,	182
Harbor Island,	4	Holbrook Island,	3
Marshall's Island,	8		
Duck Island,	6		28,646
Long Island,	114		

COUNTY OF WASHINGTON.

Towns.	Population.	Towns.	Population.
Addison,	1,052	Lubec,	2,307
Alexander,	513	Machias,	1,351
Beddington,	164	Machiasport,	834
Baileyville,	329	Marion,	281
Baring,	376	East Machias,	1,395
Calais,	2,934	Northfield,	232
Columbia,	843	Pembroke,	1,050
Cooper,	657	Perry,	1,008
Cutler,	657	Princeton,	157
Charlotte,	666	Robbinston,	822
Cherryfield,	1,003	Stouben,	884
Crawford,	300	Trescott,	793
Dennysville,	378	Topsfield,	188
Eastport,	2,876	Wesley,	255
Edmonds,	259	Whiting,	460
Harrington,	1,525	Plantation No. 23,	122
Jonesborough,	392	E. half Town'p No. 6, 2d R.	73
Jonesport,	576	Hill's Gore, 4th Range,	30

10*

COUNTY OF WASHINGTON, (CONTINUED.)

Towns.	Population.	Towns.	Population.
No. 9, 2d Range,	12	Township No. 1, 2d Range,	12
Fowler and Ely, 1st Range		Township No. 21, Eastern	
Township No. 1,	13	Division,	26
Township No 9, 4th Range,	49	Annsburg,	23
Danforth half Township, 4th		Devereaux,	30
Range,	45	Township No. 14,	153
Township No. 9, 3d Range,	48	Township No. 18,	35
Township No. 2, 2d Range,	53	Township No. 19,	62
No. 3, 2d Range,	47		
Hinkley Township No. 3, 1st			28,309
Range,	9		

COUNTY OF KENNEBEC.

Town	Pop.	Town	Pop.
Albion,	1,624	Readfield,	2,037
Augusta,	5,314	Rome,	987
Belgrade,	1,748	Sidney,	2,190
China,	2,675	Vassalborough,	2,951
Clinton,	2,818	Vienna,	891
Dearborn,	168	Waterville,	2,939
Fayette,	1,016	Wayne,	1,201
Greene,	1,406	Windsor,	1,789
Gardiner,	5,044	Winthrop,	1,915
Hallowell,	4,668	Winslow,	1,722
Leeds,	1,736	Clinton Gore,	110
Litchfield,	2,293	Wales,	656
Monmouth,	1,882	Territory North of Albion,	89
Mount Vernon,	1,475		
Pittston,	2,460		55,804

COUNTY OF OXFORD.

Town	Pop.	Town	Pop.
Albany,	691	Dixfield,	1,166
Andover,	551	Fryeburg,	1,536
Bethel,	1,994	Greenwood,	836
Brownfield,	1,360	Gilead,	313
Buckfield,	1,629	Hartford,	1,472
Byron,	219	Hebron,	945
Canton,	919	Hiram,	1,232
Denmark,	1,143	Howard's Gore,	131

COUNTY OF OXFORD, (CONTINUED.)

Towns.	Population.	Towns.	Population.
Hamlin's Grant,	80	Turner,	2,479
Lovel,	941	Waterford,	1,381
Livermore,	2,745	Woodstock,	819
Mexico,	447	Township B.,	111
Newry,	463	No. 5, 1st Range,	49
Norway,	1,786	No. 5, 2d Range,	42
Oxford,	1,246	Township C.,	29
Paris,	2,454	Andover North Surplus,	45
Peru,	1,002	Riley Township,	51
Porter,	1,133	Letter A, No. 2,	54
Roxbury,	227	No. 4, 1st Range,	4
Rumford,	1,444	Fryeburg Academy Grant,	153
Stoneham,	313	Number two,	386
Stow,	376	Batchelder's Grant.	3
Sumner,	1,269		
Sweden,	670		38,389

COUNTY OF SOMERSET.

Anson,	1,941	Norridgewock,	1,865
Athens,	1,427	Palmyra,	1,500
Bingham,	751	Pittsfield,	951
Bloomfield,	1,093	Ripley,	591
Brighton,	803	Solon,	1,139
Canaan,	1,379	St. Albans,	1,564
Cambridge,	461	Starks,	1,559
Concord,	577	Skowhegan,	1,584
Cornville,	1,140	Smithfield,	789
Chandlerville,	372	No. 1, 2d Range West	
Embden,	993	Kennebec river,	63
Fairfield,	2,198	No. 1, 2d Range, Pleasant	
Hartland,	1,028	Ridge,	167
Harmony,	1,096	No. 1, 3d Range, West	
Lexington,	564	Kennebec River,	85
Madison,	1,701	No. 1, 4th Range,	10
Maxfield,	149	No. 1, 5th Range, Forks	
Mercer,	1,432	Township,	80
Moscow,	562	Enchanted Stream,	5
New Portland,	1,620	Parlin Pond,	9

COUNTY OF SOMERSET, (Continued.)

Towns.	Population.	Towns.	Populat
Jackman's Township,	10	Spencer Stream,	
Holden Plantation, Moose		Long Pond,	
River,	65	No. 5, 2d Range, Canada	
Canada Road,	6	Road,	
Canada Line, No. 5, 3d		No. 1, 3d Range, East	
Range,	10	Kennebec River,	
No. 2, 2d Range,	139	No. 1, 4th Range, East	
No. 3, 3d Range,	106	Kennebec River,	
Flag Staff Township, No.			
4, 4th Range,	64		33

COUNTY OF PENOBSCOT.

Argyle,	527	Lagrange,	3
Bangor, city,	8,634	Lee,	7
Bradford,	1,001	Levant,	1,0
Bradley,	395	Lincoln,	1,1
Brewer,	1,736	Lowell,	25
Burlington,	350	Maxfield,	18
Carmel,	521	Mattamiscontis,	9
Corinna,	1,702	Milford,	47
Corinth,	1,318	Newburg,	9
Charleston,	1,269	Newport,	1,1
Chester,	277	Orono,	1,5
Dexeter,	1,464	Orrington,	1,5
Dixmont,	1,498	Oldtown,	2,3
Etna,	745	Passadumkeag,	3
Eddington,	595	Plymouth,	8
Edinburg,	52	Springfield,	5
Enfield,	346	Stetson,	6
Exeter,	2,052	Jarvis' Gore,	1
Garland,	1,065	Township No. 3,	
Glenburn,	664	Township No. 4,	
Greenbush,	260	Township, No. 3, Range	
Hampden,	2,665	8th,	
Hermon,	1,045	Lower Indian Township,	
Howland,	312	West Penobscot River,	
Kirkland,	351	Indian Township No. 2,	

COUNTY OF PENOBSCOT, (CONTINUED.)

Towns.	Population.	Towns.	Population.
Hopkins' Academy Grant,	3	W. half of Town'p No. 6,	187
Letter A,	29	Township No. 7,	30
Unincorporated Township,			
North of Lincoln,	147		45,705

COUNTY OF WALDO.

Towns	Population	Towns	Population
Appleton,	891	Monroe,	1,602
Belfast,	4,194	Montville,	2,153
Belmont,	1,378	Northport,	1,207
Brooks,	910	Palermo,	1,594
Burnham,	609	Prospect,	3,492
Camden,	3,005	Searsmont,	1,374
Frankfort,	3,603	Swanville,	919
Freedom,	1,153	Thorndike,	897
Hope,	1,770	Troy,	1,376
Islesborough,	778	Unity,	1,467
Jackson,	652	Vinalhaven,	1,950
Knox,	897	Waldo Plantation,	721
Liberty,	895		
Lincolnville,	2,048		41,535

COUNTY OF PISCATAQUIS.

Towns	Population	Towns	Population
Abbot,	661	Milton,	469
Atkinson,	704	Milo,	756
Barnard,	153	Parkman,	1,205
Bowerbank,	165	Sangerville,	1,197
Blanchard,	270	Sebec,	1,116
Brownville,	568	Shirley,	190
Dover,	1,597	Wellington,	722
Eliotsville,	60	Wilson,	70
Foxcroft,	926	Williamsburg,	131
Guilford,	892	Township No. 3, 3d Range,	28
Greenville,	128	Plantation No. 8,	31
Kilmarnock,	319	Letter B, 10th Range,	5
Kingsbery,	227		
Monson,	548		13,138

COUNTY OF FRANKLIN

Towns.	Population.	Towns.	Population.
Avon,	827	Weld,	1,045
Berlin,	442	Wilton,	2,198
Carthage,	522	No. 3, 2d Range,	47
Chesterville,	1,098	No. 4, 2d Range,	6
Farmington,	2,613	No. 4, 1st Range,	4
Freeman,	838	Bigelow Township,	37
Industry,	1,035	Township Letter E.,	77
Jay,	1,750	Township No. 2, 2d Range,	82
Kingfield,	671	Township No.1, 4th Range,	163
Madrid,	368	Township No. 1, 3d Range,	52
New Sharon,	1,829	Township No. 3, 1st Range,	7
New Vineyard,	927	Township No. 2, 1st Range,	9
Phillips,	1,312	Township No.2, 3d Range,	216
Salem,	561		
Strong,	1,109		20,900
Temple,	955		

COUNTY OF AROOSTOOK.

Amity,	169	Letter A, 1st Range,	177
Belfast Academy Grant,	141	Williams College Grant,	85
Hodgdon,	665	Bridgewater Acad Grant,	51
Houlton,	1,597	Framingham Acad. Grant.	16
Township No. 5, 3d Range,	9	Westfield Acad. Grant,	3
Township A, 2d Range,	6	Letter A, 5th Range,	15
Weston,	249	Benedicta, or No. 2, 5th R.	222
Township No. 2, 2d Range,	43	No. 3, 5th Range,	100
Linneus,	311	No. 4, 5th Range,	294
Township No. 11,1st Range,	66	No. 6, 5th Range,	43
Township No. 1, 4th Range,	69	Nos. 7 and 9, 5th Range,	48
Township No. 2, 3d Range,	14	No. 10, 5th R. or Masardis	140
Township No. 1, 2d Range,	104	No. 11, 5th Range,	45
Township No. 1 3d Range,	24	No. 13, 3d Range,	66
Orient Gore,	68	Letter G, 2d Range,	58
Township No. 9,	50	Letter K, 2d Range,	96
Township No. 3, 2d Range,	20	Plymouth and Eaton Grant,	63
Smyrna,	184	Letters H, and J, 1st and	
New Limerick,	123	2d Ranges,	194

COUNTY OF AROOSTOOK, (CONTINUED.)

Towns.	Population.	Towns.	Population.
Plymouth Grant,	200	Madawaska South of the	
Letter G,	27	St. John river,	1,584
Fort Fairfield, or Letter D,	26	Madawaska North of the	
Number 3, 6th and 7th		St. John river,	1,876
Ranges,	50		
No. 1, 5th Range,	22		9,413

RECAPITULATION.

Counties.	Population.
York,	54,023
Cumberland,	68,660
Lincoln,	63,512
Hancock,	28,646
Washington,	28,309
Kennebec,	55,804
Oxford,	38,539
Somerset,	33,912
Penobscot,	45,705
Waldo,	41,535
Piscataquis,	13,138
Franklin,	20,800
Aroostook,	9,413
Total,	501,796

STATE VALUATION OF 1845.

COUNTY OF YORK.

Towns	Polls.	Estate.
Acton,	294	173,9
Alfred,	246	184,3
Berwick,	274	199,2
Biddeford,	484	421,11
Buxton,	482	289,7
Cornish,	224	130,7
Eliot,	324	254,04
Hollis,	391	265,5
Kennebunk,	429	581,8
Kennebunkport,	381	400,9
Kittery,	409	242,9
Lebanon,	387	257,
Limerick,	236	166,0
Limington,	398	265,
Lyman,	241	159,
Newfield,	218	156,
North Berwick,	245	265,
Parsonsfield,	444	537,
Saco,	589	1,072,
Sanford,	381	264,
Shapleigh,	251	156,
South Berwick,	402	454,
Waterborough,	311	188,
Wells,	475	385,
York,	579	366,
	8,874	$7,642,

COUNTY OF CUMBERLAND.

Towns.	Polls.	Estate.
Auburn,	339	259,165
Baldwin,	213	125,396
Bridgton,	354	300,200
Brunswick,	840	835,786
Cumberland,	248	231,426
Cape Elizabeth,	305	152,342
Casco,	163	89,779
Danville,	221	159,336
Durham,	335	280,756
Falmouth,	369	234,133
Freeport,	508	381,593
Gorham,	477	514,348
Gray,	290	193,428
Harpswell,	281	211,966
Harrison,	240	161,529
Minot,	263	228,491
Naples,	170	85,500
North Yarmouth,	532	599,159
New Gloucester,	309	287,777
Otisfield,	188	167,882
Poland,	372	202,500
Portland,	2,445	4,076,303
Pownal,	221	181,134
Raymond,	191	103,018
Scarborough,	360	308,725
Sebago,	150	56,012
Standish,	380	292,131
Westbrook,	738	652,236
Windham,	402	304,719
	11,883	$11,627,770

COUNTY OF LINCOLN.

	Polls.	Estate.
Alna,	198	181,895
Arrowsic,	73	44,426
Bath,	736	1,388,175
Boothbay,	395	181,005

11

Bowdoin,
Bremen,
Bristol,
Cushing,
Dresden,
Edgecomb,
Friendship,
Georgetown,
Jefferson,
Lewiston,
Lisbon,
Newcastle,
Nobleborough,
Phipsburg,
Richmond,
St. George,
Thomaston,
Topsham,
Union,
Waldoborough,
Webster,
Warren,
Washington,
Westport,
Whitefield,
Wiscasset,
Woolwich,
Patricktown plantation,
Monhegan plantation,
Townsend,
West Bath,

COUNTY OF HANCOCK.

Towns.	Polls.	Estate.
Aurora,	36	24,016
Amherst,	65	27,549
Bluehill,	392	274,161
Brooksville,	200	89,526
Bucksport,	636	447,094
Castine,	212	361,878
Cranberry Isles,	55	34,931
Deer Isle,	481	162,699
Dedham,	90	45,853
Ellsworth,	495	366,711
Eden,	208	90,136
Eastbrook,	32	20,373
Franklin,	122	67,865
Gouldsborough,	237	85,864
Greenfield,	53	20,270
Hancock,	145	73,252
Mariaville,	56	27,877
Mount Desert,	328	134,274
Orland,	290	172,465
Otis,	26	14,703
Penobscot,	279	156,640
Seaville,	30	42,214
Sedgwick,	405	179,994
Sullivan,	157	75,690
Surry,	191	108,795
Swan Island,	63	13,147
Trenton,	202	103,659
Waltham,	49	29,744
Wetmore Isle,	37	22,519
	5,572	3,276,902
Wild Lands,		200,400
		$3,477,302

Wild Lands in the County of Hancock.

No. and Range.	Description.	Acres.	Value.
No. 1,	North Division,	23,040	7,000
No. 2,	do	23,040	8,000
No. 3,	do.	23,040	16,000
No. 4,	do.	23,040	16,000
	Strip N of No 3, N. Divis,	7,844	2,000
	do. do. 4, do	7,844	2,000
No. 7,	South Division,	20,475	5,000
No. 8,	do.	9,600	2,400
No. 9,	do	5,760	2,000
No. 10,	Adjoining Steuben,	23,936	8,300
No. 16,	Middle Division,	23,040	8,000
No. 21,	do	23,040	8,000
No. 22,	do	23,040	8,000
No. 28,	do	23,040	8,000
No. 32,	do	23,040	8,000
No. 33,	do	23,040	16,000
No. 34,	do	23,040	16,000
No. 35,	do	23,040	16,000
No. 39,	do	23,040	8,000
No. 40,	do	23,040	12,300
No. 41,	do	23,040	16,000
	Butter Island,	240	750
	Eagle Island,	240	1,000
	Spruce-head and Bear Isl,	172	500
	Beech Island,	96	500
	Hog Island,	75	400
	Bradbury Island,	140	500
	Pond and Western Island,	65	200
	Little Spruce-head Island,	60	200
	Pond Island,	207	1,000
	Calf Island,	256	500
	West Black Island,	150	100
	East Black Island,	300	100
	Placentia Island,	500	200
	Old Harbor Island,	150	300
	Long Island,	500	3,000
	Marshall's Island,	375	500
	Great Duck Island,	100	250
	Pickering's Island,	150	1,000
	Holbrook Island,		400
		424,835	$200,400

200	104,049
103	33,926
34	14,111
50	23,439
64	42,148
664	341,312
29	16,012
191	112,888
105	33,390
147	52,552
108	39,827
233	132,045
58	16,800
69	54,364
233	188,449
511	340,725
57	38,248
306	115,508
97	30,385
133	34,773
471	161,779
256	191,973
214	80,050
37	14,300
61	15,991
41	16,411
150	88,333
283	85,250
53	18,339
162	96,372
179	67,328
102	42,515
46	20,456
52	19,832
88	40,717
107	54,850

No. 19,	do.
No. 24,	do.
No. 25,	do.
No. 29,	do.
No. 30,	do.
No. 31,	do.
No. 36,	do.
No. 37,	do.
No. 42,	do.
No. 43,	do.
No. 5,	North Division,
No. 6,	do.
	Two mile strip N. of No. 5,
	do. do. 6,
No. 1, R. 1,	Titcomb's survey,
No. 3, R. 1,	do. do. Hinkley's,
No. 1, R, 2,	do. do. Dyer's,
No. 2, R. 2,	do. do. Waite's,
No. 3, R. 2,	do. do. Tallmadge,
N. ½ No. 1, R. 3,	
S. ½ No. 1, R. 3,	
No. 1, R. 4,	Vanceboro',
W. ½ No. 6. R. 1,	Lennox,
E. ½ No. 6, R. 1,	Vanceboro',
N.E. ¼ No. 7, R. 2,	
¾ No. 7, R. 2,	
S. ½ No. 9, R. 2,	
N. ½ No. 9, R. 2,	
No. 8, R. 3,	
No. 9, R. 3,	
No. 10, R. 3,	
No. 11, R. 3,	

Wild Lands in the County of Washington—(Contin'd.)

No. and Range.	Description.	Acres	Value.
No. 9, R. 4, No. 8, R. 4,	Danforth tract, N. of Bingham Purchase, do do	11,520 23,583 23,040	4,000 8,000 8,000
		876,036	$388,000

COUNTY OF KENNEBEC

Towns.	Polls	Estate.
Augusta,	984	1,143,885
Albion,	286	228,475
Belgrade,	311	206,291
China,	501	391,248
Clinton,	251	160,934
Clinton Gore,	25	6,722
Fayette,	205	165,921
Gardiner,	600	878,821
Greene,	208	177,803
Hallowell,	750	851,229
Leeds,	252	219,340
Litchfield,	391	256,133
Monmouth,	432	291,893
Mount Vernon,	275	177,752
Pittston,	446	469,483
Readfield,	311	363,795
Rome,	144	63,493
Sidney,	405	338,603
Sebasticook,	175	103,990
Vassalborough,	491	503,498
Vienna,	150	95,951
Waterville,	571	677,800
Wales,	111	99,654
Wayne,	165	149,549
Windsor,	274	196,348
Winthrop,	396	355,150

Wild Land.

COUNTY OF OXFO

Albany,
Andover,
Bethel,
Buckfield,
Brownfield,
Byron,
Canton,
Denmark,
Dixfield,
Fryeburg,
Gilead,
Greenwood,
Hartford,
Hebron,
Hiram,
Hanover,
Lovel,
Livermore,
Mexico,
Mason,
Newry,
Norway,
Oxford,
Porter,
Paris,
Peru,
Rumford,

COUNTY OF OXFORD, (Continued.)

Towns.	Polls.	Estate
Roxbury,	39	13,251
Sumner,	245	156,213
Sweden,	146	83,578
Stow,	80	27,888
Stoneham,	62	12,380
Turner,	458	305,995
Woodstock,	117	53,314
Waterford,	284	200,209
Hamlin's Grant,	13	2,379
Franklin plantation,	57	3,948
Milton plantation,	30	7,080
	6,756	3,935,536
Wild Lands,		86,250
		$4,021,786

Wild Lands in the County of Oxford

No. and Range	Description.	Acres.	Value
	Andover North Surplus,	15,960	2,500
No. 2,	South of Rumford,	26,165	3,750
A, No. 1,		26,880	6,250
B,		25,600	10,000
A, No. 2,		28,507	6,250
C,		21,074	6,250
C,	Surplus,	12,206	6,250
No. 4, R. 1,	West of Bingham Purchase,	24,448	6,250
No. 5, R. 1,		31,780	6,250
No. 4, R. 2,		23,040	6,250
No. 5, R. 2,		20,904	6,250
No. 4, R. 3,		21,000	3,750
No. 5, R. 3,		22,717	4,375
No. 4, R. 4,		23,040	4,375
No. 5, R. 4,		24,436	4,375
S. ½ No. 5, R. 5,		10,404	1,875
N. ½ No. 5, R. 5,		5,202	1,250
		362,363	$86,250

COUNTY OF SOMERSET.

Towns.	Polls.	Estate.
Anson,	145	86,851
Athens,	222	189,736
Brighton,	123	45,865
Bloomfield,	194	180,814
Bingham,	129	54,505
Cornville,	211	160,645
Canaan,	219	132,075
Concord,	96	27,754
Cambridge,	92	26,150
Detroit,	81	29,896
Embden,	179	105,355
Fairfield,	353	301,690
Hartland,	210	68,255
Harmony,	194	107,339
Lexington,	97	33,122
Mercer,	182	131,608
Madison,	306	230,423
Moscow,	124	44,173
Mayfield,	30	13,508
New Portland,	265	188,311
Norridgewock,	386	306,776
North Anson,	188	163,349
Palmyra,	312	123,511
Pittsfield,	218	77,993
Ripley,	132	44,615
Starks,	242	134,538
Skowhegan,	285	196,403
Solon,	247	128,126
Smithfield,	141	51,091
St. Albans,	334	134,143
	5,917	3,520,488
Wild Lands,		405,115
		$3,925,603

Wild Lands in the County of Somerset.

No. and Range.	Description.	Acres.	Value.
No. 1, R. 2,	Bing Pur. W. of Ken. riv,	13,116	3,090
No. 2, R. 2,	do. do. do	23,040	6,180
No. 1, R. 3,	do do. do.	8 883	2,060
No. 2, R. 3,	do. do. do.	24,162	10,300
No 3, R. 3,	do. do. do.	24,792	8.240
No. 4, R. 3,	do do. do N. ½	11,144	5,050
No. 1, R. 4,	do. do do.	17,800	5,050
No. 2, R. 4,	do. do. do.	25,200	10,300
No. 3, R. 4,	do. do. do	24,040	9,270
No. 4, R. 4,	do. do do	21,143	10,300
No. 1, R. 5,	do do do	29,950	10,300
No. 2, R. 5,	do. do do	22,320	12,360
No. 3, R 5,	do. do do	23,980	8,240
No. 4, R. 5,	do do. do.	23,915	8,240
No. 1, R. 6,	do. do. do	24,175	14,420
No. 2, R. 6,	do. Crocker's pt E.pt	13,040	6,180
No. 2, R. 6,	do. W K Riv , W. pt	10,000	2,060
No. 3, R. 6,	do. do. do	23,040	6,180
No. 4, R. 6,	do. do do	23,040	8,240
No. 5, R. 6,	do. do do.	23,040	8,240
No. 1, R. 7,	do do do	17,600	8,240
No. 2, R. 7,	do. do. do.	22,9-5	9,270
No. 3, R. 7,	do do do	14,600	6,180
No. 4, R. 7,	do do do.	15,144	7,210
No. 5, R. 7,	do. do. do	15,744	8,240
No. 6, R. 7,	do. do. do	16,350	4,120
No. 1, R. 3,	do. E. Ken River,	29,541	7,210
No. 2, R. 3,	do do.	23,040	14,240
No. 1, R. 4,	do. do.	23,040	14,240
No. 2, R. 4,	do. do.	24,250	12,360
No. 1, R. 5,	do. do.	12,240	4,120
No. 2, R. 5,	do. do	23,040	8,240
No. 1, R. 6,	do. do.	10,750	5,150
No. 1, R. 1,	S pt , N. of Bing. Pur	11,520	7,210
No. 1, R. 1,	N pt. N.of B P , strip north,	4,469	2,060
No. 2, R. 1,	N.B.P.,S pt Sandwich acad	11,520	6,180
No. 2, R. 1,	" N pt ,stp N.the above,	2,066	1,030
No. 3, R 1,	" Long Pond,	20,065	10,300
No. 4, R. 1,	" Moose River,	23,040	7,210
No. 5, R, 1,	"	23,040	7,210

Wild Lands in the County of Somerset—(Continued.)

No and Range.	Description.	Acres.	Value.
No. 1, R. 2,	N. B. P , Tomhegan,	18,224	10,300
No. 2, R. 2,	" Brassua,	21,960	10,300
No. 3, R. 2,	" Thorndike,	23,040	12,360
No. 4, R. 2,	" pt of, granted sold's,	17,000	7,210
No. 5, R. 2,	" Dennis,	23,040	8,240
No. 1, R. 3,	" W Middlesex,	23,040	8,240
No. 2, R. 3,	" pt of, granted sold's,	17,000	6,180
No. 5, R. 3,	" Sandy Bay,	23,040	4,120
No. 1, R. 4,	" Plymouth,	23,040	8,240
No. 2, R. 4,	" ½ of, Pittston,	7,680	5,150
No. 2, R. 4,	" ¾ of,	15,369	8,240
No. 3, R. 3,	" ¼ of East half,	5,480	3,090
No. 3, R. 4,	" ½ of,	11,040	6,180
	Seboomook,	23,040	13,055
		1,012,789	$405,115

COUNTY OF PENOBSCOT.

Towns	Polls.	Estate.
Alton,	33	9,782
Argyle,	73	19,606
Bangor,	1,549	2,016,914
Bradford,	220	59,342
Bradley,	110	57,338
Brewer,	382	257,560
Burlington,	73	14,596
Carmel,	165	71,546
Carroll,	50	13,500
Corinna,	280	112,819
Corinth,	266	137,357
Charleston,	269	104,410
Chester,	45	11,698
Dexter,	312	174,058
Dixmont,	249	142,528
Eddington,	135	75,545

14	10,147
66	19,137
144	33,700
366	169,833
155	60,124
221	100,324
80	16,322
450	294,967
183	75,525
42	22,067
77	26,422
73	27,055
156	$7,738
259	100,010
249	86,901
74	15,988
9	4,523
34	5,340
104	67,696
170	81,614
282	149,568
379	176,346
345	188,682
480	195,705
53	16,838
152	56,126
91	24,319
96	22,209
129	57,220
9,144	5,421,045
	330,525
	$5,751,570

Wild Lands in the County of Penobscot.

No. and Range.	Description.	Acres.	Value
No. 3, R. 1,	North of Bingham Purch ,	26,010	11,250
No. 4, R. 1,	do do. do.	38,424	9,000
No 5, R. 1,	do. Amherst Acad.,	11,520	5,695
No 6, R 3,	do. Bingham Purch.,	23,040	10,125
No. 7, R. 3,	do do. do.	23,040	5,625
S W¼ No 6,R.4,	do do. do.	5,760	4,500
½ No. 6, R 4,	do do. do.	17,280	9,000
No. 7, R 4,	do do. do.	23,040	12,375
No. 4,	River Township,	23,040	45,000
No. 2, R 8,	North of Waldo Patent,	23,040	9,000
E ½ No 3, R. 8,	do do do.	11,520	2,250
No. 2, R. 9,	do do do	23,040	11,250
No. 3, R. 9,	do do do	23,040	9,600
S. ¼ A, R 6,	W. from E line of State,	12,000	2,700
N. ½ A, R 6,	do. do. do.	12,000	2,700
S. ¼ No. 1, R. 6,	do. do. do.	11,520	2,250
N ½ No 1, R 6,	do. do. do.	11,520	2,250
No 2, R. 6,	do. do. do.	23,040	7,875
S. ¼ No. 3, R. 6,	do. do. do.	11,520	4,500
Pt.N.½ No.3,R.6	do. do. do.	9,520	4,500
A, R. 7,	do. do. do.	24,000	6,750
No. 1, R 7,	do. do. do.	23,040	16,875
No. 2, R 7,	do. do. do.	23,040	4,500
No. 3, R. 7,	. do. do. do.	23,040	13,500
No. 6, R. 7,	do. do. do.	23,040	11,250
No. 7, R. 7,	do. do do.	23,040	11,250
No. 1, R 8,	do. do do.	11,520	9,000
S. ¼ No 2, R. 8,	do do do.	11,520	11,250
N. ½ No.2, R. 8,	do. do. do.	11,520	5,625
E. ½ No. 3, R. 8,	do. do. do.	11,520	5,625
No. 4, R. 8,	do do do.	23,040	11,250
No 5, R 8,	do. do. do.	23,040	11,250
E. ½ No 6, R. 8,	do. do do.	11,520	6,750
Part No. 2,	Indian Purchase,	17,040	6,750
No. 3,	do. do.	23,040	13,500
No. 4,	do. do.	15,040	2,250
Z, N. No.2,	do do.	2,100	2,250
R. 8,	Hopkins Academy Grant,	11,520	5,625
	Jarvis' Gore,	15,050	4,500
		689,584	$330,525

COUNTY OF WALDO.

Towns.	Polls.	Estate.
Appleton,	311	150,000
Belfast,	755	664,474
Belmont,	206	108,000
Brooks,	172	91,000
Burnham,	112	47,000
Camden,	574	367,480
Frankfort,	633	447,000
Freedom,	188	127,200
Hope,	212	122,000
Islesborough,	171	71,000
Jackson,	135	95,000
Knox,	201	102,000
Liberty,	154	74,000
Lincolnville,	326	200,000
Monroe,	287	141,000
Montville,	295	220,000
Northport,	231	107,000
Palermo,	221	138,000
Prospect,	410	280,207
Searsmont,	318	154,000
Searsport,	388	293,648
Swanville,	178	83,000
Thorndike,	172	123,000
Troy,	242	138,000
Unity,	283	190,000
Vinalhaven,	324	124,000
Waldo,	160	65,000
	7,658	$4,702,959

COUNTY OF FRANKLIN.

Avon,	118	53,280
Carthage,	89	30,687
Chesterville,	197	121,158
Farmington,	457	468,386
Freeman,	147	71,062
Industry,	195	137,623
Jay,	281	201,526

COUNTY OF FRANKLIN, (CONTINUED.)

Towns.	Polls.	Estate.
Kingfield,	125	52,798
Madrid,	76	18,242
New Sharon,	327	257,333
New Vineyard,	108	55,624
Phillips,	285	159,897
Salem,	95	31,709
Strong,	197	158,590
Temple,	129	69,726
Weld,	188	83,479
Wilton,	362	272,231
	3,576	2,223,351
Wild Lands,		138,800
		$2,362,151

Wild Lands in the County of Franklin.

No. and Range.	Description.			Acres.	Value.
E. part No. 6,	Near Phillips,			10,000	2,400
W part. No. 6,	Walker,			10,000	2,400
N.pt. No 4, R 1,	Bingham Purchase,			18,300	3,200
No. 3, R 2,	do.	do.		26,792	4,800
No 4, R 2,	do.	do.		21,288	4,000
S. ½ No. 4, R. 3,	do.	do.		10,644	2,000
D,				20,500	4,800
F,				20,600	5,600
No. 2, R. 1,	West of Bingham Purchase,			22,080	4,800
No. 3, R. 1,	do.	do.	do.	29,440	6,400
No. 1, R. 2,	do.	do.	do	23,040	4,000
No. 2, R. 2,	do.	do.	do.	23,040	9,600
No. 3, R. 2,	do.	do.	do.	30,720	12,000
N ½ No. 1, R. 3,	do.	do.	do.	11,520	3,200
S. ½ No. 1, R. 3,	do.	do.	do.	11,520	1,600
No. 2, R. 3,	do.	do.	do.	21,000	6,400
No 3, R. 3,	do.	do.	do.	21,000	4,800
N. ½ No. 1, R 4,	do.	du.	do	11,520	6,400
S. ½ No. 1, R. 4,	do.	do.	do.	11,520	6,400

Wild Lands in the County of Franklin—(Continued.)

No. and Range.	Description.			Acres.	Value.
N ½ No. 2, R 4,	West of Bingham Purchase,			11,520	5,600
No 1, R 5,	do.	do	do.	22,080	11,200
No 2, R 5,	do.	do	do.	23,040	8,000
S ⅜ No. 1, R 6,	do	do.	do.	14,694	4,000
W. ½ No. 2, R 7,	do.	do.	do.	10,100	4,000
Gore N of Nos 2 & 3, R 6,	Dead River,			20,000	11,200
				455,966	$138,800

COUNTY OF PISCATAQUIS.

Towns.	Polls.	Estate.
Abbot,	138	46,844
Atkinson,	177	68,475
Barnard,	30	12,952
Bowerbank,	32	14,598
Blanchard,	49	12,846
Brownville,	132	48,466
Dover,	275	101,321
Eliotsville,	18	8,944
Foxcroft,	166	68,340
Greenville,	37	17,480
Guilford,	177	72,172
Kilmarnock,	67	22,237
Kingsbery,	43	20,496
Milo,	156	42,245
Monson,	120	54,111
Orneville,	80	21,470
Parkman,	251	88,956
Sangerville,	245	108,952
Sebec,	208	85,455
Shirley,	43	13,890
Wellington,	121	29,825
Williamsburg,	26	11,787

12*

No. and Range.	Description.	
No. 4, R. 8,	North of Waldo Patent,	
No. 8, R. 8,	do.	do.
No. 5, R. 9,	do.	do.
N. ½ No. 6, R. 9.	do.	do.
S. ½ No. 6, R. 9,	do.	do.
No. 3, R. 5,	Bingham Pur. E. K. R.,	
No. 2, R. 6,	do.	do.
No. 1, R. 9,	W. from E. line of State,	
No. 2, R. 9,	do.	do.
No. 4, R. 9,	do.	do.
No. 6, R. 9,	do.	do.
E. ½ A, R. 10,	do.	do.
W. ½ A, R. 10,	do.	do.
No. 1, R, 10,	do.	do.
No. 2, R. 10,	do.	do.
No. 3, R. 10,	do.	do.
E. ½ No. 5, R. 10,	do.	do.
W. ½ No 5, R. 10,	do.	do.
No. 6, R. 10,	do.	do.
S. E. ⅔ No. 7, R. 10	do.	do.
A, R. 11,	do.	do.
B, R. 11,	do.	do.
No. 1, R. 11,	do.	do.
S. ½ A, R. 12,	do.	do.
N. ½ A, R. 12,	do.	do.
S. ½ No. 1, R. 12,	do.	do.
N. ⅔ No. 1, R. 12,	do.	do.
No. 2, R. 12,	do.	do.

Wild Lands in the County of Piscataquis—(Continued.)

No. and Range.	Description.	Acres.	Value.
E. ½ No 3, R. 12,	W. from E line of State,	11,520	5,000
W. ½ No. 3, R 12,	do. do.	11,520	5,000
½ No. 4, R. 12,	do. do.	11,377	4,000
A, No. 2, R 13 and 14,	do. do.	17,925	7,000
A, R. 13,	do. do.	23,040	11,000
⅔ No 1, R 13,	do. do.	15,360	7,000
No 3, R 13,	do. do.	19,825	15,000
S.pt. No.4, R 13,	do. do.	10,126	7,000
A, R 14,	do. do.	19,164	11,000
No. 1, R 14,	do. do.	23,941	9,000
E ½ No. 3, R 14 and 15,	do. do.	19,787	11,000
W ½ No. 3, R 14 and 15,	do. do.	23,236	9,000
S E ¼ No. 4, R 14,	do. do.	6.462	4,000
No. 6, R 10,	do. do.	23,040	9,216
No 6, R 11,	do. do.	23,040	9,216
No. 6, R 15,	do. do.	23,040	9,216
N W ¼ No. 5, R 15,	do do	5,760	2,304
	Middlesex Canal,	23,040	11,000
	Day's Academy Grant,	11,520	5,000
	Sugar Island,	4,950	5,000
	Deer Island,	2,000	7,000
		854,240	$344,952

COUNTY OF AROOSTOOK.

Towns	Polls.	Estate
Amity,	34	12,141
Hodgdon,	116	47,377
Houlton,	257	113,517
Linneus,	95	15,901
New Limerick,	29	7,493

No. and Range.	Description.
No. 1, R, 1,	Gore East of Weston,
No. 9,	Greenwood's Survey,
No. 1, R. 2,	Fowler and others,
No. 2, R. 2,	Pickering,
No. 3, R. 2,	Morrill & Pickering,
R. 1,	Williams College Grant,
R. 1,	Framingham Acad. Grant,
A, R. 1,	Monticello,
R. 1,	Portland Academy Grant,
R. 1'	Bridgewater Academy Gt.,
R. 1	Mars Hill Township,
R. 1	Town of Plymouth Grant,
R. 2	Belfast Academy Grant,
B, R. 2,	W. from E. line of State,
D, R. 2,	do. do. do.
R. 2,	Deerfield Academy Grant,
R. 2'	Westfield Academy Grant
R. 2,	General Eaton Grant,
E, R. 2,	W. E. L. S.,
Part No.1, R. 3,	do. Nichols Acad.,
No. 1, R. 3,	do.
S. ½ No. 2, R. 3,	do.
N. ½ No. 2, R. 3,	do.
No. 3, R. 3,	do.
⅔ S. part Nº. 4, R. 3,	do.

Wild Lands in the County of Aroostook—(Continued.)

No. and Range.	Description.		Acres.	Value.
½ N. part No. 4, R. 3,	W. E. L. S.,		9,600	2,880
No. 7, R. 3,	do.		23,040	4,500
No. 8, R. 3,	do.		23,040	4,500
S. pt. No.1, R.4,	do.		16,520	4,956
No. 1, R. 4,	do.	N. Yarmouth Acd.	11,520	4,000
N.pt. No.1, R.4,	do.		11,520	4,000
No. 2, R. 4,	do.		23,040	6,912
No. 5, R. 4,	do.		23,040	5,000
E. ½ No. 6, R. 4,	do.		11,520	3,456
N. W. ¼ No. 6, R. 4,	do.		5,760	1,728
S. pt. A, R. 5,	do.	Camberlain,	7,680	2,560
N. pt. A, R. 5,	do.	Fisk & Bridge,	11,520	3,860
S. ½ No. 1, R. 5,	do.	do.	11,520	3,860
N. ½ No. 1, R. 5,	do.	Harvey Reed,	11,520	3,860
W. ½ No.2, R.5,	do.	Benedicta,	11,520	3,860
No. 3, R. 5,	do.		22,188	6,656
No. 5, R. 5,	do.		23,040	5,000
No. 7, R. 5,	do.		23,040	5,000
Pt. No. 6, R. 5,	do.		13,452	3,363
			690,792	$207,237

Polls.	Estates.
8,874	7,642,778
11,883	11,627,770
11,390	9,859,871
5,572	3,477,302
5,694	3,166,514
9,563	8,917,662
6,756	4,021,786
5,917	3,925,603
9,094	5,751,570
7,658	4,702,959
2,618	1,326,913
3,376	2,362,151
659	436,467
89,054	$67,219,356

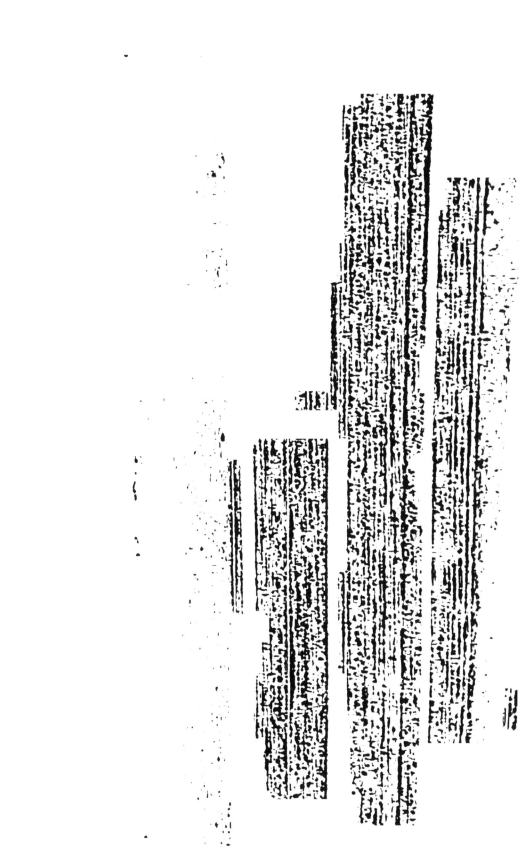

MESSAGE

OF

NOR ANDER

TO

BRANCHES OF THE LEGISLATU

OF THE

STATE OF MAINE.

HOUSE OF REPRESENT
May 15, 1846.

Read and laid on the table and one thousand copi
be printed for the use of the House.

SAMUEL BELCH

MESSAGE.

Gentlemen of the Senate
and House of Representatives :

SINCE the adjournment of the last Legislature, a period has elapsed, considerably longer than that which has usually intervened between consecutive sessions; and in conformity to the constitution of the State, as it has been amended by the people, we have assembled for the first time, upon the day designated by the recent provision.

It brings you together at a season more conducive to personal comfort, and better adapted, as I trust it will be found, to an expeditious and economical transaction of the public business.

During the recess of the Legislature, but little has occurred to interrupt the prosecution of the various pursuits, upon which the enterprise and activity of our citizens lead them to engage.

The orderly habits which prevail among the people, have protected us from the disturbances which have occasionally occurred in some of our sister states; and the invigorating influence of a healthful climate, has exempted us from those enfeebling diseases, which have visited other sections of the country.

In addition to the vigorous prosecution of their ordinary avocations, the enterprise of our citizens is also leading them to other branches of profitable labor: under the liberal policy adopted by the Legislature, numerous acts of incorporation for manufacturing purposes have been granted, and there is reason to believe, that with the increase of our population, and the accumulation of unemployed capital, our natural advantages for this species of productive industry will be gradually developed.

Nor have the benefits which result from the opening of new avenues of intercommunication between distant and important points, been overlooked or neglected. Various projects to cheapen transportation, and facilitate the public travel, have been suggested and examined, one of which, as the result wholly of private enterprise and capital, deserves to be ranked among the most magnificent and useful conceptions of the time.

Designed to connect by a continuous line of Rail Road, the principal depot upon the St. Lawrence, with so convenient and excellent a seaport as Portland, the facilities this work would afford to both the internal and external commerce of the State, can scarcely be overrated: and though the well settled policy of the State government precludes it from any active co-operation in its construction, its successful prosecution will be regarded with the highest satisfaction in every section of the State.

In the retrospect of a period distinguished by so many evidences of public prosperity, it would be strange, if there should be found no admixture of disappointment.

The partial failure of an important crop has been seriously felt, and the extraordinary floods which have prevailed during the present spring, have been productive of great inconvenience and loss: for the one however, a considerable indemnity was found in the great abundance of more valuable productions; and it is hoped, that the perseverence and energy, so strikingly characteristic of the community most deeply affected, will speedily overcome the disasters occasioned by the other.

In assembling, to enter upon the duties assigned us by the people, it is gratifying, that with the exceptions I have mentioned, we are enabled to indulge in mutual congratulations, upon the continued and growing prosperity with which we have been favored. With abundant cause to be satisfied with the past, we may also hope, that with the blessing of Him, who has so signally favored us hitherto, our progress, in all that essentially conduces to the welfare of a State, will be sufficiently rapid in the future.

The annual Reports of the Treasurer and Land Agent, the latter of which is herewith communicated, will advise you of the condition of the two most important branches of the public service.

Under the care of the able and vigilant officers who have charge of these departments, the financial concerns of the State exhibit the most satisfactory aspect.

The balance in the Treasury at the date of the last report of the Treasurer, amounted to the sum of $392,422.

There has been received into the Treasury from all

1 *

sources, and for all purposes, during the financial year, ending upon the 30th April last, the sum of $610,772.

Of this sum, there was received from the avails of the State Tax for 1844 and 1845, the sum of $215,433; from the Land Agent, $155,048, and for claims against the General Government, adjusted and paid during the year, the sum of $162,398.

There has been paid from the Treasury, during the same period, the sum of $634,210; of which $454,000 was for payment of principal and interest of the public debt, the greater part of which became due during the year. The balance in the Treasury is now $370,000; and it is estimated, that the receipts for the ensuing political year, would fully justify the immediate application of the whole of this sum, in the payment of the principal of our State debt; and it is also estimated, that with the small amount now required to defray the ordinary expenses of the State, the receipts which may be expected from the Land office, together with other sources of income, and the tax for 1846, will increase the sum which may be appropriated to the same purpose during the year.

The whole amount of the funded debt of the State is now $1,274,285; if the holders of its stock certificates would consent to receive, in anticipation of their maturity, the money now on hand, it would be reduced to the sum of $905,000.

Three years ago, our debt amounted to $1,700,000; the means are now in the Treasury, and needed for no other purpose, to reduce it to little more than half that sum.

It is but seldom, that largely indebted governments or individuals, are seriously incommoded with surplus funds. Such, however, has been our condition for two years past, and such will probably be our condition for some time to come. With the means of paying nearly a third of our whole debt, it is impossible to find, among the creditors of the State, those who will receive at any reasonable advance, the amount of principal that will be due to them ; certificates of stock are but rarely offered in any of the markets, and it has been with considerable difficulty, that the Treasurer has been able to obtain the amount redeemed during the past year ; and there seems but little probability, especially while it is known that the State itself is constantly in the market as a purchaser of its own scrip, that it will be offered for sale, upon terms which would justify its purchase. In the year 1848, there will be due the sum of $169,000 ; with that exception, there will be little which can be paid until the year 1851, and in the meantime, the large sum I have named, with the accumulation of the coming year, must remain wholly unproductive in the Treasury, or be loaned to banks at such low rate of interest as they are disposed to allow.

In this unexpected condition of our finances, what course ought the State government to adopt?

Desirable as it is to extinguish our State debt as speedily as possible, it would seem consistent with neither justice nor economy, to make a further call upon the resources of the people, without a better prospect of effecting that object, than now exists.

Under these circumstances, it would seem to me, that,

unless you should deem it practicable and expedient, to repeal or modify the Act of the last session, by which the sum of $200,000, was required to be raised for the use of the Treasury, the State Tax for the ensuing year, might be either wholly dispensed with, or so much reduced in amount, as to prevent a further accumulation of unnecessary funds.

It is somewhat unfortunate, that by the postponement of your annual session to so late a period, it became necessary to anticipate legislation, in regard to the State Tax, for so long a time; and I apprehend it will be found inconvenient in future. It is now more than a year, since the Tax Act for the current year was passed; and it was not then foreseen, either that so large a sum would be received into the Treasury from other sources, or that it would be difficult for the Treasurer, under the authority with which he was clothed, to apply its redundant means to the payment of the State debt.

The purchases of stocks which have been made during the year, have been of that class first becoming due.

With the exception of the sum I have named, as payable in 1848, it is not probable, that without some extraordinary and long continued pressure upon the money market, the stock payable on and after 1851, could be purchased under a premium of eight or ten per cent.; and sales have been made within the year, at prices considerably above that rate.

It will be perceived, that there has been received during the year, for the claims of the State against the General government, the sum of $162,398.

claims, $56,754, were for claims ari
of Washington, comprehending a
llowable under the first appropria
5,928 for military expenditures, w
 the War Department; and $19,
tive share of the land money belon
e Treaty claims due the State, ha
paid in full : of the military claims,
id.

particular accounts of the final a
 claims, at the several department
referred, with a statement of the s
 the settlement of our military acc
hed me.

ipers, with a particular statement o
; also a detailed statement of the
Fund," which I have also receiv
 before you.

a constantly increasing revenue, and it may reasonably
be hoped, that with an adherence to the same prudent
policy, the time is not distant when it will afford an income
sufficiently large to defray the expense of our State government.

The appropriations which have been made for the
construction and repair of roads in the vicinity of the
State lands, have increased the facilities of travel and
transportation, and rendered to those whose enterprise
and labor have been so profitable to the State, as well as
to the public generally, a very essential service. The
expenditure of the sums which have heretofore been
granted for those purposes, has been generally contingent
upon the expenditure of like sums by the State of Massachusetts, whose pecuniary interest is greatly promoted
by the opening of these important avenues of communication. It is to be regretted, that the expenditure of
these grants has been frequently limited for want of the
required co-operation.

Several of these roads are in want of immediate repair,
and considerable sums will be needed to render those now
opened, tolerably passable. I trust an appropriation sufficiently large to make the necessary improvements will
be made, and that the proper steps to induce the co-operation of Massachusetts will also be adopted.

The Report of the Bank Commissioners, which was
made in December last, has been printed, and copies will
be herewith laid before you.

The highly important functions which are performed

most unlimited control over our local
ding their agency into every depart-
the imperative duty of the State gov-
o see that they are subjected to wise
gislation, but to maintain over them
as will insure a strict compliance with
s by which they should be governed.

former Legislatures has been anxious-
accomplishment of these objects, and
trictions have been imposed, as with-
usefulness or efficiency, have been
it to protect the community from the
uses, to which experience has shown

ill the Banks in the State will expire
tober of next year; and although the
cessarily require your action at the
ay be proper in the meantime, to in-
operation of existing laws may have
of further legislation.

entitled to respectful consideration. They do not however contemplate any considerable innovation upon the present system; nor, with the exception of a narrower limit in the extent of their loans, do they recommend that any material restrictions should be added to those now provided. And they express their conviction, that the several acts for regulating banks and banking now in force, "though not entirely faultless, are as perfect as those of any State in the Union."

It will be perceived, that the Commissioners again invoke the attention of the Legislature to the continued infraction, by some of the banks, of that provision of the law, which limits the amount of their circulation. Neither this, nor any other habitual violation of the law, should be countenanced or permitted; if the restriction be unwise or impracticable, the law which imposes it should be repealed or amended; if it be salutary and proper, it should be rigidly enforced.

If one institution is allowed to transcend its legal limits, on the ground either of local necessity or of the undoubted ability of the Bank, it is difficult to conceive how another, no more culpable, but in which the violation may be attended with real danger, can be rebuked or punished. The same privileges should be extended to all, or all required scrupulously to conform to the prescribed limit.

The adoption of some provision, better calculated than any now in force, to remedy this continued irregularity, and which shall be also applicable to a similar excess in the amount of loans, and the liability of directors, is strongly recommended by the Commissioners, and should receive your careful attention.

It has been frequently urged, that in the annual exhibits of the condition of our Banks, there uniformly appears a much greater disproportion between their paper circulation, and the amount of specie it is intended to represent, than was either contemplated by the law, or is consistent with a sound and prudent policy; and that while this disproportion is suffered to continue, there will be a greater liability to those sudden expansions and contractions in the currency, which have heretofore produced such injurious effects upon the operations of business, and created such frequent changes in the value of property.

However this may be, an inspection of the returns for some years past, has impressed me with the apprehension, that our paper circulation is becoming less and less dependent upon a metallic basis; and that the increasing disparity which these returns exhibit, may well call for legislative consideration.

It will be seen by referring to these returns, that while our banking capital was little more than half its present amount, and the paper circulation in the same proportion, the specie means in possession of the banks, exceeded by more than two to one, the sum now in their vaults; and even since 1843, while the paper circulation has increased more than six hundred thousand dollars, the returns show an actual diminution of the coin it represents; and in the report of the present year, there will be found a circula-

2

tion, by a single bank, of eighty thousand dollars, against eight hundred in specie.

It is not to be presumed, that while the present arrangement for the redemption of their bills is adhered to by the banks, it would be regarded as necessary, that an amount of specie, bearing any near approximation to their paper circulation, would be required; that the establishment of some moderate limit, beyond which the disproportion referred to, should not extend, would seem to me but the dictate of prudent foresight; and in view of the policy, which it is probable will be adopted by the general government, may be absolutely required.

That all the banks are abundantly able to fulfil their obligations, cannot be doubted; in the opinion of the Commissioners, they are not only solvent, but remarkably prosperous, and are represented as doing a safe and profitable business.

The Reports of the Trustees and Superintendent of the Insane Hospital will be herewith laid before you.

Since the date of the last Reports from that Institution, its late able and accomplished Superintendent has retired from its service, and his place has been supplied by a gentleman, whose high professional and personal character is a sufficient guarantee, that its arduous and responsible duties will be adequately performed. Under his superintendence, the affairs of the institution have been judiciously managed; and notwithstanding a considerable reduction which was made in June last, in the charges which had previously been made for the board and attendance of patients, its pecuniary condition is quite as satisfactory as at any former period.

There will be required a small appropriation for the payment of expenses properly chargeable to the State; and in the opinion of the Trustees, the sum of $600 should be granted, to meet an anticipated deficiency for the coming year, which may grow out of the reduction in the charges before referred to, both of which, I trust, will be made.

It will be observed, by reference to the Report of the Trustees, that a very considerable increase in the number of patients has taken place within the year; and that the number of males is now as large as the present capacity of the building will enable it to accommodate; and that unless some of the present occupants should be dismissed, no new male patients could be received.

It is estimated, that there are in the State, above six hundred persons, upon whom the dreadful visitation of insanity has fallen; and it may be presumed, that this number will increase in like proportion with the increase of our population; it may therefore be reasonably anticipated, that a much larger number than have heretofore enjoyed the benefit of this Asylum, will seek to participate in its privileges. In order that they may do so, it is indispensably necessary, that the building should be enlarged, and that one wing, for the accommodation of male patients, should be added. It is not anticipated, that a very large sum will be required for this purpose; and in view of the facts above suggested, I entirely concur in the recommendation of the Trustees, that the necessary amount should be granted.

It is desirable, also, that the grounds belonging to the Asylum should be somewhat enlarged; more land for pasturage, is greatly needed; and I am advised, since the printing of the Report, that an adjacent lot, containing about twenty-six acres, lying between the river and the road, and which has always been regarded as a necessary acquisition to the lands of the institution, is now offered at a moderate price. The sum required for this purchase will be $1,050, and I recommend an appropriation for that purpose.

While this most excellent institution has been contributing to the relief and comfort of the insane, the humane and liberal provision, which the bounty of the Legislature has extended, to another unfortunate class of our fellow beings, has been silently diffusing its beneficent and salutary influence.

The appropriations for the support and education of the indigent blind, and deaf and dumb, have been sufficient to place at the Asylums at South Boston and Hartford, all the youth, of suitable age and capacity, whose parents or friends have applied for the aid of the State. Twenty-four deaf and dumb pupils are now at the Asylum at Hartford, and thirteen blind children are at the Institution at South Boston, all of whom are receiving such an education, as will not only rescue them from mental darkness, and open multiplied sources of occupation and happiness, but which will qualify them to provide for their future support.

. In a continued provision for these interesting recipients of the public bounty, you will find the indulgence of a kindly sympathy, entirely consistent with an enlightened and economical public policy.

The quarterly reports of the Inspectors of the State Prison, give a satisfactory account of the condition of that establishment. A more particular statement of its affairs will be furnished by the report of the Warden, which will be made directly to the Legislature.

. The number of convicts in the Prison is much below the general average, there being but sixty-six now in confinement; and with the exception of the salaries paid to the officers, the establishment is wholly supported from the avails of their labor. It was anticipated by the Warden, that this aid might be dispensed with; but a series of disappointments beyond his control, have rendered it necessary that the appropriations for this purpose should be used. The reports of the Inspectors are herewith transmitted.

In the annual communication I had the honor to make to the last Legislature, I expressed at considerable length, the views I entertained upon the subject of our common schools.

Lamenting the defects in the practical operation of the present system, which the slightest examination will demonstrate to exist, the attention of the Legislature was earnestly invited to the consideration of measures, which might tend to elevate these primary institutions, to that

2*

high degree of usefulness and efficiency they are entitled to possess.

That no plan, having in view this desirable object, was finally perfected, cannot have arisen from neglect or indifference to this legitimate and important subject of legislative action. Everywhere regarded as the proper objects of governmental care, the encouragement of our public schools, should be with us, a controlling and paramount obligation; and it would be matter of just and lasting reproach, if, through the apathy or neglect, either of the government or people, they should fail to accomplish the beneficent and patriotic purposes for which they were established.

That they have failed to participate in the general spirit of improvement and reform, which is characteristic of the time, is too obvious to be questioned; nor are there wanting those, who entertain the belief, that a careful examination of their actual condition, will show in some respects, a positive deterioration. It is one of the deficiencies of the present system, that no authentic means of affirming or disproving so startling an allegation, are anywhere to be found. The returns annually made to the Secretary of State, contain but meagre and scanty materials upon which to form a reliable opinion; of the abstracts which were formerly made from these returns, the publication has been for some time discontinued; and they are permitted to slumber, undisturbed and unregarded, among the obsolete files which encumber the office.

The observation and enquiries of public spirited individuals, and the evidence of remarkable proficiency in par-

ticular localities, occasionally brought to the notice of the
community through the public press, are the chief sources
of information, as to the condition of our public schools,
which now exist; and I respectfully submit, whether it is
proper, that these imperfect and casual communications,
upon a subject of such incalculable importance, should
longer constitute the sum of information within our reach.

Is it not but too probable, that a diligent investigation
into the operation of the existing system, will to a lament-
able extent, verify the apprehensions to which I have alluded; that it will disclose the same melancholy array of
incompetent teachers—dilapidated or inconvenient buildings—the same waste or perversion of the public funds—
and the same absence of intelligent and active supervision, which have been generally exhibited by similar in-
quiries in other States?

However this might be, it cannot be doubted, that such
an investigation would demonstrate the necessity of
additional legislation; that it would show in what particular parts of our present system, reformation and improvement were most needed, and how far the public
mind was prepared to countenance and sustain, the inno-
vations proposed; and if conducted by intelligent and
competent individuals, would powerfully contribute to
awaken the public attention, and to strengthen the hands,
and encourage the hopes, of those private individuals,
whose commendable exertions have already done so much
to advance the cause of popular education.

Various modes to attain this object, with but little inconvenience and expense, could be readily suggested;

but none would seem more entirely unobjectionable, than
that proposed by the Committee on Education of the
last Legislature.

By the establishment of a Board of Commissioners,
selected for their peculiar qualifications, either by the
Legislature or the Executive, the requisite information
could be easily and economically obtained; existing defects would be pointed out and exposed, and the improvements which have been introduced by the liberality and
spirit of particular communities, commended to the notice
and imitation of all.

And availing themselves of the experience of other
States, which have preceded us in this laudable undertaking, the operation of those auxiliary establishments, which
have been recently engrafted upon their respective sys-
tems, and their adaptation to the wants and capacities of
our own, might form a subject of profitable inquiry.

With the information which could be thus obtained,
the Legislature would be enabled to adapt its action to
the condition and wants of the existing system; and be
better qualified to enter upon the consideration of a more
permanent and comprehensive plan of educational improvement.

In the amount of money annually devoted to the support of our common schools, it is not believed, that we
should suffer by a comparison with other States; nor that
the improvements required would add, in any formidable
degree, to the pecuniary means we are accustomed to
allow them.

In the belief, that by introducing into our system higher elements of order, economy and uniformity, the expenditure of these means may be productive of a greater amount of good, I respectfully commend the inquiry I have suggested, to the consideration of the Legislature.

Under the resolve passed by the last Legislature, for the promotion of Education in the Madawaska settlements upon the St. John, the Agent who had superintended the expenditures of the preceding year, was again appointed to perform the duty.

Having afterwards engaged in other business, which rendered it inconvenient to discharge the duties of the office, he resigned the appointment, and in October last, another Agent was appointed, under whose superintendence, a portion of the appropriation has been expended.

There remained an unexpended balance of $700, which, as the Legislature was to convene before it would be needed, it was not deemed advisable to draw from the Treasury.

Unless, therefore, you shall consider it proper to re-appropriate that sum, there will be no means to continue the schools, and the Agency of the Superintendent will be terminated.

The Report of the Agent is herewith communicated.

In communicating the Report of the Adjutant General, I would bespeak your attention to several suggestions connected with the care of the property of the State, at the several Arsenals and Gun-houses. Much of this property is rapidly falling into decay, and some small appropriations are required to preserve it from entire ruin.

·Having upon former occasions expressed the regret with which I had witnessed the subversion of our military system, it is not now my intention, to reiterate to the Legislature, views, which however weighty they have appeared to me, have found so little favor with those to whom they were addressed.

I am aware also, that the increasing aversion which has been manifested by our citizens to the performance of military duty, may have rendered the preservation of an efficient militia, not only difficult, but perhaps impracticable; and that, unless under circumstances of imminent public danger, an attempt to revive it would probably prove unavailing.

It will appear from the report communicated, that under the present law, the militia may be considered as entirely disbanded; the returns which should be made to the Adjutant General, are either wholly omitted, or so imperfect as to be of little value; and in making the annual requisition for our quota of arms from the general government, it is necessary to resort to returns which have been made in former years.

In the annual communications I have made to former Legislatures, I have taken occasion briefly to refer to the several topics of public interest, which were then occupying the public mind.

I have done so with no view, unnecessarily to introduce into their deliberations, the irritation and excitement incident to the discussion of national politics; nor do I now desire to mingle with the local interests which require the care of the present Legislature, the disturbing questions which are properly committed to other hands.

Upon the questions to which I have referred, the public judgment has been deliberately pronounced, and the administration of the general government has passed into hands, charged with the consummation of those measures of public policy, which have constituted the leading topics of popular discussion, and upon which, the opinions of the people have been clearly expressed. My own convictions are unchanged, that in a steady adherence to the line of policy indicated by that expression, the stability of our Institutions, and the solid and enduring prosperity of the whole country, will be most effectually promoted.

But whatever importance may be attached to the adjustment by the general government, of these disputed questions of domestic policy, the unsettled and threatening aspect of our relations with foreign governments, will at this juncture, more strongly arrest the public attention.

The information which has recently reached us, renders it highly probable that with the republic of Mexico, hostilities have actually commenced; it is sincerely to be lamented, that the repeated efforts which have been made to avoid an alternative so much to be deprecated, should have proved unavailing; and that the misguided government of that unhappy country, should have compelled the adoption of measures, which must inflict the most serious evils upon its people.

The long pending controversy between the governments of the United States and Great Britain, in relation to their respective rights in the territory of Oregon, seems also to be rapidly approaching its crisis; it is most devoutly to be hoped, that it will result in a pacific and honorable settlement.

In the spirit of liberal and honorable compromise, and with a moderation which evinces the strongest desire to bring this agitating question to a speedy termination, the President of the United States has offered a nearly equal division of the territory in dispute.

That a proposition so clearly within our just rights, and which may be regarded as the limit, beyond which, in the united judgment of the country, it would be improper to go, should have been declined by the government of Great Britain, is deeply to be regretted. In the hope which is entertained, that negotiations between the two countries will be resumed, and the controversy settled upon just, and mutually satisfactory terms, I strongly participate.

As it is my purpose to retire from the office, to which the suffrages of my fellow citizens have called me, at the close of the present political year, I avail myself of this occasion, to express my grateful acknowledgments for the repeated marks of their confidence and regard, with which I have been honored; and to tender to the Legislature, in the meantime, my ready co-operation in every measure which may be calculated to promote the public good.

H. J. ANDERSON.

Council Chamber,
　Augusta, May 15, 1846.

REPORT

OF THE

TREASURER OF MAINE,

ON THE

STATE OF THE TREASURY,

APRIL 30, 1846.

~~~~~~~~~~~~~~~~~~~

AUGUSTA:

WM. T. JOHNSON,...........PRINTER TO THE STATE.

1846.

STATE OF MAINE.

TREASURER'S OFFICE,
Augusta, April 30, 1846.

To the President of the Senate
and Speaker of the House of Representatives:

The Treasurer would respectfully lay before the two houses of the legislature the following report of the state of the treasury as it existed at the close of business on the 30th day of April 1846.

Receipts of the treasury in				
Receipts of the treasury in			January, 1845,	$48,067 57
"	"	"	February, "	40,559 06
"	"	"	March, "	26,210 13
"	"	"	April,	34,148 87
"	"	"	May, "	28,017 64
"	"	"	June,	6,596 41
"	"	" ,	July,	30,465 09
"	"	"	August, "	6,148 24
"	"	"	September, "	92,582 62
"	"	"	October, "	36,130 33
"	"	"	November, "	52,141 27
"	"	"	December, "	46,420 20
"	"	"	January, 1846,	38,560 39
"	"	"	February, "	15,773 34
"	"	"	March, "	72,041 37
"	"	"	April,	37,028 93

Amount of receipts from January 1, 1845, to
April 30, 1846, inclusive,   . $610,891 46
Balance of cash in treasury, January 1, 1845,   392,422 24

$1,003,313 70

Expenditures of the treasury in January, 1845,		$6,991 41
" " " February, "		13,105 43
" " " March, "		42,999 46
.. . . April, "		119,757 66
May, "		186,822 37
.. .. June, "		19,661 48
.. .. July, ".		~7,056 54
August, "		21,199 97
" " September, ",		·1,337 68
" .· October, "		69,940 65
November, "		5,272 17
December, "		14,076 05
January, 1846,		69,686 43
.. .. February, "		15,887 61
'' '' March, "		6,616 01
" " " April, "		33,799 24
Total amount of expenditure from January 1, 1845, to April 30, 1846, inclusive .		$634,210 16
Leaving a balance in the treasury, April 30, 1846, of		$369,103 54

STATE OF MAINE *in account with* JAMES WHITE, *Treasurer.*

Dr.

Roll of accounts, No. 25, . . .	$149 24
School fund, No. 10, .	189 06
Costs in criminal prosecutions, . .	18,612 83
County taxes. Oxford county, .	86 63
" Hancock "	72 81
School fund, No. 11, .	419 70
County taxes. Franklin county, .	123 79
Cash, ...	369,103 54
Instruction in Madawaska, .	978 91
Public debt, . . .	316,646 22
Miscellaneous items, . .	1,378 67
Indian annuities, . . .	1,525 00
Agricultural productions to Penobscot Indians,	462 00
Penobscot Indian fund, . . .	5,321 55
Contingent fund of governor and council, .	2,228 51
School fund, Nos. 9 and 10, .	34 84

STATE OF MAINE *in account with* JAMES WHITE, *Treasurer.* .
Dr.

Trustees Insane Hospital, . . .	$257 00
Valuation committee, . .	2,273 00
Printing, . . .	3,137 75
Agricultural societies, . . .	1,498 07
Roll of accounts, No. 24, . .	9 80
Postage, ...	545 94
Porter and messenger, . .	202 00
Subordinate officers of state prison, . .	4,446 00
Clerks, ...	3,043 50
Binding and stitching, .	615 38
Council, . . .	3,778 00
Senate, . . .	7,988 20
House, . . .	31,809 00
Library, ...	300 00
Contingent fund of secretary, . .	200 00
Furniture and repairs, . . .	1,150 00
Indexes, . .	150 00
Stationery, .	1,400 00
Insane Hospital, . .	300 00
Military purposes, . .	3 00
Roll of accounts, . . .	8,438 57
Contingent fund of treasurer, . .	1,000 00
Deaf, dumb and blind, . .	4,688 31
School fund. No, 12, . .	25,175 17
Foreign exchanges, .	200 00
Inspectors of state prison, .	60 00
Fuel and lights, . .	400 00
Revised statutes, . .	100 00
Canada road, . .	200 00
Salaries, ...	28,607 30
Reports of judicial decisions,	780 00
Militia pensions, . .	3,102 00
Baring and Houlton road, .	300 00
Moosehead lake road, . .	500 00
County taxes. Piscataquis county, .	396 83
" Penobscot " .	4,333 08
Roll of accounts, No. 19 and 20, .	53 40
County taxes. Washington county, .	2,230 60
" Aroostook " .	2,312 44

1*

State of Maine *in account with* James White, *Treasurer.*

Dr.

County taxes. Somerset county, . .	2,169 18
Interest on public debt, . .	137,707 62
	$1,003,194 46

State of Maine *in account with* James White, *Treasurer.*

Cr.

State of Maine, ...	$392,422 24
Land Agent, . . .	135,782 33
County taxes—Oxford county, .	380 81
" Hancock "	39 36
" Franklin " . .	128 90
Duty on commissions, .	2,523 00
North eastern boundary, . .	142,382 44
Miscellaneous items, .	1,336 27
Interest on deposits in banks, .	6,510 14
State tax, 1840, . .	51 90
" 1841, .	288 35
" 1842, .	751 51
" 1843, . .	3,624 62
" 1844, . .	128,998 93
" 1845, . .	86,435 64
Penobscot Indian fund, .	50 00
Stationery, .	3 00
Bank dividends, . . .	900 00
Notes receivable, . . .	2,121 12
Distribution of sales of public lands, .	19,716 23
Permanent school fund, . . .	21,088 70
School fund, No. 13, . . .	26,090 00
Revised statutes, . .	1 00
Bank stock—Maine bank, .	375 00
" Mercantile Bank, .	3,000 00
County taxes—Piscataquis county,	739 66
" Penobscot " . .	2,252 99
School fund, No. 14, . . .	13,045 00
County taxes—Washington county,	4,348 48

STATE OF MAINE *in account with* JAMES WHITE, *Treasurer.*

Cr.

County taxes.	Somerset county,	.	.	2,654 18
"	Aroostook "	.	.	3,137 30
Interest on taxes,		.	.	2,015 36
				$1,003,194 46

Resources of the State.

Cash in the treasury, May 1, 1846, .	$369,103 54
Balance due on state tax of 1840,	144 63
" " " 1841,	412 52
" " " 1842,	545 50
1843,	756 92
1844, .	2,142 56
" 1845, .	65,501 71
Amount " 1846, .	202,583 13

BALANCE OF COUNTY TAXES.

County of Hancock, 1841, '44 and '45, .	5,089 18
" Washington, 1842, '43, '44 and '45,	3,094 93
" Oxford, 1840, '41, '42, '43, '44 and '45, . . .	1,281 91
" Somerset, 1840, '41, '42, '43, '44 and '45, . . .	1,171 66
" Penobscot, 1836, '40, '41, '42, '43, '44 and '45, . .	4,907 92
" Piscataquis, 1840, '41, '42, '43, '44 and '45, . . .	583 99
" Franklin, 1842, '43, '44 and '45,	1,957 93
" Aroostook, 1841, '42, '43, '44 and '45, ...	3,408 63
Securities in the land office, . .	232,543 88
Notes receivable in the treasury office, .	20,198 05
100 shares in the Augusta bank, . .	10,000 00
	$925,428 40

Balance of claims against the United States.

Liabilities of the State.

PUBLIC FUNDED DEBT.	
There is now due and uncalled for, . .	$2,400 00
There will become due in 1846, . .	1,500 00
" " 1847, . .	50,800 00
" " 1848, . .	169,400 00
" " 1850, . .	21,000 00
1851, . .	416,685 00
1852, . .	130,000 00
1854, . .	10,000 00
1855, . .	277,000 00
1856, . .	132,500 00
1860, . .	63,000 00
Amount of funded debt, .	$1,274,285 00
Penobscot Indian fund, . .	58,593 03
Permanent school fund, . .	78,718 21
Balance due on rolls of accounts, . .	451 29
" " school funds, .	1,358 72
Interest due, uncalled for, . .	10,455 00
Warrants unpaid, . .	2,332 79
AMOUNT DUE FOR COUNTY TAXES.	
County of Hancock, for ordinary expenses, .	998 31
" " for roads, . .	4,082 70
" . Washington, for ordinary expenses,	790 72
" " for roads, . .	1,300 00
" Oxford, for ordinary expenses, .	127 93
" Somerset, for ordinary expenses, .	527 95
" " for roads, . .	915 88
" Penobscot, for ordinary expenses, .	800 18
" " for roads, . .	1,676 07
" Piscataquis, for ordinary expenses,	793 40
" Franklin, for ordinary expenses, .	158 62
" " for roads, . .	1,776 00
" Aroostook, for ordinary expenses, .	1,367 41
Total liabilities of the State, April 30, 1846,	$1,441,509 21

Estimated Expenditures for the year 1846–7.

Interest on public debt, ...	$86,000 00
Public debt, ...	54,700 00
House, . . .	27,000 00
School fund, No. 13, . . .	26,090 00
Salaries, ...	24,000 00
Costs in criminal prosecutions, .	16,000 00
County taxes, . . .	15,315 17
Senate, ...	6,500 00
Printing, ...	5,000 00
Subordinate officers of State Prison, .	5,000 00
Penobscot Indian fund, . . .	4,000 00
Contingent fund of Governor and Council, .	4,000 00
Deaf, dumb and blind, . . .	4,000 00
Council, . .	3,000 00
Clerks, . .	2,600 00
Miscellaneous items, . .	2,500 00
Bounty on animals, .	2,000 00
Militia pensions, . .	2,000 00
Agricultural societies, . .	2,000 00
Furniture and repairs of public buildings, .	2,000 00
Indian annuities, . . .	1,500 00
Stationery, . . .	1,000 00
Contingent fund of Treasurer, .	1,000 00
Reports of judicial decisions, .	1,000 00
Bank Commissioners, . .	600 00
Postage, . .	600 00
Sheriff and Coroners, . .	600 00
Fuel and lights, . .	300 00
Inspectors of State Prison, . .	300 00
Trustees Insane Hospital, .	400 00
Library, . .	300 00
Binding and stitching, .	500 00
Bounty on silk, . .	100 00
Contingent fund of Secretary, .	200 00
Balance on rolls of accounts, .	451 29
" school funds, .	1,358 72
Warrants unpaid, .	2,332 79
	$306,247 97

Estimated Receipts for the year 1846–7.

Cash in the Treasury May 1, 1846, . .	$369,103 54
State tax, (balances,) for 1840, '41, '42, '43, '44, and '45, ...	69,503 74
State tax for 1846, ...	202,583 13
County taxes, (balances,) for 1836, '40, '41, '42, '43, '44, and '45, ...	21,496 05
Land office, . . .	60,000 00
Bank tax, ...	26,090 00
Duty on commissions, . .	1,500 00
Bank dividends, ...	600 00
Notes receivable in Treasury office, . .	1,000 00
	$751,876 46

Amount paid for claims prior to 1845.

Instruction in Madawaska, . . .	$478 91
Military purposes, ...	3 00
Salaries, ...	1,935 41
Contingent fund of Governor & Council, .	81 69
Roll of accounts, ...	212 44
School funds, . . .	643 62
Costs in criminal prosecutions, . .	1,511 49
Pensions, ...	636 00
Interest, . . .	3,999 00
County taxes, .	11,692 75
	$21,194 31

Recent laws have imposed duties upon the treasurer for public convenience, which were not originally contemplated as coming within his province; and they have so enlarged his services, and the business of his office has been increased to such an extent, that to give a " detailed account of the state of the treasury," if not in itself impracticable, would be attended with much unnecessary expense and labor.

The collection of taxes assessed by the State, and those " assessed or ordered" by county commissioners, on unincorporated townships or tracts of land, devolves upon the treasurer, and under existing laws is a service of much care and difficulty.

For the convenience of owners of land in severalty, each individual has the right to pay his proportion of every such tax, however small his interest, and thereby discharge his estate therein of all claim and lien created by reason of such assessment. And in many instances those holding from one to two hundred acres of land, the tax on which does not exceed four cents, and in some instances is not more than one, claim their right to pay their proportion and hold their interest discharged, and every form must be observed in keeping the account which is necessary in the payment and receipt of any other sum.

If a more summary method of collecting such taxes could be devised, and at the same time the rights of all persons equally well preserved, by adopting it the treasury department would be relieved—but in taxation the rights of the people should be carefully guarded, and taxes should be imposed with as little embarrassment and hardship as their character will admit of; and the power should not be exercised in a manner, either oppressive or offensive. It is a subject which demands constant oversight, and the unremitting watchfulness of the legislature, for, under color of right and legal sanction, gross wrong may be done.

County commissioners are clothed with the power of locating and altering highways in or through unincorporated townships or tracts of land, and for the purpose of making and repairing such ways they are invested with the power of assessing or ordering taxes thereon. Whenever they have assessed or ordered a tax for such purposes, notice is given to the State treasurer, and the same is credited by him to the county treasurer, and the State is thereby made liable to the county for the amount of such tax. This law in its operation indicates 'injurious consequences to the State in a two-fold respect. Proprietors and owners of land, apparently not wholly without just cause, complain that this power is exercised in such a manner as to render their property of so little value that they are inclined to suffer their lands to revert to the State. If such

complaints are well founded the interests of the State require that a
remedy should be applied without delay. It is believed that pur-
chasers of lands belonging to this State and to Massachusetts, in,
consequence of the excessive taxation to which unincorporated
lands are subject for the making of roads, are in some instances
deterred from perfecting their title—this also has an injurious effect
upon the interests of the State. Unjust taxation is equally as
oppressive as the appropriating of private property to public uses
without a just compensation; and the difference is immaterial to
the owner whether his land is taken for the public highway or his
property appropriated to make such highway convenient and passable for travelers.

In regard to the balance of cash on hand, it is so much larger
than it was estimated, at the last session of the legislature, that it
would be at the commencement of the present, it may be proper
to remark, that it has arisen from receipts of money due from the
general government, and other sources which were of an uncertain
and contingent character. There has been received on account of
the northeastern boundary, the sum of $142,382 44. And as a
large amount had been paid into the treasury the year preceding,
by the land agent, it was estimated that the receipts from the land
office would not exceed an average amount, and the sum of $60,
000, being more than the average receipts from that department for
the last ten years, was the sum which was anticipated; but the
sum actually received was $156,871 03, which greatly exceeds
the amount received in any one year, since the organization of the
government of this state, and exceeds by one third the aggregate
of all that was paid into the treasury, from that department, for five
years, from 1836 to 1840, inclusive. And there is still another
sum that was not included in the estimate of the receipts—the proceeds of the sales of public lands paid by the general government,
amounting to $19,716 28. Thus it will be seen that there has
been received, the sum of $258,969 70, which was not anticipated
in making the estimates of the year, and which is included in the
balance of cash on hand. It would not have been prudent to have

relied upon such receipts to meet the demands upon this department ; but the money is now received, and may be made availiable for such purposes as may be thought expedient and proper.

Since the adjournment of the legislature, in addition to the stock which has become due, the treasurer has taken up about $90,000, which was payable in 1848, or at some subsequent period. It was obtained with difficulty, as holders appear to have the fullest confidence in the faith and credit of the state and are little inclined to part with it. Money has been abundant for some time past, and while such is the condition of the market, Maine stock will be sought for as a permanent investment, and will command a high premium.

JAMES WHITE, *Treasurer.*

BANK COMMISSIONERS,

DECEMBER, 1845.

Published agreeably to Resolve of March 22, 1836.

AUGUSTA:

WM. T. JOHNSON,..●...PRINTER TO THE STATE.

1846.

REPORT.

To the Governor and Council of the State of Maine.

AGREEABLY to the provisions of law, the undersigned, Bank Commissioners, have made their annual examination of the several Banks in this State, and ask leave to submit the following

REPORT:

As the object of these examinations is to give the government and the public the state and condition of the several banks as ascertained to exist at the time of the examination, it is believed that that object will be best attained by presenting each institution separately.

By this course strict justice will be rendered to all; as each bank, by its statement, exhibits its own strength or weakness, and a comparison may be drawn as to their relative standing.

The banks which have surrendered their charters since 1841 may be considered to be closed so far as the public are interested. It is therefore deemed unnecessary to make a detailed report in relation to them.

The 35 banks now in active operation, are alphabetically arranged, and their state and condition at the time of our examination, together with the names of their several officers, are as follows, viz :

ANDROSCOGGIN BANK.

Capital stock,	50,000 00	Loan,	55,985 83
Circulation,	43,006 00	Bank stock,	1,000 00
Profits,	5,282 69	Real estate,	2,100 00
Due to other banks,	59 63	Bills of other banks,	895 00
Deposits,	21,616 06	Due from other bks.,	55,095 36
		Specie,	4,888 19
	$119,964 38		$119,964 38

Immediate liabilities, $64,681 69.

Immediate resources, $60,878 55.

Charles Thompson, *President;* John Barron, David Scribner, Nahum Perkins, Woodbury B. Purinton, *Directors;* John Coburn, *Cashier.*

AUGUSTA BANK.

Capital stock,	110,000 00	Loan,	193,992 61
Circulation,	91,368 00	Real estate,	10,832 51
Profits,	3,931 29	Bills of other bks.,	7,166 00
Due to other banks,	93 98	Due from other bks.,	75,978 41
Deposits,	92,644 70	Specie,	10,068 34
	$298,037 97		$298,037 97

Immediate liabilities, $184,106 68.

Immediate resources, $93,212 75.

Thomas W. Smith, *President;* Greenleaf White, Issachar Snell, James W. Bradbury, George W. Morton, Eben Fuller, *Directors;* George W. Allen, *Cashier.*

BANK OF BANGOR.

Capital stock,	100,000 00	Loan,	186,012 34
Circulation,	148,727 00	Bank stock,	33,300 00
Profits,	14,882 33	Checks and drafts,	38,346 15
Due to other banks,	4,808 41	Real estate,	3,272 62

Deposits,	62,540 06	Bills of other bks.,	3,961 96
		Due from other bks.,	58,241 65
		Bank charges,	1,567 21
		Specie,	6,285 85
	$330,957 80		**$330,957 80**

Immediate liabilities, $216,075 47.
Immediate resources, $106,785 68.

Samuel Veazie, *President;* Nathaniel Lord, John Bright, John McDonald, Samuel P. Strickland, *Directors;* William S. Dennet, *Cashier.*

BANK OF CUMBERLAND.

Capital stock,	100,000 00	Loan,	167,476 68
Circulation,	77,161 00	Real estate,	21,000 00
Profits,	6,703 15	Bank charges,	865 18
Deposits,	45,454 27	Bills of other bks.,&c.	7,961 97
		Due from other bks.,	35,738 76
		Specie,	6,255 83
	$229,318 42		**$229,318 42**

Immediate liabilities, $122,615 27.
Immediate resources, $39,976 56.

William Moulton, *President;* John Anderson, David Drinkwater, Ashur Ware, Samuel Haskell, Jonathan Tukesbury, James Todd, *Directors;* Samuel Small, Jr., *Cashier.*

BANK OF WESTBROOK.

Capital stock,	50,000 00	Loan,	70,520 16
Circulation,	37,588 00	Bank stock,	4,500 00
Profits,	1,737 05	Real estate,	3,819 56
Deposits,	11,393 72	Bank charges,	36 58
		Bills of other bks.,	6,880 63
		Due from other bks.,	12,834 50
		Specie,	2,127 34
	$100,718 77		**$100,718 77**

1*

Immediate liabilities, $46,981 72.

Immediate resources, $21,842 47.

Samuel Jordan, *President;* Samuel B. Stephens, Joseph Walker, Jr., Walker B. Goodrich, Nathan L. Woodbury, *Directors;* A. G. Fobes, *Cashier.*

BRUNSWICK BANK.

Capital stock,	75,000 00	Loan,	90,079 41
Circulation,	35,086 00	Bank stock,	2,000 00
Profits,	2,265 79	Real estate,	2,925 82
Deposits,	11,701 35	Bills of other bks.,	2,027 00
		Due from other bks.,	24,015 51
		Specie,	3,005 43
	$124,053 14		$124,053 17

Immediate liabilities, $47,787 35.

Immediate resources, $29,047 94.

Richard T. Dunlap, *President;* John C. Humphrey, Alfred J. Stone, Joseph Badger, William Barron, *Directors;* A. C. Robinson, *Cashier.*

BELFAST BANK.

Capital stock,	50,000 00	Loan,	76,353 42
Circulation,	53,913 00	Real estate,	5,693 75
Profits,	3,566 72	Bills of other banks,	6,400 00
Deposits,	25,132 11	Due from agent and	
		other banks,	40,120 60
		Specie,	4,044 06
	$132,611 83		$132,611 83

Immediate liabilities, $79,045 11.

Immediate resources, $50,564 66.

James White, *President;* Joseph Williamson, Paul R. Hazelton, James P. White, Thomas Marshall, Salathiel Nickerson, Daniel Harnden, *Directors;* N. H. Bradbury, *Cashier.*

CANAL BANK.

Capital stock,	400,000 00	Loan,	597,654 21	
Circulation,	185,828 00	Canal stock,	75,000 00	
Profits,	12,324 19	Real estate,	37,009 55	
Due to other bks.,	8,461 68	Bank charges,	895 65	
Deposits,	171,606 55	Bills of other banks,	8,434 00	
		Due from other bks.,	48,372 80	
		Specie,	10,854 21	
	$778,220 42		$778,220 42	

Immediate liabilities, $365,896 23.

Immediate resources, $67,661 01.

Charles E. Barrett, *President ;* Thomas Hammond, William Goodenow, William Kimball, Joshua B. Osgood, William W. Thomas, Nathaniel Warren, *Directors;* Josiah B. Scott, *Cashier.*

CASCO BANK.

Capital stock,	300,000 00	Loan,	453,964 25	
Circulation,	88,201 00	Real estate,	25,827 54	
Profits,	11,363 29	Stocks,	1,900 00	
Due to other banks,	2,943 98	Bills of other banks,	8,426 00	
Deposits,	125,278 88	Due from other bks.,	22,298 31	
		Specie,	15,371 05	
	$527,787 15		$527,787 15	

Immediate liabilities, $216,423 86.

Immediate resources, $46,095 05.

Eliphalet Greeley, *President ;* Nathaniel Blanchard, William Evans, St. John Smith, Charles Jones, Phinehas Varnum, Nathan Cummings, *Directors ;* John Chute, *Cashier.*

CENTRAL BANK.

Capital stock,	50,000 00	Loan,	139,104 26	
Circulation,	83,310 00	Bank stock,	11,606 86	
Profits,	10,041 67	Real estate,	29,802 47	

Deposits,	64,192 17	Bills of other banks,	517 00
		Due from other bks., 25,663 25	
		Specie,	850 00
	$207,543 84		$207,543 84

Immediate liabilities, $147,502 17.
Immediate resources, $27,030 25.

Calvin Spaulding, *President* ; John Smith, Reuel Washburn, Francis Butler, *Directors* ; one vacancy,—Artemas Leonard, *Cashier*.

COMMERCIAL BANK.

Capital stock,	50,000 00	Loan,	71,877 86
Circulation,	41,632 00	Real estate,	550 00
Profits,	1,933 13	Profit and loss,	10 95
Due to other banks,	300 00	Bills of other banks,	5,210 00
Deposits,	21,239 55	Due from other bks.,	34,288 28
		Specie,	3,167 59
	$115,104 68		$115,104 68

Immediate liabilities, $63,171 55.
Immediate resources, $42,665 87.

Jacob Robinson, *President* ; Thomas M. Reed, William Patten, Gilbert Trufant, William D. Sewall, *Directors* ; Thomas Agry, *Cashier*.

CALAIS BANK.

Capital stock,	50,000 00	Loan,	97,123 92
Circulation,	32,135 00	Real estate,	5,820 62
Profits,	1,494 66	Bills of other banks,	2,328 00
Deferred stock,	6,188 65	Due from other bks.,	2,488 81
Due to other banks,	5,369 35	Specie,	2,129 77
Deposits,	14,703 46		
	$109,891 12		$109,891 12

Immediate liabilities, $52,207 81.

Immediate resources, $6,946 58.

George Downs, *President ;* Francis Swan, Ovid Burrill, William Demming, Levi L. Lowell, *Directors ;* Joseph A. Lee,
Cashier.

———

EASTERN BANK.

Capital stock,	50,000 00	Loan,	98,581 15
Circulation,	77,036 00	Real estate,	6,175 00
Profits,	4,638 09	Bank stock,	5,000 00
Stock in trust,	1,800 18	Bills of other banks,	9,774 93
Deposits,	32,777 11	Due from other bks.,	41,342 45
		Specie,	5,377 85
	$166,251 38		$166,251 38

Immediate liabilities, $109,813 11.

Immediate resources, $56,495 23.

Amos M. Roberts, *President ;* Daniel B. Hinkley, William A.
Blake, John Bradbury, Samuel P. Strickland, *Directors ;* William H. Mills, *Cashier.*

———

FRANKLIN BANK.

Capital stock,	50,000 00	Loan,	77,879 27
Circulation,	29,555 00	Real estate,	505 00
Profits,	395 85	Bills of other bks. &c.,	3,698 93
Due to other banks,	652 10	Due from other bks.,	8,650 79
Deposits,	11,372 76	Specie,	1,241 72
	$91,975 71		$91,975 71

Immediate liabilities, $41,579 87.

Immediate resources, $13,591 44.

John Otis, *President ;* Stephen Young, E. F. Dean, Samuel
N. Cooper, Joseph Eaton, *Directors ;* Hiram Stevens, *Cashier.*

FREEMAN'S BANK.

Capital stock,	50,000 00	Loan,	86,777 78
Circulation,	45,986 00	Bills of other banks,	5,521 00
Profits,	2,727 39	Due from other bks,	27,308 19
Deposits,	25,034 88	Specie,	4,141 30
	$123,748 27		$123,748 27

Immediate liabilities, $71,020 88.

Immediate resources, $36,970 49.

Benjamin Davis, *President ;* John Mulliken, William Hunt, Watson F. Hallett, Prince B. Moores, *Directors ;* William Caldwell, *Cashier.*

FRONTIER BANK.

Capital stock,	75,000 00	Loan,	119,285 27
Circulation,	26,304 00	Real estate,	2,500 00
Profits,	3,234 53	Bank stock,	300 00
Deposits,	41,414 25	Bills of other banks,	1,868 00
		Due from other bks,	17,351 14
		Specie,	4,648 37
	$145,952 78		$145,952 78

Immediate liabilities, $67,718 25.

Immediate resources, $23,867 51.

Samuel Wheeler, *President ;* Charles H. Hayden, William M. Brooks, Lorenzo Sabine, Partman Houghton, Darius Pearce, George A. Peabody, *Directors ;* Edward Ilsley, *Cashier.*

GRANITE BANK.

Capital stock,	75,000 00	Loan,	129,685 20
Circulation,	59,567 00	Real estate,	7,121 63
Profits,	2,677 07	Due from other bks.,	8,032 41
Due to other banks,	4,042 56	Specie,	2,791 67
Deposits,	6,344 28		
	$147,630 91		$147,630 91

Immediate liabilities, $69,953 84.
Immediate resources, $10,824 08.

William Woart, *President ;* William A. Brooks, Henry Williams, Erastus Bartlett, William Thomas, *Directors ;* Silas Leonard, *Cashier.*

GARDINER BANK.

Capital stock,	100,000 00	Loan,	181,718 95
Circulation,	63,933 00	Real estate,	2,000 00
Profits,	8,235 42	Bills of other banks,	4,349 00
Due to other banks,	4,699 80	Due from other bks.,	34,897 88
Deposits,	48,929 66	Specie,	2,832 05
	$225,797 88		$225,797 88

Immediate liabilities, $117,562 46.
Immediate resources, $42,078 93.

Samuel C. Grant, *President ;* Frederick Allen, William B. Grant, Samuel B. Tarbox, Peter Grant, *Directors ;* Joseph Adams, *Cashier.*

KENDUSKEAG BANK.

Capital stock,	100,000 00	Loan,	154,108 15
Circulation,	72,300 00	Real estate,	11,170 00
Profits,	4,364 70	Bank & Bridge stock,	42,959 49
Due to other bks.,	1,661 14	Bills of other banks,	15,192 53
Deposits,	100,403 48	Due from other bks.,	44,800 23
		Specie,	10,503 92
	$278,729 32		$278,729 32

Immediate liabilities, $174,364 62.
Immediate resources, $70,496 68.

John Wilkins, *President;* Abner Taylor, George W. Pickering, Thomas H. Sandford, John Godfrey, *Directors ;* T. S. Dodd, *Cashier.*

LINCOLN BANK.

Capital stock,	100,000 00	Loan,	178,263 34
Circulation,	72,353 00	Real estate,	3,000 00
Profits,	3,598 81	Bills of other banks,	1,365 00
Due to other banks,	4,998 57	Due from other bks.,	93,433 22
Deposits,	105,963 52	Specie,	10,852 34
	$286,913 90		$286,913 90

Immediate liabilities, $183,315 09.

Immediate resources, $105,650 56.

George F. Patten, *President;* William Richardson, Levi Houghton, Joshua Page, William M. Rogers, Thomas Harwood, Samuel Gray, *Directors;* John Shaw, *Cashier.*

LIME ROCK BANK.

Capital stock,	50,000 00	Loan,	80,768 85
Circulation,	44,059 00	Real estate,	3,908 18
Profits,	1,358 73	Bills of other banks,	10,613 00
Due to other banks,	39 30	Due from other bks.,	30,300 69
Deposits,	35,489 49	Specie,	4,855 80
	$130,946 52		$130,946 52

Immediate liabilities, $79,587 79.

Immediate resources, $46,269 49.

Knott Crockett, *President;* Iddo Kimball, Charles Holmes, Joseph Hewett, John Spear, Reuben Sherer, Iddo K. Kimball, *Directors;* E. M. Perry, *Cashier.*

MANUFACTURERS' BANK.

Capital stock,	100,000 00	Loan,	150,461 98
Circulation,	68,656 00	Real estate,	6,076 34
Profits,	3,686 54	Bills of other banks,	1,258 00
Due to other banks,	787 93	Due from other bks.,	38,581 04
Deposits,	28,174 29	Specie,	4,927 40
	$201,304 76		$201,304 76

Immediate liabilities, $97,618 22.
Immediate resources, $44,766 44.

William P. Haines, *President;* Josiah Calef, Amos Chase, Tristram Jordan, Jr., David Fernald, Nathaniel M. Towle, *Directors;* S. S. Fairfield, *Cashier.*

MARINERS' BANK.

Capital stock,	50,000 00	Loan,	82,106 99
Circulation,	42,131 00	Real estate,	3,705 54
Profits,	1,598 88	Bank charges,	71 61
Due to other banks,	171 16	Bills of other banks,	3,921 00
Deposits,	22,909 72	Due from other bks.,	23,717 71
		Specie,	3,287 91
	$116,810 76		$116,810 76

Immediate liabilities, $65,211 76.
Immediate resources, $30,926 62.

Henry Clark, *President;* Wilmot Wood, William M. Boyd, Samuel Alley, James McCarty, *Directors;* S. P. Baker, *Cashier.*

MAUFACTURERS' AND TRADERS' BANK.

Capital stock,	75,000 00	Loan,	115,935 16
Circulation,	38,226 00	Real estate,	1,000 00
Profits,	3,983 34	Expenses,	374 90
Due to other banks,	1,177 33	Bills of other banks,	6,527 00
Deposits,	15,742 46	Due from other bks.,	6,569 82
		Specie,	3,722 25
	$134,129 13		$134,129 13

Immediate liabilities, $55,145 79.
Immediate resources, $16,819 07.

Joshua Richardson, *President;* Stephen Waite, Rufus Horton, Neal Dow, E. McKenney, *Directors;* E. Gould, *Cashier.*

2

MERCANTILE BANK.

Capital stock,	50,000 00	Loan,	65,764 81
Circulation,	60,889 00	Bank & Bridge stock,	34,650 00
Profits,	2,663 39	Real estate,	4,158 98
Deposits,	13,755 92	Suspended debt,	990 83
		Expenses,	445 15
		Bills of other banks,	286 00
		Due from other bks.,	17,568 96
		Specie,	3,443 58
	$127,308 31		$127,308 31

Immediate liabilities, $74,644 92.

Immediate resources, $21,298 54.

Samuel Farrar, *President ;* Oliver Frost, Asa Warren, Ebenezer G. Rawson, Moses Woodward, James Jenkins, *Directors ;* John S. Ricker, *Cashier.*

MERCHANTS' BANK.

Capital stock,	150,000 00	Loan,	296,581 29
Circulation,	93,312 00	Bank charges,	756 08
Profits,	10,826 70	Real estate,	5,000 00
Due to other banks,	8,054 33	Bills of other banks,	2,099 00
Deposits,	95,551 05	Due from other bks.,	21,810 54
		Specie,	31,497 17
	$357,744 08		$357,744 08

Immediate liabilities, $196,917 38.

Immediate resources, $55,406 71.

William Woodbury, *President ;* Philip Greeley, Jonathan Tucker, Rufus Emerson, George Warren, Josiah Dow, Charles Kimball, *Directors ;* Reuben Mitchell, *Cashier.*

MEDOMAK BANK.

Capital stock,	50,000 00	Loan,	65,445 77
Circulation,	43,043 00	Real estate,	2,555 92
Profits,	85 37	Bills of other banks,	52 00
Deposits,	7,171 45	Due from other bks.,	28,454 04
		Specie,	3,792 09
	$100,299 82		$100,299 82

Immediate liabilities, $50,214 45.
Immediate resources, $32,298 13.

James Hovey, *President ;* George D. Smouse, Frederick Cast-ner, George Sproul, John Bulfinch, Alexander Palmer, Joseph Clark, *Directors ;* Parker McCobb, *Cashier.*

MEGUNTICOOK BANK.

Capital stock,	49,000 00	Loan,	51,603 14
Circulation,	35,628 00	Real estate,	318 12
Profits,	602 25	Bank stock,	3,300 00
Deposits,	5,777 24	Bills of other bks.,	3,963 00
		Due from other bks.,	27,746 91
		Specie,	4,076 32
	$91,007 49		$91,007 49

Immediate liabilities, $41,405 24.
Immediate resources, $35,786 23.

Joseph Jones, *President ;* Samuel G. Adams, Charles R. Por-ter, J. C. Stetson, Samuel D. Carleton, Elisha Gilkey, Hosea Bates, *Directors ;* Nathaniel Dillingham, *Cashier.*

NORTHERN BANK.

Capital stock,	75,000 00	Loan,	115,739 62
Circulation,	37,702 00	Bills of other banks,	5,391 00
Profits,	3,302 28	Due from other bks.,	11,458 45

Due to other banks,	2,254 16	Specie,	1,794 89
Deposits,	16,120 52		
	$134,378 96		$134,378 96

Immediate liabilities, $56,076 68.
Immediate resources, $18,639 34.

Franklin Glazier, *President*; Isaac Aiken, Williams Emmons, B. Nason, John Gardner, Philo Sanford, David Brown, *Directors*; William M. Vaughan, *Cashier*.

SAGADAHOCK BANK.

Capital stock,	50,000 00	Loan,	73,504 64
Circulation,	35,145 00	Real estate,	188 98
Profits,	2,247 45	Bills of other banks,	1,440 00
Due to other banks,	4,129 74	Due from other bks.,	52,853 38
Deposits,	40,025 81	Specie,	3,561 00
	$131,548 00		$131,548 00

Immediate liabilities, $79,300 55.
Immediate resources, $57,854 38.

Joseph Sewall, *President*; T. D. Robinson, John Smith, William M. Reed, Lewis Blackmer, Moses Riggs, William Purington, *Directors*; D. F. Baker, *Cashier*.

SOUTH BERWICK BANK.

Capital stock,	50,000 00	Loan,	99,146 62
Circulation,	50,847 00	Real estate,	1,000 00
Profits,	5,205 83	Bills of other banks,	317 00
Deposits,	16,864 24	Due from other bks.,	20,533 65
		Specie,	1,919 80
	$122,917 07		$122,917 07

Immediate liabilities, $67,711 24.
Immediate resources, $22,770 45.

William A. Hayes, *President*; William Hight, Thomas Jewett, Benjamin Mason, Josiah W. Seaver, *Directors*; E. Norton, *Cashier*.

SKOWHEGAN BANK.

Capital stock,	75,000 00	Loan,	114,425 44
Circulation,	48,440 00	Real estate, .	2,581 54
Profits,	5,219 06	Bills of other banks,	5,652 00
Deposits,	10,402 36	Due from other bks.,	14,187 40
		Specie,	2,215 04
	$139,061 42		$139,061 42

Immediate liabilities, $53,842 36.
Immediate resources, $22,054 44.

William Allen, *President ;* Ebenezer H. Neil, Judah McLellan, Abner Coburn, Samuel Parker, John G. Neil, Edmond Pearsons, *Directors ;* Samuel Philbrick, *Cashier.*

TICONIC BANK.

Capital stock,	75,000 00	Loan,	105,746 10
Circulation,	54,936 00	Real estate,	3,317 00
Profits,	2,493 43	Bills of other banks,	6,380 00
Deposits,	15,002 90	Due from other bks.,	28,258 37
		Specie,	3,730 96
	$147,432 33		$147,432 33

Immediate liabilities, $69,938 90.
Immediate resources, $38,369 23.

Timothy Boutelle, *President ;* Moses Appleton, Jedediah Morrill, Sumner Percival, Elah Esty, *Directors ;* Augustine Perkins, *Cashier*

THOMASTON BANK.

Capital stock,	50,000 00	Loan,	60,583 70
Circulation,	46,124 00	Real estate,	2,500 00
Profits,	1,078 74	Bills of other banks,	3,676 00
Due to other banks,	512 05	Due from other bks.,	77,790 29
Deposits,	59,693 38	Profit and loss,	6,814 71
		Specie,	6,043 57
	$157,408 17		$157,408 17

2*

Immediate liabilities, $106,329 43.

Immediate resources, $87,509 76.

'Richard Robinson, *President*; Edward Robinson, William Singer, William R. Keith, Manassah H. Smith, Edwin Smith, John T. Gleason, *Directors*; John D. Barnard, *Cashier.*

YORK BANK.

Capital Stock,	75,000 00	Loan,	95,857 64
Circulation,	45,300 00	Bank stock,	780 00
Profits,	5,382 26	Real estate,	9,242 30
Deposits,	32,984 77	Bills of other banks,	1,050 00
		Due from other bks.,	45,188 41
		Specie,	6,548 68
	$158,667 03		$158,667 03

Immediate liabilities, $78,284 77.

Immediate resources, $52,786 71

Jonathan King, *President*; Horace Bacon, James M. Deering, William Smith, *Directors*; one vacancy—Henry D. Thatcher, *Cashier.*

The following table gives an abstract of the principal items in the foregoing statements of the several banks for the year 1845, together with those of the two preceding years.

	1843.	1844.	1845.
Capital stock, . .	$3,009,000	$3,009,000	$3,009,000
Immediate liabilities,	2,549,814	3,124,475	3,620,053
Immediate resources,	1,300,160	1,369,325	1,537,238
Loan, ...	4,027,335	4,492,762	4,800,110
Circulation, . . .	1,496,540	1,846,816	2,109,427
Deposits, . . .	1,053,274	1,254,915	1,455,407
Specie, ...	213,366	198,899	196,803
Bills of other banks,	257,218	144,192	154,625
Due from other banks,	829,576	1,003,082	1,184,810

This table shows that with no increase of banking capital during the last three years, there has been a gradual increase in most of our bank movements for the same period of time.

Since our last report there has been a small increase in every item, named above, except that of the specie. The banks, however, which continue to redeem their circulation in Boston, under what is denominated the Suffolk system, it is believed need very little specie at home for the redemption of their notes.

The inability of the banks to redeem their notes, is sometimes argued from the excess of their circulation over the amount of specie in their vaults. But if the banks should cease discounting and demand full payment for their notes as fast as they fall due, not only would the banks be relieved in a very few days from demands for specie in payment of their bank notes, but the debtors to the banks would find it very difficult to obtain bank notes to pay their own liabilities.

It is true that such a course would produce great embarrassment to those indebted to the banks, and to the trading community generally, but the banks would be relieved.

The strength of a bank depends much more upon the character and extent of its loan, than upon the amount of specie in its vaults. If the loan is kept within proper limits, is well secured and payments promptly enforced, the losses are most certain to be very few. If on the contrary however, the business is conducted loosely and on what is denominated permanent loans, losses are pretty certain ultimately to follow. But, notwithstanding there has been a falling off of specie, it will be seen that the banks have an abundance of immediate means to meet their immediate liabilities. Among their resources is a large amount due from other banks, most of which is due from banks in Boston, and is equivalent to specie for the redemption of their circulation.

The deposits of a bank are put down among its immediate liabilities—this is right—because they are liable to be checked out at the will of the depositors. Yet so far from being considered by bankers as an immediate liability, they are counted upon as a resource upon which the line of discounts may be extended.

In well regulated banks, the amount of individual deposits continues very equal, except under extraordinary circumstances—what one depositor draws out is usually replaced by another, and in that way the amount varies but very little for a long time.

The income of a bank is upon its loan. By the aid of the deposits and the circulation, it is enabled to extend it beyond the amount of its capital stock, and by thus increasing it the bank is enabled to pay the tax to the State and the other expenses, leaving the interest of the capital invested, to be divided among the several stockholders. It is found, by actual calculation, that the expenses of banking in this State, including the tax, amount in the aggregate to about two per cent. upon the capital stock. Of course the banks must earn eight per cent. clear of all losses, to give the stockholders six per cent. upon the capital invested.

There have been great improvements in the mode of transacting the business of banking in this State within the few years last past. It is generally conducted upon sound principles; the loans in most instances are promptly met, and a very small amount of paper is permitted to remain overdue. These improvements in banking have exerted a salutary influence upon the general business of the State. It is to be regretted, however, that the provisions of the statutes, regulating banks and banking, are not yet universally adhered to.

By reference to the state of the several banks comprehended in this report, it will be seen that the law has again been violated in several instances, but particularly in the excess of circulation.

The commissioners in their former reports have alluded to these violations of the statutes, and pointed out the delinquent banks; they regret to say, however, without seeming to impress the Legislature with the necessity of taking action to correct these violations of their own enactments.

The general apology of bank directors for these violations, and particularly that of over issues in their circulation, is that the legal restriction is too great; that the means of the banks are ample; and that the public interest requires an extension of their loans, which cannot be done without extending the circulation.

The answer to this is perfectly easy—they should petition the

Legislature for an alteration in the law restricting the circulation, or for an increase of their capital, or both. It is not a good answer for them, that they have no more capital to invest, but it is a very strong reason why they should be kept within the limits of the statute, if they have exhausted their capital.

The restriction upon the circulation is believed to be unequal, and could probably be made more favorable to the banking interest without endangering that of the public.

But we again repeat that the statutes should be either enforced or repealed. The violation of any law should be regarded as dangerous to our free institutions.

The following table gives a condensed view of the movements of the banks in this State at different periods, from the year of our separation from Massachusetts, in 1820, to this time:

YEARS.	BANKS.	CAPITAL.	CIRCULATION	SPECIE.	LOAN.
1820,	15	1,654,900	1,380,572	543,347	2,478,947
1830,	18	2,205,000	687,189	208,000	2,888,000
1835,	35	3,735,000	2,380,114	186,050	6,357,010
1838,	55	5,458,750	1,696,023	246,720	7,552,938
1840,	50	4,671.500	1,224,658	257,610	5,901,611
1842,	39	3,414,000	1,585,820	177,823	4,319,394
1845,	35	3,009,000	2,109,427	196,803	4,800,110

The above table shows that while our State has continued to increase in population, business and wealth, our banks have diminished twenty in number since 1838, and a *nominal* banking capital of about two and a half millions has been withdrawn. But although an additional banking capital may be wanting in some few portions of our State, yet we doubt not that trade is in a more healthy condition, at this time, than it was when our banking capital was five and a half millions, and our loan seven and a half millions of dollars.

We have said that our banking capital had been reduced *nominally* about two and a half millions of dollars. The actual amount, however, which has been withdrawn, is much less than that sum.

Several of the banks which have surrendered their charters, had very little actual capital at the time of their surrender, and some few of them, it is believed, had very little when they commenced operating. The present banks, however, are believed to be conducting their business upon actual capital, and so long as they restrain themselves within legal limits, are undoubtedly safe. If we take a view of the changes and fluctuations of the currency for the last thirty years, we shall cease to wonder at the commercial disasters with which the country has been visited.

It appears from official documents, that during the suspension of specie payments in 1815 and '16, the circulating medium of the country had reached to one hundred and ten millions of dollars; and that in 1819 it was reduced to forty-five millions, or 59 per cent. in four years! From that time to 1830, it was estimated to average fifty-five millions; while in 1837 it had again run up to one hundred and fifty millions, being an increase of more than 150 per cent.!

In 1838 it was suddenly reduced to one hundred and sixteen millions. In 1839 it again expanded to one hundred and thirty-five millions. In 1840 it again sunk to one hundred and seven millions. In 1841 it increased to one hundred and twenty-four millions, and in 1843 it had again sunk to forty-six millions, or nearly 63 per cent. in two years! Since that period it has increased to about eighty-five millions of dollars. Is it wonderful that with such immense changes in the currency of the country, we should have had revulsions in trade, and panics in the money market?

The most important regulator of the prices of all kinds of property, is the currency. If it is inflated, property advances in price. If it is contracted, it declines in value. A healthy and uniform state of the currency, therefore, is most conducive to a sound state of trade, and a permanent and fair value of property.

The increased rate of interest in our large cities, during the last year, shows that money has been in more demand than it was the two preceding ones. It appears, however, sufficiently abundant for all the legitimate wants of trade.

It is matter of congratulation, that notwithstanding foreign exchange has been kept so near the specie standard, the currency of the country continues so sound and uniform. This in a great measure arises from the fact, that for the last three years the balance on our foreign trade, each year, has been in our favor; and as we shall probably, hereafter, continue to export more and import less, in proportion to the increase of the trade and population of the country, the balance in our favor may long continue. Our foreign imports for the years 1836, '37 and '38, exceeded those of 1842, '43 and '44, about 155 millions of dollars; while our exports fell off during the latter period, but 39 millions; leaving a balance in favor of the last three years, over the speculative years named above, of 116 millions of dollars. But a more just comparison could be made by taking four years previous to the speculative years, and comparing them with the four years last past, viz:

YEARS.	IMPORTS.	YEARS.	IMPORTS.
1832, . .	101,029,226	1842, . .	100,162,087
1833, . .	108,118,311	1843, . .	89,260,895
1834, . .	126,521,332	1844, . .	108,435,035
1835, . .	149,895,742	1845, . .	117,254,564

By comparing the imports, as stated in the above table, it will be seen that the excess of the first four years, over that of the last four years, was in the aggregate more than seventy millions of dollars; the population of the country in the mean time having increased about one third, and its wealth probably one fourth.

The decrease in the amount of our imports may, to a considerable extent, be attributed to the steady increase in the home manufacture of many articles which had formerly been imported from abroad, and which are now not only extensively supplying our own market, but which, to some extent, are exported, thereby diminishing our indebtedness to foreign markets, and preventing the export of our specie.

With prudence, therefore, on the part of those who have the controlling power of the trade and currency of the country, we may look for a steady and prosperous business for a series of years. It seems to be conceded that paper of some kind must, to a great degree, constitute the medium of exchange in the United States. We must, therefore, take banks for better or for worse, and all those who are entrusted with the creation or management of them should direct their efforts to secure the good they are calculated to produce and to prevent the evils to which they are liable.

Solid capital and prudent management are the main pillars upon which a firm confidence in banks must rest; they never should be chartered for the purpose of creating capital, but for funding it. When the latter course is adopted they are pretty sure to be directed by able and efficient officers; for few men who invest actual capital are willing to entrust it to unskillful hands. If, therefore, banks are established upon fair banking principles, the public have very little to apprehend from their failure.

The bank charters granted by the Legislature of this State, will all expire in the year 1847, and although the several acts for regulating banks and banking are believed to be as perfect as those of any other State in the Union, experience, which is said to be the best modern legislature, has shown that they are not entirely faultless. Some amendments, therefore, it is believed, are necessary.

The bank commissioners are perfectly aware that it is not their province to legislate; they hope, however, that it will not be considered obtrusive in them to point out such defects in the statutes as have occurred to them during their several examinations, and to suggest the remedy.

It is obvious that the threatened forfeiture of charter will not deter all bank officers from transcending their legal limits in the matter of their circulation, the extent of their loan, the liabilities of their directors, and in taking, indirectly, usurous interest.

It is believed that these evils would be more effectually remedied by imposing fines of a sufficient amount to outweigh the advantages which may be derived from the several violations of the statutes.

It is believed also that very little additional security is given to the public by the present restriction upon the circulation of bank notes; that it would be more just to extend it to the amount of the capital stock of all the banks, and that such an alteration in the law would very little impair the public security; for although banks with small capitals might sometimes reach their legal limits, those with large ones could never.

If the security of the public is the object of the Legislature, a more effectual guard to a redundant circulation, would be given by further restricting the loan. By the existing law it is extended to double the amount of the capital stock paid in. There never was a time since banking was established to any considerable extent in the country, that the aggregate loan of all the banks reached that limit; nor did it ever reach it in this State, although individual banks have exceeded it.

If the loan should be restricted to seventy-five per cent. more than the capital stock of the bank, instead of one hundred per cent. as it now is, and the restriction rigidly enforced, it is believed that very little danger could be apprehended from an extended circulation, or for a want of specie to redeem it, so long as the present system of redeeming in Boston is continued.

It is suggested whether provision should not be made by law the more effectually to prevent bank note plates from falling into irresponsible hands; and also for the better security of the public against counterfeiting bank notes, by requiring the use of a uniform and superior quality of bank note paper, and plates of superior workmanship. This object would perhaps be more effectually carried out, if the notes for each bank should be furnished directly by the State.

The facility with which bank notes are imitated, demands serious Legislative attention.

It is also suggested, whether it would not be an improvement in our banking system, to grant no new charters for banks with capitals of less than one hundred thousand dollars; and in our cities, of less capital than two hundred thousand dollars.

A bank with a reasonably large capital can be conducted with very little additional expense, excepting the tax, over that of a small one.

3

There is less danger of getting up a spurious bank with a large capital than with a small one. A bank with a small capital may be owned and managed by a few individuals. Indeed, under the existing law, a bank of fifty thousand dollars may be owned by five individuals, the lowest number necessary to form a board of directors. Such a bank could do a larger amount of business in proportion to its capital, than one with a large capital, and would pay less tax to the State in proportion to the business it transacted. State policy, therefore, as well as public security, is adverse to the establishment of banks with small capitals.

We would further suggest whether provision should not also be made by law to oblige banks to protect their funds against fire and burglars, by obliging them to furnish vaults and locks of sufficient strength and guards for that purpose. While we would respectfully contend for legislative aid to protect the public and those who invest capital in banks without having a controlling power over it, we would also ask that the just rights of the banks should not be neglected. Banks we must have, and if they are too severely restricted, charters will either be entirely refused or accepted by those only who would not hesitate to violate the law to enable them to make large dividends. Something, too, is due to them for the amount which they annually contibute to the revenue of the State, and which if applied to aid the payment of our State debt, as we believe it should be, would go so far to lessen the taxes of the people.

All of which is respectfully submitted.

NATH'L MITCHELL,   *Bank*
ALPHEUS LYON,   *Commissioners.*

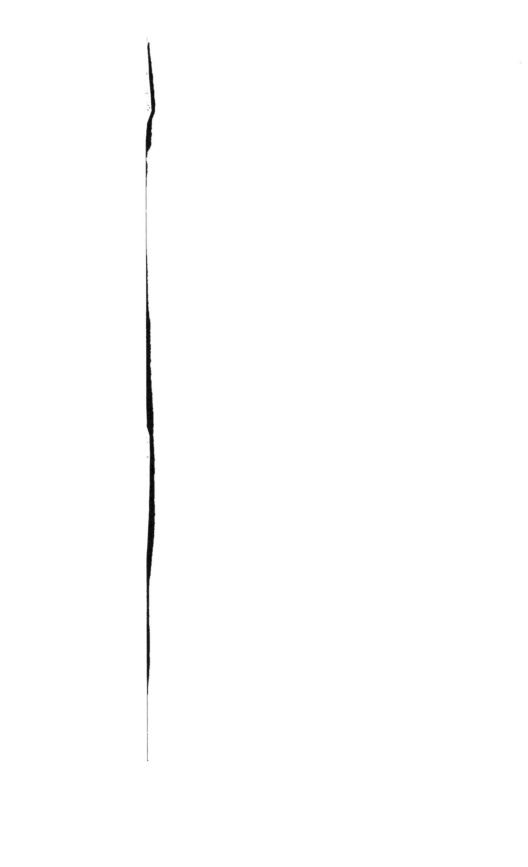

TRUSTEES, STEWARD AND TREASURER,

AND

SUPERINTENDENT

OF THE

INSANE HOSPITAL,

1845.

Published agreeably to Resolve of March 22, 1836.

AUGUSTA:
Wm. T. JOHNSON, PRINTER TO THE STATE.

1846.

REPORT

OF THE

TRUSTEES

OF THE

INSANE HOSPITAL,

1845.

Officers of the Institution.

1*

tion.

AND.

REPORT.

To the Governor and Council of the State of Maine.

THE Trustees of the Insane Hospital, in making this their annual report, have the satisfaction to state, that at the monthly, quarterly, and annual examinations the past year, they have found the situation and prospects of the Hospital equal in all, and in some respects better, than at their prior visits.

The Treasurer's accounts have been examined and settled each quarter by three of the Trustees.

At the last settlement, made November 30th, there was a balance due the Treasurer from the Hospital of $312 $\frac{31}{100}$, and the balances then due the institution were forty hundred and eighty dollars $\frac{92}{100}$, ... $4,080 92

Viz: From towns and individuals, $3,478 34
    From State for State paupers
      after deducting $300 allow-
      ed by legislature, . 602 58

From this statement, it appears that the finances of the Hospital are a little better than they were last year.

There was then due from towns and
   individuals, ... 3,334 40
And cash in treasury, fifty-three
   dollars six cents,   .   .   .   53 06
                                 —————— 3,387 46
There is now due from towns and
   individuals, ... 3,478 34
     From State,   .   .   .   602 58

                         4,080 92
Less balance due Treasurer,   .   312 31
                                 —————— 3,768 61

Being an increase of the funds of the Institution from the last year, of three hundred
   eighty-one dollars and fifteen cents, .   . $381 15

On the 10th of February last, Dr. Ray gave notice to
the chairman of the Trustees, that having been appointed
Superintendent of an Insane Hospital in a neighboring
State, he resigned the office of Superintendent of the
Maine Insane Hospital, and on the 19th of March the
board met to fill the vacancy, and elected Dr. James
Bates as Superintendent.

On the 31st of December, Dr. Smith, the Assistant
Physician, having previously resigned, Dr. Henry M. Har-
low was elected Assistant Physician.

By an order of the board the monthly visits are now
made on such days as the visitors may themselves select;
it is impossible therefore to have the Hospital prepared
for their reception, and they obtain a correct knowledge
of its management, which might not have been the case
when it was visited on set days.

The following statement gives the number of patients
that have been admitted each year, the average number

in the Hospital during each year, the number discharged, number improved, recovered, and remaining.

Year.	Admitted.	Average No.	Discharged.	Recovered.	Improved.	Remaining.	
1840,	30	–	2	1	1	Dec. 31,	28
1841,	105	–	79	33	20	"	54
1842,	87	62$\frac{1}{2}$	76	36	16	"	65.
1843,	82	65	79	31	27	Nov. 30,	68
1844,	83	70	75	32	18	"	76
1845,	99	80	90	38	22	"	85
	486		401	171	104		

From the information received by the Trustees, in reply to letters addressed by them in 1844 to all the towns
in the State, it would appear that there were then more
than six hundred insane persons within its limits; that
number has undoubtedly increased in an equal proportion
with the population; and from present appearances it
cannot be long before a considerable portion of these unfortunates will be offered at the Institution, and the largest
number that can be accommodated at the Hospital is
about one hundred, being less than one sixth of the
whole number of insane in the State.

On the 1st of June last, in conformity with a request
received from a large number of the members of the Legislature, and a recommendation of the joint standing
committee on the Insane Hospital, to which the Trustees
gave their decided approbation, the price of board was
reduced fifty cents per week for males and twenty-five
cents for females. The highest price of board for males,
including washing and medicines, is now only two dollars and fifty cents, and the lowest one dollar and fifty
cents, and for females cannot exceed two dollars and
twenty-five cents, nor be less than one dollar and twenty-

five cents. The effect of this reduction in the price of board has been to increase the number of those receiving the benefits of the institution, and our rooms in the male department are now full, the male patients having increased from fifty, the number on the 30th of November, 1844, to fifty-five, the number on the 30th of November, 1845; the females have increased during the same time from twenty-six to thirty. We have it in our power to accommodate a still larger number of females, but cannot increase the number of male patients without additional accommodations, only to be effected by an enlargement of the Hospital. The Trustees would therefore respectfully suggest to the Governor, and through him to the State, that it is highly desirable that provision should be made at the next session of the Legislature for the addition of another wing to the Hospital. When founded it was intended for the benefit of all those unfortunates that might require its aid, and as the number of its inmates increased an enlargement was undoubtedly contemplated; it would not have been just to have erected a hospital with other views. In our country, and under our form of government, public money ought not to be expended for a portion only of the community—public institutions should always be for the advantage of all our citizens, and their benefits within the reach of all that can profit by them. This will be no longer the case with the Insane Hospital unless enlarged—its male wards are now all full, and should there be any more applicants for admission, as we have every reason to believe there will be, it will become necessary either to refuse them, or to discharge some of those now within its walls. To reject the new applicants would be to deny to them the same advantages others have received, a portion of the expense of which has probably been borne by themselves. To discharge such of the present inmates as are considered incurable, and who have aided to support the institution in its infancy, will be to consign them again to shackles, dens, and cages, after having been taught to relish the air and light of heaven, and freedom from all unnecessary restraint. We shall have given them the capability of enjoying and the desire to retain these blessings, and then cruelly force them from their grasp. Some of those who now join in daily hymns of praise to their Maker, making melody in their hearts, were, when first brought to the Hospital, literally howling maniacs. We ask of the State government, will it, can it, consent to be the cause of converting these hymns again into those howlings? It should also be borne in mind that by increasing the size of the Hospital you add to its fixed, but not to its floating capital; the expense of the officers, (which is the only one paid by the State,) would not be any more. Should the patients be doubled in number no additional officers would be required, and but few additional assistants and domestics. And as the wages of the assistants and domestics constitute more than one quarter of the expense of board, if their number is but little increased by an increased number of patients, it follows that the price of board could then be still further reduced and might thus save to the people the full amount of the interest of the money the additional building would cost.

By a resolve of the Legislature of April 7th, 1845, the principal on the bond for the maintenance of Oakman Ford was released from his obligation, and the Trustees directed to discharge him from the debt. We do not deny the power thus to step between us and our debtors, but we would respectfully inquire on what principle such discharge was granted, and if our debtors are thus to be exonerated, how can it be expected the Institution will defray its expenses? What in this case renders the action of the Legislature the more extraordinary, is, that no notice was given to the officers of the Institution to enable them to appear and show cause why the prayer of the petitioners should not be granted. Should a similar application again be made we hope the Legislature will direct the petitioner to give notice to the officers of the Hospital, and if the debtor should be released an appropriation at the same time made to supply the deficiency thus created.

The Hospital the past year would have more than paid its expenses had the State made an appropriation for payment of the board of the insane State paupers, which amounts since its commencement to $902, but taxed with their support it will not be able to meet its engagements. The Trustees are therefore under the necessity of requesting an appropriation of six hundred and two dollars fifty-eight cents to cover the expense incurred in supporting the before mentioned patients directly chargeable to the State, and also the sum of six hundred dollars to aid in defraying the expenses of the Hospital the coming year, and to supply any deficiency in funds which may arise from the reduction that has been made in the price of board.

The Superintendent's and Treasurer's reports are herewith submitted, and by that of the latter it appears that the whole expense for the farming operations during the last year were—

Wages and board of one man, wages $144, board estimated at $78, ...	$222 00
Hay purchased, $9-54, ...	9 54
Manure and seed, ...	105 81
	$331 57

Expenses, brought up,		$331 57
The receipts by his estimate are, . . .		919 54

Leaving a balance in favor of the farm of .		587 97
But from this balance ought to be deducted over estimate of		
Twenty tons of hay, .	$40 00	
Two tons oat straw for fodder,	8·00	
Wheat straw, . . .	10 00	
		58 00
		529 97
Deduct also labor of one horse and its keeping, estimated at, ...		75 00
		$454 97

It appears from the above that the farm has afforded a fair profit, notwithstanding the unproductiveness of the season; it is however capable of being much improved, a large portion is even now little better than waste land, although requiring only the plough and manure to render it productive. It would have given great pleasure to the Trustees to have had some improvements made, but it could not be done without aid from the legislature, and it has been their desire to keep the institution within its own resources. Much of the labor of the patients has been laid out in grading the grounds—work which although necessary is unproductive. This work being now nearly completed, some attention can be devoted to the farm, and the amount of its hay product, now not enough for the supply of the cows and horses necessary for the use of the Hospital, increased.

The Trustees take pleasure in being able to assure the

2

Executive that they have reason to be perfectly satisfied
with the management of the Hospital ; that as far as they
have had an opportunity of judging, the officers are faithful in the discharge of their duties, and there is a care,
tenderness and mildness evinced by them in their treatment of its inmates that has given them great gratifica-
tion.

Before closing their report the Trustees would again
call the attention of the Executive to the subject of a census of the insane, and would take the liberty to suggest
that steps be taken if possible to ascertain their number
prior to the meeting of the next legislature, by directing
the selectmen and assessors to make return of the same
to the Secretary of State.

EDWARD S. JARVIS,
EDWARD KENT,
REUEL WILLIAMS,
EDWARD SWAN.

REPORT

OF THE

STEWARD AND TREASURER

OF THE

INSANE HOSPITAL,

1845.

REPORT.

THE Steward and Treasurer of the Maine Insane Hospital respectfully presents to the Board of Trustees his annual statement of the receipts and expenditures of the Institution for the year ending November 30th, 1845, which are as follows, viz :

Balance in the hands of the Treasurer November 30, 1844, ... $53 06

Amount received for board of patients and some few articles sold, ... 9,339 57

Amount received of the bequest of Hon. Bryce McLellan, ... 30 00
_____
$9,422 63

The expenditures are as follows, and have somewhat increased since the last year, which is owing to the higher price we have been obliged to pay for nearly all the articles of provision and groceries consumed in an establishment of this kind.

Paid for provisions and groceries, . . $3,810 17
" hay, ... 9 54
" medicine, ... 148 54
" clothing, which is charged in patients' accounts, ... 595 67
" books and stationery, . . . 67 59

2*

Paid for soap, ...   78 77
   "   repairs about the buildings,   .   .   410 06
   ..   fuel, ...   832 68
   "   manure and seed for farm,   .   .   105 81
   ..   oil, ...   163 07
   "   furniture, ...   587 10
   "   horse, ...   108 00
   "   miscellaneous items,   .   .   .   602 11
   "   for labor, including the work
         on the farm,   .   .   2,258 25
Forty-two dollars and $\frac{42}{100}$ of which
  was paid with property belonging
  to the Hospital,   .   .   .   42 42
                   ———— 2,215 83

                        $9,734 94

Leaving a balance against the Hospital of three hundred and twelve dollars and $\frac{31}{100}$ for moneys expended more than received during the year.

Notwithstanding the apparent deficit, by reference to the report of the financial affairs of the Hospital made Nov. 30th, 1844, you will find there was due for board of patients, &c., ... $3,334 40
And Nov. 30, 1845, there is due the Hospital
  from towns and individuals,   . $3,478 34
And the balance due for boarding
  State paupers, after deducting
  three hundred dollars allowed by
  the legislature of last winter,   .   602 58
                   ———— $4,080 92

Showing an increase of debts due the Hospital of seven hundred forty-six dollars $\frac{52}{100}$—

From which sum deduct, ... $312 31
And also fifty-three dollars and $\frac{6}{100}$, . . 53 06

$365 37

And we still have a balance in favor of the Hospital of three hundred eighty-one dollars and $\frac{15}{100}$ after paying all the expenses for the year past.

Included however in the above sum of four thousand and eighty dollars and $\frac{23}{100}$ due the institution, are near six hundred dollars of debts that are not collectable, and when we take into account the length of time the bad debts have been accumulating (more than five years), I think we have been well favored, for some losses will unavoidably occur yearly.

In making an estimate of the value and products of the farm, I would observe, that the operations have been much the same as in years past, but Providence has not smiled upon our efforts to the extent we anticipated.

The quantity and estimated value of the crops are as follows, viz:

20 tons of hay, at $12, ...	$240 00
300 bushels potatoes, at 40 cts., . . .	120 00
31 1-2 bushels wheat, at 7s. 6d, . . .	39 37
72 bushels oats, at 40 cts., . . .	28 80
20 bushels barley, at 50 cts., . . .	10
89 bushels turnips, at 33 cts., , . .	29
30 bushels beets, at 50 cts., . . .	15
25 bushels carrots, at 25 cts., . . .	6
200 bushels apples, at 25 cts., . . .	50
200 cabbage heads, at 4 cts., . . .	8
40 bushels of green peas and beans, at 75 cts.,	30
2 tons late oat straw for feed, . . .	24
3848 lbs. pork, at 6 cts., ...	230 00

510 lbs. beef, at 3 1-2 cts., ... $17 85
  10 tons oat and wheat straw, at $5,   .   .   50 00
A quantity of small vegetables,   .   .   .   20 00
                                                 ————
                                                 $919 52

The labor on the farm has been performed by the patients with the exception of the services of one man, for
which we pay twelve dollars per month and board.

J. S. TURNER, *Steward and Treasurer.*

INSANE HOSPITAL, AUGUSTA, ⎱
    November 30, 1845.   ⎰

SIXTH ANNUAL REPORT

OF THE

SUPERINTENDENT

OF THE

INSANE HOSPITAL,

1845.

REPORT.

To the honorable the Governor and Council
of the State of Maine.

GENTLEMEN :—Through the goodness of God we have arrived at the season when duty requires of us an account of our stewardship in this highly favored and prosperous Institution.

When I reflect on the qualifications of the scientific and talented gentleman, who had so long and efficiently presided here before me, I feel no small diffidence in reporting on a subject which had not, until recently, occupied any *peculiar* portion of my professional investigations.

The gradual increase of admissions and recoveries, reported from time to time, in this institution, is not only cause for thankfulness, but proof of greater confidence in those who have occasion to place their friends here.

It is believed the success of the past year will not suffer from a comparison with any which has preceded it.

It was stated in the last annual report that the admissions and discharges for that year had been proportionably less than the year previous. This year shows a decided increase of both, although several of the discharges have been prematurely made, owing to the injudicious course pursued by friends and corporations.

	Males.	Females.	Total.
The number of patients in the Hospital Nov. 30, 1844, was, ...	50	26	76
There have been admitted during the year ending 30th Nov., 1845, ...	50	49	99
Whole number that has been in the Hospital during the year, ...	100	75	175
Discharged during the year—			
Recovered, ...	21	17	38
Improved, ...	10	12	22
Unimproved, ...	9	14	23
Died, ...	5	2	7
Whole number discharged, ...	45	45	90
Remaining Nov. 30, 1845, ...	55	30	85
Largest number at any time during year, . .	.	.	89
Smallest number, ...	.	.	72
Average number, ...	.	.	80.2
Average number, 1844, ...	.	.	70

Much difference of opinion exists amongst practical men, having the superintendence of Insane Hospitals, as to the value of the statistical tables in their reports; hence the almost total difference which exists in the numerous reports annually made on this subject.

Those who object to them, are doubtless influenced by the want of distinctness of terms used, and from the uncertainty whether the facts stated, truly conform to terms, which have received general assent. For instance, one reporter will class cases of insanity as *recent*, which have existed not over a year; whilst another will only denominate those such, which have not exceeded three months. So also in stating cases "recovered," "curable," &c., much latitude may obtain with gentlemen equally learned and honest. Much more, should such a case possibly occur, where the requisite knowledge and honesty were wanting.

I shall prepare several tables with a view to show as nearly as possible the success which has attended the treatment at this Institution, so that it may be compared with that of other asylums of the kind, and with the results hereafter obtained here.

This course seems more necessary, as it will serve to explain why a less proportion of our patients are discharged *recovered*, than in those institutions where patients are obliged to remain a specified time, unless sooner cured. Besides, it may be that all the advantages to be derived from statistics on insanity have not yet been realized.

If to these reasons I add, respect for the opinions of gentlemen whose talents, worth and long experience, entitle them to entire confidence, you will pardon me for making details requiring considerable labor, both to make and examine.

Should the results be less flattering than the predictions of the sanguine led them and others to anticipate, I trust the failure will be found to have resulted from circumstances beyond the control of the officers of this institution, and not from any remissness of duty on their part.

3

[No. 1.] *Table showing the disposal and state*

No.	When admitted.	Sex.	Age.	Age at 1st attack.	Civil state.	By whom committed.	Duration of present attack before admission.
15	14 Nov., 1840.	F.	44	24	Single.	Friends.	20 years.
28	30 Dec., "	M.	37	25	do	do	12 do
29	" " "	"	32	24	do	Town.	8 do
48	25 Feb., 1841.	"	53	23	do	do	30 do
52	9 March, "	"	36	32	Married	Friends.	4 do
70	11 April, "	"	28	25	Single.	Town.	3 do
74	21 " "	"	18	16	do	Friends.	2 do
75	23 " "	"	77	50	Married.	do	5 do
79	6 May, "	"	33	30	Single.	do	3 do
118	14 Oct., "	"	17	16	do	do	1 do
126	29 " "	"	37	29	do	do	8 do
131	13 Dec., "	F.	27	23	do	Town.	4 do
133	22 " "	M.	27	21	do	Friends.	6 do
139	14 Jan., 1842.	"	48	33	do	Court.	15 do
158	23 April, "	"	44	40	Married	Friends.	4 do
167	11 May, "	"	20	18	Single.	do	2 do
188	1 July, "	F.	27	27	do	do	3 months
194	23 " "	M.	40	40	Married.	do	2 do
210	12 Oct., "	F.	51	47	do	Town.	3 years 6 months.
211	17 " "	M.	26	22	Single	do	4 years
214	28 " "	"	35	15	do	do	20 do
215	7 Nov., "	"	70	66	Married.	Friends.	4 do
229	23 Feb., 1843.	"	43	25	Single.	do	18 do
237	25 March, "	F.	38	37	Married.	Town.	7 months.
250	30 May, "	M.	32	31	Single.	Friends.	8 do
257	8 June, "	"	27	24	do	do	3 years.
260	17 " "	"	83	73	Widower.	do	10 do
289	5 Oct., "	"	41	33	Married.	Court	8 do
295	26 " "	"	53	38	do	Town.	7 months.
297	8 Nov., "	F.	27	27	do	Friends.	6 do
300	17 " "	M.	25	21	Single.	do	4 years.
304	29 " "	"	36	35	Married.	Town.	8 months.
308	22 Dec., "	"	25	24	Single.	Friends.	13 do
314	10 Jan., 1844.	"	30	26	do	do	4 years.
319	13 Feb., "	"	49	48	Widower.	do	6 months.
320	22 " "	F.	45	35	Married.	Town.	10 years.
321	" " "	"	37	34	do	do	3 do
324	26 " "	"	45	30	Single.	Friends.	3 months.
326	13 March, "	"	40	25	do	do	1 year.
332	13 April, "	M.	22	22	do	do	1 month.

of 76 patients remaining December 1, 1844.

Time spent in the Hospital.			Discharged or remain.	State now or when discharged.	Supposed prospect.	Remarks.
5 years.			Remains.	Unimproved.	Incurable.	Now by town.
4	do	11 mos.	do	do.	do	
4	do		Discharged.	Improved.	do	
4	do	9 do	Remains.	Unimproved.	do	
4	do	8 do	do	do. Epileptic	do	Now by town.
4	do	7 do	do	Unimproved.	do	
4	do	7 do	do	do	do	
4	do		Died.			Pneumonia.
4	do	6 do	Remains.	do	do	
4	do	1 do	do	do	do	
4	do		do	Improved.	do	
4	do		do	Unimproved.	do	
4	do		do	do	do	
3	do	10 do	do	do	do	
2	do	11 do	Discharged.	do	do	
3	do	6 do	Remains.	do	do	
2	do	8 do	Discharged.	Recovered.		
2	do	9 do	do	Improved.	do	
2	do	9 do	do	Unimproved.	do	
2	do		Died.			2d admission.
2	do	6 do	Discharged.	Unimproved.	do	
3	do		Remains.	do	do	
2	do	9 do	do	do	do	
2	do	2 do	Discharged.	Recovered.		
2	do	6 do	Remains.	Unimproved.	do	
2	do		Discharged.	Improved.	do	
2	do	5 do	Remains.	Unimproved.	do	
1	do	3 do	Eloped.	Recovered.		3d admission.
1	do	4 do	Discharged.	Improved.	Curable.	
1	do	3 do	do	Unimproved.	Incurable.	Since dead.
2	do		Remains.	do	do	1 at McLean.
2	do		do	do	do	
1	do	2¼ do	Discharged.	Recovered.		
1	do	10 do	Remains.	Unimproved.	do	2d admission.
1	do	2 do	Discharged.	Recovered.		
1	do	9 do	Remains.	Unimproved.	do	
1	do	9 do	do	do	do	
1	do	7 do	Discharged.	do	do	
9¼ months.			do	Improved.	Curable.	
1 year 6 months.			do	Unimproved.	Incurable.	

Table No. 1,

No.	When admitted.	Sex.	Age.	Age at last attack.	Civil state.	By whom committed.	Duration of present attack before admission.
334	24 April, 1844.	M.	60	40	Married.	Friends.	3 months.
340	14 May, "	"	50	45	do	Town.	3 years.
344	28 " "	"	35	19	Single.	do	16 do
349	17 June, "	F.	35	34	Married.	Friends.	1 do
350	26 " "	M.	57	53	Widower.	Court.	4 do
352	9 July, "	F.	30	27	Married.	Friends.	3 do
355	1 Aug., "	M.	40	39	do	Town.	3 months.
356	1 " "	"	29	28	do	do	6 do
357	12 " "	F.	32	30	Single.	do	2 weeks
358	16 " "	M.	22	19	do	do	2 1-2 years.
360	30 " "	"	44	24	Married.	Friends	3 months.
361	4 Sept., "	"	26	22	Single.	Town.	4 years.
362	5 " "	"	80	74	Married.	Friends.	3 weeks.
363	7 " "	"	50	25	do	Town.	3 do
364	11 " "	F.	29	22	Single.	do	7 do
366	12 " "	"	42	39	Married.	Friends.	3 years.
367	17 " "	M.	48	28	Single.	do	20 years.
368	20 " "	F.	34	34	Married.	do	3 months.
369	21 " "	M.	38	37	do	Town.	6 do
370	23 " "	"	17	17	Single.	do	5 do
371	27 " "	F.	23	23	do	Friends	8 weeks.
372	9 Oct., "	"	17	15	do	Town.	2 years.
374	11 " "	"	36	31	Married.	Friends.	3 do
375	14 " "	"	65	65	Widow.	Town.	2 months.
376	22 " "	"	55	37	Married.	Friends.	2 weeks
377	23 " "	M.	51	50	do	Town.	3 do
378	25 " "	F.	45	28	do	do	17 years.
379	29 " "	M.	60	41	do	Friends.	2 months.
380	7 Nov. "	F.	50	30	do	do	4 do
381	8 " "	M.	33	19	do	Town.	3 do
382	9 " "	F.	35	35	do	Friends.	3 do
383	15 " "	"	33	30	do	Town.	5 do
384	16 " "	M.	23	22	Single.	do	2 do
385	10 " "	F.	56	55	Married.	Friends.	2 do
386	23 " "	M.	63	43	do	Town.	3 do
337	24 " "	"	31	27	Single.	do	4 years.

Whole number 76.

(Continued.)

Time spent in the Hospital.	Discharged or remain.	State now or when discharged.	Supposed prospect.	Remarks.
1 year 1 week.	Discharged.	Unimproved.	Incurable.	
7¼ months.	do	Improved.	do	
1 year 5 months.	Remains.	Unimproved.	do	2d admission.
1 do 3 do	Discharged.	do	do	
1 do 5 do	Remains.	Improved.	do	
10 months.	Discharged.	do	Curable.	
5½ do	do	Recovered.		
7 do	do	do		Irish.
43 weeks.	do	do		2d admission.
1 year 3 months.	Remains.	Unimproved.	Incurable.	do
4 months.	Discharged.	Recovered.		
3¾ do	Eloped.	Unimproved.	do	do
3 do	Discharged.	Recovered.		
1 year 2 months.	Remains.	Unimproved.	do	
51 weeks.	Discharged.	Recovered.		
1 year 2 months.	Remains.	Improved.	Curable.	
1 do 2 do	do	Unimproved.	Incurable.	
1 do 2 do	do	do	do	Paralytic.
1 do 2 do	do	do	do	
7 months.	Discharged.	Recovered.		
8 do	do	do		
1 year 1 month.	Remains.	Unimproved.	do	
1 do 1 do	do	Improved.	do	
1 do 1 do	do	Unimproved.	do	
5 months.	Discharged.	Recovered.		
8 weeks.	do	do		
35 do	do	Improved.	do	
1 year 1 month.	Remains.	do	Curable.	
47 weeks.	Discharged.	do	Incurable.	
27 weeks.	do	do	Curable.	
5½ months.	do	Recovered.		
3¼ do	do	do		
1 year.	Remains.	Unimproved.	Incurable.	
8¾ months.	Discharged.	Recovered.		
7 weeks.	do	do		
22 weeks.	do	Unimproved.	do	

[No. 2.]   *Table showing the disposal and state of 99*

No.	When admitted.	Sex.	Age.	Age at 1st attack.	Civil state.	By whom committed.	Duration of present attack before admission.
388	5 Dec., 1844.	F.	28	27	Single.	Friends.	7 months.
389	11 " "	"	21	21	do.	Town.	4 do
390	11 " "	"	45	41	Married.	Friends.	9 do
391	20 " "	M.	40	40	Single.	Town.	2 weeks.
392	21 " "	F.	60	52	Married	Friends.	2 months.
393	23 " "	"	58	48	do.	do.	2 years.
394	" " "	M.	19	18	Single.	Town.	3 weeks.
395	29 " "	"	59	54	Married.	do.	4 do
396	30 " "	F.	43	24	do.	Friends.	2 months.
397	1 Jan., 1845.	M.	50	40	do.	do.	15 do
398	3 " "	"	56	44	do.	do.	1 do
399	6 " "	F.	22	22	Single.	do.	3 do
400	9 " "	M.	20	19	do.	do.	10 do
401	1 Feb., "	"	49	24	Married.	do.	2 weeks.
402	10 " "	"	52	32	Widower.	Town.	2 months.
403	5 March, "	"	19	17	Single.	Friends.	2 years.
404	17 " "	F.	48	21	do.	do.	7 weeks.
405	19 " "	M.	40	40	Married.	Town.	9 months.
406	23 " "	F.	30	29	Single.	Friends.	1 year.
407	27 " "	M.	61	58	Married.	Town.	3 years.
408	28 " "	F.	27	27	do.	Friends.	3 months.
409	30 " "	"	41	37	do.	Town.	4 years.
410	2 April, "	"	27	23	Single.	do.	2 months.
411	14 " "	"	23	21	do.	do.	2 years.
412	15 " "	"	31	31	Married.	do.	6 weeks.
413	29 " "	"	32	30	do.	do.	2 years.
414	" " "	M.	24	22	Single.	Friends.	5 weeks.
415	3 May, "	"	24	24	do.	Town.	3 do
416	1 " "	F.	24	24	do.	do.	5 do
417	10 " "	"	41	31	Married.	Friends.	6 do
418	12 " "	"	56	56	Widow.	do.	3 months.
419	" " "	M.	40	25	Married.	do.	4 weeks.
420	14 " "	"	23	18	Single.	Town.	4 do
421	" " "	F.	56	18	do.	do.	10 do
422	19 " "	M.	30	30	Married.	Friends.	6 do
423	21 " "	F.	52	49	Widow.	do.	2 years 6 months.
424	22 " "	"	66	35	Married.	do.	1 year 3 months.
425	23 " "	"	66	64	do.	do.	2 years.
426	26 " "	M.	21	18	Single.	Court.	4 months.
427	31 " "	"	37	36	do.	Town.	1 year.

patients admitted during the year ending Nov. 30, 1845.

Time spent in the Hospital.	Discharged or remain.	State now or when discharged	Supposed prospect.	Remarks.
16 weeks.	Discharged.	Unimproved	Curable.	
31 do	do	Recovered.		
10 do	do	do		
11 months.	Remains.	Unimproved	Incurable.	
36 weeks.	Discharged.	Improved	do	
22 do	do	Unimproved.	do	
23 do	do	Recovered.		
26 do	do	do		
22 do	do	do		
3 do		Died.		Suicide.
9 do	do	Recovered.		
30 do	do	Improved	Curable.	
21 do	do	Unimproved	Incurable.	
10 months.	Remains.	Improved.	Curable.	
19 weeks.	Discharged.	do	do	
9 do	do	Recovered		
7 months.	Remains.	Unimproved	do	
7 do	do	Improved.	Incurable.	
7 do	do	do	Curable	
7 do	do	Unimproved	Incurable	
10 weeks.	Discharged.	Recovered.		
24 do	do	Improved	do	
7 months.	Remains.	Cured.		
24 weeks.	Discharged.	Unimproved	Curable.	
6 months.	Remains.	Cured		
6 do	Discharged.	Unimproved	Incurable	
7 weeks.	do	Improved.	Curable.	
11 do	do	Recovered.		
7 months.	Remains.	Cured.		
6 do	do	do		
7 do	Died.			Consumption.
6 do	Discharged.	Recovered.		
5 do	do	do		
14 weeks.	do	do		
5 do	do	Improved.	Curable.	Soon recover'd
6 months.	Remains.	Unimproved.	Incurable	
16 weeks.	Discharged.	do	do	
3 do	do	do	do	
22 do	do	Recovered.		
6 months.	Remains.	Improved.	Curable.	

Table No. 2,

No.	When admitted.	Sex.	Age	Age at 1st attack.	Civil state.	By whom committed.	Duration of present attack before admission.
428	2 June, 1845.	M.	72	72	Widower.	Friends.	3 months.
429	2 " "	"	61	41	do.	do.	15 do
430	4 " "	F.	25	25	Married.	do.	2 do
431	7 " "	M.	22	22	Single.	Town.	6 weeks.
432	8 " "	"	47	46	Married.	Friends.	8 months.
433	9 " "	"	69	67	do.	do.	17 do
434	11 " "	F.	72	66	Single.	Town.	6 years.
435	12 " "	M.	26	26	Married.	do.	2 weeks.
436	13 " "	F.	66	46	do.	Friends.	9 do
437	15 " "	"	33	20	do.	Town.	1 do
438	" " "	M.	17	16	Single.	Friends.	3 do
439	16 " "	"	65	50	Married.	do.	6 months.
440	19 " "	F	23	23	do.	do.	3 weeks.
441	20 " "	M.	20	18	Single.	do.	2 years.
442	26 " "	"	31	27	do.	do.	10 days.
443	27 " "	"	27	25	do.	Town.	18 months.
444	1 July, "	F.	26	26	Married.	Friends.	4 do
445	2 " "	"	49	35	do.	do.	8 do
446	8 " "	M.	40	36	do.	Town.	9 weeks.
447	16 " "	F.	33	33	do.	Friends.	3 do
448	17 " "	"	30	30	do.	do.	5 months.
449	20 " "	M.	18	18	Single.	do.	6 weeks.
450	29 " "	"	79	37	Widower.	do.	2 years 6 months.
451	2 Aug., "	"	20	16	Single.	Town.	3 weeks.
452	7 " "	F.	59	48	Married.	Friends.	4 years.
453	7 " "	M.	34	32	Married.	Town	4 months.
454	8 " "	"	40	40	Single.	Friends.	4 weeks.
455	14 " "	"	19	10	do.	do.	6 do
456	15 " "	F.	19	19	Married.	do.	3 months.
457	19 " "	M.	25	25	Single.	Town.	3 weeks.
458	21 " "	"	46	30	Married.	Friends.	10 months.
459	22 " "	F.	32	24	Single.	do.	8 years.
460	25 " "	M.	45	35	do.	do.	10 do
461	26 " "	F.	51	47	do.	Town.	4 weeks.

(Continued.)

Time spent in the Hospital.	Discharged or remain.	State now or when discharged.	Supposed prospect.	Remarks.
6 months.	Remains.	Unimproved.	Incurable.	
6 do	do	do	do	
10 weeks.	Died.			Consumption.
6 months.	Remains.	Cured.		
2 days.	Discharged.	Unimproved.	Curable.	
6 months.	Remains.	Improved	Incurable.	
5 do	do	Unimproved.	do	
10 weeks.	Discharged	Recovered.		
14 do	do	Unimproved	do	
11 do	do	do	Curable.	
10 do	do	Recovered.		
16 do	do	Improved.	do	
7 do	do	Recovered		
5 months.	Remains.	Unimproved	Incurable.	
5 do	do	Improved.	do	
5 do	do	Unimproved	do	
5 weeks.	Discharged.	Improved.	Curable.	
6 do	do	do	do	
5 months.	Remains.	Unimproved.	Incurable.	
7 weeks.	Discharged	Improved.	Curable.	
3 do	do	Unimproved.	do	
11 do	Died.			{ Wound in throat for which he was committed.
4 months.	Remains.	Unimproved.	Incurable.	
4 do	do	Cured.		
4 do	do	Unimproved.	do	{ Paralytic. 2d admission.
4 do	do	do	Curable.	
4 do	Discharged.	Recovered.		
3 do	Remains.	Unimproved.	Incurable.	
11 weeks.	Discharged.	Recovered.		
3 months.	Remains.	Unimproved.	Curable.	
3 do	do	Improved.	do	
4 days.	Discharged.	Unimproved.	Incurable.	
9 do	do	do	do	
3 months.	Remains.	Improved.	Curable.	

No.	When admitted.		Sex.	Age.	Age at 1st attack.	Civil state.	By whom committed.	Duration of present attack before admission.
462	4 Sept., 1845.		F.	45	44	Married.	Friends.	10 months.
463	4 "	"	"	59	38	Widow.	do.	21 years.
464	5 "	"	M.	18	16	Single.	do.	17 months.
465	10 "	"	"	45	30	Married.	Court.	15 years.
466	14 "	"	F.	50	20	do.	Friends.	2 months.
467	15 "	"	M.	32	30	do.	do.	2 do
468	16 "	"	M.	58	57	Single.	do.	1 year.
469	" "	"	F.	44	24	Married.	do.	3 weeks.
470	19 "	"	"	46	28	do.	do.	6 months.
471	23 "	"	"	19	17	Single.	Town.	5 do
472	28 "	"	"	47	46	Married.	Friends.	5 do
473	1 Oct., "		M.	60	54	do.	do.	2 weeks.
474	1 " "		F.	43	22	Single.	Town.	2 months.
475	3 " "		M.	23	22	do.	Friends.	5 do
476	3 " "		"	33	33	do.	do.	6 do
477	7 " "		"	36	28	Married	Town	6 do
478	8 " "		F.	31	26	Single	Friends.	5 years.
479	14 " "		"	33	20	Married.	Town.	18 weeks.
480	" " "		"	40	30	do.	do.	3 months.
481	20 " "		M.	59	48	do.	Friends.	1 do
482	29 " "		F.	54	52	Widow.	do.	2 years.
483	31 " "		"	64	40	Single.	Town.	1 year 6 months.
484	8 Nov., "		M.	20	16	do.	Friends.	18 months.
485	14 " "		"	17	17	do.	do.	2 weeks.
486	24 " "		F.	56	37	Married	do.	10 days.

(Continued.)

Time spent in the Hospital.	Discharged or remain.	State now or when discharged	Supposed prospect.	Remarks.
3 months.	Discharged	Improved.	Curable.	
3 do	Remains.	Unimproved	Incurable	
3 do	do	do	Curable	
10 weeks.	do	do	Incurable.	
9 do	Discharged.	Improved.	do	
10 do	Remains.	Unimproved.	Curable.	
10 do	do	do	Incurable	
8 do	Discharged.	Recovered.		
8 do	Remains.	Unimproved	Curable	
8 do	do	do	Incurable	
8 do	do	Cured.		
8 do	do	Improved.	Curable.	
8 do	do	Unimproved.	do	
8 do	do	Improved.	do	
3 days.	Died.			Hæmorrhage.
7 weeks.	Remains.	Unimproved	Incurable.	
7 do	do	Improved.	Curable.	
6 do	do	Unimproved.	do	2d admission.
6 do	do	Improved.	do	
6 do	do	do	do	
5 do	do	Unimproved.	Incurable	
4 do	do	do	do	
3 do	do	Improved.	Curable.	
2 do	do	Unimproved.	do	
1 do	do	do	do	

RECAPITULATION.

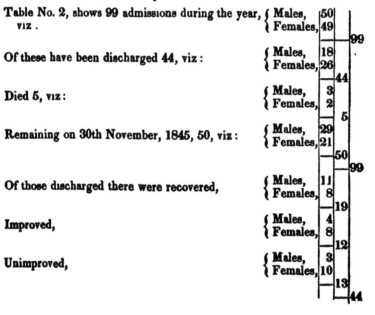

			Total.
Table No. 1, shows remaining in Hospital 1st December, 1844,	Males,	50	
	Females,	26	
			76
Of these have been discharged 39, viz :	Males,	22	
	Females,	17	
Died,	Males,	2	
Remain November 30, 1845, 35, viz ·	Males,	26	
	Females,	9	
			76
Of those discharged, there were recovered,	Males,	10	
	Females,	9	19
Improved,	Males,	6	
	Females,	4	10
Unimproved,	Males,	6	
	Females,	4	10
			39

The average time spent in the Hospital by the 19 old cases recovered, 292 days.

Table No. 2, shows 99 admissions during the year, viz .	Males,	50	
	Females,	49	
			99
Of these have been discharged 44, viz :	Males,	18	
	Females,	26	
			44
Died 5, viz :	Males,	3	
	Females,	2	
			5
Remaining on 30th November, 1845, 50, viz :	Males,	29	
	Females,	21	
			50
			99
Of those discharged there were recovered,	Males,	11	
	Females,	8	
			19
Improved,	Males,	4	
	Females,	8	
			12
Unimproved,	Males,	3	
	Females,	10	
			13
			44

Average time spent in the Hospital by the 19 new cases, 102 days, when discharged recovered.

The deaths this year have been proportionably large. Of the cases in the Hospital at the commencement of the year, one died from the effects of a long continued and certainly fatal form of disease. Another at 80 years of age—probably on account of old age. Of the admissions within the year, one committed suicide—another died from a suicidal wound, inflicted before admission. Two women in confirmed pulmonary consumption died of that disease soon after admission. One man was brought here laboring under hemorrhage from the bowels, of which he died within three days.

It will be seen by the tables that 17 have been discharged considered curable. Ten of these spent an average of less than 60 days in the Hospital.

The whole 17 remained much below the average time required for the cure of the whole number who have been discharged recovered, since the Hospital went into operation.

This is one of the evils which it has been thought most prudent not to remedy, by stipulating a period, before which patients should not be removed, uncured, until the house should be filled.

The reputation of the establishment, both at home and abroad, has not only suffered from this circumstance, but those who have been prematurely removed have not received the benefits the Institution was every way competent to afford.

Our annual reports compare poorly with those of many other institutions simply because we had no power to retain our patients until a reasonable time was afforded for recovery.

Our present situation will not only justify, but I think imperatively demands the correction of this evil.

Some of the best regulated and most successful Retreats in the United States will receive no patient for a less term than six months, unless sooner cured.

As our greatest anxiety should be the establishment of such rules of admission as will afford the greatest possible good to the greatest number, the time required to be spent here should be regulated with a sole view to such a result.

Before closing this branch of the subject it may be proper to observe, that from no source does a well regulated asylum for the insane suffer so much in its reputation, as from the false representations of patients prematurely removed.

It is peculiarly interesting and gratifying to observe the kind feelings and gratitude expressed by those who leave the Hospital perfectly cured, towards those who have had the charge of them : whereas those who go away still insane, remember with bitterness every restraint and denial they have experienced.

All this would be harmless, but for the morbid sympathy which induces some persons to place more reliance on the evil reports of an insane man, than the truth from the best citizen in the community.

There were in the Hospital on the 30th November, six patients, *cured*, who were waiting for their friends to remove them.   Had these been removed, our list of recoveries, instead of 38, would have shown 44.

The whole number of admissions since 14th October, 1840, has been

Males,	276
Females,	210—486

CIVIL STATE.

Married,	Males,	- - - - -	122
Single,	"	- - - - -	137
Widowers,	"	- - - - -	17
			276
Married,	Females,	- - - - -	117
Single,	"	- - - - -	76
Widows,	"	- - - - -	17
			210
			486
Of these discharged,	Recovered,	- - -	171
	Improved,	- - - -	104
	Unimproved,	- - -	100
	Died,	- - - -	26
			401
Remain,	- - - - - - - -		85
Of those discharged,	were Males,	- - -	213
	Females,	- - -	162
			375
Of those who died,	were Males,	- - - -	18
	Females,	- - -	8
			26
			401

Average time spent in the Hospital by the 171 discharged recovered, 140 days.

It seems desirable to convince the public of two very important facts, viz: that patients should be brought to the Hospital as soon as it is *certain* they are insane—and secondly, that they remain there until all *reasonable* prospect of recovery is past.

With a view to establish the first point, a table is prepared showing the results of early and late admissions. Also one to show the average time required for the recovery of that portion of each class discharged cured.

[No. 3.]   Table showing the results of early and late admissions.

	MALES, 231.												FEMALES, 170.												Total.
	Three months and under.				Over 3 and not over 12 months.				Over 12 months.				Three months and under.				Over 3 and not over 12 months.				Over 12 months.				
	Recovered.	Improved.	Unimproved.	Died.	Recovered.	Improved.	Unimproved.	Died.	Recovered.	Improved.	Unimproved.	Died.	Recovered.	Improved.	Unimproved.	Died	Recovered.	Improved.	Unimproved.	Died.	Recovered.	Improved.	Unimproved.	Died.	
	68	24	8	7	21	13	16	4	11	19	33	7	49	20	5	5	16	12	14	1	6	16	24	2	401

RECAPITULATION.

Recovered.	Three months and under,	117
	Over three and not over twelve months,	87 }—171
	Over twelve months,	17
Improved.	Three months and under,	44
	Over three and not over twelve months,	25 }—104
	Over twelve months,	35
Unimproved.	Three months and under,	13
	Over three and not over twelve months,	30 }—100
	Over twelve months,	57
Died.	8 m.=12 —3 m. to 12=5.—Over 12 m.=9,	28 }—401

It will be seen that of those admitted within 3 months, 62.9 per cent. recovered. Of those 3 to 12 months, 38 per cent. recovered. Of those over 12 months, 14 per cent. recovered.

It will naturally be asked why we do not cure 80 to 90 per cent. of our recent cases? The answer is found, in part at least, in there having been removed from the Hospital 56 such cases, considered *curable*. The average time these were in the institution, was far below that required for the restoration of those in the same class, who were discharged recovered.

[No. 4.] *Table showing the time spent in the Hospital by each class, discharged cured.*

Duration of disease before admission.	Three months and under.	Over 3 and not over 12 mos.	Over 12 mos.
Average No. of days in the Hospital.	130	164	280

It is hoped that no stronger proof than the above will be required to convince the public of the propriety and utility of an early resort to, and reasonable continuance in, our Institution, and the Trustees of the necessity of designating some appropriate time of residence, before which, patients shall not be removed, unless sooner recovered.

Although it is impossible to obtain correct information on a subject, which many persons consider as one of delicacy, if not involving reputation of family, we have always sought it, in relation to hereditary predisposition. In some families this is very evident. In one case, a father and two sons have been here; in two, the mother and daughter; in one, a man and his nephew and niece, at the same time. Of 486 admissions, 211 are repre-

sented by their friends as having insane ancestry or blood
relatives in that condition.

When we add to these, foreigners and others concerning whom little information can be obtained, there can be
little doubt more than one half are hereditarily predis-
posed to that state of brain of which insanity is a symptom.

The comparative liability of persons at different ages
to attacks of insanity has formed an interesting subject
of inquiry. It is evident in a community like ours, nothing accurate in all its details can be arrived at.

In the following tables will be shown at what age the
first attack took place in 486 cases, as nearly as could be
ascertained, divided into decades.

Secondly, the probable number of each sex now insane
in the State in each decade; assuming three hundred of
each sex as the aggregate; which number approaches, as
is believed, very near the truth—taking the admissions
here as the basis of the calculation.

Thirdly, showing the proportion of these to the whole
population of the same sex and age according to the last
census.

[No. 5.]   *Table showing the age at which the first attack*
took place.

Sex.	10 to 20 ys.	20 to 30.	30—40.	40—50.	50—60.	60—70.	70—80.	Aggregate
Males,	55	90	62	37	23	6	5	278
Females,	30	78	48	35	12	5		208
								486

[No. 6.] *Table showing the distribution of 600 cases,
supposed to exist, into the same classes.*

Sex.	10 yrs to 20	20 to 30.	30—40.	40—50,	50—60.	60—70.	70—80.	Aggregate
Males,	59	97	67	40	25	7	5	300
Females,	43	113	70	50	17	7		300

[No. 7.] *Table showing the number of inhabitants of the
different ages and sexes according to the estimate in
Table 6, to one insane person.*

Sex	10 yrs. to 20.	20—30.	30—40.	40—50.	50—60.	60—70.	70—80.
Males,	1 to 1007	535	445	498	502	1058	1062
Females,	1 to 1348	373	415	400	723	1100	

It is evident from the above table that males under
twenty furnish a fearful proportion of the insane, and I
am sorry to add, many of the most hopeless cases, the result of their voluntary misconduct.

In the next ten years the disease is much more prevalent among females.

It also appears that in advanced age as well as in youth
males are most liable to attacks for the first time.

I have given no table showing the actual age of all our
patients at the time of admission. In tables 1 and 2 the
disparity on this point is shown as correctly as our inqui-
ries enable us to do it.

Liability to recurrence of insanity is fully shown from
the facts, that 32 of our patients have been once or more
at the McLean Hospital, and two at Worcester. That
one patient is here for the sixth and one for the fifth time.
Six have been admitted three times and thirty-nine twice.

As most of our male patients are farmers, and our females house keepers, our records do not enable us to

show any very obvious effect of occupation on the cases which come under our observation. The case is different in those institutions located near large cities and manufacturing towns, where confinement within doors, and sedentary habits give a decided predisposition to this form of disease.

The use of medicines in this institution, so far as I am informed, does not materially differ from that in other similar Retreats. We endeavor to avoid extremes in this, as in all other means adopted for the recovery of those entrusted to our care. My predecessor so clearly stated his views on the subject, that I deem any observations on that point wholly uncalled for at this time. With one exception, the moral means are the same as have been heretofore in use. On taking charge of the Hospital, I caused family worship to be daily attended by the household and as many inmates as were in a condition to behave with decorum.

I have not only found a hearty co-operation in every officer, but an undiminished interest in those who are in a state to join in the solemnity. Several of our patients assist in singing the hymns, and evince both interest and taste in the performance.

How much is due to habit or how much to reverential feeling on these occasions, it is not easy to determine, but one thing is certain, they not only have the power of self-control, but exercise it to a degree not surpassed by an equal number, in the most exemplary community.

The clergymen of Augusta and Hallowell have kindly attended our sabbath evening services whenever circumstances permitted. Their ready and cheerful acquiescence in our wishes in this respect, entitles them to the gratitude of all concerned.

Instead of receiving visitors at improper and inconvenient hours, we have adopted a different course, and prohibited visits on the Sabbath entirely.

Since the middle of September we have had more patients than rooms in the male wing of the building. Should applications increase as they have the year past, we must either refuse to take curable cases, or send away some of our incurables, who have been long with us.

It is fondly hoped the people and their public servants will take the earliest measures to make provision for their accommodation.

There would be great physical and moral advantages to our convalescents, from an increase of furniture in their galleries and rooms. Many of our patients have been accustomed to better furnished rooms at home, and should not be surrounded with less cheerful accommodations here. In this respect our establishment does not compare favorably with similar institutions in this country.

The number of newspaper publishers who have gratuitously furnished their periodicals has annually increased. They are not only entitled to our thanks, but would find themselves in some measure compensated could they see their papers, after having been so perfectly read *through* as to be *perforated* in a hundred places.

The Olive Branch, Boston Cultivator, Christian Mirror, Eastern Argus, Portland Transcript, Maine Democrat, Maine Cultivator, Maine Farmer, State Signal, Bangor Courier, Yankee Blade, and Cold Water Fountain, have made us a weekly visit for all or most of the year. The publishers of the Age and Journal of this town have furnished us with hundreds of the exchange papers received by them. Several individuals have forwarded papers and pamphlets, and I wish particularly to remember the kindness of a late patient, Mrs. M. G. M. of B., in this respect.

Our library has been increased by the addition of over one hundred and fifty small volumes, purchased by the interest arising from the donation of the late Hon. Bryce McLellan.

I have great pleasure in acknowledging the prompt and efficient assistance I have received from every officer and attendant since the day I entered the house. The uniform kindness to myself, my family and those over whom they are placed, entitles them to my entire approbation and grateful acknowledgments and the confidence of their employers.

JAMES BATES, *Superintendent.*

Extract from the "Regulations" of the Hospital.

ADMISSION OF PATIENTS.

Patients admitted to the institution must come provided with at least two strong cotton shirts—a coat, vest, and pantaloons, of strong woolen cloth—two pairs of woolen socks or stockings—one black stock—a hat or cap—and one pair of shoes or boots.

The females must have at least the same quantity of under clothes, including shoes and stockings, a decent bonnet, and two substantial dresses. In both cases, the articles must be new and in good condition. The woolens must be of a dark color.

The patients offered for admission must be perfectly neat and clean in their persons, and free from vermin and infective diseases.

The price of boarding, washing, medicines and attendance, shall vary according to the trouble and expense incurred, in the judgment of the superintendent, not to exceed three dollars, nor be less than two dollars for males; not to exceed two dollars and fifty cents, nor be less than one dollar and fifty cents, for females, per week.

Before any patient shall be received into the institution, except when sent by towns, a good and sufficient bond will be required for the payment of all expenses that may be incurred for each patient, including board, and such articles of clothing as it may become necessary to furnish.

For the admission of patients sent by towns, a written request for such admission, signed by the overseers of the poor, will be required.

FORM OF BOND.

KNOW ALL MEN BY THESE PRESENTS, That we, ——
——, of ——, in the county of ——, as principal, and
—— ——, of —— in the county of ——, as sureties,
are held and bound unto —— ——, steward of the Insane
Hospital, at Augusta, or to his successor in said office, in
the sum of —— ——, to the payment of which sum,
well and truly to be made to him, the said —— ——, or
to his successors in said office, we bind ourselves, our
executors and administrators, firmly by these presents.

Sealed with our seals, and dated at ——, this ——
day of ——, A. D. ——.

The condition of the above obligation is such, that
whereas —— ——, of ——, in the county of ——, is
about to be admitted as a boarder and patient to the institution aforesaid, now if the said —— —— shall pay to
said —— ——, or to his successor in said office, such
sum per week, for the board, washing, medicine and attendance, according to the trouble and expense incurred
for said patient, in the judgment of the superintendent
for the time being, [not to exceed three dollars, nor be less
than two dollars for males; not to exceed two dollars and
fifty cents, nor be less than one dollar and fifty cents
for females;] and pay for all such necessary articles of
clothing as shall be furnished said —— —— by the said
—— ——, or his successor, and remove the said ——
—— from said institution, whenever they shall be thereto
in writing requested by the superintendent for the time
being—and shall also pay a further sum, not exceeding
fifty dollars, for all damages that may arise from injury
to the furniture and other property of said institution, by
said —— ——, and the reasonable charges that may be
incurred in case of the elopement of said —— ——;
payments to be made semi-annually and at the time of
removal, with interest on the amount after it becomes due
as aforesaid: then this obligation to be null and void—
otherwise to remain in full force and virtue.

OF

STOCKHOLDERS,

(With the amount of Stock held by each, Jan. 1, 1846,)

IN THE

BANKS OF MAINE.

Prepared and published agreeably to a Resolve of the Legislature, approved March 21, 1839.
By EZRA B. FRENCH, Secretary of State.

AUGUSTA:
WM. T. JOHNSON, PRINTER TO THE STATE.

1846.

STATE OF MAINE.

Resolve requiring the Secretary of State to publish a List of the Stockholders of the Banks in this State

RESOLVED, That the Secretary of State be and hereby is required annually to publish a list of the Stockholders in each Bank in this State with the amount of Stock owned by each Stockholder agreeably to the returns made by law to the Legislature of this State, and it shall be the duty of the Secretary of State to distribute to each town in this State, and also to each Bank in this State, one copy of such printed list ; and it shall be the duty of the Secretary of State to require any Bank, which may neglect to make the returns required by law to the Legislature, to furnish him forthwith, with a list of the Stockholders of such Bank, and also the amount of Stock owned by each Stockholder.

[*Approved March* 21, 1839.]

LIST OF STOCKHOLDERS.

Androscoggin Bank, (Topsham.)

Names	Residence.	Amount of Stock.
Androscoggin Bank,	Topsham,	1,000
Betsey N. Baker, guardian,	Roxbury, Mass.,	1,000
John Barron,	Topsham,	2,500
William Barron,	do.	2,500
Jeremiah Clough,	do.	300
John Curtis,	Harpswell,	400
Sophia Chick,	Topsham,	1,100
William Dennett,	do.	1,000
John Given, Jr., (deceased,)	Brunswick,	500
Crispus Greaves,	Topsham,	200
Priscilla Hallett,	Augusta,	400
Peletiah Haley,	Topsham,	1,000
Benjamin Hasey,	do.	3,100
Joshua Haskell,	do.	2,000
Guardian of Samuel Hunter,	do.	1,000
Lithgow Hunter,	do.	1,000
Hannah Hunter,	do.	1,000
Mary Holbrook,	do.	100
Collamore Mallet,	do.	700
Isaac Mallett,	do.	300
James McKeen,	do.	1,000
Charity Mustard,	do.	500
Jabez Perkins,	Brunswick,	2,000
Nahum Perkins,	Topsham,	1,000
Ezekiel Purinton, (deceased,)	do.	600
Samuel Perkins,	do.	500
Woodbury B. Purinton,	do.	1,000
Sarah Purinton,	do.	3,000
Hannah E. Purinton,	do.	300
David Scribner, guardian,	do.	700

Androscoggin Bank, (Continued.)

Names.	Residence.	Amount of Stock
David Scribner,	Topsham,	2,400
Ann E. Thompson,	do.	2,100
Charles Thompson,	do.	10,000
Francis Tucker, (deceased,)	do.	500
Samuel Thompson,	do.	1,300
Nathaniel Walker,	do.	2,000
		$50,000

Augusta Bank.

William Allen, Jr.,	Norridgewock,	1,600
Est. Francis Bowles,	Wayne,	500
Cony Female Academy,	Augusta,	3,000
Anna Child,	do.	2,500
Cashier Boston Bank,	Boston,	10,000
Isaac Coffin,	Wiscasset,	500
Martha Curtis,	Boston,	1,200
James L. Child,	Augusta,	1,600
Hannah P. Dillingham,	do.	600
American Education Society,		400
Elisha Folgier,	Sidney,	1,400
Francis M. Folgier,	do.	300
Lydia H. Blake,	Monmouth,	300
Est. Joshua Gage,	Augusta,	2,000
Est. James Hall,	do.	2,000
S. A. Hitchcock,	Boston,	5,700
State of Maine,		10,000
John McLellan,	Woodstock, Vt.,	2,800
Judah McLellan,	Skowhegan,	200
George W. Morton,	Augusta,	1,000
Susannah Rockwood,	do.	600
Roxana Rockwood,	Hallowell,	300
Mary Ann Rockwood,	Waterville,	200
Hannah G. Rockwood,	do.	200
Hannah Sanford,	Augusta,	100
Sarah F. Lambard,	do.	300
Thomas Rice,	Winslow,	1,000

Augusta Bank, (Continued.)

Names.	Residence.	Amount of Stock.
Issachar Snell,	Augusta,	2,200
T. W. Smith,	do.	5,500
John Smith,	Readfield,	1,700
Eliza P. Vose,	Augusta,	5,000
Zilpha Williams,	do.	200
Reuel Williams,	do.	3,400
Sarah L. Williams,	do.	1,800
Sarah Williams,	do.	100
Abby Williams,	do.	100
Helen Williams,	do.	100
Greenlief White,	do.	500
Willard Sayles,	Boston,	5,800
David White,	Solon,	400
Joseph D. Emery,	Augusta,	300
Samuel E. Smith, (Adr.,)	do.	800
Nathan Weston,	do.	3,500
Benjamin Davis,	do.	600
Elizabeth L. Sawtelle,	Norridgewock,	800
Sarah H. Snell,	Augusta,	100
Joseph H. Williams,	do.	400
Susan B. Cony,	do.	2,800
P. B. Weston,	do.	2,000
Abby G. Ingraham,	do.	2,500
John H. Ingraham,	do.	500
Betsey Eustes,	Boston,	100
Benj. Ellis,	Carver, Mass.,	3,000
Alvah Moulton,	Ossipee, N. H.,	500
A. G. Dole,	Alna,	400
Carlton Dole,	Augusta,	400
Mary M. Smith,	Warren,	400
E. Dole, C. Dole & A. G. Dole,	Augusta,	400
Sophronia Randall,	do.	100
Lucretia G. Fuller,	do.	800
Standish & Woodbury,	Boston,	600
William Hunt,	Augusta,	1,000
H. W. Fuller,	Boston,	100
Samuel E. Smith,	Wiscasset,	300
Benj. A. G. Fuller, trustee,	Augusta,	400
Eliza W. Fuller,	do.	100
E. G. Fuller.	do.	800

1*

Augusta Bank (*Continued.*)

Names.	Residence.	Amount of Stock.
Sarah J. Rockwood,	Augusta,	200
G. W. Stanley,	do.	6,000
J. W. Bradbury,	do.	900
E. Hathaway, Jr.,	Hobarttown,	100
Dudley Haines, guardian,	Readfield,	1,300
John Mullikin,	Hallowell,	200
Judith F. Jones,	Augusta,	500
		$110,000

Bank of Bangor.

Samuel Veazie,	Bangor,	20,000
Jones P. Veazie,	do.	4,300
Timothy Crosby,	do.	600
Bank of Bangor,	do.	33,300
Frances A. Lord,	do.	5,000
John Bright,	do.	100
Stephen J. Bowles,	Roxbury,	2,000
Nathaniel L. Williams,	Boston,	7,100
Stephen Williams,	do.	7,200
Wildes P. Walker,	do.	20,000
John McDonald,	Bangor,	200
Samuel P. Strickland,	do.	200
		$100,000

Bank of Cumberland, (*Portland.*)

John Anderson,	Portland,	520
John Anderson, trustee,	do.	2,560
Isaac Adams,	Gilead,	240
Joseph Badger,	Brunswick,	400
Rufus Burnham,	Unity,	600
James W. Bradbury,	Augusta,	200
Charles Brooks,	Boston,	400

Bank of Cumberland, (Continued.)

Names.	Residence.	Amount of Stock.
James Bradbury, (deceased,)	Unknown,	160
J. J. Brown,	Portland,	80
John Barron,	Topsham,	360
William Barron,	do.	200
Thomas Browne,	Portland,	240
Clarissa Brooks,	do.	440
Mary Bradbury,	Standish,	2,600
Amelia Bradbury,	Unknown,	360
Thadeus Brown,	do.	560
John Curtis,	Gorham,	200
Thomas Crocker,	Paris,	800
Asa Clapp,	Portland,	360
Parker Cleaveland,	Brunswick,	160
Thomas P. Coburn,	Unknown,	160
Mary Cleaves,	do.	1,200
Rufus Emerson,	Portland.	560
E. N. Chaddock,	Boston,	480
Rebecca K. Chesley,	Westbrook,	360
Olive Dennet,	Standish,	200
Emeline Dennet,	do.	200
David Drinkwater,	Portland,	880
Benjamin Day,	Unknown,	240
Charles S Daveis,	Portland,	400
Ann and Eunice Deering,	do.	200
Ezekiel Day, (deceased,)	do.	520
Asa Dresser,	do.	400
Mary L. Deering,	Westbrook,	400
M. O. and E. C. Emerson,	Portland,	240
Nicholas Emery,	do.	1,440
William Evans,	do.	760
Eben'r Everett,	Brunswick,	520
Henry S. Edwards,	Portland,	280
James L. Farmer,	do.	480
C. D. French,	Unknown,	360
W. P. Fessenden,	Portland,	400
Joseph Goold,	do.	400
R. G. Greene, (deceased,)	do.	320
Daniel Goold,	do.	120
Susan Goold,	do.	80
Samuel C. Grant,	Gardiner,	1,000

Bank of Cumberland, (Continued.)

Names.	Residence.	Amount of Stock.
Mary Garland,	Unknown,	120
Stephen Gale,	Portland,	240
Mary Hyde,	Cornish,	400
Charles Hunt, (deceased,)	Gorham,	1,000
Samuel Haskell,	Portland,	280
John Heard,	Boston, Mass.,	120
James Hasty, (deceased,)	Standish,	400
William Hackett,	Kennebunk,	400
Joseph Hale,	Unknown,	200
Rufus Horton,	Portland,	480
Charles Holden,	do.	360
Joseph Howard,	do.	160
Eleanor W. Head,	do.	920
Augustine Haines,	do.	560
Ann Jameson,	Unknown,	240
William Kimball,	Portland,	400
Moses Kittredge,	Unknown,	400
Joseph M Kellogg,	Portland,	120
Frances F. Kimball,	Unknown,	200
Littlehale & Co.,	Boston,	1,800
Eliab Latham, (deceased,)	Unknown,	400
Joseph Leavitt,	Portland,	200
Isaac Lincoln,	Brunswick,	1,000
Benjamin Lord,	Falmouth,	200
Eliza Little,	Windham,	90
John D. McCrate,	Wiscasset,	40
Moses Mason,	Unknown,	480
Isaac Merriam,	do.	600
Parker McCobb,	Portland,	1,920
Esther Mussey,	do.	400
William Moulton,	do.	2,960
Dolly Mussey,	Standish,	400
Matthias Meserve,	Scarborough,	80
Edmund Mann,	Gorham,	280
Rufus Nichols,	Saco,	120
Joshua B. Osgood,	Portland,	320
Ocean Insurance Co.,	do.	1,720
Simeon Pease,	Cornish,	2,480
Clarissa A. Parsons,	Bridgton,	40
Albion K. Parris,	Washington,	600

Bank of Cumberland, (Continued.)

Names	Residence	Amount of Stock
Hannah Pierce,	Gorham,	200
Geo. W. Pierce, (deceased,)	Portland,	400
Lucy Pritchard,	do.	200
Barnabas Palmer,	Kennebunk,	1,000
Mark Pease,	Cornish,	200
President and Trustees Bowdoin College,	Brunswick,	4,000
P.D.& Co. Bank of Cumberland,	Portland,	8,800
do. Merchants' Bank,	do.	400
do. Brunswick Bank,	do.	2,000
do. Casco Bank,	do.	280
do. Canal Bank,	do	560
do. Man. & Traders' Bk.,	do.	2,600
Jacob Rolfe,	do.	520
Charles Rogers,	do.	80
Lucy Russell,	do.	240
James F. Rawson,	Unknown,	200
C. D. Robinson,	do.	200
J. T. Reeves,	Portland,	280
Samuel Small, Jr.,	do.	1,400
Eliza Sawyer,	Unknown,	80
Horatio Southgate,	Portland,	800
Samuel Staples,	do.	200
Ether Shepley,	do.	1,440
Nathaniel Shaw,	do.	440
Joseph Stevens,	do.	200
M. P. Sawyer,	Boston,	3,960
Isaac Sturdivant,	Cumberland,	160
Ephr. Sturdivant,	do.	760
Diana E. Shaw,	Oxford,	1,080
Cornelia E. Shaw,	do.	1,080
Saco and Biddeford Institution for Savings,	Saco,	840
Wm. B. Sewall,	Kennebunkport,	600
Isaac Stevens,	Unknown,	240
James Todd,	Portland,	800
Jonathan Tukesbury,	do.	800
Eliza C. Turner,	do.	360
Nancy B. Thatcher,	Unknown,	160
Calvin Thomas,	do.	3,200

Bank of Cumberland, (Continued.)

Names.	Residence.	Amount of Stock.
John Webb,	Windham,	1,000
Daniel Winslow,	Portland,	240
David Winslow,	Westbrook,	600
Levi Woodbury,	Unknown,	6,000
N. L. Woodbury,	Portland,	680
Jabez C. Woodman,	Minot,	40
Ashur Ware,	Portland,	1,600
Lydia Whitten,	Augusta,	480
Harriet S. Woodbury,	Unknown,	240
C. W. Waite,	Falmouth,	200
Samuel Wells,	Portland,	1,000
		$100,000

Bank of Westbrook.

Oliver Buckley,	Westbrook,	800
S. B. Stevens,	do.	1,000
Samuel Jordan,	do.	2,000
Rufus Morrill,	do.	2,000
Jos. Walker, Jr.,	do.	1,200
William Kimball,	Portland,	500
Asa Clapp,	do.	1,000
Charles Bartlett,	Westbrook,	900
Walter B. Goodrich,	do.	300
P. D. & Co. Bk. of Cumberland,	Portland,	1,000
Rebecca K. Chesley,	Westbrook,	600
Almyra Broad,	do.	500
Solomon H. Chandler,	New Gloucester,	800
P. D. & Co. Bk. of Westbrook,	Westbrook,	7,800
Ann Jameson,	Portland,	200
John J. Brown,	do.	200
John F. Anderson,	do.	600
P. D. & Co. Casco Bank,	do.	400
Joseph Ilsley,	do.	200
Ashur Ware,	do.	1,300
Charles Holden,	do.	1,000

Bank of Cumberland, (Continued.)

Names.	Residence.	Amount of Stock.
Elizabeth Nichols,	Unknown,	800
N. S. Littlefield,	Bridgton,	500
William Bartlett,	Westbrook,	300
Dana Bridgham,	do.	300
Moody F. Walker,	Portland,	500
Benjamin Walker,	Bridgton,	500
James Furbish, guardian,	Portland,	3,500
John Anderson, trustee,	do.	2,500
John Anderson,	do.	600
Susan Watson,	Unknown,	600
James Ellison,	Boston,	2,000
Calvin Thomas,	Unknown,	7,800
P. D. & Co. Merchants' Bank,	Portland,	1,400
Samuel Wells,	do.	1,000
John Anderson, guardian for E. W. Morton,	do.	3,400
		$50,000

Belfast Bank.

Hugh J. Anderson,	Belfast,	1,100
David Alden, Jr.,	Northport,	200
Adams & Gay,	Castine,	1,000
Ann Avery,	Belfast,	500
Hiram O. Alden,	Belfast,	200
Elisha Ames, estate,	Islesborough,	400
Amos Atkinson,	Boston,	1,000
Alden & Crosby,	Belfast,	100
Benjamin Brown,	do.	100
Joseph Bean,	Montville,	200
Jonathan Bean,	do.	400
Francis Bean,	do.	800
Elizabeth A. Barns,	Belfast,	100
Hannah Bean,	Montville,	300
Isaac C. Brown,	Boston,	1,000
Elizabeth Barns,	Belfast,	200

Belfast Bank, (Continued.)

Names.	Residence	Amount of Stock.
Enoch Clements,	Knox, ·	200
Mercy E. Dyer,	Unknown,	200
Estate of Philip Eastman,	Belfast,	200
Josiah Farrow,	do.	900
Estate of Samuel French,	do.	200
Jane Bishop,	do.	300
D. B. Buller,	Freedom,	100
James Gammans,	Belfast,	200
Jonathan Gilmore,	Searsport,	100
Charles Gordon,	Belfast,	800
Oliver K. Gordon,	Brooklyn, N. Y.,	800
Eliza A. Gordon,	do.	700
Oliver H. Gordon,	do.	700
Nathaniel Gurney,	Waldo,	1,500
Prescott Hazeltine,	Belfast,	200
Paul R. Hazeltine,	do.	2,200
Benjamin Hazeltine,	do.	500
Paoli Hewes,	do.	600
John Haraden,	do.	500
John Haraden & Son,	do.	500
Daniel Haraden,	do.	500
John Hathaway,	Boston,	2,000
S. W. Hall,	do.	500
Elizabeth Hosmer,	Castine, ·	100
Horatio H. Johnson,	Belfast,	100
Anson Johnson,	Ohio,	2,000
John S. Kimball,	Belfast,	600
Susan S. Kimball,	Salem, Mass.,	500
Isabella G. Kimball,	Belfast,	200
Nathaniel M. Lowney,	do.	800
John McArthur,	Brooks,	200
Elizabeth McGregor,	Derry, N. H.,	200
Hollis Monroe,	Belfast,	500
Thomas Marshall,	do.	1,000
Edmund Muzzy,	Unity,	500
Thomas Morton.	Jackson,	500
Susanna T. Mitchell,	Bridgewater, Mass.,	600
Margaret Mead,	Castine,	100
Abigail L. Mead,	do.	100
Pauline Moody,	Belfast.	1,500

Belfast Bank, (Continued.)

Names.	Residence.	Amount of Stock.
Salathiel Nickerson,	Belfast,	2,000
Lemuel R. Palmer,	do.	1,200
Robert Patterson,	do.	300
Rebecca Prentiss,	do.	600
Hale Parkhurst,	Unity,	200
Reuben Sibley,	Belfast,	200
William Sibley,	Freedom,	500
Eliza Sumner,	Hope,	500
Moses True,	Montville,	500
Paul True,	do.	1,000
Ezekiel True,	do.	600
John Thurston,	Unknown,	100
Robert Treat,	Frankfort,	800
Martin P. White,	Belfast,	400
William White,	do.	200
James P. White,	do.	2,100
James White,	do.	1,000
Joseph Williamson,	do.	1,500
Wm. D. Williamson, adm'r,	Bangor,	2,200
H. G. O. Washburn,	Belfast,	400
Charlotte M. Washburn,	do.	200
Samuel A. Whitney,	Lincolnville,	200
Joseph Wescott,	Castine,	1,100
Lydia A. White,	Hallowell,	400
		$50,000

* Brunswick Bank.

Wm. Allen,	Northampton, Ms.,	1,000
Joseph Badger,	Brunswick,	4,000
Charles Boardman,	Boston, Mass.,	100
Elizabeth Brumigion,	Brunswick,	100
Brunswick Bank,	do.	2,000
Bowdoin College,	do.	4,100
J. & W. Barron,	Topsham,	3,000
James Carey,	Brunswick,	300
Parker Cleaveland,	do.	200

2

Brunswick Bank, (Continued.)

Names.	Residence.	Amount of Stock.
Asa Clapp,	Portland,	1,000
A. W. H. Clapp,	do.	1,000
James Cowing,	Brunswick,	100
William Curtis,	do.	500
Patrick Clark,	Unknown,	500
Nathaniel Davis,	Brunswick,	500
William Dennett,	Topsham,	300
R. T. Dunlap,	Brunswick,	100
Robert H. Dunlap,	Boston,	5,000
Ebenezer Everett,	Brunswick,	1,000
Mary W. Green,	Topsham,	500
Delia Gross,	Brunswick,	100
John C. Humphreys,	do.	4,200
Jeremiah Hunt,	do.	300
L. T. Jackson,	do.	1,000
Thomas Knowlton,	do.	500
Adam Lemont,	do.	100
Isaac Lincoln,	do.	100
John D. Lincoln,	do.	100
Joseph McKean,	do.	800
Jos. McLellan,	do.	400
Moses E Merrill,	Unknown,	200
Samuel R. Merrill,	do.	300
Henry Merritt,	Brunswick,	300
Mary Mosley,	do.	200
James Otis,	do.	300
John Owen,	do.	1,900
Nathaniel Robbins,	do.	500
George F. Richardson,	Topsham,	4,000
James Sampson,	Bowdoinham,	300
David Scribner,	Topsham,	1,000
David Shaw,	Brunswick,	200
Stephen Snow,	do.	200
Humphreys Snow,	do.	300
Nathaniel Springer,	do.	300
Wm. Stanwood,	do.	1,500
A. J. Stone,	do.	1,000
Daniel P. Stone,	Boston,	3,300
Wm. P. Story,	Brunswick,	100
Charles Thomson,	Topsham,	2,000

Brunswick Bank, (Continued.)

Names.	Residence.	Amount of Stock.
John F. Titcomb,	Brunswick,	10,000
Trustees of Brunswick School Fund,	do.	400
Thomas C. Upham,	do.	2,500
Sarah Wilson,	do.	100
Nathaniel Walker,	Topsham,	2,500
George Woodside,	Brunswick,	300
Jordan Woodard,	do.	100
Nathan Woodard,	do.	300
Wildes P. Walker,	Boston, Mass.,	1,000
John Dunlap,	Brunswick,	7,000
		$75,000

Canal Bank, (Portland.)

John Anderson,	Portland,	2,200
Mehitable Alden, trustee,	do.	500
Charles E. Barrett,	do.	5,800
Olive Barron,	Gorham,	200
Thomas Beck,	Deceased,	5,000
Thomas Browne,	Portland,	6,600
Joseph Barbour,	Gorham,	900
Dorcas Bagley,	Portland,	400
Theodore Bradbury,	Standish,	1,800
Caroline M. H. Bradbury,	do.	100
Maria Bradbury,	do.	1,900
Wm. G. Brooks, trustee,	Boston,	2,500
Charles Brooks, guardian,	do.	1,200
John C. Brooks,	Portland,	500
Benjamin D. Bryant,	Deceased,	3,000
Brazier & Hall,	Portland,	300
George L. Bradbury,		100
John Bartels,	Portland,	200
Angeline Bradbury,		100
James Bradbury,		100
Hannah Chase,	Danville,	1,100
Asa Cummings,	Portland,	500

Canal Bank, (Continued.)

Names.	Residence.	Amount of Stock.
Asa Clapp,	Portland,	6,500
Samuel Chadwick,	do.	6,600
Charity Fund, 1st Parish,	do.	200
Benjamin P. Chamberlain,	Salem,	8,200
Nathan Cummings, adm'r,	Portland,	1,100
B. T. Chase,	Buxton,	300
Betsy Sewall Cross,		1,000
Mary M. P. Cram,		500
Ellen E. Crocker,		500
Oliver Carlton,		3,000
Warren E. Chase,	Portland,	1,000
Marshall Cram,	Bridgton,	500
Louisa Dennet,		500
Abagail Dennet,		500
John A. Douglass,	Waterford,	1,600
Charles S. Daveis,	Portland,	1,800
Lucy Deane,	Standish,	1,800
Nathan Dane, Jr.,		200
Jacob Drummond,		1,100
Henry S. Edwards,	Portland,	500
Jacob Eaton,		500
Rufus Emerson,	Portland,	2,200
William Evans,	do.	1,100
Nicholas Emery,	do.	5,400
Margaret Emery,		300
Nathan Elden,	Buxton,	600
Hannah Elden,	do.	1,100
Ed. C. and Mary O. Emerson,	Minors,	4,300
John Fox,	Portland,	6,300
Stephen Frothingham,	do.	100
Female Orphan Asylum,	do.	2,100
C. D. French,		300
Phebe C. Freeman,	Minor,	200
Charles M. Freeman,	do.	200
Charles Freeman,	Limerick,	600
Joseph Frost,		600
First Parish,	Kennebunk,	500
Grand Lodge of Maine,		2,000
Grand Royal Arch Chapter of Maine,		100

Canal Bank, (Continued.)

Names.	Residence.	Amount of Stock.
Joseph M. Gerish,	Portland,	700
William Goodenow,	do.	1,200
Stephen Gale,	do.	700
Byron Greenough,	do.	500
John D. Gardner,	Boston,	3,000
Melbury Green,	Minor,	300
Joseph Green,	do.	300
Sarah M. Gilman,		100
Augustus Gilman,	Minor,	200
Sarah H. Gilman,	do.	200
Samuel Goddard, Ex. in trust,		2,000
Eliphalet Greeley,	Portland,	300
Moses Gould,	Bridgton,	500
Mary Garland,	Ohio,	500
Frances Gould,	do.	500
Joseph T. Gilman,	do.	4,300
Daniel Goodenow,	Alfred,	700
Moses Hall,	Westbrook,	1,000
Esther C. Horton,	do.	1,100
James Hall,	Portland,	400
Thomas Hammond,	do.	5,700
Joel Hall,	do.	9,400
Polly Hobart,	Deceased,	1,500
Simeon Hall,	Portland,	700
Eleanor W. Head,	Minor,	1,300
W. A. Hayes,	South Berwick,	800
Chester Holbrook,		4,000
Enoch F. Higgins,	Deceased,	1,000
Joseph E. Hatch,		600
Isaac and Elizabeth Hopkins,	New Portland,	1,100
Mary Caro & J. D. Higgins,	Minors,	2,000
John Hamilton,	Portland,	1,400
Sophia E Hamilton,		500
Abigail S. Hill,	Phipsburg,	500
Edward Howe,	Portland,	1,800
S. Hubbard, B. Grant and W. T. Green, trustees,	Boston,	3,600
Isaac Illsley,	Portland.	4,200
Ann Jameson,	do.	500
James C. Jordan,	Minor,	900

2*

Canal Bank, (Continued.)

Names.	Residence.	Amount of Stock.
Ruth Jewett,	Portland,	1,000
William Kimball,	do.	1,300
Elijah Kellogg,	Deceased,	1,100
Joseph M. Kellogg,	Portland,	300
James Lunt,	Westbrook,	1,600
Sarah Lunt,		700
Phebe Lord,		4,300
Elizabeth Langdon,		200
Zenas Libby,	Portland,	500
Luther Libby,	Scarborough,	1,300
Benjamin Lord,	Falmouth,	1,500
Josiah Little,	Newburyport,	1,400
Paul Langdon,		2,100
Josiah Little,		2,000
Ann Libby,		100
Sarah M. Mayo,	Portland,	800
Clarissa Minot,	Deceased,	300
Dolly Mussey,	Standish,	2,000
Esther Mussey,	Portland,	2,000
Nancy Moseley,	New Gloucester,	600
Mary Mills,		300
Isabella Mead,	Minor,	600
Jane G. Mead,		600
Sarah G. Moore,		600
Thomas McLellan,	Portland,	500
Edward Motley,	do.	1,300
Caroline M. Mellen,		500
Eleazer McKenney,	Portland,	900
George G. Minot,	do.	200
Roger Merrill,		100
Joseph McKeen, treas.,	Brunswick,	100
Albert Newhall,	Cumberland,	5,000
Ichabod Nichols,	Portland,	2,200
Frederick S. Nichols,	Minor,	100
Charles G. Nichols,	do.	100
Nicholas G. Nichols,	do.	100
Prentiss M. Nichols,	do.	100
Joseph Noble,	Boston,	900
Noah Nason,	Westbrook,	1,600
Joshua B. Osgood,	Portland,	800

Canal Bank, (Continued.)

Names.	Residence.	Amount of Stock.
Richard Odell,	Portland,	1,500
Edward Oxnard,	do.	2,300
Ocean Insurance Company,	do.	24,200
Lucy Phinney,	Gorham,	800
Thomas Perley,	Deceased,	2,000
John P. Perley,		600
Augustus Perley,	Bridgton,	600
Sarah Perley,		1,500
Portland Marine Society,	Portland,	1,000
Proprietors Portland Athenæum,	do.	2,700
Nathan Pope,	Windham,	700
Oliver Pope,	do.	500
Lydia C. Pease,	Westbrook,	900
Portland Mutual Ins. Co.,	Portland,	1,200
Eleanor J. Pote,		300
Mary Plummer,		300
Phelps, Dodge & Co.,		1,000
P. D. & Co., Bank of Portland,	Portland,	100
do. Canal Bank,	do.	10,900
do. Casco Bank,	do.	8,300
do. Merchants' Bank,	do.	3,900
do. York Bank,	Saco,	1,300
do. Brunswick Bank,	Brunswick,	1,500
Albert G. Pollard,		600
Susannah Partridge, (deceased,)		1,500
Elizabeth P. Peters,		300
Ann Quincy,	Portland,	4,400
Mary L. Quincy,	do.	600
Thomas B. Ripley,		500
Lucy Russell,		400
John F. Reeves,	Portland,	1,500
John W. Reeves,	Minor,	1,000
Mary C. Robinson,	Portland,	500
Charles D. Robinson,	Minor,	600
Toppan Robie,	Gorham,	1,000
Israel Richardson,	Portland,	2,500
Isaac Sturdivant,	do.	12,400
Josiah B. Scott,	do.	1,400
William Swan,	do.	800
Lucy Sewall,	Kennebunk,	500

Canal Bank, (Continued.)

Names.	Residence.	Amount of Stock.
Nathaniel Shaw,	Portland,	600
Smith & Brown,	do.	2,000
St. John Smith,	do.	1,500
Elizabeth Stevens,		700
Sarah Stockman,		100
Caroline Stockman,		100
Martha J. Stockman,		100
Eben'r Sumner,	Portland,	600
W. B. Sewall,	Kennebunk,	1,800
W. B. Sewall, in trust,	do.	100
Narcissa Sewall,	do.	500
Eveline Sewall,	do.	500
Gideon L. Soule,		300
Matilda Sewall,	Winthrop,	500
Benjamin Smith,		1,000
Dolly C. Smith,		1,200
W. H. Smith,		900
Ether Shepley,		1,700
Nicholas E. Smart,		600
Miranda Stone,		1,000
Mary E. Stone,		2,000
Cornelia Shaw,	Minor,	800
Priscilla P. Smith,	Portland,	1,900
Saco and Biddeford Sav. Ins.,		2,000
R. M. Stratton, agent,		1,300
Nancy Smith,		1,800
Elias Thomas,	Portland,	11,600
W. W. Thomas,	do.	6,900
Martha Trask,	do.	1,500
Samuel Trask,	do.	1,500
Franklin Tinkham,	do.	500
Martha Tappan,	Deceased,	300
Trustees N. Yarmouth School Fund,	North Yarmouth,	900
Trustees N. Yarmouth Acad.,	do.	2,000
do. Min. Fund, 1st Parish,	do.	1,300
do. do. do.	Gorham,	1,300
do. Portland Academy,	Portland,	1,200
Trustees Charity Fund Mt. Vernon Chapter,		1,000

Canal Bank, (Continued.)

Names.	Residence.	Amount of Stock.
Trustees Ancient Landmark Lodge Charity Fund,		200
Thomas C. Upham,	Brunswick,	2,000
Phinehas Vanum,	Portland,	2,300
J. & N. Warren,	Do. & Westbrook,	3,500
Nathaniel Warren,	Portland,	2,100
Nathaniel Warren, guardian,	do.	1,100
Jeremiah Winslow,	France,	6,200
Benjamin Willis,	Boston,	8,500
Benjamin Willis, Jr.,	do.	3,500
Leonard White,	Haverill,	4,300
Phebe Wadlin,		1,300
Adam Wilson,	Portland,	600
Levi Woodbury,		4,300
Warren & King,	Westbrook,	100
Ashur Ware,	Portland,	2,900
William Woodbury,	do.	500
Harrison Whitman,	do.	300
Hezekiah Winslow,	do.	2,500
Charlotte Wilson,	do.	300
William Willis,	do.	1,500
		$400,000

Casco Bank, (Portland.)

John Anderson, trustee,	Portland,	1,100
John Anderson,	do.	1,300
Edward Anderson,	Windham,	500
Abraham W. Anderson,	Gray,	1,900
Ann W. Anderson,	Portland,	1,000
Nathaniel Blanchard,	do.	900
Nathaniel Blanchard, guard.,	do.	4,000
Hannah P. Buxton,	Cumberland,	100
Hannah Buxton,	do.	200
Julia Buxton,	do.	500
Maria Bradbury,	Sandish,	2,400
Caroline M. Bradbury,	do.	2,400

Casco Bank, (Continued.)

Names.	Residence.	Amount of Stock.
Mary Blake,	Portland,	500
Elizabeth M. Bennett,		100
Mary E. Bennett,		100
Theophilus Boyd,		100
William Buxton, deceased,		600
Clarissa Brooks,	Portland,	400
Olive Barron,	Topsham,	100
Ellen E. Crocker,	Westbrook,	500
Parker Cleaveland,	Brunswick,	1,500
Hannah Chase,	Danville,	300
Emily Cummings,	Portland,	7,600
Nathan Cummings,	do.	600
Asa Clapp,	do.	17,000
Samuel Chadwick,	do.	10,000
Dorcas Deblois,	do.	1,000
Charles W. Dennison,	do.	500
Neal Dow,	do.	1,200
Eunice Day,	do.	500
Edward II. Daveis,	do.	500
Charles S. Daveis,	do.	2,100
James Deering,	do.	2,400
William Evans,	do.	7,500
Eben. Everett,	Brunswick,	300
E. C. & M. O. Emerson, minors,	Portland,	400
Nicholas Emery,	do.	1,700
William P. Fessenden,	do.	600
Erastus Foote, guardian,	Wiscasset,	100
Daniel Gould,	Portland,	600
Moses Gould,	do.	600
Susan Gould,	do.	600
Eliphalet Greeley,	do.	3,500
Daniel Goodenow,	Alfred,	2,600
Sarah M. Gilman,	Portland,	200
Joseph T. Gilman,		800
John T. Gilman, guardian,	Portland,	1,300
Mary Garland,		600
Joseph Howard,	Portland,	300
Elenore W. Head, minor,	do.	500
Alexander Hubbs,	do.	2,000
Polly Hobert, estate of,	do.	2,300

Casco Bank, (Continued.)

Names.	Residence.	Amount of Stock.
Benjamin Hasey,	Topsham,	1,300
Edward Howe,	Portland,	200
Samuel Hanson,	do.	1,400
Horton & Towbridge,	do.	500
Isaac Ilsley,	do.	19,200
Parker Ilsley,	do.	1,300
Ann Jameson,	do.	4,100
James C. Jordan, minor,	do.	500
Jones & Hammonds,	do.	200
Charles Jones,	do.	200
Josiah Little, Jr.,		1,500
Josiah S. Little,	Portland,	4,000
Eliza P. Lewis, minor,	do.	700
Sarah R. Lewis, minor,	do.	700
C. C. Mitchell,	do.	200
Penelope Martin,	do.	200
Catharine Martin,	do.	200
Esther Mussey,	do.	3,300
John Mussey,		500
Eben. McIntosh,	Portland,	400
Matthias Meserve,	Cape Elizabeth,	300
Daniel Mountfort, estate of,	Portland,	1,000
Almira Merrill,	do.	1,000
Elizabeth Merrill,	do.	300
N. Doane, McLellan,	do.	700
Albert Newhall,	Cumberland,	1,100
Joshua B. Osgood,	Portland,	500
Martha P. Oxnard,	do.	300
Mary C. D. G. Oxnard, minor,	do.	400
John R. Philbrick,	Standish,	600
Abby Pierce,	Portland,	300
Susan Purinton,	do.	600
William P. Preble,	do.	5,000
Esais Preble,	York,	200
Hannah Preble,		600
David Pettingill,	Portland,	1,500
Ann Quincy,	do.	2,600
Mary L. Quincy,	do.	1,200
Clarissa A. Robie,	Gorham,	1,100
Toppan Robie,	do.	1,500

Casco Bank, (Continued.)

Names.	Residence.	Amount of Stock.
Mary Rea,	Portland,	400
Isaac Sturdivant,	North Yarmouth,	11,500
Dolly Stockman,	Portland,	2,700
Martha J. Stockman,	do.	1,500
Caroline Stockman,	do.	600
Rebecca Strong,	do.	1,000
Elizabeth Stevens,	do.	600
Anna Stevens,	do.	200
St John Smith,	do.	500
Nancy Smith,	Boston,	1,000
Benjamin Smith,	Kennebunk,	1,300
Eben Storer,	Gorham,	200
Martha Smith, deceased,		1,400
William B. Sewall,	Kennebunk,	400
Sarah Sargent,	Portland,	200
C. & D. E. Shaw,	Oxford,	1,900
Elizabeth L. Storer, deceased,		500
Calvin Thomas,		1,700
Samuel Trask,	Portland,	1,500
Martha Trask,	do.	500
Martha Tappan,		200
James Todd,	Portland,	300
Jane C. Thayer,	do.	300
Jonathan Tucker,	do.	500
William Titcomb,	North Yarmouth,	1,000
Tho. C. Upham,	Brunswick,	2,000
Phinehas Varnum,	Portland,	3,000
Joshua Wingate, Jr., estate,	do.	16,500
Levi Woodbury,	Portsmouth, N. H.,	6,000
Benjamin Willis,	Boston,	15,000
Christopher Wright,	Portland,	1,000
Sarah Webb,	do.	400
John Waterhouse, deceased,		1,200
Joseph H. Wardwell,	Rumford,	600
Ulitta Wood,	Portland,	100
Hanah N. Wenberg,	do.	400
Nathan Winslow,	do.	1,000
Timothy Walker,	do.	300
Casco Bank.	do.	26,600
Merchants' Bank,	do.	700

Casco Bank, (Continued.)

Names.	Residence.	Amount of Stock.
Ocean Insurance Company,	Portland,	12,800
Mutual Fire Insurance Co.,	do.	1,000
Institution for Savings,	Saco & Biddeford,	700
Bowdoin College,	Brunswick,	18,200
Maine Missionary Society,		1,500
N. Yarmonth School Fund,		800
Cumberland School Fund,		500
Grand Lodge of Maine,		1,000
Mt. Vernon Charity Fund,	Portland,	300
Anc. Land Mark Charity Fund,	do.	1,600
Portland Relief Society,	do.	300
Portland Academy,	do.	1,800
First Parish Charity Fund,	do.	1,000
		$300,000

Central Bank, (Hallowell.)

Merritt Coolidge,	Hallowell,	58 82
Thomas M. Andrews,	do.	58 17
J. F. Hill,	Massachusetts,	2,058 83
A. V. Smith,	Unknown,	2,352 94
T. Coolidge,	Massachusetts,	588 24
Reuel Williams,	Augusta,	588 24
Lucy Emerson's estate, dec'd,	Hallowell,	588 24
Peleg Sprague,	Boston,	1,764 70
F. G. Butler,	Farmington,	882 35
F. Butler, deceased,	do.	1,470 58
Reuel Washburn,	Livermore,	588 24
Oliver Otis, estate of,	Hallowell,	1,294 11
C. Spaulding,	do.	58 82
A. Leonard, cashier, in trust,	do.	647 06
Central Bank,	do.	6,470 60
J. M. Leonard,	Illinois,	1,294 11
J. E. Leonard,	do.	1,294 11
F. W. Leonard,	do.	1,294 11
Isaac Leonard,	do.	10,000
M. Andrews,	R. Island,	9,764 71

3

Central Bank, *(Continued.)*

Names.	Residence.	Amount of Stock.
M. Andrews, in trust,	R. Island,	5,235 29
Vassalboro' Quarterly Meeting,	Vassalborough,	235 30
John Smith,	Readfield,	588 24
Artemas Leonard,	Hallowell,	823 53
		$50,000

Calais Bank.

Barnard & Pike,	Calais,	100
Manufac. Insurance Co.,	Boston,	5,000
Lane & Reed,	do.	1,000
James M. Robbins,	do.	1,450
John G. Faxon,	do.	3,600
Titus Welles,	do.	1,000
Austin D. Barnard,	do.	50
F. E. & J. L. Barnard,	do.	50
Eagle Bank,	do.	5,000
Catherine Robbins,	Cambridge,	300
Franklin Ins. Company,	Boston,	3,000
Thomas Vose,	do.	500
Lemuel P. Grosvenor,	Pomfret, Ct.,	6,000
Henry Rice,	Boston,	100
Charlotte W. Seaver,	do.	350
Catharine F. Seaver,	do.	250
Mary Ann P. Seaver,	do.	200
Martha W. Seaver,	do.	200
Hubbard Winslow,	do.	2,000
Waldo Flint,	do.	350
Waldo Flint, guardian,	do.	1,500
Otis Daniell,	do.	850
Robert Farley,	do.	850
Theodore Prentice,	do.	250
Daniel Denney,	do.	250
Hugh R. Kendall, guardian,	do.	1,000
Robert Farley, in trust,	do.	2,000
James Longley,	do.	1,250
M. P. Sawyer,	do.	800

Calais Bank, (Continued.)

Names.	Residence.	Amount of Stock.
Levi L. Lowell,	Calais,	150
John Tucker,	Boston,	1,300
Scudder Cordis & Co.,	do.	800
William Deering,	Calais,	100
Calais Bank,	do.	1,300
Francis Swan,	do.	50
Thomas Robitson,	do.	100
George Downes,	do.	1,200
Daniel Hume,	do.	150
Downes & Cooper,	do.	50
Stephen Emerson,	do.	50
Phinehas Nevins,	St. Stephens,	1,250
Robert Watson, trustee,	do.	250
John Dickinson,	Amherst, Mass.,	500
Thomas Child,	U. S. Army,	100
Greenwood C. Child,	Augusta,	2,500
Ovid Burrill,	East Machias,	500
Abel Brooks, Jr.,	Robbinston,	150
Frederick Hobbs,	Bangor,	250
		$50,000

Commercial Bank, (Bath.)

Hannah S. Allen,	Bath,	500
Sarah A. T. Allen,	do.	200
Samuel G. Bowman, guard.,	Deceased,	400
Timothy Bachelder,	Phipsburg,	1,500
Rachel L. Bachelder,	do.	100
B. C. Bailey,	Bath,	500
Freeman Clark,	do.	600
Zacheus Crooker,	do.	500
Wm. Crawford,	do.	200
Daniel F. Coombs,	West Bath,	100
Jno. Corliss,	Woolwich,	500
Mary Chandler,	Bath,	500
Robert Dresser,	Portland,	200
Thomas S. Bowles,	Bath,	300

Commercial Bank, (Continued.)

Names.	Residence.	Amount of stock.
Wm. Donnell,	Bath,	400
Lucy P. Donnell,	Litchfield,	300
Mary A. French,	Camden,	100
Mary Farnham,	Woolwich,	200
E. W. K. Groton,	Bath,	400
Zina Hyde,	do.	800
James Hall's estate,		3,000
Samuel Hunter,	Topsham,	1,800
Benjamin Hasey,	do.	1,000
Eliza A. Haggett,	Unknown,	100
Eleanor Kittridge,	do.	1,000
Adam Lemont, estate,		400
William Ledyard,	Bath,	700
Eliza Lenox,	Wiscasset,	200
Parker McCobb,	Portland,	7,500
John Masters,	Bath,	500
John Parsons,	Phipsburg,	1,500
Wm. Potter,	Arrowsic,	500
Caroline C. Porter,	Camden,	200
Rachel Patten,	Massachusetts,	400
Estate of Ezekiel Purinton,	Topsham,	1,400
Wm. Patten,	Richmond,	300
Caroline C. Prescott,	Bath,	700
Joshua Page,	do.	100
Mary J. Patten,	Topsham,	200
Charles T. Patten,	Illinois,	100
Jacob Robinson,	Bath,	4,600
Jeremiah Robinson,	do.	2,800
Thomas M. Reed,	Phipsburg,	2,200
William M. Reed,	Bath,	300
Mary E. Robinson,	do.	500
Sarah A. Robinson,	do.	500
Ann M. Robinson,	do.	500
Daniel Robbins, Jr.,	do.	400
Geo. Shepherd,	do.	1,000
Wm. D. Sewall,	do.	1,600
Joseph Sewall,	do.	900
John Smith,	do.	100
Samuel Stanwood,	do.	200
Joseph Sewall, adm'r,	do.	200

Commercial Bank, (Continued.)

Names.	Residence.	Amount of Stock.
Polly Sewall,	Bath,	200
Gilbert Trufant,	do.	500
Samuel Tarbox,	Westport,	500
Thomas Wilson,	Greene,	2,500
Seneca White,	Massachusetts,	400
Estate of Charles C. Waldron,		200
		$50,000

Eastern Bank, (Bangor.)

John Bradbury,	Bangor,	50
Amos M. Roberts,	do.	1,950
Lucy Adams,	Boston,	4,000
Henry W. Fuller, estate,	Augusta,	500
William A. Blake,	Bangor,	1,000
Sally Henderson,	Warren,	100
James Henderson,	do.	100
Ann Henderson,	do.	50
Susan Henderson,	do.	50
Dunbar Henderson,	do.	50
Joseph A. Ballard,	Boston,	10,000
William Henderson,	Warren,	50
Reuel Williams,	Augusta,	2,000
Daniel B. Hinkley,	Bangor,	300
Samuel P. Strickland,	do.	2,000
Beal, Jenkins & Vinal,	Situate, Mass.,	1,300
A. M. Roberts, trustee,	Bangor,	350
Eastern Bank,	do.	12,150
M. M. Ballou,	New York,	9,000
E. D. Peters & Co.,	Boston,	5,000
		$50,000

Franklin Bank, (Gardiner.)

Names.	Residence.	Amount of Stock.
George W. Bachelder,	Gardiner,	200
Eben. F. Deane,	do.	2,100
Nathaniel Kimball,	do.	1,000
Pelham Harden,	do.	1,000
George Evans,	do.	200
Mrs. Nancy Mitchell,	do.	1,000
Gardiner Savings Institution,	do.	500
Rebecca Gould, guardian,	do.	1,500
Augustus Ballard,	do.	600
Richard Stuart, deceased,	do.	2,000
Robert H. Gardiner,	do.	1,000
Wm. Purinton,	Bowdoinham,	1,500
Nathaniel Stone,	Gardiner,	600
Dorcas Bowman,	do.	1,700
Joseph Mustard,	Bowdoinham,	1,800
Wm. Stevens, 2d,	Pittston,	1,200
Christopher Jackins, deceased,	do.	400
James N. Cooper,	do.	300
Betsey G. Cooper,	do.	2,200
Stephen Young,	do.	2,500
Caleb Curtis, trustee,	Boston,	10,000
John Smith,	Readfield,	1,000
John Hiscock,	Nobleborough,	500
Lucy Ann Farley,	Bath,	500
Joseph Eaton,	Winslow,	3,700
Elizabeth Call,	Dresden,	800
Maria H. Sanford, under the guardianship of H. Flagg,	Bangor,	500
John Henry,	Bath,	1,000
John Otis,	Hallowell,	400
Betsey Otis,	do.	5,000
Solomon Eaton,	Bowdoin,	1,000
Wm. V. Kent,	Boston,	1,800
Joseph H. Sanford,	do.	500
		$50,000

Freeman's Bank, (Augusta.)

Names.	Residence.	Amount of Stock.
Benjamin Davis,	Augusta,	3,900
Prince B. Moore,	Vassalborough,	2,000
William Hunt,	Augusta,	2,400
John Mulliken,	Hallowell,	1,700
Watson F. Hallett,	Augusta,	200
James W. Bradbury,	do.	600
Bradbury & Rice,	do.	100
John Smith,	Readfield,	2,000
Francis Butler, deceased,	Farmington,	1,000
Reuel Washburn,	Livermore,	2,000
Daniel Page, deceased,	Augusta,	600
Henry Flagg,	Bangor,	1,000
Daniel Gage, estate,	Augusta,	600
Jacob Sleeper,	Massachusetts,	3,000
J. & W. Odlin,	New Hampshire,	100
Sam'l Wells and Isaac Gage, } executors,	Portland and Augusta,	1,500
Williams Emmons,	Hallowell,	500
Nathan Hovey,	Augusta,	500
Bethuel Perry,	do.	500
Gilbert Newall,	Massachusetts,	3,800
Jesse Aiken,	Hallowell,	500
Grand Lodge,		500
Abigail W. Rogers,	Massachusetts,	200
Arno Bittues,	Augusta,	1,500
L. W. Lithgow,	do.	1,000
Jabez Gay,	Farmington,	600
George Evans,	Gardiner,	500
G. W. Morton,	Augusta,	800
Wm. Caldwell, cashier,	do.	2,000
John Atkins,	Hallowell,	200
Benjamin Ellis,	Massachusetts,	1,000
Daniel Blaisdell,	Sidney,	400
Eliza P. Vose,	Augusta,	1,000
Sally Fletcher,	Norridgewock,	1,000
Cullen Sawtelle,	do.	500
Alden Sampson,	Hallowell,	500
W. G. Pool,	Massachusetts,	300
R. Pope,	Hallowell,	500
Loring Cushing,	Augusta,	1,900

Freeman's Bank, (Continued.)

Names.	Residence.	Amount of Stock.
R. Goodenow,	Farmington,	500
Benjamin Hasey,	Topsham,	1,300
Alvah Moulton,	N. Hampshire,	800
J. & W. Barron,	Topsham, '	1,000
Samuel Wells,	Portland,	1,000
Samuel L. Rogers,		1,000
Issachar Snell,	Augusta,	100
James Bradbury,	New Hampshire,	500
Henry R. Smith,	Augusta,	1,500
S. B. Moores,	Vassalboro',	2,000
		$50,000

Frontier Bank, (Eastport.)

Estate of Nathaniel Ames,	St. Andrews, N. B.,	975
Isaac Ames,	Machias-port,	450
Issac L. Bedell,	St. John, N. B.,	450
William Bell,	Trescott,	450
Henrietta B. Brewer,	Robbinston,	975
Estate of Jona. Buck,	Eastport,	150
Ann O. Buck,	do.	1,500
William M. Brooks,	do.	1,500
Charles Brooks,	do.	450
Jerry Burgin,	do.	150
James M. Balkam,	Robbinston,	375
Lewis Bliss,	Halifax, N. S.,	1,950
Joseph H. Claridge,	Eastport,	300
John C. Crookshank,	St. John, N. B.,	1,050
Charles S. Carpenter,	Eastport,	375
George W. Crocket,	Boston,	375
Louis A. Cazenove, trustee,	Alexandria, D. C.,	375
Meletiah Calkin,	Eastport,	975
Greenwood C. Child,	Augusta,	6,975
Chase & Grew,	Boston,	450
Samuel K. Dawson,	U. S. Army,	450
Charles F. Eaton,	Boston,	1,500
Becke Fairbanks,	do.	150

Frontier Bank, (Continued.)

Names.	Residence.	Amount of Stock.
J. D. Farnsworth,	Boston,	375
John Beckford,	Eastport,	300
Mowe & Co.,	do.	300
J. B. Ricketts,	U. S. Army,	750
Frontier Bank,	Eastport,	300
David Fullam,	Boston,	3,975
Edward Gilligan, estate,	Eastport,	300
Peter Gilligan,	do.	1,050
Estate of Jesse Gleason,	do.	900
Frederick Hobbs,	Bangor,	1,050
Archibald Heney,	Deer Isle, N. B.,	150
Paoli Hewes,	Belfast,	600
Jane Hammond,	St. John, N. B.,	975
Estate of Aaron Hayden,	Eastport,	3,000
Aaron Hayden,	do.	375
Partmon Houghton,	do.	600
Edward Ilsley, cashier, trustee,	do.	2,100
John Kilby,	Dennysville,	975
John Kerr,	St. John, N. B.,	1,050
Theodore Lincoln, Jr.,	Dennysville,	525
Samuel A. Morse,	Machias,	1,500
William Maybee,	Eastport,	525
Charles Merritt,	St. John, N. B.,	975
P. J. Nevins,	New York,	2,700
Jacob R. Nevins,	do.	900
Ocean Insurance Company,	Portland,	900
Darius Pearce,	Eastport,	1,575
Hannah F. Porter,	do.	150
John J. Robinson, trustee,	Campo Bello, N. B.	3,000
Thomas Reed,	St. John, N. B.,	450
James M. Robbins,	Milton, Mass.,	975
Isaac Ray,		1,800
Samuel Root, estate,	Lubec,	1,950
Stevens & Peabody,	Eastport,	1,800
Abel Stevens,	do.	150
J. Shackford,	do.	450
Wm. Shackford,	do.	450
Lorenzo Sabine,	do.	300
David S. Townsend,	Boston,	1,050

Frontier Bank, (Continued.)

Names.	Residence.	Amount of Stock.
Samuel Tuttle, estate,	St. Stephens, N. B.,	2,025
John V. Thurger, trustee,	St. John, N. B.,	1,950
Bela Wilder,	Pembroke,	300
Ebed Wilder,	do.	300
Samuel Witherell,	Eastport,	525
Samuel Wheeler,	do.	2,025
Samuel Wheeler & Sons,	do.	975
Loring F. Wheeler, estate,	do.	1,050
Jas. Whitney,	St. John, N. B.,	300
Amos Seaman,	Manudia, N. S.,	1,950
		$75,000

Granite Bank, (Augusta.)

Joseph R. Abbot, guardian,	Augusta,	1,575
Mary Andrews,	R. Island,	7,500
Charles G. Bachelder,	Hallowell,	150
William A. Brooks,	Augusta,	1,500
James W. Bradbury,	do.	525
Susannah Brooks,	do.	75
John S. R. Brown,	New Hampshire,	2,025
Albert F. Barnard,	Unknown,	75
James R. Bachelder,	Readfield,	375
Arno Bittues,	Augusta,	375
David Brown,	Readfield,	450
Francis Butler's estate,	Farmington,	1,500
Erastus Bartlett,	Augusta,	150
Mary Chandler,	Unknown,	600
Cony Female Academy,	Augusta,	1,800
J. & M. A. Chandler,	do.	300
Estate of John A. Chandler,	do.	225
James Child's estate,	do.	750
James L. Child,	do.	225
Abigail S. Caldwell,	do.	300
Lois Carlton,	Unknown,	375
Carleton Dole,	Augusta,	900
Albert G. Dole,	Alna,	2,850

Granite Bank, (Continued.)

Names.	Residence.	Amount of Stock.
Carleton Dole and others, trust.,	Alna and Augusta,	900
Estate of John Dole,	do.	150
F. M. A. Davis,	Unknown,	825
Isaac Downing,	do.	300
H. Weld Fuller,	Massachusetts,	1,950
Esther G. Fuller,	Augusta,	900
Lucretia G. Fuller,	do.	825
Jabez Gray,	Farmington,	600
Timothy Goldthwait,	Augusta,	75
John Goldthwait,	do.	600
Timothy Goldthwait, Jr.,	do.	450
Thomas Goldthwait,	Unknown,	675
Elizabeth Goldthwait,	Augusta,	75
A. S. Harris,	Unknown,	525
Gardiner Savings Institution,	Gardiner,	150
James Hall's estate,	Bath,	8,025
Margaret Hamlin,	Augusta,	300
Llewellyn W. Lithgow,	do.	750
Dexter W. Hahn,	Unknown,	300
J. C. Howe & Co.,	do.	2,325
Silas Leonard,	Augusta,	2,475
Alfred Marshall,	China,	975
George W. Morton,	Augusta,	975
Laura A. Morse,	Massachusetts,	675
Charlotte M. Morse,	do.	675
Elisha Prescott,	Readfield,	2,250
Alexander Parris,	Massachusetts,	4,125
Samuel Redington,	Vassalborough,	1,425
P. Rogers,	Unknown,	75
Daniel Stone,	Wiscasset,	75
Elizabeth W. Stanwood,	Boston,	75
Mary M. Smith,	Warren,	900
Joshua Sears,	Massachusetts,	1,500
Manasseh H. Smith,	Warren,	225
Robert G. Shaw,	Massachusetts,	750
David Stanley,	Winthrop,	375
Lydia Stone,	Unknown,	525
James Starr,	Jay,	750
Samuel E. Smith,	Wiscasset,	750
Moses Safford, Jr.,	Augusta,	75

Granite Bank, (Continued.)

Names.	Residence.	Amount of Stock.
William Thomas,	Augusta,	975
Nathan Weston,	do.	2,250
Greenlief White,	do.	900
William Woart,	do.	750
Henry Williams,	do.	1,125
Henry Winslow,	do.	225
Israel Webster,	N. H.,	450
Church Williams,	Augusta,	525
Hiram Wheelock, guardian,	Massachusetts,	675
Willard Walcott,	Augusta,	525
Samuel Wells,	Portland,	300
Wingate & Allen,	Waterville and Augusta,	750
Nathaniel M. Whitmore,	Gardiner,	600
		$75,000

Gardiner Bank.

Names.	Residence.	Amount of Stock.
Lucy Adams,	Farmington,	500
Frederick Allen,	Gardiner,	500
Sophia Bond,	Hallowell,	1,300
Charles E. Bradstreet,	Pittston,	3,000
William Bradstreet,	Gardiner,	2,300
Mary H. Bridge,	Boston, Mass.,	300
Henry B. Bradstreet,	Gardiner,	500
Joseph H. Bradstreet,	do.	500
George W. Bachelder,	do.	500
S. J. Bridge & N. W. Bridge, trustees,	Boston,	300
Caleb Curtis, trustee,	do.	3,600
Susan B. Cony,	Augusta,	1,500
Caleb Curtis, trustee,	Boston,	15,000
Episcopal Church,	Gardiner,	400
R. H. Gardiner, trustee,	do.	300
Gardiner, Wild and Bridge, trustees,	do. and unk.,	800

Gardiner Bank, (Continued.)

Names.	Residence.	Amount of Stock.
Emma J. Gardiner, deceased,	Gardiner,	500
R. H. Gardiner, trustee for Mrs. Caldwell, deceased,	do.	10,000
Gardiner Savings Institution,	do.	3,100
Mary Gay, deceased,	do.	400
Dorcas P. Gay,	do.	300
Peter Grant,	do.	2,000
Nancy Grant,	do.	2,500
Samuel C. Grant,	Hallowell,	6,700
Thomas Grant,	Gardiner,	700
Samuel G. Johnson, guard.,	Dresden,	100
Wm. B. Grant,	Gardiner,	5,900
Abby G. Ingraham,	Augusta,	1,500
Enoch Jewett,	Pittston,	3,700
E. Lord,	Gardiner,	8,600
Meltiah Lawrence,	do.	1,000
John Merrick,	Hallowell,	2,000
Thomas Agry, trustee,	Bath,	500
William Purinton,	Bowdoinham,	1,000
William Purinton, guardian,	do.	1,300
John Stone,	Gardiner,	1,000
Edward Swan,	do.	2,000
Edward Swan, trustee,	do.	200
William Stevens, 2d,	Pittston,	500
Stephen Titcomb,	Farmington,	500
Samuel B. Tarbox,	Gardiner,	5,100
Eleazer Tarbox, deceased,		1,000
Petty Vaughan, trustee,	London, Eng.,	2,000
Samuel Wells,	Portland,	900
H. P. Worcester and M. O. Worcester,	Gardiner,	700
Sarah L. Williams,	Augusta,	1,500
Paulina B. Weston,	do.	1,500
		$100,000

* *Lincoln Bank, (Bath.)*

Names.	Residence.	Amount of Stock.
Bath Academy,	Bath,	2,000
Jonathan Belden, heirs,	Hallowell,	1,000
F. E. Bond,	Bangor,	200
S. S. Couillard,	Phipsburg,	200
Eben. Clapp,	Bath,	100
Bowdoin College,	Brunswick,	3,000
Charles Davenport,	Bath,	900
William Donnell,	do.	7,500
David Dunlap, heirs,	Brunswick,	2,000
Ebenezer Everett,	do.	800
Francis Elwell,	New York,	500
J. W. Ellingwood,	Bath,	2,000
Mary Ann French,	do.	100
Francis Gage,	Springfield,	200
Samuel Gray,	Bowdoinham,	200
Hannah F. Gray,	Topsham,	800
Jonathan Hyde,	Bath,	4,000
Thomas Howard,	do.	2,000
Zina Hyde,	do.	2,400
Henry Hyde,	do.	500
Levi Houghton,	do.	2,500
Andrew Heath,	do.	1,200
John Henry,	do.	1,000
Joshua Haskell,	Topsham,	500
A. M. T. Hyde,	Bath,	500
Priscilla Hallett,	Augusta,	1,100
Priscilla P. Lunt,	Bowdoinham,	100
Adam Lemont, trustees,	Bath,	600
Thomas Lambard,	do.	1,300
William Ledyard,	do.	1,200
Parker McCobb,	Portland,	5,000
Ammi R. Mitchell,	Bath,	100
John Masters,	do.	4,200
James F. Mustard,	Topsham,	100
Elmira Merritt,	Brunswick,	300
James F. Patten,	Bath,	2,000
H. E. Purrington,	Bowdoinham,	800
Eunice Purrington,	do.	200
Nathaniel Purrington,	do.	200
Sarah Purrington, trustee,	Topsham,	600

Lincoln Bank, (Continued.)

Names.	Residence.	Amount of Stock.
Charity M. Jameson,	Topsham,	100
Abel Merrill,	do.	1,000
Isaac Merritt,	Bath,	500
James McKeen,	Topsham,	1,500
Joseph McKeen,	Brunswick,	500
Noble Maxwell,	Boston,	1,800
Asa Palmer,	Gorham,	3,000
Joshua Page,	Bath,	5,000
George F. Patten,	do.	10,000
John Patten,	do.	5,000
William Patten,	Richmond,	1,300
William Purington,	Bowdoinham,	2,300
John Parsons,	Phipsburg,	1,000
Isabella Parsons,	Unknown,	800
Samuel Perkins,	Topsham,	900
William Richardson,	Bath,	1,000
William M. Rogers,	do.	700
Daniel Robbins, Jr.,	do.	600
Thomas M. Reed,	Phipsburg,	1,000
Joseph Sewall, guardian,	Bath,	200
Joseph Sewall,	do.	100
Elizabeth Stetson,	do.	1,500
Jacob Smith,	Wiscasset,	300
John Smith,	Bath,	200
Charles Thompson,	Topsham,	1,000
Ezekiel Tarbox,	Westport,	1,800
Cornelius Tarbox,	do.	500
Samuel Tarbox,	do.	500
Paul C. Tibbetts,	Lisbon,	1,000
Senaca White,	Marshfield,	1,000
		$100,000

Kenduskeag Bank, (Bangor.)

Names.	Residence.	Amount of Stock.
Abner Taylor,	Bangor,	500
John Wilkins,	do.	100
G. A. Pierce, trustee,	Frankfort,	1,300
Wiggins Hill,	Bangor,	300
Maria H. Sandford,	do.	300
John Godfrey,	do.	100
Charles Stetson,	do.	700
G. W. Pickering,	do.	17,800
Timothy Crosby,	do.	300
S. Rich, Jr.,	do.	2,000
Kenduskeag Bank,	do.	54,300
Humphrey Hight,	Wayne,	200
A. L. Vaughan,	Unknown,	100
J. P. Veasie,	Bangor,	500
Jerusha Head, adm'x,	Portland,	1,000
Hannah Robinson,	Union,	200
S. J. Bowles,	Roxbury, Mass.,	4,000
Jotham Moulton,	Bucksport,	2,000
Silas Pierce & Co.,	Boston,	2,000
Joseph Hay,	do.	2,000
James Longley,	do.	2,000
Traders' Bank,	do.	1,500
John Fiske,	Bangor,	300
James Brooks,	Orrington,	300
Amasa Bartlett,	do.	200
Samuel Bartlett,	do.	200
Nathaniel B. March,	Portsmouth, N. H.,	1,500
Izette Shaw,	do.	1,000
Joshua Blake,	Boston,	1,200
Samuel Moody,	Newburyport,	300
Mary J. Moody,	do.	300
Eunice Moody,	do.	300
Sarah B. Moody,	do.	300
Sophronia L. Moody,	do.	300
John H. Moody,	do.	200
John Balch,	do.	300
Thomas Burton,	Warren,	100
		$100,000

Lime Rock Bank, (Thomaston.)

Names.	Residence.	Amount of Stock.
Michael Achorn,	Thomaston,	500
Philip Achorn,	do.	300
L. B. Allen,	do.	400
Butler & Kimball,	do.	100
Anson Butler,	do.	400
Wm. Branton,	do.	300
Ephraim Barrett,	do.	100
John S. Coburn,	do.	300
Joseph Condon,	do.	500
John H. Counce,	Warren,	500
Nancy Creighton,	do.	700
William Cole,	Thomaston,	500
Knott Crockett,	do.	4,200
Benj. Crabtree,	Vinalhaven.	1,000
Jesse Calderwood,	do.	300
Oliver Crockett,	do.	100
James Crockett,	do.	900
Rebecca Crockett,	Thomaston,	300
Daniel Day,	Newcastle,	1,000
Nathan Daniels,	Union,	200
Joseph Daniels,	do.	100
Edmund Daggett,	Camden,	500
Mary T. Fogg,	Thomaston,	100
John Gregory, Jr.,	do.	500
Hanson Gregory,	Camden,	400
William Gregory,	do.	800
Susan Glover,	Vinalhaven,	200
Margaret George	Thomaston,	500
William Hovey.	Warren,	200
Elijah Glover,	Vinalhaven,	1,000
Joseph Gilchrist,	Thomaston,	400
John M. Hunt,	do.	1,000
Charles Holmes,	do.	500
Joseph Hewett,	do.	1,200
P. A. Hewett,	do.	200
Susan F. Huse,	Warren,	200
Ann M. Huse,	do.	200
Jona. Huse,	do.	100
Coit Ingraham,	Thomaston,	400
Joseph Ingraham, 2d,	do.	1,000

4*

Lime Rock Bank, (Continued.)

Names.	Residence.	Amount of Stock.
Barnard Ingraham,	Thomaston,	200
Patrick Keagan,	Boston,	500
Iddo Kimball,	Thomaston,	2,500
Iddo K. Kimball,	do.	600
Samuel Libby,	do.	800
Eliza Lovejoy,	do.	600
Eliza A. Lovejoy,	do.	500
John G. Lovejoy,	do.	500
H. C. Lowell,	do.	600
John Lermond,	Warren,	1,000
Lewis Leadbetter,	Vinalhaven,	300
Reuben Leadbetter,	do.	500
Jno. Little,	Union,	400
Nancy Lermond,	do.	800
William Malcom,	Cushing,	400
Wm. McLoon,	Thomaston,	1,000
S. F. Morse & Co.,	Boston,	1,300
Jno. Payson,	Union,	500
James Partridge,	Thomaston,	300
Jno. Pillsbury,	do.	1,000
Hezekiah Prince's estate,	do.	200
Jno. G. Paine, estate,	do.	500
Nathaniel Robbins,	Union,	500
Aaron Starrett,	Warren,	300
William Singer,	do.	500
Orrin O. Stewart,	Union,	200
Israel Snow,	Thomaston,	700
Isabella Starr,	do.	100
Edward Spear,	Warren,	300
Henrietta Prince,	do.	300
A. G. Spear,	Thomaston,	300
Reuben Shearer,	do.	1,500
John Spear, Jr.,	do.	1,700
A. G. Spaulding,	do.	400
Wm. F. Tilson,	do.	800
George Thomas,	do.	700
Peggy Thomas,	do.	500
Jno. Tolman,	Camden,	100
Samuel Tolman,	do.	500
White, Stedman & Co.,	Boston,	200

Lime Rock Bank, (Continued.)

Names.	Residence.	Amount of Stock.
Josiah Tolman,	Thomaston,	1,000
Charles Thorndike,	do.	300
Barnabas Webb,	do.	500
Jno. Whitmore,	Hope,	500
Lydia Wooster,	Vinalhaven,	700
Jane Wooster,	do.	100
H. L. & P. Wooster,		200
		$50,000

Manufacturers' Bank, (Saco.)

Trustees of Thornton Acad,	Saco,	1,300
George H. Adams,	Biddeford,	500
Alvan Bacon,	Scarborough,	200
Samuel Batchelder,	Cambridge, Mass.,	5,300
Moses Bradbury,	Biddeford,	1,000
Edward R. Bradbury,	Saco,	1,000
John A. Berry, executor,	do.	200
John A. Berry,	do.	100
John C Bradbury,	do.	700
Alvan Bacon, Jr.,	Boston,	1,000
Sarah Bacon,	Scarborough,	500
John D. Boothby,	Limington,	1,000
John M. Batchelder,	Saco,	100
Thomas Bickford,	do.	100
Edward R. Cogswell,	Unknown,	1,200
Margaret E. Cogswell,	do.	600
John Cranch,	do.	200
Barnabus E. Cutter,	Saco,	300
Josiah Calef,	do.	100
Amos Chase,	do.	200
Mary A. Cutts,	do.	300
Thomas Cutts, estate,	do.	100
Abraham Cutter,	do.	300
Bracy Curtis,	Kennebunk,	500
Mehitable Curtis,	do.	500

Manufacturers' Bank, (Continued.)

Names.	Residence.	Amount of stock.
Wm. R. K. Douglass and Alex. Gordon, executors,	London, Eng.,	1,800
Isaac Deering,	Waterborough,	500
Benjamin Day,	New York,	1,300
Wm. Deering,	Saco,	200
Nathan Elden,	Buxton,	400
Hannah Elden,	do.	800
Samuel Emery, Jr.,	Biddeford,	600
Ralph Emery,	do.	300
Sarah S. Emery,	Boston, Mass.,	400
David Fernald,	Saco,	1,300
Loring French,	do.	3,400
Albert W. Fisk,	Unknown,	600
John W. Foster,	Portsmouth, N. H.,	200
Mary A. Foster,	do.	1,500
Frances Fernald,	do.	800
Henry Flagg,	Bangor,	600
Elizabeth Goldthwait,	Biddeford,	400
Elizabeth M. Goodwin,	do.	100
Ellen W. Goodwin,	Unknown,	200
J. Goodwin,	Somersworth, N.H.,	2,000
Philip Greely,	Portland,	300
Lucia A. Greene,	Cambridgeport, Ms.,	400
Hugh W. Greene,	do.	900
Davis Googins,	Saco,	600
Mary E. Gilpatrick,	do.	100
Haven & Co.,	New York,	2,000
John Haven, estate,	Portsmouth, N. H.,	2,000
A. W. & E. W. Haven, trustees,	do.	500
Elisha Hill,	do.	2,000
Ezekiel Hurd,	Dover, N. H.,	500
Francis B. Hayes,	Boston,	1,700
Elizabeth Hooper,	Saco,	900
Wm. P. Haines,	do.	
Robert Jameson,	do.	100
Tristram Jordan,	do.	300
Tristram Jordan, Jr.,	do.	500
Rebecca Kittridge,	Portsmouth, N. H.,	300
		500

Manufacturers' Bank, (Continued.)

Names.	Residence.	Amount of Stock.
Samuel Lord and J. W. Foster, trustees,	Portsmouth, N. H.,	1,500
Oliver Libby,	Parsonsfield,	500
Rebecca McCobb,	Portland,	500
Mutual Fire Insurance Co.,	Saco,	200
William Murch,	Biddeford,	1,000
Asaph Moody,	Kennebunkport,	1,000
Marine Society,	Newburyport,	3,000
Sarah and Elizabeth Moody,	Saco,	200
Dorcas Merrill,	do.	200
Sarah P. Moulton,	do.	100
Eunice C. Nye,	do.	1,000
Abel L. Pierson,	Salem, Mass.,	1,000
Wm. Pike's estate,	Saco,	1,200
Horatio N. Perkins,	Charlestown, Mass.,	1,000
Eliphalet Perkins' estate,	Kennebunkport,	2,000
Eunice Perkins,	do.	500
Jott S. Perkins,	do.	500
Stephen Pearse,	Portsmouth, N. H.,	1,000
Susan Parker,	do.	500
M. W. & J. W. Pierce,	do.	2,000
William Rice,	do.	2,600
James Rundlett,	do.	2,500
James Sheafe's estate,	do.	4,000
George Scammon,	Saco,	100
Hannah Smith,	do.	100
James Smith,	Biddeford,	500
Samuel Storer,	do.	100
Alfred Smith,	Durham, N. H.,	200
Miranda Stone,	Kennebunkport,	1,000
Mary E. Stone,	do.	2,000
Maria H. Sandford,	Unknown,	400
Isaac Sturdivant,	Portland,	1,200
Olive Sawyer,	Saco,	100
Saco & Biddeford Savings Ins.,	do.	4,800
Nancy B. Thatcher,	Newburport,	800
Sarah Thornton, estate,	Saco,	3,400
Mary C. Thornton,	do.	1,400
David Tompkins,	Dover, N. H.,	1,000
George Toppan,	Saco,	500

Manufacturers' Bank, (Continued.)

Names.	Residence.	Amount of Stock.
Nathaniel M. Towle,	Saco,	1,100
Twambley & Smith,	Portsmouth, N. H.,	500
Levi Woodbury,	do.	1,800
Sarah Williams,	Wayland, Mass.,	500
George A. Williams,	do.	500
Estate of Lewis Wakefield,	Saco,	1,400
Samuel Whitten,	do.	600
James Weston,	Unknown,	200
		$100,000

Manufacturers' and Traders' Bank, (Portland.)

Frances Baker,	Portland,	150
Clarissa Brooks,	do.	100
Henrietta L. Brooks, minor,	do.	250
Eleanor T. Brooks, minor,	do.	250
Elizabeth M. Brooks, minor,		250
Henry T. Brooks, minor,	do.	250
Benjamin Chadbourne,	Standish,	100
Benj. P. Chamberlain,	Salem, Mass.,	1,000
Asa Clapp,	Portland,	1,100
Charity Fund, First Parish,	do.	250
Neal Dow,	do.	1,400
Cyprus Eustis,	Dixfield,	150
John D. Gardner,	Boston,	750
Joseph B. Gardner,	New York,	150
Deborah Gardner,	Exeter, N. H.,	250
Jane Gardner,	Portland,	200
Sarah M. Gilman,	do.	50
A. & S. H. Gilman, minors,	do.	150
Sophia Gilpatrick,	Kennebunk,	250
Frances Gould,	do.	150
Samuel M. Gould,	Norristown,	2,700
William E. Greeley,	Boston,	250
Pamela Hanford, estate,	St. John,	700
Horace Harvey,	Portland,	150
Polly Hobart, deceased,		1,750

Manufacturers' and Traders' Bank, (Continued.)

Names.	Residence.	Amount of Stock.
Rufus Horton,	Portland,	2,800
Horton & Towbridge,	do.	750
Isaac Ilsley,	do.	1,250
Parker Ilsley,	do.	750
Maria W. Jones,	Philadelphia,	500
Caleb Jones,	Unknown,	250
Moses F. Kimball,	Rumford,	300
Joseph Leavitt,	Portland,	200
Mary J. Lewis,	Gorham,	250
Harriet S. Libby,	Portland,	50
Barak Littlefield,	do.	50
Solomon Loring, minor,	Cumberland,	100
Albert Loring, minor,	do.	150
Emma Loring, minor,	do.	100
Anna G. Loring, minor,	do.	100
J. McKeen and E. Everett, ex'rs,	Brunswick,	400
Sarah Martin,	Portland,	800
Pamela Martin,	do.	800
Eleazer McKenney,	do.	100
Lucy McLellan,	do.	500
Maria A. Mead, minor,	Gorham,	500
Caroline M. Mellen,	Unknown,	200
Henry B. Minot,	Portland,	100
Happy Morss,	do.	600
F. S. Nichols, C. G. Nichols, N. G. Nichols and P. M. Nichols,	do.	150
Mutual Insurance Co.,	do.	400
Ocean Insurance Co.,	do.	8,150
Samuel Paine,	Gorham,	250
Samuel Parris,	Washington, D. C.,	750
Ann L. Paysen,	Portland,	750
Lydia C. Pease,	Westbrook,	150
Catharine B. Pease, minor,	do.	550
Plummer & Moor,	Portland,	250
William P. Preble,	do.	1,600
Mary Preble,	do.	1,500
Lucy Phinney,	Gorham,	600
Bowdoin College,	Brunswick,	5,550
Canal Bank,	Portland,	600

Manufacturers' and Traders' Bank, (Continued.)

Names.	Residence.	Amount of Stock.
Merchants' Bank,	Portland,	500
Casco Bank,	do.	1,050
Manufac. and Tra. Bank, trust.,	do.	7,450
Joshua Richardson,	do.	1,100
Eunice Richardson,	Salem, Mass.,	2,100
Toppan Robie,	Gorham,	1,650
Thomas S. Robie, minor,	do.	250
Benj. A. Robie, minor,	do.	250
Lucinda E. Robie, minor,	do.	250
Charles G. Robinson, minor,	Portland,	200
Lucy Sewall,	Kennebunk,	150
Narcissa Sewall,	do.	150
Eveline Sewall,	do.	150
Harriet M. Smith,	Portland,	500
Isaac Sturdivant,	Unknown,	750
Susan Sumner,	Portland,	100
Portland Benevolent Society,	do.	1,050
Marine Society,	do.	1,000
American Education Society,		400
Maine Missionary Society,		350
Samuel Trask,	Portland,	500
Helen Trask,	Calais,	500
Martha Trask,	Portland,	500
Jonathan Tucker,	do.	1,250
Phinehas Varnum,	do.	1,150
Stephen Waite's estate,	do.	200
Stephen Waite,	do.	300
Nathan Winslow,	do.	150
George Warren,	do.	1,000
Samuel Weed,	do.	100
Ezekiel Whitman,	do.	250
Benjamin Willis,	Boston,	3,000
Christopher Wright,	Portland,	600
Ashur Ware,	do.	500
		$75,000

Mariners' Bank, (Wiscasset.)

Names.	Residence.	Amount of Stock.
Samuel Alley,	Dresden,	600
Edward H. Hall,	do.	400
Charles Thayer,	do.	200
Nathaniel Stone,	Gardiner,	500
Hannah Miller,	Wiscasset,	200
Isaac Coffin,	do.	500
Elisha J. Taylor,	do.	200
William Elmes,	do.	200
Wilmot Wood,	do.	400
Tempe Lee's estate,	do.	1,000
Henry Clark,	do.	300
Silas L. Young,	do.	100
William Stacy,	do.	100
Philip E. Theobald,	do.	200
Lydia T. Wood,	Hallowell,	400
Barker Neal,	Wiscasset,	100
Patrick Lenox,	do.	400
Isaac Lincoln's estate,	do.	100
John and Wm. R. Young,	do.	100
Wiscasset Female Asylum,	do.	500
Isabella Coffin,	do.	100
Lydia R. and Lucy Smith,	do.	600
Mary Plummer,	do.	200
Samuel E. Smith,	do.	700
Freeman Parker,	do.	300
John Brooks,	do.	1,800
S P. Parker, cashier,	do.	4,000
Martha W. Barrett,	do.	400
Jonathan Pierce,	Boothbay,	400
Silas Lewis,	do.	500
Allen Lewis,	do.	400
Ebenezer Hodge,	Edgecomb,	200
William Hodge,	do.	200
Thomas Parsons,	do.	100
John H. Sheppard,	Boston,	7,000
R. H. McKown,	Bath,	1,000
Addison D. Fisher,	Arrowsic,	500
Lincoln Webb,	Woolwich,	200
Wm. & Andrew Adams,	Boothbay,	100
Robert Sproul,	do.	200

5

Mariners' Bank, (Continued.)

Names.	Residence.	Amount of Stock
Spencer Clefford,	Edgecomb,	400
Jane F. Richards,	Wiscasset,	100
Elisha Palmer,	Unknown,	500
Martha Hedge,	Woolwich,	500
Thomas Hodgdon,	Boothbay,	300
Samuel Tarbox,	Westport,	900
James McCarty,	do.	600
Sarah Knight,	do.	100
Martha Jane McCarty,	do.	200
Abaline R. Greenleaf,	do.	300
Stephen Lewis,	Whitefield,	400
Thaddeus Weeks,	Jefferson,	1,500
Jane Decker,	Alna,	500
Joseph Decker,	do.	300
Jotham Donnell,	do.	1,200
Oakes Rundlett's estate,	do.	1,000
Mashall S. Hagar,	Richmond,	1,000
Seneca White,	Marshfield,	1,200
C. & W. B. Wilkins,	Boston,	400
Theophilus P. Kendall,	do.	500
Sargent S. Littlehale,	do.	1,000
Joseph Langdon,	Wiscasset,	300
Joseph Ballister,	Boston,	200
Atkins & Stedman,	do.	200
Isaac Richardson,	Unknown,	10,000
Bernard C. Bailey,	Bath,	400
Sarah Hager,	Littleton, Mass.,	500
G. W. Philbrick,	China,	100
		$50,000

Mercantile Bank, (Bangor.)

Amos M. Roberts,	Bangor,	550
John Hodgdon,	Hodgdon, Me.,	50
Samuel Farrar,	Bangor,	7,150
Henry Warren,	do.	3,650
Oliver Frost,	do.	7,150

Mercantile Bank, (Continued.)

Names	Residence.	Amount of Stock.
E. Gilman Rawson,	Bangor,	50
Moses Woodward,	do.	50
James Jenkins,	do.	5,000
S. K. Howard,	do.	1,250
John S. Kimball,	do.	1,250
Isaac H. Parker,	Boston,	2,500
Mercantile Bank,	Bangor,	19,300
Asa Warren,	Guilford,	1,900
John Mills, treasurer,	Bradley,	150
		$50,000

Merchants' Bank, (Portland.)

Joseph S. Adams,	Hebron, N. H.,	6,150
John Anderson, guardian,	Portland,	225
Portland Academy,	do.	375
John Anderson, trustee,	do.	975
Fayette Bartlett,	New Bedford, Mass.	1,200
Francis Baker,	Portland,	150
Thomas Browne,	do.	750
Joseph Barbour,	Gorham,	1,500
Harrison Brazier,	Portland,	750
Dorcas Bagley,	do.	150
Portland Benevolent Society,	do.	375
Samuel Chadwick,	do.	7,500
Samuel Chase,	do.	375
Charity Fund, First Parish,	do.	2,025
Edward F. Cutter,	Warren,	375
Bowdoin College,	Brunswick,	1,500
Eben D. Choate,	Portland,	300
Harriet Capen,	do.	150
Moses Clark,	do.	225
C. S. Daveis,	do.	750
Phinehas Drinkwater,	do.	2,250
Josiah Dow,	do.	1,950
Neal Dow,	do.	1,800
Ezekiel Day's estate,	do.	1,425

Merchants' Bank, (Continued.)

Names.	Residence.	Amount of Stock.
Nicholas Emery,	Portland,	1,050
Rufus Emerson,	do.	1,950
William Evans,	do.	750
Female Charitable Society,	do.	525
Thomas Forsaith,	do.	750
James Furbish, guardian,	do.	1,200
Eliphalet Greely,	do.	1,350
Philip Greely,	do.	1,800
Ministerial Fund,	Gorham,	450
Jonathan Greely,	Cumberland,	150
Sarah Greely,	Portland,	1,275
Byron Greenough,	do.	75
Mary Garland,		375
William Goodenow,	Portland,	525
Polly Hobart's estate,	do.	7,500
Martha C. Hall,	do.	525
Joel Hall,	do.	450
Elizabeth W. Howard,		2,775
Isaac & Elizabeth Hopkins,	New Portland,	750
Samuel Hanson, guardian,	Portland,	1,200
Augustine Haines,	do.	225
Thomas Hammond,	do.	450
Daniel Hood,	do.	300
Isaac Ilsley,	do.	3,600
Mary C. Jordan,	do.	375
James C. Jordon,	do.	225
Sarah Jewett,	do.	1,425
Ruth Jewett,	do.	1,275
Joseph S. Jewett,	Gorham,	750
Ocean Insurance Company,	Portland,	11,700
Portland M. Fire Ins. Co.,	do.	2,025
Charles Jordan,	do.	225
Charles Kimball,	do.	450
Stephen Longfellow,	do.	750
Elizabeth P. Lewis,	do.	150
Sarah K. Lewis,	do.	75
Isaac Lincoln,	Brunswick,	2,175
David Morton,		225
Daniel Mountfort,	Portland,	750
Eben. McIntosh,	do.	375

Merchants' Bank, (Continued.)

Names.	Residence.	Amount of Stock.
Portland Marine Society,	Portland,	1,125
Thomas S. Minot,	do.	300
Robert A. Merrill,	Falmouth,	375
Lucy S. Moody,	Portland,	300
P. D. & Co. Merchants' Bank,	do.	750
P. D. & Co. Manufacturers' and Traders' Bank,	do.	1,050
Eliza Mayo,	do.	450
Hannah Martin,	do.	300
Sarah Martin,	do.	375
Pamela Martin,	do.	375
Trustees Ministerial Fund,	North Yarmouth,	300
Joshua B. Osgood,	Portland,	825
Elizabeth G. Oxnard,	do.	450
Harriet C. Oxnard,	do.	450
Ann M. Oxnard,	do.	450
Martha P. Oxnard,	do.	225
Edward Oxnard,	do.	1,875
Richard K. Porter,	do.	1,725
Barrett Potter,	do.	2,025
John Potter,	Augusta,	600
Ann Quincy,	Portland,	1,350
Mary L. Quincy,	do.	450
Israel Richardson,	do.	3,300
Chandler Rackleff,	Westbrook,	375
Mary C. Robinson,	Portland,	675
Charles D. Robinson,	do.	1,125
Toppan Robie,	Gorham,	4,275
Edward Robie,	do.	525
Lucinda A. Robie, minor,	do.	
Thomas A. Robie, minor,	do.	375
Benj. A. Robie, minor,	do.	
Susan Sumner,	Portland,	450
Isaac Sturdivant,	Cumberland,	4,875
Elizabeth Stevens,	Portland,	750
William Swan,	do.	900
Horatio Southgate, trustee,	do.	4,950
Jona. Stephens,	do.	300
Horatio Southgate,	do.	900
Jona. Tucker,	do.	4,725

5*

Merchants' Bank, (Continued.)

Names.	Residence.	Amount of stock.
Heirs of George Titcomb,	Cumberland,	600
Helen Trask,	Portland,	1,650
Martha Trask,	do.	750
George Turner,	do.	1,200
Thomas C. Upham,	Brunswick,	1,500
William Woodbury,	Portland,	2,325
George Warren,	do.	1,575
Stephen Waite's estate,	do.	525
Joshua Wingate, Jr.'s estate,	do.	1,125
Mary C. Webster,	do.	375
Adam Wilson,	do.	525
Joseph Weeks,	do.	750
Ezekiel Whitman,	do.	1,500
Benjamin Willis,	Boston,	2,400
Mary Webb,	Portland,	150
Harrison Whitman,	do.	675
Ashur Ware,	do.	1,200
Deacons 1st Church in York,	York,	375
		$150,000

* Medomak Bank, (Waldoborough.)

James Hovey,	Waldoborough,	10,000
George Sproul,	do.	1,000
John Bulfinch,	do.	2,500
Frederic Castner,	do.	500
William Groton,	do.	4,000
Samuel Morse,	do.	1,700
Christian Schwier,	do.	600
Charles Miller,	do.	500
Martin Demuth,	do.	500
Gorham P. Smouse,	do.	300
J. & R. Miller,	do.	300
Rebecca Elwell,	do.	200
George Benner,	do.	300
Henry Kennedy,	do.	500
George D. Smouse,	do.	2,600

Medomak Bank, (Continued.)

Names.	Residence.	Amount of Stock.
Charles M. Reed,	Boston,	1,200
James Herbert,	Waldoborough,	200
Sarah Suckforth,	do.	200
Alexander Palmer,	do.	200
Cephas Cole,	do.	200
James Hovee, trustee,	do.	300
Samuel Porter,	Philadelphia,	400
Edward Benner,	Waldoborough,	500
Jacob Sprague,	do.	100
Benjamin Wellman,	Bremen,	100
Frederic Hahn,	do.	200
John Seiders,	Waldoborough,	300
John Kaler, Jr.,	do.	500
Ezekiel Winslow,	do.	500
James N. Stimson,	Boston,	200
Avery Trouant,	Bremen,	200
William H. Miller,	Friendship,	100
Frederic Benner,	Waldoborough,	100
William H. Little's estate,	Bremen,	100
Charles Benner, 2d,	Waldoborough,	100
Thomas Johnson,	Bremen,	1,000
John Studley,	Friendship,	600
Benjamin Eugely,	Nobleborough,	300
John T. Castner,	Waldoborough,	500
Jacob Bornheimer, Jr.,	do.	200
Deborah Burge,	New Hampshire,	300
Josiah A. Winslow,	Nobleborough,	400
Anna Johnson,	Bremen,	1,000
William Kennedy,	Jefferson,	200
Sawyer & Williams,	Boston,	100
Charles Welt,	Waldoborough,	300
Mary Groton,	do.	300
Charles L. Kaler,	do.	200
John Kaler, Jr.,	do.	500
Rhoda Little,	Bremen,	200
James Hovey, trustee,	Waldoborough,	1,400
Harriet A. Levensaler,	do.	100
Joseph Bornheimer,	do.	200
Dorothy Eugely,	do.	100
Arthur Child,	Unknown,	1,000

Medomak Bank, (Continued.)

Names.	Residence.	Amount of Stock.
Mary J. Morse,	Waldoborough,	400
Rebecca Hovey,	Dracut, Mass.,	5,000
Seville Starrett,	Unknown,	200
Christian Borheimer, Jr.,	Waldoborough,	300
Moses Studley,	Friendship,	200
Gilbert Wellman,	Bremen,	100
William Jordan,	Friendship,	100
Francis Gracia,	Cushing,	500
Charles P. & J. H. Willett,	Waldoborough,	200
Peter Mink,	do.	200
Sally G. Elwell,	do.	300
Sarah E. Allen,	do.	200
David M. Mitchell,	Portland,	200
Andrew Sides,	Waldoborough,	300
Henry Robinson,	Friendship,	100
Joseph Clark,	Waldoborough,	300
James Hovey, adm'r,	do.	1,500
John Robinson,	Friendship,	100
Otis Miller,	Waldoborough,	200
		$50,000

Megunticook Bank, (Camden.)

Samuel G. Adams,	Camden,	2,000
Joseph Ames,	Matinicus,	400
John Athearn,	Hope,	1,000
Nathan Brown,	Camden,	500
Nathan Barrett,	New York,	500
William Blake,	Camden,	200
Hosea Bates,	do.	100
Samuel Bragdon,	do.	100
Jonathan Corthell,	do.	400
Benjamin Crabtree,	do.	500
Benjamin Cushing,	do.	500
James Calderwood,	do.	100
Silas Clark,	do.	500
David Conner,	Montville,	200

Megunticook Bank, (Continued.)

Names.	Residence.	Amount of Stock.
Robert Chase,	Camden, .	200
William Carleton's estate,	do.	2,800
Samuel D. Carleton,	do.	300
Charles A. Carleton,	do.	700
Boyce Crane,	Hope,	200
Charles Drinkwater,	Northport,	100
Joseph H. Esterbrook,	Camden,	200
Abigail S. Eells,	do.	100
Nathaniel T. Eaton,	do.	300
Samuel Emerson,	do.	200
Joel Fay,	Boston,	700
Elijah Glover,	Camden,	500
John Glover,	do.	200
Erastus Gurney,	Hope,	400
Isaac Hobbs,	Hope,	100
Jonas Howe,	Camden,	100
Robert Harkness,	do.	200
Joseph Jones,	do.	1,800
Benjamin Jones,	Lincolnville,	100
George's Insurance Co.,	Thomaston,	1,700
Abram T. Jacobs,	Vinalhaven,	100
Jonas Knight,	Lincolnville,	200
Bezealer Knight, treas. 2d Par.,	Camden,	900
Betsey Knight,	Lincolnville,	300
William Kidder,	do.	200
David Lane's estate,	Camden,	200
John Moody,	Searsmont,	300
Joseph W. Moody,	do.	300
Patience Moody,	do.	200
Daniel Moody,	Appleton,	500
Deborah Norwood,	Camden,	500
Megunticook Bank,	do.	6,300
Isaac Pendleton,	do.	1,400
Charles Pendleton,	do.	300
Abigail S. Piper,	Camden,	200
Charles R. Porter,	do.	300
James Richards,	do.	500
John Pickens,	Boston,	1,900
Lemuel Rich,	Hope,	400
Benjamin P. Richardson,	Boston,	800

Megunticook Bank, (Continued.)

Names.	Residence.	Amount of Stock
J. Richardson & Brothers,	Boston,	500
Deborah Robbins,	Union,	200
N. Sylvester & Sons,	Lincolnville,	1,000
Reuben Safford, Jr.,	Hope,	1,400
Benjamin Safford,	do.	500
James P. Safford,	do.	500
Ignatius Sherman,	Camden,	1,200
William Simonton, estate,	do.	100
William Simonton,	do.	1,100
Abram Simonton,	do.	300
Joseph Sherman,	do.	2,000
Joseph C. Stetson,	do.	1,000
James Sherman,	Islesborough,	500
William M. Stedman, & Co.,	Boston,	1,500
Jonathan Thayer,	Camden,	300
Betsey Thomas,	do.	200
Jacob Trafton,	do.	500
John Whitmore,	Lincolnville,	500
Samuel A. Whitney,	do.	1,000
Wetherell & Whitney,	Boston,	400
James White,	Belfast,	600
		$49,000

Northern Bank, (Hallowell.)

John Agry,	Hallowell,	1,500
Jesse Aiken,	do.	1,000
Augustus Alden,	do.	500
James Blish,	do.	1,500
Smith C. Cox,	do.	1,000
Nathaniel Davenport,	do.	300
W. Emmons,	do.	700
A. W. Fuller,	Boston,	1,000
F. Glazier,	Hallowell,	1,300
Julia Glazier,	do.	800
Samuel C. Grant,	do.	2,000
John Gardner,	do.	100

Northern Bank, (Continued.)

Names.	Residence.	Amount of Stock.
S. Kendall,	Hallowell,	300
Augustine Lord,	do.	100
Andrew Masters,	do.	2,500
Richard Macy,	Vassalborough,	200
B. Nason,	Hallowell,	500
Henry Nason,	New York,	2,700
Oliver Otis, estate,	Hallowell,	500
William Holly,	Farmington,	500
John S. R. Brown,	Loudon, N. H.,	5,000
Fanny Bartlett,		2,000
R. K. Page.	Hallowell,	2,000
Enoch Jewett,	Pittston,	3,000
P. Sanford,	Hallowell,	500
Alden Samson,	do.	1,000
Lydia A. White,	do.	300
Martha W. Whittier,	do.	1,000
Samuel Wells,	Portland,	1,100
L. A. Wells, wife of S. Wells,	do.	1,000
Sarah Vaughan,	Hallowell,	1,400
Hallowell Academy,	do.	1,800
Sam'l Wells and Isaac Gage, executors,	Portland and Augusta,	1,600
Alfred Alley,	Vassalborough,	2,500
Robert Alley,	do.	200
Jacob Abbot,	Farmington,	4,500
David Brown,	Readfield,	100
Caroline P. Bement,	Bangor,	500
Lucretia F. Bond,	do.	1,000
John Collins,	New York,	1,900
Isaac Coffin,	Wiscasset,	500
C. Curtis,	Boston,	1,000
R. Richards, Jr.,	do.	2,500
P. Sprague,	do.	500
Gardiner Savings Institution,	Gardiner,	5,400
Nancy Grant,	do.	3,400
Judah McLellan,	Bloomfield,	100
John McLellan,	Connecticut,	900
E. Pettengill,	Livermore,	500
Hannah Robinson,	Mt. Vernon,	200
S. Sewall,	Winthrop,	4,100

Northern Bank, (Continued.)

Names.	Residence.	Amount of Stock.
H. Sewall, estate,	Augusta,	400
John Stratton,	Boston,	1,900
W. G. Brooks,	do.	300
Petty Vaughan,	London, Eng.,	900
James Fillebrown,	Readfield,	500
Mary Chandler,	Bath,	500
		$75,000

Sagadahock Bank, (Bath.)

Names.	Residence.	Amount of Stock.
Joseph Berry,	Georgetown,	1,200
James Bowker.	Phipsburg,	300
Lewis Blackmer,	Bath,	2,600
J. & W. Barron,	Topsham,	3,000
Thomas S. Bowles,	Bath,	600
James Cushing.	Phipsburg,	200
Jeremiah Clough,	Topsham,	500
William Crawford,	Bath,	700
Mary Chandler,	Unknown,	600
William Dennett,	Topsham,	1,600
James Drummond,	Phipsburg,	600
William Donnell,	Bath,	1,200
A. R. Delano,	Georgetown,	500
Caleb Fuller,	Unknown,	500
Mary A. French,	do.	100
Willard Gray,	do.	3,800
E. W. K. Groton,	Bath,	400
John Henry,	do.	1,000
Edward A. Hodgkins,	do.	300
Jonathan Hyde,	do.	400
A. M. T. Hyde,	do.	1,000
S. S. Hawes,	do.	200
Joshua Haskell,	Topsham,	1,500
E. Kittredge,	Unknown,	1,000
Eunice D. Knight,	do.	100
William Ledyard,	do.	100
Abner Lowell,	Phipsburg,	200

Sagadahok Bank, (Continued.)

Names.	Residence.	Amount of Stock.
M. J. Ledyard,	Bath,	400
Palmer & Ledyard,	do.	400
James McClellan,	do.	300
W. V. & O. Moses,	do.	1,300
Henry Merrit,	Harpswell,	200
Eunice Purington,	Unknown,	500
Wm. Purington, for the B. V. Church Bowdoinham,	Bowdoinham,	500
Charles W. Patten,	Georgetown,	200
William Purington,	Bowdoinham,	3,300
Caroline C. Prescott,	Bath,	400
Humphrey Purington,	Bowdoinham,	1,200
William Richardson,	Bath,	1,100
James Riggs,	Georgetown,	500
William M. Reed,	Bath,	700
Benjamin Riggs,	Georgetown,	1,800
Moses Riggs,	do.	500
Thomas D. Robinson,	Bath,	900
D. Robbins,	do.	300
George Rogers,	Topsham,	200
James M. Soule,	Unknown,	200
Joseph Sewall,	Bath,	1,300
John Smith,	do.	1,700
Jacob Smith,	Wiscasset,	500
D. Scribner,	Topsham,	2,000
Isaiah Snow,	Harpswell,	400
Mary P. Snow,	do.	400
Joanna Torrey,	Bath,	700
Charles Thompson,	Topsham,	2,000
Samuel Thompson,	do.	1,100
J. Winslow, Jr.,	Bath,	1,300
E. Waldron,	Wiscasset,	200
L. Webb,	Woolwich,	300
		$50,000

South Berwick Bank.

Names.	Residence.	Amount of Stock.
Hannah Brown,	South Berwick,	200
Margaret E. Cogswell,	Portland,	500
Edward R. Cogswell, minor,	do.	1,000
Samuel Fernald,	Kittery,	600
Jordan Goodwin's estate,	South Berwick,	1,300
Ruth Griffin,	Durham, N. H.,	100
George Goodwin,	South Berwick,	900
Sarah Hayman,	do.	650
Philip Hall,	North Berwick,	500
Hannah Silsbee Hoag,	do.	1,500
Abby M. Hoag,	do.	550
James Hobbs,	South Berwick,	700
Albert J. Hoag,	Philadelphia,	1,300
Wm. A. Hayes,	South Berwick,	250
William Hight,	do.	950
Nathaniel Hobbs,	North Berwick,	1,500
Elisha Hill,	Portsmouth, N. H.,	750
Francis B. Hayes,	Boston,	3,750
Joseph Hilliard's estate,	Berwick,	500
Jeremiah Goodwin,	Somersworth,	1,200
T. F. & T Jewett,	South Berwick,	100
Edwin Leigh,	Bristol, R. I.,	1,250
Nancy Leigh,	do.	1,750
Benjamin Nason,	South Berwick,	250
Olivia S. Nason,	do.	850
Mary Ann C. Norton,	do.	1,100
Ministerial Fund, 1st Parish, in Berwick,	Berwick,	700
John Plummer,	South Berwick,	1,500
Samuel Parks,	do.	500
Samuel Pray,	Lebanon,	500
Joshua W. Pierce, trustee,	Greenland, N. H.,	2,000
Portsmouth Savings Bank,	Portsmouth, N. H.,	5,000
Estate of Thomas Savage,	York,	500
Josiah W. Seaver,	South Berwick,	1,150
Theda Smith's estate,	Danvers, Mass.,	500
Sally M. Sargent,	Newburport,	2,000
Ether Shepley,	Portland,	2,500
Charles Trafton,	South Berwick,	1,250
Sarah S. Thatcher,	Unknown,	500

South Berwick Bank, (Continued.)

Names.	Residence.	Amount of Stock.
Daniel Wood,	Lebanon,	250
Helen M. Wallingford,	Kennebunk,	300
Sophia C. Wallingford,	do.	100
James W. Ward,	Abington, Mass.,	1,000
Elizabeth Walker,	Portsmouth, N. H.,	2,000
Mark Walker,	do.	1,000
Moses Varney,	Somersworth, N.H.,	700
Ebenezer Yeaton,	do.	1,150
Ministerial Fund, 1st Parish,	South Berwick,	1,000
		$50,000

Skowhegan Bank.

Charles Avery,	New Brunswick,	500
William Allen,	Norridgewock,	1,400
Charles F. Allen,	Unknown,	500
Stephen Allen,	do.	400
Elizabeth T. Abbott,	Norridgewock,	200
Sarah Anderson,	Unknown,	100
William Atkinson,	Madison,	300
Susan Bowtelle,	Bloomfield,	300
Betsey Bosworth,	Norridgewock,	1,300
Bloomfield Academy,	Bloomfield,	3,100
George Bixby,	Athens,	200
Ephraim Bigelow,	Bloomfield,	400
John H. Bigelow,	do.	200
Cromwell Barnard,	do.	300
Simon Bean,	New Brunswick,	1,000
E. Coburn & Sons,	Bloomfield,	4,500
Abner Coburn, guard.,	do.	400
Congregational Parish,	do.	500
Benjamin Cushing, 2d,	Camden,	300
John Colby,	Madison,	1,000
James B. Dascomb,	Bloomfield,	2,000
Caroline F. Dole,	Unknown,	500
Arthur Drinkwater,	do.	500
Sally Fletcher,	Norridgewock,	1,800

Skowhegan Bank, (Continued.)

Names.	Residence.	Amount of Stock.
Mary Fletcher,	Norridgewock,	500
Eunice Farnsworth,	do.	100
Sarah G. Gilman,	Skowhegan,	300
Joseph Jenkins,	Madison,	1,400
Holman Johnson, 2d,	St. Albans,	300
Nathan Jewett, Jr.,	Solon,	300
Thomas P. Kendall,	Andover, Mass.,	1,500
Joseph Locke,	Bloomfield,	800
Joseph L. Locke,	Savannah, Ga.,	1,300
Daniel Lord, guardian,	Athens,	200
James Lord,	do.	300
James T. Leavitt,	Skowhegan,	400
John Mendell,	Fairfield,	1,000
Peter Malbon,	Skowhegan,	500
Henry McClellan,	Bloomfield,	100
Judah McClellan,	do.	700
John McClellan,	Woodstock, Ct.,	2,000
Lucy McIntire,	Unknown,	100
John G. Neil,	Skowhegan,	3,400
Eben H. Neil,	do.	200
Polly Norton,	Unknown,	100
Sarah Neil,	Skowhegan,	600
Elizabeth L. Neil, deceased,	do.	300
Hélen Neil, Deceased,	do.	300
Lydia Nuth,	Bloomfield,	200
Henrietta O. Pearson,	Exeter, N. H.,	100
Edmund Pearson's estate,	do.	800
Edmund Pearson,	Bloomfield,	3,200
John R. Philbrick,	Waterville,	3,000
Joseph Philbrick,	Bloomfield,	200
William Philbrick,	Exeter, N. H.,	1,600
John Pierce,	Solon,	200
Luther Pierce,	do.	100
Luther Pierce, Jr.,	do.	200
Samuel Parker,	Bloomfield,	1,900
Bryce M. Pratt,	Unknown,	300
Edward D. Peters,	Boston,	3,000
William Rowell,	Bingham,	300
Samuel Robinson,	Skowhegan,	500
Silvina L. Stanley,	Unknown,	400

Skowhegan Bank, (Continued.)

Names.	Residence.	Amount of Stock.
Mary A. Stanley,	Unknown,	400
Calvin Selden,	Norridgewock,	1,000
Betsey Smith,	Bloomfield,	100
Cullen Sawtelle,	Norridgewock,	500
Solomon Steward,	Bloomfield,	200
Galen Soule,	Fairfield,	800
Daniel Snow, Jr.,	Bloomfield,	1,500
Daniel Steward,	Anson,	1,200
Elvira F. Thayer,	Unknown,	3,200
Abraham Tinkham,	do.	300
John S. Tenney,	Norridgewock,	300
Hanover Trefethern,	Cornville,	100
Trustees Ministerial Fund,	Skowhegan,	400
Trustees Ministerial Fund,	Bloomfield,	200
Lydia Titcomb,	Unknown,	200
Nancy Titcomb,	do.	100
S. & J W. Weston,	Bloomfield,	1,000
Joseph Weston, 2d,	do.	200
John Ware,	Athens,	1,000
Joseph B Webb,	Bloomfield,	400
Joshua Woodman,	Cornville,	1,200
Abel Wood,	Norridgewock,	1,200
Nathan Weston,	Augusta,	2,000
Samuel Woodman,	Cornville,	300
Salmon White,	Bloomfield,	1,400
Nancy White,	do.	600
Sibyl Wood,	Unknown,	100
Daniel Wells,	Bloomfield,	100
Ira Whittier,	Dover,	100
Joseph Whittier,	Cornville,	200
William Whittier,	do.	100
John Woodman,	do.	200
		$75,000

Ticonic Bank, (Waterville.)

Names.	Residence.	Amount of Stock.
Timothy Boutelle,	Waterville,	4,900
Moses Appleton,	do.	500
Mary Dalton,	do.	1,500
Waterville Lodge,	do.	300
Harriet Redington,	do.	2,100
Clymene Mathews,	do.	1,000
Mary Esty,	do.	1,000
Ann E Mathews, minor,	do.	900
Fidelia Stevens,	do.	100
Ruth J. Stevens,	do.	100
Elah Esty,	do.	100
Jediah Morrill,	do.	4,400
W. & D Moor, Jr.,	do.	800
John Mathews,	do.	2,000
Heirs of Wm. Phillips,	do.	100
Samuel Plaisted,	do.	1,300
James Stackpole,	do.	4,500
Estate of Isaac Stevens,	do.	300
James Shores,	do.	2,400
Alfred Burleigh,	do.	1,300
Samuel Redington,	do.	200
Sumner Percival,	do.	400
James M. West,	do.	100
Abel Hoxie, estate,	Fairfield,	3,000
Arnold Hoxie,	do.	600
Reuben Jones,	do.	600
John Mendall,	do.	3,000
Elizabeth Whiting,	do.	500
Benjamin Bowman,	do.	500
Allen Wing,	do.	400
Daniel Blaisdell,	Sidney,	1,500
Silas H. Delano,	do.	500
Silas L. Hoxie,	do.	700
Daniel Tiffany,	do.	500
Margaret Tiffany,	do.	300
Samuel S. Tiffany,	do.	200
David P. Tiffany,	do.	200
Cullen Sawtelle,	Norridgewock,	500
Caroline Fletcher,	do.	500
Mary Fletcher,	do.	500

Ticonic Bank, (Continued.)

Names.	Residence.	Amount of Stock.
Sarah Sawtelle,	Norridgewock,	500
Turner Allen,	Vassalborough,	500
Charles Cushman,	Winslow,	300
Lucy Cushman,	do.	800
Thomas Rice,	do.	1,500
Samuel B. Tarbox,	Gardiner,	500
William Mathews,	do.	1,200
Jesse B. Tozer,	do.	600
Daniel R. Wing,	do.	400
Eleazer Tarbox,	do.	500
Christiana Whitney,	Boston,	500
Elbridge G. Crowell,	Canaan,	2,000
John G. Neil,	Skowhegan,	1,000
Skowhegan Bank,	Bloomfield,	4,000
Judah McClellan,	do.	300
Asbur Hinds,	Sebasticook,	500
Thomas P. Kendall,	Athens,	500
Nathan Weston,	Augusta,	2,500
Nathaniel Gilman,	New York,	1,000
John McClellan,	Woodstock, Ct.,	3,000
Sarah N. Nickels,	Pittston,	2,000
Francis W. Pattison,	Kentucky,	500
George E Shores,	Waterville,	600
Stephen Stark,	do.	500
Emily Heath,	Belfast,	1,000
Henry Nourse,	Waterville,	500
James Stackpole, Jr.,	do.	1,000
William M. Phillips,	do.	200
Elizabeth Barney,	Fairfield,	200
Joseph Eaton,	Winslow,	1,000
Octavia Brackett,	China,	400
Charles A. Brackett, minor,	do.	400
John A. Brackett, minor,	do.	100
Horace W. Brackett, minor,	do.	100
Clarissa Holman,	Canaan,	600
		$75,000

Thomaston Bank.

Names.	Residence.	Amount of Stock.
Boynton & Miller,	Thomaston,	200
William Cole,	do.	500
Nancy Creighton,	do.	500
Sullivan Dwight,	do.	1,450
Georges Insurance Company,	do.	2,200
Jane Gleason's estate,	do.	200
Sarah Henderson,	do.	500
Susan Henderson,	do.	200
Ann Henderson,	do.	200
Dunbar Henderson,	do.	100
Oliver Jordan, guardian,	do.	300
Iddo Kimball,	do.	6,000
W. R. Keith,	do.	100
Lincoln Bap. Benev. Society,	do.	350
Thomas McLellan,	do.	2,000
Sarah C. Cushing,	do.	100
Snow Paine.	do.	600
Hannah C. Thomas,	do.	100
John H. Robbins,	do.	100
Edward Robinson,	do.	700
Richard Robinson,	do.	900
Daniel Rose's estate,	do.	700
Reuben Sherrer,	do.	700
William Singer,	do.	700
Ephraim Burrett,	do.	300
John H Gleason,	do.	1,300
John Spear, Jr.,	do.	1,000
Barnabus Webb,	do.	500
Robert Walsh,	do.	400
Lydia Burton,	Warren,	100
John H. Counce,	do.	2,000
John Creighton,	do.	300
Kesiah Creighton,	do.	200
A. H. Hodgman,	do.	300
Joshua Lermond,	do.	1,000
Edward O'Brien,	do	500
John Robinson's estate,	do.	1,000
Edwin Smith, trustee,	do.	5,300
Edwin Smith,	do.	500
M. H. Smith,	do.	400

Thomaston Bank, (Continued.)

Names.	Residence.	Amount of Stock.
Trustees of Warren School Fund,	Warren,	400
M. M. Smith,	do.	3,500
Nancy Copeland,	do.	100
St. George's Lodge,	do.	500
Elizabeth Miller,	do.	300
Eliza Vaughan,	do.	100
Hannah Vaughan,	do.	100
Lucy Lowry,	do.	200
John Little,	Union,	800
Hannah Robinson,	do.	100
William Thompson,	do.	200
Isaac Coffin,	Wiscasset,	1,500
Samuel E. Smith,	do.	1,300
L. R. Smith,	do.	500
Daniel Day,	Newcastle,	500
E. Wilder Farley,	do.	200
Lincoln Academy,	do.	1,000
Rufus B. Allyn,	Belfast,	1,500
James Barter,	St. George,	400
Sally Benner,	Waldoborough,	200
James Hovey,	do.	400
Second Lincoln Baptist Benevolent Society,	do.	350
Abigail Clark,	Boston,	100
S. F. Morse & Co.,	do.	300
Elsa Kelleran,	do.	300
F. C. Head,	do.	650
Joel Fay,	do.	600
Phebe Jordan,	Unknown,	100
Olivia Smith,	do.	200
H. E. Smith,	do.	700
Olive S. Smith,	do.	400
		$50,000

York Bank, (Saco.)

Names.	Residence.	Amount of Stock
Stillman B. Allen,	Sanford,	525
Samuel Batchelder,	Cambridge, Mass.,	2,250
Eugene Batchelder,	do.	75
Horace Bacon,	Biddeford,	525
P. D & Co. York Bank,	Saco,	3,975
Edward E. Bourne,	Kennebunk,	300
Emily E. Barstow,	Manchester, N. H.,	75
Margery Boothby,	Saco,	75
John Chadwick,	do.	1,200
Daniel Cleaves,	do.	6,000
Mary Cleaves,	Washington, D. C.,	7,950
Hannah D. Cutts,	Saco,	150
Charles F. Cutts,	do.	150
Hannah D. Cutts & C. F. Cutts,	do.	75
Charles Dummer,	Washington, D. C.,	1,650
Isaac Deering,	Waterborough,	150
Orinda Deering,	do.	150
James M. Deering,	Saco,	75
William Deering,	do.	225
Moses Dunn,	Hollis,	450
Lucia Ela,	Washington, D. C.,	450
Isaac Emery,	Boston,	75
Samuel Emery,	Biddeford,	1,725
Sarah S. Emery,	Boston,	300
Isaac Furbish,	Kennebunk,	525
Benjamin F. French,	Lowell, Mass.,	825
First Parish,	Kennebunk,	1,125
Dorothy Gilpatrick,	do.	1,200
Joseph M. Hayes,	Saco,	375
Joseph Hatch,	Kennebunk,	1,425
Daniel L. Hatch,	do.	900
William P. Hooper,	Biddeford,	675
Mary Hooper,	do.	375
Samuel Hartley,	Saco,	1,500
R. F. C. Hartley,	do.	600
Jonathan King,	do.	750
Dorcas K. Leland,	Hanover, N. H.,	1,200
Nathan Lord,	do.	825
William Lord,	Kennebunk,	2,250
J. M. Leland, wife of R. Reed,	Goffstown, N. H.,	1,200

York Bank, *(Continued.)*

Names.	Residence.	Amount of Stock.
Samuel W. Lord,	Effingham, N. H.,	1,200
Sarah L. Mason,	Kennebunkport,	750
Samuel Merrill's estate,	Biddeford,	1,500
Eliphalet Perkins' estate,	Kennebunkport,	1,125
Joshua Maxwell,	Portland,	150
Edmund Parker,	Nashua, N. H.,	825
Israel Pinkham,	Biddeford,	' 75
William Richardson,	Bath,	825
John Ricker,	Saco,	450
Apphia H. Sawyer,	do.	450
Ether Shepley,	Portland,	7,500
John Shepley,	Saco,	750
Abby F. Shepley,	do.	75
Dolly C. Smith,	Kennebunk,	1,875
Samuel Storer,	Biddeford,	225
Robert Smith,	Kennebunkport,	1,350
William Smith,	Biddeford,	375
Sarah Smith,	Tuftonboro', N. H.,	75
Hannah Stone,	Kennebunk,	675
Benjamin Smith,	do.	375
Alfred Smith.	Durham, N. H.,	975
Isaac D. Smith,	Tuftonboro', N. H.,	375
Saco and Biddeford Savings Institution,	Saco,	375
Thornton Academy,	do.	1,200
Nancy B. Thatcher,	Roxbury,	1,875
Mary Titcomb,	Wells,	525
Almira Towne,	Kennebunkport,	225
John Tarbox,	do.	150
Abigail Titcomb,	Kennebunk,	900
George P. Titcomb,	do.	375
William Titcomb,	do.	375
Lucy W. Titcomb,	do.	375
Lewis Wakefield's estate,	Saco,	2,025
Elizabeth A. Wight,	Hollis,	300
		$75,000

NOTE.—The returns from the Banks bearing this mark (*) were not sworn to by the Cashiers.

RETURNS OF CORPORATIONS,

MADE TO THE OFFICE OF THE SECRETARY OF STATE,

IN JANUARY, 1845,

FOR THE YEAR

1845.

Prepared and published agreeably to a Resolve of the Legislature, approved March 24, 1843.
By EZRA B. FRENCH, Secretary of State.

AUGUSTA:

WM. T. JOHNSON,..........PRINTER TO THE STATE.

1846.

STATE OF MAINE.

~~~~~~~~

Resolve authorizing the printing of the Returns of Clerks of Corporations.

RESOLVED, That the Secretary of State is hereby directed to cause the printing of four hundred copies of the returns of the several corporations (excepting banks,) of this State, comprising the name, residence, and amount of stock owned by each stockholder, and furnish each city, town and plantation, with a copy of the same.

[*Approved March* 24, 1843.]

LIST OF STOCKHOLDERS.

THE following comprises a list of all the returns of clerks of corporations that have been received at the office of the Secretary of State, for the year 1845. The abstracts of the returns of such corporations as are marked (*) did not specify the value of shares or the amount of their capital stock, nor is such information found in their acts of incorporation.

Casco Manufacturing Company.

Names.	Residence.	No. of shares.	Am't of stock
Asa Clapp,	Portland,	60	6,000
Albert Newhall,	Cumberland,	48	4,800
Samuel Chadwick,	Portland,	36	3,600
John Mussey,	do.	48	4,800
John Rand,	do.	17	1,700
Julia C. Wingate, executrix,	do.	12	1,200
John R. Larrabee,	Gorham,	12	1,200
Francis Skinner & Co ,	Boston,	7	700
		240	$24,000

*Cumberland Marine Railway Company.

Isaac F. Sturdivant,	Portland,	10	
Isaac Sturdivant,	North Yarmouth,	160	
Charles Deake,	New Orleans,	10	
Joseph Drown,	do.	10	
Benjamin Deake,	Cape Elizabeth,	10	
		200	

Machias Water Power and Mill Company.

Names.	Residence.	No. of shares.	Am't of stock
Daniel Harwood,	Machias,	466	46,600
Wm. B. Smith,	do.	60	6,000
Nathan Longfellow,	do.	90	9,000
Wm. F. Penniman,	do.	50	5,000
Geo. Burnam,	do.	73	7,300
Samuel A. Morse,	do.	58	5,800
Ignatius Sargent,	do.	5	500
William Freeman,	Cherryfield,	4	400
John G. Deane,	Portland,	84	8,400
Eliphalet Case,	do.	50	5,000
Thomas Darling,	Boston, Mass,	95	9,500
A. G. Peck & Co.,	do.	62	6,200
Thayer & Bates,	do.	30	3,000
Ebenezer T. Andrews,	do.	194	19,400
Ebenezer Smith, jr.,	do.	67	6,700
Alonzo Crosby,	do.	159	15,900
Jonathan M. Dexter,	do.	126	12,600
Jona. Jones,	do.	15	1,500
Henry Cutter,	do.	20	2,000
William Savage,	do.	279	27,900
John E. Kimball,	do.	1	100
Elliot P. Tucker,	Cambridge,	135	13,500
Joshua Tucker,	Boston,	573	57,300
Rufus Shattuck,	E Cambridge, Mass.,	9	900
Stephen Goodhue,	Boston, Mass.,	15	1,500
Thomas P. Goodhue,	do.	15	1,500
S & T. P. Goodhue,	do.	1	100
Peter 'C. Bacon,	Oxford, Mass.,	80	8,000
Wm. M. Towne,	Springfield, Mass.,	53	5,300
Salem Towne,	Charlton, Mass ,	126	12,600
Assignees Fessenden & Co.,	Brattleboro', Vt.,	2	200
Peter Harwood,	Barre, Mass.,	100	10,000
Bailey Cobb,	Boston,	50	5,000
Cushing Otis,	Scituate, Mass.,	26	2,600
Machias W P & Mill Co.,	Machias, Me.,	48	4,800
Wm. P. Tewksbury,	Boston,	21	2,100
Geo. A. Trumbull,	Worcester, Mass.,	8	800
Thomas R. Sewall,	Boston, Mass.,	25	2,500
Isaac Sweetser,	do.	2	200
Charles Haynes,	do	7	700
Thomas G. Wells,	do.	35	3,500
James H Barnes,	do.	16	1,600
Robert Farley, in trust,	do.	145	14,500

Machias Water Power and Mill Company, (Continued.)

Names.	Residence.	No. of shares.	Am't of stock
James Hunnewell,	Charlestown, Mass.,	20	2,000
		3,500	$350,000

Mousam Manufacturing Company.

John Chickering's estate,	Newburyport, Mass.,	3	1,500
David S. Brown,	Philadelphia,	127	63,500
George T. Peabody,	do.	6	3,000
Robert F. Walsh,	do.	12	6,000
Benj. T. Tredick,	do.	12	6,000
Daniel Dagget,	Newburyport, Mass.,	1	500
William Lord,	Kennebunk,	6	3,000
Jabez Smith,	do.	2	1,000
Ivory Lord,	do.	2	1,000
		171	$85,000

Ocean Insurance Company.

Joseph Adams,	Unknown,	3	300
John Anderson, trustee,	Portland,	3	300
John Anderson, guardian,	do.	1	100
John Anderson,	do.	3	300
Thomas Browne,	do.	16	1,600
George Bartol,	do.	41	4,100
Phinehas Barnes,	do.	4	400
Nath'l Blanchard,	do.	15	1,500
Brunswick Bank,	Brunswick,	10	1,000
Sarah Barnes,	Portland,	1	100
Samuel Chadwick,	do.	43	4,300
B. P. Chamberlain,	Salem, Mass.,	10	1,000
Asa Clapp,	Portland,	30	3,000
Freeman Cummings,	do.	3	300
Samuel Chase,	do.	10	1,000
Casco Bank,	do.	5	500
Thomas Chadwick,	do.	5	500
Eliphalet Clark,	do.	5	500

1*

Ocean Insurance Company, (Continued.)

Names.	Residence.	No. of shares.	Am't of stock
Phinehas Drinkwater,	Portland,	5	500
Charles S. Daveis,	do.	13	1,300
James Deering,	Westbrook,	5	500
Ezekiel Day,	Deceased,	2	200
Asa Dresser,	Portland,	10	1,000
Edward H. Daveis,	do.	5	500
Rufus Emerson,	do.	5	500
Ebenezer Everett,	Brunswick,	10	1,000
E. C. & M. O. Emerson,	Portland,	5	500
Charles O. Emerson,	York,	10	1,000
Luther Fitch,	Portland,	5	500
Thomas Forsaith,	do.	12	1,200
James Furbish, guardian,	do.	4	400
Philip Greely,	do.	35	3,500
Eliphalet Greely,	do.	20	2,000
Sarah Greely,	Boston, Mass.,	3	300
John D Gardner,	do	15	1,500
Jos B Gardner,	New York,	10	1,000
Polly Hobart,	Deceased,	20	2,000
Alex. Hubbs,	Portland,	10	1,000
John Hamilton,	do.	10	1,000
Joel Hall,	do.	10	1,000
Thomas Hammond,	do.	10	1,000
Rufus Horton,	do.	5	500
Pamelia Hanford,	Unknown,	5	500
Samuel Hanson, guardian,	Portland,	4	400
Samuel Hanson,	do.	10	1,000
Noah Hinkley, ex'r & trustee,	Boston, Mass.,	5	500
Moses Hall,	Westbrook,	10	1,000
Isaac Ilsley,	Portland,	15	1,500
Charles Jordan,	do.	5	500
William Kimball,	do.	4	400
James Lunt,	Westbrook,	5	500
Ammi Loring,	North Yarmouth,	12	1,200
Richmond Loring,	do.	2	200
Parker McCobb,	Portland,	20	2,000
Merchants' Bank,	do.	10	1,000
Albert Newhall,	Cumberland,	10	1,000
William Oxnard,	Portland,	5	500
John Oxnard,	do	5	500
Israel Richardson,	do	5	500
John Robinson,	Cape Elizabeth,	5	500
John W. Rich,	Gorham,	5	500

Ocean Insurance Company, (Continued.)

Names.	Residence.	No. of shares.	Am't of stock
Charles D. Robinson,	Portland,	10	1,000
Mary C. Robinson,	do.	10	1,000
George W. Smith,	do.	5	500
Smith & Brown,	do.	10	1,000
William Swan,	do.	10	1,000
Caroline Stockman,	do.	10	1,000
M. P. Sawyer,	Boston,	20	2,000
H. Southgate, trustee,	Portland,	3	300
Mary S. Smith,	do.	11	1,100
Priscilla P. Smith,	Unknown,	10	1,000
Isaac Sturdivant,	Portland,	9	900
Jona. Tucker,	do.	10	1,000
George Turner,	do.	15	1,500
Elias Thomas,	do.	10	1,000
Margaret Thayer,	do.	6	600
Lucy Thorndike,	do.	1	100
Martha Tappan,	Unknown,	3	300
John R Vinton,	do.	25	2,500
Phinehas Varnum,	Portland,	6	600
William Woodbury,	do.	12	1,200
Ch'r Wright,	do.	5	500
Thomas Warren,	do.	5	500
George Warren,	do.	5	500
John & N. Warren,	do.	5	500
Benjamin Willis,	Boston,	16	1,600
Benjamin Willis, jr.,	do.	10	1,000
Hezekiah Winslow,	Portland,	40	4,000
Jeremiah Winslow,	France,	102	10,200
Rufus E Wood,	Portland,	5	500
Wm. Wood,	do.	2	200
Ocean Insurance Company,	do.	20	2,000
		1,500	$150,000

*Laconia Company.

Eben. T. Andrews,	Boston,	12	
Augustus Aspenwall,	do.	4	
Atkins Adams,	Fairhaven,	5	
Wm. R Austin,	Dorchester,	10	

Laconia Company, (Continued.)

Names.	Residence.	No. of shares.	Am't of stock
Nathaniel W. Appleton,	Boston,	10	
Alfred T. Appleton,	Salem,	13	
Charles T. Appleton,	B⬛⬛.	3	
Abel Adams,	do.	6	
John Aiken,	Lowell,	2	
John Anderson,	Portland,	6	
John R. Adun,	Boston,	6	
Joshua Aribin,	Amesbury,	3	
Samuel Batchelder,	Saco,	13	
Ezra A. Bourne,	Boston,	6	
Charles Bradbury,	do.	10	
Charles Bradbury, trustee,	do.	2	
Susan Burley,	do.	11	
Elisha Bartlett,	Lowell,	2	
Joseph Balch,	Boston,	12	
Joseph Balch, trustee,	do.	2	
I. T. Bigelow,	do.	2	
Jacob Bigelow,	do.	6	
John Bryant,	do.	12	
Nabby and Anne Balch,	do.	1	
Enoch Baldwin,	do.	3	
Homer Bartlett,	Lowell,	3	
George Bragdon,	do.	1	
John Belknap,	Boston,	10	
W. B. Brown,	Lowell,	1	
Sally Bachelder,	Hingham,	1	
Charles W. Cartwright,	Boston,	12	
Edward Clark,	Northampton,	5	
Eliphalet Clark,	Portland,	1	
John Clark,	Lowell,	10	
Pliny Cutler,	Boston,	1	
Ebenezer Chadwick,	do.	13	
John P. Cushing,	Watertown,	12	
Thomas Cole,	Salem,	.8	
Charles P. Curtis,	Boston,	7	
Thomas B. Curtis,	do.	4	
Jona. Chapman,	do.	15	
R. M. Chapman,	Saco,	1	
Josiah Calef,	do.	1	
Charles Cunningham,	Boston,	6	
Charles Cunningham, trustee,	do.	6	
James Dennie,	Saco,	6	
Tucker Daland, trustee,	Salem,	5	

Laconia Company, (Continued.)

Names.	Residence.	No. of shares.	Am't of stock
Charles S Daveis,	Portland,	4	
Nathaniel H. Emmons,	Boston,	7	
John S. Ellery,	do.	13	
Moses Emery,	Saco,	1	
Samuel Fales,	Boston,	6	
Ebenezer Francis,	do.	13	
Wm. Frost,	New Orleans,	1	
John Freeman,	Boston,	1	
Sarah Freeman,	do.	4	
Ozias Goodwin,	do.	10	
Benj. Gorham,	do.	6	
Amos Greene,	Lowell,	1	
Frederic T. Gray,	Boston,	1	
John T. Gilman, trustee,	Portland,	3	
Henry Hall,	Boston,	2	
Benj. Humphreys,	do.	10	
Otis Holmes,	Biddeford,	6	
Jeremiah Hall,	Boston,	2	
Frederic Howes,	Salem,	4	
Wm. B Howes,	Boston,	1	
Hercules M. Hayes,	New York,	10	
Robert Hooper,	Boston,	8	
John Hooper, jr.,	Marblehead,	4	
Dudley Hall,	Medford,	4	
Dudley C. Hall,	New Orleans,	2	
Wm. Haskell,	Biddeford,	1	
Eliza, Geo. W., and Henry S. Hallett, trustees,	Boston,	5	
George W. Hallett,	do.	1	
R. M. Hutchinson,	Lowell,	2	
Jerome G. Kidder.	Boston,	5	
Henry Lawrence,	New York,	12	
Amos Lawrence,	Boston,	25	
Abbot Lawrence,	do.	64	
James Lawrence,	do.	6	
Wm. Lawrence,	do.	15	
Samuel Lawrence,	Lowell,	6	
Wm. G. Lambert,	Boston,	5	
Elijah Loring,	do.	6	
Benj. Loring,	do.	8	
Benj. Loring & Co.,	do.	3	
Caleb Loring,	do.	4	
George Lee,	Cambridge,	13	

Laconia Company, (Continued,)

Names.	Residence.	No. of shares.	Am't of stock
Henry Lee,	Boston,	30	
Sargent S. Littlehale,	do.	5	
John A. Lowell,	do.	20	
Thomas Lamb,	do.	4	
T. C. Leeds,	do.	2	
Wm. P. Matchett,	Brighton,	7	
Thomas Motley,	Boston,	2	
Robert W. Morville,	Lowell,	3	
Abby A. Means,	Boston,	1	
Parker McCobb,	Portland,	6	
Sarah E. Miles,	Boston,	2	
Thaddeus Nichols,	do.	5	
Rufus Nichols,	Saco,	2	
Mary Nelson, trustee,	Newburyport,	5	
Mary Nelson,	do.	1	
John B. Nelson,	do.	2	
Cheever Newhall,	Saco,	2	
Pratt & Emery,	do.	3	
Edward Pickering,	do.	1	
Charles H. Parker,	do.	6	
Isaac Parker,	do.	3	
J. W. Peele,	Salem,	13	
George Pitnam,	Roxbury,	3	
Lemuel Pope,	Boston,	4	
Paschel P. Pope,	do.	7	
Wm. D. Parkman,	Salem,	20	
Richard Picket,	Beverly,	2	
Charles Pelham,	Boston,	3	
Wm. P. Perkins,	do.	5	
Mary Parker,	do.	1	
Rice & Thaxter,	do.	8	
Henry Rice,	do.	3	
Benj. Rich,	do.	4	
Edward S. Rand,	Newburyport,	6	
Wm. W. Stone,	Boston,	6	
Samuel W. Swett,	do.	2	
Elizabeth B. Swett,	do.	2	
Elizabeth L. Swett,	do.	2	
Joseph C. Swett,	do.	3	
Wm. B. Swett,	do.	3	
Samuel Swett,	do.	4	
Wm. Sturgis,	do.	13	
Henry Sigourney,	do.	18	

Laconia Company, (Continued.)

Names.	Residence.	No. of shares.	Am't of stock
Joshua Sears,	Brookline,	9	
Nath'l Silsbee, jr.,	Salem,	15	
Nathaniel Tracy,	Boston,	2	
Samuel Tenney,	do.	4	
Isaac P. Townsend,	do.	2	
Waterston & Pray,	do.	15	
Francis Watts' estate,	do.	1	
Israel Whitney,	do.	5	
Wm. F. Whitney,	do.	2	
John Williams,	do.	4	
Benj. C. Ward,	Baltimore,	4	
Thomas B. Wales,	Boston,	20	
Thomas B. Wales, jr.,	do.	5	
George W. Wales,	do.	2	
Joshua H. Walcott,	do.	25	
Thomas I. Wigglesworth,	do.	10	
Nath'l White,	Amesbury,	2	
Edward Wigglesworth.	Boston,	6	
Stephen M. Weld,	Roxbury,	3	
Wm. F. Weld,	Boston,	13	
John Wright,	Lowell,	2	
Hugh Wallace,	Saco,	2	
Hezekiah Winslow,	Portland,	2	
Arnold Welsh,	Lowell,	1	
Alex. Young,	Boston,	3	
Willard C. Welch,	Lowell,	1	
		1,000	

Palmer and Machias-port Rail Road.

Names.	Residence.	No. of shares.	Am't of stock
John W. Trull,	Boston,	300	
M. Healy,	do.	16	
Bela Hunting,	do.	258	
Daniel Hammond,	do.	263	
James Cunningham,	Dorchester,	80	
S. R. M. Holbrook, in trust,	do.	48	
C. Reed,	Boston,	20	
E. Pickering,	do.	8	
B. A. Tufts,	do.	7	
		1,000	

Portland Marine Railway.

Names.	Residence.	No. of shares	Am't of stock
Zilpha Andrews,	Bridgton,		1,000
Belinda Andrews,	do.		1,000
Caleb Adams,	Brunswick,		200
Geo. Bartol,	Portland,		200
Thomas Browne,	do.		1,000
Nath'l Blanchard,	do.		1,600
Fayette Bartlett,	New Bedford,		400
Henrietta Brooks, in trust,	Portland,		200
Samuel Chase,	do.		400
Sam'l Chadwick,	do.		2,200
Hannah Chase,	Lewiston,		400
Phineas Drinkwater,	Portland,		800
Charles S Daveis,	do.		1,400
Rufus Emerson,	do.		2,000
William Evans,	do.		1,400
John Emery,	do.		200
Daniel Fox, guardian,	do.		400
Edward Fox,	do.		200
Phebe E. Freeman,	Limerick,		400
Charles M. Freeman,	do.		400
Charles Freeman,	do.		200
John Fox,	Portland,		400
Philip Greeley,	do.		1,200
Eliphalet Greeley,	do.		1,800
Pamela Hanford,	do.		1,000
Thomas Hammond,	do..		2,200
John Hamilton,	do.		200
Polly Hobart's estate,	do.		1,200
Samuel Holbrook,	Freeport,		600
Elizabeth Halliday,	do.		200
Ocean Insurance Company,	Portland,		1,600
Isaac Ilsley,	do.		800
Geo. Knight, jr.,	do.		200
H J. Little,	do.		600
Thomas R. Jones,	do.		600
Charles Jones,	do.		200
James Lunt,	Westbrook,		600
Hannah Little,	Portland,		1,200
David Mountfort,	do.		1,200
Merchants' Bank,	do.		1,200
Albert Newhall,	Cumberland,		8,060
Ichabod Nichols,	Portland,		400
B. R. Nichols,	do.		400

Portland Marine Railway, (Continued.)

Names.	Residence.	No. of shares.	Am't of stock
Joseph Noble,	Boston,		600
Geo. L. Nevins,	do.		200
John Oxnard,	Portland,		1,200
Israel Richardson,	do.		400
Mary C. Robinson,	do.		200
John F. Reeves,	do.		200
Joshua Richardson,	do.		200
Isaac Sturdivant,	do.		1,200
Martha J. Stockman,	do.		200
M. P. Sawyer,	Boston,		800
William Swan,	Portland,		1,000
Jonathan Tucker,	do		800
George Turner,	do.		600
George Warren,	do.		400
Joshua F. Weeks,	do.		600
Joseph Weeks,	do.		800
Rufus E. Wood,	do.		200
Warren O. Hersey,	do.		600
William Woodbury,	do.		2,400
Jeremiah Winslow,	Havre, France,		600
			$55,000

Saccarappa Manufacturing Company.

Noah Nason,	Westbrook,	21	2,100
J. & N. Warren,	do.	180	18,000
Ira Crocker,	Portland,	10	1,000
Josiah Pierce,	Gorham,	15	1,500
Casco Bank,	Portland,	86	8,600
Franklin Partridge,	Westbrook,	14	1,400
Nathaniel S. Partridge,	Newton, Mass.,	2	200
Daniel Carpenter,	Westbrook,	5	500
William B. Sewall,	Kennebunk,	13	1,300
Canal Bank,	Portland,	59	5,900
Samuel B. Stevens,	Westbrook,	22	2,200
Abner Coburn,	Bloomfield,	5	500
Zophar Reynolds,	Portland,	2	200
Thomas Hammond,	do.	25	2,500
Charles Robie,	Gorham,	4	400

2

Saccarappa Manufacturing Company, (Continued.)

Names.	Residence.	No. of shares.	Am't of stock
Manufact. & Traders' Bank,	Portland,	14	1,400
Thomas Jameson,	Gorham,	11	1,100
Robinson & Hyde,	Portland,	8	800
Philip Eastman,	Harrison,	1	100
Francis Blake,	do.	4	400
S. R. Lyman,	Portland,	7	700
B. M. Edwards,	Westbrook,	6	600
Franklin Tinkham,	Portland,	25	2,500
James Phiney, Jr.,	Gorham,	10	1,000
Jeremiah Winslow,	France,	11	1,100
Eben'r M'Intosh,	Portland,	8	800
Nathan Winslow,	do.	3	300
Jno. P. Boyd, guardian,	do.	3	300
Benjamin Day,	do.	10	1,000
Samuel Trask,	do.	4	400
Sarah Jane Robinson,	do.	3	300
John Dow,	do.	8	800
		600	$60,000

Saco Water Power Company.

Ebenezer T. Andrews,	Boston,	16
Nathan W. Appleton,	do.	6
John Anderson,	Portland,	10
Charles Bradbury,	Boston,	30
Charles Bradbury, in trust,	do.	3
Wm. Burns,	New York,	22
Joseph Balch,	Boston,	9
Joseph Balch, trustee,	do.	4
Joshua Blake,	do.	13
Frances Bundy,	do.	2
Samuel Batchelder,	Cambridge,	20
Ezra A. Bourne,	Boston,	5
Andrew E. Belknap,	do.	23
Thomas Bartlett,	do.	3
Peter C. Books, Jr.,	do.	10
Jeremiah Burns,	Matteawan,	2
Nabby and Ann Balch,	Boston,	2
Francis Boott,	do.	1

Saco Water Power Company, (Continued.)

Names.	Residence.	No. of shares.	Am't of stock
Rebecca B. Bradlee,	Boston,	1	
Solomon C. Buzel,	W. Northwood, N.H.	4	
Mary Brown,	Boston,	1	
Susan Burley,	do.	18	
John M. Batchelder,	Saco,	5	
Horace Batchelder,	do.	3	
Enoch Baldwin,	Boston,	2	
Eliphalet Clark,	Portland,	1	
A. & C. Cunningham,	Boston,	2	
City Bank,	do.	20	
John Chapman,	do.	5	
Thomas Cole,	Salem,	6	
Thomas B. Curtis,	Boston,	2	
Edward Clark,	do.	10	
R. M. Chapman,	Biddeford,	3	
Pliny Cutler,	Boston,	9	
Catharine Davenport,	do.	2	
Joanna Davenport,	do.	1	
Thomas Dwight,	do.	9	
Charles S. Daveis,	Portland,	2	
Tucker Daland, trustee,	Salem,	2	
John W. Edmunds,	Boston,	4	
John S. Ellery,	do.	25	
Nathaniel H. Emmons,	do.	7	
Moses Emery,	Saco,	1	
Samuel Fales,	Boston,	20	
Eben'r Francis,	do.	10	
Caleb Foote,	Salem,	2	
John J. Fiske, guardian,	New York,	1	
Sarah Freeman,	Boston,	1	
John Gray,	do.	2	
Lydia D. Gillis, adm'x,	Salem,	2	
Augustus Heard,	Boston,	20	
Robert Hooper,	do.	2	
Benjamin Humphrey,	do.	12	
Mary Hedge,	do.	1	
Hercules M. Hayes,	New York,	16	
Samuel Hopkins,	Saco,	3	
Dudley Hall,	Medford,	10	
Otis Holmes,	Saco,	2	
E. G. W. & H. S. Hallet,	Boston,	5	
Jeremiah Hill,	do.	4	
Eben'r Hale,	Newburyport,	3	

Saco Water Power Company, (Continued.)

Names.	Residence.	No. of shares.	Am't of stock
Wm. P. Hooper,	Biddeford,	2	
Wm. P. Haines,	Saco,	2	
Frederick Howes,	Boston,	13	
Wm. B. Howes,	do.	2	
Mary Huntington,	do.	2	
Abbott Lawrence,	do.	10	
Amos Lawrence,	do.	6	
Micajah Lunt,	do.	3	
Benjamin Loring,	do.	40	
John A. Lowell,	do.	10	
Benjamin Loring & Co.,	do.	6	
Francis L. Lee,	do.	3	
Elijah Loring,	do.	9	
George Lee,	Cambridge,	19	
James Longley,	Boston,	10	
Henry Lee,	do.	10	
S. S. Littlehale,	do.	10	
Henry Loring, trustee,	do.	5	
Henry Lee, guardian,	do.	11	
Henry & Tho's Lee, trustee,	do.	2	
William P. Matchett,	Brighton,	14	
Parker McCobb,	Portland,	20	
Samuel Merrill,	Biddeford,	1	
Thomas Motley,	Boston,	4	
Thaddeus Nichols, Jr.,	do.	8	
John B. Nelson,	do.	5	
Mary Nelson,	do.	2	
Mary Noyes,	do.	2	
Rufus Nichols,	Saco,	16	
Mary Nelson, trustee,	do.	15	
Isaac C. Pray,	Boston,	6	
Horatio N. Perkins,	do.	2	
George Putnam,	Roxbury,	4	
Provident Institution,	Boston,	30	
Isaac Parker,	do.	5	
William Pickering,	Greenland, N. H.,	6	
Rice & Thaxter,	Boston,	7	
Edward S. Rand,	Newburyport,	6	
Elizabeth B. Swett,	Boston,	11	
Israel M Spelman,	do.	1	
Elizabeth Swett,	do.	6	
Henry Sigourney,	do.	5	
Joseph C. Swett,	do.	6	

Saco Water Power Company, (Continued.)

Names.	Residence.	No. of shares.	Am't of stock
Samuel Swett,	Boston,	23	
William B. Swett,	do.	6	
Samuel W. Swett,	do.	2	
William Savage,	do.	3	
Joshua Sears,	do.	7	
Saco & Biddeford Savings Institute,	Saco,	10	
John B. Swett,	Exeter, N. H.,	9	
William Savage,		3	
Suffolk Bank,	Boston,	2	
Hitty Stephens,	Beverly,	3	
Rosa A Scull,	Havana,	11	
Henry B. Smith,	Boston,	5	
Thomas B. Wales, Jr.,	do.	4	
Sayles, Merriam & Brown,	do.	9	
William Smith,	Saco,	2	
Nathaniel Tracey,	Boston,	2	
Albert Thorndike,	Beverly,	3	
Daniel Treadwell,	Cambridge,	6	
Joshua H Walcott,	Boston,	4	
Phebe Winslow,	do.	1	
John Williams,	do.	1	
Israel Whitney,	do.	8	
Benjamin M. Watson,	do.	5	
Francis Watts,	do.	1	
Waterston & Pray,	do.	11	
Robert Waterston,	do.	6	
Thomas B. Wales,	do.	10	
Edward B. Warren,	do.	2	
John Ware,	do.	7	
Henry Warren,	do.	2	
Titus Welles,	do.	1	
Parker, Wilder & Parker,	do.	5	
Hezekiah Winslow,	Portland,	5	
Hugh Wallace,	Saco,	8	
C. B. Ward,	Boston,	7	
Rufus E. Wood,	Portland,	2	
George Wales,	Boston,	2	
Charles E. Ware,	do.	1	
York Bank,	Saco,	.2	
		1,000	

2*

Springvale Manufacturing Company.

Names.	Residence.	No. of shares.	Am't of stock
Alexander Dewitt,	Oxford, Mass.,	313	28,170
A. H. Boyce,	Sanford, Me.,	63	5,670
John T. Paine,	do.	75	6,750
Theodore Willard,	do.	15	1,350
C. S. Emery,	do.	10	900
B. F. Hodgdon,	do.	10	900
Andrew Cooper,	do.	10	900
David Fall,	do.	2	180
John Montelius, Jr.,	do.	5	450
A. F Howard,	do.	12	1,080
Jacob Ford,	Dover, N. H.,	2	180
S V. Loring,	Athens, Me.,	3	270
D. & S. Ward,	Kennebunk, Me.,	7	630
Olive Allen,	Alfred,	1	90
		528	$47,520

York Manufacturing Company.

Eben T. Andrews,	Boston,	20
Charles W. Cartwright,	do.	10
Pliny Cutler,	do.	3
Samuel Fales,	do.	25
Samuel Johnson,	do.	15
Benjamin Loring,	do.	40
Elijah Loring,	do.	5
Samuel W. Swett,	do.	3
Atlantic Bank,	do.	3
Robert Hooper,	do.	12
Enoch Baldwin,	do.	2
Nathaniel Tracy,	do.	2
John Williams,	do.	1
Eagle Bank,	do.	1
Andrew E. Belknap,	do.	5
Jeremiah Hill,	do.	4
Solomon C. Buzzell,	do.	1
Titus Wells,	do.	4
John Ware,	do.	7
James Longley,	do.	13
Joseph Hall,	do.	6

York Manufacturing Company, (Continued.)

Names.	Residence.	No. of shares.	Am't of stock
John S. Ellery,	Boston,	40	
Benj. M. Watson,	do.	5	
Thomas Bartlett,	do.	3	
Israel Whitney,	do.	8	
Thaddeus Nichols,	do.	8	
Thomas B. Wales,	do.	14	
Ozias Goodwin,	do.	10	
Columbus Tyler,	do.	1	
Edward S. Rand,	Newburyport, Mass.,	10	
Sarah S. Dunn,	Boston,	1	
Samuel Torrey,	do.	2	
Nathaniel H. Emmons,	do.	7	
George H. Loring,	do.	3	
John Hooper, jr.,	do.	6	
Abby M. Loring,	do.	2	
Cornelia W. Loring,	do.	2	
Samuel Davis,	do.	1	
Joshua Sears,	do.	7	
Halleburton Fales,	do.	3	
Wm. W. Cutler,	S. Reading,	3	
Thomas B. Wales, jr.,	Boston,	2	
Henry Lee, guard. and trust.,	do.	3	
Susan Inches,	do.	2	
Elizabeth Inches,	do.	7	
Benj. Loring & Co.,	do.	6	
Epes Sargeant,	do.	2	
Joseph C. Swett,	do.	5	
Wm. B. Swett,	do.	5	
Elizabeth B. Swett,	do.	7	
Charles Bradbury,	do.	20	
Charles Bradbury, trustee,	do.	3	
Caleb Curtis,	do.	3	
Joshua Blake,	do.	13	
Elizabeth L. Swett,	do.	5	
James B. Bradlee,	do.	3	
Mary Brown,	do.	1	
Edward Clark,	do.	5	
Benj. Humphrey,	do.	16	
Peter C. Brooks, jr.,	do.	10	
Charles Cunningham,	do.	3	
Henry Sigourney,	do.	6	
Mary E. Low,	do.	5	
Jonathan French, jr.,	do.	3	

York Manufacturing Company, (Continued.)

Names.	Residence.	No. of shares.	Am't of stock
Isaac Parker,	Boston,	3	
James Cunningham, trustee,	do.	2	
Nabby and Anne Balch,	do.	2	
John S. Copley Greene,	do.	5	
Henry Loring, trustee,	do.	5	
Daniel Treadwell,	Cambridge,	3	
Union Bank,	Boston,	10	
Charles E. Ware,	do.	1	
Philip Marrett,	do.	2	
Dudley C. Hall,	do.	2	
Phebe Winslow,	do.	1	
John B. Swett, trustee,	do.	1	
George Burroughs,	do.	3	
John Gray,	do.	2	
Samuel Swett,	do.	23	
Eben. Francis,	do.	10	
J. M. Spelman,	do.	1	
Paschal P. Pope,	do.	5	
J. B. Swett,	do.	10	
Henry and Thos Lee, trust.,	do.	1	
Nathaniel W. Appleton,	do.	12	
Nath'l W. Appleton, trust.,	do.	2	
Abbot Lawrence,	do.	20	
John W. Edmonds,	do.	6	
Joshua H. Walcott,	do.	7	
Samuel R. Putnam,	do.	6	
John A. Lowell,	do.	10	
Eben. Chadwick,	do.	5	
Ezra A. Bourne,	do.	5	
Sargent S. Littlehale,	do.	4	
Jeremiah Lee, trustee,	do.	2	
Catharine Ward,	do.	2	
Charles A. Kilham,	do.	1	
George Lee,	do.	20	
Charity Pickens,	do.	2	
Mary, Elizabeth, and Sarah P. Pratt,	do.	10	
Louisa F. Pickens,	do.	1	
Matilda Pickens,	do.	1	
Henry B. Smith,	do.	4	
P. G. Munro,	do.	2	
Edward Warren,	do.	1	
George T. Bigelow,	do.	3	

York Manufacturing Company, (Continued.)

Names.	Residence.	No. of shares.	Am't of stock
Mary Huntington,	Boston,	2	
Theodore Metcalf,	do.	2	
Washington Bank,	do.	1	
Susan M. Fales,	do.	5	
Caleb Loring,	do.	4	
Samuel Salisbury,	do.	2	
Rebecca B. Bradlee,	do.	1	
Elijah Loring, adm'r,	do.	25	
Francis Watts,	do.	1	
George Homer,	do.	3	
Catharine Putnam,	do.	2	
Joseph S. Cabot,	Salem,	3	
James M Thompson,	do.	1	
Benjamin French, jr.,	Boston,	1	
Wm. F. Weld,	do.	10	
Isaac Emery,	do.	2	
John A. Lowell, trustee,	do.	12	
Abel Adams,	do.	1	
Albert Clark,	do.	1	
Wm. T. Andrews,	do.	6	
Francis L. Lee,	do.	1	
John Fox,	Charlestown,	1	
Dudley Hall,	Medford,	10	
Tucker Dalund,	Salem,	2	
Francis Boardman,	do.	1	
Hiram Hosmer,	Watertown,	10	
Elizabeth Storey,	Newburyport,	2	
Benj. C. Ward,	Baltimore,	3	
Mary Nelson,	Newburyport,	3	
Susan Cushing,	Newton,	1	
William Burns,	New York,	7	
Wm. P. Matchett,	Brighton,	7	
Hitty Stephens,	Beverly,	3	
Albert Thorndike,	do.	3	
Dwight Boyden,	Waltham,	17	
Mark W. Pierce,	Portsmouth,	4	
Russell Glover,	New York,	6	
Lydia D. Gillis, adm'x,	Salem,	2	
John Harvey,	Northwood, N. H.,	3	
John J. Fiske, guardian,	New York,	1	
George Putnam,	Roxbury,	1	
Thomas Cole,	Salem,	3	
Hercules M. Hayes,	New York,	16	

York Manufacturing Company, (Continued.)

Names.	Residence.	No. of shares.	Am't of stock
Susan Burley,	Gloucester,	2	
Hezekiah Winslow,	Portland,	10	
Nashua Bank,	Nashua,	18	
Stephen M. Weld,	Roxbury,	1	
Samuel Batchelder,	Cambridge,	20	
Luther V. Bell,	Charlestown,	1	
Henry Hooper,	Marblehead,	4	
George Wilson,	do.	4	
Joanna Davenport,	Milton,	1	
Catharine Davenport,	do.	1	
James M. Thompson,	Salem,	1	
Sarah E Miles,	Roxbury,	1	
Charles T. Appleton,	Lowell,	4	
Parker McCobb,	Portland,	8	
Rosa A Scull,	Havana,	11	
Ebenezer Hale, guardian,	Newburg,	1	
John B. Nelson,	Newburyport,	4	
Josiah Calef,	Saco,	5	
Catharine Hunt,	Watertown,	1	
Tyler Bigelow,	do.	4	
J. P. Dabney,	Salem,	1	
William R. Rodman,	New Bedford,	2	
Charles H. Bigelow,	U. S. A.,	3	
Mary Nelson, trustee,	Newburyport,	12	
William Frost,	New Orleans,	1	
John Andrews, jr.,	Newburyport,	2	
Sarah P. Pratt,	Boston,	3	
Ellen Hallet,	Roxbury,	1	
Maria Hallet,	do.	1	
Almira Hallet,	do.	1	
Frances Hallet,	do.	1	
Harriet Hallet,	do.	1	
Georgianna Hallett,	do.	1	
Samuel D. Ward,	Hadley,	1	
William C. Appleton,	Boston,	5	
		1,000	

Kennebec Company.

Names.	Residence.	Am't of stock	Am't paid.
Chace, Motley & Mills,	Boston,	22,500	9,000
Reuel Williams,	Augusta,	20,000	8,000
Reuben S. Denny,	Clappville, Mass.,	2,500	900
Allen Lambard,	Augusta,	2,500	900
Carlton Dole,	do.	1,500	600
George W. Morton,	do.	1,000	400
Nathan Weston,	do.	1,500	600
Joseph D. Emery,	do.	1,000	400
James W. Bradbury,	do.	1,000	400
Benj. A. G. Fuller,	do.	1,000	400
James L. Child,	do.	1,000	400
Henry Williams,	do.	1,000	250
John Mulliken,	Hallowell,	1,000	250
Llewelyn W. Lithgow,	Augusta,	1,000	400
Benjamin Davis,	do.	1,000	400
Wm. R. Smith,	do.	1,000	400
James Rogers,	do.	1,000	250
Joseph H. Williams,	do.	1,000	400
Greenlief White,	do.	500	200
Richard D. Rice,	do.	500	200
Dillingham & Bicknell,	do.	500	200
John H. Ingraham,	do.	500	250
Edmund Munroe,	Boston,	4,000	1,000
Chester Clark,	New York,	5,000	2,000
Thomas J. Lobdell,	Boston,	1,500	600
Thomas R. Sewall,	do.	500	125
Samuel J. Bridge,	do.	2,000	400
Ezra C. Hutchings,	do.	3,000	
Alfred Redington,	Augusta,	7,500	
Abner H. Bowman,	Boston,	500	200
Henry W. Fuller,	do.	500	200
William Woart,	Augusta,	500	
Nathaniel Kimball,	Gardiner,	500	200
Severance & Dorr,	Augusta,	500	200
Israel G. Johnson,	do.	500	200
Lewis P. Mead & Co.,	do.	500	125
Joseph E. Ladd,	do.	500	200
Loring Cushing,	do.	500	200
Willard Wolcott,	do.	500	50
Daniel Hewins,	do.	500	200
J. G. Phinney & Co.,	do.	500	125
B. Rust & J. A. Thompson,	do.	500	200
Francis M. Folger,	do.	500	200

Kennebec Company, (Continued.)

Names.	Residence.	Am't of stock	Am't paid.
Freeman Barker,	Augusta,	500	200
T. Smith & A. A. Bittues,	do.	500	200
George Cox,	Vassalborough,	500	200
James V. Hadley,	Augusta,	500	200
Elisha Folger,	Sidney,	500	200
Estate of John Dutton,	Vassalborough,	500	125
B. Stackpole & M. H. Pettingill,	Augusta,	500	200
James Sturgess,	Vassalborough,	500	200
Samuel Kendall,	Augusta,	500	200
Henry B. Hovey & J. Arnold,	do.	500	200

Kennebec and Boston Steam Packet Company.

Jeremiah Arnold,	Waterville,	50	50
William Brown,	do.	50	16
Noah Boothby,	do.	50	
E. D. Balkcom,	do.	100	
B. C. Benson,	do.	50	50
William Branch,	do.	50	
Abner Chick,	do.	50	
Nathan Faunce,	do.	100	100
George Gilman,	do.	100	
Otis Getchell,	do.	100	17
James Hasty,	do.	150	50
John Hanscom,	do.	50	
William H. Hatch,	do.	50	33
Esty & Kimball,	do.	100	100
John Kendall,	do.	50	50
David Leighton, jr,	do.	50	
W. & D. Moore, jr.,	do.	250	250
Enoch Merrill,	do.	50	50
Silas S. Morey,	do.	50	
John Matthews,	do.	50	50
Henry Nourse,	do.	100	
S. Plaisted,	do.	100	100
Augustus P. Stevens,	do.	100	
Ripley T. Simpson,	do.	50	

Kennebec and Boston Steam Packet Company, (Continued.)

Names.	Residence.	Am't of stock	Am't paid.
Leonard Stanley,	Waterville,	50	
Nathaniel Stedman,	do.	50	
E. L. Smith,	do.	100	5
J. O. Simpson,	do.	50	
Charles G. Tozier,	do.	50	15
Charles J. Wingate,	do.	250	
J. M. West,	do.	100	100
Alfred Winslow,	do.	50	50
Cyrus Williams,	do.	50	50
C. & J. Williams,	do.	50	50
Isaac Britton,	Winslow,	100	100
A. H. Davis,	do.	150	150
David Garland,	do.	50	50
Charles F. Paine,	do.	50	5
Franklin H. Whitney,	do.	50	
James D. Brown,	Clinton,	50	50
D. & J. Piper,	do.	50	50
Dudley Sinkler,	do.	50	16
Albert Sinkler,	do.	50	33
Philander Soule,	do.	50	50
Ambrose H. Abbot,	China,	50	50
Jeremiah Crowell,	do.	50	50
O. N. Doe,	do.	50	33
Nelson Russell,	do.	50	17
Freeman Shaw,	do.	50	50
O. W. Washburn,	do.	50	50
David Wait,	do.	50	50
Benjamin Reed,	Boothbay,	250	
Thomas Carlton,	Vassalborough,	50	50
Joseph Bowman,	do.	50	50
Enoch Brown,	do.	100	100
George Cox,	do.	300	300
John Dutton,	do.	100	100
Ebenezer Frye,	do.	100	100
Martha Hedge,	do.	100	100
Prince Hopkins,	do.	100	100,
D. P. Howland,	do.	50	50
William Lewis,	do.	50	5
Prince B. Mooers,	do.	100	100
Richard Macy,	do.	100	100
Hiram Pishon,	do.	100	100
David Robinson,	do.	100	100
Ira D. Sturgess,	do.	100	100

Kennebec and Boston Steam Packet Company, (Continued.)

Names.	Residence.	Am't of stock	Am't paid.
Jonas R. Slack,	Vassalborough,	50	32
James Sturgess,	do.	50	50
John S. Sturgess,	do.	100	100
Benj W. Whitehouse,	do.	50	50
William P. Whitehouse,	do.	50	17
Joseph E. Wing,	do.	100	76 30
Henry Weeks,	do.	100	100
Stackpole, Pope & Co.,	do.	100	100
John C. Persley,	do.	50	
William H. Doe,	Sebasticook,	50	16
Livona C. Norcross,	do.	50	34
Shubael Baker,	Sidney,	100	33
D. L Purrinton & Co.,	do.	50	
Bradford Sawtelle,	do.	100	100
William Bacon,	do.	50	50
E. B. Blackwell,	Fairfield,	50	17
Cannon & Burgess,	do.	50	33
S. W. Hodges,	do.	50	50
O. S. Holbrook,	do.	50	
S. W. Coburne,	Bloomfield,	50	50
Samuel Parker,	do.	100	100
Abraham Wyman,		100	100
U. R. Penny,	Canaan,	100	66
Willis Currier,	Skowhegan,	50	50
Albert Fuller,	do.	50	50
William McLellan,	do.	100	100
Edward McLellan,	do.	50	50
Eben H. Neil,	do.	50	50
John G. Neil,	do.	50	50
Samuel Philbrick,	do.	50	50
Joseph W. Robinson,	do.	50	50
Reuel Weston,	do.	50	50
John M. Pollard,	Cornville,	100	68
Benjamin Weston, jr.,	Madison,	100	100
Daniel Steward,	North Anson,	100	100
Hapgood & Brown,	do.	50	50
Benjamin Steward,	do.	50	50
Thomas C. Jones,	Norridgewock,	100	34
William Allen,	do.	150	150
Margaret Weeks,	do.	100	100
Edward Rowe,	do.	100	100
Moses H. Pike,	do.	200	133
John C. Page,	do.	50	33

Kennebec and Boston Steam Packet Company, (Continued.)

Names.	Residence.	Am't of stock	Am't paid.
Sally Fletcher,	Norridgewock,	50	50
Hanson Hight,	do.	50	50
Archibald Landers,	Kingfield,	50	20
Hannibal Ingalls,	Mercer,	50	50
Amasa Fisher,	do	50	
Joseph Rollens,	Belgrade,	50	50
D. D. Blunt,	do.	50	
Robert T. Whitten,	do	100	100
Lewis Davis,	Readfield,	50	50
Jacob S. Graves,	do.	500	500
Barnabas Hedge,	do.	100	100
Catharine Hedge,	do.	50	50
Daniel Craig,	do.	1,000	1,000
Joshua Lane,	do.	100	100
John Smith, jr.,	do.	50	50
H. B. Lovejoy,	do.	50	50
Benjamin Pike,	do.	200	200
William Wells,	Vienna,	100	
George Smith,	Wayne,	100	100
Blanding & Dyer,	New Sharon,	50	50
Blanding & C. W. Dyer,	do.	50	50
Joshua Bullen,	do.	50	50
Jason Chandler,	do.	100	33
Daniel Hale,	do.	200	131
Thomas Lancaster,	do.	50	50
Samuel Prescott,	do.	50	34
Jonathan Rust,	do	50	50
Charles G. Smith,	do.	100	67
John Trask, jr,	do	50	16
Samuel Wyman,	do.	50	32
Joshua M. Hopkins,	do.	50	50
John W. Sanburne,	Chesterville,	100	100
Otis Blabun,	do.	50	17
Aaron Cooledge,	Livermore,	200	200
Jefferson Cooledge,	do.	100	100
Levi Lyford,	do	50	
Elisha Pettingall,	do.	250	250
Comfort Pettingall,	do.	100	100
John Smith,	do.	100	100
Adam Wilbur,	do.	100	100
Andrew Barrows,	Canton,	50	50
Cornelius Holland,	do.	50	50
Ezekiel Treat, jr.,	do.	100	100

Kennebec and Boston Steam Packet Company, (Continued.)

Names.	Residence.	Am't of stock	Am't paid
Issac D. Atwood,	Farmington,	50	33
Boardman & Cutter,	do.	200	100
T. F. Belcher,	do.	100	
Francis Butler,	do.	400	134
L S. Caswell,	do.	100	67
Thomas Croswell,	do.	100	100
Thomas Chase,	do.	50	5
F. P. Fairbanks,	do.	50	50
Rhoda Huse,	do.	50	50
H. B. & J. A. Stoyle,	do.	300	300
S. F. Stoddard,	do.	50	33
L. M. Williams,	do.	100	80
John W. Perkins,	do.	100	
Joseph Johnson & Son,	do.	50	50
James Blaisdell,	Rome,	50	
Benjamin H. Mitchell,	do.	50	
Jeremiah Mitchell,	do.	50	
Samuel Alley,	Dresden,	250	250
Philip Larrabee,	Wales,	500	
Simon Willey,	Litchfield,	50	
Ephraim Ballard,	Augusta,	100	63
Charles H. Beck,	do.	300	300
Freeman Barker,	do.	200	
Samuel Cole,	do.	200	
Loring Cushing,	do.	100	100
Gardiner H. Cushing,	do.	100	100
James L. Child,	do.	200	200
Greenwood C. Child,	do.	1,000	1,000
Nehemiah Flagg,	do.	100	100
Benjamin Hodges,	do.	200	200
E. W. Hilton,	do.	50	
Jonathan Hedge & Co,	do.	100	100
Alvah Josselyn,	do.	200	200
Joseph Knowlton,	do.	50	32
William Kennedy,	do.	50	34
Nathaniel Lincoln,	do.	50	
Lewis P. Mead & Co.,	do.	50	50
U. L. Pettingill,	do.	50	50
John A. Pettingill,	do.	50	50
Joseph Piper,	do.	50	50
James Rogers,	do.	500	500
B. C. Robinson,	do.	50	
Thomas W. Smith,	do.	500	500

Kennebec and Boston Steam Packet Company, (Continued.)

Names.	Residence.	Am't of stock	Am't paid.
Charles Savage,	Augusta,	50	25
Tillinghast Springer,	do.	50	
James A. Thompson,	do.	100	100
William Thomas,	do.	200	200
William Wendenburg,	do.	100	100
Rufus Whitten,	do.	50	50
Greenlief White,	do.	500	500
Horace Waters,	do.	100	100
Reuel Williams,	do.	500	500
William H Wheeler,	do.	50	50
James Atkins,	Hallowell,	100	100
Ira Buswell,	do.	50	
Joseph Barrett,	do.	100	67
F. L. Ball,	do.	50	
Andrew Brown,	do.	500	
Merritt Coolidge,	do.	100	67
Samuel Currier,	do.	1,000	650
Webber Furbish,	do.	50	
Eben. Horn,	do.	50	50
John N. Hovey,	do.	100	
Zenas King,	do.	50	
Sullivan Kendall,	do.	100	100
E. S. Loomis,	do.	50	50
Ambrose Merrill,	do.	200	200
Mark Means,	do.	100	67
John Parker,	do.	100	
Phinehas Sweetser,	do.	100	100
Jarvis Wilson,	do.	200	50
Samuel Walker,	do.	200	134
Samuel Watts,	do.	1,000	1,000
Aaron H. Davis,	do.	50	50
William Bradstreet,	Gardiner,	5,000	5,000
Baxter Bowman,	do.	100	
J. H. Edwards,	do.	50	
Archibald Horn,	do.	50	50
Sumner Knight,	do.	50	17
Davis Lawrence,	do.	100	
E. C. Rafter,	do.	50	50
Isaac Sheppard,	do.	50	50
John Meader,	do.	100	50
E. K. Blake,	Monmouth,	100	100
John Safford, 2d,	do.	200	100
Thomas Lancaster,	Winthrop,	50	

3*

Kennebec and Boston Steam Packet Company, (Continued.)

Names.	Residence.	Am't of stock	Am't paid.
Josiah Little, jr.,	Winthrop,	50	50
T. W. Stevens,	do.	50	50
Daniel Merritt,	Jay,	50	50
Josiah D. Haley,	Bath,	200	150
B. C. Bailey,	do.	2,500	500
G. L. Pease,	East Wilton,	100	100
James Bailey,	Pittston,	400	160
Daniel Brookings,	do	100	67
John Blanchard,	do.	250	250
William Cooper,	do	200	200
James N. Cooper,	do.	750	500
John Jewett,	do	250	250
S. W. McKown,	Bristol,	1,000	500
Rice King,	Whitefield,	50	50
Benjamin King,	do.	50	50
Luther M. Kennedy,	do.	50	50
Abraham Preble,	do.	50	50
Joseph King,	do.	50	50
Thomas Cushing,	Phipsburg,	200	66 67
Thomas Kelley,	do.	100	
James Boland,	Newcastle,	150	150
Albert Glidden,	do.	150	150
Daniel Day,	do.	1,000	500
Eben Farley,	do.	1,000	1,000
E. Wilder Farley,	do.	300	300
John Glidden,	do.	500	500
Simeon Handley,	do.	500	500
Josiah Myrick,	do	200	200
William Hitchcock,	do.	500	346 45
I. L. Kenney,	do.	250	166
Samuel Beals,	Arrowsic,	100	
Timothy Eaton,	West Cambridge,	50	50
John Tilton,	Woburn,	300	
John S. Watts,	Portland,	500	
John Brooks,	Wiscasset,	100	100
H. & F Clark,	do.	250	83 33
Philip Gafrey,	do.	100	
Alexander Johnston,	do.	250	250
John Johnston,	do.	250	250
Patrick Lennox,	do.	250	166 67
Philip E. Theobald,	do.	50	50
Wilmot Wood,	do.	250	
Benjamin Bailey,	do.	100	

Kennebec and Boston Steam Packet Company, (Continued.)

Names.	Residence.	Am't of stock	Am't paid.
Goold & Spooner,	New Portland,	50	50
James Carney, jr.,	Richmond,	100	100
Bracket & Rowe,	Boston,	250	166 67
Samuel L. Cutter,	do.	1,000	1,000
Francis Day,	do.	100	100
J. L. Hanson,	do.	100	100
Francis Milliken,	do.	100	100
George Meacham,	do.	200	200
George Nason,	do.	250	250
Aden Patridge,	do.	100	100
A. Edson,	do.	500	500
J. F. Woodman,	do.	50	50
Levi Whitney,	do.	400	400
E. Gunnison,	do.	300	300
Joseph T. Huston,	do.	500	500
R. R. Waldron,	do.	500	500
Frederick Kidder,	do.	100	100
Thomas Boyd,	do.	500	
Ichabod S. Conner,	do.	500	
George Henchman,	do.	100	
Levi Jennings,	do.	1,000	
D. C. Parkhurst,	do.	100	
Greenleaf Page,	do.	100	
John Stratton,	do.	100	
Ephraim Whitney,	do.	200	
		$49,900	37,401 69

Portland, Saco and Portsmouth Rail Road.

Capital Stock of the Company, 12,000 shares at $100—$1,200,000.

		No. of shares.
Nathan Appleton,	Boston,	65
E. T Andrews,	do.	27
Abner Austin,	Lynn,	4
A. B. Adams,	Newburyport,	7
B. L. Atkinson,	do.	6
Betsey Atkinson,	do.	1

Portland, Saco and Portsmouth Rail Road, (Continued,)

Names.	Residence.	No. of shares.	Am't of stock
Dan'l Abbot,	Nashua, N H.,	22	
Atkins Adams,	Fairhaven,	30	
John Anderson,	Portland,	5	
C H Atherton,	Amherst,	85	
Samuel Adams,	York,	24	
G M. Adams,	Saco,	3	
P. D Allen, (minor,)	Salem,	25	
John Archer,	do	10	
Nancy Andrews, ex'x,	do.	35	
Samuel P Andrews,	do.	7	
Anna G. Alvord,	do.	9	
John Ashton,	Newburyport,	10	
E G. Atwood,	Boston,	4	
I. D Akerman,	Portsmouth,	2	
J. F Andrews,	Salem,	35	
J. W. Andrews,	do.	35	
Abel Adams,	Boston,	34	
John Bryant,	do.	100	
D. C Bacon,	do.	73	
Benjamin Bangs,	do	50	
Bates & Co,	do.	53	
Josiah Bradlee,	do.	115	
J. B Bradlee,	do.	33	
Geo Bond, treas'r,	do.	20	
Charles Bradbury,	do	1	
W. H Boardman,	do.	50	
Francis Bassett,	do.	30	
Jotham Bush,	do.	2	
Isaiah Breed,	Lynn,	20	
Nathan Breed,	do.	5	
Jona. Batchelder,	do	5	
Isaac Bassett,	do.	28	
John Bertram,	Salem,	19	
J. B. Brigs,	do.	30	
Williams Brown,	Newburyport,	9	
Lucy Bagley,	do.	1	
M. Boyd,	Salisbury,	4	
Jona. Barker,	Portsmouth,	5	
Samuel Batchelder,	Saco,	55	
J. M. Batchelder,	Biddeford,	5	
Cyrus Butler,	Providence,	100	
C. E Barrett,	Portland,	30	
J. P. Blanchard, trustee,	Boston,	13	

Portland, Saco and Portsmouth Rail Road, (Continued.)

Names.	Residence.	No. of shares.	Am't of stock
F. H. Bradlee,	Boston,	10	
J. W. Barron,		44	
F. Boardman,	Salem,	25	
Goold Brown,	Lynn,	16	
Eben'r Brown,	do.	14	
Nathan Brown,	Newburyport,	1	
Mary Bradlee,	Boston,	8	
W. G. Blacklee,	Marblehead,	4	
James Barr,	Salem,	10	
Ann Baldwin,	Boston,	8	
W. S. Bartlett,	do.	10	
W. S. Bartlett, trustee,	do.	9	
Jona. Batchelder,	Beverly,	6	
N. Batchelder, 2d,	do.	3	
David Batchelder,	Amesbury,	10	
James A Bray,		7	
Brown Bro. & Co.,	Boston,	59	
Anstis S Barstow,	Salem,	7	
C.. Booth, jr.,	Boston,	5	
Barnard Adams & Co.,	do.	14	
John Barnard,	do.	6	
Catharine Bartlett,	Salem,	3	
C. A. Bartlett,	Boston,	13	
S Farrar and C. Brockway, trees.,	do.	5	
Wm. B. Bannister, treas ,	Newburyport,	30	
Charles Brooks,	Boston,	10	
G. B. Blake,	do.	75	
Edward Clark,	do.	53	
Casco Bank,	Portland,	50	
C. P. Curtis,	Boston,	50	
E Chadwick,	do.	70	
E. Chadwick, trustee,	do.	30	
A. Cunningham, treas ,	do.	25	
C. Cunningham,	do.	55	
T. B. Curtis,	do.	53	
Samuel Cabot,	do.	3	
Thomas Crehore,	do.	16	
F. B. Crowningshield,	do.	50	
do trustee,	do.	3	
Caleb Chase,	do.	20	
J. P. Cushing,	do.	100	
S. A. Chase,	Salem,	80	

Portland, Saco and Portsmouth Rail Road, (Continued.)

Names.	Residence.	No. of shares.	Am't of stock
J S. Cabot,	Salem,	28	
Hannah Caldwell,	Ipswich,	2	
Thomas Cook,	Newburyport,	2	
Josiah Calef,	Saco,	25	
Daniel Cleaves,	Biddeford,	15	
Samuel Chadwick,	Portland,	20	
T H. Cushing,	Dover, N. H.,	30	
N D Chase,	Lynn,	75	
Isaiah Chase,	do.	6	
J N. Crehore,	Dorchester,	13	
S. Chadwick,	Charleston, S. C.,	60	
Mary H Cutts,	Portsmouth,	13	
B W. Crowningshield,	Boston,	47	
P. S Coffin,	Portsmouth,	50	
C. W. Clark,	Boston,	20	
Eunice A. Currier,	Newburyport,	2	
Benjamin Cutts, treasurer,		7	
C A. Cheever,	Portsmouth,	15	
Susan C Cabot,		3	
Abijah Chase,	Salem,	42	
Annis W. Clark,	do.	5	
Mehitable Choate,	do.	82	
Rachel Crocker,	do.	11	
William Clark,	Fryeburg, Me.,	4	
Addison Cogswell,	Essex, Mass.,	1	
Margaret E Cogswell,	Portland,	10	
Mary Cheever,	Salem,	3	
W. E. Chase,	Portland,	14	
S. E Cowes,	Portsmouth,	36	
Asa Clapp,	Portland,	100	
C H S Cowes,	Boston,	10	
S. E. Cowes, Ex.,	Portsmouth,	15	
Stephen Codman,	do	5	
Patrick Canavan,	Dover, N. H.,	12	
Thomas Dixon,	Boston,	100	
James Dishon,	do.	26	
T. Downing, guardian,	Salem,	11	
William Dean,	do.	20	
Daniel P. Drown,	Portsmouth,	5	
E Dean,	Biddeford,	10	
William Dennett,	do.	45	
Edward Dearborn,	Seabrook,	6	
J. Devereaux,	Salem,	40	

Portland, Saco and Portsmouth Rail Road, (Continued.)

Names.	Residence.	No. of shares	Am't of stock
Richard Davis,	Salem,	20	
T. Brown, cashier,	Boston,	5	
P. Dodge,	Salem,	3	
Sarah Dunlap,	do.	10	
Mary Davis,	do.	7	
J. S. Elery,	Boston,	100	
George B. Emerson,	do.	20	
C. M. Endicott, treasurer,	Salem,	25	
E India Marine Society,	do.	5	
F. Emerson,	Boston,	5	
William Estes,	Lynn,	8	
J. M. Forbes,	Boston,	150	
M. H Foster,	Salem,	4	
T. Fisher,	do	11	
E. Francis,	Boston,	100	
Samuel Theobald,	Eliot,	20	
C. H. Fabens,	Salem,	5	
Betsey A. Faulkner,	Bluehill, Me.,	6	
A. W. Fisk,	Scarborough,	3	
Fanny Ford,	Beverly,	13	
R. B. & J. M. Forbes, trust.,	Boston,	51	
Eliza L Follen,	do.	10	
C. Foote,	Salem,	5	
C. D. Fitch,	Amherst, N. H ,	5	
F C. Gray,	Boston,	45	
Wm. H. Gardner, trustee,	do.	35	
B Gorham,	do	70	
I. Goodwin,	Portsmouth,	48	
William Goodenow,	Portland,	20	
Mary Goddard,	Boston,	50	
N. Griffin,	Salem,	15	
D. P. Galloup,	do.	2	
A Garney,	Lynn,	4	
J. L. Gardner,	Boston,	33	
J. T Gilman, trustee,		20	
L. D. Gillis, adm'r,		7	
Joseph Gray,	Milton, Mass.,	3	
Wm. Graves,	Newburyport,	5	
Hannah Hodges,	Salem,	9	
F. Homer,	Boston,	100	
Miss E. Hodges,	Salem,	12	
R. Hooper, trustee,	Boston,	45	
B. Hale,	Newburyport,	40	

Portland, Saco and Portsmouth Rail Road, (Continued.)

Names.	Residence.	No. of shares.	Am't of stock
W. Healey,	Hampton Falls,	25	
R. Henderson,	Portsmouth,	4	
W. H. Y. Hackett,	do.	5	
J M. Hayes,	Saco,	5	
W. P. Hooper,	Biddeford,	5	
D. S. Hooper,	do.	5	
William Haskell,	Saco,	2	
Otis Holmes,	do.	5	
John Hooper,	Marblehead,	50	
D. Hall,	Medford, Mass ,	30	
John Houston,	Exeter, N. H.,	37	
James Hall,	Portland,	35	
Miss P. Henry,	Charlestown, Mass.,	50	
Samuel Hopkins,	Saco,	22	
William Hill,	North Berwick,	19	
Mary Hardy,	Portsmouth,	2	
Betsey Hill,	Biddeford,	1	
Benjamin Howard,	Boston,	25	
J. M. Hunt,	Nashua, N. H.,	2	
E. Hopkins,	Northampton,	22	
L. S Hopkins,	do.	20	
Jno. Hunt,		37	
William Hunt,		26	
F. B. Hayes,		16	
A W. Haven,	Portsmouth,	34	
Mary M. W. Harris,	do.	9	
J. L. Hayes,	do.	23	
Charles Hurd,	Londonderry, N. H.,	20	
G. W. Haven,	Portsmouth,	12	
Charles Hurd, jr.,	Londonderry, N. H.,	4	
Jos. Hurd,	Reading, Mass.,	4	
Hamilton Bank,	Boston,	106	
Miss P. Howard,	Salem,	15	
Eben. B. Houston,	Boston,	5	
E. Hill,	Portsmouth,	13	
John Howard, Jr.,	Salem,	20	
B. W. Hinkley, adm'r,	Bluehill, Me.,	13	
J. T. Howe,	Beverly,	4	
Moses Hunt,		5	
Samuel Hyde, jr.,		5	
A. R. Hatch, treasurer,		5	
William Hawkes,	Lynn,	3	
D. Hood,	Portland,	5	

Portland, Saco and Portsmouth Rail Road, (Continued.)

Names.	Residence.	No. of shares.	Am't of stock
C. C. Jackson,	Portsmouth,	5	
E. Johnston,	Boston,	22	
T. Jordan, jr.,	Saco,	1	
W. & S. B. Ives,	Salem,	5	
O. Johnson,	Lynn,	10	
E. Johnson,	do.	2	
S. S. Jelley,		12	
Jos. Johnson,	Newburyport,	2	
Anna P. Jones,		13	
Anna P. Jones, trustee,		2	
Sally Jewett,	Portland,	1	
N. Kinsman,	Salem,	30	
Jona. King,	Saco,	10	
E. Kilham,	Beverly,	20	
Miss L. Killham,	do.	11	
A. Kimball,	Salem,	5	
J. S. Kimball,	do.	5	
E. Kimball, jr.,	Wenham, Mass.,	10	
Mark Kimball,	do.	3	
Edward King,	Newport, R. I.,	30	
Rebecca Kittridge,	Portsmouth.	38	
James King,	Salem,	17	
Mary J King,	do.	20	
James B. King,	do.	2	
S. S. Littlehale,	Boston,	1	
G. P. Low,	Gloucester, Mass.,	15	
Lydia G. Lancaster,	Newburyport,	1	
Daniel Libby,	Saco,	10	
Hannah Ladd,	Portsmouth,	27	
John D. Lang,	N. Berwick,	20	
Lynn Mechanics' Ins. Co.,	Lynn,	20	
George Long,	Portsmouth,	7	
J.C. Lee & H.Wheatland, tr.,	Salem,	7	
J. C. Lee,	do.	30	
Porter Lambert,	do.	10	
George Lee,	W. Cambridge,	50	
F. T. LaHey,	Portland,	5	
Charles Lyon,		10	
R. Nichols,	Saco,	32	
F. S & H. Newhall,	Lynn,	16	
F. B Noyes,	Newburyport,	8	
F. V. Noyes,	do.	10	
George Newhall,	E. Cambridge,	10	

4

Portland, Saco and Portsmouth Rail Road, (Continued:)

Names.	Residence.	No. of shares.	Am't of stock
Henry Newman,	Roxbury,	28	
Marine Society,	Newburyport,	6	
J' G. Naylor,	Portsmouth,	12	
Mirriam Newhall,	Lynn,	2	
N Church Salem,	do.	1	
Charles Nelson,	Salem,	6	
G. R. Noyes,	Cambridge,	6	
James Oliver,	Lynn,	5	
J. B. Osgood,	Salem,	14	
T. H. Perkins,	Boston,	130	
T. H. & S G. Perkins, tr.,	do.	10	
T. H. Perkins and others, tr.,	do.	20	
Peter Peduzzi,	Portsmouth,	19	
S. Philbrick,	Brookline, Mass.,	35	
S. R. Putnam,	Boston,	50	
W. P. Perkins,	do.	50	
William Perkins, 3d,	do.	4	
M. C. Pratt,	Lynn,	20	
W. D. Pickman,	Salem,	40	
D. L. Pickman,	do.	50	
A. L. Pearson,	do.	10	
J. S. Pickering,	do.	10	
N. B. Perkins,	do.	8	
Eben Plummer,	Newburyport,	12	
J. Prescott,	do.	4	
Alex. Perry,	Bristol,	7	
E. N. Perkins,	Boston,	43	
John Percival,	do.	27	
Plummer & Mayo,	do.	100	
Israel Pinkham,	Biddeford,	1	
N. Pierce, jr.,	Salem,	11	
Wm. Pickman,	do.	20	
Richard Pickering,	Newington,	6	
M. T. Pickman,	Salem,	2	
C C. Perkins,	Boston,	50	
G. W. Pease,	Salem,	9	
W. F. Parrott,	Portsmouth,	35	
J. S. Perkins,	Kennebunkport,	4	
J. Putnam,	Salem,	30	
A. W. Putnam,	Danvers,	5	
Martha P. Putnam,	do.	5	
F. Peabody,	Salem,	63	
George Peabody,	do.	34	

Portland, Saco and Portsmouth Rail Road, (Continued.)

Names.	Residence.	No. of shares.	Am't of stock
T. Popkin, trustee,	Boston,	10	
J. Phillips,	do.	50	
John Parsons,	Rye, N. H.,	15	
C. Prescott,	Boston,	1	
W. H. Prince,	do.	6	
Isaac Parker,	do.	10	
Aaron Perkins,	Salem,	5	
W. Pickering,	Greenland,	5	
M. Purrington,	Lynn,	8	
A. Purrington,	do.	10	
Rebecca C. Reed,	New York,	1	
B. T. Reed,	Boston,	50	
F. C. Raymond,	do.	12	
Amos Rhoades,	Lynn,	4	
Charles Roundy,	Salem,	61	
John Robinson,	do.	180	
E. S. Rano,	Newburyport,	50	
J. S. Rummery,	Saco,	3	
W. A. Reed,	Salem,	1	
J. W. Rogers and others, tr.,	do.	55	
S. Robinson,	South Kingston, R. I.	3	
J. M. Robbins,		20	
Robert Rantoul,	Beverly,	10	
John Riley,	Dover, N. H.,	5	
Sarah Rea, ex.,	do.	5	
Isaac Ray,	Boston,	5	
C. A. Read,	do.	5	
J. M. Rice,	do.	4	
Ann Ricdell,	do.	6	
Caroline Richards,	Portsmouth,	5	
Abigail Ropes,	Salem,	10	
Hannah H. Ropes,	do.	10	
Harriet Rose,	do.	10	
William Sturgis,	Boston,	100	
L. Saltonstall, &c., tr.,	Salem,	50	
Benjamin Seaver, guard.,		2	
William Savage,	Boston,	50	
D. P. Stone,	do.	111	
R. G. Shaw,	do.	100	
Samuel Swett,	do.	60	
N. Silsbee, jr.,	Salem,	66	
Daniel Smith,	Newburyport,	8	
John Stevens,	Portsmouth,	5	

Portland, Saco and Portsmouth Rail Road, (Continued.)

Names.	Residence.	No. of shares.	Am't of stock
Samuel Storer,	Biddeford,	4	
William Smith,	do.	5	
Seth Scammon,	do.	2	
Saco and Biddeford Sav. Ins.,	Saco,	30	
J. C. Stimpson,	Biddeford,	3	
Charles Sweetser,	Saugus, Mass.,	10	
Stephen Salisbury,	Worcester, Mass.,	53	
Charles Saunders,	Salem,	37	
Jeremiah Lee, trustee,	do.	11	
J. & D. W. Leland,		36	
D. W. Leland,		3	
Robert Lash,	Boston,	6	
Samuel May,	do.	100	
W. P. Mason,	do.	50	
Parker McCobb,	Portland,	20	
Henry Merrill,	Newburyport,	5	
John P. Mellen,	Saco,	5	
Manufacturers' Bank,	do.	50	
Merchants' Bank,	Boston,	20	
do. do.	do.	31	
E. R. Mudge,	Lynn,	20	
G. W. Mudge,	do.	5	
N. B. March,	Portsmouth,	20	
Asaph Moody,	Kennebunkport,	5	
Mary Mifflin,	Boston,	10	
Harriet Mills,	do.	33	
Manufacturers' Ins. Co.,	do.	10	
John Marshall,	Salem,	16	
Mary Moody,	Newburyport,	2	
Rebecca Moody,	do.	2	
Merchants' Bank,	do.	50	
M. Mulliken, jr.,	do.	1	
F. Mitchell,	Ipswich,	25	
G. M. Marsh,		10	
M. E. Merrill,	Saco,	10	
W. Moulton, president,	Portland,	15	
W. W. Munroe,		25	
John Newhall,	Lynn,	21	
D. A. Neal, guardian,	Salem,	73	
Neal & Co.,	do.	243	
Samuel Nichols,	Newburyport,	25	
Miss C. Saltonstall,	Salem,	23	
S. Stodard,	Northampton,	5	

Portland, Saco and Portsmouth Rail Road, (Continued.)

Names.	Residence.	No. of shares	Am't of stock
W. C. Spalding,	Newburyport,	5	
J. M. Sargent,	Portsmouth,	36	
E. A. Shaw,	Quincy,	7	
M. H. Simpson,	Boston,	86	
A. F. Symonds,	Saco,	5	
Samuel Small, jr.,		50	
Z. W. Sanderson,	Philadelphia,	21	
Eliza P Spaulding,		5	
H O. Stone,	Salem,	9	
R. O. Stone,	do.	2	
N. F. Safford,	do.	4	
W. Sargent,	do.	10	
Eliza W Stone,	do.	6	
Robert Stone,	do.	20	
Samuel Simonds,	do.	37	
J. H. Stone,	do.	2	
Mrs. M Silsbee,	do.	5	
J E Salter,	Portsmouth,	6	
J. M. Schillinger,	Portland,	1	
W. H. Stephenson,	do.	3	
Harriet M. Smith,	do.	10	
M. & Ann Savage,	Salem,	3	
G F Saunders,	do.	40	
J. E Sprague,	do.	12	
Salem Female Char. Society,	do.	5	
William Silsbee,	do.	5	
N Silsbee, trustee,	do.	20	
Sarah Shattuck,	do.	4	
L Saltonstall and others, tr.,	do.	140	
Lucy C. Sheafe, guardian,	do.	1	
C. P. & E. S. Saltonstall,	do.	4	
J. A Southworth,		5	
M. Titcomb,	Newburyport,	12	
Helen Tracy,	do.	3	
L. L. Tracy,	do.	8	
J. W. Treadwell,	Salem,	10	
Jno. E. Thayer & Bro., tr.,	Boston,	100	
Jno. E. Tayer & Bro.,	do.	30	
George Tappan,	Saco,	6	
W. H. Turner,	Salem,	4	
Trustees 1st Parish, Bluehill, Me.,	Bluehill,	2	
Trustees Bluehill Academy,	do.	2	

4*

Portland, Saco and Portsmouth Rail Road, (Continued.)

Names.	Residence.	No. of shares.	Am't of stock
A. Thorndike,	Bluehill,	30	
Francis Todd,	Newburyport,	50	
Caroline Tuck,		20	
J. Tilden,	Boston,	100	
Mrs. J. P. Tuckerman,	do.	1	
Esther Tarbox,		9	
Samuel Trask,	Portland,	6	
Isaac Varney,	North Berwick,	14	
P. Varnum,	Portland,	21	
T. W. Ward,	Boston,	90	
J. G. Ward & Co.,	do.	20	
Charles Woodbury,	Beverly,	5	
Stephen Woodbury, jr.,	do.	5	
Thomas Wigglesworth,	Boston,	10	
W. D. Waters,	Salem,	20	
Hannah Wilson,	Boston,	5	
Samuel Walton,	Salisbury,	2	
G. A. Williams,	E. Bridgewater,	10	
G. D. Williams,		1	
Samuel Whittier,	Portland,	5	
W. P. Winchester,	Boston,	50	
Henry Wilder,	Lancaster,	10	
Nathaniel Warren,	Portland,	10	
W. P. Winchester & others, trustees,	Boston,	330	
John Wheeler,	Burlington, Vt.,	13	
Benj. Wheatland,	N. Market, N. H.,	10	
S. P. Webb, trustee,	Salem,	5	
J. H. Wheeler,	Dover, N. H.,	10	
Lydia R. Ward,	Salem,	3	
Susan Ward,	do.	5	
Ashur Ware,	Portland,	35	
P. W. Warren,	Boston,	38	
B. & G. Wheatland, ex.,	Salem,	10	
S. G. Wheatland,	do.	10	
S. G. Ward,	do.	20	
R. R. Waldron,	do.	5	
A. H. Wildes,	Boston,	5	
Alice Watt,	Lynn,	5	
F. A. Whitwell,		10	
J. W. Ward,		11	
L. D. Wells, trustee,		25	
H. Whitwell, trustee,		40	

Portland, Saco and Portsmouth Rail Road, (Continued.)

Names.	Residence.	No. of shares.	Am't of stock
Samuel Wells,	Portland,	20	
Levi Woodbury,	Portsmouth,	50	
Almira M. Wilcox,	Bluehill, Me.,	3	
Harrison Whitman,	Boston,	17	
F. Williams,	Newburyport,	13	
York Bank,	Saco,	51	
		11,275	

Atlantic and St. Lawrence Rail Road Company.

Names.	Residence.	No. of shares.	Am't of stock
William H. Ayres,	Portland,	2	
James Aiken,	do.	5	
John Anderson,	do.	100	
Samuel Allen,	do.	2	
Joseph Adams,	do.	10	
John Ayres,	do.	1	
Abiezer Andrews,	do.	2	
William Allen,	do.	2	
Elijah Adams,	do.	1	
Moses M Allen,	do.	1	
William S. Allen,	do.	2	
William Akerman,	do.	5	
E. W. Appleton,	do.	2	
William Anson,	do.	10	
Joseph Adams,	do.	10	
Daniel F. Adams,	do.	1	
Moses Adams,	do.	2	
James Appleton, jr.,	do.	3	
Elijah Adams,	do.	1	
William Arnold,	do.	1	
Elvira Allen,	do.	3	
Samuel J. Anderson,	do.	1	
Mahlon Ahers,	do.	1	
Ancient Brothers Lodge,	do.	5	
John Averill,	do.	5	
Ancient Land Mark Lodge,	do.	10	
Ebenezer Armstrong,	do.	1	
L. W. Bradley,	do.	5	
H. Brazier,	do.	5	

Atlantic & St. Lawrence Rail Road Company, (Continued.).

Names.	Residence.	No. of shares.	Am't of stock
F. Bradbury,	Portland,	10	
Jos. R. Brazier,	do.	1	
Joseph Brooks,	do.	3	
Ira Brett,	do.	10	
W. A Bean,	do.	1	
Cornelius B Butler,	do.	1	
J. & C. J. Barbour,	do.	10	
J. O. Bancroft,	do.	5	
Thomas Brown,	do.	5	
Samuel Blanchard,	do.	6	
Alfred Butler,	do.	1	
H. C. Barnes,	do.	2	
Henry H. Boody,	do.	10	
William C. Bradley,	do.	5	
Elbridge Bacon,	do.	3	
A. M. Baker,	do.	4	
John B. Brown,	do.	100	
Charles E. Barrett,	do.	35	
John P. Boyd,	do.	10	
Boothby & Harmond,	do.	2	
Stillman Barbour,	do.	2	
E. P. Burbank & Co.,	do.	5	
Clarissa Branscomb,	do.	1	
John W. Burk,	do.	10	
Beckett & Ingraham,	do.	5	
George Brock,	do.	2	
Martha Brock,	do.	3	
Nathaniel Blanchard,	do.	66	
Charles Blake,	do.	6	
George H. Blanchard,	do.	2	
William Briggs,	do.	2	
Hiram Beal,	do.	2	
Charles Baker,	do.	5	
Nathaniel Brown,	do.	2	
Benjamin Brock,	do.	1	
S. Bolton,	do.	2	
John Bartels,	do.	10	
Phinehas Barnes,	do.	7	
J. J. Brown,	do.	5	
George Burnham,	do.	2	
Boyd & Hanson,	do.	6	
Asa Bailey,	do.	5	
John Bradford,	do.	2	

Atlantic & St. Lawrence Rail Road Company, (Continued.)

Names.	Residence.	No. of shares.	Am't of stock
George L. Bradbury,	Portland,	2	
Edward Burnham,	do.	1	
Joseph Bradford,	do.	1	
Eunice Bradford,	do.	1	
Wm. Boyd,	do.	1	
Charles H. Boyd,	do.	1	
Henry Bradbury,	do.	2	
E. D. Branscomb,	do.	1	
A. H. Branscomb,	do.	3	
Edward P. Banks,	do.	2	
Nathan Barker,	do.	1	
Robert A. Bird,	do.	2	
John C. Baker,	do.	1	
George H. Babcock,	do.	2	
Zebulon Black,	do.	1	
James Bradley,	do.	1	
Alexander Barbour,	do.	3	
Henry B. Burns,	do.	2	
Hiram Brooks,	do.	3	
Thomas H. Brown,	do.	1	
Mary E. Barbour,	do.	1	
Greenleaf Bibber,	do.	5	
John Bond,	do.	2	
James H. Baker,	do.	2	
John B. Bagley,	do.	1	
Stephen B. Bowles,	do.	1	
Sarah Barnes,	do.	3	
George Bartol,	do.	10	
Augustus Blanchard,	do.	2	
Albus R. Blanchard,	do.	2	
Leonard Billings,	do.	1	
Clarissa Brooks,	do.	5	
Mary Blake,	do.	5	
John C. Brooks,	do.	20	
Mrs. H. L. Brooks,	do.	3	
Thomas Bolton,	do.	5	
Edward W. Baker,	do.	2	
Edward Baker,	do.	2	
J. & J. S. Brooks,	do.	2	
Nathaniel Blake,	do.	10	
William Bartlett,	do.	10	
William Briggs,	do.	1	
Charles E. Beckett,	do.	2	

Atlantic & St. Lawrence Rail Road Company, (Continued.)

Names.	Residence.	No. of shares.	Am't of stock
S. S. Beckett,	Portland,	2	
William H. Barnes,	do.	1	
Charles Blake,	do.	4	
Arnold Burroughs,	do.	2	
G. S. Bastow,	do.	2	
E. P. Burbank & Co,	do.	5	
Joseph Barnes,	do.	1	
Mary Bartol,	do.	5	
Louisa Baker,	do.	1	
Daniel Brazier,	do.	2	
John B Buttrick,	do.	1	
James L. Baker,	do.	2	
Charles E. Bennett,	do.	1	
Asa M. Bond,	do.	2	
Phinehas Barnes,	do.	1	
Charles Baker,	do.	1	
J. & C J Barbour,	do.	5	
L. W Bradley,	do.	5	
A. Bradish,	do.	2	
John B. Bagley,	do.	1	
Charles H Blake,	do.	1	
William Buxton,	do.	1	
Arnold Burrough,	do.	3	
Elias Banks,	do.	2	
James Bradley,	do.	1	
Isaac Bartlett,	do.	1	
Isaac H. Brown,	do.	1	
Hiram Brooks,	do.	2	
J. & J S Brooks,	do.	3	
Nathaniel Brown,	do.	3	
Elias Banks,	do.	1	
Henry Bradbury,	do.	3	
James Barbour,	do.	1	
H. V. Bartol,	do.	5	
John B. Buttrick,	do.	1	
Henry C Baker,	do.	1	
John P. Boyd,	do.	10	
H. Brazier,	do.	5	
J. J. Brown,	do.	10	
Samuel Blanchard,	do.	4	
Boyd & Hanson,	do.	4	
Edward P. Banks,	do.	1	
George Bartol,	do.	5	

Atlantic & St. Lawrence Rail Road Company, (Continued.)

Names.	Residence.	No. of shares.	Am't of stock
Hiram Covell,	Portland,	10	
Dudley Cammett,	do.	5	
Mary Card,	do.	1	
Abel Chase, jr ,	do.	2	
Emery Cushing,	do.	1	
Caleb Crockett,	do.	5	
George Cushing,	do.	1	
John Chase,	do.	3	
J. C Churchill,	do.	10	
A. H. & C. W. Cutter,	do.	4	
S. H. Colesworthy,	do.	5	
Lemuel Cobb, jr ,	do.	5	
J. B. Condit,	do.	5	
John Crockett,	do.	1	
Thomas B. Cook,	do.	2	
Samuel Chadwick,	do.	50	
Sumner Cummings,	do.	12	
Edwin Churchill,	do.	20	
Eliphalet Clark,	do.	10	
John B. Cummings,	do.	10	
Walter Corey,	do.	5	
Nathan Chapman,	do.	5	
S. T. Corser,	do.	10	
Charles Carle,	do.	2	
William Chase,	do.	3	
Nathan Cleaves,	do.	1	
F. G. Cummings,	do.	11	
M. M. & M. A. Cobb,	do.	4	
Charles Q. Clapp,	do.	10	
Charles Cobb,	do.	10	
Eliphalet Case,	do.	20	
Cram & Minot,	do.	3	
Charles H. Carruthus,	do.	2	
Samuel Chase,	do.	10	
Samuel Chase & Son,	do.	10	
Thomas Cummings,	do.	10	
John Conner,	do.	5	
W. W. Carr,	do.	1	
Oliver Clapp,	do.	2	
J. B. Cahoon,	do.	10	
N. O. & C. H. Cram,	do.	15	
Chamberlain & Hatch,	do.	10	
Thomas Chadwick,	do.	15	

Atlantic & St. Lawrence Rail Road Company, (Continued.)

Names.	Residence.	No. of shares.	Am't of stock
Asa Cummings,	Portland,	5	
Henry T. Cummings,	do.	2	
Hannah Cummings,	do.	1	
Sarah M. N. Cummings,	do.	1	
Ralph W. Cummings,	do.	1	
John W. Chickering,	do.	2	
N. P. Cushman,	do.	5	
Richard Crockett,	do.	5	
Nathaniel Crockett,	do.	2	
John Chute,	do.	5	
J. M. Coolbroth,	do.	5	
Samuel Chesley,	do.	2	
Philip Cassidy,	do.	3	
J. W. Chadbourne,	do.	1	
Matthew Cobb,	do.	2	
George Clark,	do.	2	
William Cammett,	do.	1	
Antonio Cook,	do.	1	
George Colman,	do.	1	
Ambrose Colby,	do.	5	
Charles W. Child,	do.	5	
Judah Chandler,	do.	10	
Edward T. Cushman,	do.	1	
Solomon Crockett,	do.	1	
Stanley Covell,	do.	1	
J. B. Coyle,	do.	3	
George W. Cobb,	do.	1	
John Carter,	do.	1	
David Chandler,	do.	1	
John W. Chase,	do.	4	
Samuel Clark,	do.	5	
Levi Cram,	do.	1	
Martha Cumpston,	do.	1	
Rufus Cushman,	do.	3	
Nathan Cummings,	do.	10	
R. A. L. Codman,	do.	10	
Thomas Cobb,	do.	1	
Ira Crockett,	do.	16	
Warren E. Chase,	do.	1	
Charles W. Cahoon,	do.	5	
S. Curtis,	do.	5	
Hannah Collins,	do.	5	
A. W. H. Clapp,	do.	12	

Atlantic & St. Lawrence Rail Road Company, (Continued.)

Names.	Residence.	No. of shares.	Am't of stock
Sewall C. Chase,	Portland,	3	
Ruth Cutter,	do.	10	
Silas A. Cummings,	do.	2	
John Conley,	do.	1	
Daniel Cummings,	do.	2	
Mary H. Cummings,	do.	3	
Harriet Capen,	do.	1	
John R. Corey,	do.	2	
Thomas F. Cummings,	do.	1	
Francis Cook,	do.	5	
Alvan Cushman,	do.	2	
J. B. Cummings, jr.,	do.	1	
Ammi G. Cutter,	do.	5	
Louis J. de Creney,	do.	2	
Artemus Carter & Son,	do.	2	
James Crie,	do.	1	
Cumberland Tent,	do.	10	
John Crease,	do.	1	
J. W. Crowther,	do.	1	
Moses Clark,	do.	1	
Leonard Crockett,	do.	1	
Albert Collee, jr.,	do.	5	
D. H. Chandler,	do.	2	
John Crockett,	do.	2	
Jacob Cheever, jr.,	do.	1	
Fred. A. de Creney,	do.	1	
Samuel Cobb,	do.	1	
Frances E. Cummings,	do.	1	
Benjamin Cobb,	do.	1	
Charles E. Carle,	do.	1	
Alvan Cushman,	do.	2	
H. E. Chadwick,	do.	1	
C. M. Chadwick,	do.	1	
Mary Chadwick,	do.	1	
Martha Cahoon,	do.	3	
Mary E. Cahoon,	do.	1	
Charlotte D. Cahoon,	do.	1	
B. Cushman,	do.	5	
Catharine Cushman,	do.	1	
Arthur Cleasby,	do.	2	
Thomas Chadwick,	do.	5	
A. L. E. Clapp,	do.	2	
Charles H. Carruthers,	do.	1	

5

Atlantic & St. Lawrence Rail Road Company, (*Continued.*)

Names.	Residence.	No. of shares.	Am't of stock
Philip Cassidy,	Portland,	2	
P. G. Chase,	do.	1	
Wm. F. Chadwick,	do.	1	
Samuel Chadwick, jr.,	do.	1	
George H. Chadwick,	do.	1	
Sumner Cummings,	do.	5	
Walter Corey,	do.	5	
Charles C. Cole,	do.	2	
Charlotte A. Cummings,	do.	1	
Hiram Covell,	do.	5	
N. O. & C. H. Cram,	do.	5	
R. O. Conant,	do.	5	
A. H. Cutter & Co.,	do.	2	
Joseph Curtis,	do.	2	
Charles O. Cole,	do.	1	
Ruth Cutter,	do.	10	
S. H. Colesworthy,	do.	5	
William Coolidge,	do.	5	
George Clark,	do.	3	
Caroline Chase,	do.	1	
William Collagan,	do.	5	
James C. Churchill,	do.	2	
D. F. Chase,	do.	10	
H. A. Curtis,	do.	10	
J. M. Colbroth,	do.	5	
Samuel Chase,	do.	10	
Lemuel Cobb, jr.,	do.	5	
Charles F. Correy,	do.	1	
Emery Cushing,	do.	1	
Sewall C. Chase,	do.	2	
F. & F. Cummings,	do.	10	
Daniel Cummings,	do.	2	
Daniel Carr,	do.	1	
Thomas Conner,	do.	1	
Abel Chase, 2d,	do.	2	
Oliver Dennett,	do.	5	
Eben E. Drake,	do.	1	
O. E. Durgin,	do.	5	
Dexter Daniels,	do.	3	
Benjamin Deake,	do.	2	
Thomas A. Deblois,	do.	5	
Jeremiah Dow,	do.	8	
Josiah Dow & Son,	do.	10	

Atlantic & St. Lawrence Rail Road Company, (Continued.)

Names.	Residence.	No. of shares.	Am't of stock
Lemuel Dyer,	Portland,	40	
William Duren,	do.	5	
Phineas Drinkwater,	do.	2	
Joshua Dyer,	do.	2	
James E. Davis,	do.	2	
James Dyer,	do.	5	
William H. Dyer,	do.	2	
George R. Davis,	do.	5	
O. E. Durgin,	do.	5	
John Dow,	do.	30	
Eunice Day,	do.	10	
Oliver Dennett,	do.	20	
C. Davidson,	do.	3	
C. G. Downes,	do.	2	
Dexter Daniels,	do.	5	
Dunn & Osborne,	do.	2	
M. & A. P. Darling,	do.	2	
Jeremiah Dow,	do.	10	
H. W. & A. Deering,	do.	5	
Edward H Daveis,	do.	5	
Charles S. Daveis,	do.	10	
Woodbury S. Dana,	do.	5	
M. G. Deane,	do.	5	
Jas. R. Dockray,	do.	2	
Gardner Dyer,	do.	1	
Nathan J. Davis,	do.	2	
Henry Dyer,	do.	1	
B. F. Demerritt,	do.	3	
C. M. Davis,	do.	3	
Andrew T. Dole,	do.	5	
William S. Davis,	do.	2	
John S. Dunlap,	do.	1	
Josiah Duren,	do.	1	
William Duren,	do.	5	
A. M. Dresser,	do.	5	
William Dyer,	do.	5	
Charles Day,	do.	3	
Josiah Dow & Son,	do.	20	
Nathaniel H. Dana,	do.	1	
Luther Dana,	do.	6	
Stephen O. Danielson,	do.	2	
David Drinkwater,	do.	5	
Levi F. Drake,	do.	3	

Atlantic & St. Lawrence Rail Road Company, (*Continued.*)

Names.	Residence.	No. of shares.	Am't of stock
Harris Dresser,	Portland,	1	
Greene S. Deguil,	do.	2	
Hiram H. Dow,	do.	5	
Benjamin Dodge,	do.	1	
Edward Deering,	do.	2	
Lemuel Dyer,	do.	45	
Joseph W. Dyer,	do.	5	
Noah Deering,	do.	1	
Day & Lyon,	do.	10	
Bradbury Dearborn,	do.	5	
Daniel G. Drew,	do.	1	
Robie Davis,	do.	1	
George W. Dam,	do.	2	
Christopher Dyer,	do.	1	
E. Daniels,	do.	5	
Robertson Dyer,	do.	3	
Thomas A. Deblois,	do.	5	
James R. Dockray,	do.	2	
Mary F Dow,	do.	1	
Caroline E. Dow,	do.	1	
Simon A. Dyer,	do.	1	
Peter Duran,	do.	1	
David Drinkwater,	do.	5	
John W. Dick,	do.	2	
J B. Duroy,	do.	2	
Eunice Day,	do.	10	
John J. Davis,	do.	2	
Andrew Dooley,	do.	2	
Charles Dehan,	do.	2	
Patrick Dehan, 3d,	do.	3	
Lewis Dela,	do.	1	
Robert Dresser,	do.	3	
Mark P Emery,	do.	5	
N. Ellsworth,	do.	7	
Rufus Emerson,	do.	5	
Emery & Waterhouse,	do.	10	
John E. Elder,	do.	1	
William Evans,	do.	60	
Charles P. Evans,	do.	1	
Daniel Evans,	do.	10	
C. R. Edwards,	do.	5	
H. S. Edwards,	do.	5	
John Edwards,	do.	1	

Atlantic & St. Lawrence Rail Road Company, (Continued.)

Names.	Residence.	No. of shares.	Am't of stock
S. W. Eaton,	Portland,	5	
Francis Edmond,	do.	5	
George B. Eaton,	do.	1	
Joshua Emery,	do.	1	
Samuel Emery,	do.	9	
N. W. Ellsworth,	do.	3	
William Evans,	do.	10	
John Elder,	do.	5	
Stephen Emerson,	do.	3	
William E. Edwards,	do.	1	
M. P. Emery,	do.	5	
Otis C. Edwards,	do.	1	
Samuel Elder,	do.	1	
John Elder,	do.	5	
Eastern Star Encampment,	do.	5	
Rufus Emerson,	do.	5	
S. W. Eaton,	do.	5	
Emery & Waterhouse,	do.	5	
Noah Edgcomb,	do.	2	
Stephen Frothingham,	do.	8	
Edwin Fernald,	do.	10	
Fobes & Wilson,	do.	10	
Benjamin C. Fuller,	do.	1	
James L. Farmer,	do.	25	
James Furbush,	do.	10	
Benjamin Furlong,	do.	1	
Hersey Freeman,	do.	1	
Wm. Fives,	do.	2	
John Fox,	do.	30	
Gideon Foster,	do.	8	
O. G. Fessenden,	do.	5	
Daniel Fox,	do.	10	
Edward Fox,	do.	10	
D. & A. L. Fox,	do.	5	
Samuel R. Fernald,	do.	1	
Luther Fitch,	do.	10	
Horace Felton,	do.	5	
Henry Fox,	do.	2	
Alexander Foss,	do.	2	
Thomas Forsaith,	do.	2	
Daniel Freeman,	do.	5	
U. H. Furlong,	do.	3	
Charles H. Foye,	do.	1	

5*

Atlantic & St. Lawrence Rail Road Company, (Continued.)

Names.	Residence.	No. of shares.	Am't of stock
Stephen Furbish,	Portland,	5	
Samuel Fessenden,	do.	5	
Wentworth P. Files,	do.	1	
Thomas Files,	do.	1	
Fernald & Co.,	do.	3	
Lydia Ferrin,	do.	1	
Franklin Fox,	do.	1	
Thomas J. Furlong,	do.	1	
Thomas Fabyan,	do.	1	
Isaac Fickett,	do.	4	
Antonio Frates,	do.	2	
Gilbert Fowler,	do.	2	
Benj. Fogg,	do.	1	
R. Follansbee,	do.	1	
D. H. Furbish,	do.	1	
Daniel Fox,	do.	10	
Michael Foley,	do.	3	
John J. & C. R. Frost,	do.	5	
Nathan Fessenden,	do.	1	
Ellen W. Fox,	do.	5	
Mary K. Farrington,	do.	2	
Stephen Frothingham,	do.	4	
Thomas Forsaith,	do.	1	
Luther Fitch,	do.	10	
Benjamin Fogg,	do.	1	
Edwin Fernald,	do.	5	
Oliver G. Fessenden,	do.	5	
Edward Fox,	do.	2	
John Fox,	do.	20	
Fobes & Wilson,	do.	2	
Philip Greeley,	do.	25	
William Goold,	do.	3	
Joshua Gordon,	do.	3	
Jotham Grant,	do.	5	
Oliver Gerrish,	do.	5	
Ephraim Gammon,	do.	3	
William Graves & Son,	do.	2	
Eliza D. Griffith,	do.	1	
J. & M. Griffith,	do.	2	
Eliphalet Greeley,	do.	50	
Henry Goddard,	do.	25	
Gerrish & Edwards,	do.	10	
Byron Greenough,	do.	20	

Atlantic & St. Lawrence Rail Road Company, (Continued.)

Names.	Residence.	No. of shares.	Am't of stock
John T. Gilman,	Portland,	5	
Joseph Gray,	do.	3	
C. W. Goddard,	do.	1	
Edward Gould,	do.	5	
Moses Gould,	do.	5	
Daniel Gould,	do.	5	
Daniel Green,	do.	5	
William Goodenow,	do.	10	
Samuel Gooding,	do.	3	
Joseph M. Gerrish,	do.	20	
E. P. Gerrish,	do.	1	
F. A. & A. F. Gerrish,	do.	2	
Joseph Goold,	do.	10	
Amos Grover,	do.	5	
N. J. Gilman,	do.	1	
Gammon & Huntress,	do.	4	
Edwin C. Greeley,	do.	1	
George H. Greeley,	do.	5	
William Gorham,	do.	2	
Abel Grover,	do.	2	
Peter Graffam,	do.	2	
Samuel P. Gerts,	do.	5	
Ephraim Gammon,	do.	2	
Elijah Guilford,	do.	2	
William Griffin,	do.	1	
Nathaniel Gordon,	do.	3	
Nathaniel Gordon, jr.,	do.	1	
John Gooding,	do.	1	
Joseph G. Gilman,	do.	2	
Martin Gore,	do.	7	
Charles M. Gore,	do.	5	
Ellen Gerrish,	do.	1	
W. Scott Gerrish,	do.	1	
William Gould,	do.	2	
Joseph Goold,	do.	10	
Eliza D. Griffith,	do.	3	
Stephen Gale,	do.	1	
Moses Gould,	do.	5	
Richard Gooding,	do.	2	
Edward Gooding,	do.	3	
Sarah N. Gardner,	do.	1	
Mrs. Eliza L. Goddard,	do.	5	
Daniel Gould,	do.	5	

Atlantic & St. Lawrence Rail Road Company, (Continued.)

Names.	Residence.	No. of shares.	Am't of stock
David Griffin,	Portland,	1	
James Greenough,	do.	2	
Mary P. Goddard,	do.	1	
Alphonso S. Godfrey,	do.	1	
Oliver Gerrish,	do.	5	
Charles Gould,	do.	1	
E. E Gould,	do.	1	
Sarah N. Gardner,	do.	1	
Abner G. Green,	do.	1	
Elijah Guilford,	do.	2	
James Gould,	do.	1	
Edward Gould,	do.	5	
Henry W. Goddard,	do.	8	
George Gray,	do.	1	
John T. Gilman,	do.	2	
Simon Gross,	do.	5	
Peter Graffam,	do.	2	
P. Greeley,	do.	15	
Joseph M. Gerrish,	do.	10	
Byron Greenough,	do.	20	
William Gulliver,	do.	1	
Martin Gore,	do.	3	
William Goodenow,	do.	10	
Daniel Gould,	do.	5	
Moses Gould,	do.	5	
Andrew Griffin,	do.	1	
William Hoyt,	do.	5	
Charles Holden,	do.	10	
Alfred Haskell,	do.	2	
Elizabeth Halliday,	do.	4	
Edward Harlow,	do.	2	
J. E. Hodgkins,	do.	1	
Horace Harvey,	do.	2	
Hosea Harford,	do.	1	
Edward Howe,	do.	20	
Simeon Hall,	do.	5	
George Hall,	do.	8	
S. N. & W. & al Haskell,	do.	6	
Joshua Hobbs,	do.	8	
Washington Hartshorn,	do.	5	
H. B. Hart,	do.	5	
Orrin Hobbs,	do.	2	
Thomas H. Haskell,	do.	3	

Atlantic & St. Lawrence Rail Road Company, (Continued.)

Names.	Residence.	No. of shares.	Am't of stock
V. C. & L. D. Hanson,	Portland,	5	
Abner Howard,	do.	1	
Thomas Hammond,	do.	50	
Augustine Haines,	do.	10	
Winslow Hall,	do.	5	
Samuel Hanson,	do.	30	
T. C. Hersey,	do.	10	
Samuel Haskell,	do.	5	
Solomon Hawkes,	do.	2	
Hanson M. Hart,	do.	5	
John K. Hooper,	do.	2	
William Hammond,	do.	5	
Amos J. Haskell,	do.	1	
Hall & Conant,	do.	30	
Edward Hamblin,	do.	10	
Rufus Horton,	do.	15	
Hannah Harding,	do.	4	
Seth B. Hilborn,	do.	1	
James Hall,	do.	50	
Elihu Hasty,	do.	5	
William A. Hyde,	do.	8	
Rufus W. Hyde,	do.	1	
George T. Hedge,	do.	1	
John Hasty,	do.	2	
William Hyde,	do.	5	
Hammond & Nash,	do.	5	
Joseph Howard,	do.	10	
Joseph B. Haskell,	do.	2	
Mehitable M Hicks,	do.	2	
S. B. Haskell,	do.	2	
Elisha Hinds,	do.	5	
Charles C. Hull,	do.	3	
Joseph Hay,	do.	2	
Joseph F. Hay,	do.	1	
Walter Hatch,	do.	1	
George S. Hay,	do.	3	
Charles H. Ham,	do.	2	
Sarah W. Hooper,	do.	1	
Lazarus Harlow,	do.	3	
Apollo Howe,	do.	1	
James Hindle,	do.	1	
Mehitable Hindle,	do.	1	
Charles O. Hindle,	do.	1	

Atlantic & St. Lawrence Rail Road Company, (Continued.)

Names.	Residence	No. of shares.	Am't of stock
Benjamin Harmon,	Portland,	1	
A. D. Hall,	do.	2	
H. H. Hinkley,	do.	1	
Ann Hatch,	do.	3	
Joel Hall,	do.	10	
H H Hay,	do.	1	
Ellen Hall,	do.	1	
Sarah T. Hall,	do.	1	
James R Hawkes,	do.	3	
Catharine M. Hyde,	do.	1	
Ellen T. Hyde,	do.	1	
Harriet L. Howe,	do.	2	
Elizabeth F. Howe,	do.	1	
Ruth Howe,	do.	1	
Nathan Howe,	do.	1	
Daniel Hamblet,	do.	1	
Stephen D. Hall,	do.	2	
Caleb S. Hatch,	do.	1	
David Hodson,	do.	2	
William H. H. Hatch,	do.	3	
William Hoit,	do.	5	
Lydia Hancock,	do.	1	
Daniel Hood,	do.	14	
Hosea Harford,	do.	1	
James H Harford,	do.	1	
Henry B. Hussey,	do.	2	
Joseph Hale,	do.	2	
Obed Hall,	do.	2	
Otis Harward,	do.	5	
Charles C. Hall,	do.	5	
Almira Hasty,	do.	1	
Elihu T. Homan, jr.,	do.	1	
Augusta Hall,	do.	2	
Mary P. Hanson,	do	4	
Alexander Hobbs,	do.	4	
H. K. Hinkley,	do.	1	
Higgins & Libby,	do.	4	
Solomon Hawkes,	do.	1	
Simeon H. Higgins,	do.	2	
Andrew P. Holmes,	do.	1	
Daniel Hood,	do.	1	
J. E. Hodgkins,	do.	1	
Orrin Hobbs,	do.	1	

Atlantic & St. Lawrence Rail Road Company, *(Continued.)*

Names.	Residence.	No. of shares.	Am't of stock
William Hatch,	Portland,	2	
F. P. Haines,	do.	1	
John Haggerty, jr.,	do.	1	
Greely Hannaford, jr.,	do.	1	
V. C. & L. D. Hanson,	do.	3	
Hartshorn & Payson,	do.	2	
Joshua Haskell,	do.	5	
Thomas Harkin,	do.	1	
Hammond & Nash,	do.	5	
Winslow Hall,	do.	5	
H. B & H. M. Hart,	do.	5	
C M. Harris,	do.	2	
Daniel Hawkes,	do.	5	
Caleb S. Hatch,	do.	2	
Almira Hasty,	do.	4	
Horace Harvey,	do.	1	
Samuel Hanson,	do.	10	
T C. Hersey,	do.	5	
Edward Howe,	do.	5	
Samuel Hanson,	do.	10	
Lazarus Harlow,	do.	1	
Joseph Hill,	do.	3	
Joseph Howard,	do	10	
Joel Hall,	do.	30	
Simeon Hall,	do.	2	
Charles Harding,	do.	2	
W. P. Harmon,	do.	5	
Henry W. Hersey,	do.	2	
Henry A. Jones,	do.	3	
Edward Ingraham,	do.	5	
Thomas R. Jones,	do.	10	
Ruth Jewett,	do.	5	
Sarah Jewett,	do.	2	
George Jewett,	do.	4	
Luther Jewett,	do.	4	
Charles P. Ingraham,	do.	5	
Hiram Jordan,	do.	10	
Winthrop T. Jordan,	do.	1	
Deering Johnson,	do.	2	
James Jewett,	do.	2	
Nathan Ilsley,	do.	1	
Benjamin Ilsley,	do.	1	
Holt Ingraham,	do.	1	

Atlantic & St. Lawrence Rail Road Company, (Continued,)

Names.	Residence.	No. of shares.	Am't of stock
Jedediah Jewett,	Portland,	5	
Clement Jordan,	do.	1	
Margaret Jones,	do.	1	
Caroline Jones,	do.	1	
Mary Jones,	do.	1	
Charles Jones,	do.	15	
William Jacobs,	do.	2	
James D. Jackson,	do.	1	
Albert Jewett,	do.	5	
James Jack,	do.	2	
Moses C. Jewett,	do.	5	
Henry Jackson,	do.	2	
Alice Ilsley,	do.	1	
Theophilus Ilsley,	do.	1	
Edward P. Jumper,	do.	3	
George B. C. Ingraham,	do.	1	
Joseph Johnson,	do.	2	
George T. Ingraham,	do.	2	
Everett H. Jones,	do.	1	
Tristram Jordan,	do.	1	
Edward B. Jack,	do.	1	
Ruth Jewett,	do.	3	
Sarah Jewett,	do.	2	
John M. Jordan,	do.	1	
Margaret Jones,	do.	2	
Charles Jordan,	do.	20	
Samuel Johnson,	do.	1	
Benjamin Ilsley,	do.	1	
John Jackson,	do.	1	
Charles Jones,	do.	5	
Nathaniel Ilsley,	do.	2	
Alden Jackson,	do.	2	
Ann F. Jones,	do.	1	
Frederic Ilsley,	do.	5	
Thomas R. Jones,	do.	5	
Jedediah Jewett,	do.	1	
Isaac Ilsley,	do.	30	
William H. Knight,	do.	1	
William Kimball,	do.	10	
Hannah Kilborn,	do.	1	
Mary A. Kilborn,	do.	1	
Reuben Kent, jr.,	do.	4	
Isaac Knight,	do.	5	

Atlantic & St. Lawrence Rail Road Company, (Continued.)

Names.	Residence.	No. of shares.	Am't of stock
Jacob Kimball,	Portland,	5	
Thomas E. Knight,	do.	3	
David Keazer,	do.	5	
William C. Kimball,	do.	1	
George Knight,	do.	3	
William Kinsman,	do.	2	
Benjamin Kingsbury, jr.,	do.	5	
Angela Kinsman,	do.	1	
Eunice Kellogg,	do.	1	
Joseph M. Kellogg,	do.	1	
Sarah Killgore,	do.	5	
R. W. Kennard,	do.	2	
Joshua Knight,	do.	1	
Charles T. Knight,	do.	1	
Joshua Knight,	do.	1	
William Kimball,	do.	2	
Jos. L. Kelley & Co.,	do.	3	
George Knight, jr.,	do.	2	
Bethany W. Knight,	do.	2	
David Kelley,	do.	2	
Reuben Kent, jr.,	do.	2	
C. M. Kingsbury,	do.	1	
J. T. Lewis,	do.	2	
Lowell & Senter,	do.	5	
Hall J. Little,	do.	20	
R. W. Lincoln,	do.	5	
Zenas Libby,	do.	5	
Samuel Lincoln,	do.	1	
J. R. Lufkin,	do.	3	
H. J & F. O. Libby,	do.	8	
Benjamin Larrabee, 2d,	do.	2	
John A. Larrabee,	do.	2	
Benjamin Longley,	do.	4	
Josiah S. Little,	do.	25	
S. R. Lyman,	do.	5	
Stephen Longfellow,	do.	10	
Edward M. Leavitt,	do.	1	
Joseph Leavitt,	do.	5	
Samuel R. Leavitt,	do.	5	
Mathias Libby,	do.	2	
N. W. Lefavor,	do.	2	
Sylvanus Ling,	do.	5	
John Leavitt,	do.	5	

6

Atlantic & St. Lawrence Rail Road Company, (Continued.)

Names.	Residence.	No. of shares.	Am't of stock
Nahum Libby,	Portland,	2	
Alexander W. Longfellow,	do.	5	
Elijah Long,	do.	2	
William Lord,	do.	5	
William D. Little,	do.	3	
Ancient L. M. Lodge,	do.	10	
Mary Lunt,	do.	1	
Charles Littlejohn, jr.,	do.	2	
Aaron D. Lowell,	do.	2	
Benjamin Littlefield,	do.	1	
Alpheus Libby,	do.	3	
Samuel Lowell,	do.	1	
John Lewis,	do.	1	
Nahum Littlefield,	do.	1	
M. Landers,	do.	1	
Follet T. Lally,	do.	10	
Abba P. Little,	do.	2	
Ligonia Lodge,	do.	10	
George Lord,	do.	2	
John F Leavitt,	do.	2	
John Lynch,	do.	2	
J. R. Lufkin,	do.	2	
J. S. Lewis,	do.	1	
J. B. Libby,	do.	2	
W. D. Little,	do.	1	
U. T. Ling,	do.	1	
Philip Larkin,	do.	1	
H. J. Little,	do.	10	
Benjamin Longley,	do.	1	
Abner Lowell,	do.	3	
Samuel S. Lufkin,	do.	2	
John Leavitt,	do.	5	
George McLellan,	do.	4	
J. A. Montgomery,	do.	1	
Eben McIntosh,	do.	5	
Lemuel Moody,	do.	2	
Seward Merrill,	do.	3	
Gabriel Mark,	do.	3	
Isaac Milliken,	do.	1	
Mary M. Mountfort,	do.	6	
Elias Mountfort,	do.	3	
Peter Merrill,	do.	2	
D. M. Mitchell,	do.	5	

Atlantic & St. Lawrence Rail Road Company, (Continued.)

Names.	Residence.	No. of shares.	Am't of stock
Thomas McLellan,	Portland,	20	
Moses Morrill,	do.	3	
Reuben Mitchell,	do.	20	
Jonathan K. Morse,	do.	1	
Joshua Maxwell,	do.	5	
John Mussey,	do.	100	
Daniel Mussey,	do.	3	
John M. Milliken,	do.	4	
P. W. Morrill,	do.	5	
Thomas S. Minot,	do.	5	
James B. Moore,	do.	2	
William C. Means,	do.	2	
Moody & Swift,	do.	5	
William Moulton,	do.	5	
Benjamin McKenney,	do.	1	
Joseph R. Matthews,	do.	5	
James Mayberry,	do.	2	
T. L. Merrill,	do.	1	
L. U. Merrill,	do.	1	
L. D. Mason,	do.	5	
Simon Merrill,	do.	4	
J. N. Morrill & Co.,	do.	6	
Maine C. M Association,	do.	20	
Charles Morrill,	do.	2	
Charles Moody,	do.	2	
Albert J. Merrill,	do.	2	
Nathan Mayhew,	do.	5	
Sylvanus D. Merrill,	do.	2	
Thomas Murphey,	do.	2	
John Mahan,	do.	5	
Nathan S. Mitchell,	do.	1	
Esther Mussey,	do.	5	
Godfrey Mark,	do.	3	
E. McKenney,	do.	5	
Enoch Moulton,	do.	1	
Joshua C. Morse,	do.	2	
C. C. Mitchell & Son,	do.	5	
Jacob McLellan,	do.	10	
J. R. Milliken,	do.	5	
Maria Mariner,	do.	2	
George McAllister,	do.	3	
Dennis McCarty,	do.	1	
Moses L. McCarty,	do.	1	

Atlantic & St. Lawrence Rail Road Company, (Continued.)

Names.	Residence.	No. of shares.	Am't of stock
John F. Milliken,	Portland,	1	
James L. Merrill,	do.	2	
Jas. L. Merrill, for children,	do.	2	
Charles E. Marwick,	do.	3	
Albert Marwick,	do.	3	
Hannah Marwick,	do.	3	
Pamela Martin,	do.	1	
Sarah Martin,	do.	1	
James Mountfort,	do.	5	
Thomas Mallard,	do.	1	
Stephen C. Munsey	do.	1	
Edwin Merrill,	do.	2	
Maine Lodge No. 1, O. F.,	do.	20	
William Merrill,	do.	5	
J. W. Mighels,	do.	5	
Joseph Mountfort,	do.	5	
Moses Merrill,	do.	2	
James S. Merrill,	do.	1	
George W. Means,	do.	1	
Seward Merrill,	do.	2	
Peter Mugford,	do.	1	
George G. Minot,	do.	2	
Thomas Murry,	do.	1	
Seth Mason,	do.	2	
Seth C. Mason,	do.		
Daniel Mussey,	do.	2	
Thomas McLellan,	do.	10	
Esther Mussey,	do.	8	
Harriet T. Mussey	do.	5	
Margaret J. Mussey,	do.	5	
Lucy McLellan,	do.	2	
N. Doane McLellan,	do.	2	
Eliza Mayo,	do.	5	
J. K. Morse,	do.	1	
J. W. & S. Mansfield,	do.	1	
Machigonne Encampment,	do.	10	
Mutual Fire Insurance Co.,	do.	100	
William Moulton,	do.	15	
Mount Vernon Chapter,	do.	15	
Michael Patrick Mackin,	do.	1	
Michael McBride,	do.	2	
Benjamin McGill,	do.	2	
J. S. Merrrill,	do.	1	

Atlantic & St. Lawrence Rail Road Company, (Continued.)

Names.	Residence.	No. of shares.	Am't of stock
Patrick Murphy,	Portland,	2	
Mary M. Mountfort,	do.	1	
Eleazer McKenney,	do.	5	
Edward Mason,	do.	5	
Edward Motley,	do.	10	
James Mountfort,	do.	3	
Rufus Morrill,	do.	5	
Reuben Mitchell,	do.	10	
Sewall Mitchell,	do.	2	
J. R. Millikin,	do.	1	
Thomas McLellan,	do.	30	
Ebenezer McIntosh,	do.	5	
James Maxwell,	do.	5	
James B. Moore,	do.	1	
Noyes, Ilsley & Rolfe,	do.	3	
Robert Noble,	do.	2	
John Neal,	do.	30	
Ward Noyes,	do.	1	
Amos Nichols,	do.	1	
Thomas Norton,	do.	2	
Julia M. Norton,	do.	1	
Mary E. Norton,	do.	1	
Harriet A. Norton,	do.	1	
Mighel Nutting,	do.	1	
R. C. Neal,	do.	5	
S. B. Newbegin,	do.	1	
E. A. Norton,	do.	5	
Abraham W. Niles,	do.	1	
P. W. Neal,	do.	1	
Ichabod Nichols,	do.	10	
William Noyes,	do.	1	
Joshua B. Osgood,	do.	30	
Thomas W. O'Brien,	do.	10	
Thomas Owen,	do.	2	
John Oleson,	do.	2	
Samuel Osgood,	do.	2	
William Oxnard,	do.	18	
Frederic Oxnard,	do.	1	
Clarissa Oxnard,	do.	1	
Edward Oxnard,	do.	20	
John Oxnard,	do.	10	
A. A. Osgood,	do.	2	
Ervin Orcutt,	do.	5	

Atlantic & St. Lawrence Rail Road Company, (Continued.)

Names.	Residence.	No. of shares.	Am't of stock
Charles Oxnard,	Portland,	5	
Thomas W. O'Brien,	do.	1	
John Oleson,	do.	3	
Edward Oxnard,	do.	2	
Edward P. Oxnard,	do.	1	
Mary A. Oxnard,	do.	1	
Martha A. Oxnard,	do.	1	
Patrick O'Sullivan,	do.	2	
Edward Oxnard,	do.	10	
Frederic Oxnard,	do.	1	
William Oxnard,	do.	8	
A. A. Osgood,	do.	1	
William Oxnard,	do.	5	
John Oxnard,	do.	6	
George Owen,	do.	1	
George Parsons,	do.	3	
E. N. Perry,	do.	2	
Josiah Pennell,	do.	3	
N. L. Purrington,	do.	5	
John Purinton,	do.	4	
A. H. Putney,	do.	10	
Edwin Parsons,	do.	2	
James Poole,	do.	1	
F. E. Pray,	do.	1	
William P. Preble,	do.	100	
Mary Preble,	do.	50	
Eliza R. Pettingill,	do.	1	
Moses J. Plummer,	do.	10	
Winslow H. Purinton,	do.	5	
J. H. Perley,	do.	3	
Oliver Parsons,	do.	2	
Clement Pennell,	do.	10	
Poor & Jose,	do.	10	
William P. Preble, Jr.,	do.	5	
Mary W. Pollies,	do.	4	
Trist. G. Prince,	do.	2	
Increase Pote,	do.	1	
Edward M. Patten,	do.	2	
Jere. Proctor,	do.	1	
W. W. Polleys,	do.	1	
H. Packard,	do.	2	
A. S. Poole,	do.	1	
J. C. Poole,	do.	1	

Atlantic & St. Lawrence Rail Road Company, (Continued.)

Names.	Residence.	No. of shares.	Am't of stock
J. H. Perley,	Portland,	4	
Daniel Plummer,	do.	2	
S. W. Porter,	do.	10	
M. Patterson,	do.	2	
A. P. Pennell,	do.	2	
J. T. Pike,	do.	3	
C. Pennell, Jr.,	do.	2	
L. Peters,	do.	1	
R. C. Pennell,	do.	3	
G. H. Pearson,	do.	1	
J. F. Purinton,	do.	1	
Enoch Paine,	do.	1	
Phebe Paine,	do.	1	
E. A. Paine,	do.	1	
A. M. Paine,	do.	1	
Winslow H. Purinton,	do.	5	
M. M. Powell,	do.	1	
Francis Pennell,	do.	3	
Giles Porter,	do.	10	
H. H. Phinney,	do.	2	
Lydia Parks,	do.	3	
C. W. Pennell,	do.	2	
G. W. Pennell,	do.	1	
Josiah Pennell,	do.	1	
Mary Preble,	do.	50	
Jonathan Pennell,	do.	1	
James Prentiss,	do.	1	
C. B. Pettingill,	do.	4	
D. Pettingill,	do.	2	
David Pettingill,	do.	3	
W. Parker,	do.	1	
Portland Relf. Soc.,	do.	10	
J. K. Pierce,	do.	2	
Jane Paine,	do.	1	
L. F. Pingree,	do.	3	
R. B. Paine,	do.	1	
Wm. Phinney,	do.	2	
C. W. Prime,	do.	1	
C. Pennell,	do.	5	
S. W. Porter,	do.	5	
Theodore Paine,	do.	1	
A. Poole,	do.	1	
Winslow H. Purinton,	do.	5	

Atlantic & St. Lawrence Rail Road Company, (Continued.)

Names.	Residence.	No. of shares.	Am't of stock
P. Quinn,	Portland,	3	
H. Quincy,	do.	5	
F. A. Quimby,	do.	5	
W. A. Quincy,	do.	1	
Henry Quincy,	do.	10	
William Porter,	do.	7	
M. K. Porter,	do.	1	
N. L. Purinton,	do.	5	
Fanny Putney,	do.	1	
S. W. Porter,	do.	5	
Poor & Jose,	do.	5	
Daniel Plummer,	do.	1	
William H. Purinton,	do.	5	
Hannah Robinson,	do.	2	
John F. Reeves,	do.	20	
Robinson & Hale,	do.	5	
Charles H Ross,	do.	5	
Nathaniel Ross,	do.	10	
Charles Rogers,	do.	5	
J. T. Rogers,	do.	5	
Albus Rea,	do.	5	
Samuel Robinson,	do.	2	
Zophar Reynolds,	do.	10	
Nathaniel Redlon,	do.	1	
Mary C. Robinson,	do.	1	
John Russell, Jr.,	do.	5	
L. O. Reynolds,	do.	2	
Rufus Read,	do.	5	
Marshall Rood,	do.	2	
Samuel Rolfe,	do.	3	
Moses Russell,	do.	2	
Ezra Russell,	do.	2	
R. D. Roberts,	do.	2	
William Ross,	do.	5	
Nehemiah Ryerson,	do.	5	
C. T. Ryerson,	do.	1	
R. S. Randall,	do.	10	
Edward M. Rand,	do.	1	
George D. Rand,	do.	1	
Stephen Ricker,	do.	2	
John C. Remick,	do.	3	
Thomas Randall,	do.	1	
J. W. Russell,	do.	1	

Atlantic & St. Lawrence Rail Road Company, (Continued.)

Names.	Residence.	No. of shares.	Am't of stock
R. R. Robinson,	Portland,	3	
R. J. Robison,	do.	5	
J. J. W. Reeves,	do.	5	
John Rand,	do.	10	
C. W. Roberts,	do.	2	
David Ross,	do.	5	
William H. Roberts,	do.	1	
James Rackleft,	do.	5	
Roberts & Black,	do.	4	
Israel Richardson,	do.	30	
Elizabeth C. Rounds,	do.	1	
W. D. Robinson,	do.	1	
Hannah Robinson,	do.	1	
James A. Roach,	do.	1	
Rolfe, Cole & Co,	do.	5	
Rufus Read,	do.	3	
J. & J. Russell,	do.	5	
Mrs. J. Richardson,	do.	2	
Ann H. Richardson,	do.	1	
D. Robinson, jr.,	do.	2	
H. Robinson,	do.	1	
John Rounds,	do.	5	
Joshua Richardson,	do.	10	
Orrin Ring,	do.	1	
Robinson & Hale,	do.	1	
Arthur S. Ricker,	do.	1	
David Robinson,	do.	1	
Ezra Russell,	do.	2	
Duncan M. Ross,	do.	1	
Thomas H Richardson,	do.	2	
E. T. Russell,	do.	1	
Joseph Ring,	do.	1	
R. R Robinson,	do.	3	
John Rand,	do.	8	
Aug. Randall,	do.	1	
N. P. Richardson,	do.	3	
Zophar Reynolds,	do.	5	
Alfred Randall,	do.	1	
Charles Rogers,	do.	5	
Margaret W. Reeves,	do.	5	
Charles Richardson,	do.	2	
Charles P. Rolfe,	do.	2	
Bethuel Sweetser,	do.	4	

Atlantic & St. Lawrence Rail Road Company, (Continued.)

Names.	Residence.	No. of shares.	Am't of stock
John Sargent,	Portland,	3	
George Smith,	do.	6	
Edward Shields,	do.	5	
Hez. E. Sargent,	do.	2	
Cyrus Sturdivant,	do.	5	
O. E. Silsbee,	do.	5	
William Swan,	do.	20	
Jonathan Stevens,	do.	5	
Albert Shaw,	do.	1	
Andrew S Sawyer,	do.	1	
John Stilworthy,	do.	5	
L. L. Sadler,	do.	5	
Stephen Swett,	do.	1	
St. J. Smith,	do.	100	
Abner Shaw,	do.	20	
Woodbury Storer,	do.	20	
Sanborn & Carter,	do.	20	
Aretas Shurtleff,	do.	2	
C. B Smith,	do.	1	
Nathaniel Shaw,	do.	5	
Philip Shaw,	do.	5	
Joshua Stevens,	do.	5	
John W Smith,	do.	4	
William Small,	do.	2	
Levi Sawyer,	do.	10	
Charles Staples,	do.	5	
J. B Scott,	do.	10	
Charles E. Sawyer,	do.	5	
Charles F. Safford,	do.	5	
Ebenezer Steele,	do.	20	
W. P. Smith,	do.	5	
Samuel Small, jr,	do.	5	
William F. Spear,	do.	1	
Sevey & Libby,	do	5	
E. Scammon,	do.	5	
Joseph S. Smith,	do.	2	
Mary S. Smith,	do.	3	
A. K. Shurtliff,	do.	4	
T. & W. H. Shaw,	do.	2	
Edward Shaw,	do.	2	
M. E. & M Staples,	do.	2	
William Steward,	do.	2	
Joseph Stevens,	do.	5	

Atlantic & St. Lawrence Rail Road Company, (*Continued.*)

Names	Residence.	No. of shares.	Am't of stock
J. M. Stevens,	Portland,	3	
William F. Safford,	do.	5	
William E. Short,	do.	2	
Thorndike H Sawyer,	do.	1	
E. D. Seavey,	do.	2	
Francis Sweetsir,	do.	5	
R. H. Stickney,	do.	5	
Edward L. Stevens,	do.	2	
James P. Stetson,	do.	1	
George Sumner,	do.	3	
George F. Shepley,	do.	2	
William B. Stevens,	do.	3	
Thomas T. Sawyer,	do.	2	
James Simonton,	do.	2	
William H. Simonton,	do.	2	
Rufus Stanley,	do.	2	
Jabez M Stevens, 2d,	do.	1	
Henry H. Starbird,	do.	1	
Greenleaf Sawyer,	do.	1	
John W. Smith,	do.	5	
Paul M. Snow,	do.	3	
Rebecca Stinchfield,	do.	1	
E. C. Stevens,	do	5	
William H. Sweetsir,	do.	5	
Daniel Stevens,	do.	2	
Joseph F. Springer,	do.	3	
Mrs. H. M. Smith,	do.	2	
James Sawyer,	do.	1	
William T. Smith,	do.	5	
Samuel Sargent,	do.	1	
Micah Sampson,	do.	1	
Fitz E. Sargent,	do.	1	
O. E. Silsby,	do.	5	
Simeon Skillins,	do.	2	
Abel Sawyer,	do.	3	
George Symes,	do.	1	
Horatio Southgate,	do.	20	
Abiel Somerby,	do.	1	
John H. Short,	do.	2	
Louisa P. Smith,	do.	2	
E. W. Simmons,	do.	1	
Philip Shaw,	do.	3	
Thomas J. Sparrow,	do.	1	

Atlantic & St. Lawrence Rail Road Company, (Continued.)

Names.	Residence.	No. of shares.	Am't of stock
Josiah Spafford,	Portland,	2	
Warren Sparrow,	do.	2	
William E. Slayton,	do.	5	
William W. Sweat,	do.	1	
Nathaniel Shaw,	do.	5	
William H. Simonton,	do.	3	
E. C. Stevens,	do.	5	
George E. Small,	do.	1	
Tristram Simpson,	do.	2	
William H. Smith,	do.	2	
George W. Simonton,	do.	1	
John M. Simonton,	do.	1	
Theoph. Skillings,	do.	1	
Simeon B. Skillings,	do.	1	
Mary G. Souther,	do.	1	
L. D'M. Sweat,	do.	5	
Charles Staples, jr.,	do.	2	
Albert Staples,	do.	2	
M. H. & C. W. Sweetsir,	do.	1	
Alexander Stephenson,	do.	1	
Joseph Symonds,	do.	1	
J. S. Sargent,	do.	2	
Jere. Swett,	do.	1	
Ebenezer Steele,	do.	10	
George Smith,	do.	2	
J. T. Safford,	do.	4	
Susan B. Staples,	do.	1	
Charles B. Staples,	do.	1	
Levi Sawyer,	do.	5	
William H. Sweetsir,	do.	3	
Elizabeth F. Stevens,	do.	5	
Horace P. Stevens,	do.	2	
Samuel O. Smith,	do.	2	
George F. Shepley,	do.	2	
Strout & Mathews,	do.	3	
J. H. Stickney,	do.	1	
Sanborn & Carter,	do.	10	
John Sparrow,	do.	5	
G. W. Seavey,	do.	1	
Samuel Small,	do.	5	
Mary S. Smith,	do.	2	
Elias Thomas,	do.	75	
R. W. Thaxter,	do.	5	

Atlantic & St. Lawrence Rail Road Company, (Continued.)

Names.	Residence.	No. of shares.	Am't of stock
Jonathan Tewksbury,	Portland,	5	
J. G. Tolford, and als.,	do.	5	
James Todd,	do.	5	
H. F. Thompson,	do.	1	
Joseph Thompson,	do.	5	
Samuel Trask,	do.	8	
O. P. Thorp,	do.	5	
George Turner,	do.	100	
Franklin Tinkham,	do.	9	
John F. Tinkham,	do.	1	
Samuel True,	do.	10	
T. F. & C. C. Tolman,	do.	10	
William Thorndike,	do.	1	
O. L. Towle,	do.	3	
Elisha Trowbridge,	do.	4	
Brown Thurston,	do.	4	
Charles W. Thomas,	do.	1	
George A Thomas,	do.	1	
Ebenezer True,	do.	5	
Henry Trefethren,	do.	2	
Joseph M. Thompson,	do.	2	
D. J. True,	do.	5	
Rhuhames Trow,	do.	1	
Esther Tucker,	do.	1	
Joshua Tolford,	do.	1	
Timo. B. Tolford,	do.	5	
Joseph C. Turner,	do.	2	
D. M. Thurston & Co.,	do.	2	
Jonathan Tucker,	do.	10	
William Thorndike,	do.	1	
A. W. Tinkham,	do.	3	
Charles G. Thayer,	do.	5	
J. Tukesbury & Co.,	do.	5	
S. L. Treat,	do.	2	
James Treat,	do.	1	
H. E Trowbridge,	do.	1	
J. R. Thompson,	do.	2	
Brown Thurston,	do.	1	
Joseph Thomes,	do.	2	
C. S. True,	do.	2	
E. S. True,	do.	1	
M. M. Tukesbury,	do.	1	
Thomas Tracey,	do.	1	

7

Atlantic & St. Lawrence Rail Road Company, (Continued.)

Names.	Residence	No. of shares.	Am't of stock
Ebenezer Turner,	Portland,	3	
D. M. Tolford,	do.	1	
James Todd,	do.	2	
Samuel Trask,	do.	4	
Moses Turner,	do.	1	
Elisha Trowbridge,	do.	2	
W. W. Thomas,	do.	20	
T. F. Tolman,	do.	5	
J. A. Tolman,	do.	1	
C. C. Tolman,	do.	2	
E. E. Tolman,	do.	1	
S. C. Tolman,	do.	1	
Elias Thomas,	do.	25	
Jonathan Tucker,	do.	5	
H. Trefethren,	do.	2	
F. Talbot,	do.	1	
Edward R. Upham,	do.	1	
P. F. Varnum,	do.	30	
George Veazie,	do.	2	
Ph. Varnum,	do.	10	
George Veazie,	do.	1	
C. B. Varney,	do.	1	
William Woodbury,	do.	10	
Eliphalet Webster,	do.	1	
J. F. Weeks,	do.	2	
Samuel Waterhouse, jr.,	do.	2	
Seth Winship,	do.	3	
William Wood,	do.	10	
J. M. Waterhouse,	do.	3	
John Webb,	do.	2	
William M. Wiswell,	do.	1	
Eli Webb,	do.	3	
A. Winslow,	do.	5	
George W. Woodman,	do.	10	
W. W. Woodbury,	do.	5	
J. M. Waterhouse,	do.	2	
Nathaniel Warren,	do.	40	
Nathaniel Walker,	do.	2	
George Warren,	do.	15	
M. F. Walker,	do.	10	
Joseph Walker,	do.	10	
Eben Wilson,	do.	5	
H. Winchester,	do.	6	

Atlantic & St. Lawrence Rail Road Company, (Continued.)

Names.	Residence.	No. of shares.	Am't of stock
Josiah Williams,	Portland,	2	
W. H. Williams,	do.	1	
Levi Weymouth,	do.	5	
George Worcester,	do.	2	
Adam Wilson,	do.	5	
A. B. Waite,	do.	2	
A. Wilson,	do.	1	
R. E. Wood,	do.	20	
A. Witham,	do.	2	
F. A. & W. H. Waldron,	do.	2	
N. L. Woodbury,	do.	10	
A W. Whitmore,	do.	5	
Thomas Warren,	do.	25	
M. E. Warren,	do.	2	
Williams & McLellan,	do.	20	
Thomas Wright,	do.	1	
J. N. Winslow,	do.	2	
Willis & Fessenden,	do.	10	
Stephen Waite,	do.	5	
Ed. Waite,	do.	5	
S. Waterhouse,	do.	2	
J. G. Warren,	do.	4	
A. Woodman,	do.	5	
Eleazer Wyer,	do.	10	
R. C. Webster,	do.	1	
Daniel Winslow,	do.	15	
Samuel Whittier,	do.	10	
Nathan Winslow,	do.	10	
Octavia Woodard,	do.	5	
Charles Woodard,	do.	5	
Henry Woodard,	do.	5	
Frances Woodard,	do.	5	
Patrick Wogan,	do.	1	
Winship & Paine,	do.	5	
Nathan Whitten,	do.	3	
Oliver C. Waterman,	do.	3	
Benjamin Webb,	do.	5	
Martha Webster,	do.	1	
John F. Winslow,	do.	2	
F. E. Webster,	do.	1	
S S. Webster,	do.	1	
Chris. Wright,	do.	10	
W. L. Wilson,	do.	3	

Atlantic & St. Lawrence Rail Road Company, (Continued.)

Names.	Residence.	No. of shares.	Am't of stock
A. W. Whitmore,	Portland,	5	
S. A. Whittier,	do.	3	
Samuel Whittier,	do.	5	
H. Winchester,	do.	4	
Samuel Wells,	do.	5	
Francis Witham,	do.	1	
Green Walden,	do.	3	
F. H. Woods,	do.	1	
W. L. Witham,	do.	1	
Josiah Whitman,	do.	2	
Julia C. Wingate,	do.	2	
Harriet Winslow,	do.	1	
Francis Witham,	do.	1	
Calvin Whiting,	do.	5	
Mark Walton, jr.,	do.	1	
Calvin Woodman,	do.	1	
Isaac De Wolfe,	do.	3	
Eliab Ward,	do.	5	
William M. Wiswell,	do.	1	
S. R. Webber,	do.	1	
Daniel Winslow,	do.	5	
James L. Whittier,	do.	2	
William Wallace,	do.	1	
William S. Waterhouse,	do.	1	
Joseph Walker,	do.	5	
Edmund, Windship,	do.	3	
M. F. Whittier,	do.	1	
Eliza Weeks,	do.	2	
James Williams,	do.	2	
David Wiggin,	do.	1	
Manasses Ward,	do.	1	
Darius White,	do.	1	
Edward Wheeler, jr.,	do.	2	
William Wood,	do.	5	
Nathan Winslow,	do.	1	
Willis & Fessenden,	do.	10	
Joshua F. Weeks,	do.	1	
Thomas Warren,	do.	25	
William Walker,	do.	2	
Enos Woodard,	do.	10	
Jacob S. Widher,	do.	1	
Rufus E. Wood,	do.	10	
Stephen Waite,	do.	5	

Atlantic & St. Lawrence Rail Road Company, (Continued.)

Names.	Residence.	No. of shares.	Am't of stock
George Worster,	Portland,	1	
Minus Ward,	do.	1	
Nathaniel Warren,	do.	10	
Christ. Wright,	do.	5	
Green Walden,	do.	7	
William Woodbury,	do.	5	
Catharine B. Warren,	do.	2	
Sarah J. Warren,	do.	2	
Henry B. Wright,	do.	5	
George Warren,	do.	5	
W. W. Woodbury,	do.	2	
Albert Winslow,	do.	1	
N. L. Woodbury,	do.	5	
John Yeaton,	do.	5	
John O York,	do.	1	
William R. York,	do.	5	
Robert H Kimball,	Limington,	2	
Walter Higgins, jr.,	do.	3	
James Walker,	Lovell,	5	
George Johnson,	Westbrook,	5	
George Slemons,	do.	5	
Caleb Bradley,	do.	5	
John Warren,	do.	10	
Lathrop Libby,	do.	2	
Moses K Haskell,	do.	2	
Sewall Polisler,	do.	2	
J. F. Randall,	do.	2	
Chandler Rackleft,	do.	5	
Robert Allen,	do.	1	
J. R. Sawyer,	do.	2	
J. N. Read,	do.	1	
George Libbey,	do.	5	
Warren Harmon,	do.	1	
John Lowell,	do.	1	
Arthur Milliken,	do.	1	
Samuel Jordan,	do.	5	
Levi Morrill,	do.	10	
Josiah H. Beals,	do.	1	
William Adie,	do.	5	
Moses Hall,	do.	5	
Henry Weeks,	do.	1	
Jane Weeks,	do.	10	
Daniel Ilsley,	do.	1	

7*

Atlantic & St. Lawrence Rail Road Company, (*Continued.*)

Names.	Residence.	No. of shares.	Am't of stock
James Knight,	Westbrook,	1	
L. B. Stevens,	do.	5	
Rufus Morrill,	do.	5	
James Dearing,	do.	100	
Samuel Blake,	do.	5	
Joseph Stevens,	do.	3	
Daniel Woodman, jr.,	do.	10	
John Randall,	do.	2	
Archelaus Lewis,	do.	2	
Charles Bartlett,	do.	4	
Cornelius A. Davis,	do.	2	
Joseph Brackett,	do.	5	
Alexander Pride,	do.	1	
H. A. Lambert,	do.	1	
Thomas Seal,	do.	1	
Alford Dyer,	do.	1	
Isaac Randall,	do.	2	
Thomas Seal, jr.,	do.	1	
Jane Weeks,	do.	5	
Henry Weeks,	do.	5	
E. D. Woodford & Co.,	do.	5	
Otis Trickey,	do.	1	
Alex'r Bailey,	do.	2	
G. W. Turney,	do.	3	
Jona. Smith,	do.	5	
F. O. J. Smith,	do.	30	
Walcher & Graffam,	do.	4	
C. P. Graffam,	do.	1	
Gerry Cook,	do.	5	
Dan'l Woodman, jr.,	do.	9	
Ch. G. Woodman, jr.	do.	1	
John T. Brock,	do.	2	
Adam Libby,	do.	2	
John L. Hancock,	do.	2	
Fred'k W. Clark,	do.	2	
Chesley & Nason,	do.	2	
Archelaus Lewis,	do.	1	
Levi Morrell,	do.	5	
Samuel Jordan,	do.	5	
John Randall,	do.	1	
Wm. H. Small,	do.	2	
Samuel Davis, jr.,	do.	2	
Peter G. Winslow,	do.	5	

Atlantic & St. Lawrence Rail Road Company, (Continued.)

Names.	Residence.	No. of shares.	Am't of stock
John Warren,	Westbrook,	5	
James Lunt,	do.	5	
James Deering,	do.	100	
Daniel Paine,	Pownal,	1	
Richard Dresser,	do.	1	
William Randall,	do.	2	
Joseph Lufkin,	do.	5	
Moses Richards,	do.	1	
Silas B Osgood,	do.	2	
Benj. Mitchell,	do.	1	
Wm. V. Jordan,	do.	1	
John Noyes,	do.	2	
Arthur Thompson,	do.	4	
Edward Thompson,	do.	3	
True Tuttle,	do.	1	
Henry J Warren,	do.	2	
Joseph Small,	do.	5	
Benj. Randall,	do.	2	
G. P. Thompson,	do.	3	
Samuel Bliss,	do.	5	
Dennis Soule,	do.	2	
Jeremiah Austin,	do.	4	
George Bibber,	Falmouth,	1	
Charles H. Marston,	do.	2	
Benj. M Marston,	do.	1	
Peter N Marston,	do.	1	
Samuel N. Merrill,	do.	1	
Jeremiah Hall,	do.	5	
Paul E. Merrill,	do.	5	
Ephraim Merrill,	do.	1	
Ralph Kelley,	do.	5	
Samuel Moody,	do.	5	
Alfred B Marston,	do.	2	
Bucknam Noyes,	do.	1	
Edward P. Merrill,	do.	2	
Nathaniel Locke,	do.	1	
Mary Williams,	do.	1	
George W. Davis,	do.	2	
William Y. Jones,	do.	2	
Samuel Prince,	do.	3	
J. E. Donnell,	do.	5	
Adam Winslow,	do.	2	
Ingraham E. Huston,	do.	1	

Atlantic & St. Lawrence Rail Road Company, (Continued.)

Names.	Residence.	No. of shares.	Am't of stock
Adam Winslow,	Falmouth,	3	
Samuel Hicks,	do.	4	
Adams Merrill,	do.	2	
Royal Leighton,	do.	5	
Frances Field,	do.	1	
Charles W. Waite,	do.	5	
Robert Knight,	do.	2	
Paul E Merrill,	do.	1	
Samuel Long,	do.	2	
Fred'k Merrill,	do.	2	
Benjamin Lunt, jr.,	do.	4	
Reuben Allen,	do.	5	
William Prince,	do.	2	
Daniel E Noyes,	do.	2	
Nancy Blackstone,	do.	1	
Joseph Lambert,	do.	2	
Bucknam Noyes,	do.	1	
Samuel Prince,	do.	3	
Benjamin P. Butler,	Minot,	2	
Charles Millet,	do.	7	
William Cobb, jr.,	do.	1	
S. F. Waterman,	do.	2	
Isaac Dwinel,	do.	2	
Jacob Dwinel,	do.	2	
J. G. Hawke,	do.	2	
Albert Valentine,	do.	1	
Benjamin Sanborn,	do.	1	
A. B Dwinel,	do.	2	
Thayer & Vosmes,	do.	1	
Nathaniel Cushman, jr.,	do.	1	
J. C. Woodman,	do.	2	
Isaiah Perkins,	do.	2	
Amos Chipman,	do.	1	
Simon Thayer,	do.	1	
Jonathan Bartlett,	do.	1	
William Dale,	do.	1	
William R. Pottle,	do.	1	
Isaac Currier,	do.	1	
Samuel Stearns, jr.,	do.	2	
Samuel Stearns,	do.	1	
Isaiah Woodman,	do.	1	
Sullivan Woodman,	do.	1	
Daniel Freeman,	do.	1	

Atlantic & St. Lawrence Rail Road Company, (Continued.)

Names.	Residence.	No. of shares.	Am't of stock
Eben Whitehouse,	Minot,	1	
Cyrus Bridgham,	do.	2	
Charles Moody, jr.,	do.	1	
Calvin Bridgham,	do.	0	
Enos Bradbury,	do.	1	
Charles Millet,	do.	3	
B. P. Butler,	do.	1	
Rebecca T Whitehouse,	do.	1	
Ephraim Sturdevant,	Cumberland,	5	
James Hamilton, jr.,	do.	5	
H. P. Buxton,	do.	4	
Albert Newhall,	do.	20	
Benjamin Henley,	do.	5	
P A. Merrill,	do.	2	
J. G. Merrill,	do.	1	
Enos Blanchard,	do.	3	
Isaac Merrill,	do.	1	
Simeon Clough,	do.	2	
A. G. Blanchard,	do.	2	
Tristram Pittee,	do.	1	
John Merrill,	do.	1	
S. C. Kilborn,	do.	1	
Israel True,	do.	2	
William Read,	do.	2	
David S Merrill,	do.	1	
Charles P. Merrill,	do.	1	
S. T. Merrill,	do.	1	
D B. Wilson,	do.	1	
J. Whitney,	do.	1	
A. Leighton,	do.	1	
R. Prince,	do.	1	
L. Clough,	do.	1	
N. Rideout, jr.,	do.	1	
M. Thomas,	do.	1	
J. Blanchard,	do.	1	
J. T. Merrill,	do.	1	
A. G. Mitchell,	do.	1	
Cum'd School Fund,	do.	6	
Solomon Thayer,	Lubec,	16	
Caroline Whipple,	Gorham,	2	
J. Lindsey,	do.	2	
D. Jordan,	do.	10	
J. Barbour,	do.	10	

Atlantic & St. Lawrence Rail Road Company, (Continued.)

Names.	Residence.	No. of shares.	Am't of stock
Toppan Robie,	Gorham,	10	
B Skillings,	do.	1	
B. Manchester,	do.	1	
J Pierce,	do.	5	
E. Mann,	do.	5	
J. Johnson,	do.	5	
S. Elder,	do.	3	
J Phinney,	do.	5	
J. Cresey,	do.	1	
Martha Hight,	do.	1	
M. C. Maybery,	do.	1	
J. & J. Parker,	do.	2	
T. H. Hersey,	do.	1	
W. Hall,	do.	1	
Joshua E. Hall,	do.	1	
W. C. Whitney,	Norway,	10	
Nathaniel Bennett,	do.	8	
Henry Rust,	do.	7	
L Hathaway,	do.	8	
E. F. Beal,	do.	5	
Eben. Hobbs,	do.	3	
Levi Whitman,	do.	3	
S. Millett,	do.	5	
B. Tucker, jr.,	do.	3	
Jere. Hobbs,	do.	1	
E. C. Shackley,	do.	2	
A. Danforth,	do.	2	
D. Noyes,	do.	1	
N Pike,	do.	2	
C. Soule,	do.	2	
T. J. Tenney,	do.	2	
L. W. Pingree,	do.	3	
Thomas Witt,	do.	3	
Ich'd Bartlett,	do.	2	
Elliot Smith,	do.	1	
E. H. Brown,	do.	2	
Simon Noble,	do.	1	
Solomon Noble,	do.	2	
Jonathan Swift,	do.	1	
Ar. Bennett,	do.	2	
George Frost,	do.	1	
Amos J. Holt,	do.	1	
Jacob Bradbury,	do.	1	

Atlantic & St. Lawrence Rail Road Company, (Continued.)

Names.	Residence.	No. of shares.	Am't of stock
Joel Millet,	Norway,	1	
John H. Millet,	do.	1	
George P. Whitney,	do.	2	
Moses G. Dow,	do.	2	
James N. Hall,	do.	2	
Ephraim Briggs,	do.	3	
Samuel L Preble,	do.	1	
Richard Evans,	do.	1	
Nathan K. Noble,	do.	1	
Ansel Dinsmore,	do.	1	
Horatio G. Cole,	do.	3	
Samuel Lord,	do.	1	
James Crockett,	do.	1	
Benjamin Tucker,	do.	2	
Prescot L. Pike,	do.	1	
Jesse Howe,	do.	1	
Jere. Howe,	do.	1	
Benson Hawkins,	do.	1	
Thomas Higgins,	do.	1	
William P. Witt,	do.	2	
Solomon S. Hall,	do.	1	
Luther F. Foster,	do.	1	
Lee Mixer,	do.	1	
Robert Noyes,	do.	1	
William Stowell,	do.	1	
G J. Odway,	do.	5	
Lavina Smith,	do.	1	
Mark P. Smith,	do.	1	
William Evans,	do.	1	
Jarias S. Chipman,	do.	1	
Henry R. Cushman,	do.	1	
William E. Goodenow,	do.	1	
William W. & D. S. Millett,	do.	2	
Jonathan S. Millett,	do	1	
Daniel F. Millett,	do.	1	
T. O. Brown, jr.,	do.	1	
Orrin Wilbur,	do.	1	
Eben J. Pottle,	do.	2	
Stephen Berry,	do.	1	
Joshua B. Richardson,	do.	1	
Laura Smith,	do.	1	
Daniel Young,	do.	1	
Rodolphus Young,	do.	1	

Atlantic & St. Lawrence Rail Road Company, (Continued.)

Names.	Residence.	No. of shares.	Am't of stock
Ezra Tubbs,	Norway,	1	
Nathan Millett,	do.	2	
Levi Millett,	do.	1	
Jonathan S. Millett, jr ,	do.	1	
John Richardson, jr.,	do.	1	
Alanson M. Dunham,	do.	1	
James Bennett,	do.	1	
William P. Merrill,	do.	1	
Oliver A. Hall,	do.	1	
William R. Danforth,	do.	1	
Moses Ames,	do.	1	
F. A. Young & D. W. Beal,	do.	1	
Peter B. Frost,	do.	1	
Asa Thayer, jr.,	do.	1	
Joshua Crockett,	do.	1	
Amos F. Noyes,	do.	1	
William Frost, 3d,	do.	2	
Samuel Favor,	do.	1	
William Hayes,	do.	1	
Simon Stevens,	do.	1	
Dresser Stevens,	do.	1	
William Cox,	do.	2	
Wellington Hobbs,	do.	1	
James Flint,	do.	1	
Lorenzo D. Hobbs,	do.	1	
Andrews Mills,	do.	1	
Solomon Millett, jr.,	do.	1	
Jonathan B. Smith,	do.	1	
Greenville L. Reed,	do.	1	
Osgood Perry,	do.	1	
A. C. Dennison,	do.	2	
Benjamin Tucker,	do.	2	
C. A. Noyes,	do.	1	
C. W. & M. W. Hobbs,	do.	1	
Aaron Wilkins,	do.	1	
E. L. Knight,	do.	1	
J. K. Deering,	do.	1	
Horatio G. Cole,	do.	2	
Moses A. Young,	do.	1	
Loren H. Wesley,	do.	1	
Benjamin Tucker, 3d,	do.	1	
George A Noyes,	do.	2	
J. W. Hobbs,	do.	1	

Atlantic & St. Lawrence Rail Road Company, (Continued.)

Names.	Residence.	No. of shares.	Am't of stock
A. D. L. Hawkins,	Norway,	1	
Luther P. Tucker,	do.	1	
Jacob Parsons,	do.	1	
William H. Lovejoy,	do.	2	
Amos Young,	do.	1	
E. F. Beal,	do.	3	
P B. Frost,	do.	1	
Robert Noyes,	do.	1	
John A. Bolster,	do.	1	
Eben. Hobbs,	do.	1	
John Dearing,	do.	1	
Jeremiah Howe,	do.	1	
Nathaniel Bennett,	do.	2	
Ephraim Briggs,	do.	2	
Joanna Pike,	do.	1	
Jonathan Swift,	do.	1	
Nancy Blackstone,	Falmouth,	1	
Joseph Lambert,	do.	2	
Buckman Noyes,	do.	1	
Samuel Prince,	do.	3	
Thomas Crocker,	Paris,	20	
Alanson Mellen,	do.	5	
Mary Cummings,	do.	10	
E. L. Cummings,	do.	5	
Hersey & Brothers,	do.	10	
Simeon Cummings,	do.	5	
Moses Hammond,	do.	10	
Levi Stowell,	do.	5	
Stephen Emery,	do.	5	
Ansel Field,	do.	5	
Seth Morse,	do.	3	
Elisha Morse,	do.	2	
R. K. Goodenow,	do.	1	
America Thayer,	do.	2	
E. W. Clark,	do.	2	
Warren Hersey,	do.	1	
James Deering,	do.	2	
H. R. Parsons,	do.	2	
G. G. Waterhouse,	do.	5	
A. Hall,	do.	5	
Leonard Shurtliff,	do.	1	
Charles W. Bemis,	do.	1	
William Gallison,	do.	1	

8

Atlantic & St. Lawrence Rail Road Company, (Continued.)

Names.	Residence.	No. of shares.	Am't of stock
Joel B. Thayer,	Paris,	1	
George F. Emery,	do.	5	
Cyrus Hutchins,	do.	1	
Cyprian Hall,	do.	1	
Asa Mathews,	do.	1	
E. L. Porter,	do.	2	
Asaph Kittridge,	do.	2	
Joseph D. Cole,	do.	5	
Eben Drake,	do.	5	
Ransom Ripley,	do.	5	
Reuben Chandler, jr.,	do.	1	
Virgil D. Parris,	do.	5	
John Porter,	do.	5	
William K. Kimball,	do.	5	
J. B. Stowell,	do.	5	
Hiram Hubbard,	do.	3	
Nathan M. Marble,	do.	2	
Asa Woodbury,	do.	1	
James E. Poor,	do.	1	
Thomas H. Brown,	do.	3	
Alvah Shurtliff, jr.,	do.	1	
Caleb Cushman,	do.	2	
Ziba Thayer,	do.	1	
J. H. Merrill,	do.	2	
Orrin Hall,	do.	1	
Aaron Dunn, jr.,	do.	1	
George W. Young,	do.	1	
Phineas Morse,	do.	2	
Benjamin T. Royal,	do.	1	
William B. Royal,	do.	1	
America Thayer,	do.	2	
S. M. Newhall,	do.	1	
John Parsons, jr.,	do.	2	
Eben B. Humphrey,	do.	1	
America Thayer,	do.	2	
S. M. Newhall,	do.	1	
Silas Merriam,	Norway,	1	
John Deering,	do.	2	
Hiram Millett,	do.	3	
Luther F. Pike,	do.	2	
Joel Howe,	Greene,	3	
George E. Smith,	do.	1	
Ezra Smith,	do.	1	

Atlantic & St. Lawrence Rail Road Company, (Continued.)

Names.	Residence.	No. of shares.	Am't of stock
Gardner G. Hoit,	Greene,	1	
Enoch Bartlett,	do.	1	
Cyrus Bartlett,	do.	2	
Elkanah Bartlett,	do.	1	
George E. Smith,	do.	1	
C. H. & W. R. Howe,	Sumner,	2	
Eli Howe,	do.	1	
Benjamin F. Howe,	do.	1	
Edwin W. Howe,	do.	1	
Dennis Thayer,	Oxford,	10	
Henry Hawkins,	do.	1	
Jairus S. Keith,	do.	2	
James Woodbury,	do.	3	
Charles McFadden,	do.	1	
Joseph Freeman,	Poland,	1	
Daniel Waterman,	do.	2	
John Valentine,	do.	1	
Rufus Hayes,	do.	1	
Giles Shurtleff,	do.	1	
Samuel Cousens,	do.	1	
Nathan Cobb,	do.	1	
Nelson Valentine,	do.	1	
David Waterhouse,	do.	1	
Hiram Waterhouse,	do.	1	
W. F. & M. S. Haskell,	do.	2	
Lydia Crocker,	do.	1	
Aaron Merrow,	do.	1	
Lowell Valentine,	do.	1	
John S. Barrows,	do.	1	
Samuel Cousens,	do.	1	
Benj. Waterhouse,	do.	1	
Daniel Pearce,	do.	1	
William Cousens,	do.	1	
George Bridgham, jr.,	do.	1	
Zenas Briggs,	do.	1	
Jairus Dennen,	do.	2	
Wm. Davis, jr.,	do.	1	
Brackett Marston,	do.	1	
Moses Bray,	do.	1	
Robert Martin,	do.	1	
Alfred Woodman,	do.	2	
Rufus Haskell,	do.	1	
Washington Haskell,	do,	1	

Atlantic & St. Lawrence Rail Road Company, (Continued.)

Names.	Residence.	No. of shares.	Am't of stock
Jacob Rowe,	Poland,	2	
Cyrus Green,	do.	1	
Thomas Frank,	do.	1	
Josiah J. Knight,	Woodstook,	5	
Gideon Cushman,	Hebron,	1	
Moses Allen,	do.	2	
Timothy Walker,	Rumford,	10	
Lyman Rawson,	do.	3	
Otis C. Bolster,	do.	4	
Alonzo Holt,	do.	1	
Aaron Stevens,	do.	2	
Jeremiah Wardwell, jr.,	do.	1	
Peter C. Virgin,	do.	1	
P. H. & W. W. Virgin,	do.	1	
William Moody,	do.	1	
Hez. Hutchins, jr.,	do.	2	
Jonathan Virgin,	do.	1	
Sophia Stevens,	do.	3	
Susan Adams,	do.	1	
Rufus Virgin,	do.	1	
Porter Kimball,	do.	3	
Aaron Graham,	do.	1	
Timothy Walker,	do.	5	
J. H. Wardwell,	do.	5	
Colman Goodwin,	do.	1	
Asa Kimball,	do.	1	
John M. Adams,	do.	1	
Jonathan A. Virgin,	do.	1	
Daniel Farnam,	do.	1	
Thomas Roberts,	do.	5	
P. M. Wheeler,	do.	1	
Daniel Martin,	do.	1	
Jesse Putnam,	do.	1	
Henry C. Rolfe,	do.	3	
Alvin Bolster,	do.	5	
James H. Farnum,	do.	1	
Jere. Richardson,	do.	1	
Ephraim Carter,	do.	1	
Ebenezer Virgin,	do.	1	
Cyrus Small,	do.	1	
Charles A. Kimball,	do.	1	
John Akley,	do.	1	
Jere. Martin,	do.	1	

Atlantic & St. Lawrence Rail Road Company, (Continued.)

Names.	Residence.	No. of shares.	Am't of stock
David Kimball,	Rumford,	1	
John Rolfe,	do.	1	
William J Abbot,	Letter B,	1	
Albert Harmon,	Boston,	3	
William H. Grueby,	do.	3	
Mary A. Grueby,	do.	1	
Susan F. Grueby,	do.	1	
D. A. Neal,	do.	25	
Benjamin Willis,	do.	20	
B. T. Reed,	do.	10	
Daniel C. Bacon,	do.	10	
William Shepardson,	do.	5	
Albert Huse,	do.	1	
George W. Bazin,	do.	10	
Joseph Noble,	do.	20	
Henry Poor,	do.	5	
John R. Dow & Co.,	do.	10	
Greeley & Guild,	do.	20	
Charles Brooks,	do.	10	
Whiton, Meserve & Co.,	do.	5	
John Dodge,	do.	1	
Daniel Burrows,	do.	5	
Albert Harmon,	do.	2	
Oliver B. Dorrance,	do.	10	
Luke Bicknell,	Livermore,	1	
Alfred Pettingill,	Freeport,	1	
Henry F. Cram,	do.	1	
Robert S. Soule,	do.	3	
H. W. Bailey,	do.	1	
Jedediah Burbank,	Bethel,	4	
Henry Ward,	do.	4	
Charles Frost,	do.	2	
M. B. Bartlett,	do.	1	
Tyler P. Towne,	do.	1	
Moses Mason,	do.	2	
Thomas Peabody,	do.	2	
John Grover,	do.	5	
Abernethy Grover,	do.	1	
Tallyrand Grover,	do.	2	
George Chapman,	do.	1	
D. P. Burbank,	do.	1	
John Harris,	do.	1	
Timothy Chapman,	do.	2	

8*

Atlantic & St. Lawrence Rail Road Company, (Continued.)

Names.	Residence.	No. of shares.	Am't of stock
Timothy H. Chapman,	Bethel,	1	
Gilman Chapman,	do.	1	
William Frye,	do.	1	
Eben. Eames,	do.	2	
R. A. Chapman,	do.	2	
Elbridge Chapman,	do.	1	
William Goddard,	do.	1	
Elias M. Carter,	do.	1	
Hiram Holt, 2d,	do.	1	
Israel Kimball,	do.	1	
Ira C. Kimball,	do.	5	
A. W. Crowinshield,	Charlestown, Mass.,	5	
John Hooper,	Marblehead,	20	
John M. Frye,	Lewiston,	5	
Samuel Pickard,	do.	10	
David Davis,	do.	2	
Nathan Reynolds,	do.	10	
Alonzo Garcelon,	do.	10	
John B. Jones,	do.	1	
John H. Randall,	do.	1	
James C. Foss,	do.	1	
Mark Lowell,	do.	5	
V. E. Litchfield,	do.	2	
Daniel Holland,	do.	5	
Stephen Davis,	do.	2	
Eben Ham,	do.	2	
Wm R. Frye,	do.	3	
Sam'l Litchfield,	do.	1	
Archibald Wakefield,	do.	1	
Calvin Gorham,	do.	5	
Thomas Thorn,	do.	1	
Barker Brooks,	do.	2	
Stephen H. Read,	do.	3	
Temple Tibbets,	do.	1	
Ezra F. Bucknam,	do.	1	
James L. Foster,	do.	1	
Stephen Field,	do.	1	
Jacob Golder,	do.	3	
John Nash,	do.	5	
Jos. B. Harding,	do.	2	
E. P. Tobie,	do.	2	
John Farnham,	do.	1	
James Carrill,	do.	2	

Atlantic & St. Lawrence Rail Road Company, (Continued.)

Names.	Residence.	No. of shares.	Am't of stock
Clarence P. Griffin,	Lewiston,	2	
Sewall Merrill,	do.	1	
Edward Little,	Danville,	10	
Jona. Raynes,	do.	2	
Edward P. Weston,	do.	1	
Charles Clark,	do.	2	
James Dingley,	do.	1	
E. D. Townsend,	do.	1	
David R. Loring,	do.	2	
John Penley,	do.	10	
Enoch Penley,	do.	1	
Rufus Penley,	do.	2	
Horace C. Briggs,	do.	2	
Increase B. Kimball,	do.	1	
Samuel Gorham,	do.	1	
Josiah Penley,	do.	1	
Edward T. Little,	do.	4	
James F. Davis,	do.	2	
J. H. Ronk,	Auburn,	5	
Jas. Nash for Dan'l Morrell,	do.	8	
James Goff, jr.,	do.	5	
Jos. Chamberlain,	do.	1	
John R. Merrill,	do.	1	
Henry McKenney,	do.	1	
George F. Gould,	do.	1	
John Briggs,	do.	1	
David Strout,	do.	1	
Charles Briggs,	do.	5	
Hiram Briggs,	do.	5	
Freeman Newell,	do.	1	
Richmond Bradford,	do.	3	
James S. Nash,	do.	1	
Mary Ann Raynes,	do.	1	
A. W. Allen,	do.	1	
Zebina Briggs,	do.	2	
Daniel Briggs,	do.	3	
Noah Packard,	do.	1	
Eliphalet Packard,	do.	3	
Ann W. Whitman,	do.	2	
Zenas Whitman,	do.	1	
Enoch Littlefield,	do.	2	
Daniel Carey,	Turner,	2	
John Blake,	do.	2	

Atlantic & St. Lawrence Rail Road Company, (Continued.)

Names.	Residence.	No. of shares.	Am't of stock
William B. Bray,	Turner,	2	
James Webster,	Gray,	1	
B. F. Colley,	do.	1	
Th. W. O'Brien,	do.	3	
Th. W. O'Brien,	do.	6	
Silo. Blanchard,	North Yarmouth,	10	
Cushing Prince,	do.	3	
Jere. Baker,	do.	10	
R. L. Cutter,	do.	5	
Allen H. Weld,	do.	5	
Albion Seabury,	do.	3	
Joseph Chandler, jr.,	do.	2	
Barnabas Freeman,	do.	2	
Levi Blanchard,	do.	3	
Reuben Prince,	do.	3	
Timo. Pratt,	do.	5	
George Humphrey,	do.	1	
Alfred Seabury,	do.	2	
George Dunham,	do.	3	
Paul Prince,	do.	2	
Levi Lane, jr.,	do.	2	
Philip Torrey,	do.	2	
Charles Armstrong,	do.	5	
Nath'l Haynes,	do.	1	
Samuel Sweetsir,	do.	5	
Reuben Cutter,	do.	1	
M. McClanning,	do.	1	
Rufus R. York,	do.	1	
Joseph Stanley,	do.	5	
Asa Sears,	do.	2	
Jere. Loring 3d,	do.	2	
Francis W. Seabury,	do.	2	
Benj. Oakley,	do.	2	
Ezekiel Merrill,	do.	1	
J. N. Merrill,	do.	1	
Daniel Coffin,	do.	1	
David Mitchell,	do.	2	
David Trickey,	do.	4	
Hosea J. Chase,	do.	1	
P. H. Kimball,	do.	5	
Asa Bisbee,	do.	1	
Thomas Chase,	do.	1	
Wm. T. Baker,	do.	5	

Atlantic & St. Lawrence Rail Road Company, (Continued.)

Names.	Residence.	No. of shares.	Am't of stock
Reuben Chandler,	North Yarmouth,	5	
Jos. Woods, jr ,	do.	1	
Jos. Hayes,	do.	2	
Amos Osgood,	do.	1	
Eleazer Burbank,	do.	3	
David True,	do.	10	
Huldah Blanchard,	do.	1	
Jacob Hill,	do.	2	
Cushing Prince,	do.	3	
Gardner M. Sturdevant,	do.	2	
Reuben Chandler,	do.	1	
James Merriman, 4th,	Harpswell,	2	
Paul R. Thomas,	do.	2	
Charles Merriman,	do.	2	
Thomas Eaton,	do.	1	
Albert S. Merriman,	do.	1	
Norton Stover, 2d,	do.	2	
Johnson Stover,	do.	1	
George Haskell,	do.	1	
Thomas Pholand,	do.	2	
Paul C. Merryman,	do.	1	
Joshua Webber,	do.	2	
Nath'l Pinkham,	do.	1	
Francis Haskell,	do.	1	
John Conley,	do.	1	
Joseph A. Bartlett,	Augusta,	1	
Joseph Day,	Matanzas,	10	
H. J. Robinson,	do.	5	
Wm. H. Foster,	Salem,	3	
Richard P. Waters,	do.	10	
Harriet Adams,	do.	5	
Stephen A. Chase,	do.	5	
Isaiah Breed,	Lynn,	5	
Jeremiah O'Brien,	Machias,	20	
Obadiah Hill,	do.	20	
Daniel Harwood,	do.	3	
S. A. Morse,	do.	3	
William B. Smith,	do.	1	
William C. Holway,	do.	1	
Moses Gould,	Bridgton,	10	
Marshall Cram,	do.	10	
Mary M. P. Cram,	do.	10	
Samuel Pond,	Cambridgeport,	2	

Atlantic & St. Lawrence Rail Road Company, (Continued.)

Names.	Residence.	No. of shares.	Am't of stock
Sarah B. Richardson,	Hiram,	1	
Nathan A. Bradbury,	Sweden,	1	
Luther F. Powers,	do.	1	
Benjamin Webber,	do	5	
Benjamin Webber,	do.	5	
Cotton Lincoln,	Cornish,	5	
Mark Pease,	do.	25	
Simeon Pease,	do	50	
John O'Brien,	do.	6	
John O'Brien,	do.	4	
Simeon Pease & Co.,	do.	10	
Mark Pease,	do.	10	
Cotton Lincoln,	do.	5	
George Gwinn,	Cape Elizabeth,	5	
John M. Cummings,	do.	2	
Charles F. Hartman,	do.	2	
Silvanus Higgins,	do.	6	
Elisha Brown,	do.	1	
Woodbury Dyer,	do.	1	
John Lovett,	do.	1	
David Lovett,	do.	1	
Enoch Lovett,	do.	1	
George Lovett,	do.	1	
John Thurston,	do.	1	
Alfred Thasher,	do.	1	
Jos. Thurston,	do.	1	
Samuel Willard, jr.,	do.	1	
John Lovett,	do.	1	
Silvanus Higgins,	do.	4	
Levi Strout,	do.	1	
Wm. Low,	do.	3	
Wm. Kingman, jr.,	Waterford,	3	
John A. Douglass,	do.	5	
Eliakim Maxfield,	do.	2	
Ephraim Blake,	New Gloucester,	1	
Mary Blake,	do.	1	
Ephraim Blake,	do.	1	
Seth L. Haskell,	do.	1	
Joseph Cross,	do.	2	
E. H. Merrill,	Baltimore,	10	
P. H. & S. M. Baker,	Windham,	5	
Levi Hawks,	do.	2	
Humphrey Cousins,	do.	5	

Atlantic & St. Lawrence Rail Road Company, (Continued.)

Names.	Residence.	No. of shares.	Am't of stock
Peter Trickey,	Windham,	2	
Jefferson Maybury,	do.	1	
Enoch Maybury,	do.	1	
Samuel R. Hawks,	do.	2	
Peter Trickey,	do.	1	
Benj. Hawks,	do.	1	
Ruth Hawks,	do.	1	
Geo. R. Furbish,	do.	1	
Daniel Furbish,	do.	1	
David L. Furbish,	do.	1	
James Hall,	do.	3	
Amos Anthoine,	do.	1	
Levi Hawkes,	do.	1	
Edward B. Forest,	do.	1	
Samuel Freeman,	do.	5	
Elisha Jones,	do.	2	
John Eveleth,	do.	2	
Mary Anthoine,	do.	1	
Daniel Furbish,	do.	1	
N. B. D. Whitman,	New York,	5	
Wm. Thirlwall,	do.	2	
Moses Pattee,	Albany,	10	
Joseph T. Sawyer,	Raymond,	2	
John Brown,	do.	1	
Nath'l J. Miller,	Hollis,	10	
Cyrus Thompson, jr.,	Hartford,	2	
Daniel Harmon,	Scarborough,	5	
John N. Waterhouse,	do.	2	
Sewall Millikin	do.	2	
Matthias Meserve,	do.	5	
John Sweetsir,	do.	2	
Asa Dresser,	do.	5	
Samuel N. Tarbox,	Parsonsfield,	2	
Wm. Clark,	Concord, N. H.,	5	
A. L. Came,	Buxton,	5	
Charles Atkinson,	do.	1	
John Atkinson,	do.	1	
David Kimball, jr.,	do.	3	
Edwin W. Wedgwood,	do.	5	
Joseph Hobson, jr.,	do.	5	
Almon L. Hobson,	do.	5	
J. Jones,	Camden,	5	
Samuel P. Ingraham,	do.	3	

Atlantic & St. Lawrence Rail Road Company, (Continued.)

Names.	Residence.	No. of shares.	Am't of stock
John & Minot H. Tolman,	Camden,	5	
William B. Sewall,	Kennebunk,	15	
Barnabas Palmer,	do.	15	
Horace Porter,	do.	10	
Abigail Titcomb,	do.	5	
George P. Titcomb,	do.	5	
William Titcomb,	do.	5	
Lucy W Titcomb,	do.	5	
Joseph Titcomb,	do.	3	
Abigail Grant,	do.	1	
Daniel Nason,	do.	5	
Lucy Sewall,	do.	1	
Narcissa Sewall,	do.	1	
Daniel Nason, jr.,	do.	2	
William Fitch,	Sebago,	5	
Solomon Nason, jr.,	Standish,	1	
Hannah Cresey,	do.	2	
John Paine,	do.	1	
James Weston,	do.	10	
Hobson & Came,	do.	5	
Horatio Merrill,	W. Newbury,	1	
John B. Hudson,	Bath,	2	
Benj. Goodridge,	Naples,	5	
Hannah Pierce,	Baldwin,	5	
Charles Freeman,	Limerick,	2	
Nath'l Eaton,	Trinidad, Cuba,	10	
Nath'l Eaton,	do.	10	
Lemuel W. Crabtree,	Savannah,	5	
George Crabtree,	do.	5	
Henry Ganahl,	do.	10	
Henry Proctor,	Lisbon,	2	
Josiah Starling,	Union,	5	
Sylvanus Poor, jr.,	Andover,	2	
Nath'l B. Crockett,	do.	1	
Lewis Crockett,	do.	3	
Mary Frye Poor,	do.	1	
J. W Talbot,	do.	1	
Farnum Abbott,	do.	1	
Caleb F. Poor,	do.	1	
Wm. W. Abbott,	do.	1	
E. E. Merrill,	do.	1	
Elbridge Poor,	do.	1	
James Stevens, jr.,	do.	1	

Atlantic & St. Lawrence Rail Road Company, (Continued.)

Names.	Residence.	No. of shares.	Am't of stock
Jane L. Knight,	Webster,	1	
Eben M. Winslow,	Saco,	5	
Josiah Calef,	do.	10	
Samuel Bachelder,	do.	10	
Tristram Jordan, jr.,	do.	3	
Nathaniel M. Towle,	do.	5	
S. S. Fairfield,	do.	2	
Thomas Cutts,	do.	3	
Ezra Deane,	do.	4	
Moses E. Merrill,	do.	1	
Jere. Gordon,	do.	1	
Rufus Nichols,	do.	5	
Rufus Banks,	do.	1	
S. Hopkins,	do.	2	
Jarvis Williams,	do.	5	
Loring French,	do.	5	
Sewall Libby,	Durham,	2	
James H. Eveleth,	do.	1	
William Gerrish, jr.,	do.	1	
Jonathan C. Merrill,	do.	2	
William Gerrish,	do.	1	
John Nason,	do.	2	
Edmund H Williams,	Winthrop,	1	
Charles A. Stackpole,	Bangor,	1	
Jabez True,	do.	5	
Rufus Dwinel,	do.	5	
Ephraim Moulton,	do.	5	
Joseph Bryant,	do.	4	
William H. McCrillis,	do.	3	
Henry V. Poor,	do.	5	
John A. Poor,	do.	4	
Laura E. Poor,	do.	1	
Emily S. Hill,	do.	5	
J. B. Hill,	do.	3	
William T. Hilliard,	do.	5	
Thomas H. Shaw,	do.	2	
Samuel Lowder,	do.	2	
Jacob A. Smith,	do.	2	
Elisha H. Allen,	do.	2	
William A. Dresser,	do.	1	
Ezra Jewell,	do.	5	
James Jenkins,	do.	5	
William C. Bruce,	do.	3	

9

Atlantic & St. Lawrence Rail Road Company, (Continued.)

Names.	Residence.	No. of shares.	Am't of stock
Simeon Hall,	Bangor,	1	
George W. Smith,	do.	1	
George B. Moody,	do	1	
David Mosman,	do.	1	
Nathaniel Hatch,	do.	1	
Jairus Dunning,	do.	1	
Ira Pitman,	do.	1	
Ellen Dale,	do.	1	
Mary E. Wood,	do.	1	
Hall & Young,	do.	1	
J. J. Dearborn,	do.	1	
Edward Kent,	do.	1	
John McDonald, jr.,	do.	1	
William J. McDonald,	do.	1	
Henry E. Prentiss,	do	1	
Allen Haines,	do.	1	
Joseph Treat,	do.	1	
C K. Miller,	do.	1	
Henry F. Merrill,	do.	1	
Frederick Lambert,	do	1	
Warren Brown,	do	1	
Horatio Foster,	do	1	
Roscoe F Hersey,	do.	1	
George W. Tasker,	do	4	
Benjamin F. Brown,	do	1	
W. P. Wingate,	do.	2	
Cyrus S. Clark,	do.	5	
William Jewell,	do.	1	
Franklin Adams,	do.	5	
Samuel Smith,	do	10	
William H. Mills,	do	1	
S W Robinson,	do	2	
S. Parsons & Co,	do.	1	
Davis Wasgatt,	do.	1	
S. H Jackson,	N. Berwick,	3	
John D. Lang,	do.	10	
William H. Webb,	Havana,	10	
J. S Thrasher,	do	10	
J Cohen, jr.,	Charleston, S. C,	5	
John Goddard,	Orono,	4	
John Goddard, jr,	do.	2	
Charles Goddard,	do	2	
Eliza P Goddard,	do.	2	

Atlantic & St. Lawrence Rail Road Company, (Continued.)

Names.	Residence	No. of shares.	Am't of stock
Caroline A Babcock,	Orono,	1	
Julia E. Babcock,	do	1	
Elizabeth C. Babcock,	do.	1	
Albert Dole,	do	1	
Hiram Emery,	Bradley,	3	
William Gooch,	Wells,	8	
Jott S. Perkins,	Kennebunkport,	5	
Orlando Perkins,	do.	3	
Eliphalet Perkins,	do.	5	
William F. Moody,	do.	1	
J. G. Perkins,	do	3	
B F Mason,	do	2	
S. H. Gould,	do.	2	
William Jefferds,	do.	2	
Robert Towne,	do.	2	
Asaph Moody,	do.	6	
Sophia Moody,	do	1	
Sally Moody,	do.	1	
Lois Jones,	Brunswick,	1	
Daniel S. Hooper,	Biddeford,	2	
William Smith,	do	2	
Otis Holmes,	do.	5	
William P. Hooper,	do.	1	
George A. Warren,	do.	1	
James Smith,	do	1	
Thomas Quinby,	do	1	
William H. Hutchins,	do	1	
Daniel Carlton,	do	1	
W. H. Hanson,	do.	1	
Calvin Starrett,	Washington,	10	
Edward Tobey,	do.	1	
William Young,	do.	3	
George Gray,	do	1	
		10,137	

lation

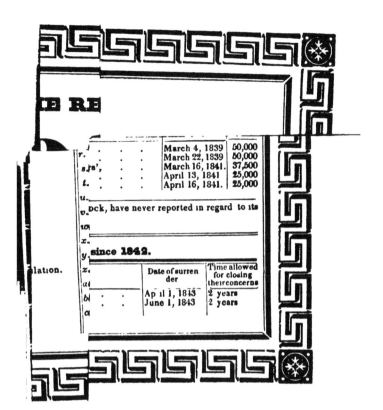

r.	.	.	.	March 4, 1839	50,000
				March 22, 1839	50,000
s. s',	.	.	.	March 16, 1841.	37,500
t.	.	.	.	April 13, 1841	25,000
				April 16, 1841.	25,000

u.

v. ock, have never reported in regard to its

w.

x.

y. **since 1842.**

lation. z.

			Date of surrender	Time allowed for closing their concerns
a.				
b.	.	.	Ap il 1, 1843	2 years
a.	.	.	June 1, 1843	2 years

REPORT

OF THE

ADJUTANT GENERAL

OF THE

MILITIA OF MAINE,

MAY 12, 1846.

Published agreeably to Resolve of March 22, 1836.

AUGUSTA:

WM. T. JOHNSON,..........PRINTER TO THE STATE.

1846.

STATE OF MAINE.

ADJUTANT GENERAL'S OFFICE,
Augusta, May 12, 1846.

His Excellency, HUGH J. ANDERSON,
   Governor and Commander-in-Chief,

SIR:—In my annual report, transmitted to you December, 1843, I had occasion to present my views somewhat at length, in regard to our Militia system. Those views, which were based substantially upon the law of 1834, did not command the approval of the Legislature.

In my last annual report transmitted to you December, 1844, I presented no views upon this subject, but proposed to furnish some *projet* to the proper committee of the legislature. In pursuance thereof, I prepared and presented a draft of a law, placing our militia upon the volunteer system, reducing its number to about seven thousand, requiring the State to furnish the soldiers with arms and equipments, with a small compensation for their services, and providing for an annual inspection, two annual trainings and an annual review. This draft was reported to the legislature without substantial alteration, by the committee on the militia, and received the sanction of the senate, but was lost in the house by a decisive majority. It was presented by me, not because I had reason to change the opinions expressed in my report of 1843, but because I supposed it to be the only practicable recommendation in the then existing aspect of popular opinion. Although now entertaining all the views expressed in that report, and although confident that these views have lost none of their force from the late and present appearance of our foreign relations, I forbear to *press* them, from the apprehension that it might be deemed, under the circumstances of the case, importunate and disrespectful to the legislature who are the ultimate and responsible judges of what is due to the public interest in this matter.

Several projects for a general re-organization of the militia of the United States are now pending before congress. The military committee of the popular branch of congress have reported a bill embodying one of these projects. The main features of this bill appear worthy of approval; but I fear there is little ground to hope its enactment as a law. Indeed, the local circumstances and local opinions of the several states are so diversified, and in many respects, so antagonistical, that there is no good ground to expect congress will act at all in reference to this subject, except under the pressure of some imminent and absolute necessity.

It remains to be seen whether, in the judgment of congress, such a necessity will be deemed to exist in the present condition of our public affairs. That it is the duty of congress to act in this matter, appears to me unquestionable, and I respectfully suggest the propriety of an expression of an opinion by the legislature, in favor of the establishment by congress, of some uniform and efficient militia system. In the meantime, the duty of the state is equally clear as that of congress; and it does not seem to be the part of wisdom to await an action elsewhere, which is, at the best, uncertain, when we have the means of useful legislation in our own hands, and when the confessedly prostrated condition of our militia calls so loudly for immediate and effectual organization.

In the event of a failure of the legislature to establish a better system, I would respectfully recommend the adoption, with slight modifications, of the volunteer system, which was acted upon by the legislature of 1845. This system will incur but a trifling expense, would be more effective in its operation, and infinitely more honorable to the state, than the present law, which must be regarded as virtually inoperative.

The condition of our foreign relations imperatively demands that something should be done to revive the military vigor of the State, and I am satisfied that what I have recommended is far short of what would be justified by the patriotic impulses of our people. War is now imminent and apparently unavoidable, upon our south western frontier, and its duration and consequences cannot be foreseen. The government of Mexico is feeble and its people are distracted by internal feuds. But against a foreign foe they will present an united front. Long inured to the habits of military life, and sustained by the courage and obstinacy of the Spanish blood, they may maintain a tedious and harrassing warfare. In this warfare, they may have a still more formidable ally in the powerful nation with which we are now contesting the title to a magnificent territory on the Pacific ocean. At such a time and under such circumstances, Maine ought not to remain voluntarily disarmed, bereft of even the shadow of a military organization, and condemned to a self-imposed condition of helpless impotence. The high spirit of her people, as well as the dictates of foresight, revolts at a state of things like this, which is as unworthy as it is hazardous. They do not wish to be out-run in the race of patriotism, by their sister states; and they will esteem no sacrifice too great, which will restore them to a sense of honorable security under the safeguard of a well organized citizen soldiery.

Very few resignations of officers have occurred during the past year, but from information which reaches me from various quarters, I am satisfied that they have only been delayed by a hope that the legislature may speedily adopt some measure calculated to restore vitality to the militia system.

The returns made to this office during the past year, have been too imperfect to enable me to comply with the act of congress which requires an annual exhibit of the number of soldiers enrolled in each state, as the basis of apportioning the annual supply of arms to the militia of the union. I have, therefore, transmitted to the war department at Washington, a copy of the returns from this office, of December 1844.

The condition of the several gun houses in the state, and of the artillery now stored in them, will require the attention of the legis-

1*

lature.   This valuable property is exposed to dilapidation and decay, is unprotected by suitable care, and answers no beneficial purpose whatever.

If the militia law remains as it now is, I recommend that these gun houses be sold, and that the ordnance and ordnance stores which they contain be transferred to the arsenals at Portland and Bangor.

It is the judgment of the keepers of those arsenals, as well as my own, that some appropriations for labor upon arms and equipments under their charge, are absolutely necessary the present season.

The amount deemed necessary for labor in Portland arsenal is	$75 00
For labor in Bangor arsenal, . . .	75 00
For removal and repairs of the gun house at Portland,	40 00
For transportation, and repairs of gun houses,	300 00
The keeper of the Bangor arsenal reports that an appropriation is necessary for the erection of an arsenal fence recently blown down, and estimates the expense at	50 00
For whitewashing the same, . .	20 00
For repairs of the slating on the roof,	15 00
The same keeper also recommends an appropriation for painting the arsenal buildings at Bangor, and estimates the expense at	200 00

I have the honor to be,
Very respectfully,
Your obedient servant,
ALFRED REDINGTON.
Adjutant General.

No.	Description.	Remarks.
38	42 lbs. Shot.	.
226	32 " "	
1548	24 " "	
808	18 " "	
1034	12 " "	
819	9 " "	
1031	6 " "	
2123	4 " "	
728	3 " "	
1836	Double headed Shot.	
21	Cases Grape "	
1	" 32 lb. Strap "	
1	" 8 " Howitzer Shot.	
708	13 inch Shells.	
341	9½ " "	
134	8 " "	
276	6½ " "	
187	5½ " "	
214	4½ " "	
1800	Hand Grenades.	
9	Cases fixed ammunition.	
52	" Musket "	
1	Keg " "	
4	Kegs Powder.	
3	Boxes fixed hand Grenades.	
19	" Lead Balls.	1800 each.
1	Iron 42 pdr. Cannon.	Unmounted.
4	" 32 " "	"
22	" 24 " "	"
4	" 18 " "	"
3	" 12 " "	"
2	" 9 " "	"
8	" 6 " "	"
3	" 4 " "	"
1	" 18 " "	Old, mounted.

SCHEDULE of *Public Property*—(*Continued.*)

No.	Description.	Remarks.
2	Iron 12 pdr. Cannon.	Old, mounted.
2	" 12 " "	New, "
4	" 6 " "	" "
1	" 4 " "	Old,
1	" 3 " "	" "
1	10 inch Howitzer.	Unmounted.
2	Brass 12 pdr. Cannon.	Mounted.
7	" 6 " "	"
2	Brass 6 inch Howitzer.	Unmounted.
2	" Eprovetts.	
13	Ship Gun Carriages.	
2	Sea coast Gun Carriages.	
40	Trucks for " "	
3	18 pdr. Gun "	Old.
1	6 " "	"
1	3 " "	"
4	6 " " "	
8	Elevating Screws.	
11	Ammunition Boxes.	
7	Sponge Buckets.	
6	Tar "	
34	Trail Handspikes.	
165	Bricoles.	
12	Tompions.	
11	Drag Ropes.	
13	Buckets.	
12	Prolongs.	
13	Vent Covers.	
29	Tompions, Collars and Straps.	
47	Sponges and Rammers.	
45	Ladles and Worms.	
18	Sponge Covers.	
3	Sea Sponges.	
29	Implement Straps.	
	Lot of Wads.	
1	Tumbril.	
6	Packing Boxes.	
6	Towhooks.	
5	Tongs and Ladles.	For Hot Shot.
3	Tarpaulins.	

Schedule of Public Property—(Continued.)

No.	Description.	Remarks.
1	12 pdr. Caisson.	
6	Tangent Scales.	
6	Vent Punches.	
5	Powder Monkeys.	
23	Tube Pouches.	
21	Portfire Clippers.	
26	Priming Horns.	
17	Thumbstalls.	
27	Lint Stocks.	
100	Artillery Swords.	
7	Implement Belts.	
18	Pairs of Trace Chains.	
1	Swingle Tree.	
1	Pair Pole Straps.	
10	Breechings.	
50	Pairs Hames.	
24	Back and Belly Bands.	
571	Hall's Rifles.	1 at Augusta.
571	Bayonets.	
571	Wipers.	
571	Screw Drivers.	
571	Spare Flint Caps.	
57	Spring Vices.	
571	Pouches.	
570	Buff Bayonet Belts and Plates.	
570	" Waist Belts.	
50	Extra Springs.	
29	Implement Straps.	
	Lot of Wads.	
1	Tumbril.	
6	Packing Boxes.	
6	Towhooks.	
6	Worms and Staves.	
51	Haversacks.	
16	Portfire Cases.	
21	" Stocks.	
48	Priming Wires.	
19	Gunners' Gimblets.	
8	Yards Match Rope.	
1 00	Sword Belts.	

SCHEDULE *of Public Property—(Continued.)*

No.	Description.	Remarks.
4	Whiffletrees.	
9	Sets Lead Bars.	
21	Pairs Trace Spreads.	
8	Buck Saddles.	
14	Horse Collars.	
4	Head Stalls.	
240	Short Bright Rifles.	
240	Bullet Moulds.	
240	Wipers.	
24	Screw Drivers.	
24	Ball Screws.	
36	Powder Flasks.	
40	Pouches.	
40	Straps.	
57	Bullet Moulds.	
570	Buff Pouch Belts.	
570	Bayonet Scabbards.	
570	Belt Plates.	
570	Copper Flasks.	
760	Johnson's Rifles.	Bronzed.
760	Wipers.	
760	Screw Drivers.	
660	Spare Flint Cases.	
76	Ball Screws.	
76	Spring Vices.	
66	Bullet Moulds.	
239	Johnson's Rifles.	
6642	Muskets.	
55	Old English Muskets.	
3	Drums.	
4	Fifes.	
402	Bayonet Belts.	
365	Musket Locks.	
147	Sabres.	
250	Pistols.	
101	Field Tents.	
	Lot Tent Poles, Pins and Toggles.	
347	Mallets.	
6	Standard Impressions.	
1	Box Flints.	

SCHEDULE *of Public Property—(Continued.)*

No.	Description.	Remarks.
59	Sabre Belts.	
20	Lances.	
14¾	Dozen Iron Spoons.	
69	Tin Camp Kettles.	
12	Sheet Iron "	
149	Tin Pans.	
349	" Dippers.	
6	" Basons.	
63	" Plates.	
6	Wheel Barrows.	
29	Hand "	
78	Bill Hooks.	
1	Pick Axe.	
1	Tin Fuse.	
464	Screw Drivers.	
340	Spare Flint Covers.	
68	Ball Screws.	
36	Powder Flasks.	
40	Pouches.	
40	Straps.	
6642	Bayonets.	
55	"	
4	Fifes.	
300	Bayonet Scabbards.	
1	Box Flints.	
59	Sabre Belts.	
20		
1	Marquee.	
2	Signal Lanterns.	
2	Long handled Fry Pans.	
14	Fry Pans and Spiders.	
1	Iron Kettle.	
47	Coffee Pots.	
2	Tea "	
5	Skimmers.	
3	Toast Pans.	
166	Flat Square Pans.	
1	Crow and Bar.	
1	Rake.	
4	Hatchets.	

SCHEDULE *of Public Property—(Continued.)*

No.	Description.	Remarks.
37	Handspikes.	
24	Shovels.	
6	Spades.	
1	Traveling Forge.	
	Lot of cut Spikes.	
1	Desk and sundry Books.	
1	Water Pot.	
2	Bench Vices.	
2	Iron Bit-stocks.	
1	Hand Saw.	
3	Seives.	
2	Tackle Blocks.	
2	Slings.	
2	Ensigns.	
1	State Brand.	
1	Copper Adz.	
1	Wooden Bowl.	
1	Large Bullet Mould.	
1	Drawing Knife.	
1	12¾ inch Former.	
4	Formers.	
1	Tool Chest.	
1	Large Chair.	
1	Box Brimstone.	
1	Pendant Halyards.	
1	Auger and Gimblet.	
2	Pairs old Shears.	
1	Gun Rimmer.	
1	Sling Cart.	
16	Blank Books.	
6	Standard Impressions.	
1	Stove and Funnel.	
1	Polishing Lathe.	
1	Hand Vice.	
1	Grindstone.	
2	Small Saws.	
2	Oil Cannisters.	
1	Tackle and Fall.	
1	Standard Plate.	
4	Day Flags.	

SCHEDULE *of Public Property*—(*Continued.*)

No.	Description.	Remarks.
	Lot of Sheet Lead.	
6	Powder Measures.	
	Set Brass Seals and Weights.	
1	Pair Shoe Pincers.	
2	Hammers.	
1	Portfire Mould.	
1	Pair Steelyards.	
	Bench Tools, Chisels and Gouges.	
1	Ladder.	
2	High Steps.	
1	Iron Ladle.	
1	Set Callipers.	
1	Gin.	
1	Gun Searcher.	
2	Boxes Steel.	
1	Saltpetre Mill.	
1	Sheep Skin.	
234	Cartridge Box Woods.	
2	Camp Kettles.	
1	Old Signal Lantern.	
600	Unfinished Powder Horns.	
3	Old Drums.	
	Lot of Old Spikes and Nails.	
1	Paste Brush.	
2	Old White-wash Brushes.	
1	Pair Smith's Tongs.	
	Part of an old Gin.	
	Lot of old Boxes and Barrels.	
10	Empty Bullet Boxes.	
	Lot of old Standard Impressions.	

SCHEDULE *of Public Property in the State Arsenal at Bangor.*

No.	Description.	Remarks.
2	12 pdr. Iron Guns.	With Carriages.
1	Baggage Wagon.	Canvas Cover.
2	18 pdr. Iron Guns.	
2	9 " " "	And Carriages.
2	3 " Brass "	" "
2	4 " Iron "	" "
4	6 " Brass "	"
1	Powder Proof.	
1	Iron Howitzer.	Mounted.
1	12 pdr. Caisson.	
3	6 " "	
112	12 " Round Shot.	
154	6 " " "	
302	3 " " "	
510	4 " " "	
965	Hand Grenades.	
12	Panes Window Glass.	
1	Lot of Old Nail Casks.	
1	Stove and Funnel.	
1	Forge and Bellows.	
4	Emery Wheels.	
1	Man Drill.	
1	Screw Plate, Wench and 6 Taps.	
5	Drills for Lathe.	
2	Gimblets.	
10	Files.	
11	Screw Drivers.	
1	Bench Hammer.	
1	Varnish Brush.	
1	Glue Brush.	
4	Stone Jugs.	
2	Iron Rods.	
1	Old Tea Kettle.	
1	Oil Barrel, and small quantity of Oil.	
8	Paint Pots.	
1	Keg Powder.	
6	Drum Woods.	
22	Horse Chains.	
1	Set State Brands.	
2	Iron Ladles.	

SCHEDULE *of Public Property—(Continued.)*

No.	Description.	Remarks.
1	Flesh Fork.	
4	Draw Knives.	
5	Hand Saws.	
1	Iron Square.	
6	Copper Powder Measures.	
1	Broom.	
1	Dust Brush.	
3155	Muskets.	With Bayonets.
74	"	Without "
494	Hall's Rifles.	With "
73	Bayonets.	
86	Cavalry Pistols.	
200	Johnson's Rifles.	
1	Box containing apparatus for a 12 Pounder.	
700	Sabres.	
100	Bill Hooks.	
34	Boxes containing Cartridges.	In Packs.
13	" 24 lb. Case Shot.	6 to the Box.
27	" 18 " " "	6 " "
11	" 12 " " "	18 " "
12	" 9 " " "	12 " "
12	" 6 " " "	28 " "
5	" 3 " " "	27 " "
8	" 4 " " "	24 " "
14	" 12 " " "	10 " "
19	" 6 " Fixed "	18 " "
3	" 4 " Strapped Shot.	
21	" Grape Shot.	
19	" Bullets, 100 lbs. each.	18 to the pound.
1	" Buck Shot.	
1	" Loose Bullets.	Various sizes.
2100	Scabbard Belts.	In good condition.
98	" "	Out of repair.
427	Ball Pouches.	In good condition.
24	6 lb. Cannister.	Not fixed.
16	Ball Pouches.	Out of repair.
351	Rifle Belts.	
314	Sword "	
184	Sabre "	

Schedule *of Public Property—(Continued.)*

No.	Description.	Remarks.
2	Tin Tube Boxes.	
2587	Cartridge "	
5	Yards Match Rope.	
1	Box Flints.	
11	Gross Priming Wires and Brushes.	
1	Signal Lantern.	
5	Portfire Clippers.	
58	Portfires.	
9	Artillery Priming Wires.	
4	Gunners' Gimblets.	
8	Fifes.	
3	Drums.	
54	Bricoles.	
8	Gunners' Haversacks.	
6	Amunition Bags.	
9	Powder Horns.	7 with Belts.
6	Portfire Cases.	
459	Copper Powder Flasks.	
95	Tin Powder Flasks.	
4	Tube Cases and Belts.	
17	Priming Wires and Brushes.	
1	Box containing loose Musket Balls.	
345	Flint Caps.	
22	Rifle Bullet Moulds.	
17	" Spring Vices.	
19	Musket " "	
35	Buckets.	
267	Artillery Tubes.	
576	Musket Wipers.	
248	Rifle "	
30	Ball Screws.	
51	Iron Tent Pins.	
225	Rifle Screw Drivers.	
58	Musket " "	
152	Knives and Forks.	
2	Carving Knives.	
1	" Fork.	
74	Old Forks.	
1	Pair Brass Candlesticks.	
3	" Tin "	

SCHEDULE *of Public Property—(Continued.)*

No.	Description.	Remarks
440	Pint Dippers.	
17	½ " "	
1	Pepper Box.	
1	Shaving Dish.	
4	Tin Lanterns.	
21	Skimmers.	
186	Tin Pails.	
35	" Tumblers.	
2	Wash Dishes.	
1	Tinder Box.	
2	Lamp Trimmers.	
20	Square Bake Pans.	
633	Tin Mess Pans.	
136	Table Spoons.	
9	Tea "	
2	Lead Aprons and Straps.	
21	Lint Stocks.	
6	Portfire "	
1	Bench Vice.	
1	Iron Ladle.	
6	Tarpaulins.	
36	Spades.	4 damaged.
156	Iron Shovels.	9 old and damaged.
62	Company Tents.	
2	Broad Axes.	
15	Narrow "	
20	Handbarrows.	
6	Horse Shoes.	
30	Pick Axes.	
1	Grub Hoe.	
812	Wooden Canteens.	Worthless.
10	Crowbars.	
1	Box Wooden Tent Pins.	
2	Wood Buckets.	
1	Box, containing 79 Carpenters' Mallets.	
10	Drag Ropes.	
4	Boarding Pikes.	
54	Hand "	
1	Garden Rake.	

SCHEDULE *of Public Property*—(*Continued.*)

No.	Description.	Remarks.
71	Artillery Rammers, Sponges, Ladles and Worms.	
89	Tent Poles.	
22	Sheet Iron Camp Kettles.	
1	Steamer.	
1	Coffee Mill.	
27	Fry Pans.	
4	Tea Kettles.	
100	3 pint Tin Basins.	
1	Bread Pan.	
336	Tin Canteens.	Imperfect.
2	Cast Steel Drills.	
1	Back and Belly Band.	
1	Stone Hammer.	
2	Tompions and Straps.	
12	Camp Blankets.	Old.
5	Augers.	
478	Square Mess Pans.	
1	Tea Cannister.	
400	Bricks.	
6	Orderly Books.	
1	6 pdr. Brass Gun.	Without Carriage.
1	Barrel two thirds full of Grape Shot.	
	The following received from Fort Kent in damaged condition.	
59	Cartridge Boxes.	
44	Ball Pouches.	
22	Rifle Belts.	
59	Scabbard and Belts.	

SCHEDULE *of Public Property in the Arsenal at Bath.*

No.	Description.	Remarks.
1	9 Pound Iron Cannon.	
1	9 " Cannonade.	
3	3 " Iron Cannon.	
1	Tumbril and Harness.	
80	3 lb. Round Shot (less a few delivered to Troops).	
20	9 lb. Case Shot.	
33	6 " " "	
48	3 " " "	
40	3 and 6 lb. Cannister Shot.	
9840	Musket Ball Cartridges.	
23000	" Balls.	
12	Sets Harnesses for one Horse.	
2	Pairs Trace Chains.	
8	Halters extra of Harness sets.	
4	Ladles and Worms.	
5	Rammers and Sponges.	
4	Prolongs.	
65	Bricoles.	
4	Drag Ropes.	
9	Haversacks.	
8	Lintstocks.	
8	Portfires.	
3	Priming Horns and Belts.	
1	Pair Pincers.	
3	Hand Saws.	
2	Axes.	
1	Tube Box and Belt.	
3	Tompions on Guns.	
4	Lead Aprons.	
4	Swab Buckets.	
8	Tin Camp Kettles.	
1000	Pistol Flints.	

SCHEDULE *of Public Property at Augusta.*

No.	Description	Remarks.
2	Muskets and Bayonets.	
1	Old English Musket and Bayonet.	
2	Rifles and 1 Bayonet.	
2	Pistols.	
2	Swords.	
509	Tin Canteens.	
	Lot Tents, Tent Poles, Pins, &c.	

REPORT

OF THE

LAND AGENT

OF THE

STATE OF MAINE,

DECEMBER 31, 1845.

Published agreeably to Resolve of March 22, 1836.

AUGUSTA:

WM. T. JOHNSON,..........PRINTER TO THE STATE.

1846.

REPORT.

LAND OFFICE, DEC. 31, 1845.

To the Governor and Executive Council:

HEREWITH I have the honor to lay before you an account of the land department for the past year.

I have sold of the lands held by the state of Maine in severalty, forty nine thousand seven hundred and ten acres, for $25,041 64, a schedule of which is herereunto annexed, marked A.

One fourth part of the purchase money has, in all cases, been received; and in some instances, where small lots have been sold, they have been fully paid for.

It will be perceived by reference to the schedule, that no whole township has been sold, but detached parcels, not reckoned among the most valuable lands.

Of lands once sold and reverted to the state, I have sold ten thousand nine hundred and seven acres, for $4,798 96, as per schedule marked B.

Of the lands held in common with Massachusetts, I have sold twenty one thousand five hundred and fifty eight and a half acres, amounting to $23,767 88, agreeably to schedule marked C.

The lands set off by the commissioners, to settlers upon the undivided lands on the St. John river, have been conveyed by the agents of Maine and Massachusetts jointly, and the deeds, after being recorded in the land offices of both states, have been delivered, through the agency of Gen. Webber, to the respective claimants.

In June 1843, I sold to Hiram Hall, Esq., lot number three, in township letter H, range 2, containing 157 acres, for one dollar an acre. Alexander Cochran occupied at the time, two lots adjoining said lot No. 3, and had for some years resided thereon. He had, unknown to me, cut a few trees on said lot No. 3, before the lines of the lots were run, but I never heard of his making any claim to it before the summer of 1844.

It does not appear to have been understood by the commissioners, that this lot had been sold, and as Cochran was an ancient settler, they set this off to him with the two lots which he occupied. The joint commission expired before the report of the commissioners was made in this state; and it was too late for them to make any alteration.

I have endeavored to get some proposition from Cochran for an adjustment of the difficulty and release of his claim, but without success. Hall has some ten or twelve acres nearly cleared on said lot, intended for crops next season. Cochran has threatened to use violence, if Hall attempts to occupy it further.

Under the circumstances, I suggest that some person might be appointed to settle the difficulty, by purchasing the claim of the one or the other. At the time this lot was sold, there was no road within ten miles of it, and but one family besides Cochran's, in the township. A road was opened in the summer and autumn of the same year, to and through this township and upon the line of this lot. There has also been built on an adjoining lot, an excellent saw and grist mill, which has very much enhanced the value of this lot.

It is very desirable that the question of title should be settled, that some one put the land in crop, without molestation.

It is the only difficulty which has occurred of the kind, in the settlement of the claims by the commissioners.

There has been expended on the military road, under the superintendence of John Rollins, Esq., $930 23. On the Moosehead Lake road, under the superintendence of Philip S. Lowell, Esq., $500. On the Houlton and Baring road, under the superintendence of David Dow, Esq., $300. On the Aroostook road, under the superintendence of John Rollins and Ira Fish, $455 82, one half of which last sum, has been paid by Massachusetts.

By a resolve of Feb. 12, 1844, I was authorized to expend $3,000 in improving the eastern Aroostook road, provided Massachusetts should expend an equal amount. Massachusetts authorized her agent to expend $1,500 when in funds. The work was delayed for want of agreement between the agents, until last January, when a contract was made with Reuben Whittier, Jr., of Palermo, to build a bridge across the Little Madawaska river—open 12 miles of road between the Little Madawaska and the St. John river, by cutting it three rods wide, and grubbing and leveling twenty feet. The bridge has been built, the road opened, and about six hundred rods of causeway built. Mr. Whittier's accounts are not settled, but the expense will be about $3,800, chargeable to both states.

One thousand dollars, chargeable one half to Maine and one half to Massachusetts, have been expended on the road leading from the Presque Isle of the Aroostook, to No. 11, range 5.

This is a very important thoroughfare, and our legislature authorized a much more generous expenditure, but Massachusetts would not consent to a larger expenditure. With this however, we were enabled to causeway such parts of the road as were before impassable.

The lumbering operations of the past year have terminated generally very successfully, and arrangements were early made for extensive operations the ensuing year ; but the extravagant prices of stumpage, on the St. John waters, and subsequent rise of those articles which are largely consumed by lumbermen, will considerably lessen the operations in that quarter; and the receipts on account of timber will probably be considerably less the ensuing year, than they have been the past.

I have formerly urged the importance of a liberal expenditure upon the main roads leading through the public lands in the county of Aroostook. It is unnecessary for me to repeat the reasons heretofore urged in favor of the policy. The public lands north of the monument line, extend from north to south, about one hundred miles, and from east to west, about the same distance.

2

A large portion of this territory is more easy of access from the province of New Brunswick, than from the settled parts of Maine; and it cannot be doubted that the interest of the state will be promoted by a liberal and judicious expenditure of money on the great leading roads.

A survey of undivided lands in the north part of the state, has been made during the past summer and autumn. It was commenced at the north west corner of township numbered 15, in the 7th range, from which a line was extended west to the boundary line; and all of the territory north of said line surveyed into twenty one townships. Seven townships south of said line extending up the river St. John, have been partially surveyed, leaving about seventy townships of the undivided lands unsurveyed. The season has been very unfavorable for surveying in consequence of the frequent and long continued rains through the summer and autumn; yet it is believed that the expenses have not exceeded that of former surveys in more favorable seasons. I recommend (if Massachusetts concur) a continuance of the survey next season.

The new boundary line crosses some of the townships surveyed on the head branches of the Penobscot, Moose and Dead rivers, leaving parts of them in the province of Lower Canada. I recommend that such of these townships as belong to Maine, be resurveyed, and the quantity remaining to us, determined.

I have paid into the treasury, during the year, $155,048 63, and there remains a balance in my hand, of $3,042 60.

LEVI BRADLEY, Land Agent.

Dr. STATE OF MAINE, in account with LEVI BRADLEY, Land Agent for the Year ending December 31, 1845.

For amount paid for postage, . .	45 27	
See sheet No. 1.		
For amount paid for Office rent at Bangor,	100 00	
See sheet No. 2.		
For amount paid for Bills of Cost, . .	25 00	
See sheet No. 3.		
For amount paid for incidental expenses,	396 86	
See sheet No. 4.		
For amount paid Assistant Land Agent, .	1,000 00	
See sheet No. 5.		1,567 13
For amount paid for surveying timber on the public lands, ...	1,280 60	
See sheet No. 6.		
For half amount paid for surveying timber and other expenses on account of the undivided land,	2,247 83	
See sheet No. 7.		
For half amount paid for surveying undivided lands,	109 61	
See sheet No. 8.		3,638 04
For amount endorsed on notes given for settling lands, having been received in labor opening and making roads under the law of 1838, and for labor received under Resolves of March 24, 1835, and February 22, 1844, . .	2,944 46	
See sheet No. 9.		2,944 46
For half amount expended on the Aroostook Road, per Resolve approved . . .	227 91	
See sheet No. 10.		
For half amount expended on the Eastern Aroostook Road, per Resolve approved February 12, 1844, ...	42 19	
See sheet No. 11.		
For amount expended on the Military Road, per Resolve approved April 4, 1845, and Act approved March 22, 1844, . . .	930 23	
See sheet No. 12.		1,200 33
For amount paid "Commissioners to locate grants, and determine the extent of possessory claims under the late treaty with Great Britain, per Resolve approved February 21, 1843, .	4,041 46	
See sheet No. 13.		4,041 46
For amount paid into the Treasury on account of the permanent School Fund, under the provisions of the Act of February 23, 1828, . .	21,088 70	
For other money paid into the Treasury, .	133,959 33	
See sheet No. 14		155,048 03
For amount of notes given up per Resolve approved March 17, 1845, . . .	121 00	
For amount allowed and abated on J. G. Folsom's note, being for timber cut on his land in 1842, which was erroneously credited to timber,	14 31	
		135 31
For amount of cash expended on the Madaceunk		

Dr. STATE OF MAINE in account with LEVI BRADLEY, Land Agent for the Year ending December 81, 1845.

Road, included in the Madaceunk Road Fund, being part of the amount transferred to the credit of the State of Maine, December 30, 1843,	164 00	
		164 00
For amount of notes taken for lands which have become forfeited to the State, transferred to account of "lands reverted," See Schedule.	3,465 79	3,465 79
For amount paid Geo. W. Coffin balance of accounts	63 15	
" " " John Webber " " "	1,118 52	
" " " Samuel Smith " " "	1,052 14	
" " " C. S. Clark, " " "	1,822 00	
" " " S. P. & H. Strickland " "	268 05	
		4,323 86
For amount of securities, funds, &c., on hand, viz:		
Notes in the office,	176,041 77	
Bonds in the office,	50,567 95	
Executions in the office,	1,542 79	
Demands in the hands of Attorneys,	16,946 61	
School Fund,	5,954 16	
Public Lots, No. 2, Range 2, Titcomb's Survey,	94 99	
Road Fund, (Madaceunk)	158 97	
" " No. 4, R. 5,	463 57	
" " " 6, R. 5,	19 32	
" " " 8, R. 5,	996 52	
" " " 10, R. 5,	764 52	
" " " 11, R. 5,	1,781 35	
" " " 12, R. 5,	179 49	
" " " 9, R. 6,	2,204 96	
" " " 11, R. 6,	431 84	
" " " 2, Old Indian Purchase,	214 33	
" " " F., R. 2,	1,107 94	
" " " D., R. 1,	581 95	
For amount paid Isaac S. Small, advance,	2,044 87	
" " " Andrew Dwinel, "	25 00	
" " " John B. Wing, "	86 74	
" " " Samuel Furlong, "	18 00	
" " " John Webber, "	200 00	
" " " Daniel W. Bradley, "	328 59	
" " " Moses Greenleaf, "	1,972 00	
" " " Reuben Whittier, Jr., advance,	3,293 32	
" " " Zeb. Ingersoll, "	1,000 00	
Cash on hand,	3,042 58	
		271,994 ▮
		$448,5▮2 ▮

Cr. STATE OF MAINE in account with LEVI BRADLEY, Land Agent for the Year ending December 31, 1845.

By balance in the hands of the Land Agent, December 31, 1844, viz:		
Notes in the office,	175,073 18	
Bonds in the office,	37,983 55	
Executions in the office,	892 19	
Demands in the hands of Attorneys,	17,356 66	
School Fund,	4,687 15	
Public Lots, No. 2, R. 2, Titcomb's Survey,	94 99	
Road Fund, (Madaceunk)	666 78	
" " No. 4, R. 5,	534 82	
" " " 6, R. 5,	19 32	
" " " 8, R. 5,	1,202 38	
" " " 10, R. 5,	2,320 75	
" " " 11, R. 5,	2,574 85	
" " " 12, R. 5,	396 99	
" " " 5, R. 6,	134 86	
" " " 9, R. 6,	2,234 98	
" " " 11, R. 6,	431 84	
" " " 1, River Township,	75 00	
" " " 2, Old Indian Purchase,	136 39	
" " F, R. 2,	1,308 85	
" " D, R. 1,	658 66	
By amount due for repair of the Military Road advanced in 1843,	3,319 17	
By amount due from sundry persons for advances,	3,215 65	
By Cash,	5,566 97	
		260,885 98
By amount received for sales of land,	25,041 64	
Per schedule A.		
By amount received for sales of "forfeited lands,"	4,798 96	
Per schedule B.		
By half amount received for sales of undivided land	23,767 88	
Per schedule C.		53,608 48
By amount received in advance for permits and for timber cut on the public lands,	58,034 34	
Per schedule D.		
By half amount received in advance for permits and for timber cut on the undivided lands,	63,046 19	
Per schedule E.		
By amount received for timber cut by trespassers upon the public land,	70 00	
		121,150 53
By amount received on demands transferred to the account of "lands reverted",	306 61	
		306 61
By amount received for interest on demands due the State,	10,942 11	
By amount of interest received in labor on Road Fund notes,	373 03	
By amount of interest included in executions embraced in the account of Bills Receivable,	184 32	
		11,499 46

Cr. **STATE OF MAINE** in account with **LEVI BRADLEY,** Land
Agent for the Year ending December 31, 1845.

By amount received for bills of cost, included in executions embraced in the account of Bills Receivable, ...	56 23	
By half amount received of sundry individuals in part payment for sundry tracts of undivided land sold at auction, which by the conditions of sale is forfeited to the State, . .	1,000 00	
By amount received for medicine, &c., at Fort Fairfield, ...	15 25	
		1,015 25
		$448,522 54

RECEIPTS of Money from all sources during the year ending December 31, 1845.

Balance from last year, . . . , . .	5,566 97
For trespass timber, ...	70 00
For timber cut on the public lands, . . .	40,900 07
For half amount for timber cut on the undivided land, .	50,150 99
For sales of land, ...	7,187 38
For half amount for sales of undivided lands, . .	4,753 60
For forfeited lands, ...	2,302 80
For bills receivable, principal, ...	52,819 26
" " " interest, ...	10,942 11
For advance for repair of the Military road in 1843, refunded,	3,319 17
For advances to sundry persons refunded, . .	3,581 11
For half amount of forfeiture for sale of undivided lands,	1,000 00
For sales of public property at Fort Fairfield, . .	15 25
For receipts from undivided lands for Massachusetts, .	37,422 42
	$220,030 13

DISBURSEMENTS of Money during the year ending Dec. 31, 1845.

Postage, ...	45 27
Office Rent, ...	100 00
Bills of cost, ...	25 00
Charges for incidental expenses, ...	396 86
Assistant Land Agent, ...	1,000 00
Surveys of timber, ...	1,280 60
Surveys of timber on undivided land, &c., . .	2,247 83
Surveys of undivided land, ...	109 61
Aroostook Road, ...	227 91
Eastern Aroostook Road, ...	42 19
Military Road, ...	930 23
Madaceunk Road, ...	164 00
Commissioners to locate grants, &c., . . .	4,041 46
Sundry persons, balance due on account, . . .	4,323 86
Road fund, F. R. 2, (transferred,) . . .	135 05
" " No. 10, R. 5, " . . .	35 31
" " No. 2, Old Indian Purchase, (transferred,) .	77 94
Moses Greenleaf, advance, ...	1,972 00
Reuben Whittier, Jr., advance, ...	3,293 32
Z. Ingersoll, "	1,000 00
I. S. Small, "	2,044 87
Sundry persons on account, ...	1,023 79
State Treasury, ...	155,048 03
Geo. W. Coffin, ...	37,422 42
Cash on hand, ...	3,042 58
	$220,030 13

TRIAL BALANCE, December 31, A. D. 1845.

Accounts.	Debit footings	Credit foot'ngs	Debit balances	Credit bal'nces
Geo. M. Chase,	177 61		177 61	
I. S. Small,	2,044 87		2,044 87	
Andres Dwinel,	25 00		25 00	
Surveys of land in Co.,	219 22	109 61	109 61	
Asst. Land Agent,	1,000 00		1,000 00	
Aroostook Road in Co.,	455 82	227 91	227 91	
Office rent,	100 00		100 00	
Madaceunk Road,	411 55		411 55	
Hodgdon & Rawson,	360 37		360 37	
Frederick Hobbs,	3,684 09	650 60	3,033 49	
Road fund No. 12, R. 5.,	396 99	217 50	179 49	
Road Fund, No. 10, R. 5.,	2,356 06	1,591 54	764 52	
Road Fund, No. 6, R. 5,	19 32		19 32	
Howard & Osgood,	100 00		100 00	
Joseph A. Wood,	112 89		112 89	
Road Fund No. 8, R. 5,	1,242 66	246 14	996 52	
Road Fund F., R. 2,	1,443 90	335 96	1,107 94	
Road Fund D, R. 1,	658 66	76 71	581 95	
Road Fund No. 11, R. 6,	431 84		431 84	
Road Fund No. 11, R 5,	2,598 62	867 27	1,731 35	
Road Fund No. 9, R. 6,	2,234 98	30 02	2,204 96	
Madaceunk Road Fund,	666 78	507 81	158 97	
Executions,	1,542 79		1,542 79	
Bonds,	63,437 57	12,869 62	50,567 95	
John B. Wing,	86 74		86 74	
Road Fund No. 2, O. I. P.,	231 33	17 00	214 33	
Roads No 8, R. 5,	246 14		246 14	
Roads No. 2, O. I. P.,	547 75		547 75	
Roads No. 10, R. 5,	169 65		169 65	
Roads No. 11, R. 5,	971 50		971 50	
Roads No. 9, R. 6,	50 40		50 40	
Public Lots No.2, R.2, T.S.	94 99		94 99	
Roads F., R. 2,	270 46		270 46	
Roads D., R. 1,	86 44		86 44	
Roads No. 5, R. 6,	143 50		143 50	
Trespass,		70 00		70 00
John Hodgdon,	7,043 61		7,043 61	
Charges in Co.,	4,495 65	2,247 82	2,247 83	
Surveys of Timber,	1,280 60		1,280 60	
Samuel Furlong,	18 00		18 00	
E. A. Road, in Co.,	84 37	42 18	42 19	
Postage,	45 27		45 27	
John Webber,	4,666 36	4,466 36	200 00	
Abatements,	135 31		135 31	
State Treasury,	155,048 03		155,048 03	
Sales of land in Co.,		23,767 88		23,767 88
State of Maine,	4,487 86	261,901 23		257,413 37
D. W. Bradley,	1,125 98	797 39	$28 59	
Notes,	211,461 69	35,419 92	176,041 77	
Joseph Carr, Jr.,	702 64		702 64	
Comm'rs to locate grants, &c.	7,337 37	3,295 91	4,041 46	

TRIAL BALANCE---(Continued.)

Accounts	Debit footings	Credit footings	Debit balances	Credit bal'nces
Timber in Co.,	4,105 27	67,151 46		63,046 19
Bills of Cost.	25 00	56 23		31 23
Sales of land,		25,041 64		25.041 64
Timber,		58,034 34		58,034 34
School Fund,	32,881 84	26,947 68	5,934 16	
Military Road,	930 23		930 23	
Lands reverted,	3,465 79	5,105 57		1,639 78
John McDonald,	2,177 68		2,177 68	
James W. Bradbury,	3,238 32		3,238 32	
Road Fund, No. 4, R. 5,	534 82	71 25	463 57	
Interest,		11,499 46		11,499 46
Moses Greenleaf,	1,972 00		1,972 00	
Reuben Whittier, Jr.,	3,293 32		3,293 32	
Z. Ingersoll,	1,000 00		1,000 00	
Charges,	396 86		396 86	
Cash,	220,030 13	216,987 55	3,042 58	
Roads No. 4, R. 5,	47 07		47 07	
	760,651 56	760,651 56	440,543 89	440,543 89

[A.]

SALES OF LAND, *during the year 1845.*

Date.	Purchasers.	Township.	Lot.	Acres.	Amount received Dollars.	Cts.	Remarks.
1845.							
Jan. 4,	Moses Thurlow,	11, R. 6, W.E.L.S.	30 and 31	304	76	00	L. C.
Jan. 4,	John T. Pike,	H, R. 2,	66	152 40/100	38	10	"
Jan. 4,	Watson R. Starbird,	do.	75	180	45	00	"
Jan. 4,	John A. Hubbard,	do.	83	152 40/100	38	10	"
Jan. 6,	W. & W. Getchell,	2 R. 2, W.B.K.P.	Reserved,	320	48	00	U. D.
Jan. 7,	Sam. Smith & al.,	W. ½ 2 R. 11 W.E.L.S.		9,533	8,740	32	C. D.
Jan. 7,	Wm. McCrillis & al.,	N. ½ 8 R. 7 do.		10,506	6,045	60	"
Jan. 14,	Cephas Sampson,	H. R. 2,	28	157 38/100	39	42	L. C.
Jan. 14,	Hiram Hines,	do.	36, 37, 42, 47	647	161	75	"
Feb. 17,	D. F. Adams,	do.	23	153	39	50	"
Feb. 17,	F. A. Williams,	do.	13	172	43	00	"
Feb. 17,	John Williams,	do.	31	168	42	00	"
Mar. 21,	Jos. W. Haines,	D. R. 1,	87, 92, 94, 101, 102, 110	808			Resolve.
June 11,	Hazon Walker,	11 R. 5, do.	71	133	33	25	L. C.
June 12,	Town of Passadumkeag,	Unsold Land,		1,301¾			Resolve.
June 17,	Geo. Atwood & al.,	No. 1, I. P.	72	116	58	00	C. D.
June 20,	Jos. B. Hall,	H. R. 2, W.E.L.S.	84	160	40	00	L. C.
June 20,	John A. Hubbard,	do.	87	170½	42	62	"
July 1,	Asa Smith,	1 I. P.	2 and 3	9 44/100	18	00	U. D.
July 1,	Town of Burlington,	Burlington,	Sundry lots,	4,695			Resolve.
July 3,	Ira Wadleigh,	1 R. 13, W.E.L.S.	3 and 9	1,303 7/100	424	77	C. D.

Date	Name	Location	Lot / Section	No. acres	$ cts.	Fund
Aug. 8.	Abram Parsons,	H, R. 2, do. Reserved,	70	167	41 75	L. C.
Aug. 13,	Jabez True,	2 R. 3, E. of Ken. river,	3 R. 4	320	50 00	U. D.
Sept. 18,	J. P. & Elisha Gubtail,	Enfield,		290	81 20	C. D.
Sept. 19,	Ira Fish & al.,	11 R. 6, W.E L.S. Sundry lots,		3,736¼	2,337 80	"
Sept. 19,	Wm. H. McCrillis,	same, same,		7,929¾	2,946 70	L. C.
Oct. 6,	Wm. A. Vaughan,	H, R. 2, W.E.L.S.	1 and 6	335	83 75	C. D.
Oct. 6,	Sam. S. Collins,	do.	12, 17, 16, 22	681	170 25	L. C.
Oct. 13,	Ira Fish,	9 R. 6,	Sec. 30	619	309 50	"
Oct. 18,	James Cunningham,	4 R. 5,	E ¼ Sec. 23	161	40 25	"
Oct. 18,	Jacob Greeley,	do.	34	162	40 50	C. D.
Oct. 18,	E. D. W. Murphy,	do.	32	163	40 75	"
Oct. 15,	Fuller and Remick,	1, I. P.	71	173¾	73 90	L. C.
Oct. 28,	Samuel Brailey & al.,	8, R. 7, W.E.L.S. Sundry lots,		3,124	2,717 88	"
Nov. 10,	John Bell,	4, R. 5,	Part of 23	161½	20 18	L. C.
Nov. 26,	Francis Kean,	F, R. 2,	8	157¼	39 30	"
Dec. 12,	Thomas Field,	D, R. 1,	34	158	39 50	"
Dec. 12,	John B. Raymond,	Ripley,	13 and 14	224	35 00	C. D.
				49,710 33/100	25,041 64	

[B.]

SALES OF REVERTED LANDS, *A. D.* 1845.

Date.	Purchasers.	Township.	Lot.	Acres.	Amount. Dollars. Cts.	Remarks.
1845.						
Jan. 6,	Bearce & Foss,	Bradley,	12	596	119 20	C. D.
Jan. 6,	Pratt & Hammond,	No. 1, I. P.	152	139	55 60	"
Jan. 7,	Wm. Paine,	Bradley,	Gore 2	30)	46 05	U. D.
Jan. 7,	Isaac Webber,	4, R. 5, W. E. L. S.	W. ½ 5 and 6	162	30 38	"
Jan. 7,	Wm. Young,	do.	E. ½ 5 and 6	162	30 50	"
Jan. 7,	Jas. Cunningham,	do.	E. ½ 7 and 8	162	31 12	"
Jan. 7,	Wm. Lovejoy,	do.	40	162	20 31	"
Jan. 7,	Samuel H. Chesley,	do.	41 and 42	328	41 08	"
Jan. 9,	Rufus Lord,	Topsfield,	5	153	38 25	L. C.
May 17,	Anthony Woodard,	Bradley,	20	579	250 00	C. D.
May 20,	Sylvanus Hatch,	Chester,	24	618	16 58	U. D.
May 27,	Peleg T. Jones,	Springfield,	1, R. 2	100	50 00	"
May 28,	Edmund T. Canney,	Masardis,	16	174	60 90	"
June 3,	John Moore,	Topsfield,	123	199¾	49 94	L. C.
June 18,	William Black,	Greenbush,	34	102	52 00	U. D.
June 20,	T. C. Burleigh,	Springfield,	11, R. 5	71	35 25	"
June 20,	Samuel Millett,	do.	14, R. 3	100	60 00	"
July 1,	Samuel W. Coombs,	No. 1, I. P.	42	54 48/100	27 24	"
July 1,	Asa Smith,	do.	88	169 66/100	60 00	"
July 3,	Rendol Whidden,	Topsfield,	64, 73, 82, 83, 84 and 85	884 33/100	442 17	C. D.
July 21,	Josiah Garland,	Ellsworth,	N. ½ 179	80	22 00	U. D.

Date	Purchaser	Township	Lot	Acres	Amount	Code
July 21,	G. & R. R. Woods,	Greenbush,	63	100	103 25	U. D.
Aug. 1,	William Foster,	do.	20	71	42 94	"
Aug. 1,	Stephen B. Parker,	do.	64	155	77 50	C. D.
Aug. 11,	Phineas Foss,	No. 1, I. P.	19, 20, & 35	254	167 38	C. D.
Aug. 12,	Elias Whittier,	Enfield,	30	100	75 00	U. D.
Aug. 20,	Gardner & Stetson,	No. 5, R. 6,	94	164	41 00	L. C.
Aug. 26,	Lucretia H. Eldridge,	Greenbush,	29	93¾	100 00	U. D.
Sept. 1,	Dan Pineo,	Topsfield,	101	113	56 50	C. D.
Sept. 11,	Joseph Hammond,	No. 1, 1. P.	74	122½	122 50	"
Sept. 12,	David Fox,	Lowell,	8, R. 5	100	96 25	U. D.
Sept. 15,	Eben'r Martin,	Topsfield,	102	103½	50 16	C. D.
Sept. 15,	A. F. Hunnewell.	do.	103	98	49 00	"
Sept. 15,	Benj. McCorrison,	Burlington,	6, R. 5	100	50 00	"
Sept. 16,	Gilman Weeks,	Wellington,	56	160	75 00	U. D.
Sept. 16,	James Butterfield,	Springfield,	19, R. 5	75	37 50	C. D.
Sept. 16,	Peter M. Chase,	do.	14, R. 2	100	50 00	"
Sept. 18,	W. Weatherbee,	do.	16, R. 4	100	25 00	U. D.
Sept. 19,	Lyman Bradford,	4, R. 5,	E. ½ 11, & 12	166	41 48	"
Oct. 3,	Saml. C. & Philip Page.	Burlington,	5, 6 & 7, R. 6	300	213 00	C. D.
Oct. 3,	James Butterfield,	Springfield,	16, R. 3	100	30 00	"
Oct. 7,	Hezekiah Lombard,	Lincoln,	B, R. 4	220	40 00	U. D.
Oct. 13,	Samuel Wiggin,	No. 1, I. P.	25 & 41	320	160 00	"
Oct. 13,	Ira Fish,	Lincoln,	50	129	32 25	"
Oct. 21,	Elias G. Riggs,	Greenbush,	6, 7, 8, 9 & 10	500	250 00	"
Oct. 24,	Samuel Briggs,	No. 1, I. P.	98	110	55 00	C. D.
Oct. 27,	Andrew Woodman,	Burlington,	11 & 12, R. 6	200	400 00	"
Oct. 30,	Charles Jarvis,	Ellsworth,	284	160	56 26	U. D.

[B.]

SALES OF REVERTED LANDS, *A. D.* 1845—(*Continued.*).

Date.	Purchaser.	Township.	Lot.	Acres.	Amount. Dollars. Cts.	Remarks.
1845.						
Nov. 3,	E. B. Hodgkins,	No. 10, I. P.	28	100	60 00	U. D.
Nov. 17,	Asa Smith,	No. 1, I. P.	27	4 $\frac{83}{100}$	48 30	"
Nov. 17,	D. Brown & al.,	No. 10, I. P.	4, 11, 29 and meadow, 1	500	100 00	C. D.
Nov. 18,	B. F. Brown,	No. 1, I. P.		68	50 00	"
Nov. 26,	John Goddard,	Chester,	57 & 58	320	224 00	"
Nov. 27,	Rendol Whidden,	Topsfield,	25 & 100	304¼	231 12	"
Dec. 9,	Nathaniel Coffin,	Lowell,	7, R. 2	100	50 00	"
				10,907 $\frac{81}{100}$	$4,798 96	

[C.]

SALES OF UNDIVIDED LANDS, A. D. 1845.

Date.	Purchasers.	Township or tract.	Acres.	Amount received. DOLLARS. CTS.	Remarks.
1845.					
Jan. 3,	S. P. & H. Strickland,	S. W. ¼ No. 5, R. 10,	2,654	1,340 25	C. D.
Jan. 3,	Samuel Smith,	No. 8, R. 9,	10,999	16,498 50	"
Aug. 7,	Wm. H. McCrillis, et al.	¼ No. 5, R. 15,	7,905½	5,929 13	"
			21,558½	$23,767 88	

(D.)

AMOUNT RECEIVED A. D. 1845, *for Timber cut on Lands assigned to Maine.*

Date.	Of whom received.	Township.	Amount. Dollars. Cts.
1845.			
April 15,	Samuel Smith,	11, R. 6, W. E. L. S.,	389 75
May 26,	same,	15, R. 6, "	50 00
May 30,	Allen Crane,	Lincoln,	86 85
June 3,	J. S. Elliott,	F, R. 2, W. E. L. S.,	12 50
June 23,	I. Farrar & Co.,	Burlington,	214 89
June 25,	Willey & Harthorn,	4, R. 5, W. E. L. S.,	222 43
July 11,	Joph Connell,	E, R. 1, "	50 00
"	same,	K, R. 2, "	50 00
"	Geo. W. Towle,	10, R. 3, "	50 00
"	W. A. Vaughan, et al.,	14, R. 3, "	50 00
"	S. B. Pattee,	16, R. 3, "	50 00
"	G. W. Towle,	11, R. 4, "	50 00
"	same,	13, R. 4, "	50 00
"	Cl....les H. Shepard,	15, R. 4, "	50 00
"	Z. Ingersol,	14, R. 5, "	50 00
"	Oliver Frost,	16, R. 5, "	50 00
"	G. L. Boynton,	13, R. 6, "	50 00
"	C. S. Clark,	15, R. 6, "	50 00
"	Ira Fish,	12, R. 7, "	50 00
"	Samuel Smith,	14, R. 7, "	50 00
"	C. S. Clark,	16, R. 7, "	50 00
"	Dennis Fairbanks,	12, R. 3, "	50 00

Date	Name	Location	Amount
July 12,	C. H. Shepard,	15, R. 4, W. E. L. S.,	2,185 86
July 15,	Samuel Smith,	2, R. 11, "	672 33
August 1,	Barnes & Carrick,	Springfield, "	15 75
August 13,	Ira Fish,	9, R. 6, W. E. L. S.,	50 00
August 29, "	same,	14, R. 7, "	7,826 32
August 30,	me,	9, R. 6, "	668 06
September 3,	thos M. Roberts,	7, R. 6, "	843 38
"	Milton & Run,	X & 2, R. 13, "	2,081 90
"	Willey & Harthorn,	6, R. 5, "	42 73
"	Wi fan,	W. ⅓ 3 R. 4, "	50 00
"	Willey & Harthorn,	7, R. 4, "	50 00
"	J. H. Pillsbury,	7, R. 6, "	50 00
"	Samuel Brailey,	4, R. 7, "	50 00
"	T. J. Grant,	2, R. 13, "	50 00
"	Horace ss,	X, R. 14, "	50 00
September 4,	Mes Rose et als.,	F, R. 2, "	172 50
September 24,	Samuel Soule,	6, R. 1, W. B. K. P.,	50 00
"	Joph B. Wbb,	R. 6, "	50 00
October 10,	C. Ruberts,	Passadumkeag,	53 00
October 27,	Jeb Lowell,	2, R. 6, W. B. K. P.,	50 00
October 28,	Ines Tibbetts,	16, R. 3, W. E. L. S.,	1,291 75
"	Samuel Smith,	12, R. 7, "	5,368 83
"	same,	16, R. 7, "	1,887 64
"	Benjamin Dyer,	11, R. 6, "	1,634 50
"	S. B. Bearce,	11, R. 6, "	284 31
October 30,	James McCann,	11, R. 5, "	137 15
"	Samuel Sterling,	10, R. 5, "	474 40

(D.)

AMOUNT RECEIVED A. D. 1845, *for Timber cut on Lands assigned to Maine*—(Continued.)

Date.	Of whom received.	Township.	Amount. Dollars. Cts.
1845.			
October 30,	S. G. Burpee,	12, R. 5, W. E. L. S.,	2,176 68
"	William Connell,	16, R. 5, "	2,207 94
"	Joseph Connell,	K, R. 2, "	2,158 00
"	same,	E, R. 1, "	956 49
"	Benjamin Rackliff,	F. R. 2, "	200 00
"	Samuel Smith,	12, R. 7, "	6,159 74
"	same,	15, R. 6, "	582 35
"	Jabez S. Currier,	14, R. 3, "	586 03
"	Dennis Fairbanks,	12, R. 3, "	634 57
"	Oliver Frost,	12, R. 5, "	50 00
"	Eliphalet Watson,	14, R. 3, "	12 00
"	J. P. Longley,	3, R. 11, "	50 00
"	James Jenkins,	3, R. 11, "	221 36
"	Samuel Soule et als.,	6, R. 1, W. B. K. P.,	2,909 70
"	same,	1, R. 8, "	2,588 17
November 5,	George W. King et al.,	6, R. 2, N. B. K. P.,	193 21
November 13,	Hewey Reed et al.,	4, R. 7, W. E. L. S.,	320 57
December 19,	Timothy Crane et al.,	7, R. 4, "	2,284 34
December 22,	William Towle et al.;	10, R. 3, "	1,687 00
December 24,	same,	13, R. 4, "	1,681 40
"	same,	11, R. 4, "	2,508 03
			$58,034 34

(E.)

AMOUNT RECEIVED A. D. 1845, *for Timber cut on the Undivided Lands.*

Date	Name	Location	Amount
April 15,	Leonard Jones & Co.,	7, R. 13, W. E. L. S.,	$240 65
June 27,	Thomas Berebee,	St. John River,	50 42
"	Charles Pelletier,	"	33 91
"	Lus Michaud,	"	43 04
"	B. ell,	"	353 16
"	D. & M. Savage,	"	303 84
July 10,	Paul Michaud,	"	20 00
"	Has E. Perley,	G, R. 1, W. E. L. S.,	25 00
"	same,	L, R. 2, "	25 00
"	Samuel Sterling,	M, R. 2, "	25 0
"	H. Sad,	17, R. 3, "	25 00
"	J. B Wing,	18, R. 3, "	25 0
"	E. P. Whiting,	17, R. 4, "	25 00
"	Has E. Perley,	18, R. 4, "	25 0
"	same,	18, R. 5, "	25 00
"	C. H. al,	17, R. 6, "	25 00
"	Hiram Hunt,	18, R. 6, "	25 00
"	Ira Fish,	17, R. 7, "	25 00
"	John Glazier,	R, .7, "	25 0
"	same,	St. John River,	25 00
"	Samuel Smith,	17, R. 5, W. E. L. S.,	25 00
"	B Beverage,	St. John River,	25 00
"	Thomas Picard,	"	25 00
"	Samuel Smith,	"	25 00
"	Jewett & Mh,		2500

(E.)

AMOUNT RECEIVED A. D. 1845, *for Timber cut on the Undivided Lands*—(*Continued.*)

Date.	Of whom received.	Township.	Amount. DOLLARS. CTS.
1845.			
July 10,	Samuel Smith,	St. John River,	25 00
"	S. D. Ward,	"	25 00
"	same,	"	25 00
"	same,	"	25 00
"	same,	"	25 00
"	C. Jewett,	"	25 00
"	C. S Clark,	"	25 00
"	Thomas E. Perley,	16, R. 10, W. E. L. S.,	25 00
"	C. Jutt,	16, R. 11, "	25 00
"	Joseph Carleton,	16, R. 12, "	25 00
"	Samuel Smith,	8, R. 8, "	25 00
July 17,	D. Pingree,	5, R. 13, "	734 57
August 6,	Jas. Jenkins,	{ 7, R. 8, / E. ½ 7, R. 9, / 4, R. 11, "	50 00
"	C. S. Clark,	¾ 4, R. 14, "	50 00
"	C. for,	5, R. 11, "	25 00
"	J. Wadleigh,	7, R. 15, "	25 00
"	C. E. Dole,	¾ 7, R. 14, "	25 00
"	same,	8, R. 15, "	25 00
"	Jas. Thissell,	4, R. 18, "	25 00
"	E. Gulliver,	5, R. 16, "	25 00

Date	Name	Location	Amount
August 9,	T. H. Dillingham & Co.,	7, R. 8, W. E. L. S.,	377 50
August 28,	Samuel Brailey,	E. ½ 7, R. 9, W. E. L. S.,	438 48
August 30,	A. M. ...s,	7, R. 11,	2,201 47
"	...a,	5, R. 11, "	869 08
September 8,	John H. Pills ...by,	7, R. 11, "	25 00
September 9,	Samuel Smith,	17, R. 5, 6 and 7,	6,127 88
"	...e,	St. John River,	4,697 43
September 11,	same,	5, R. 12, W. E. L. S.,	500 00
October 18,	...iel Lunt,	4, R. 11, "	25 00
October 20,	J. M. & H. ...he,	4, R. 17 and 18, W. E. L. S.,	303 77
"	Iohn Goddard,	6, R. 13, W. E. L. S.,	25 00
October 28,	Samuel Smith,	5, R. 12, "	208 23
"	same,	17, R. 5, "	1,053 65
"	Amos Rines,	St. Francis,	367 81
"	Thas E. Perley,	18, R. 5, W. E. L. S.,	2,144 26
"	I ...wis Heustis,	18, R. 4, "	1,938 17
"	...e,	17, R. 4, "	505 72
"	Charles Perley,	L, R. 2, "	869 27
"	...el Smith,	17, R. 3, "	655 60
"	...e,	G, R. 1, "	685 85
"	Thomas E. Perley,	18, R. 6, "	4,500 00
"	J. & S. ...ler & Co.,	St. John River,	1,168 67
"	...nes ...ok,	"	1,000 00
"	R. & B. Kilborn,	"	558 14
"	Benjamin ...d,	"	289 50
"	Jacob McKean,	"	767 72
	S. Tapley,		

(E.)

AMOUNT RECEIVED A. D. 1845, *for Timber cut on the Undivided Lands*—(*Continued.*)

Date.	Of whom received.	Township.	Amount. Dollars.	Cts.
1845.				
October 28,	R. R. Ketchum,	St. John River,	1,285	61
"	J. ?ir & Co.,	"	69	17
"	Thas E. Perley,	"	67	53
"	John Baker,	"	342	00
"	Hhas E. Perley,	"	464	15
October 30,	John Shea,	"	084	40
"	John B. Wing,	18, R. 3, W. E. L. S.	188	98
"	Samuel Smith,	17, R. 5, "	1,439	69
?er 31,	Shepard ?Gy,	St. John River,	627	70
"	W. H. Smith,	? 7, R. 14, W. E. L. S.,	25	00
"	William ?ell,	17, R. 7,	0?8	55
?er 4,	B. Hunnewell,	St. John River,	307	37
?er 6,	H. R. & W. N. Soper,	5, R. 12, W. E. L. S.,	25	00
?er 1?,	?ett & ?h,	St. John River,	4,538	96
?er 2,	Levi Young,	5, R. 9, W. E. L. S.,	25	00
?er 8,	Samuel Smith,	5, R. 13, "	25	00
?er 22,	?nes Jenkins,	4, R. 12, "	582	69
December 24,	?el F. Smith,	5, R. 11, "	981	32
"	Newell Avery et als.,	7, R. 15, "	986	02
"	?nes Thissell et als.,	8, R. 15, "	842	87
"	I?m Wadleigh et als,	6, R. 13, "	433	10
"	?????,	7, R. 14,	1,774	48

T. H. Dillingham et als.,	7, R. 8, W. E. L. S.,	576 57
Stephen Glazier et als.,	18, R. 7, "	52 31
Shepard Cary et als.,	Black River,	5,135 90
D. W. Bradley,	17, R. 5, W. E. L. S.,	549 03
		$63,046 19

STATE OF MAINE.

HOUSE OF REPRESENTATIVES, June 3, 1846.

A majority of the committee on elections ask leave to report, in the case of Messrs. Colburn and Hersey, each claiming a seat in the House of Representatives, from the town of Belfast, the following statement of facts, and the accompanying resolve.

Henry Colburn was duly elected representative of the town of Belfast, on the fifteenth day of September, 1845. On or about the first day of November, he went to New York to make arrangements to enter into business. On the twenty eighth day of November, he again left for New York, taking with him his wife and two children, leaving in Belfast one son in the employment of a Mr. Kimball. He also carried with him a large part of his furniture, leaving in Belfast furniture enough to fill one chamber in the house of Thomas Marshall, expressly declaring, that he should return in the spring, to reside there. After his arrival at New York, he kept house and formed a co-partnership with Judkins & Adams. He was again in Belfast, with his family on the fifth day of April, 1846. Never having (so far as it appeared from the evidence before us) altered or changed his determination to continue his residence in Belfast.

One witness for Mr. Hersey "inferred that Mr. Colburn would have remained in New York if business had proved good, but could not say that Mr. Colburn had ever so said or written." Mr. Colburn

Wm. T. Johnson, Printer to the State.

also resigned the office of town clerk, before he went away in November, stating as a reason for so doing, "That it might involve the title to personal property mortgaged and recorded if the records should be kept by his son during his absence." A warrant was issued by the selectmen of Belfast, and a meeting was held in conformity thereto, on the sixth of April last, at which time Mr. S. S. Hersey received a majority of the votes thrown. Thomas Marshall and B. F. Blackstone were called, by Mr. Hersey, to prove these facts, and the reason for issuing their warrant. Mr. Marshall said "he was opposed to signing the warrant for the meeting of April sixth, and did not think there was a vacancy," but he signed it because there was an "implied solicitation for a meeting—there was a call from one of the papers." Mr. Blackstone said he signed the warrant "because Mr. Colburn was absent, but did not undertake to decide at that time that there was a vacancy, but thought the legislature could settle that matter right." The question to be decided is, whether, with this statement of facts, Mr. Colburn did lose his residence or not. That he had been five years a citizen of the United States; that he was twenty one years of age; that he had been a resident in the state one year, and in the town of Belfast for three months next preceding his election, has not been disputed or doubted. It was proved that he had resided in Belfast thirty years. It is also admitted and proved that he has been a resident of Belfast since the sixth day of April, 1846, up to this time. We have the testimony of three respectable and apparently intelligent witnesses that Mr. Colburn did, directly and unequivocally, say that he should return to Belfast in the spring. And they further show that these declarations were made at three several times; one on the day before he started, one on the very day on which he started, and the other in Boston, while on his way to New York. Here we have the intention to return and an actual return, and surely that settles the residence.

In the case of Richmond vs. Vassalborough it was held good law, that when a man went from one town to another with a conditional resolution *not to return*, but did return, his residence was in the town he came from and returned to. How much stronger the present case of expressed intention to return and actual return, makes Mr. Colburn's claims to a continued residence, your committee must leave you to determine.

RICHARD ROGERS, *Chairman.*

STATE OF MAINE.

RESOLVED, That Henry Colburn is duly elected and
2 entitled to a seat in this House as representative for
3 the town of Belfast.

MINORITY REPORT.

The minority of the committee on Elections, having had the case of Messrs. Colburn and Hersey, claimants of the seat of representative from the town of Belfast, under consideration, are unable to coincide with the majority of said committee, and ask leave to give their reasons for such disagreement in the following

REPORT.

Messrs. Colburn and Hersey both appeared before your committee, claiming to be representatives from Belfast. Each had credentials signed by the town officers in due form.

Now as the town of Belfast is entitled to but *one* representative; and as it was incumbent upon your committee to decide between them, an investigation was commenced.

The claimants stated to your committee, that there was certain evidence in the town of Belfast, which would be useful and necessary; and upon making a corresponding report to the house, an order was granted, authorizing your committee to send for persons and papers.

Accordingly the parties with their witnesses, appeared before your committee on the 29th ult.

It appeared in evidence, that Mr. Colburn was elected representative from Belfast, in September last—that in the early part of November following, he went to New York for the purpose of completing certain arrangements which he was making with a gentleman, preparatory to entering a partnership there, in the lumber business—that he soon returned; and the latter part of the same month (November), broke up housekeeping, resigned the office of town clerk, and delivered up the books and papers to the selectmen —dissolved all his business connections with the town of Belfast, and taking with him all his family (except one son, a young man who *had been* for some time previous, and still continues to be, absent from his father, as an assistant in a store,) and also taking his furniture and other property (except such things as were not worth removal, which were left in the custody of his brother-in-law, Thomas Marshall,) he proceeded to the city of New York, became a member of the aforementioned firm, and *set up housekeeping*. He remained in this situation till the 5th of April last, when he returned to the town of Belfast.

A short time previous to his return, however, the same board of selectmen which called and presided at the town meeting at which Mr. Colburn was elected—Thomas Marshall, the particular friend and brother-in-law of said Colburn, being chairman—issued their warrant calling a town meeting the 6th of April, to elect a new representative ; it being a very general opinion, that by his contin-ued absence, Mr. Colburn had vacated his seat. At this town meeting, which was well attended by both political parties, Mr. Hersey was elected and received the usual certificate of such election.

It also appeared by the evidence of three or four individuals, who casually inquired of Mr. Colburn previous to his departure in the fall, what they should do for a representative, that he stated in reply, he should be back.

It further appeared, from the evidence of his most *intimate friend* and brother-in-law, the aforementioned Thomas Marshall, that he had a conversation with Mr. Colburn, relative to his removal, last fall ; and that Mr. Colburn then told him that certain proposals had been made to induce him to go to New York, and embark as a lumber merchant there. That Colburn said that if he found the business equalled his expectations and hopes, he should remain there ; if it did not, he should return. This same witness kept up an active correspondence with his brother-in-law, Mr. Colburn—receiving from him no less than a half a dozen letters, during the four or five months of his residence in New York—and who to use his own language, said, he " probably knew as much about his affairs, as Mr. Colburn did himself,"—stated that he *inferred* from these letters, that his friend and correspondent would not return to Belfast if his business succeeded in New York; that he had *no doubt* from what *he knew*, that his continuance in that city depended upon a *contingency*, viz: the prosperity of his lumber business. This witness further stated, in reply to a cross examination, that no letter previous to the 20th of March, mentioned any thing about Mr. Colburn's return to Belfast—that the letter of that date, *did* mention the subject of his return, and inquired if he, the witness, could procure him a house. It also stated as the reason of his return to Belfast, that his business operations had not succeeded to his mind.

The above, the minority of your committee consider to be a fair, unvarnished statement of the facts in the case, as it appeared in evidence before them.

Now it must be apparent to the mind of every one, that the main, indeed the only point at issue, is, whether Mr. Colburn, by a four or five months residence in New York, at the time and under the circumstances named, rendered himself, constitutionally, ineligible to a seat in this House?

The minority of your committee, according to what they deem the true construction and apparent meaning of the constitution, cannot decide otherwise, than that Mr. Colburn has by such breaking up his residence in Belfast, become ineligible.

Art. 4, part 1st, sec. 4, of the constitution of Maine, reads as folllows :

" No person shall be a member of the house of representatives, unless he shall at the commencement of the period for which he is elected, have been five years a *citizen* of the United States—have arrived at the age of twenty-one years—have been a *resident* in this state one year, or from the adoption of this constitution ; and for the three months next preceding the time of his election shall have been, and during the period for which he is elected, shall continue to be a *resident* in the town or district which he represents."

We cannot but believe that the framers of the constitution intended that there should be a material difference between the words " citizen " and " resident," as they are used in this short section.

Among the qualifications for a representative, above enumerated, are, that he must be a "citizen" of the United States, and a "resident" (one *actually residing*) of this State for the period of one year.

Now it is the confident opinion of the minority of your committee, that Mr. Colburn, by his removal and absence, till the fifth day of April, under the circumstances mentioned, had not been a "resident" in this State, "one year" according to the meaning and true intent of the constitution.

We believe, that that instrument requires that any man, to be eligible to a seat in this House, must, *at the commencement of the period* for which he is elected, not only have been a "*citizen*" of the United States for five years, but must also have been a "*resident*" of this State, one entire year without interruption, "at the commencement of the period for which he is elected." It is a well settled point in law, that a man's residence is established in the place or town where his family resides, except in cases where his family has abandoned him.

And further, that when a man leaves a town, with his *family* and *property*, for an indefinite period, and dissolves his business connections with that town, he loses his "residence," and begins to acquire a new one, in the town to which he may remove.

In the case of Green vs. Windham, reported in the thirteenth volume of the Maine Reports, the Supreme Court decided, that " whoever removes into a town for the purpose of remaining there an indefinite period, thereby establishes his domicil (or place of residence) in that town. It is not necessary that he should go with a fixed resolution to spend his days there. He might have in contemplation, many contingencies which would induce him to go elsewhere. Some persons are more restless in their character, and migratory in their habits, than others; but they may and do acquire a domicil wherever they establish themselves for the time being, with an intention to remain, until inducements may arise to remove."

With regard to the evidence before your committee, we are induced to lay much stress upon that of Thomas Marshall. He testified with evident reluctance; and such admissions as were at all unfavorable to Mr. Colburn, were made only in answer to rigid questioning.

In every case where evidence is admitted, the minority of your committee believe that a just discrimination should be used in summing up that evidence; that there should be taken into the account, not only the witness's general standing and character for veracity, but that we should also include his known, openly avowed feelings, and relative position to the parties. In a case where a witness is known to be an intimate family connection—a *political* friend, as well as a *personal* one—it is but justice to allow that every admission of his, which militates against the interests of the party, in favor of which he is naturally prejudiced, possesses *double force* to what it would if his prejudices—his political and personal sympathies, were enlisted on the opposite side.

This Thomas Marshall was chairman of the board of selectmen, which issued the warrant for a new election; was in close correspondence with Mr. Colburn, the whole time he was in New York; was his intimate and very particular friend; knew all about his business and intentions; and with all these opportunities for knowing the actual state of affairs, and well knowing how injurious his movements would be to the claims of his friend, (if indeed, at *that time*, Mr. Colburn or his friends entertained any notion of claiming his seat, which we very much doubt,) he proceeded *voluntarily* to call a town meeting to choose a representative to fill the vacancy. Neither of the selectmen, nor indeed, did any other person, so far as we can learn, remonstrate against, or make any opposition to the meeting. Each party nominated a candidate and supported him with their votes. Mr. Marshall himself, voting for the candidate which his party supported, in opposition to Mr. Hersey.

Upon a careful, somewhat extended, and as we think, candid examination of the subject, your committee are irresistably compelled to conclude that the *acts* of Thomas Marshall, especially when connected with his verbal testimony, furnish evidence of the strongest and most conclusive character, against the claims of Mr. Colburn.

JABEZ D. HILL.
AMOS PITCHER.
HORATIO G. RUSS.

STATE OF MAINE.

RESOLVED, That Samuel S. Hersoy, having been
2 duly elected, is entitled to a seat in this House as
3 representative from the town of Belfast.

STATE OF MAINE.

REPORT.

The Joint Standing Committee on Agriculture, to which was referred an order in relation to flowage, have had that subject under consideration, and respectfully

REPORT:

That in 1836, the same was brought to the notice of the legislature by numerous petitions, now on the files of the Senate. In 1838, a Joint Select Committee reported a bill to repeal so much of the Acts for mills as related to flowage, with an able report, wherein it is stated, that flowing is at common law in the states of New Hampshire, Vermont, Connecticut, New York, New Jersey, Pennsylvania, Delaware, Maryland, Ohio, Indiana, South Carolina and Georgia. See documents, 1838.

As expressed by the late C. J. Parker, in 1814, the committee are of opinion that the act on flowage was incautiously copied from a provincial statute of 1713, passed to encourage the building of mills, then much wanted to promote the settlement of the country, when lands liable to be flowed were of little value. In like manner, after the separation, the same act was incautiously continued among the other statutes of Maine.

In the report of the commissioners for the revision of the statutes, this principle was made to stand alone in a chapter separated from

Wm. T. Johnson, Printer to the State.

that on mills, apparently to facilitate an after repeal. When first
enacted in 1713, there existed no declaration of rights, such as
stands at the head of the Constitution of Maine, declaring that
private property shall not be taken for public use without just compensation, nor unless the public exigencies require it. At this day,
mills stand in about the same relation to public use with stores,
wharves and hotels.

In a short time, flowing by dams gives to a prime alluvial tract
of meadow the appearance of a drowned bog. Without any previous enquiry, chapter 126 gives to any man, however interested, a
right to erect and maintain a dam, and flow, no matter whose land,
no matter of what quality, to what purpose appropriated, or how
much, subject only to such yearly damages and limitations as can
be got by law, at a heavy expense. The land owner is compelled
to seek his remedy through mud and mire, after the fair face of his
land has been destroyed, and perhaps under water.

This unlimited right to flow, prevents from being into good grass
a great amount of rich meadow land, for want of drainage. The
courts have ruled that under the principle of chapter 126, flowing
to create reservoirs is protected, no matter about the miles that may
intervene between the reservoir and mills, whereby some meadows
are also subject to injury from water let down from above, perhaps
in hay time, as such is a season of probable demand on the reservoir, when small sluggish streams are apt to be much choked up
by vegetation. The value of many farms depends much on an
unfailing resource for hay from lands liable to be affected by dams.

Men differ very much in opinion, as to the value of lands thus
flowed. It is easy for mill owners to hunt up witnesses, who believe
and will honestly testify that such lands are worth very little; hence
a fair jury are very liable to, and do in fact, often, perhaps generally, set the yearly damage so low that the owner had better
given up his land as lost. Others again consider much of the
liable to be overflowed by dams, as the best land in the
In places where the matter is well understood, after such I
put under improvement, they are rarely sold, except from n
and then command the highest prices.

As to future erections, the bill herewith reported, is calculated to restore flowage to common law, as it is and always has been, in nearly all the northern and middle states, giving to the courts a salutary power for the protection of dams now erected.

Generally the cases of flowage from dams now erected, liable to occasion much trouble and expense in future, as they have done in times past, would be quietly compromised by the parties at home, as they could do, if so disposed, better than any courts or juries could do for them. To make a proper arrangement, both parties would then lie under strong motives, knowing that the court could compel right to be done—such motives as cannot exist where one party has an undue advantage over the other.

If applied to, the Judge would ordinarily cite or order the parties to appear before him, in term time or out of term time, as might be convenient. By the complaint and written answer, and by oral admissions, the Judge would soon see about what the case required, and in the way of friendly advice, would indicate something of his opinion and thus set wide open the door for adjustment by compromise, having stopped, by injunction, actions at law and abatement of dams during the time required to look into the matter. If a trial must be had, the Judge would direct a view and report from a civil engineer or from a committee, and frame his final decree according to the peculiar circumstances of each case. By thus dispensing with jury trials, and also cutting off a fruitful source of law questions, much litigation would be cut up by the roots and much time and expense be saved, not to the parties only, but to all others attending court.

Statutes ought not to be such as to encourage lawsuits, as this flowing principle does in a high degree. Suppose chapter 126, to remain and the public sentiment to take a turn, as is natural when a prevailing error comes to be understood, and juries should give fair, perhaps heavy damages, numerous claims of damage for flowing would start up, now dormant from a dread of expense, and of inadequate damages. There is no end to the law questions that may be raised under chapter 126, as is usual when a statute thus breaks in upon the common law. Let not " too much legislation " be said of this bill, designed to clear off the too much legislation from a subject plain, if not so incumbered.

BENJAMIN B. THOMAS, *Chairman.*

STATE OF MAINE.

IN THE YEAR OF OUR LORD ONE THOUSAND EIGHT HUNDRED AND
FORTY-SIX.

AN ACT to repeal Chapter one hundred and twenty six of the Revised Statutes.

Be it enacted by the Senate and House of Represent-
2 *atives in Legislature assembled,* as follows:

3 SECTION 1. Chapter one hundred and twenty
4 six of the Revised Statutes is hereby repealed, re-
5 serving in force so much thereof as may be necessary
6 for the recovery, as therein provided for, of damages
7 incurred before this Act shall take effect, and cost.

SEC. 2. The Judges of the District Courts shall
2 severally, in their respective Districts, have the
3 power of a Court of Equity as to flowage, over all
4 cases arising from dams now erected and maintained,
5 including power to protect such dams from abatement
6 and to prevent actions at law, and generally in relation
7 to such dams as to flowage to make decrees to promote
8 the ends of justice, and to issue writs of injunction to
9 prevent injustice, so as to grant an equitable and ad-
10 equate relief to the parties.

SEC. 3. Said Judges are authorised to execute the
2 powers given in the preceding section out of term

3 time, provided the parties be heard or neglect to be
4 heard after due notice. If required, the party com-
5 plaining shall give a bond to the satisfaction of such
6 Judge to pay all cost he may order such party to pay;
7 and the same or so much thereof as he may direct shall
8 be taxed in the bill of cost in favor of the prevailing
9 party. A record of all such proceedings shall be
10 made by the clerk under the direction of the court in
11 the county where the dam is situated.

Sec. 4. No length of time during which lands
2 may have been flowed by dams erected for working
3 water mills before this Act shall take effect, shall
4 be evidence of a grant or licence to flow such lands,
5 or make up any part of the twenty years limitation
6 provided for in Chapter one hundred and forty seven
7 of the Revised Statutes.

STATE OF MAINE.

House of Representatives, June 3, 1846.

Ordered, That this report and the bill accompanying the same, be printed for the use of the Legislature.

SAMUEL BELCHER, *Clerk.*

TWENTY-SIXTH LEGISLATURE.

STATE OF MAINE.

In SENATE, June 3, 1846.

THE Joint Standing Committee on the Militia to whom was referred the Report of the Adjutant General and also so much of the Governor's Message as relates to the Militia, have had the same under consideration and ask leave to report a Bill, which is herewith submitted.

JOHN J. PERRY, Chairman.

Wm. T. Johnson, Printer to the State

STATE OF MAINE.

AN ACT in addition to the sixteenth chapter of the Revised Statutes.

Be it enacted by the Senate and House of Represent-
2 *atives in Legislature assembled,* as follows :

3   SECTION 1.   Every able bodied white male citizen,
4 resident within this State, who is, or shall be of the
5 age of eighteen years, and under the age of forty five
6 years, excepting persons enlisting into volunteer com-
7 panies, persons already exempt from the performance
8 of military duty by the sixteenth chapter of the Revis-
9 ed Statutes, idiots, lunatics, common drunkards, vag-
10 abonds, paupers, and persons convicted of any infa-
11 mous crime in this or any other State, shall be enroll-
12 ed in the militia.

   SEC. 2.   It shall be the duty of the assessors of cities,
2 towns and plantations within this State, to prepare a
3 list annually of all persons liable to be enrolled, living
4 within their respective limits, and said assessors shall

5 annually place a list of such persons in the hands of
6 the clerk of every city, town or plantation in this State,
7 and it shall be the duty of every such clerk to preserve
8 such list of names in his office, and make an annual
9 return of the militia thus enrolled to the office of the
10 Adjutant General in the month of May or June.

SEC. 3.   The militia thus enrolled shall be subject to
2 no active duty whatever, except in case of insurrection,
3 war, invasion, to prevent invasion, or other public
4 danger or emergency ; in such case the governor and
5 Commander-in-Chief is hereby authorised and required
6 to order out from time to time, by draft or otherwise,
7 as many of the militia as the necessity of the case may
8 require.   The militia when called into actual service,
9 shall be governed and trained according to the laws
10 of the United States and this State.

SEC. 4.   If necessary, the order of the Commander-
2 in-Chief may be made and directed to the mayor and
3 aldermen of any city, the selectmen of any town, or
4 the assessors of any plantation within this State.   And
5 whenever such order is made and directed as aforesaid,
6 it shall be the duty of the mayor and aldermen, the
7 selectmen or assessors aforesaid, to appoint a time and
8 place of parade for the militia, in each city, town or
9 plantation, and to order them to appear at the time

10 and place by leaving a written or printed notice at the
11 usual place of residence of each soldier within their
12 respective limits, and then and there proceed to draft
13 as many thereof, or to accept as many volunteers as
14 is required by the order of the Commander-in-Chief;
15 and the mayor and aldermen, selectmen or assessors
16 shall notify the Commander-in-Chief forthwith that
17 they have performed the aforesaid duty, by returning
18 to the Commander-in-Chief an alphabetical list of
19 those drafted or volunteered. And whenever any
20 person thus ordered out, detached or drafted, shall
21 neglect or refuse to appear at the time and place
22 designated by the mayor and aldermen, selectmen or
23 assessors as aforesaid, and shall not within twenty-four
24 hours after he shall have been notified, pay to the
25 mayor and aldermen, selectmen or assessors, the sum
26 of fifty dollars, or procure an able bodied man in his
27 stead, such person, on being ordered to march to the
28 place of rendezvous, shall be considered a soldier be-
29 longing to the detachment, and shall be dealt with
30 accordingly.

SEC. 5. All civil officers named in this act, who
2 shall neglect or refuse, at any time, to obey the pro-
3 visions thereof, shall forfeit and pay not less than
4 twenty dollars, nor more than five hundred dollars for

1*

5 each and ever offence, to be recovered in any court
6 of competent jurisdiction, for the use and benefit of
7 the State.

Volunteer Militia.

Sec. 6. The active militia of this State shall consist
2 and be composed of volunteers, or companies raised
3 at large without limitation or restriction as to the
4 numbers in the standing companies within whose
5 bounds they may be enlisted, and in all cases shall first
6 be ordered into service to suppress riots, invasions, or
7 to aid civil officers in the execution of the laws of the
8 State.

Sec. 7. The whole number of volunteers shall not
2 exceed five thousand men, and shall be divided or
3 apportioned to each division of the militia throughout
4 the State, according to the number enrolled, in such
5 manner however, as to retain all the volunteer com-
6 panies, with their officers, now raised and organized.

Sec. 8. If any division shall neglect or refuse for
2 the term of two years to raise at large their quota of
3 volunteers according to the provisions of this act, the
4 Commander-in-Chief may grant petitions to citizens
5 in any other division to raise at large the prescribed
6 number of volunteers as herein provided.

Organization.

SEC. 9. The Commander-in-Chief with advice of
2 Council, may grant petitions for raising companies at
3 large not to exceed one hundred and four companies,
4 including those already raised.

SEC. 10. Whenever forty-eight men shall have been
2 enlisted according to the provisions of this act, an
3 election of officers may be ordered, upon notification
4 being given by one or more of the petitioners, attested
5 by the mayor and aldermen of any city, the selectmen
6 of any town, or the assessors of any plantation in the
7 State, to the Commander-in-Chief.

SEC. 11. The several volunteer companies of cav-
2 alry, artillery, light infantry and riflemen in each divis-
3 ion, shall be numbered and a record made of such
4 numbers in the Adjutant Generals' office : and when
5 they exist in sufficient numbers in any one division,
6 shall compose battalions, and regiments, and be put
7 under the command of such regimental, brigade and
8 division officers as the Commander-in-Chief may desig-
9 nate ; and when not attached to any battalion or regi-
10 ment, to remain in command of its captain or com-
11 manding officer, subject to the orders of the brigadier
12 general of the brigade to which the company is
attached.

Sec. 12. Every non-commissioned officer and soldier of any company raised at large, shall be holden to do duty therein for the term of five years from his enlistment, unless disability after enlistment should absolutely incapacitate him to perform such duty, or he should be regularly discharged by the proper officer.

How Officered.

Sec. 13. To each company of light infantry or riflemen there shall be one captain, one first and one second lieutenant, four sergeants, four corporals, one or more fifers or buglers, and one or more drummers. To each company of artillery one captain, one first and two second lieutenants, five sergeants, four corporals, one or more fifers, one or more drummers, and three drivers. To each company of cavalry, one captain two lieutenants, one cornet, five sergeants, four corporals, one saddler, one farrier, and one or more trumpeters.

Articles furnished.

Sec. 14. Each company of light infantry and riflemen, raised at large, shall be furnished with muskets or rifles, and every company of cavalry with sabres, belts and pistols, and every company of artillery with swords and belts and musketoons, whenever the State may have them on hand, on application to the acting

7 quartermaster general and producing to him satis-
8 factory evidence that said company is organized and
9 uniformed agreeably to the provisions of this act and
10 that a suitable armory or place of deposit for such
11 muskets or rifles, swords, sabres, pistols and belts, has
12 been provided by the city or town within which said
13 company is situated or otherwise; which arms so
14 furnished, shall be carefully kept by said city or town
15 in the armory so 'provided for the use of the company
16 for military purposes only. The Commander-in-Chief
17 may from time to time require any officer to examine
18 any armory provided as aforesaid, and report to him
19 the condition thereof, and of the arms therein deposit-
20 ed. And the several cities and towns in the State are
21 hereby required to raise money to be expended in
22 providing armories, or places of deposit, as above
23 provided, or otherwise provide the same. And when-
24 ever any arms are furnished as aforesaid, to any com-
25 pany formed from different towns and plantations, the
26 same shall be deposited in the town within which the
27 greatest number of the members of said company may
28 vote to establish their armory. And any city, town or
29 plantation furnishing any such amory shall have the
30 right to recover of the severals towns and plantations
31 where the members of such company reside and have

32 their home, their proportion of the expenses of such
33 armory according to the number of members of such
34 company residing in such towns and plantations re-
35 spectively.   And the cities and towns in which said
36 arms are so deposited are hereby made responsible to
37 the State for their safe keeping and return, when re-
38 quired by the Commander-in-Chief, and are hereby
39 authorized to exercise full control over said arms at
40 all times except when required for the purposes afore-
41 said by the commanding officer of the company for
42 whose use they were assigned.   But such cities, towns
43 and plantations shall not be held responsible for any
44 damage or loss done or happening to such arms while
45 in the use of such companies.

SEC. 15. Each company of artillery, light infantry
2 and riflemen shall be furnished with a drum and fife
3 or bugle horn, and each company of cavalry with a
4 trumpet, and all of them with more, or other instru-
5 ments, as the Commander-in-Chief shall order.

Discipline, inspection, trainings, reviews, and com-
pensation.

SEC. 16.   The system of discipline and field exercise
2 which are ordered to be observed by the regular army
3 of the United States in the different corps of cavalry,
4 artillery, light infantry and riflemen, or such other

5 system as may at any time hereafter be directed for
6 the volunteers and militia, by the laws of the United
7 States, shall be observed by the companies raised at
8 large in this State, in the discipline and exercise of
9 said corps respectively.

SEC. 17. Every commanding officer of a company
2 raised at large, shall parade his company on the last
3 Wednesday in May, annually, at one o'clock, in the
4 afternoon, for the purpose of inspecting, examining,
5 and taking an account of all the equipments of his
6 men, in order that a thorough inspection may be made
7 of all the volunteer companies in the State. Every
8 commanding officer of a company shall exercise and
9 discipline as well as inspect his company on said day.
10 Every commanding officer as aforesaid, shall in addi-
11 tion thereto, parade his company for exercise and dis-
12 cipline, on two other days, at the hour aforesaid, by
13 his own order.

SEC. 18. There shall also be an inspection and re-
2 view in each year; and the commanding officer of
3 each division within which such volunteer corps may
4 be located, shall order such troops to parade in the
5 month of September annually, at such time as he shall
6 deem expedient, regard being had to the scattered or
7 compact situation of the troops. The commanding

8 officer of the brigade shall appoint the place and give
9 notice thereof to the commanding officer of the divis-
10 ion.   But if the troops to be inspected compose a
11 regiment or battalion, the commanding officer thereof
12 shall appoint the place and give notice to the com-
13 manding officer of the brigade; and the place ap-
14 pointed for inspection and review shall be as central,
15 as in the judgment of the officer appointing the place,
16 may be convenient; *provided*, that no officer, non-
17 commissioned officer or private shall be obliged to
18 travel more than twenty miles from the armory of the
19 company to which he belongs to any review of a regi-
20 ment or less body of men, and that no larger body
21 than a brigade be ordered to parade at the same time
22 and place except by order of the major general.

SEC. 19.   Each and every company of the volunteer
2 militia—which for any year shall have performed all the
3 duties required by this act, shall have had, at all the
4 several trainings, reviews and inspections required by
5 this act, at least fifty officers, non-commissioned of-
6 ficers and privates present in uniform, duly equipped,
7 and doing duty—shall be entitled to receive from the
8 State the sum of one hundred dollars as a reward for
9 meritorious services, to the use of such company, and
10 by them to be disposed of in such manner as a major-

11 ity thereof may determine. And the Governor and
12 Council on receiving satisfactory evidence that the
13 services and conditions required by this section have
14 been performed and complied with by any such com-
15 pany, shall draw their warrant on the Treasurer of
16 State in favor of the treasurer of any such company
17 for the sum aforesaid. And any such company
18 at any meeting of the same by a majority of the votes
19 of the company may choose by ballot a treasurer who
20 shall give a bond to the members of said company
21 with sufficient surety or sureties for the faithful perform-
22 ance of his duties and shall hold his office during the
23 pleasure of the company and until another treasurer
24 is chosen, on whom shall devolve the care of the funds
25 of the company, and keeping all proper accounts re-
26 lating to the same. The commanding officer of the
27 company shall preside at the election of the treasurer
28 of his company, and shall give him a certificate of his
29 election.

Sec. 20. It shall be the duty of the commanding
2 officers of all volunteer companies on or before the
3 first day of November annually to make out and certify
4 to the Adjutant General a list of all persons belonging
5 to their respective companies, describing the duties
6 performed by each individual in his company through-

2

7 out the year, and in all cases where the reward for
8 meritorious services is claimed under the provisions of
9 this act, there shall be a return made to the Adjutant
10 General as aforesaid setting forth the several days on
11 which said company were ordered on duty either for
12 inspection, ordinary trainings or review, with the
13 number of officers, non-commissioned officers and
14 privates present in uniform duly equipped and doing
15 duty on each of said days required by this act.

SEC. 21.   Any commanding officer of a company
2 who shall make any false return in relation to such
3 service with the intent thereby to authorise the receiv-
4 ing from the State treasury the aforesaid reward, such
5 officer on conviction thereof by a court martial, shall
6 be deprived of his commission, and deemed disquali
7 fied ever after from holding a commission under the
8 State, and shall also be liable in action of debt to an-
9 swer to the State for all money drawn from the treas-   .
10 ury thereof by reason of any such false return.

Fines and Penalties.

SEC. 22.   Every non-commissioned officer, musician,
2 or private, who shall unnecessarily neglect to appear
3 on the days, at the times and places appointed for
4 such duty, agreeably to the provisions of this act,
5 shall pay two dollars for each and every such neglect.

Sec. 23. Whenever any volunteer company, which
2 has received any arms or equipments from the acting
3 Quartermaster General, shall de disbanded, the acting
4 Quartermaster General is required to receive said
5 arms and equipments, on presentation of the same by
6 the officers of said company or their agents.

Sec. 24. No Adjutant shall be entitled to any pay for
2 services, excepting such Adjutants as are attached to
3 and do duty in such regiments and battalions as may be
4 formed out of the volunteer militia provided for by this
5 act.

Sec. 25. It shall be the duty of the Adjutant Gen-
2 eral to furnish the necessary blanks for all returns
3 required by this act.

Sec. 26. An act to repeal the forty-second section
2 of the sixteenth chapter of the Revised Statutes, ap-
3 proved March 11, 1842, and an act to govern and
4 discipline the militia, approved March 22, 1844, are
5 hereby repealed, and so much of the sixteenth chapter
6 of the Revised Statutes and the act to amend the six-
7 teenth chapter of the Revised Statutes, approved
8 March 24, 1843, as was repealed by said act approved
9 March 22, 1844, and is not inconsistent with the pro-
10 visions of this act, are hereby revived.

STATE OF MAINE.

In SENATE, June 3, 1846.

Laid on the table, and 500 copies ordered to be printed for the use of the Legislature.

DANIEL T. PIKE, *Secretary*.

TWENTY-SIXTH LEGISLATURE.

To the members of the Senate
      and House of Representatives:

I herewith lay before the Legislature a copy of a communication addressed to me by the Secretary of War dated upon the 19th ult., requesting "upon the part of the President of the United States, that I would cause to be enrolled and held in readiness for muster into the service of the United States, a volunteer corps consisting of one regiment of Infantry." A copy of the Act of Congress providing for the prosecution of the existing war between the United States and the Republic of Mexico, passed upon the 13th ult., together with a "memorandum of the organization of Volunteer Corps," under said act, accompanying the same, are also herewith transmitted.

In pursuance of this requisition from the President, I have issued a proclamation, inviting the services of volunteers for the purpose therein specified; and promulgated by a general order, the regulations which will be observed in the organization of said corps.

Sufficient time has not yet elapsed, since the publication of these documents, to enable me to determine with entire certainty, whether, with the inducements which are now held out, the number of men necessary to constitute the Regiment required, can be enlisted with the promptitude and despatch with which it is desirable the requisition of the General Government should be met. The officers and privates composing the company of Bangor City Greys, have promptly tendered their services; and applications have been received from several individuals, asking for authority to recruit, in different sections of the State. With these exceptions, the indications have not been as favorable as could be desired, and considering the remoteness of our position from the theatre of active operation,

Wm. T Johnson, Printer to the State.

and that the call is made at a season of the year when all classes of our fellow citizens are actively engaged in their various avocations, it may be doubted whether some additional inducements will not be needed, to command the immediate services of those whose patriotic feelings would otherwise impel them, at this juncture, to engage in the military service of the country.

Without authority from the Legislature, I have not deemed it within my province to offer any pecuniary compensation, either for the services of persons engaged in recruiting, or any emolument, either to officers or privates, other than that provided in the Act of Congress herewith communicated.

As that Act makes no provision for the payment of any expenses preliminary to the acceptance of their services by the President of the United States, and as the process of enlistment and organization must necessarily precede such acceptance, it would seem to be indispensable, that some means should be provided by which these unavoidable expenses should be defrayed.

In order to secure the services of suitable individuals who may be disposed to exert themselves in forming companies, it will probably be necessary to make some pecuniary allowance for the time and expense necessarily incurred : when formed into companies, some time will be required for meetings for the choice of officers, and still more for the subsequent meeting of company officers, at some central point, for the election of regimental officers in the manner required by law.

In addition to these expenses, it is possible that some further inducement, in the form of pay or bounty, may be required to facilitate the progress of enlistments, and to enable the Executive promptly to comply with the requisition of the President. I have been thus particular in enumerating the expenses which will probably arise, in order, that if it be the pleasure of the Legislature to authorize the employment of the necessary means, as I doubt not it will, the mode and manner of their expenditure may be pointed out with as much particularity as the nature of the case will permit.

Although it is not probable that any immediate call will be made for the quota of troops required from this State, every consideration of patriotism and duty should impel us to have them in readiness when the necessities of the National Government may require their services; and as I am sure that the Legislature fully participates in this sentiment, I cannot doubt that such measures as may be deemed best calculated to secure that object, will be readily considered.

I beg leave also, to call your attention to that provision of the Act of Congress accompanying this communication, which provides for the employment of the State Militia. In the present condition of our Militia, if a call were made under the provision of the Act of Congress, it would be impossible to comply with it.

There is reason to believe that even the slight duty required by the present law is almost wholly neglected; and as I stated in my communication at the opening of the session, both the enrolment and the returns are generally omitted.

In the present attitude of our foreign relations, we are liable at any moment to a call for the services of this arm of our national security and defence; and I cannot but hope, that some measure, calculated to remedy this obvious defect in the operation of the existing law, will commend itself to the judgment of the Legislature.

H. J. ANDERSON.

Council Chamber,
Augusta, June 11, 1846.

[copy.]

War Department, May 19, 1846.

Sir

I have the honor to enclose a copy of an Act of Congress, authorizing the President to accept the services of volunteers.

It will be perceived that all the officers with volunteers taken into the service of the United States under this act, are to be appointed and commissioned, or such as have been appointed and commissioned, in accordance with the laws of the State from whence they are taken; and that the volunteers received into the service are to have the organization of the army of the United States. For this exact organization so far as relates to companies and regiments, please see the memorandum appended to the law herewith, to both of which, particular attention is requested. Under the discretion allowed to him, the President has decided that the number of *privates* in all volunteer companies, shall be limited to sixty-four.

On the part of the President, I have to request your Excellency to cause to be enrolled and held in readiness for muster into the service of the United States, the following Volunteer Corps:

ONE REGIMENT OF INFANTRY.

Due notice will be given to your Excellency when their services will be required, at which time, an officer or officers of the army will be sent to muster them into the service, at such place or places as may be designated, and where the inspecting and mustering officers will be instructed to receive no man under the rank of commissioned officer, who in years, is apparently over forty-five, or under eighteen, or who is not in physical strength and vigor.

It is respectfully suggested that public notice of these requirements of law may prevent much disapointment to the zealous and patriotic citizens of your State, multitudes of whom, the President cannot doubt, will be eager to enrol themselves.

The Department desires the earliest information of the progress of enrolment.

Very respectfully,

Your Obt. Sert.,

W. L. MARCY,

Secretary of War.

To his Excellency, the GOVERNOR OF MAINE, Augusta, Maine.

AN ACT providing for the prosecution of the existing war between
the United States and the Republic of Mexico.

WHEREAS by the act of the Republic of Mexico, a state of war
exists between that Government and the United States,

*Be it enacted by the Senate and House of Representatives of
the United States of America, in Congress assembled,* That for
the purpose of enabling the Government of the United States to
prosecute said war to a speedy and successful termination, the
President be, and he is hereby authorized to employ the militia,
naval and military forces of the United States, and to call for and
accept the services of any number of volunteers, not exceeding
50,000, who may offer their services, either as cavalry, artillery, infantry, or riflemen, to serve twelve months after they shall have arrived
at the place of rendezvous, or to the end of the war, unless sooner
discharged, according to the time for which they shall have been
mustered into service; and the sum of ten millions of dollars out
of any moneys in the treasury, or to come into the treasury, not
otherwise appropriated, be, and the same is hereby appropriated for
the purpose of carrying the provisions of this act into effect.

SEC. 2. *And be it further enacted,* That the militia when called
into the service of the United States by virtue of this act, or any
other act, may, if in the opinion of the President of the United
States, the public interest requires it, be compelled to serve for a
term not exceeding six months after their arrival at the place of
rendezvous, in any one year, unless sooner discharged.

SEC. 3. *And be it further enacted,* That the said volunteers
shall furnish their own clothes, and if cavalry, their own horses,
and horse equipments; and when mustered into service, shall be
armed at the expense of the United States.

SEC. 4. *And be it further enacted,* That said volunteers shall,
when called into actual service, and while remaining therein, be
subject to the rules and articles of war, and shall be in all respects,
except as to clothing and pay, placed on the same footing with

similar corps of the United States army, and in lieu of clothing, every non-commissioned officer and private in any company, who may thus offer himself, shall be entitled, when called into actual service, to receive in money, a sum equal to the cost of clothing of a non-commissioned officer or private (as the case may be) in the regular troops of the United States.

SEC. 5. *And be it further enacted*, That the said volunteers, so offering their services, shall be accepted by the President in companies, battalions, squadrons, and regiments, whose officers shall be appointed in the manner prescribed by law in the several States and Territories to which such companines, battalions, squadrons, and regiments shall respectively belong.

SEC. 6. *And be it further enacted*, That the President of the United States be, and he is hereby, authorized to organize companies so tendering their services into battalions or squadrons; battalions and squadrons into regiments; regiments into brigades; and brigades into divisions, as soon as the number of volunteers shall render such organization, in his judgment, expedient, and the President shall, if necessary, apportion the staff, field, and general officers among the respective States and Territories from which the volunteers shall tender their services; as he may deem proper.

SEC. 7. *And be it further enacted*, That the volunteers who may be received into the service of the United States by virtue of the provisions of this act, and who shall be wounded or otherwise disabled in the service, shall be entitled to all the benefit which may be conferred on persons wounded in the service of the United States.

SEC. 3. *And be it further enacted*, That the President of the United States be, and he is hereby, authorized forthwith to complete all the public armed vessels now authorized by law, and to purchase or charter, arm, equip and man such merchant vessels and steamboats as, upon examination, may be found fit, or easily converted into armed vessels fit for the public service, and in such number as he may deem necessary for the protection of the seaboard, lake coast, and the general defence of the country.

SEC. 9. *And be it further enacted*, That whenever the militia or volunteers are called and received into the service of the United States, under the provisions of this act, they shall have the organization of the army of the United States, and shall have the same pay and allowances; and all mounted privates, non-commissioned officers, musicians and artificers shall be allowed 40 cents per day for the use and risk of their horses, except of horses actually killed in action; and if any mounted volunteer, private, non-commissioned officer, musician, or artificer shall not keep himself provided with a serviceable horse, the said volunteer shall serve on foot.

[Approved May 13, 1846.]

MEMORANDUM *of the organization of the Volunteer Corps under the act of* 13*th May,* 1846.

A company of Cavalry or mounted men, will consist of—
1 Captain ;
1 First Lieutenant ;
1 Second Lieutenant,
4 Sergeants ;
4 Corporals ,
2 Buglers ,
1 Farrier and Blacksmith ;
64 Privates ; as established by order of the President

A regiment of Cavalry or mounted men, will consist of—

Field and Staff Officers. {
1 Colonel ;
1 Lieutenant Colonel ,
1 Major ;
1 Adjutant, (a Lieutenant in addition to the Lieutenant of the corps.)'

Non-commissioned Staff. {
1 Sergeant Major ,
1 Quartermaster Sergeant ;
1 Principal Musician ;
2 Chief Buglers ; and
10 Companies, for the organization of which see above.

A company of Infantry (or Riflemen) will consist of—
1 Captain ;
1 First Lieutenant ;
1 Second Lieutenant ;
4 Sergeants ;
4 Corporals ;
2 Musicians ;
64 Privates ; as established by the order of the President.

A regiment of Infantry (or Riflemen) will consist of—

Field and Staff Officers.
> 1 Colonel;
> 1 Lieutenant Colonel;
> 1 Major;
> 1 Adjutant, (a Lieutenant of one of the companies, but not in addition.)

Non-commissioned Staff.
> 1 Sergeant Major;
> 1 Quartermaster Sergeant;
> 2 Principal Musicians; and
> 10 Companies, for the organization of which see above.

STATE OF MAINE.

~~~~~~~~~~~

In Senate, June 11, 1846.

Ordered, That 300 copies of the foregoing Message, with the accompanying documents, be printed for the use of the Senate.

DANIEL T. PIKE, *Secretary*.

STATE OF MAINE.

Secretary's Office,
Augusta, June 12, 1846.

To the President of the Senate :

IN compliance with an order of the Senate of the 18th ult.; I herewith lay before you an abstract from the returns of the Clerks of the Courts, "of the proceedings in the Courts of their respective counties, since the first day of August, 1841, under the thirty-sixth chapter of the Revised Statutes, concerning innholders, common victualers and retailers of spirituous liquors."

I have the honor to be,
Very respectfully,
Your ob't serv't,

E. B. FRENCH, *Secretary of State.*

Wm T Johnson, Printer to the State

STATE OF MAINE.

SECRETARY'S OFFICE, Augusta, June 12, 1846.

ABSTRACT *from the returns of the Clerks of the Judicial Courts, made to this office, in pursuance to an order of the Senate passed May 18, 1846.*

COUNTIES.	No. of indictments found, including appeals from Justices of the Peace	No not pros'd	No pleaded guilty or nolo contend	No of trials	No of verdicts of acquittal	No of verdicts of guilty	No of indictments, including appeals from Justices of Peace, under said act, now standing continued	Whole amount of fines imposed	Amount of fines actually and really paid by the respondents	Whole amount of costs taxed and allowed against the State	Amount of the costs repaid by the defendants
York,	73	54	31	10		10	2	260 00	160 00	888 42	648 71
Cumberland,	247	71	61	82	26	49	18	3,127 00	340 00	5,398 36	1,830 19
Lincoln,	94	43	24	4	1	3	11	1,265 00	460 00	1,813 88	769 95
Hancock,	9	4		1	1		4			239 56	19 95
Washington,	12	7	1	4	4	3		120 00	120 00	384 31	243 82
Kennebec,	127	64	17	21		17	25	1,155 00	830 00	1,642 18	183 10
Oxford,	8	2	3							218 65	77 10
Somerset,	12	4	1	1		1	4	50 00		207 99	28 54
Penobscot,	174	12	2	25	6	15	114	100 00		1,930 57	279 34
Waldo,	23	10					13			547 44	200 89
Franklin,	16	14	2				1	50 00		143 08	137 43
Piscataquis,	none.										
Aroostook,	none.										
	786	285	149	149	86	98	192	$6,127 00	$1,910 00	$13,414 44	$4,419 02

STATE OF MAINE.

In SENATE, June 12, 1846.

Ordered, That 800 copies of the foregoing communication and accompanying abstract, be printed for the use of 'the Legislature.

DANIEL T. PIKE, *Secretary.*

TWENTY-SIXTH LEGISLATURE.

No. 9.   SENATE.

ANNUAL REPORT

OF THE

WARDEN OF THE STATE PRISON.

To the Honorable the Senate
and House of Representatives :

Agreeably to law, the undersigned most respectfully submits the following, as the annual report of the Maine State Prison for the term of one year and four months, ending 30th of April, 1846.

There are now confined in the Prison, 60 convicts and they are employed as follows, viz :

In the Quarry,	12	In the Smith Shops,	4
" Shoe Shop,	24	" Wheelwrights' Shops,	7
" Tailors,	3	In the Hospital,	3
Washers,	2	Lumpers,	2
Waiters,	1		—
Cooks,	2	Aggregate,	60

The last annual report was made to the Legislature, 31st of December, 1844. By reference to that report, it will be seen there was then in confinement, 75 prisoners, and a decrease since that time, of fifteen in number, or twenty per cent. We should be glad to believe that crime had also decreased in the same proportion. It must be a happy reflection, when we are informed that our State, numbering 500,000 inhabitants, has in our State Prison, no more than 60 prisoners. Other States, we are sorry to say, are not so fortunate. Some of them have in their State Prisons, some three

Wm. T. Johnson, Printer to the State.

and four, and even as high as fifteen hundred prisoners, besides a large number in Houses of Correction.

The condition of our Prison as it regards health and comfort, never was better. Our former anticipations in this matter are fully realized. Now all of the convicts have good warm and dry beds to sleep in. The new Prison has been in operation about eighteen months, and the comfort which the prisoners must have enjoyed during the two cold winters, is worth all the expense of erecting it.

The finances of the Prison are in a good condition, as much so as could reasonably be expected, when we take into account, that it is sixteen months since my last report, which includes two winters. In the winter, our expenses are much more than in the warmer part of the year. In looking at the general account, a large item of expense will be seen in the article of wood. Before the erection of the new Prison our expenses in winter were more than in summer, and since that time have been increased, as we consume a larger quantity of wood in the new Prison, fires being kept during the night, to warm the prisoners. The price of wood for the last year has been much higher than for many years. There is another cause for enhancing our expenses, which is the scarcity and high price of potatoes, as well as that of corn, &c.

In my last report, I then ventured to predict that the Prison would not need an appropriation for any thing, including officers' salaries; but the reasons just given, I trust, will be sufficient to show that we have needed and received the salary of officers. In addition to the above reasons, is one more, and a stronger one. At the time I last reported, a large portion of our convicts were under contract to Samuel Bigelow, of Boston, for five years. After having them some five or six months, he failed, and his contract was stopped, leaving a debt due the Prison for the labor of convicts.

A suit was instituted, and prosecuted to judgment, against Bigelow and his bondsman, a part of which, only as yet, has been received. If this contract had been carried out in good faith, as we had reason to believe it would, we should not have needed even the salaries of the officers.

The Prison now owes $8,395 00, and has due $12,089 78,

leaving a balance in favor of Prison, of $3,694 78. Some portion of this sum will not be collected, as in all such demands a portion will be worthless. A large portion of the Prison liabilities are due to individuals trading with the Prison, which are arranged for and all its debts are paid at maturity. We have in stock and tools on hand, at this time, $17,437 89, which is an increase from last year of $4,215 59. The Prison has paid all its expenses during the last sixteen months, and $1,822 80 towards officers' salaries.

The question is now asked, as it has been before, if the Prison pays its way, why call for the salary of officers? The answer is, the surplus of $3,694 78, added to $17,437 89 in stock, and the new Prison of $13,177 44, you have the sum of $34,310 11, and about $9,000, occasioned by fire, &c., in 1841 ; in this you have $43,310 11. The State has paid in appropriations and subordinate officers at the Prison, since 26th of April, 1839, the sum of $41,014 59. The stock on hand, on the 26th of April, 1839, was $9,554 28, to be added, which is $50,568 87 ; from this deduct $43,310 11, and you have $7,258 76, total loss or expense more than income, in seven years and four days, since the present incumbent took charge and has been in charge since, except one year.

There are some $2,000 00 more to be deducted from the $7,258 76, that the Prison has in property on hand, such as new lime kiln sheds, and other repairs of real estate about the Prison, and making over the entire fence about the yard, &c., &c. Then the whole expense will be $5,258 76. I have thought proper to be thus particular in making plain this statement, as some persons who look at the tables or general account, do not readily understand them. I have no doubt that the Prison will be able to go along this year, by receiving the salary of officers from the State. I am in hopes to reduce the liabilities of the Prison this year, and shall endeavor to square them all off, by the collection of dues from those indebted to the Prison. I am of the opinion that the Prison will soon cease to be a drain upon the treasury, although it cannot be expected to pay as well with our small number of convicts, as it would with a much larger number. We are thankful that the number is small, yet the same number of officers is required to take care of 60 that it would, if there were 160 prisoners.

There is now pending in the Massachusetts' court, a suit brought by the Prison, for non-fulfillment of contract made in 1840. If this case is decided in favor of the Prison, which we have reason to suppose it will, it will make quite a difference, as the sum in suit is some $1,700 00, besides several hundred dollars already paid out in prosecuting that suit. If on the other hand, it should be decided against the Prison, it will make the difference of cost, interest, &c.

I have nothng new to advance to the Legislature, as I believe we now have as good a Prison as there is in the Union, though not so costly. I am so informed by persons who have made it their business to examine all, and they give ours the preference. I am fully satisfied now, that our Prison is no longer a disgrace to the State, except to those who are unfortunate enough to be confined in it. It is clean, healthy and comfortable, and but one thing lacking to make it more comfortable, and that is the Hospital to which I alluded in my last report. The Hospital now used is unfit and always must be, located as it is. It needs fresh air.

Perhaps I should apologise to the Legislature for the omission in not making my report as heretofore, on the 31st December, 1845. It will be recollected that an act passed at the last session of the Legislature closing the political year on the 30th of April, as the time of the meeting of the Legislature was altered to May and as the law requires the Warden of the Prison to report to the Legislature. I failed to attend to that duty in December last, therefore my report contains sixteen months' operations of the Prison, instead of twelve months as heretofore. I found when it was too late that the political year ended on the 31st of December, last year, and on the 30th of April after that time. I am not aware that any evil grows out of the omission, as the Legislature were not in session to receive my communication, and a considerable expense must have accrued in taking an account of stock in December last, without any profit to the State. The subordinate officers of the Prison are faithful and attentive to duty and take an interest in its welfare and discipline. I am happy to say that nothing has transpired since my stay at the Prison, between the subordinate officers and the Warden and Inspectors, of an unpleasant kind, but all has been harmony.

The Inspectors are frequent in their visits, vigilant in their duty, always rendering aid to the Warden in the discharge of his duty, which enables him to be the more serviceable to the unfortunate inmates.

I trust you will have the necessary information in regard to the treatment of the convicts, from the Inspectors, and as they are familiar with these matters, I leave it for them to inform you, through the Governor.

BENJAMIN CARR.

Thomaston, May 11, 1846.

1*

The State Prison in account with the State of Maine.

Dr.			Cr.		
1844			**1846**		
Dec. 31. For stock and Tools on hand,	13,222	30	April 30. By stock and Tools on hand,	17,437	89
" paid Officers' salaries,	5,783	83	By cash received from visiters,	144	49
" Convicts discharged,	439	04	By cash received of convicts admitted,	6	45
" Clothing,	1,021	28	By rec'd and chg'd for Clothing,	385	76
" Fuel and Light,	1,185	79	Fuel and Lights,	24	16
" Lime Quarry,	1,034	25	Lime Quarry,	2,811	05
" Wheelwrights,	2,589	62	Wheelwrights,	3,889	60
" Building and Repairs,	681	61	Build'g & repairs	35	22
" Team,	779	12	Team,	669	33
" Subsistence,	3,954	72	Subsistence,	589	47
" Shoemaking,	9,776	97	Shoemaking,	10,678	14
" Expense account transporting Convicts, &c.	1,215	68	Expense account.	101	24
" Blacksmithing,	943	19	Blacksmithing,	1,944	52
			By Balance,	3,961	03
	$42,628	35		$42,628	35

BENJAMIN CARR.

LINCOLN, ss.—May 11, 1846.

Personally appeared, Benjamin Carr, and made oath that the above account is true to the best of his knowledge and belief.

BEFORE ME, GEORGE A. STARR, *Justice of the Peace.*

Examined and compared with vouchers, and found correct.

BENJ. F. BUXTON,
GEORGE A. STARR, } *Inspectors.*
STEPHEN BARROWS,

Convicts.

Number of Convicts, December 31, 1844,	75
Received since,	29
	104
Discharged on expiration of sentence,	38
Pardoned,	4
Died,	2
	44
Remaining number, April 30, 1846,	60

Whole number of commitments since July 2, 1824,	881
Discharged on expiration of sentence,	654
Died,	134
Escaped and not taken,	26
	7
Present number, April 30, 1846,	60
	881

Crimes.

Rape,	1	Murder sentence commuted,	1
Assault with intent to kill,	1	Murder awaiting sentence of death,	1
Larceny,	37	Murder in the second degree,	1
Arson,	4	Forgery,	3
Bigamy,	5	Lewd and lascivious cohabitation,	1
Adultery,	4		
Passing counterfeit money,	1		60

Convicts in the State Prison, April 30, 1846.

County	Names.	Sentence.	Crimes.	When committed.	Place of Birth.	Age.	No. com
Lincoln,	Akers, Nathaniel	Life.	Arson.	Sept. 24, 1841.	Gorham.	30	3
do.	Alexander, James	5 years.	Larceny.	Oct. 29, 1844.	Northport	40	2
Cumberland,	Allen, John T. G.	2 years.	do.	Oct. 11, 1845.	Deerfield.	32	
Waldo,	Ball, Benjamin	15 years.	do.	Dec. 1, 1834.	Boston.	31	3
Washington,	Brannick, William	Life.	Burglary.	Aug. 1, 1842.	Ireland.	28	
Cumberland,	Blackstone, Edward	4 years.	Adultery.	Dec. 3, 1842.	England.	60	2
Penobscot,	Brown, Joshua,	2 years.	Larceny.	Oct. 11, 1844	Greene.	24	
Cumberland,	Brown, George Jr.	4 years.	do.	March 26, 1844	Portland.	24	
Lincoln,	Cremer, Israel	10 years.	Arson.	Sept. 25, 1843.	Waldoborough	35	
Penobscot,	Cornelius, Thomas	4 years.	Larceny.	Oct. 26, 1843.	N. Brunswick.	28	2
Cumberland,	Cole, Isaiah	5 years.	do.	March 26, 1844.	Philadelphia.	29	
do.	Carleton, George W.	3 years.	Adultery.	May 5, 1844.		41	
York,	Cole, Elisha	5 years.	Passing counterfeit money.	Oct. 11, 1845.	Buxton.	41	
Cumberland,	Dyer, Martha A.	10 years.	Larceny.	Oct. 17, 1839.	Pittsfield.	38	3
do.	Davis, James	5 years.	do.	June 29, 1844.	Portland.	18	
Penobscot,	DeBoice, James	3 years.	do.	June 25, 1845	Woodstock.	21	5
do.	Donegan, William	2 years.	do.	Oct. 30, 1844.	Ireland.	36	
Oxford,	Drew, Nathan B	2 years.	Burglary.	Nov. 15, 1845.	Livermore.	18	
Kennebec,	Daly, James	2 years.	Larceny.	June 25, 1845.	Hampden.	18	
do.	Drew, Smith	1 year, 6 months.	do.	Jan. 3, 1846.	Augusta.	22	
Oxford,	Briggs, Philip H.	1 year.	do.	June 27, 1845.	Minot.	20	
Penobscot,	Bailey, George	1 year, 6 months.	do.	Nov. 3, 1845.	Italy.	35	
Kennebec,	Fogg, Elijah	Life.	Arson.	Oct. 20, 1838	Gorham.	28	
Lincoln,	Fox, Robert	2 years.	Forgery.	Sept. 17, 1844.	England.	45	
Waldo,	Fletcher, Stephen	3 years.	do.	Dec. 21, 1844.	Prospect.	28	
Cumberland,	Finney, Edward	1 year.	Lewd & lascivious cohab'n.	July 10, 1845.	Ireland.	30	
Waldo,	Glenn, Henry	6 years.	Larceny and Arson.	April 1, 1844.	Baldwin.	19	
	Otter	Life.	Adultery. Arson.	Dec. 20, 1845. June 28, 1842.	England.		

County	Name	Sentence	Crime	Date	Nativity	Age
Kennebec,	Wilson, John	5 years.	lay.	Aug. 27, 1845.	Alna.	47
Penobscot,	Horton, William	1 year, 6 months.	do.	Nov. 3, 1845.	England.	23
do.	Hurd, Newhall	1 year.	do.	June 25, 1845.	Hampden.	18
Cumberland,	Hunt, William H.	1 year, 6 months.	do.	Oct. 25, 1845.	New York.	19
Waldo,	Kennedy, Michael	4 years.	do.	April 2, 1844.	Ireland.	35
Washington,	Lysle, Samuel	4 egrs.	do.	Oct. 9, 843.	England.	20
Penobscot,	Leavett, Eliphalet	5 egrs.	do.	Oct. 26, 1843.	N. Hampshire.	31
Kennebec,	Lewis, John E	2 years.	do.	Aug. 26, 845.	England.	27
Penobscot,	Mahoney, Charles	2 egrs	do.	Feb. 19, 1846.	Ireland.	38
Me. Dis U.S	... John	2 yrs. & $25 fine	Assault to kill.	Oct. 21, 1845.	N. York.	27
Cumberland,	Nickerson, Freeman	3 years.	...ly,	Mch 22, 1845.	Cape Cod.	45
Washington,	Owen, Walter	1 year.	Adultery	Aug. 4, 1845.	Lubec.	23
Cumberland,	Owen, Thomas Jr.	5 years.	Larceny.	May 29, 846.	Portland.	19
do.	Pinkham, Nicholas	12 egrs.	Rape.	May 2, 1846.	Freeport.	60
Lincoln,	Richardson, Oliver D.	7 years.	Larceny.	July 1, 1843.	Otisfield.	37
Penobscot,	Spencer, Isaac	Life.	Burglary.	Sept. 25, 1843.	Wayne.	27
...,	Sharkey, Thomas	Life.	Murder, commuted.	Feb 24, 1836.	Orono.	21
Lincoln,	Smith, Robert	2 years.	Burglary.	Aug. 1, 1842.	Ireland.	22
...,	..., Russell F.	2 years.	Adultery.	Aug. 9, 1844.	Ireland.	23
Cumberland,	Sweetser, Charles	4 eg.	...ny	April 29, 846.	...	24
Waldo,	Starr, Arthur	5 years.	do.	April 1, 1844.	Portland.	19
Penobscot,	Sawyer, Henry	To be hanged	la,	... 19, 1846.	Ireland.	29
Cumberland,	Thorn, Thomas	2 years.	Murder.	May 17, 1843.	Saco.	38
do.	Thompson, Otis	2 years.	Larceny.	N. 7, 1844.	Long Island.	24
Somerset,	Wheeler, Samuel	4 egrs	do.	April 11, 1845.	Portland.	17
Oxford,	Willis, Isaiah	2 egrs.	Forgery.	May 31, 1845.	Cannan.	32
...,	Wilson, James	4 egrs.	Larceny.	Mch 22, 1845.	Middleboro'.	67
do.	Murray, James	5 egrs.	do.	Mch 29, 1846.	Derby.	50
Penobscot,	Varney, Richard	1 year.	Murder, 2d degree.	Feb. 23, 1846.	Ireland.	23
Cumberland,	White, Lewis	Life.	Larceny.	...20, 1845.	England.	47
		5 eg.		June 29, 1844.	Portland.	17

STATE OF MAINE.

In Senate, June 9, 1846.

Laid on the table, and 300 copies hereof ordered to be printed for the use of the Senate, and 50 additional copies for the use of the Warden of the State Prison.

DANIEL T. PIKE, *Secretary.*

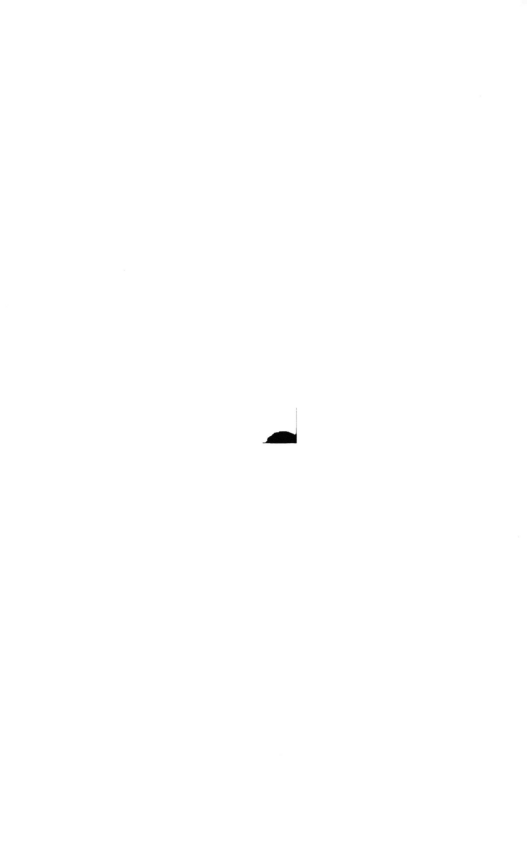

STATE OF MAINE.

THE committee on Education, to whom was referred the memorial of Amos Brown, Philip Eastman, Alpheus S. Packard, and Samuel P. Benson, a committee appointed by a State convention of the friends of education, praying for the establishment of a board of education in this State, and for the adoption of other measures for improving' the' free school system, have had the same under consideration, and ask leave to report, that five hundred copies of said memorial be printed for the use of the Legislature.

E. M. THURSTON, Chairman.

IN SENATE, June 12, 1846.

Read and accepted.
    Sent down for concurrence.

DANIEL T. PIKE, Secretary.

IN HOUSE OF REPRESENTATIVES, }
June 13, 1846.   }

Read and concurred.

SAMUEL BELCHER, Clerk.

Wm. T. Johnson, Printer to the State.

MEMORIAL.

To the Honorable the Legislature
of the State of Maine.

In the month of January last, a convention of instructors and of the friends of popular education, was held in Augusta. The object of that convention was to consider the defects in our system of popular education, and to suggest measures for their removal. Lectures were delivered by gentlemen appointed for that purpose by a committee of a previous convention, and discussions were had, in which some of the prominent defects in our system, or in the operation of it, were exposed, and remedies suggested.

The convention found, that they could not come to a definite result on the various points, which were presented for their consideration ; and it was accordingly concluded, that the whole subject of our State system of popular education, should be submitted to a committee consisting of five individuals, who should inquire into its defects and their remedies, and address a memorial to the next Legislature on the subject, containing such suggestions as they might judge advisable.

This committee had one session in the month of February. They took a general view of the defects in our system of popular instruction, and having divided among themselves the most important topics, they aggreed to address the public through the public journals on the several subjects, which had, or might, come under their notice, in order that their fellow citizens at large might be informed of what is in agitation, and might direct their attention to the topics thus presented to them. The committee are not given to a love of change ; but they are persuaded that much is needed to give efficiency to our system of free schools, even as it is. They know that our State is falling behind most of the New England States in the cause of popular education, and their own state pride, as well as a desire to promote the ends of a system of public instruction, has prompted them to make, in obedience to a call of a respectable meeting of the friends of education, an effort to excite the attention of our community to the more prominent defects in our free school system, or in the proper execution of the system as it already exists.

In presenting their memorial, the committee beg leave to state to the Legislature what they consider some of the defects in our system of popular education, and in compliance with the wishes of the aforesaid convention, to suggest how these defects may be remedied. They also beg leave to state some of the circumstances and reasons, which have led them to feel the importance and necessity of the subject, and which have determined them to offer to the Legislature the propositions, which they now lay before them.

The following are the more prominent defects in our system, as they were brought under review in the convention, or subsequently in the committee :

1. Serious evils in our system of common schools arise from the multiplying of school districts. Parents wish their school to be near their own door, and for this reason alone, school districts are often divided. The town money drawn by one of the school districts in this State, was recently one dollar and fifty cents; by another, two dollars and fifty cents. There was doubtless in each of the cases a great saving of time and exercise to the children in walking to school: but was it on the whole good economy? It is a fair question whether a child would not be better to walk, even in winter, a mile and a half to a school of three or four months continuance, than ten rods to a school kept only six weeks ?

2. Great evils arise from the prevalent inefficiency of school committees. Sometimes no committee is chosen, and the town thinks it good economy to pay the fine laid by law for such neglect, rather than to pay the expenses of a school committee. School committees are often chosen without suitable care to select com-

petent men. Often, moreover, the committee do not discharge faithfully their duty as examiners of candidates for teachers, or as inspectors of the schools. No system of schools, will be effectual without vigilant inspection.

3. The want of suitable qualifications in teachers, is a great source of evil. Ignorant or inefficient teachers are employed, and even immoral men. Cheapness is often the best recommendation a candidate can offer.

4. The want of a proper classification in our schools, is a serious evil: whether it arises from the multiplication of school books, or from the want of system in the course of study. Something like a course of study with the proper text books, should be marked out and recommended by competent committees, and then the time and energies of the teachers would not be wasted, as they now are, by a great number of text books and a minute subdivision into classes. In most branches, the teaching is most effective with a number of pupils.

5. The great defect after all, is the want of a general interest in our free schools. They are not visited except in the way of office, and scarcely so. We take but little pride in them. We are not aware of their importance. A plan, which will certainly be for their advancement, may be rejected, because it may cost a community of 500,000 inhabitants, a few hundred dollars more or less, or increase the tax of an individual a cent more. These are serious defects in our State system of instruction. They may be easily remedied. Badly executed however as the system is, it is doubtless of great value. What would be its value if it were to have the full operation which was designed? Is it not worth the while to attempt to infuse into it some energy? Suppose it should cost the State something in addition to what is already paid, would not the State receive a good return in the end?

To two or three of these defects, your memorialists beg leave to refer more at large.

The duties of school committees, as provided by law, are to examine candidates for teaching, to visit the schools, and superintend the instruction and discipline pursued in them. They may prescribe the books to be used; they may dismiss incompetent teachers and refractory pupils. They are to make report to the town of the state of the schools; and for all their services are to receive compensation. The law is a good one, and if executed in the spirit of it, and with intelligence and vigor, *so far* it will ensure good schools. But these are important conditions. If those who offer themselves as candidates to teach are thoroughly examined by competent men in regard to their qualifications to instruct and to govern, we may generally be sure of competent teachers. If the schools are regularly visited by active, intelligent committees, well versed in the duties of their office, fearless and independent, and anxious to exert the influence which their office gives, we may anticipate well managed and successful schools. But what are the facts in the case?

Are school committees carefully selected from citizens, who cherish a lively interest in the welfare of our schools, and of such weight of character as will command respect and confidence; or in the majority of cases, is the choice of the school committee, (a body of officers certainly as important to the town as any other) left to a few who happen to remain at the close of a town meeting, and who care but little who are chosen? Are school masters carefully and thoroughly examined, and do the committee, without regard to the wishes of friends or neighbors, or to their own personal feelings, fearlessly and conscientiously reject such as they believe to be incompetent? Are our schools regularly visited?—The law requires all this, and all this is essential to the ends for which our free school system was established. The object of the law on this subject is to secure for our public schools vigilant, thorough inspection. Without such inspection the best system of schools, will fail of its end.—No seminary of any kind, can long enjoy a vigorous prosperity, without the stimulus of a competent visitorial power. Every human being needs the impulse of a sense of responsibility. How much our law fails of its object through incompetency, or unfaithfulness is well known. There are towns, which have omitted altogether to choose school committees. The fine imposed by law for this neglect, has been paid again and again on the score of economy. It was stated in convention at Augusta, that one town had instructed their school committee to discharge all their duties *except that of visiting the schools,* and this, it is probable, to save the expense of such visitation.

Again, as it regards the examination of teachers, in how many towns is this examination a mere farce? In how many do they omit even the form of examination? So long as this is so, it is useless to speak of a standard of qualification for teachers,—there is no such standard. Many teachers are employed in this State, who are wholly incompetent to teach any one branch usually taught in our schools. It could not be so, if the law, even as it is, were executed.

We have provided, that public instruction shall be *general,* but that does not ensure its being *good.* The *diffusion* of education is one thing, its *quality,* another. The law requires that candidates for teaching "shall be well qualified to instruct youth in reading, in writing the English language grammatically, in arithmetic and other branches usually taught in public schools." What is it to be well qualified? It is idle for a person to attempt to teach a branch with which he is not familiar. A stammering, blundering reader, is not qualified to teach boys to read; one who has merely *ciphered* through an arithmetic, is not qualified to teach arithmetic,—nor is one, who has passed through Pope's Essay, of course qualified to teach grammar. The teacher should have mastered his branch so that he can promptly detect the difficulties which embarrass the scholar—and readily and skillfully illustrate and explain. His ear should be as quick to detect an error in reading, or grammar, &c., as the ear of a musician a discord. The teacher should be far above his pupils in knowledge, or he will not command their respect. No parent would send his son to learn carpentry of a man who has but half learned his trade. Yet teachers are often employed, who have not half learned the branches they profess to teach. This is a fatal evil in our system of schools. No laws, no influence will make a good school, if the teacher be incompetent. And this evil will continue to weaken the efficiency of our schools,

so long as half taught young men and women, can procure certificates.

What are the evils of having incompetent teachers? The public
money is wasted. The money is raised for the purposes of instruction, which, under incompetent teachers, the children do not receive. Errors are inculcated. An incompetent teacher will teach
his scholars many things which they will be obliged to unlearn.
Under such a teacher, the children will not be stimulated—there
can be no progress. Pupils must of course be shut up to the field
of the knowledge of the teacher—their minds then will be cramp-
ed—there can be no advance or expansion among them. The
condition of the school, moreover, will act upon the district. You
may judge of the one by the other. A district or town which has
badly managed schools, will soon make that defect manifest to the
passers by. Now if we would ensure vigorous intellectual growth
in a school and in a community, *(for the character of a community
depends on that of its schools,)* we must, for one thing, have competent teachers.

But the great evil arising from incompetent teachers is that they
bring the free school system into contempt. The object of our free
school system is to educate the public mind. It should furnish an
education sufficient for the wants of the community at large. But
the pernicious practice of cutting up a town into small districts—
and of employing incompetent teachers (and this last practice is a
direct and unavoidable consequence of the former) injures the public schools—and gives rise to private schools. Short *public schools
and poor teachers render it necessary (for those who are able,) to
employ private teachers in all our towns and villages.* The consequence is, that the children of the poor are kept in the free
schools, while those of the more wealthy are sent to private schools.
Before long, we shall have the great mischief become general, of a
separation between the rich and the poor, springing out of the mis-
management of our free school system. This ought not, it must
not be. It makes education more expensive, without making it in
reality any better, than is designed by our free school system.

During the last century some of the best men Scotland could boast of, were reared in the parish schools. In many towns in New England, the public schools now give as good an education, as is to be obtained in any private school.

Allusion has not yet been made to the moral qualifications of a teacher. What parent would send his children to a school, where the teacher was known to have an infectious disease? Better do that, than place them under one that is low, vulgar and impure. If the teacher is corrupt, however fair may be his appearance and manner, his corruption will show itself, and will affect his pupils. Says Mr. Mann: "if none but teachers of pure taste, of good manners, of exemplary morals, had ever gained admission into our schools, neither the school rooms, nor their appurtenances would have been poluted, as some of them now are, with such ribald inscriptions and with the carving of such obscene emblems, as would make a heathen blush."

Again, every practical teacher knows that he can teach better, and pupils will learn faster, when his school is properly classed. Any one may preceive that if any instructor should undertake to teach his pupils one by one, he would expend both time and labor at great disadvantage. The advantages of system in a school are quite as important as in a manufactory. But what system can avail much with a teacher, if he has as many separate recitations, as there are pupils? A man can instruct a dozen with more ease to himself and with more effect on his pupils than he can the dozen, one by one. The instruction given to one will answer just as well for a dozen, with this advantage, that in the latter case it is given with more spirit and vivacity. A teacher, that is stupid with a bright and intelligent class before him, must be a dolt. In all our higher institutions, they teach in classes. Why not so in our common schools? The first object then of parents and committees should be to aid the teacher in classifying his school. He will then work to the best advantage.

But how is it? Here is a school where there are half a dozen reading books, as many spelling books, as many arithmetics, as many geographies. What classification can be effected in that school? Would it not be decidedly better to have all of the same rank in arithmetic and geography and grammar, placed in the same class, that they may stimulate each other, and receive the benefit of the undivided attention of the teacher to that particular branch, at a particular hour? If the six in one branch have different text books, they manifestly can each have, at most, but one sixth of the attention from the teacher, which they would have if they all recited together. "Without *uniformity* in books," says Mr. Mann, "*classification is impossible, and whatever defeats classification, destroys the power of the teacher.*"

Such are a part only of the defects which might be enumerated. They are however important defects, which cripple, and which, if uncorrected, must eventually destroy an instrumentality that is fraught with the richest blessings to our whole community. The schools of our cities and of some of our larger towns, it is admitted, constitute to a good degree, exceptions to the whole class throughout the State. Within a few years, this portion of them have made advancement and have undergone valuable changes. In the aggregate, these however, are but an inconsiderable portion of the whole number. Generally, our free schools remain unimproved and apparently unregarded. Especially is this true of those situated in the remote and poor and thinly peopled districts. "But the buds of genius are scattered as bountifully in these remote districts as elsewhere. On the rough hills and among the sterile fields, the noblest of plants, the human soul, springs with as divine capacities, and if kindly and skillfully nurtured, will expand with as large and vigorous a growth, as in any of the most favored regions; nay more, the very absence of the softness and luxuries of life will give an inward vigor and sturdiness most favorable to the highest talents and the best virtues. But a kindly nurture they require. Good schools they must have. How shall these schools be reached?"

That something should be done to render effective the means of education now in use in the State, and to provide increased facilities to promote it, is a sentiment very generally admitted. This we infer from the fact that repeated recommendations of legislative action on this subject, by different governors of the State, have been favorably regarded ; from the instructions of the pulpit and the press ; from public addresses on education, and from resolutions emanating from conventions held at different times and places to consider and mourn over deficiencies which they could do but little to remedy. And that this life-giving and life-infusing process must originate in legislation of some sort, is probably a sentiment equally prevalent with the former.

In these sentiments, we believe the Legislature most deeply sympathize. We dare not impute to them the inconsistency of making a liberal provision for the development of the material resources of the State, in its mineral and vegetable treasures, and yet remaining indifferent to the infinitely greater treasures, the whole intellectual and moral resources of its future population. What agency, if we except that of religion, is of equal value to man with education, whether it be positively or relatively considered ? Positively considered, it early impresses man with a sense of human dignity , rescues him from that state of degradation to which he is doomed unless redeemed by it, unfolds his physical, intellectual and moral powers, and fixes his eye on that moral worth, which through the narrow vista of human nature, leads him to catch distant glimpses of an almighty and infinite goodness. Or expressed in another form, man is the creature of habit ; by practice, he becomes fitted for spheres of action for which he was previously unfitted. Exercise developes, strengthens and beautifies his powers. It enlarges his conceptions, expands his memory and invigorates his judgment ; it elevates reason and gives energy to conscience. It is not however, random practice, nor every kind of exercise, that accomplishes these results ; but exercise put forth in accordance with the laws of mind ; well directed, well timed and well proportioned exertion. Whatever then, mind itself is worth in its capacities to conceive, remember, reason and reflect ; to feel, to enjoy and to will, that is education, positively considered, worth.

Relatively considered, a comparison of the savage that roams through the forest, with an enlightened inhabitant of a civilized country, would be a brief, but an impressive representation of its importance. Well disciplined mind subserves our interests and our happiness. It traces out and elucidates those principles which form the basis of those rules that regulate practice. It constructs sciences, promotes the arts, stimulates to industry, and furnishes motives to economy and virtue. As then, we prize the great principles of religion and of morality; of law and of civil polity; of music and painting and poetry; as we prize the arts of navigation, manufactures, and agriculture; as we value well regulated society and well administered laws; an appropriate and a refined language, cultivated taste and polished manners, so ought we to prize education in this latter sense—in its importance to the State. Certainly is this true in a government like ours, where the people is the sovereign power; where the will of the people is the law of the land; which will is openly and directly expressed; and where every act of the government may justly be called the act of the people. Our republic may justly be said to be founded on the intelligence and virtue of the people. With much propriety has Montesquieu said, "in a republic the whole force of education is required."

In their recent report to the Legislature of that State, the board of education in Massachusetts express themselves to this effect: If you would make the citizens of the State virtuous and happy, educate. If you would promote commerce, agriculture and manufactures, educate. If you would give stability to law, and prevent those hurtful mistakes into which men so often fall in the conduct of their affairs, whether civil, ecclesiastical, or domestic, educate.

The soundness of these views is susceptible of illustration, and they apply to ourselves no less directly, than to those for whom they were originally intended. Already to a great extent, the people of Maine are a mechanical people; and from our position, the character of our climate and soil, from the fact that peculiar advantages of various descriptions exist for this species of industry, it may be safely inferred that we shall become yet greatly more so. "Our pecuniary well being as a people, the individual competence and independence of our citizens, will depend more and more upon this department of industrial labor." There is that witholdeth more than is meet and tendeth to poverty, and there is that scattereth and yet increaseth. It is idle to believe that any outlay of money for the proper education of our youth would be treasure lost, like water spilt on the ground. Such an investment of their means would be the most profitable which our citizens could make, yeilding them some thirty, some sixty, and some an hundred fold.

Fortunately we are not left to conjecture, nor speculation in this matter. The art of printing was invented at about the commencement of the fourteenth century. In speaking of the period preceding that time, Dr. Priestly remarks: "If we only for a moment, imagine ourselves in the place of our ancestors, we cannot help fancying it to be almost impossible for us to have lived with any comfort." The best method of making ourselves fully sensible of -the real value which we derive from improvements in the sciences and the arts, is to endeavor to form clear ideas of the condition of mankind before these improvements took place.

We think ourselves very happy when we have a comfortable fire in a private sitting room or bed chamber; but we should think ourselves much more so, if we considered how lately it is that any such convenience could be had; and that in all times of antiquity, there was only one hearth belonging to any house, placed in the middle of a large hall, from which the smoke, ascending in the middle, went out of a hole in the top of the room; and particularly, if we considered that all the habitations of the English were formerly nothing better than the huts of the Scotch Highlanders and the Irish peasantry, at this day. Chimneys were not general till about the time of Elizabeth. In the fourteenth century, candles were reckoned an article of luxury—shirts were made of serge— linen worn only by persons of distinction, and there were no such things as either chimneys or stoves. The first coach was seen in England in the reign of queen Mary.

One of the chief sources of the great wealth of England is her manufactories, and the connection of philosophy with the improvement of these, is shown by the following fact: From 1771 to 1780, before the invention of the spinning jenny, the amount of raw cotton annually imported into England, was on an average, 5,735,000 pounds only; but from 1817 to 1821, the amount was

2

about 144,000,000 pounds, of which 130,000,000 were worked up in that country. To which increase, the invention of the spinning jenny is supposed to have contributed entirely.

It is but a little more than two hundred years since the soil of Massachusetts was covered with a dense forest—the abode of savage beasts and more savage men; but these have passed away. In the place of the forest, have sprung up flourishing cities and towns and villages containing a population more distinguished for intelligence, and all that subserves our various wants, than any other people on the globe. In that state more than eighty five thousand persons are engaged in manufactures and trades, which number represents a population of at least three hundred thousand, or six-fifteenths of all the inhabitants of the commonwealth, the annual income of whose labor is about $90,000.000.

We marvel at such results; but they are not causeless. Among the first settlers of that colony, were men of sagacity and of far reaching prudence; men who loved their race, and who could forego, if need be, a present enjoyment for a greater future good. Then men taxed themselves for the support of learning in the commonwealth to a degree, which tried by the standard of modern benevolence, seems to us like an imaginary tale.

For the support of her common schools, Massachusetts expended the last year $1,000,000. With a territory many times larger, and a population about equal, we expended during the same time, for the same cause, probably not more than $300,000.

As a people we are largely engaged in navigating the ocean; consequently in foreign and domestic commerce; and to the successful performance of these branches of *business* is needful a familiar knowledge of the sciences of navigation, geometry and book-keeping. We are likewise extensively a farming community; and that our soil may be made to produce the largest amount with the least labor, an acquaintance with the sciences of chemistry, geology, mineralogy and botany, is essential.

In ancient times, in certain countries bordering on the Mediterranean and Red seas, the people had attained to a high state of intellectual advancement. These nations were also skilled in many of the arts, and to a considerable degree in husbandry. About the fifth century of the Christian era, the Roman empire, which had for more than five hundred years extended over the known world, was destroyed. Consequent upon which, a thousand years of depression and ruin overspread society; in which scarcely a vestige of human effort remains worthy the attention or imitation of succeeding ages. Now respecting this deplorable result, Mr. Hallam writes: "In tracing the decline of society from the subversion of the Roman empire, we have been led, not without connection, *from ignorance to superstition, from superstition to vice and lawlessness, and from thence to general rudeness and poverty.*"

What is not seen may be thought not to exist, and causes which produce the most beneficial results, are oftentimes the least noticed.

Few can connect the present with the past, and see in what is, that which has been. To many, doubtless, the revival of learning and the invention of printing, seem to be events of ordinary importance only, limited in their influence to the period of their origin —at all events, to the few whose thoughts are exercised chiefly by such matters. "When ignorance is bliss, 'tis folly to be wise."

Well would it be however if the want of knowledge could prevent the evil consequences resulting from it.

At the period when so great was the ignorance which prevailed, that persons of the most distinguished rank could neither read nor write; when even many of the clergy did not understand the breviary, which they were daily accustomed to recite, and which some of them could scarcely read; when history was but a record of legendary and of fabulous tales, and philosophy but a medley of scholastic jargon;—at this period precisely, it was, we are told, that the "*culture of the land was very imperfect,*" *and that commerce had scarcely an existence.*

Priestly, in his lectures on history, says: "It is but since queen Elizabeth's time, that the English have had any settled notions about agriculture." Mr. Hartlib, to whom Milton dedicated his treatise on education, says, that old men in his days, remembered the first gardeners who came over to Surry and sold turnips, carrots, parsnips, early peas and rape, which were then a great rarity, being imported from Holland. They introduced at that time, the planting of cabbages and digging the ground for garden stuffs.   Cherries and hops were first planted in the reign of Henry VIII; and apples were still brought from France, also onions from Spain.

In the beginning of the fourteenth century, the inhabitants around the Mediterranean sea, first steered into the Atlantic ocean, towards England and France.   What diverted almost the whole course of trade out of its former channel, and makes the most remarkable revolution in the whole history of commerce, says the writer last mentioned, was the discovery of a passage to the East Indies round the Cape of Good Hope by the Portuguese, and to America by the Spaniards.   These discoveries they were enabled to make by means of the COMPASS, which then (about the year fourteen hundred) first began to be applied to navigation.

Your memorialists might proceed to illustrate this close connection so evidently subsisting between an increase of learning and that of temporal gain, gratifications and security, in other kindred relations;—to show that education is one of the principal sources of civilization—that it is the handmaid of religion, and in fact the very pillar of social organization, since it discovers the rules of justice and practically gives them their sanction;—to show also, its influence in promoting domestic order, purity and bliss; in curtailing crime, in breaking down factitious distinctions, in elevating woman, and in harmonizing interests, which are too often conflicting and discordant.

But not to press this train of remark, they would turn the attention of the Legislature, to what may be done to remedy the evils which have been by them set forth.

What shall the remedy be?

If in efforts to promote education, Maine has done less, than some of her sister States; for the wisdom of most of her statute regulations touching this matter, there is, nevertheless, good cause of congratulation.

These regulations seem to us deficient, that is, limited within too narrow a sphere, rather than erroneous, either in their principles or in their practical tendencies.   And moreover, we are impressed with the conviction, that it is not so much the formation of a new system of education, which is now requisite to answer the ends of legislation on this subject, as the enlargement and improvement of that which already exists.

The convention of Education in Augusta, the last winter, passed for substance, the following resolution : That the time has come for the establishment of a board of education in the State, and that its establishment should be demanded of the Legislature, with a power and energy which will not be resisted. The language employed in this resolution by the convention, is expressive of their deep sense of the utility of the measure which they recommend. They evidently regarded it as a fundamental measure ; as the measure upon which the utility of others, tending to the same effect, will mainly depend. From the opinion of the convention, the committee cannot dissent ; and they are induced to propose the resolution to the Legislature, asking for it deliberation.

Nor must the language in which it is couched, be understood as intending to cast invidious reflections on past legislation, or to be in any way disparaging to ourselves. It was intended to be only, the earnest expression of fact.

The time has come, say the convention. As a state we have existed scarcely more than a quarter of a century ; and to have imposed burdensome taxes upon the people at the outset, for the support of a good cause even, would doubtless have proved impolitic. Besides, means of advancing the cause of learning, which a few years since were considered of doubtful tendency, have been found to be highly advantageous. Instead therefore of attempting to advance by the uncertain light of untried theory, we may now do so by the light of theory justified by experiment.

The time has come, the convention repeat, when those who have the power to act must be urgently solicited to act.

The arguments in favor of this measure, have some of them, been already adduced. They are found in the defects of the practical operations of our school system, and also in the positive and relative worth of education itself.

That these arguments will be appreciated, we confidently believe. "We believe, that upon the importance of free schools—an institu-

2*

tion, which in its action, comes home to the mind of every child in
the State; which does or may do more than any other, to bring out
his powers, to furnish him with good knowledge, to form his character, to give him noble aims, and to fit him in all ways for his
duties as a citizen and a man, and for his whole future existence—
any statement we could make would fall far short of the truth, and
of the convictions of the wise and patriotic citizens who represent
the people of the State."

If the foundation be insecure, how shall the fabric stand? and,
if other interests of far less value, are deemed of sufficient importance to engage the attention and efforts of persons designated to
the service, why shall this be treated with less respect, and be left
to a more casual or uncertain supervision?

Another argument in favor of this measure is, that wherever a
board of education has been established, whether in Europe or this
country, it has proved to be highly beneficial. Prussia, in respect
to her schools, is the admiration of all intelligent travelers. The
same is true to a degree, of France and Holland. In Prussia, as
early as the reign of Elector Joachim the second (1546), visitors
were appointed to inspect the town schools of the electorate, with
express directions to report in relation to the measures deemed
necessary for their improvement. These appointments have been
renewed by succeding rulers, at various times, till the present.

Referring to this and kindred exertions in that country, President
Bache, who had for a considerable time resided there, inquires:
' What is the real social result of all this? How has it affected
the population—for good or for ill? How is it likely to affect them
for the future? The narratives given by Pestalozzi, De Fellenberg,
Oberlin, and Pere Girard, of the singular revolution, mental and
moral, I may also add physical, effected by the application of their
system of teaching on a hitherto ignorant and vicious population,
though admitted to be isolated experiments, ought not the less to
be considered evidences of the intrinsic force of the instrument
itself, and of its power to produce similar results wherever and
whenever fairly tried, without reference to country or numbers;
that is, whenever applied with the same earnestness, honesty, and

skill in other instances as in theirs. And of this portion of Prussia, of the Rhenish province, it may be surely averred, that it has now been for some time, under the influence of this system, and that during that period, whether resulting from such influence or not, its progress in intelligence, industry and morality—in the chief elements of virtue and happiness, has been steadily and strikingly progressive. In few parts of civilized Europe is there more marked exemption from all crimes of violence than in this happy land; not only from those graver delinquencies which stain the calenders of the more luxurious states of Europe, but even from those minor offenses against the person, such as riot, assault, &c., from which none scarcely are to be wholly excepted. The safety of the public roads, contrasted with their notorious insecurity in many parts of England, is supported by unequivocal facts. The same abstinence from offenses against property is conspicuous in towns. I have already had occasion to refer to the comparative rarity of theiving amongst the lower classes, especially to the diminution of the offense in that very class and age most subject to it in England, and most likely to be influenced by the want or supply, the badness or goodness of education. There is not only little amount of crime and juvenile offenders, but this amount and number are progressively diminishing. Doubtless much of this most gratifying result may be ascribed to comfort and employment. But this again must be ascribed to some still higher cause. There is comfort because there is frugality; there is employment because there is the desire and search and love of it. There is industry, incessant, universal, in every class, from high to low; because there are the early habits of useful occupation, and there are these habits, because there is sound and general education. In all those relations of life where truth, honor, confidence, and mutual kindness are most required—where fraud is most easy, but most injurious—where reciprocal good faith is of such import, but so easily disturbed—in all pecuniary, especially in all commercial transactions, the "Deutsche Treue" is more than ever proverbial. A promise is a bond—a word, an oath. The clergyman admitted that his flock had not become worse christians for becoming more intelligent men; the officer, that his men had grown more obedient, as they had grown more instructed—a word now led where a cane formerly was insufficient; the farmer, for the increased profits of his farm, as the manufacturer for those of his factory, thanked the school. Skill had increased and conduct had improved with knowledge; profits with both. Even household management had reaped its advantage, when the first vanity and presumption arising out of the partial nature of instruction had worn off—when it had become general, sound, and appropriate. The servant, especially the female servant, was not less faithful, and had become far more useful than before.

In Massachusetts, a board of education has existed for a period of about eight years. At recent interviews with intelligent gentlemen of that State, the following have been stated as some of the beneficial results of that organization.

An increased interest in the subject of education among the people of the State generally. As an evidence of this, works on education are more read than formerly; lectures on this subject are more popular; schools are more the topic of conversation at social gatherings and in public conveyances; they have assumed greater importance in the transaction of town affairs; school committees are selected with more caution, the election usually turning in favor of the most intelligent, discreet, and high minded men; schools are more often visited by parents and others; the office of teacher is more respected. Another result is, that the qualification of teachers has been greatly advanced and greater pains are taken by teachers to keep themselves informed on all matters relating to their employment. The government of schools is more effective, at the same time its severity has been greatly diminished; teaching is more practical and thorough; a better classification of scholars and greater uniformity of text books, have been secured. Through the influence of district libraries, a taste for appropriate and useful books has been extensively induced; *the length of schools has been increased on an average one month;* school houses have been essentially improved. In some of the more populous towns, elegant edifices have been erected for this use, at an expense of eight and ten thousand dollars each. And, what is worthy of remark, all these results have followed, while yet the taxes for the support of schools have not been materially increased.

A board of supervision has also for some time existed in New York; and assurances are given by many of the most intelligent and influential men there, that this agency has effected results no less important in New York than in Massachusetts. Similar reports are made of the effects of this instrumentality in Ohio and in Rhode Island.

Two questions respecting the subject of the establishment of a State board of education, claim brief attention; to which the further consideration of the Legislature is respectfully solicited.

The first. What shall be the duties of this agency when elected? And the second; by what method shall it be elected?

The duties of the board cannot be legislative, but must be suggestive, advisory and executive entirely. The board must be a servant, acting from derived powers, and not from those which are self-originated; or if at all so, to a very limited extent. A specification of its duties might include the following: The devising of means for the improvement of teachers, and for the formation of better teachers; the imparting of instruction to those interested on these subjects—on the position, construction and furniture of school houses, and the recommending of ways by which schools may be encouraged. It might also come within the duties of the board, to make suggestions upon the subjects of discipline, classification, &c.; and in these respects as well as others, to endeavor to secure among the several schools of the State, concert of action; to collect and present to the Legislature, the experience of other States, and foreign countries on subjects interesting to the common schools.

"From a knowledge of the condition and wants of the agricultural and manufacturing population of the State, the board could do much towards enabling the Legislature to determine the question whether any thing can be done, better to adapt the instruction given in common schools to their wants, or whether separate institutions may with advantage, be established. The board might also determine the questions, whether further instruction in the useful arts can be introduced into all our schools; and whether a higher

moral influence can be exercised, thus to do something more to
prevent the crimes, which it now costs the State so much to
punish."

The second and third sections of the law of 1837, on the subject
of the duties of the Massachusetts' board of education, read thus:
" The board of education shall prepare and lay before the Legislature
in a printed form, on or before the second Wednesday of January.
annually, an abstract of the school returns received by the secretary of the commonwealth, and the said board of education may
appoint their own secretary, who shall receive a reasonable compensation for his services, and who shall, under the direction of the
board, collect information of the actual condition and efficiency of
the common schools and other means of popular education, and
diffuse as widely as possible throughout every part of the commonwealth, information of the most approved and successful methods
of arranging the studies and conducting the education of the young,
to the end that all children in this commonwealth who depend upon
common schools for instruction, may have the best education, which
those schools can be made to impart.

" The board of education annually, shall make a detailed report
to the Legislature of all its doings, with such observations as their
experience and reflection may suggest, upon the condition and efficiency of our system of popular education, and the most practicable means of improving and extending it."

What should be the mode of electing a State board of education,
is an important question.

On this point we may be permitted, we hope, to speak freely,
we would not be misunderstood. In nothing, which we say, do we
intend to impeach in the slightest degree, either the wisdom or the
fidelity of those, who now, in any manner, represent the government.

The first qualification of men elected to this office should be fitness to discharge the duties of it, alike as it respects their literary
qualifications, their ability to think calmly, and to judge discretely,
and their deep interest in the cause, which it is made their duty to
superintend.

A second qualification should be freedom from political bias, and from sectarian tendency, to that degree certainly, which will give security that the board shall never be prostituted, in any sense, to party purposes.

The objection to entrusting this electing power to the Governor and Council, or to the Legislature, would be, that, in many minds a suspicion would be raised that it might not always be judiciously exercised, and that the board might at length degenerate into an organ of church, or of State, perhaps both.

If the choice were made by the popular vote immediately, no greater certainty could be afforded of obtaining judicious and interested persons for the office.

Should the board be empowered to perpetuate itself, its independency might deprive it of sympathy.

A mode of electing this body, to which many would give preference, among others the Hon. H. Mann, secretary of the board of education of Mass., would be to refer the election to persons, who had been themselves elected by the people specifically for that object. The electors might be the chairmen of the school committees of the several towns, who might be empowered and required to meet annually, or at longer intervals, at some central place in each county to discharge their duty.

Besides to a good degree, obviating objections, to which the other modes seem liable, there would be advantages connected with this, which could not attach to them. There are, in the State, thirteen counties, containing in all about three hundred and sixty towns. By this method, consequently, there would be annually collected, or as often as might be thought best, more than three hundred men in thirteen distinct associations.

Now if these gatherings occurred in different years, or at different periods of the same year, opportunity would be given for the agent of the board to be present at each of them, when he might accurately ascertain by reports, or otherwise, the actual condition of towns respecting their educational efforts, and when having got this knowledge, he might impart valuable suggestions, and advice as to methods of greater improvements, or of removing apathy.

These assemblies might be empowered to decide many important questions pertaining to the welfare of the schools in their several counties. Such as for example, the branches of studies to be pursued in schools; books to be recommended, in what branches teachers shall be examined; how such examinations shall be conducted, and what shall be considered necessary qualifications of a teacher.

They might also discuss subjects pertaining to the districting of towns; to raising of moneys for the support of schools; and numberless others of a kindred nature.

These occasions would likewise afford convenient opportunities for holding county conventions of education, when teachers and others interested in the advancement of learning, might come together to devise ways and means for the fulfilment of their desires.

Moved by these considerations, your memorialists respectfully pray you to consider the expediency of appointing a board of education, and of devising such other means as in your wisdom shall seem best, for the benefit of our free school system.

AMOS BROWN.
PHILIP EASTMAN.
A. S. PACKARD.
SAMUEL P. BENSON.

STATE OF MAINE.

IN THE YEAR OF OUR LORD ONE THOUSAND EIGHT HUNDRED AND
FORTY-SIX.

AN ACT in relation to fugitives from justice.

Be it enacted by the Senate and House of Represent-
2 *atives in Legislature assembled,* as follows:

3   SECTION 1.   Whenever any person shall be found
4 within this State, charged with any offence committed
5 in any other State or territory and liable, by the con-
6 stitution and laws of the United States, to be deliv-
7 ered over upon the demand of the Executive of such
8 other State or territory, any court or magistrate, au-
9 thorized to issue warrants in criminal cases, may, upon
10 complaint under oath, setting forth the offence and
11 such other matters as are necessary to bring the case
12 within the provisions of law, issue a warrant to bring
13 the person so charged before the same or any other
14 court or magistrate, within the State, to answer to
15 such complaint, as in other cases.

Wm. T. Johnson, Printer to the State

Sec. 2. If, upon the examination of the person
2 charged, it shall appear to the court or magistrate,
3 that there is reasonable cause to believe that the com-
4 plaint is true, and that such person may be lawfully
5 demanded of the Executive, he shall, if charged with
6 an offence, bailable by the laws of this State, be re-
7 quired to recognize with sufficient sureties, to appear
8 before such court or magistrate, at a future day, al-
9 lowing a reasonable time to obtain the warrant of the
10 Executive, and to abide the order of the court or
11 magistrate ; and if such person shall not so recognize
12 he shall be committed to prison, and be there detained
13 until such day, in like manner as if the offence
14 charged had been committed within this State ; and
15 if the person so recognizing shall fail to appear,
16 according to the condition of his recognizance, he
17 shall be defaulted, and the like proceedings shall be
18 had, as in the case of other recognizances entered
19 into before such court or magistrate ; but if such per-
20 son be charged with an offence not bailable by the
21 laws of this State, he shall be committed to prison,
22 and there detained until the day so appointed for his
23 appearance before the court or magistrate.

Sec. 3. If the person so recognized or committed
2 shall appear before the court or magistrate, upon the

3 day ordered, he shall be discharged, unless he shall be
4 demanded by some person authorized by the warrant
5 of the Executive to receive him, or unless the court
6 or magistrate shall see cause to commit him, or to re-
7 quire him to recognize anew, for his appearance at
8 some other day, and if, when ordered, he shall not so
9 recognize, he shall be committed and detained as
10 before; *provided*, that whether the person so charged
11 shall be recognized, committed or discharged, any
12 person, authorized by the warrant of the Executive,
13 may at all times take him into custody, and the same
14 shall be a discharge of the recognizance, if any, and
15 shall not be deemed an escape.

SEC. 4. The complainant, in any such case, shall
2 be answerable for all the actual costs and charges,
3 and for the support in prison, of any person so com-
4 mitted, to be paid in the same manner as by a creditor
5 for his debtor committed on execution; and if the
6 charge for his support in prison shall not 'be so paid,
7 the jailer may discharge such person, in like manner
8 as if he had been committed for debt on an execution.

SEC. 5. This act shall take effect from and after its
2 approval by the governor.

STATE OF MAINE.

HOUSE OF REPRESENTATIVES, June 13, 1846.

Ordered, That 350 copies of the foregoing bill, reported from the committee on the judiciary, be printed for the use of the Legislature.

SAMUEL BELCHER, *Clerk*.

ANNUAL REPORT

OF THE

INSPECTORS OF MAINE STATE PRISON.

To the Governor and Executive
Council of the State of Maine.

The Inspectors of the Maine State Prison respectfully present the following

REPORT:

The present number of convicts is sixty, being a decrease of fifteen since the last annual report. This is a very small number, taking into consideration the population of the State. If this may be taken as proof that crime has diminished, some cause should be assigned for this diminuation; and it is but fair to conclude that the temperance reform has exerted a strong influence in preventing crime, and that the attention to the moral discipline of convicts while in prison has induced many to abandon their former habits of idleness and dissipation, and apply themselves to some useful employment after being discharged, where they soon find that it is not difficult, again to obtain the confidence of their neighbors and the public, and establish for themselves a character that will entirely obliterate the disgrace of their former conduct.

The almost universal inquiry in regard to the prison has been concerning its pecuniary situation; but seldom have any questions been asked in relation to the health and discipline of its inmates, nor has it been considered of much importance, that frequently a convict while serving his term of punishment, has obtained for himself a good trade, and although he may have been of but little or no pecuniary advantage to the State, is enabled after being discharged, to procure good employment: thus keeping him from his former haunts of idleness and dissipation, and preventing his return to prison after a short absence.

It appears from the records of punishment that during the last sixteen months, the whole time spent by the convicts in solitary confinement for punishment, amounts to two hundred and twenty six days, equal to about three days to each prisoner; and this is the only punishment that has been inflicted, with the exception of a single case of whipping, which was inflicted upon a convict after having spent at different times, in solitary confinement, sixty days. It must be evident from this, that the conduct of the prisoners has been good, and goes far in establishing the advantage of kind treatment, and encouragement of convicts, over the old system of discipline.

Experience shows very plainly that mild and humane treatment does much towards improving the disposition of the vicious, and encouraging those who are anxious for reformation; while prisoners are treated with harshness and cruelty by their officers, without receiving from them one encouraging word or look, feeling themselves as the subjects of revenge, and outcast from society, with no prospect or hope of meeting with a kind friend after serving their term of confinement, there is but little reason to expect that a salutary and permanent reformation of character will be the result, but the fair presumption is that they will improve the first opportunity to gratify the feelings of revenge, which during their confinement has been suppressed, but not subdued, and their return to prison may be daily expected. But let the prisoners be well clothed, fed, and lodged; let proper attention be paid to cleanliness, and every means taken to preserve their health; place them in a situation, when received into the prison, to learn a trade; let them be kindly instructed and encouraged by their overseers, and be made to feel if possible, that by applying themselves to such trade, they may still make useful members of society, when discharged; let them be well supplied with useful books to occupy the time while in their cells, with suitable moral and religious instruction; and in many cases a thorough and permanent reformation in their character will be the result; and although the immediate result may not be so much to the State in dollars and cents, yet crime will diminish, the number of prisoners be reduced, jails relieved, and the criminal dockets in the courts of justice very much lessened.

The Inspectors are satisfied from a careful examination at their frequent visits, that since the prisoners have occupied the new building, where they can enjoy the privilege of sleeping in clean, dry and warm beds, and have good light enabling them to read the bible and other useful books, with which the cells are supplied, that thay have been more obedient and willing to perform their work to the satisfaction of their overseers, than they were after having spent the night in the cold and wet cells or pit-holes of the old prison; and consequently but little punishment has been required.

When convicts are seen by those visiting the prison, busily engaged in the shops, they think it strange that the returns from the different departments show but a small amount as the earnings of each convict; but when it is remembered that a large number of them are almost wholly ignorant of the business at which they are engaged, and that in making the returns from the departments, the proceeds of the labor of those who are good workmen are to be divided with those who are entirely ignorant, and whose labor has been of no profit, it will readily be seen that a large daily income cannot be expected from the whole number. In addition to this, there are many who are too old, or infirm, to do any work to advantage, but must be employed, and generally are returned as being engaged in some of the income departments, as they are unfit for cooks, waiters, or washers.

The whole amount of stock in the various departments is $17, 437 89, to which should be added the sum of $225, expended in rebuilding prison fence, and $475, in building lime shed and kiln, as these sums have been charged to building and repairs, and to the quarry, but have not been included in the account of stock. Without thus accounting for these sums, the actual situation of the departments to which they are charged would not be shown.

It was found absolutely necessary to rebuild a part of the fence, as the old one had become entirely unsafe from decay. The new kiln was built for the use of those who manufacture the rock from the prison quarry. By affording facility for burning the rock, a much larger quantity of it finds a market, and the rent for the use of the kilns makes them a source of profit.

The expenditures since December 31, 1844, appear proportionately larger, and the receipts less than for the last few years; but this is readily accounted for, when it is recollected that the time embraces two winters, which must necessarily increase the expenses of support, and diminish the proceeds of labor. It requires a large quantity of wood to warm the prison and shops during the cold weather, and this has been much higher than usual for the last season. The working time of the prisoners is much less during the short days of winter, than in the summer; besides this, many convicts are taken from the quarry where their labor yields a profit, and placed in some of the shops, where from their entire ignorance of the work, they pay little or nothing.

During the last winter so many of the convicts had to be placed in the shoe shop, that it became necessary to employ an additional overseer to look after them, while the other was cutting and fitting their work and attending to the other duties of his situation. The expense of subsistence has been increased on account of the high price of corn and the impracticability of procuring potatoes, which are generally very much used by the convicts, and the want of which has been very seriously felt during the past season.

The expense account is larger than it otherwise would have been, owing to the amount which has been paid in conducting a suit commenced some time since, in Massachusetts, to recover an amount due for limerock delivered on contract. This suit is still pending, although the Warden has used every exertion to have it brought to a close.

The Wardens of the prison have at various times, made contracts with individuals for labor to be performed by the convicts, with the expectation of receiving the pay for it when accomplished. In all such cases, the Wardens seem to have fulfilled their part of such contracts in good faith, agreeably to the spirit and letter of their agreement; but instead of receiving the pay for it, this amount is accounted for, year after year, either as stock on hand or amount due from individuals, but after a while is put into the hands of an attorney for collection, where it is constantly a bill of expense, and after a series of years, perhaps after it has been abandoned on the books as worthless, or otherwise disposed of, may return in the form of an execution, which in its turn, requires constant attention and some expense to keep it alive.

If individuals would pay their liabilities to the prison, with any thing like reasonable promptness, there would be no need of calling upon the treasury even for officers' salaries. The Inspectors are confident that under the prudent management of the present Warden, the prison could meet every demand from its own resources, were it not for the time, trouble and expense, that is too frequently spent in collecting debts; but still it will not do to abandon the barter trade, as the sales for cash alone would be exceeding small.

It will be necessary, in the course of the present season, to rebuild the northern gateway leading into the prison yard, as the old one is very rotten; and the Inspectors would advise that a permanent stone gateway be erected instead of the present wooden one. The dwelling house must soon be repaired, as it is very leaky, and its durability and safety would be much increased by covering the roof with slate instead of wood. So long as buildings and fences are constructed of wood, the State must be at constant expense in keeping them in repair.

It appears from the present situation of the prison, that its income has paid its expenses and $2,522 40 towards the officers' salaries, which amounts to $5,783 83 for the last sixteen months. There has been received from the treasury the sum of $5,681 for the payment of salaries (except the Warden's); but $1,235 of this amount was for the quarter ending December 31, 1844; the amount of salaries for the quarter ending in March, 1846, has not been received. In addition to the above sum paid toward of-

1*

ficers' salaries, should be added the amount paid for conducting the
suit in Massachusetts; then taking into consideration the increased
expense for fuel for two winters, while the profits of the summer
cannot be shown, the pecuniary situation will be good.

The report of the Chaplain will present the manner in which
the religious services have been conducted during the past year.

The attention of the different officers to their various duties, has
been such as to meet the entire approval of the Inspectors.

In the amount due to individuals on books, in the annexed tables,
is included the balance due to Mr. Carr, the Warden, amounting
to $2,641 69.

BENJ. F. BUXTON, } *Inspectors of*
GEORGE A. STARR, } *Maine*
STEPHEN BARROWS, } *State Prison.*

Maine State Prison, May 11, 1846.

To the Inspectors of the Maine State Prison:

GENTLEMEN:—During the past year, religious services have been performed in the chapel twice on the Lord's day—one at eight A. M. the other at three P. M.,—and I am happy to say, that attention and good order have generally characterized those devotional seasons. While it is to be feared, that some of the unfortunate inmates, "have sold themselves to work wickedness," yet others I have reason to believe, have under the word preached, felt a restraining and enlightning influence which cannot fail to benfit them, both for time and eternity; having found the "way of the transgressor hard," they feel determined to reform.

Our Sabbath School has been conducted as usual, in which nearly one half are brought under instruction.

The present construction of the Prison gives me a good opportunity for personal conversation with them at the door of their cell, which seasons have been deeply interesting to myself, and I trust, not without profit to them.

My visits to the sick in the Hospital, have been thankfully received.

As many of them appear interested in reading, I would respectfully recommend an addition to the Prison library.

In humble reliance on Divine aid to assist me in this unpromising field of ministerial labor, and cheered with a hope that my past services have not been altogether in vain, but at the last great day, I shall meet some who will regard this Prison as the place where they began to "think of their ways, and turn their feet into the divine testimonies."

I remain, respectfully yours,

JOB WASHBURN,
Chaplain of the Maine State Prison.

Thomaston, May 7, 1846.

Statement of Receipts and Expenditures in the various Departments from Dec. 31, 1844, to April 30, 1846.

	Wheelwright Department.		
1844. Dec. 31,	To stock and tools on hand, To charged to department since,	4,579 40 2,589 62	
1846. April 30,			7,169 02
	By stock and tools on hand, By credit to department,	5,370 84 3,889 60	
			9,260 44
	Balance in favor,		$2,091 42
	—		
	Shoemaking Department.		
1844. Dec. 31,	To stock and tools on hand, To charged to department since,	1,810 40 9,776 97	
1846. April 30,			11,587 37
	By stock and tools on hand, By credit to department,	4,781 91 10,678 14	
			15,460 05
	Balance in favor,		$3,872 68
	—		
	Blacksmiths' Department.		
1844. Dec. 31,	To stock and tools on hand, To charged to department since,	982 80 943 19	
1846. April 30,			1,925 99
	By stock and tools on hand, By credit to department,	1,286 53 1,944 52	
			3,231 05
	Balance in favor,		$1,305 06
	—		
	Lime Quarry Department.		
1844. Dec. 31,	To stock and tools on hand, To charged to department since,	2,675 14 1,034 25	
1846. April 30,			3,709 39
	By stock and tools on hand, By credit to department,	1,875 11 2,811 05	
			4,686 16
	Balance in favor,		$976 77

Statement of Receipts and Expenditures—(Continued.)

	Team Department.		
1844. Dec. 31,	To stock and tools on hand, To charged to department since,	325 33 779 12	
			1,104 45
1846. April 30,	By stock and tolls on hand, By credit to department,	465 00 669 33	
			1,134 33
	Balance in favor,		$29 88
	Subsistence Department.		
1844. Dec. 31,	To stock on hand, To charged to department since,	890 42 3,954 72	
			4,845 14
1846. April 30,	By stock on hand, By credit to department,	1,275 39 589 47	
			1,864 86
	Balance against,		$2,980 28
	Fuel and Lights Department.		
1844. Dec. 31,	To stock on hand, To charged to department since,	59 15 1,183 79	
			1,242 94
1846. April 30,	By stock on hand, By credit to department,	111 30 24 16	
			135 46
	Balance against,		$1,107 48
	Clothing Department.		
1844. Dec. 31,	To stock on hand, To charged to department since,	985 42 1,021 23	
			2,006 65
1846. April 30,	By stock on hand, By credit to department,	1,252 86 335 76	
			1,588 62
	Balance against,		$418 03

Statement of Receipts and Expenditures—(Continued.)

	Expense Account Department.		
1844. Dec. 31,	To stock on hand,	914 64	
	To charged to department since,	1,215 68	
			2,130 32
1846. April 30,	By stock on hand,	1,018 95	
	By credit to department,	101 24	
			1,120 19
	Balance against,		$1,010 13

Balance in various Departments.

Balance in favor of Wheelwright department,	2,091 42	
Balance in favor of Shoemaking department,	3,872 68	
Balance in favor of Blacksmiths' department,	1,305 06	
Balance in favor of Lime Quarry department,	976 77	
Balance in favor of Team department,	29 88	
		8,275 81
Balance against Subsistence department,	2,980 28	
Balance against Fuel and Lights department,	1,107 48	
Balance against Clothing department,	418 03	
Balance against Expense Account department,	1,010 13	
		5,515 92
Balance in favor of Income department,		$2,759 89

Receipts and Expenditures not included in above tables.

Received from visitors, ...	144 49	
" convicts admitted, . . .	6 45	
" building and repairs, . . .	35 22	
		186 16
Expended for convicts, discharged, . . .	439 04	
" building and repairs, . . .	684 61	
		$1,123 65

Statement of Stock and Tools.

1844.			
Dec. 31,	Amount of stock and tools as per stock book,		13,222 30
1846.			
April 30,	Amount of stock in Wheelwright Depart'nt,	5,370 84	
	" " Shoemaking "	4,781 91	
	" " Blacksmiths' "	1,286 53	
	" " Lime Quarry "	1,875 11	
	" " Team "	465 00	
	" " Subsistence "	1,275 39	
	" " Fuel and Lights "	111 30	
	" " Clothing "	1,252 86	
	" " Expense account "	1,018 95	
			17,437 89
	Balance in favor of this year,		$4,215 59

Statement of Notes and Accounts.

1844. Dec. 31,	Amount due from individuals on notes and accounts, ...		9,308 58
	Amount due to individuals on notes and accounts, ...		3,118 18
	Balance in favor of prison, . . .		$6,190 40
1846. April 30,	Amount due from individuals on notes, .	1,070 02	
	Amount due from individuals on books, .	11,019 76	
			12,089 78
	Amount due to individuals on notes, .	2,606 41	
	Amount due to individuals on books, .	5,788 59	
			8,395 00
	Balance in favor of prison, . .		$3,694 78

Statement of Convicts.

Number of convicts in prison Dec. 31, 1844, ...	75	Whole number of convicts received since July 2, 1824, . .	881
Received since, ...	29		
	104		
Discharged on expiration of sentence, . . .	38	Discharged on expiration of sentence, . . .	654
Pardoned, ...	4	Pardoned, . . .	134
Died, ...	2	Died, . . .	26
	— 44	Escaped and not retaken, .	7
	—	Remaining number, .	60
Remaing number, .	60		— 881

Crimes.

Adultery, ...	4	Murder, 2d degree, . . .	1
Assault to kill, ...	1	Murder, sentence commuted, .	1
Arson, ...	4	Murder, awaiting sentence of death,	1
Burglary, ...	5	Passing counterfeit money, .	1
Forgery, ...	3	Rape, ...	1
Larceny, ...	37		—
Lewd and lascivious cohabitation,	1	Total, ...	60

Ages of Convicts when committed.

From 10 to 20 years, . . . 11	From 50 to 60 years, . . . 3
From 20 to 30 years, . . . 25	From 60 to 70 years, . . . 1
From 30 to 40 years, . . . 12	
From 40 to 50 years, . . . 8	Total, ... 60

Term of Sentence.

During life, ... 7	For 3 years, ... 5
For 15 years, ... 1	For 2 years, ... 14
For 12 years, ... 1	For 1 year, 6 months, . . . 4
For 10 years, ... 2	For 1 year, ... 5
For 7 years, ... 1	Sentenced to be hanged, . . 1
For 6 years, ... 1	
For 5 years, ... 11	Total, ... 60
For 4 years, ... 7	

Number of days occupied by Convicts in different Departments from Dec. 31, 1844, to April 30, 1846.

In Quarry, ... 3,207	Washers, ... 537
In Smiths' Shop, . . . 1,673	Waiters, ... 673
In Shoe Shop, . . . 13,200	Lumpers, ... 1,310
In Wheelwrights' Shop, . 2,964	Hospital, ... 1,141
Tailors, ... 1,412	In solitary confinement for pun-
Cooks, ... 872	ishment, ... 226

STATE OF MAINE.

House of Representatives, June 19, 1846.

Ordered, That 350 copies of the Report of the Inspectors of the State Prison be printed for the use of the Legislature.

SAMUEL BELCHER, *Clerk*.

TWENTY-SIXTH LEGISLATURE.

STATE OF MAINE.

IN THE YEAR OF OUR LORD ONE THOUSAND EIGHT HUNDRED AND
FORTY-SIX.

AN ACT to incorporate the Georges Canal Company.

Be it enacted by the Senate and House of Represent-
2 *atives in Legislature assembled,* as follows :

3   SECTION 1.   John Miller, Atwood Levensaler, Ben-
4 jamin Carr, John O'Brien, Rufus C. Counce, Lewis
5 Bachelder, Francis Keating, William Keating, Samuel
6 Atkinson, John C. Knowlton, Gideon Richards, and
7 Daniel McCurdy, their associates, successors, and as-
8 signs, are hereby made and constituted a body politic
9 and corporate by the name of the Georges Canal
10 Company ; with all the powers and privileges incident
11 to similar corporations so far as may be necessary
12 to carry into effect all the purposes of this act ; to have
13 a common seal and to change the same ; and to make
14 any by-laws for the management of their affairs not

Wm. T. Johnson, Printer to the State.

15 repugnant to the laws of this State. And the said
16 corporation are hereby authorized and empowered to
17 survey, locate, construct and finally complete, alter
18 and keep in repair, such canals, locks, flood gates,
19 docks, sluices, embankments, basins, piers, dams,
20 wharves and other works, as may be necessary or
21 convenient for the purpose of rendering the Gorges
22 river, and the ponds through which it runs, or with
23 which it is connected, navigable for boats from the tide
24 waters below the village in the town of Warren, to
25 Stevens' pond in the town of Liberty, including
26 the waters of Quantebacook pond in the town of
27 Searsmont and the stream connecting the same with
28 Georges river ; and they shall have power to use and
29 employ as much of the water of said river and ponds
30 or of the streams which may be connected therewith,
31 as may be necessary or convenient for the use of said
32 locks and canals, and also to take and use such land
33 along the course of said river, ponds, locks and ca-
34 nals as shall be necessary for the purposes hereinafter
35 expressed, acquiring the same title thereto as is ac-
36 quired by the public to lands appropriated for public
37 highways, paying a just compensation therefor, and
38 also for all damages caused to any lands by means of
39 flowing occasioned by any of the said canals, locks,

40 dams or other works erected or made by said company,
41 as hereinafter provided.

Sec. 2. When the said corporation cannot agree
2 with any other corporation or individual over or
3 through whose lands any of the aforesaid works may
4 be constructed or which may be damaged by flowing
5 occasioned by any of said dams, canals, locks or other
6 works, then in that case, the damages shall be esti-
7 mated by three disinterested arbiters to be agreed up-
8 on by the parties; or if they cannot agree upon such
9 arbiters, then in that case the district court for the
10 county in which any of such lands lie, upon the ap-
11 plication of either party, and on due notice to the
12 adverse party, shall cause the damages to be ascer-
13 tained by a committee of three disinterested persons
14 to be appointed by said court, whose duty shall be
15 to view the premises, estimate the damages, and make
16 report thereof to said court; and if the same be not
17 objected to, it may be approved, and shall be final as
18 to the matter inquired of by said committee. But
19 if either party is dissatisfied with such report and
20 desires that the damages may be ascertained by
21 the verdict of a jury, said court may on such request
22 submit the question of damages and any other matter
23 of fact which may be raised by the pleadings or brief

24 statements of the parties, to a jury, to be empanneled
25 to try the cause, whose verdict shall be final on all such
26 matters of fact submitted to them; and on such trial
27 the report of the committee shall be *prima facie* evi-
28 dence of the amount of damages, but may be im-
29 peached by other evidence. And the notice to the
30 adverse party herein required shall be by causing him
31 to be served with an attested copy of such application,
32 fourteen days at least prior to the sitting of the court
33 at which such committee is to be moved for; and
34 such application may be filed in vacation in the clerk's
35 office of said court, whose duty shall be to issue an
36 order of notice thereon returnable to the next suc-
37 ceeding term thereof.

Sec. 3.   The said corporation may tender, either be-
2 fore or after such application to the court, a reasonable
3 compensation for damages, or tender a default there-
4 for; and if the final determination shall not exceed
5 the amount so tendered or named in such offer, all
6 costs arising, after such tender or offer, shall not bar
7 the party making it from showing that a less amount
8 or no damages at all have arisen or may arise to the
9 party making claim thereto. And the said court
10 shall have power to award execution for the amount
11 of damages when ascertained as aforesaid, and also

12 for costs to the party entitled thereto ; *provided also*,
13 that if the party objecting to the report of the com-
14 mittee shall not succeed in obtaining a verdict more
15 favorable to him, he shall pay the costs of such trial
16 to the adverse party.

Sec. 4. If any person or persons shall willfully and
2 maliciously take up, remove or injure any part of said
3 canal, dams, locks, sluices, or other works or append-
4 ages thereof, or divert the water from said canal or
5 locks or the streams supplying the same, such person
6 or persons for every such offense shall forfeit and pay
7 to said corporation treble damages, to be sued for in
8 a special action of the case and recovered in any
9 court of competent jurisdiction ; and shall be further
10 liable to indictment for such offense, and on convic-
11 tion thereof before the supreme judicial court, shall
12 be sentenced to fine or imprisonment at the discretion
13 of the court.

Sec. 5. A toll is hereby granted to said corporation
2 according to the rates following, viz : through all the
3 locks and canals which may be necessarily constructed
4 for the purposes heretofore expressed between the
5 head of the Seven Tree pond, in Union, and the
6 head of the tide in Warren, for all plank, boards,
7 joists, or other sawed stuff, in rafts or otherwise, forty

1*

8 cents for every thousand feet, board measure.   For
9 clapboards and staves per thousand, forty cents.   For
10 shingles per thousand, twenty cents.   For hard wood
11 and bark per cord, thirty cents.   For spruce, hemlock,
12 and other soft wood, twenty cents per cord.   For all
13 timber and masts, thirty cents per ton.   For all other
14 lumber, in proportion to the above rates.   For all
15 kinds of goods, wares or merchandise in boats or on
16 rafts, fifty cents per ton.   For lime casks or other bar-
17 rels, two cents each.   For lime, eight cents per cask.
18 For live stock, to wit: for cattle, twenty cents per
19 head; for sheep, calves or hogs, six cents each.   For
20 all passengers in freight boats or passage boats, six
21 cents each.   For all boats or rafts, twenty cents in
22 addition to the above.   Which toll shall commence
23 and become payable when the said river shall have
24 been made navigable for boats from Seven Tree pond
25 in Union to the head of the tide in Warren.   And
26 the said corporation shall have a lien upon the same
27 articles, and shall have the power to detain the same
28 for the toll aforesaid, until the same shall be paid;
29 and at the expiration of ten days from the time said
30 toll shall become due, may raise the same by public
31 or private sale of so much of said articles as will pay
32 the amount due for said toll, and the expenses for

33 collecting the same, or the corporation may sue for
34 and recover the same by an action of debt in any
35 court proper to try the same. And said corporation
36 may by their directors, establish and fix the rates of
37 toll for transportation on said canal and through said
38 locks which shall be constructed above said Seven
39 Tree pond and above said town of Union, in accord-
40 ance with the above rates and not to exceed the same
41 rate for the same number of locks; which when so
42 established shall be recoverable in the same manner
43 as herein provided. And they may also by their di-
44 rectors establish from time to time a less toll than is
45 herein provided, on any article or articles, and appor-
46 tion the toll among the several locks or sections of
47 said canal or waters; and also establish a proportional
48 toll on every article not herein enumerated.

SEC. 6. If said corporation shall not make and
2 complete said canal, locks and dams, so that the said
3 waters shall be navigable for boats from said Seven
4 Tree pond to the head of the tide in Warren, within
5 three years from the passage of this act, then this act
6 shall be void.

SEC. 7. Said corporation may build or purchase
2 and hold or sell such boats and rafts as they judge
3 best—to be propelled by steam or other power, for

4 the purpose of navigating said ponds and river, and
5 of conveying goods, merchandise and other property
6 and passengers in the same ; and for performing such
7 services, they shall have the right to demand and re-
8 ceive such sums as may have been agreed on by the
9 parties, or as may be just and reasonable, and may
10 establish such wharves, depots, and warehouses as
11 may be necessary for the convenient management of
12 their business aforesaid.

SEC. 8.   The capital stock of said corporation shall
2 consist of not less than fifty thousand nor more than
3 one hundred thousand dollars, to be divided into shares
4 of fifty dollars each.   And the immediate government
5 and direction of the affairs of said corporation shall
6 be vested in five, seven, nine or eleven directors,
7 who shall be chosen by the members of said corpora-
8 tion in the manner hereinafter provided, and shall hold
9 their offices until others shall have been duly elected
10 and qualified to take their places, a majority of whom
11 shall form a quorum for the transaction of business ;
12 and they shall elect one of their number to be presi-
13 dent of the board, who shall also be the president of
14 the corporation ; and said stockholders shall have au-
15 thority to choose a clerk, who shall be sworn to the
16 faithful discharge of his duty ; and also a treasurer

17 who shall give bonds to the corporation, with sureties,
18 to the satisfaction of the directors, for the faithful dis-
19 charge of his trust. Any three of the persons named
20 in the first section of this act may call the first meet-
21 ing of said corporation, by giving notice in any
22 newspaper printed in Thomaston, of the time, place,
23 and purposes of such meeting, at least ten days before
24 the time mentioned in such notice, at which meeting
25 a board of directors shall be chosen. The annual
26 meeting of the members of said corporation shall be
27 holden on the second Monday in January, or such
28 other day as shall be determined by the by-laws, at
29 such time and place as the directors for the time
30 being shall appoint, at which meetings, the directors
31 shall be chosen by ballot, each proprietor by himself
32 or proxy being entitled to as many votes as he holds
33 shares, provided however no person shall be entitled
34 to more than twenty votes, and the directors are here-
35 by authorized to call special meetings of the stock-
36 holders, whenever they deem it expedient and proper,
37 giving such notice as the corporation by their by-laws
38 shall direct.

SEC. 9. Every person who shall have subscribed for
2 the capital stock in said company shall be holden by
3 such subscription to pay to the directors or treasurer

4 of said company fifteen dollars on every share sub-
5 scribed for, at such time or times as the directors may
6 order, and thereafterwards further instalments or
7 assessments may be laid to an amount not exceeding
8 in the aggregate on each share said sum of fifty dol-
9 lars.

Sec. 10.   Said corporation shall be subject to the
2 laws now existing, and such as hereafter shall be made,
3 regulating the salmon, shad, and alewive fisheries on
4 Georges river.

Sec. 11.   This act shall be in force from and after
2, its approval.

STATE OF MAINE.

House of Representatives, June 22, 1846.

Ordered, That 350 copies of the foregoing Bill, reported from the committee on Interior Waters, be printed for the use of the Legislature.

SAMUEL BELCHER, *Clerk.*

STATE OF MAINE.

LAND OFFICE, June 18, 1846.

To the Speaker of the House of Representatives:

IN compliance with an order of the House of Representatives, dated yesterday, I have made a hasty examination of the books of this office and of the public documents relating to the subject of inquiry, and submit the following statements.

During the last ten years, the State of Maine has expended in making and repairing roads, $81,455 36, as follows, viz:—

Military road between Lincoln and Houlton,	14,108 73
Canada road between the N. line of Bingham's Kennebec purchase and Canada line,	3,200 00
Road leading from Blanchard to Moosehead Lake,	500 00
Road leading from Wilson to Moosehead Lake,	1,650 00
Road leading from the N. W. bay of Moosehead Lake to the Canada road,	3,556 63
Road leading from Houlton to township G, R. 2, on the Aroostook river,	845 83
Road leading from G, R. 2, to the Madawaska settlement on the St. John river,	4,997 60
Aroostook road leading from the military road to township No. 11, R. 5, on the Aroostook river,	44,662 92
Fish River road leading from No. 11, R. 5, to Fort Kent on the St. John river,	4,733 65

Wm. T. Johnson, Printer to the State

Machias road leading from No 11, R. 5, to township

   F, R. 2,   500 00

Houlton and Barring Road,   2,700 00

I cannot state definitely what amount Massachusetts has expended, but find satisfactory evidence that she has expended during the same time, $58,950 80.

The State of Maine owns thirty-six townships and parts of seven other townships of the divided lands. How much of the divided lands is now held by Massachusetts, I am unable to state, but she has probably about half as much as Maine.

Of the undivided lands, there are fifty two townships and six parts of townships, unsold; and the unsurveyed territory is estimated to be equal to about seventy townships of six miles square, or about one million, six hundred thousand acres.

The receipts for timber, for the ten years past have been, by the State of Maine, $348,740 57.

The amount received by Massachusetts not known.

The order directs me to give the value of the lands. In regard to the larger portions of the land, it has not been so thoroughly examined as to enable me to form an opinion of its value, and a mere speculative opinion would be neither satisfactory nor useful to the Legislature. I hope therefore, that I may be excused from the expression of any opinion at present, on this subject.

The question proposed in regard to the policy of Massachusetts, is one of difficult solution. She undoubtedly regards her lands in Maine, merely as a source of revenue, and by the articles of separation, she has secured to herself the protection of her property, without its being subject to taxation. Our courts are open to her, as well as the courts of the United States within our State. Her property enjoys the benefit of government and we look in vain for any provision enabling us to call on her to contribute any portion of the expenses of the government that protects it. It is easy to come to the conclusion that we made a very poor bargain, but not easy to devise a remedy.

It is presumed that the Legislature of Massachusetts know little of the situation of that part of Maine, where their lands are situated, nor of the effect of holding large tracts of land which contribute nothing towards public improvement. Looking upon those lands merely as a source of revenue, she has contributed to the making of such roads as would most clearly enhance the value of her lands and timber; and she has been benefited without doubt, already in her lands and timber sold, to a large amount beyond her expenditures.

The Agent of Massachusetts has recently directed the expenditure of fifteen hundred dollars on roads over the public lands in Aroostook county, provided this State expends an equal sum, and declines doing any more this year, not because a larger expenditure would not be profitable, but because of the difficulty in making a Massachusetts Legislature understand that an expenditure of money here, will increase her resources.

Whatever may appear to us objectionable in the policy of Massachusetts, seems naturally to have grown out of the different relations of the two parties to the lands in question, and I know of no remedy unless Massachusetts will consent to make a new contract.

LEVI BRADLEY, *Land Agent.*

STATE OF MAINE.

In House of Representatives,
June 22, 1846.

Ordered, That 500 copies of the foregoing communication be printed for the use of the Legislature.

SAMUEL BELCHER, *Clerk.*

STATE OF MAINE.

RESOLVE providing for an amendment of the Constitution, in relation to the choice of Representatives to the Legislature.

Resolved, Two thirds of both branches of the Leg-
2 islature concurring, that the Constitution of this State
3 shall be amended in the fifth section of the first part
4 of the fourth article, by striking out the words "and
5 the same proceedings shall be had at every future
6 meeting until an election shall have been effected,"
7 and inserting the words, and the same proceedings
8 shall be had at said meeting, and the person having
9 the largest number of votes shall be elected. But in
10 case the highest candidates have an equal number of
11 votes, the same proceedings shall be had at every fu-
12 ture meeting until some person shall have been elect-
13 ed by obtaining the largest number of votes as afore-
14 said.

Wm. T. Johnson, Printer to the State.

Resolved, That the aldermen of cities, the selectmen of
2 the several towns, and the assessors of the several plan-
3 tations in this State, are hereby empowered and direct-
4 ed to notify the inhabitants of their respective cities,
5 towns and plantations, in manner prescribed by law, at
6 the annual meeting in September next to give in their
7 votes upon the amendment proposed in the foregoing
8 resolve; and the question shall be, shall the Constitu-
9 tion be amended as proposed in the foregoing resolve,
10 providing that in case no person is elected represent-
11 ative to the Legislature at the first trial by a majority
12 of votes, that the person having the largest number
13 of votes at the second trial shall be elected. But in
14 case the highest candidates have an equal number of
15 votes, the same proceedings shall be had at every
16 future meeting until some person shall have been
17 elected; and the inhabitants of said cities, towns and
18 plantations, shall vote by ballot on said question, those
19 in favor of said amendment expressing it by the word
20 "yes" upon their ballots, and those opposed to the
21 amendment expressing it by the word "no" upon
22 their ballots; and the ballots shall be received, sorted,
23 counted and declared, in open ward, town and plan-
24 tation meetings, and lists shall be made out of the
25 votes by the aldermen, selectmen and assessors, and

26 clerks of the several cities, towns and plantations,
27 and returned to the office of the secretary of state,
28 in the same manner as votes for senators, and the
29 governor and council shall count the same and make
30 return thereof to the next Legislature, and if a ma-
31 jority of the votes are in favor of said amendment,
32 the Constitution shall be amended accordingly.

Resolved, That the secretary of state shall prepare
2 and furnish the several cities, towns and plantations
3 blank returns in conformity to the resolves, accom-
4 panied with a copy of these resolves.

STATE OF MAINE.

In Senate, June 23, 1846.

Ordered, That 350 copies of the foregoing Resolve be printed for the use of the Legislature.

DANIEL T. PIKE, *Secretary.*

PETITION.

To the Honorable Senate and House of Representatives of the State of Maine in Legislature assembled.

To you, gentlemen, next to Divine Providence, we should look for protection and safety. Inasmuch as you have been appointed to legislate for the benefit and welfare of the State of Maine, which, we think, includes the whole population; and among these, one half we suppose are females, and a majority of the whole population may reasonably be supposed to be children. Now, gentlemen, we pray you to interpose your influence in behalf of the whole population, and *more especially* on account of those not directly represented in your honorable body, viz: women and children, and save us from the destructive influence of intemperance. Did you but realize the grief, fear and torment that await many families in this State on the arrival of a husband or father intoxicated, we think you would listen to this our earnest prayer to you for relief. We know there are a vast number of mothers within this State who have no other hope but in the reformation of their deluded husbands. Those poor mothers are cast down too low to petition, or even hope for relief; they are too broken hearted to think of better days; they have not the wherewith to clothe themselves; their children are half starved and half naked; they cannot send them to school, to meeting, or to any other place of mental improvement. Their lot is a hard one indeed. We will not pretend to describe the various steps that brought them down, but *rum* was the "*Alpha*,"

Wm. T. Johnson, Printer to the State.

and will be the "*Omega*" of their misery, unless the powerful arm
of government interpose in their behalf. Gentlemen, you all know
of some cases of the kind which cannot be exaggerated by a
description made on paper. O ! how it pains the heart of a mother
to know that he whom she has ever looked to for *protection* and
support is senseless and prostrate in the gutter, or a raving maniac
at a grog shop : and how our destinies are linked together ; all of
us have relations or acquaintances more or less involved in the general
ruin that threatens to prostrate the best energies of the State,
and utterly to annihilate thousands of families and their descendants
for all time to come—*all of whom might be saved ;* and *you,* gentlemen,
might save them ! We therefore pray you to abolish the
sale and *use* of ardent spirits in this State by your votes ! and make
it a penal transgression to *sell* or *use* it as a *beverage.* The absolute
necessity of industry, frugality and economy in this cold country
calls loudly for such a reformation. The salvation of the *soul* calls
still *louder* for such a reformation. The present policy of the nation
by which we shall doubtless be frequently involved in war
with other nations, admonishes us, as a State, to abandon the use
of that *maddening* stimulant.

  Maine like all other countries will be wealthy and respected if
she is temperate ; if not, whole families of "*Maine folks*" may
be seen ere long traveling in misery in a foreign land, as the Canadian
is found here. Gentlemen, are you not interested, either
personally or relatively, in this reform ? Will fifty years pass by
and no poor, ragged, worthless *inebriate* stammer out his anathema
on his ancestors by saying, "my father was a senator in '46," or
" my uncle was a representative," " or my grandfather was a
governor " ? We beseech you again, in behalf of all living—and
further, in behalf of your children yet unborn, to stamp an *indelible*
annihilation on the infernal trade. Let this " first summer session"
crown themselves with unfading laurels ; let the songs of all future
time chant a requiem to their memory when they are blessed in heaven
; let them forever enjoy the highest seat in the pantheon of eternal
repose. Then grant our prayer. O ! give the daughters of this
State kind and sober husbands ; give them dutiful and temperate

sons, and fill their hearts with joy, and the blessing of millions of maids and mothers will pour upon you like a golden shower, and the "first summer session" be a lullaby of their cradle through all time to come.

LYDIA MERRILL,
JAMES MERRILL.

Whitefield, Lincoln Co., June 15, 1846.

STATE OF MAINE.

House of Representatives, June 23, 1846.

Ordered, That 300 copies of the foregoing Petition be printed for the use of the House.

SAMUEL BELCHER, *Clerk.*

REPORT.

IN SENATE, June 24, 1846.

THE Joint Standing Committee on Education, to whom was referred so much of the governor's message as relates to the subject of education; also the memorial of Amos Brown, Philip Eastman, Alpheus S. Packard and Samuel P. Benson, a committee appointed by a State convention of the friends of education, praying that a board of education may be established by the Legislature —have had these subjects under consideration, and ask leave to

REPORT:

The emphatic language of the governor's message on the subject of public education and the recommendation of improvements suggested by him, are fully in accordance with the tenor of many other executive communications to the Legislature. In repeated instances, under former administrations, the executive has proposed and recommended a comprehensive and systematic method of increasing the usefulness of common schools, by the establishment of a board of education

These repeated executive recommendations must be supposed to rest in a very considerable degree, upon a general and popular conviction, that the school system as now established by the constitution and laws of the State, is susceptible of higher practical development and fitness for the wants of the people, than have yet been attained.

The memorial before the committee proceeded from a very re-

Wm. T. Johnson, Printer to the State.

sponsible assemblage of the friends of education, and expresses with great clearness and urgency, the judgment of the convention, and of the memorialists themselves, upon the necessity and the advantage of establishing a board of education at the present time.

A majority of the States of New England, have already established some general supervisory system for the great department and interest of public instruction. The State of New York has long been distinguished for her wise and enlightened central administration of her public school affairs. There may be reason to apprehend, that unless the State of Maine shall speedily adopt the examples thus placed before her, she may be the last of the northern States in entering upon a policy of improvement, in respect to this great interest, where the genius of her constitution and the absolute necessities of her people might well have placed her among the foremost.

It is not only the force of example and of authorised recommendation, that has induced the committee to advise the establishment of a board of education in this State, but a deliberate survey of the actual condition of things among ourselves, has brought them to a unanimous conviction of its propriety, its necessity and its practicability.

The state of public sentiment is so far propitious for the attempt, that at least, it may be very difficult to predict a more favorable opportunity than the present session, for an undertaking so worthy, so long expected, and so certain to create and increase new confidence and new hope.

The duties of a board of education are simple in theory and practice. The conclusions of the committee upon that head, are succinctly stated in the draft of a bill which they have unanimously agreed to report. The committee have carefully abstained from entrusting to the board any executive or legislative power over the subjects or persons within the scope of their action. The existing common school system will continue subject only to the control of the Legislature, under the constitution, and its local administration will be in the hands of the local authorities. The duties of the board will be to investigate, to reflect, to devise and to recommend; to impart information, to exhibit models and means of improvement, to encourage parents and teachers, to unfold and quicken and satisfy the capacities and the aspirations of the young, and to enliven the whole existing system with new energy and spirit.

In regard to the method of electing the board of education, the committee suggest a plan, which they are satisfied, is both practical and highly appropriate. Considerations which might otherwise be embarassing, are removed by placing the election, as strictly as possible, within the popular control, and by requiring all the sections of the State to co-operate in the choice. Deriving their powers thus directly from the people, the members of the board will be in the closest communication with those persons to whom the inhabitants of the several towns entrust their local school interests, and the labors of the board will immediately react upon the several parts of the State which they represent.

With these explanations, the committee present the bill which is submitted with this report.

E. M. THURSTON, *Chairman.*

STATE OF MAINE.

IN THE YEAR OF OUR LORD ONE THOUSAND EIGHT HUNDRED AND
FORTY-SIX.

AN ACT to establish a Board of Education.

Be it enacted by the Senate and House of Represent-
2 *atives in Legislature assembled,* as follows:

3 SECTION 1. A board of education is hereby estab-
4 lished in this State, to consist of one member from
5 each county; who shall be elected in the manner
6 hereinafter provided.

SEC. 2. The superintending school committees of
2 the several towns in each county, are hereby required
3 to assemble, annually, at the times and places herein-
4 after designated, and when so assembled in each
5 county, to choose, by the majority of those present,
6 one person, a resident of the county, who shall be
7 the member of the board of education for such coun-
8 ty, and shall hold his office until a successor is duly
9 chosen and qualified. The county meetings afore-
10 said shall be organized by the choice of a chairman

1*

11 and clerk, who shall severally certify the election of
12 the member chosen, and transmit one copy of such
13 certificate to the secretary of state, and one copy to
14 the person chosen.

Sec. 3.   A quorum of such county meeting shall
2 consist of one or more members of the superintend-
3 ing school committees from a majority of the towns
4 in each county; but if any town or city shall have a
5 superintending school committee consisting of more
6 than five members, such committee shall appoint del-
7 egates from their own number, not exceeding five,
8 which delegates shall exercise the duties and powers
9 herein provided.

Sec. 4.   The county meetings aforesaid shall be held
2 at the shire town in each county, and at Wiscasset in
3 the county of Lincoln, at the times following;
4 York; third Tuesday of September;
5 Cumberland; Friday next after the the third Tuesday
6   of September;
7 Oxford; fourth Tuesday of September;
8 Franklin; first Tuesday of October;
9 Somerset; Friday next after the first Tuesday of Oc-
10   tober;
11 Piscataquis; second Tuesday in October;

12 Penobscot; Friday next after the second Tuesday in
13   October;
14 Aroostook; Third Tuesday in October;
15 Washington; Friday next after the third Tuesday in
16   October;
17 Hancock; fourth Tuesday in October;
18 Waldo; first Tuesday in November;
19 Lincoln; Friday next after the first Tuesday in No-
20   vember;
21 Kennebec; second Tuesday in November.
22   And each meeting shall be held at eleven o'clock
23 on the days aforesaid.

    Sec. 5. The members of the board of education
2 thus chosen, shall hold their first meeting on the first
3 Wednesday of May in each year, at Augusta, and
4 may meet thereafter, at such times and places as they
5 shall by vote determine. They shall appoint a chair-
6 man and clerk from their own number. Five mem-
7 bers shall be a quorum for the transaction of business.
8 In case of any vacancy in the board, or if in any
9 county an election shall not have been effected at the
10 county meeting herein provided, the members of the
11 board actually elected and in office, may fill such va-
12 cancy and supply such failure, for any county where
13 the same may occur.

Sec. 6.　The board of education first chosen, shall
2 meet for organization, and for the choice of the sec-
3 retary hereinafter provided, on the third Wednesday
4 of December next, at Augusta, and shall hold their
5 offices until the first Wednesday of May, 1848, and
6 the term of each new board of education, thereafter
7 shall commence on the first Wednesday of May, an-
8 nually.

Sec. 7.　The board of education shall, at their first
2 meeting in each year, elect by ballot, one person, who
3 shall be styled the secretary of the board of education,
4 and shall hold his office for one year, and until an-
5 nother shall be chosen.　But the secretary first elect-
6 ed, shall hold his office, until the first Wednesday of
7 May 1848.　In case of a vacancy in the office of sec-
8 retary, it shall be the duty of the board, as soon as
9 may be, after the occurrence of such vacancy, to elect
10 another for the remainder of the year.

Sec. 8.　The members of the board, and the secre-
2 tary, shall severally be sworn to the faithful perform-
3 ance of their respective duties, before any magistrate
4 authorized to qualify civil officers.

Sec. 9.　It shall be the duty of the board of educa-
2 tion, and especially of the secretary to devote them-
3 selves assiduously to examine the practical operation

4 of those parts of the constitution and laws of the State,
5 which provide for public education, and the diffusion
6 of knowledge among the people. In pursuance of
7 this object, the secretary shall, as far as practicable,
8 attend the county meetings herein provided for the
9 election of members of the board, and communicate
10 with the superintending school committees there as-
11 sembled, and with teachers and the friends of public
12 instruction generally. And the board of education,
13 directly, or through the agency of the secretary, are
14 authorized and required to collect and disseminate in-
15 formation in regard to the location and construction
16 of school houses, on the arrangement of school dis-
17 tricts and the use of the best school apparatus, to
18 consult with superintending school committees and
19 school agents on the best and cheapest method of in-
20 troducing uniform school books, and on the practica-
21 bility and expediency of establishing school district
22 libraries, to inquire and report upon the advantages
23 of normal schools, or schools for the education of
24 teachers, to consider the best methods of aiding and
25 promoting education in the new settlements of the
26 State, to devise improvements in teaching the branch-
27 es of instruction now pursued in the common schools,
28 and for the introduction of such other branches of

29 useful knowledge as may be practicable, and general-
30 ly to consult with school committees, school agents,
31 and other authorities and inhabitants of the State, for
32 the purpose of ascertaining, recommending and pro-
33 moting all such improvements in the common school
34 system as may be consistent with the constitution and
35 laws of the State, and the welfare of its inhabitants.
36 And it shall be the duty of the board in the month of
37 April, annually, to prepare a report of their doings,
38 and the results of their investigations during the pre-
39 ceeding year, which shall be presented to the gov-
40 ernor, and by him laid before the Legislature.

SEC. 10. The secretary of state is hereby author-
2 ized, under the direction of the governor and council,
3 to furnish such blank forms for returns respecting
4 schools, as the board of education may recommend.
5 And all such returns may be addressed to the secre-
6 tary of state.

SEC. 11. The members of the board of education
2 shall each receive for their travel from their several
3 places of residence to the place of their several meet-
4 ings, ten cents per mile, and one dollar for each day's
5 attendance at any meeting, but not exceeding in the
6 aggregate thirty days in each year.

SEC. 12. The secretary of the board of education

2 shall receive an annual salary of one thousand dollars,
3 payable in quarterly payments.

SEC. 13. The board of education, at such times as
2 they may appoint, shall make up their pay roll for
3 travel and attendance, which, when examined and
4 allowed by the governor and council, shall be paid to
5 them, out of any money in the treasury not otherwise
6 appropriated.

SEC. 14. For the purpose of providing for the or-
2 ganization of the first board of education, the gov-
3 ernor, with the advice of council, is hereby author-
4 ized to appoint, before the first day of August next, a
5 provisional school agent for the State, whose duty it
6 shall be to communicate with the superintending
7 school committees of the several towns respecting the
8 duties required by this act, to make such arrange-
9 ments as may be necessary for the first county meet-
10 ings herein provided, and to obtain, from the returns
11 now in the office of the secretary of state, and from
12 other sources, such information respecting the actual
13 condition of common schools within this State, as may
14 be usefully laid before the county meetings, and the
15 board of education, at their first organization, to ena-
16 ble them to enter without delay upon the discharge of
17 their duties. The duties of such agent shall continue

18 until the board of education is organized; and he
19 shall receive therefor such compensation as shall be
20 allowed by the governor and council, not exceeding
21 two hundred and fifty dollars.

Sec. 15. This act shall take effect from and after
2 its approval by the Governor.

STATE OF MAINE.

In Senate, June 24, 1846.

Ordered, That 1,000 copies of the foregoing Report and accompanying Bill, be printed for the use of the Legislature.

DANIEL T. PIKE, *Secretary.*

STATE OF MAINE.

IN THE YEAR OF OUR LORD ONE THOUSAND EIGHT HUNDRED AND FORTY-SIX.

AN ACT relating to hawkers and pedlers.

Be it enacted by the Senate and House of Representatives in Legislature assembled, as follows:

SECTION 1. Every hawker, pedler or petty chap-
2 man, or other person, not having been five years a
3 citizen of this State, who shall hereafter travel from
4 town to town or place to place, on foot or with a
5 horse, carriage, or otherwise, carrying to sell or ex-
6 posing to sale, any goods, wares or merchandise, shall
7 forfeit a sum not exceeding fifty dollars nor less than
8 twenty dollars, to be recovered by complaint or indict-
9 ment, and all articles and merchandise aforesaid, one
10 half to the town where the offence is committed, and
11 the other half to the prosecutor.

SEC. 2. Any justice, on complaint made to him,
2 may cause the arrest of the party accused, and the

Wm. T Johnson, Printer to the State

3 seizure of such goods, and detain the same until trial;
4 and in case of conviction of the offender, the same
5 shall be decreed forfeited to the uses aforesaid and
6 sold in the same manner as goods seized on execution
7 for debt.

    SEC. 3.   Any person who shall hereafter travel from
2 town to town, or place to place, in the State, for the
3 purpose of vending any goods, wares or merchandise,
4 shall first obtain a license therefor, from the county
5 commissioners of the county in which he resides, and
6 pay therefor, a certain sum for the use of the State.
7 to wit: every person who shall travel on foot for the
8 purpose aforesaid, shall pay the sum of ten dollars.
9 Every person who shall travel with any carriage drawn
10 by one animal, for the purpose aforesaid, shall pay the
11 sum of fifteen dollars; and if drawn by two horses or
12 other animals, twenty dollars.   Any person who shall
13 transport or convey any goods or merchandise by
14 water, in any boat or other water craft, for the pur-
15 pose of vending the same as aforesaid, shall first ob-
16 tain a license therefor, as above specified, and shall
17 pay the sum of ten dollars for the use of the State:
18 and all licenses granted as aforesaid, shall expire in
19 one year from the time of granting the same. *Pro-*
20 *vided* that every person who shall travel as aforesaid,

21 for the purpose of vending any jewelry or playing
22 cards shall be subject to all the penalties and liabili-
23 ties provided in the first and second sections of this
24 act.

SEC. 4. No person shall receive license under the
2 provisions of this act, until he shall have proved to
3 the satisfaction of the county commissioners, that he
4 sustains a good moral character; that he has been
5 five years a citizen.of this State, and that he has re-
6 sided in some city, town, or plantation in the county
7 where he shall apply for license as aforesaid, for the
8 term of one year next preceding the time of such
9 application.

SEC. 5. Any person who shall transgress any of the
2 provisions of the third section of this act, shall forfeit
3 and pay a sum not exceeding double the amount re-
4 quired to be paid for such license as he is bound to
5 obtain by the provisions of said preceding section;
6 and all fines and forfeitures for the transgression of
7 the foregoing provisions or requirements, shall be re-
8 covered in an action for debt, before a justice of the
9 peace, in any county where the offense may be com-
10 mitted, by any person who may prosecute for the
11 same, for the use of the county where such offense
12 shall be committed.

Sec. 6.   Any person who shall travel for the pur-
2 poses aforesaid, shall exhibit his license at any and all
3 times, when required to do so by any justice of the
4 peace, or any constable of any city, town or planta-
5 tion, and a refusal to exhibit such license when re-
6 quired as aforesaid, shall be deemed as evidence of
7 not having such license; and if prosecuted after such
8 refusal to show his license, the production of his
9 license at the time of trial shall not avail him in the
10 defense of such prosecution, and the person so refus-
11 ing, shall be dealt with as is provided in the fifth sec-
12 tion of this act.

-Sec. 7.   The carriages, goods, wares and merchan-
2 dise of any such person as is described in the third
3 section of this act, who refuses to exhibit his license
4 as provided in this act, may be seized by warrant
5 from any justice of the peace, and detained until such
6 justice shall decide whether such person is liable to
7 any fine imposed by this act, and until such fine, if
8 any, shall be paid.

Sec. 8.   Every person who shall apply to the county
2 commissioners for the purpose of obtaining a license
3 as aforesaid, shall present to said commissioners a
4 certificate of his good moral character, signed by the
5 selectmen of the town where he has his residence, as

6 aforesaid, which shall be attached to the license
7 granted.

SEC. 9.   Nothing in this act shall be construed to
2 prevent any citizen of this State from selling any fish,
3 fruit or provisions or from vending any farming uten-
4 sils or other articles manufactured in this State—
5 playing cards and jewelry excepted.

SEC. 10.   The act entitled an act relating to hawk-
2 ers and pedlars, approved March twenty-third, in the
3 year of our Lord one thousand eight hundred and
4 forty-three—and all other acts and parts of acts, in-
5 consistent with the provisions of this act, are hereby
6 repealed.

STATE OF MAINE.

HOUSE OF REPRESENTATIVES, July 1, 1846.

Ordered, That 350 copies of the foregoing bill, reported by Mr. Gould of Wilton, from the Joint Select Committee, to which was referred sundry petitions praying for the suppression of hawking and peddling, be printed for the use of the Legislature.

SAMUEL BELCHER, *Clerk.*

STATE OF MAINE.

IN THE YEAR OF OUR LORD ONE THOUSAND EIGHT HUNDRED AND
FORTY-SIX.

AN ADDITIONAL ACT relating to the Kennebec Log Driving Company.

Be it enacted by the Senate and House of Represent-
atives in Legislature assembled, as follows;

SECTION 1. Whenever the directors of the Kenne-
2 bec Log Driving Company shall judge it for the in-
3 terest of the owners of logs and other timber remain-
4 ing in the booms or in any place exposed to loss, after
5 the first day of October in any year, to collect and
6 deposit in suitable and convenient places and proper-
7 ly secure the same; they are hereby authorized so to
8 collect and deposit such logs and timber thus situated,
9 and to use all reasonable care safely to keep the same,
10 until removed by the owners thereof, or are otherwise
11 disposed of in the manner provided in this act.

SEC. 2. Upon all logs and other timber thus col-

Wm. T. Johnson, Printer to the State.

2 lected and deposited, the directors shall assess the ex-
3 pense actually incurred thereon, with such additional
4 sums as may be deemed necessary to cover necessary
5 future expenditures upon them while in their charge;
6 and the method of proceeding for the collection of
7 assessments thus made, shall be the same as provided
8 by law in relation to assessments for driving logs upon
9 Kennebec River; and said company shall have a lien
10 upon the logs and other timber for the full payment
11 of all expenses; or the treasurer may recover such
12 assessments, and all other assessments made by virtue
13 of an act relating to said company approved March
14 third, A. D. 1843, in an action of debt in the name of
15 the Kennebec Log Driving Company, in any court
16 competent to try the same; and no action shall abate
17 by reason of all the owners not being joined as defend-
18 ants; and the owners of all logs and other timber thus
19 deposited, upon the full payment of the sums thus as-
20 sessed upon their respective marks, shall be at liberty
21 to take the logs and other timber thus deposited be-
22 longing to them respectively.

  Sec. 3.   If any logs or other timber shall remain in
2 the depositories upon the first day May next ensuing,
3 upon which the assessments have not been paid, the
4 directors may immediately thereafter advertise for

5 three weeks successively in some newspaper printed
6 in each of the towns of Augusta, Gardiner and Bath,
7 notifying all owners of logs and other timber, deposit-
8 ed under this act, to remove the same within thirty
9 days from said first day of May ; and all logs not re-
10 moved prior to that time, and upon which the assess-
11 ments have not been paid, may be sold at public auc-
12 tion, and the proceeds thereof, after deducting all un-
13 paid assessments and necessary expenses of sale, shall
14 be paid upon demand by the treasurer of the company
15 to the owners of logs and other timber thus sold, and
16 all logs and other timber not removed by the owners,
17 by virtue of this act, remaining in said depositories
18 upon the first day of June, shall be at the expense of
19 the owners thereof.

Sec. 4. A committee shall be chosen at each annual
2 meeting, who shall be authorized, whenever they shall
3 judge the interest of the log owners to require it, to
4 collect and secure all logs and other timber which
5 may drift below the Chops (so called) on said river,
6 and for all expenses incurred by said committee, a
7 lien is hereby created upon all logs and other timber
8 so secured, and said committee shall be authorized to
9 assess upon all such logs and timber, a tax sufficient
10 to pay such expense ; and if such tax is not paid or

11 secured, and the logs removed prior to the first day of
12 August, they may proceed to sell at public auction, in
13 Bath, all such logs and other timber not previously
14 removed and the assessments thereon paid ; and prior
15 to proceeding to such sale, notice thereof shall be
16 published three weeks successively, in some newspa-
17 per printed in each of the towns of Augusta, Gardiner
18 and Bath, and the proceeds of such sales, after de-
19 ducting all necessary charges, shall be paid by the
20 treasurer of said company, on demand, to the owners
21 of such logs and other timber thus sold.

SEC. 5. So much of the eighth section of an act
2 relating to this company, approved March the third, A.
3 D. 1843, as relates to the publishing a list of marks
4 of logs, with the amount assessed upon each mark, is
5 hereby repealed, and in lieu thereof, the treasurer
6 shall be required to give notice of the time and place
7 of sale of all logs referred to in said section, without
8 giving each mark separately, in all other respects
9 complying with the provisions of said section.

SEC. 6. The fourth and twentieth sections of the
2 act relating to the Kennebec Log Driving Company,
3 approved March third, A. D. 1843, and also the whole
4 of the act extending the authority of this company,
5 approved March seventeenth, A. D. 1845, are hereby

6 repealed; and this act shall take effect and be in
7 force, from and after the date of its approval by
8 the governor.

STATE OF MAINE.

House of Representatives, July 2, 1846.

Ordered, That 350 copies of the foregoing bill reported from the Committee on Interior Waters, be printed for the use of the Legislature.

SAMUEL BELCHER, *Clerk*.

STATE OF MAINE:

IN THE YEAR OF OUR LORD ONE THOUSAND EIGHT HUNDRED AND FORTY-SIX.

AN ACT to promote the improvement of the navigation of the Penobscot river.

Be it enacted by the Senate and House of Represent-
2 *atives in Legislature assembled,* as follows:

3 SECTION 1. William Moor and Daniel Moor, jr.,
4 their associates and assigns are hereby authorized
5 to improve the navigation of the Penobscot river
6 above Oldtown—and for this purpose are authorized
7 to deepen the channel thereof—to cut down and
8 remove any gravel or ledge bars, rocks or other
9 obstructions in the bed thereof—to erect in the
10 bed, upon the shore or bank of said river, suitable
11 dams and locks with booms, piers, abutments, break-
12 waters and other erections to protect the same—to
13 build upon the shore or bank of said river any canal

Wm T Johnson, Printer to the State

14 or canals to connect the navigable parts of said river,
15 or (in case it should be deemed the preferable mode
16 of improvement) any rail road for the like purpose.

SEC. 2.   They are authorized to take and hold so
2 much land along the bank and shore of said river
3 or in the bed thereof as may be necessary for the lo-
4 cation, construction and repair of their aforesaid im-
5 provements, and to take and use the gravel, stone and
6 earth upon the land so taken—and the damages for
7 the real estate so taken when not agreed upon by the
8 parties, shall be ascertained and determined by the
9 County Commissioners of Penobscot County, under
10 the same limitations and restrictions as are by law
11 provided in case of damage by laying out highways,
12 and the damage for flowage created by any dam erec-
13 ted for the above specified purpose, shall be ascer-
14 tained and determined in the same manner as is pro-
15 vided in the one hundred and twenty-sixth chapter of
16 the Revised Statutes, for flowage created by mill
17 dams—Provided, that no claims for damage shall be
18 sustained unless made and prosecuted within two
19 years from the time of the alleged injury.

SEC. 3.   The above grant is upon the condition,
2 that the said William Moor and Daniel Moor, Jr.,
3 their associates, and assigns, shall within five years

4 from the date hereof, improve the navigation of said
5 river from Oldtown to Piscataquis Falls, and from
6 Piscataquis Falls to the foot of the Five Island rips,
7 and shall build and run over said route a steamboat,
8 and shall within said five years, or within a reasonable
9 time afterwards, build a canal and lock round said
10 falls, or a railroad to connect the route above with the
11 route below said falls.   •

SEC. 4. If said William Moor and Daniel Moor,
2 jr., their associates and assigns shall perform the
3 conditions of this grant as contained in the last
4 preceding section, the sole right of navigating said
5 river by boats propelled by steam, from said Oldtown
6 as far up as they shall render the same navigable, is
7 hereby granted to them for the term of twenty-five
8 years from and after the completion of the improve-
9 ment, as provided in the third section of this act, pro-
10 vided, however, that the said William Moor and Dan-
11 iel Moor, jr., their associates and assigns, in the exer-
12 cise of said right of navigation, or in the erection of
13 works they may make to promote the same, shall not
14 obstruct the running of any logs, rafts or lumber
15 down said river, which are usually driven or floated
16 therein.

SEC. 5. The said William Moor and Daniel Moor,

2 jr., their associates and assigns, are hereby created
3 a body corporate, by the name of the *Penobscot*
4 *River Navigation Company*, with the powers inci-
5 dent to corporations described and defined in the
6 seventy-sixth chapter of the Revised Statutes, and at
7 common law, provided that they shall at any time
8 during the continuance of the above grant, elect by
9 the vote of a majority in interest, and proceed to or-
10 ganise under and according to the provisions of said
11 chapter of the Revised Statutes; and if they shall so
12 organise, they shall not be subject to the operation
13 of the twenty-third section of said seventy-sixth chap-
14 ter of the Revised Statutes.

STATE OF MAINE.

HOUSE OF REPRESENTATIVES, }
July 2, 1846. }

Ordered, That 350 copies of this bill, reported by the Committee on Interior Waters, be printed for the use of the Legislature.

SAMUEL BELCHER, *Clerk.*

STATE OF MAINE.

IN THE YEAR OF OUR LORD ONE THOUSAND EIGHT HUNDRED AND
FORTY-SIX.

AN ACT to incorporate the Mousam Navigation Company

Be it enacted by the Senate and House of Represent-
2 *atives in Legislature assembled,* as follows:

SECTION 1.   Daniel Remich, William B. Sewall,
2 William Lord, Jabez Smith, Barnabas Palmer, James
3 Osborn, John Osborn, William Hacket, Joseph Tit-
4 comb and Wm. F. Lord, their associates, success-
5 ors and assigns, are hereby constituted a body politic
6 and corporate by the name of the Mousam Navigation
7 Company, and by that name shall have all the powers,
8 privileges and immunities which are or may be neces-
9 sary to carry into effect the objects and purposes of
10 their association as herein set forth, and subject to
11 such liabilities and restrictions as are incident by law
12 to similar corporations, except as herein after express-

Wᵐ T Johnson, Printer to the State.

13 ed, and said corporation is hereby authorized to build
14 a dam across the present river or canal, so called, as
15 it now runs, at any place between the mouth thereof
16 and the head of tide water, and to turn the present
17 course of said river so that it may run into the sea at
18 any place between the present mouth of the river and
19 its mouth as it formerly run ; to cut off any bends at
20 any point on said river, or to straighten it in any part
21 thereof; and to build any other dam or dams or raise
22 any embankments on the present river which may be
23 deemed necessary to promote the objects authorized
24 by this act; to build wharves, piers, monuments,
25 buoys, or any other necessary fixtures at such points
26 as said corporation may consider expedient; and for
27 this purpose the said corporation shall have the right
28 to take and hold so much of the land or other real
29 estate of private persons, as may be necessary for the
30 improvements contemplated and provided for by this
31 act. And in case the corporation cannot agree with
32 the owners of the estate thus taken, they shall pay
33 such damages as shall be ascertained and assessed by
34 the county commissioners for the county of York.
35 And no application to said commissioners to estimate
36 said damages shall be sustained, unless made within
37 three years from the time of taking such land or es-
38 tate.

SEC. 2. The capital stock of said company shall
2 consist at first of twenty five hundred dollars, with
3 power to increase the same to twenty-five thousand
4 dollars when the company shall find it expedient.
5 The stock shall be divided into shares of twenty-five
6 dollars each, and no assessments shall be made on any
7 share beyond that sum. The immediate government
8 and direction of the affairs of said company shall be
9 vested in such a number of directors as may be deter-
10 mined at the first meeting of the corporation. And
11 said directors shall elect one of their number to be
12 president of the board, who shall also be president of
13 the corporation. And they shall also appoint the
14 clerk of their board and of the company, and also
15 treasurer, and any other officer, agent or agents they
16 may find necessary for the convenient management
17 of the concerns of the company.

SEC. 3. A toll is hereby granted and established for
2 the sole benefit of said corporation, upon all boats and
3 vessels or other craft of ten tons and upwards, which
4 may enter said river after the new entrance shall be
5 opened for navigation. And said company may im-
6 pose and collect a reasonable wharfage upon all such
7 vessels as may improve, use or occupy their wharves
8 or places of landing.

SEC. 4. The corporation hereby established shall
2 have the exclusive right of steam navigation on said
3 river for the term of thirty years, from the time the
4 same shall be made navigable, as herein provided for.
5 But this corporation shall not be subject to any of the
6 provisions, liabilities, fines or penalties contained in
7 an act relating to steam navigation corporations
8 passed March 31, 1845; nor shall the stockholders in
9 the corporation hereby established, be liable in any
10 manner whatever, to an amount beyond the amount
11 of stock owned by each individual, for the debts of
12 the corporation.

SEC. 5. An act passed March 8, 1826, authorising
2 a canal for the improvement of Mousam river, is
3 hereby repealed.

SEC. 6. This act shall take effect and go into oper-
2 ation from and after its approval by the Governor.

STATE OF MAINE.

HOUSE OF REPRESENTATIVES, }
July 2, 1846, }

Ordered, That 350 copies of the foregoing Bill, reported from
the Committee on Interior Waters, be printed for the use of the
Legislature.

SAMUEL BELCHER, *Clerk.*

TWENTY-SIXTH LEGISLATURE.

No. 23.   SENATE.

STATE OF MAINE.

IN THE YEAR OF OUR LORD ONE THOUSAND EIGHT HUNDRED AND
FORTY-SIX.

AN ACT to incorporate the Saint Croix River Canal Company.

Be it enacted by the Senate and House of Representatives in Legislature assembled, as follows:

SECTION 1.   George Downes, Nehemiah Marks,
2 Anson G. Chandler, William Porter, Seth Emerson,
3 George M. Porter, William P. Trott, Noah Smith, jr.,
4 Levi L. Lowell, Ferdinand Tinker, Japheth H. Mc-
5 Allister, William Todd, jr., Abner Hill, Daniel Hill,
6 Gilman D. King, Miriam Lindsay, David Upton, Wil-
7 liam Eaton, William Pike, Frederick A. Pike, John
8 Stickney, Abner Sawyer, Ephraim C. Gates, Elijah
9 D. Green, Wm. H. C. Stevens, Francis Swan, Jere-
10 miah Bradbury, James S. Pike, Edward Clough, An-
11 sel Dailey, Columbus Bacon, Rendol Whidden, their

Wm. T. Johnson, Printer to the State.

12 associates, successors and assigns, are hereby de-
13 clared to be a body politic and corporate, by the
14 name of the Saint Croix River Canal Company,
15 with all the rights, liabilities, powers and privileges
16 incident to corporations by the common law and
17 by the seventy-sixth chapter of the laws of Maine,
18 for the purpose of opening and perfecting a water
19 communication by means of a canal and other im-
20 provements, from such points on the head waters or
21 streams of said river, and also of the western branch
22 thereof, as said company may deem advisable, and
23 thence down along said river and the western branch
24 thereof, and their lakes, to the tide way at the lower
25 bridge across the same.

Sec. 2.   Said company shall have the right, privi-
2 lege and power to improve said river, western branch,
3 streams and lakes, within the points named, by flow-
4 age and by removing obstructions, by making exca-
5 vations and embankments thereon, and to make,
6 excavate, build, construct and erect a canal and sec-
7 tions of slackwater therein and upon their borders,
8 and for this purpose may make all necessary excava-
9 tions, embankments, locks, gates, dams, pathways,
10 booms, piers, inclined planes, wharves, sluices, and
11 all other things which they may deem necessary and

12 expedient for the convenient attainment of their ob-
13 ject—for drifting or floating thereon logs, timber or
14 other lumber, and for passing up and down, merchan-
15 dise and other things, with greater facility than can
16 now be done, and for making the same boatable,—
17 and may and shall, for all said purposes, control said
18 river and canal and all their works, in such way and
19 manner as said company shall deem proper; and said
20 company may diverge with said canal, from said river,
21 western branch, lakes and streams, and again connect
22 it with the same at such places as they may deem
23 expedient.

Sec. 3.   The capital stock of said company shall
2 consist of two hundred thousand dollars and be divid-
3 ed into such number of shares of such amount as
4 said company shall direct.   Ten per cent of said
5 capital stock shall be paid in within three years from
6 the passage of this act, and the residue at such times
7 and in such sums as said company shall from time to
8 time direct.   In the management of the affairs of said
9 company, every stockholder shall have as many votes
10 as he may possess shares.

Sec. 4.   The company shall, in addition to the pro-
2 visions herein made for the collection of toll, have a
3 lien therefor, on all boats, lumber, or other things

4 subject to toll, passing through or over said canal or
5 improvements.

SEC. 5.   If any person shall willfully or maliciously
2 destroy, injure, impair or obstruct any of the rights,
3 privileges or property of said company, such person
4 shall forfeit and pay to said company treble damages,
5 with cost of suit, to be recovered by action of trespass,
6 in any court of competent jurisdiction; and if any
7 person shall by boat, raft, lumber, or otherwise, will-
8 fully or unnecessarily delay or obstruct the approach-
9 ing, entering, passing or repassing of any lock,
10 wasteway, inclined plane, sluice, or other avenue or
11 passageway, or do any other act or thing whereby the
12 operations of said company, or the transportation,
13 floating or passage of any lumber, merchandise or
14 other thing, in, over or upon said canal or any of their
15 improvements shall be hindered, obstructed or delayed,
16 he shall, for every such offense, forfeit and pay double
17 damages, with costs of suit, to be recovered in an
18 action on the case, in any court of competent juris-
19 diction.

SEC. 6.   The first meeting of said company shall
2 be called in the mode prescribed in section seventh of
3 chapter seventy-six of the Revised Statues of Maine,
4 but the notice therein named shall be signed by seven
5 at least, of the persons herein named.

Sec. 7.   Said company shall have no right to retain,
2 keep back or divert the water of said river, western
3 branch, streams or lakes, to the detriment of any mills
4 or machinery now erected, or which may hereafter be
5 erected thereon, and every owner of land used or
6 interfered with by said company or their works, by ·
7 virtue of this act, may still use the same in the same
8 way and manner he ever could, he leaving the works
9 of said company in as good condition as they were
10 before.

Sec. 8.   Every person shall have the right, under
2 the direction and control of said company, or its
3 agents, to use the said works and improvements for
4 the purpose for which they were erected and designed,
5 at all proper and suitable times, according to the
6 regulations of said company, upon paying therefor
7 the usual and legal toll or compensation.

Sec. 9.   Said company may occupy and use any
2 lands necessary to be occupied and used for the ac-
3 complishment of their purpose, but not until they
4 shall have paid to the owner thereof, his damages or
5 a full compensation therefor, to be ascertained by
6 agreement of said owner and company, or by such
7 arbitration as they may agree upon, if they choose so
8 to settle it; and in default of either of these modes,

1*

9 by petition, stating the cause of claim and the amount
10 claimed, to the district court in the county where the
11 land lies, and the amount of damages or compensation,
12 if any, shall be determined by the jury, on the de-
13 nial of said company of said petitioners right to
14 recover, or of his right to the amount claimed. Said
15 company shall pay for all earth, sand, gravel, stone or
16 wood they may take in their natural state, from the
17 lands adjoining their work, which they are hereby
18 authorized so to take, so far as may be necessary for
19 their said purposes, they first giving the owner written
20 notice of their intention, not injuring, interfering
21 with or impeding the access to any house, doing as
22 little damage as may be, and repairing all breaches
23 they may make in any enclosure. Said company
24 shall pay for all damages they may occasion to any
25 lands by flowage, or otherwise than is above named,
26 the amount in all cases herein named, to be deter-
27 mined in the manner above in this section named.
28 The claimant shall in all cases where he recovers any
29 damages or compensation, recover also his full cost.
30 The jury shall on petition for damages for flowage,
31 settle the amount to be paid in each future year, as
32 well as what has already arisen, to the rendition of
33 the verdict, which amount for each future year, if

34 not paid on or before the last day of July in each
35 year, may be recovered of said company by an action
36 on the case, before any court of competent jurisdic-
37 tion. Either party may from time to time, petition
38 said court for an increase or dimunition of said year-
39 ly sums, so determined by the jury to be paid in future,
40 which shall be heard and tried as above specified,
41 and the cost thereon shall follow the verdict in the
42 case; said petition in any case herein named, may be
43 served before entry by leaving a copy attested as a
44 true copy by the officer, with the adverse party, as
45 other copies are left with like adverse parties.

SEC. 10.   Said company by its officers, servants or
2 agents, may demand and receive of and from tho
3 owner or owners, or any person or persons having
4 the charge or direction of any boat, craft or other
5 vessel, timber, wood, logs, bark, shingles, staves, lath-
6 wood, boards, plank, deals, scantling, goods, wares
7 or merchandise, live or dead stock, or other things
8 whatsoever, passing through said canal or part there-
9 of, the rates of toll which shall be established by said
10 company, and the said company may bring suit for the
11 said toll, against the owner, shipper, supercargo, cap-
12 tain, controler or director of such vessel or other
13 said article before any competent tribunal.

Sec. 11. Any collector of said toll may stop or
2 prevent the passage of any person or property of any
3 kind, for or in respect of which toll ought to be paid,
4 whenever said toll shall not be paid as it should be,
5 and may seize and detain said property ; and in case
6 said toll shall not be paid, together with the expense
7 of seizure, detaining and advertising the same, within
8 the space of five days, said collector may and shall
9 sell the same, or so much thereof as may be necessary,
10 tendering the residue and overplus of the proceeds
11 of said sale, if any, after deducting the cost and ex-
12 pense of seizing, detaining, advertising and selling
13 such property, to the owner or owners thereof, which
14 the owner shall receive at the place where said col-
15 lector has it.

Sec. 12. Said company shall so make said canal,
2 as not to obstruct or impede the use and passage of
3 any public way or road which may cross the same;
4 and where said canal shall interfere with or cross any
5 such road, or any which may hereafter be located, it
6 shall be the duty of the company to make a good and
7 sufficient causeway or bridge over said canal, and the
8 same to keep in good repair ; and if said company
9 shall neglect to make said bridge as soon as practica-
10 ble, or when made to keep the same in repair, the

11 person, town or other corporation, on whom would,
12 but for this section, devolve the making or repairing
13 the same, may make and erect said bridge, or make
14 said repairs, and after notice to said company of the
15 expense thereof and demand on said company there-
16 for, and their refusal or neglect to pay double the
17 cost thereof, may sue for and recover of said com-
18 pany, said double cost, in an action of the case in
19 any court of competent jurisdiction.

SEC. 13. The owner of any land through which
2 said canal may pass, or on which any improvements
3 may be made, shall not be prevented from making
4 bridges over the same for their use and convenience,
5 nor shall such person be requested so to erect bridges
6 as to accommodate boats with masts.

SEC. 14. Said company shall complete their works
2 for the floating or driving down said river and west-
3 ern branch and streams and lakes, logs, timber and
4 other lumber, without boats, within four years from
5 the passage of this act, or all authority by this act for
6 that purpose shall cease; and said company shall
7 complete their said work for all other purposes, within
8 eight years from the passing of this act, or all author-
9 ity by this act, for all the said other purposes, shall
10 cease and become void.

STATE OF MAINE.

In Senate, July 7, 1846·

Ordered, That 350 copies of the foregoing Bill, reported from the Committee on Interior Waters, be printed for the use of the Legislature.

DANIEL T. PIKE, *Secretary·*

STATE OF MAINE.

IN THE YEAR OF OUR LORD ONE THOUSAND EIGHT HUNDRED AND
FORTY-SIX.

AN ACT to authorise school districts to borrow money for certain purposes.

*Be it enacted by the Senate and House of Represent-
atives in Legislature assembled,* as follows:

SECTION 1.   Any school district, at a legal meeting
2 called for that purpose, shall have power to borrow
3 money for the purpose of erecting a school house
4 and of purchasing land on which the same may stand.

SEC. 2.   Every such loan shall be made for a term
2 of time not exceeding five years and shall be payable
3 in equal annual instalments.

SEC. 3.   When any school district shall vote to bor-
2 row money for such purpose, the clerk shall forthwith
3 certify such vote to the assessors and treasurer of
4 the town in which such district is located, if wholly

5 within the limits of any one town, otherwise to the
6 assessors and treasurer of the oldest town out of
7 which any part of such district is taken.

Sec. 4. The district may appoint an agent or
2 agents to contract a loan as aforesaid, who are au-
3 thorized to bind the district therefor, and to give the
4 necessary evidence of debt therefor, and a copy of
5 such evidence of debt shall be, by such agent or agents,
6 filed with the town clerk of the town aforesaid and
7 shall be entered on the town records.   The money
8 procured on such loan shall be received by the treas-
9 urer of the town before mentioned, and shall be ap-
10 plied and paid out for the purposes aforesaid, in the
11 same manner as is now or may hereafter be provided
12 in case of money raised for building school houses,
13 by taxation.

Sec. 5. ·At each annual assessment of town taxes,
2 after the receipt of such money by the treasurer of
3 the town as aforesaid, the assessors of that town shall
4 assess the amount of the instalment and interest pay-
5 able in that year, upon the polls and estates of such
6 district, in the same manner as is now provided for
7 the assessment of moneys voted to be raised by any
8 school district, by taxation.   And such annual instal-
9 ments assessed as aforesaid, shall in like manner be

10 collected and paid to the treasurer of the town afore-
11 said. And the treasurer shall pay the amount of each
12 instalment and interest, as the same becomes payable,
13 on demand of the person to whom the same may be
14 lawfully due.

SEC. 6. The assessors, collector and treasurer em-
2 ployed as aforesaid, shall be under the same liabilities
3 and shall have the same authority and compensation
4 in respect to the services so performed by them for
5 any school district, as is now or may be provided by
6 law, in case of raising money by a school district, by
7 taxation.

SEC. 7. When any school district shall have ob-
2 tained money on loan as herein provided, the limit of
3 such district shall not be altered in any manner, until
4 after the last assessment shall have been made for the
5 payment of such loan.

SEC. 8. After the passage of this act, no school
2 district shall be authorized to borrow money, except
3 for the purposes and under the regulations prescribed
4 by this act.

STATE OF MAINE.

HOUSE OF REPRESENTATIVES, July 11, 1846.

Ordered, That 350 copies of the foregoing bill, reported by Mr. Barnes of Portland, from the Committee on *Education,* be printed for the use of the Legislature.

SAMUEL BELCHER, *Cerlk.*

TWENTY-SIXTH LEGISLATURE.

STATE OF MAINE.

IN THE YEAR OF OUR LORD ONE THOUSAND EIGHT HUNDRED AND
FORTY-SIX.

AN ACT to incorporate the Telos Canal Company.

Be it enacted by the Senate and House of Representatives in Legislature assembled, as follows:

SECTION 1.   Rufus Dwinel and Calvin Dwinel, their
2 associates and assigns, are hereby incorporated a body
3 politic by the name of the Telos Canal Company, with
4 all the powers, rights and privileges of similar cor-
5 porations.

SEC. 2.   Said corporation shall have the right, and
2 it shall be their duty, to construct, maintain and keep
3 open and in repair, a proper sluiceway or canal with
4 suitable dams, gates and other erections for the pas-
5 sage of water, logs and lumber, between Telos lake
6 and Webster pond, on township number six in the
7 eleventh range, in the county of Piscataquis, and to
8 afford a safe and convenient passage for all logs and

Wm. T. Johnson, Printer to the State.

9 lumber which the owner or owners of said lumber
10 may desire to pass through said sluiceway. And said
11 corporation shall have the right to preserve a free
12 passage for logs and lumber from Chamberlin lake to
13 the said canal or sluiceway, and it shall be their duty
14 to suffer said logs and lumber to pass down from said
15 Chamberlin lake to said sluiceway without any hind-
16 rance or obstruction whatever. And said corporation
17 shall have the right to demand and receive as a toll,
18 the sum of twenty-four cents for each and every
19 thousand feet, board measure, of all logs and lumber
20 which may pass through said sluiceway, to be ascer-
21 tained and fixed by the scale usually denominated the
22 Woods scale. And said corporation shall have a lien
23 on all logs and lumber which shall pass through said
24 cut, and on all lumber manufactured therefrom,
25 whether the same remain in the possession of said
26 corporation or not, until the full amount of toll due
27 on all the logs of the owner or any particular mark,
28 shall be paid. And if not paid within ten days after
29 said logs or lumber arrive at the Penobscot boom, or
30 within ten miles of said boom, said corporation may
31 sell at public auction, after ten days public notice in
32 some newspaper printed in the county of Penobscot,
33 so much of said logs or lumber as may be sufficient
34 to pay said toll and incidental charges.

Sec. 3. That there may be a sufficient depth of
2 water in said sluiceway, for tho passage of lumber
3 therein, said corporation are hereby empowered to
4 keep and maintain a dam on Allegash stream in town-
5 ship number seven in the thirteenth range. And
6 whereas a dam has already been erected on said Alle-
7 gash stream between the Chamberlin lake and Heron
8 lake so called, it shall be the duty of said corporation
9 to take said dam and site, and to keep and maintain
10 the same in good repair and of sufficient height to
11 cause the water to flow through said sluiceway, so as
12 to afford a safe, easy and commodious passage for all
13 logs and lumber through the same. And said corpo-
14 ration shall pay to the owner or owners of said dam
15 for the same, the reasonable value thereof; and if the
16 parties cannot agree upon the price of said dam, the
17 owner may have the same remedy for his damages on
18 application to tho county commissioners for the coun-
19 ty of Piscataquis, in the same manner and under the
20 same conditions and limitations as as are by law
21 provided in case of damages in laying out public
22 highways. Provided, however, that the measure of
23 damages shall be the just and reasonable value of the
24 construction.

Sec. 4. Any individual or individuals authorized by
2 the land agent of this State, or any company in-

3 corporated by the Legislature, may make such im-
4 provements and construct all necessary machinery,
5 gates and canals on said dam, and use the same for
6 the transportation of logs and lumber from the lakes
7 and streams north and east of said dam, into the
8 Chamberlin lake and water south and west of said
9 dam; and shall pay therefor, to the owner thereof,
10 such yearly sum as the land agent or Legislature shall
11 determine.

Sec. 5. Provided nevertheless, and this charter is
2 granted upon the condition, that the said Rufus Dwinel
3 and Calvin Dwinel, and their associates and assigns,
4 shall accept this charter and organise their corpora-
5 tion on or before the first day of October next; so
6 that there shall be an ample passage way for the tran-
7 sit of lumber, between said lake Telos and Webster
8 pond, and shall also take said dam and site on said
9 Allegash stream, and keep and maintain the same so
10 as to cause the water to flow through said sluiceway,
11 and pay for said dam to the owner or owners thereof,
12 within ninety days after the award and determination
13 of the county commissioners in the premises. And
14 if said company shall fail to fulfill the conditions
15 aforesaid, by the time limited, this act shall have no
16 further validity or effect.

STATE OF MAINE.

AN ACT to incoporate the Lake Telos and Webster
Pond Dam and Sluiceway Company.

*Be it enacted by the Senate and House of Represent-
atives in Legislature assembled,* as follows:

SECTION 1. William H. Smith, Daniel M. Howard,
2 Warren Brown and Theodore H. Dillingham and their
3 associates and assigns, are hereby created a body pol-
4 itic by the name of Lake Telos and Webster Pond
5 Dam and Sluiceway Company, by which name they
6 may contract, sue and be sued, defend suits at law,
7 have and use a common seal, and change the same
8 at pleasure, make by-laws not repugnant to the laws
9 of this state, for the convenient management of their
10 corporate affairs, take and hold any estate, real, per-
11 sonal or mixed, to an amount not exceeding thirty
12 thousand dollars, and sell or convey or otherwise dis-
13 pose of the same, and have and enjoy all the rights,

1*

14 powers and privileges necessary to carry into effect
15 the object of this corporation.

SEC. 2. The said corporation are hereby authorised
2 and empowered to make, construct and maintain a
3 sluiceway from lake Telos to Webster pond, other-
4 wise called Penobscot pond, on township number six,
5 in the eleventh range, in the county of Piscataquis,
6 sufficiently wide and deep for the passage of timber and
7 lumber of all kinds, which may be expedited to the pub-
8 lic market through that channel. And they are author-
9 ised to erect and maintain any dam or dams on said
10 sluiceway, or any stream or waters which may be con-
11 nected therewith on said township, which may be nec-
12 essary to render the transit of lumber more easy and
13 effectual, and to keep open a passage way for all logs
14 or lumber, on the waters between Chamberlin lake
15 and said sluiceway. And they are further authorised to
16 enter upon and take such land, property or material in
17 said township, as they may find it necessary to make
18 said canal or sluiceway, or upon which to locate their
19 dam or dams, and such as may be necessary along the
20 margin of their sluiceway for the use and accommo-
21 dation of persons employed in driving lumber through
22 the same. *Provided however*, that said corporation
23 shall pay the proprietor or proprietors of said town-

24 ship number six, for land, property or material so tak-
25 en and used for their sluiceway and dam or dams, with
26 a necessary and convenient margin, and for keeping
27 an open and free passage on the waters between said
28 Chamberlin lake and said sluiceway, such price as
29 they and said proprietor or proprietors may agree
30 upon. And in case said parties shall not otherwise
31 agree, then said corporation shall pay such damages as
32 shall be ascertained and determined by the County
33 Commissioners for the county of Piscataquis, in the
34 same manner and under the same conditions and lim-
35 itations as are by law provided in the case of damage
36 by the laying out of public highways; with the same
37 right to either party aggrieved by the doings of said
38 Commissioners, in estimating damages, to have a jury
39 to determine that matter on their petition; unless said
40 party shall agree with the other party in interest to
41 have the same determined by a committee to be ap-
42 pointed under the direction of said Commissioners.
43 And no application shall be made to said Commission-
44 ers to estimate damages unless made within two years
45 from the time of taking said land, property and mate-
46 rials.

SEC. 3.   And whereas said proprietor or proprietors
2 of said township number six, in the eleventh range,

3 have already cut a sluiceway on said township, from
4 said lake Telos to said Webster Pond, which has be-
5 come to some extent available for the passage of lum-
6 ber, and the proprietor or proprietors of said town-
7 ship instead of applying for their damages as provided
8 for, in the second section of this act, may at their
9 election, at any time within two years from the taking
10 of said land, property or materials, apply to said Coun-
11 ty Commissioners at any regular term of said court,
12 claiming to be paid the reasonable costs and expenses
13 of making said sluiceway and dam upon said township
14 number six in the eleventh range. And thereupon
15 said court shall issue due notice to said corporation,
16 requiring them to appear before said court, and an-
17 swer to said complaint. And said corporation shall
18 pay such sum as damages, as shall be ascertained and
19 determined by said County Commissioners, to be the
20 reasonable cost and expenses in making and construct-
21 ing said sluiceway and dam or dams, on said township
22 number six, of the said eleventh range, but if damages
23 are awarded under this section of this act, no further
24 or other damages shall be allowed said proprietor or
25 proprietors.

SEC. 4. There shall be allowed to said corporation
2 as toll for the passage of every thousand feet, board

3 measure of lumber, according to the Woods scale,
4 through their sluiceway, a sum not exceeding ten
5 cents; excepting such lumber as may be cut on town-
6 ship number six, of the eleventh range, which shall be
7 allowed a free passage through said sluiceway, with-
8 any payment whatever. And to secure to the corpor-
9 ation the toll granted by this act, they shall have a
10 lien on all the lumber, subject to the payment of toll,
11 and if the same is not paid within ten days after the
12 arrival of said lumber at Penobscot boom, or within
13 ten miles of said boom, the corporation may advertise
14 the sale of so much thereof as may be necessary to
15 pay said toll and expenses, in one of the newspapers
16 printed in Bangor, the publication to be at least ten
17 days before the day appointed for such sale; and if
18 payment is not made before the time appointed, may
19 proceed to sell so much of said lumber as may be re-
20 quired to pay said toll and expenses.

SEC. 5. That there may be a sufficient depth of
2 water in said sluiceway for the passage of lumber
3 therein, said corporation are hereby empowed to take
4 the dam now erected on Allegash stream, in township
5 number seven, in the thirteenth range, with the land
6 on which the same is situate. And if the parties can-
7 not agree upon the price, the owner may have the

8 same remedy for his damages on application to the
9 county commissioners for the county of Piscataquis as
10 is provided in the second section of this act, and shall
11 pay therefor the expenses and cost of its construction.
12 And said corporation are empowered to flow the con-
13 tiguous lands as far as may be necessary to accomplish
14 their object, paying the owners damage therefor; and
15 if the parties cannot agree upon the amount of dam-
16 ages, the said corporation shall not be liable to any
17 action at common law for the same; but any person
18 injured may have a remedy by a complaint for flowing,
19 in which the same proceeding shall be had, as where a
20 complaint is made under a statute of this State for
21 flowing lands occasioned by the raising of a head of
22 water necessary for the working of mills.

, SEC. 6· When said corporation shall have been re-
2 imbursed by tolls received, for their reasonable costs
3 and expenses in making their sluiceway and dams to-
4 gether with all damages by them paid, with lawful in-
5 terest thereon, said sluiceway shall become open and
6 free for the use of the public generally without the
7 payment of tolls.

SEC. 7. Any individual or individuals authorised by
2 the land agent of this State may make such improve-
3 ments and construct all necessary machinery and

4 gates on said dam and use the same for the transpor-
5 tation of logs and lumber from the lakes and streams
6 north and east of said dam into the Chamberlin lake
7 and waters south and west of said dam ; subject at
8 all times to the control and regulation of the Legis-
9 lature.

Sec. 8.   One half part of the reasonable cost and
2 expenses in making said sluiceway and dams, together
3 with the damages by them paid, with legal interest
4 thereon, may be collected in tolls at ten cents per
5 thousand feet board measure, from timber cut on
6 lands of proprietors, and the other half part from tim-
7 ber which may be cut from lands now owned by the
8 commonwealth of Massachusetts and State of Maine.

Sec. 9.   Provided nevertheless, that if the Telos
2 Canal Company created at the present session of the
3 Legislature, shall provide and establish an ample and
4 sufficient passage way for the transit of lumber be-
5 tween said lake Telos and Penobscot pond, in the time
6 limited in the fifth section of an act to incorporate
7 said company, and shall duly organise under and
8 exercise the powers granted by their charter, then the
9 powers and privileges granted by this act, shall be
10 vacated and of no effect; but if said Telos Canal
11 Company shall not discharge the duties imposed on

12 them by their charter on or before the time limited
13 in their charter, then the company hereby established
14 are invested with all the powers and privileges and
15 subject to all the duties imposed upon them by this
16 act.

    SEC. 10.   The Legislature reserves to itself the
2 right to alter, amend or repeal this charter at pleasure.

STATE OF MAINE.

IN SENATE, July 11, 1846.

Ordered, That 350 copies of the foregoing Bills, reported from the Committee on Interior Waters, be printed for the use of the Legislature.

                 DANIEL T. PIKE, *Secretary.*

STATE OF MAINE.

IN THE YEAR OF OUR LORD ONE THOUSAND EIGHT HUNDRED AND
FORTY-SIX.

AN ACT granting appeals from the decisions of county commissioners.

*Be it enacted by the Senate and House of Represent-
atives in Legislature assembled,* as follows:

SECTION 1.   Any person or corporation aggrieved
2 by any decision of any court of county commissioners,
3 on an application to lay out, alter or discontinue any
4 highways, may appeal to the district court held in the
5 county where the location, alteration or discontinuance
6 is prayed for, under the limitations and restrictions
7 contained in this act.

SEC. 2.   The parties, petitioners or respondents may
2 enter their appearance before the county commission-
3 ers on any such application, either jointly or severally;

Wm. T. Johnson, Printer to the State

4 and any party so entering an appearance may take
5 an appeal from the decision of said county commis-
6 sioners within thirty days after said decision shall be
7 entered on record, and not afterwards; provided,
8 however, that if the person or corporation so appeal-
9 ing shall neglect to prosecute the appeal, any other
10 person or corporation, a party of record, may prose-
11 cute the same; and thereupon all proceedings shall
12 be stayed in said county commissioners' court until a
13 decision shall be had in the district court, from which
14 decision there shall be no appeal; and all persons or
15 corporations claiming such appeal, shall be held joint-
16 ly and severally liable for all costs that may be ad-
17 judged against them.

SEC. 3. In all cases of appeal from the judgment
2 of the county commissioners in any county, pending
3 in the district court in said county, it shall be lawful
4 for the court to appoint a special committee of three
5 disinterested persons, whose duty it shall be, after
6 giving such notice as the court shall order, to proceed
7 to view the route named in the original petition; and
8 after a hearing of the parties and their witnesses, to
9 report at the next term of said district court in said
10 county, whether in their opinion, the judgment of the
11 county commissioners should be, in whole or in part,

12 affirmed or reversed; and such committee shall be
13 sworn to the faithful performance of their duty.

SEC. 4. Upon the acceptance of such report, judg-
2 ment shall be entered accordingly, by the district
3 court, including judgment for costs as hereinafter
4 provided; and the same shall be forthwith certified to
5 the court of county commissioners. If such judg-
6 ment shall be wholly against the location, alteration
7 or discontinuance in question, no farther proceedings
8 shall be had thereon by the county commissioners;
9 but if otherwise, then the county commissioners shall
10 proceed to lay out, alter or discontinue such highway,
11 in whole or in part, as the judgment may be; and in
12 the manner and according to the regulations and lim-
13 itations provided by law, where no appeal is taken.

SEC. 5. The special committee above provided,
2 shall be paid by the county, for their time and travel,
3 such compensation as is now or may be provided by
4 law, for the county commissioners when acting upon
5 original petitions for the same purpose, subject, how-
6 ever, to the decision of the district court as to the
7 number of days attendance to be allowed said com-
8 mittee; and in case the judgment of the county com-
9 missioners shall be affirmed in whole or in part, the
10 party prosecuting the appeal, shall if so adjudged by

11 the district court, pay all costs that have arisen since
12 the appeal, and the county commissioners shall issue
13 their warrant therefor, in the same manner as is now
14 provided for the collection of costs awarded against
15 petitioners for a road.   The district court shall have
16 discretionary power to allow costs to be paid out of
17 the county treasury to the prevailing party in any
18 such appeal.

Sec. 6.   In case no person appears to prosecute the
2 appeal provided for in this act, the case may be dis-
3 missed by the court; but it may be again restored,
4 upon application to the court within a reasonable time,
5 if in the opinion of said court justice requires it.

Sec. 7.   If the judgment, upon appeal, shall be
2 wholly against the laying out, altering or discontinu-
3 ing of the road prayed for, no petition praying sub-
4 stantially for the same action, shall be entertained by
5 the county commissioners, within two years from the
6 rendition of such judgment on appeal.

Sec. 8.   This act shall take effect from and after its
2 approval.

STATE OF MAINE.

HOUSE OF REPRESENTATIVES, July 13, 1846.

Ordered, That 350 copies of the foregoing bill, reported by Mr. Getchell of North Anson, from the Committee on the Judiciary, be printed for the use of the Legislature.

SAMUEL BELCHER, *Clerk.*

STATE OF MAINE.

IN THE YEAR OF OUR LORD ONE THOUSAND EIGHT HUNDRED AND
FORTY-SIX.

AN ACT to restrict the sale of intoxicating drinks.

*Be it enacted by the Senate and House of Represent-
atives in Legislature assembled,* as follows :

SECTION 1. No person shall be allowed at any time,
2 to sell by himself or his clerk, servant or agent, di-
3 rectly or indirectly, any wine, brandy, rum or other
4 spirituous liquors, or any liquors a part of which is
5 spirituous, except as hereafter provided.

SEC. 2. The provisions of this act shall not extend
2 to wine or spirituous liquors, which shall have been
3 imported into the United States from any foreign port
4 or place, when sold in quantities of twenty-eight gal-
5 lons and over, and delivered and carried away at one
6 time.

SEC. 3. The selectmen, clerk and treasurer of ev-

W T. Johnson, Printer to the State.

2 ery town, shall annually meet on the first **Monday** of
.3 May, or on the succeeding day, or both, and at such
4 place in said town as they may appoint, by posting up
5 notices in two or more public places therein, at least
6 seven days previously, stating the purposes of the
7 meeting, and at such meeting, shall license under
8 their hands, and under such rules and regulations as
9 they may deem necessary, one person of good moral
10 character, if any such shall appear and request it, for
11 every town having less than one thousand inhabitants,
12 two for every town having over one thousand and
13 less than three thousand, and three for every town
14 having more than three thousand inhabitants, to be
15 sellers of wine, brandy, rum or other strong liquors,
16 in said town, to be used for medical and mechanical
17 purposes, and no other; provided however that no
18 such license shall be granted, until the person to be
19 licensed shall have executed and delivered to said
20 treasurer a bond with two good and sufficient sureties,
21 in the sum of six hundred dollars, in substance as
22 follows:

23 Know all men, that we — as principal, and — as
24 sureties, are holden and stand firmly bound to the in-
25 habitants of the town of — in the sum of six hundred
26 dollars, to be paid them, to which payment well and

27 truly to be made, we bind ourselves, our heirs, exec-
28 utors and administrators, firmly by these presents.
29 Sealed with our seals, and dated this — day of —,
30 A. D. —. The condition of the foregoing obligation
31 is such, that whereas the above bounden — has been
32 duly licensed to sell within the said town, wine, bran-
33 dy, rum, and other strong liquors, to be used for
34 medical and mechanical purposes, in quantities of
35 twenty-eight gallons and under (or over, as the case
36 may be), until the first Monday of May next; now if
37 the said — shall in all respects conform to the provis-
38 ions of the law relating to the business for which he
39 is licensed, and to such rules and regulations as shall
40 be from time to time established by the board grant-
41 ing the license, in reference thereto, then this obliga-
42 tion to be void; otherwise, to remain in full force.

SEC. 4. The said licensing board may at any other
2 time, at a meeting called and notified as aforesaid,
3 grant such licenses, but in no case shall they license a
4 greater number than is allowed by the foregoing sec-
5 tion; and all such licenses shall expire on the said
6 first Monday of May, annually, and the clerk shall
7 make a record of all the licenses granted.

SEC. 5. If any person by himself, clerk, servant or
2 agent, shall at any time, sell any wine or spirituous

3 liquors, or any mixed liquors, a part of which is spir-
4 ituous, in violation of the provisions of this act, he
5 shall forfeit and pay for each offense, not less than
6 one, nor more than twenty dollars.

Sec. 6. Any forfeiture or penalty arising under the
2 above section, may be recovered by an action of debt,
3 on complaint, before any justice of the peace or
4 judge of any municipal or police court in the county
5 where the offense was committed. And the action
6 may be brought in the name of the person prosecut-
7 ing, or the town where the offense was committed.
8 One half the forfeiture so recovered shall enure to the
9 prosecutor or complainant, and the other half to the
10 town; and the prosecutor or complainant shall be
11 admitted as a witness at the trial. And if any two of
12 the licensing board shall approve of the commence-
13 ment of any such suit, by endorsing their names upon
14 the writ, the defendant shall in no event recover any
15 cost.

Sec. 7. And if any person shall claim an appeal
2 from a judgment rendered against him, by any such
3 judge or justice, on the trial of such action or com-
4 plaint, he shall, before the appeal shall be allowed,
5 recognize in a sum not less than fifty dollars, with two
6 good and sufficient sureties, to prosecute his appeal

7 and to pay all costs, fines or forfeitures that may be
8 recovered against him, upon a final disposition of
9 such suit or complaint.   And if such appellant shall
10 not within forty-eight hours (Sunday excepted) after
11 such judgment is rendered, so recognize, the appeal
12 shall not be allowed, and the said judge or justice
13 shall enter up judgment in the same manner as though
14 no such appeal had been claimed ; and the appellant
15 shall be held to advance the jury fees and all other
16 fees that may arise after the appeal.

SEC. 8.   If any person, after having been once con-
2 victed of a violation of the provisions of this act,
3 shall be guilty, and upon complaint convicted, of a
4 like offense, he shall be punished by a fine of not
5 less than five dollars, nor more than twenty dollars,
6 and shall give a bond to the inhabitants of the town
7 where the offense was committed, with two good and
8 sufficient sureties, to the acceptance of the judge or
9 justice before whom the complaint may be tried, in a
10 sum not less than fifty dollars conditioned that he will
11 not, during the term of six months then next following,
12 violate the provisions of this act, and shall stand
13 committed until the sentence shall be complied with.
14 And the thirty days named in the one hundred and

15 seventy-fifth chapter of the Revised Statutes, shall not
16 begin to run till thirty days after the commitment.

Sec. 9. The licensing board of said town, when-
2 ever complaint shall be made to them that a breach
3 of the condition of the bond given by any person
4 licensed by them, has been committed, shall notify
5 the person complained of, and if upon a hearing of
6 the parties it shall appear that any breach has been
7 committed, they shall revoke and make void his li-
8 cense. And whenever a breach of any bond given
9 to the inhabitants of any town in pursuance of any
10 of the provisions of this act, shall be made known
11 to said licensing board or the town agent, or in any
12 manner come to their knowledge, they, or some one
13 of them, shall, at the expense and for the use of the
14 town, cause the bond to be put in suit, in any court
15 proper to try the same.

Sec. 10. No action shall be maintained upon any
2 claim or demand, whether it be note, account, bond,
3 order, draft, acceptance or other security or evidence
4 whatever, made, had or given in whole or in part, for
5 any wine, brandy, rum or other strong or spirituous
6 liquors, or mixed liquors, a part of which is spirituous,
7 sold in violation of the provisions of this act; pro-

8 vided, however, that this section shall not extend to
9 negotiable paper in the hands of holders bona fide,
10 and for a valuable consideration without notice ex-
11 pressed or implied, of the illegality of the consider-
12 ation.

    SEC. 11. If any payment or compensation for any
2 such liquor hereafter sold, in violation of this law,
3 shall be received by the seller, his clerk, servant, agent
4 or attorney, whether in money, labor, or other prop-
5 erty, real or personal, the amount so received, shall
6 be held and considered to have been received in vio-
7 lation of law and without consideration, and held
8 against law and equity and good conscience, and may
9 be recovered back any time within six years from
10 the receiving thereof, by the purchaser, his guardian,
11 executors or administrators, or by any of his creditors,
12 such money in an action for money had and received,
13 and such labor, goods or other property in an action
14 of trover, in special action on the case, for the value
15 thereof, in any court proper to try the same ; and the
16 plaintiff in such action, shall within three days after
17 the commencement of such suit, give notice thereof,
18 by filing an abstract of the declaration, with the date
19 of his writ, in the office of the clerk of the town
20 where the defendant resides. And when such suit

21 shall be commenced by a creditor, the purchaser may
22 be a witness for the plaintiff, at the trial of the action,
23 and such actions and cause of action shall survive.

SEC. 12.   All payments received within the six years,
2 may be embraced in one general count, and shall
3 alledge that the money, or other thing, was received
4 by the defendant, for liquor sold in violation of law,
5 and amendments may be made to the writ and declar-
6 ation, as matter of right, and without terms in any
7 stage of the proceedings. And when the defendant
8 shall rely upon having had the legal license, or upon
9 the liquor sold having been imported, the burden of
10 proof shall be and continue upon him. The custom
11 house certificates of importation and proof of marks
12 on the cask corresponding thereto, may be received
13 as evidence that the liquor specified in said certificate
14 was once imported in said cask, but shall not be evi-
15 dence that the liquor sold in or from such cask, was
16 the same liquor once imported therein. And it shall
17 be no objection to the suit, that the payment was re-
18 ceived for the joint use of the defendant and any
19 other person or persons, or that the defendant was
20 under the age of twenty-one years, or a married
21 woman.

SEC. 13.   When the money or other thing shall have

2 been received by any clerk, servant, agent or attorney,
3 the action may be maintained against him, if he had
4 knowledge or previous notice that it was for liquor
5 sold in violation of law. And if any action which is
6 authorized by this act, be brought in the district court,
7 and the plaintiff prevail therein, full costs shall be
8 allowed, though the amount of damages recovered
9 be less than twenty dollars.

SEC. 14. The defendant shall not be allowed, on
2 the trial of any action against him, under any of the
3 provisions of this act, any claims or demands he may
4 have against the plaintiff or person to whom the liquor
5 was sold or furnished, either in set off, payment or
6 otherwise; nor shall the action of any creditor be
7 defeated by any assignment of the claim by the pur-
8 chaser.

SEC. 15. No discharge, release, receipt, settlement
2 or admission made by a purchaser, shall defeat or
3 hinder the suit, if it appear that the claim allowed to
4 the purchaser by this act, has not been actually paid
5 in good faith, to its full value and amount; and the
6 giving a negotiable note or other obligation, shall not
7 be deemed a payment.

SEC. 16. Any plaintiff suing under the tenth sec-
2 tion of this act, may, at the trial, tender his oath in

2

3 writing, which shall be received as evidence, unless
4 the defendant shall in writing, make oath that he did
5 not, within six years before the commencement of
6 the suit receive any payment or compensation, for
7 any such wine or strong liquor sold to the plaintiff, or
8 to any person whom the plaintiff represents, contrary
9 to the provisions of the law, as alledged in the dec-
10 laration.

Sec. 17.   When a plaintiff suing under any of the
2 provisions of this act, in order to prove the facts
3 which he has alledged, shall wish to avail himself of
4 the defendants knowledge, relating to the subject
5 matter of the suit, he may, in his declaration, ask for
6 a disclosure of the same upon the oath of the defend-
7 ant, in writing, and the disclosure, if made, may be
8 submitted to the 'court and jury with the other evi-
9 dence in the case; but if the defendant neglects or
10 refuses to make such disclosures, or if when made, it
11 does not absolutely and without qualification, deny
12 that he did sell the liquor and receive the money or
13 other property, therefor, as alledged in the declaration,
14 and prevails in the action he shall not receive any
15 costs.

Sec. 18.   No answers or disclosures made by a de-
2 fendant under the provisions of this act, shall ever be

3 used against him in any penal action or criminal
4 prosecution.

SEC. 19.   Moneys which are by this act, to be re-
2 covered back, may when recovered by a guardian,
3 executor or administrator, be applied at the discretion
4 of the guardian, executor or administrator, in whole
5 or in part, to meet the debts of the purchaser, or to
6 relieve his wife or widow and children, and parents,
7 in such proportions as the guardian, executors or ad-
8 ministrators may deem suitable, and when recovered
9 by a creditor, it shall be appropriated to the payment
10 of his debt against the purchaser and his costs; and
11 if any balance remains, one moiety thereof to acrue
12 to the plaintiff, and the other to be paid to the pur-
13 chaser, his guardian. executor or administrator, to be
14 appropriated by them, in the same manner as moneys
15 recovered under this act by them.   And if any guar-
16 dian, executor or administrator, neglect to pay all
17 said moneys, he and his sureties shall be liable for the
18 same in his official bond.

SEC. 20.   Whenever a judgment shall be recovered
2 against any person on account of a violation of this
3 act, the execution which shall be issued thereon, shall
4 run against the body of the execution debtor, whether
5 the amount recovered, exclusive of costs, be more or

6 less than ten dollars ; and the justice or clerk issuing
7 said execution, shall note on its margin that it was
8 issued on a judgment obtained on account of intoxi-
9 cating liquors sold in violation of law.

SEC. 21.   If such execution debtor shall be arrested
2 on such execution, he shall bo committed to prison,
3 and shall not be permitted to give any of the bonds
4 provided in the one hundred and forty-eight chapter
5 of the Revised Statutes for the liberation of his per-
6 son.   And in case he shall apply to take the oath
7 described in the twenty-eighth section of said chap-
8 ter, no notice to the creditor shall be issued until fif-
9 teen days after the commitment.   Provided, however,
10 that no person shall be imprisoned on more than one
11 warrant issued upon any judgment, recovered on ac-
12 count of a violation of the provisions of this act, at
13 the same time.

SEC. 22.   The keepers of the prisons shall be enti-
2 tled to receive the same compensation now allowed
3 by law, for the support of poor debtors imprisoned
4 for the support of persons committed on execution
5 recovered under the provisions of this act, to be al-
6 lowed and paid by the treasurer of the county where
7 such person stands committed, under the direction of
8 the county commissioners.

SEC. 23. All the provisions of this act, relating to
2 towns and their treasurers and clerks, shall be appli-
3 cable to cities and plantations, and the treasurers
4 and clerks thereof; and those relating to selectmen
5 shall also be applied to aldermen of cities and asses-
6 sors of plantations.

SEC. 24. If any person shall sell, give, or in any
2 manner, directly or indirectly furnish any person, *non*
3 *compos* or any Indian, or any person named in the
4 seventh section of the one hundred and tenth chapter
5 of the Revised Statutes, any wine, brandy, rum or other
6 spirituous liquors, or any mixed liquors a part of which
7 is spirituous, for any purpose whatever, unless in case
8 of sickness, under the direction of a regular practis-
9 ing physician, he shall be subject to all the liabilities,
10 forfeitures and penalties, provided by this act.

SEC. 25. So much of the seventeenth section of
2 the thirty-sixth chapter of the Revised Statutes as af-
3 fixes a penalty for being a common seller of liquors
4 by retail, and all other parts of said thirty-sixth chap-
5 ter, and all other acts and parts of acts, so far as they
6 are inconsistent with the provisions of this act, are
7 hereby repealed, saving and reserving all indictments,
8 prosecutions and suits which have been already com-
9 menced.

STATE OF MAINE.

House of Representatives, July 11, 1846.

Ordered, That 500 copies of the foregoing bill, reported by Mr. Davis of Stow, from the Joint Select Committee to which were referred sundry petitions for the suppression of drinking houses and tippling shops, be printed for the use of the Legislature. Also 500 additional copies for the use of the House.

SAMUEL BELCHER, *Clerk*.

In Senate, July 13, 1846.

Ordered, That 500 additional copies of the foregoing bill be printed for the use of the Senate.

DANIEL T. PIKE, *Secretary*.

AMENDMENT to a bill entitled "an act to repeal chapter 126 of the Revised Statutes."

Strike out all after the enacting clause, and insert as follows:

SECTION 1. The provisions of the one hundred
2 and twenty-sixth chapter of the Revised Statutes shall
3 not be extended, except as herein provided, to any
4 case where a new mill dam shall hereafter be erected
5 upon a site not before occupied for such purpose, nor
6 to any case where a mill dam shall hereafter be re-
7 built or repaired, and by means of such rebuilding or
8 repairing, the water above such dam shall be flowed
9 higher than it was usually before flowed by means of
10 any dam upon the same site.

SEC. 2. Any person who may propose hereafter to
2 erect, rebuild, or repair any such mill dam as is men-
3 tioned in the preceding section, whereby the land of
4 any other person will be flowed, shall present his
5 petition to the district court holden within the county

W. T. Johnson, Printer to the State.

6 where said mill site may be, praying for authority
7 therefor; and if the site of the proposed dam is in
8 more than one county, then the petition may be in
9 either county. The court shall order such notice as
10 it may deem expedient, upon any such petition, and
11 on the return thereof shall inquire and adjudge wheth-
12 er such erection, rebuilding or repairing will be of
13 public use, and whether any damages by flowing will
14 be caused thereby. For that purpose, the court shall
15 appoint three commissioners who shall be duly sworn.

SEC. 3.   It shall be the duty of such commissioners
2 to view and describe the premises, and after notice to
3 all parties interested, to hear such evidence as may be
4 adduced on the prayer of the petition. Any person
5 interested adversely to such petition, may enter an
6 appearance thereto, at the term at which notice shall
7 be returnable, and shall have process for the taking
8 testimony before the commissioners and shall be heard
9 by the commissioners and the court.

SEC. 4.   At the term next after the appointment of
2 commissioners, unless further time is granted on the
3 application of the petitioners, they shall make their
4 report and shall state therein whether the dam prayed
5 for, and the mills that may be erected thereon, will be
6 of public use, and shall also report the annual value
7 of such dam and mills and the annual damage that

8 will be caused to all the lands liable to be flowed
9 thereby. If the report shall find that such annual
10 damage will be equal to or greater than the annual
11 value of such dam and mills thereon, in that case, the
12 prayer of the petition shall not be granted; but if
13 such values are found otherwise, and the commission-
14 ers shall report that the dam will be of public use,
15 then the court shall grant authority for the erec-
16 tion, rebuilding or repairing prayed for; and such
17 dam may thereafter be maintained and kept up, with
18 all the privileges and subject to all the liabilities per-
19 taining to dams erected under the provisions of the
20 one hundred and twenty-sixth chapter of the Revised
21 Statutes, except as the same are hereinafter modified.

SEC. 5. The costs on any such petition and inquiry
2 shall in all cases be paid by the petitioners, before the
3 prayer of the petition shall be granted, or the court
4 may issue its warrant therefor, and in its discretion
5 may order any part of such costs to be paid to any
6 adverse party of record. The commissioners ap-
7 pointed on such petitions shall receive the same com-
8 pensation as is provided in cases of commissioners
9 appointed to make partition of lands.

SEC. 6. No person shall be allowed, under the
2 provisions of this act, or of the one hundred and

3 twenty-sixth chapter of the Revised Statutes, to flow
4 the land of another by means of a dam erected or
5 raised for the purpose of creating a reservoir for the
6 use of any mill or machinery on any other dam; and
7 in estimating the annual value of any dam as pro-
8 vided in this act, no account shall be made of its value
9 for the purpose of creating such reservoir.

Sec. 7. Any person whose land shall be flowed by
2 means of any such dam as is authorized by this act,
3 may recover compensation therefor, by such com-
4 plaint and process as are provided in the said one
5 hundred and twenty-sixth chapter of the Revised
6 Statutes, subject to such modifications of the same
7 as are expressed in this act.

Sec. 8. Upon any complaint hereafter commenced
2 to obtain compensation for damages caused by flow-
3 ing, or to obtain increased compensation, the ·court
4 may order such notice as may be reasonable and
5 practicable to all persons owning or occupying the
6 dam complained of, and no such complaint shall be
7 abated or dismissed on any plea or allegation that any
8 person named therein is not an owner of such dam,
9 nor for any cause of nonjoinder of parties; but all
10 such complaints, in which the dam is distinctly de-
11 scribed and on which due notice has been given, shall

12 be heard on default or otherwise, so as to ascertain
13 the injury suffered by the complainant. And in any
14 stage of the proceedings before the acceptance of the
15 report of commissioners, the court may order further
16 notice.

Sec. 9. In all cases of complaint to recover any
2 damages caused by flowing, the complainant, after
3 the report of the commissioners is made, may have
4 the right of trial by jury; but the report of the com-
5 missioners, if accepted by the court, shall be final
6 against any owner or occupant of the dam com-
7 plained of, or any mill thereon; nor shall a trial by
8 jury be allowed to any owner or occupant of a dam
9 who shall bring a complaint for diminution of any
10 damages before awarded against him. In all cases of
11 complaint, costs shall not be allowed against the
12 owner of land injured by flowing, except at the dis-
13 cretion of the court.

Sec. 10. Whenever judgment shall be rendered for
2 any damages caused by flowing, and for yearly dam-
3 ages, the court shall order at what time in each year
4 such yearly damages shall be paid. If the judgment
5 for damages sustained prior to the complaint, shall
6 not be paid within thirty days from the date of such
7 judgment, or if the yearly damages shall not be paid

8 in each year, at or before the time of payment deter-
9 mined by the court, then, in either case, the owner or
10 owners of the dam complained of, and the occupants
11 of the same, shall have no benefit of any of the priv-
12 ileges granted by this act, or by the chapter of the
13 Revised Statutes aforesaid ; and the complainant shall
14 be entitled to his remedy at common law and in
15 equity, for redress and satisfaction of the damage by
16 him sustained.

SEC. 11.   Nothing contained in this act, or in the
2 one hundred and twenty sixth chapter of the Revised
3 Statutes shall authorize any person or persons to
4 erect, raise or keep up any dam, by means of which
5 any state road, highway or town way, or any railroad,
6 bridge, turnpike or canal, shall be overflowed, or in
7 any manner, injured or impaired.

SEC. 12.   No length of time during which any lands
2 may have been flowed by any dam erected by any
3 person or corporation, before or after the passage of
4 this act, shall be taken as evidence, or afford any
5 presumption of a grant or license to flow such lands
6 or be taken to make up any part of the limitation of
7 twenty years, provided in the one hundred and forty
8 seventh chapter of the Revised Statutes.

SEC. 13.   All acts and parts of acts, inconsistent

2 with the provisions of this act, are hereby repealed;

3 and this act shall take effect and be in force from and

4 after the fifth day of November next.

STATE OF MAINE.

HOUSE OF REPRESENTATIVES,
July 17, 1846.

Ordered, That 350 copies of the foregoing amendment, offered by Mr. Barnes of Portland, to bill entitled "an act to repeal chapter 126 of the Revised Statutes," be printed for the use of the Legislature.

SAMUEL BELCHER, *Clerk.*

STATE OF MAINE.

RESOLVES providing for amendments to the constitution in relation to the meeting of the legislature, and the term of office of the governor and other officers.

Resolved, That the constitution of this State be
2 amended, in article second, section fourth; article
3 fourth, section fifth, part first; article fourth, section
4 fifth, part second; article fourth, section first, part
5 third; article fifth, section second, part second; arti-
6 cle fifth, section first, part third; article fifth, section
7 first, part fourth; article ninth, section fourth; article
8 tenth, section fourth, by substituting in each of said
9 articles and sections, the word *biennial,* for the word
10 "annual"; and article fifth, section second, part first,
11 shall be amended by substituting the words *two years,*
12 for "one year", and *next after the biennial election,*
13 for "in each year"; and article fifth, section second,
14 part first, shall be amended by substituting *two years*

W T. Johnson, Printer to the State.

15 for "one year", and *biennial* for " annual"; so that
16 each of the officers named in said sections shall be
17 elected for and hold their offices two years instead of
18 one year, and the legislature meet biennially instead
19 of annually.

 Resolved, That the aldermen of cities, selectmen of
2 the several towns and assessors of the several planta-
3 tions in this State, are hereby empowered and direct-
4 ed to notify the inhabitants of their respective cities,
5 towns and plantations, in the manner prescribed by
6 law, at the annual meeting in September next to give
7 in their votes upon the amendments proposed in the
8 above resolve; and the question shall be submitted
9 in the following words: "shall the constitution be
10 amended by adopting the above resolve for the
11 amendment of the constitution, passed by the legis-
12 lature, proposing to elect the governor, members of
13 the legislature and other State officers for the term of
14 two years, and that the legislature shall meet once in
15 two years?" And the ballots shall be received in sep-
16 arate boxes; those in favor of said amendments voting
17 "yes", and those opposed voting "no"; and the
18 ballots shall be received, sorted, counted and declared,
19 and lists made out of the votes, by the clerks, and
20 returned to the office of the secretary of state, in the

21 same manner as votes for senators; and the governor
22 and council shall count the same, and make return
23 thereof to the next legislature, and if a majority of
24 votes are in favor of said amendment, it shall become
25 a part of the constitution.

Resolved, That the secretary of state shall prepare
- 2 and furnish the several cities, towns and plantations,
3 blank returns in conformity to these resolves, accom-
4 panied with a copy of the resolves.

STATE OF MAINE.

House of Representatives, July 18, 1846.

Ordered, That 350 copies of the foregoing resolves, reported by Mr. Stuart of Hollis, from the Joint Select Committee to which were referred sundry petitions for biennial sessions of the legislature, &c., be printed for the use of the legislature.

SAMUEL BELCHER, *Clerk.*

REPORT.

The Committee on banks and banking, having had under consideration the petitions of sundry banks for a renewal of charter, ask leave to

REPORT:

That by the existing laws of the State, the charters of all banks expire the first day of October, one thousand eight hundred and forty-seven, and that justice to them as well as to the business community, would seem to require, at the present session of the legislature, an indication of the future policy of the State upon this important subject.

The use of paper money has become so associated with the habits and prejudices of the people that a return to the constitutional currency, however desirable, would at this time and under existing circumstances, be utterly impracticable. The several States claim and exercise the right of incorporating banks within their limits, for the purpose of furnishing a paper currency. Until the constitution shall have been revived and this immense power ceded to the general government, the effort of individual States to correct the evils incident to our banking system, will be unavailing.

The committee do not question the fact so often demonstrated that a paper currency gives a fictitious value to all the exchangeable products of a nation. That it sooner or later neutralizes the effect of discriminating duties upon domestic manufactures by ad-

Wm. T Johnson, Printer to the State.

vancing the price of all the agents of production, and that its inevitable tendency is to turn the balance of trade against a nation, by enhancing the price of articles of export, thereby enabling others to undersell it in the markets of the world. They are also aware that a paper system is subject to sudden contractions and expansions, which change to a ruinous degree, the relative conditions of debtor and creditor; but at the same time, they cannot forget the utter inability of a single State to regulate the currency of the Union. The most we can hope to do is, to ensure the redemption of the bills of our own banks, and impose such restrictions as will check local fluctuations.

The committee are of opinion that our present banking laws are comparatively safe, and experience shows that no losses to bill-holders have occured the last fifteen years, where a reasonable discretion was exercised by the legislature in granting charters. The Revised Statutes contain several salutary provisions not embraced in the banking law of eighteen hundred thirty-one, and it is believed, with a due vigilance on the part of bank commissioners, and a rigid enforcement of the proposed law, the redemption of all bills will be effectually secured.

To guard against local fluctuations, the committee have deemed it expedient to introduce a clause providing that all banks shall have always on hand, one dollar in specie, to every three dollars in bills they may issue beyond fifty per cent. of the capital stock. It will be seen by looking over the returns of banks, a few years past, that fifty per cent. of the capital stock is a very moderate circulation, and up to that point no specific specie balance is required.

In some parts of the State, this provision would, in practice, have very little effect; but in those sections most inclined to inflations, it would operate as a serious check. The average circulation of the banks of Maine, in April last, amounted to about seventy-five per cent upon their capital stock, and the specie on hand, if equally distributed, would have been very nearly the sum now contemplated. In some sections, however, with a small amount of specie, the circulation was up to, and even beyond the chartered limits, and would have received a salutary check from the operation of the law herewith submitted.

The banks can have no reasonable cause for complaint on account of these new restrictions; and the community, it is believed, when they consider the difficulties attending all sudden changes in the currency, will be satisfied with the law here proposed, establishing as it does, the principle of a specie basis, which may, if necessary, be hereafter enlarged.

All of which is respectfully submitted.

JOHN HODGDON, *Chairman.*

STATE OF MAINE.

IN THE YEAR OF OUR LORD ONE THOUSAND EIGHT HUNDRED AND
FORTY-SIX.

AN ACT additional in relation to banks and banking,

*Be it enacted by. the Senate and House of Represent-
atives in Legislature assembled,* as follows:

SECTION 1. The charters of all banks now incor-
2 porated or which may hereafter be incorporated
3 within this State, are hereby extended to the first day
4 of October in the year of our Lord one thousand
5 eight hundred and fifty-seven, subject to the provisions
6 of this act and all existing acts upon the subject of
7 banks and banking.

SEC. 2. All banks accepting a renewal of charter,
2 subject to the restrictions, limitations and penalties of
3 this act, shall give written notice of such acceptance,
4 to the secretary of State, on or before the first day of
5 May, in the year of our Lord one thousand eight
6 hundred and forty-seven.

SEC. 3. No bank now incorporated or which may

2 hereafter be incorporated within this State, shall issue
3 and put in circulation as money, bills to the amount
4 of more than fifty per cent. of its capital stock actual-
5 ly paid in, unless said bank shall have in its vault, at
6 the time of such issue, one dollar in specie for every
7 three dollars in bills so issued, over and above fifty
8 per cent. of its capital stock; nor shall the circula-
9 tion of any bank within this State, at any time, exceed
10 the amount of its capital stock paid in, and the specie
11 in its vault.

Sec. 4. Weekly balances shall be made by the
2 cashiers of banks, exhibiting the amount of specie
3 on hand and the amount of bills in circulation; and
4 it shall be the duty of the bank commissioners, at
5 their annual examination to note all over issues shown
6 by such balances, and report the same to the govern-
7 or and council.

Sec. 5. Every bank now incorporated or which
2 may hereafter be incorporated in this State, shall for-
3 feit and pay for the use of the State, ten per cent.
4 upon the amount of bills it shall at any time wilfully
5 and with intent to evade the provisions of this act,
6 put in circulation over and above the amount author-
7 ized by the third section of this act; and said forfeit-
8 ure may be sued for and recovered in the name of

9 the treasurer in an action on the case, in the supreme
10 judicial court.

Sec. 6. Whenever by the annual report of the bank
2 commissioners or otherwise, it shall appear that any
3 bank has put in circulation a larger amount of bills
4 than authorized by this act, it shall be the duty of the
5 secretary of State to notify the attorney general of
6 the fact, who upon the receipt of said notice, shall
7 forthwith commence an action against the president,
8 directors and company of such delinquent institution,
9 to recover the penalty established by the fifth section
10 of this act.

Sec. 7. The thirty-second section of the seventy-
2 seventh chapter of the Revised Statutes is hereby
3 repealed.

STATE OF MAINE.

IN SENATE, July 22, 1846.

Ordered, That 350 copies of a bill entitled "an act additional in relation to banks and banking," together with the report made by the committee on banks and banking, be printed for the use of the Legislature.

DANIEL T. PIKE, *Secretary.*

HOUSE OF REPRESENTATIVES, July 23, 1846.

Ordered, That 300 copies of the foregoing bill be *printed* for the use of the House.

SAMUEL BELCHER, Clerk.

REPORT

OF THE

Joint Standing Committee on the Insane Hospital,

A. D. 1846.

THE committee on the Insane Hospital, to whom was referred so much of the governor's message as relates to the Insane Hospital, together with the reports of the trustees, treasurer, steward and superintendent of said Hospital, have had the same under consideration and ask leave to submit the following

REPORT:

Your committee, in accordance with the usual custom, have made their annual visit to the Hospital, and have examined with much care, the treatment of the patients and the various accommodations of the institution, for their comfort and recovery.

The Hospital under the superintendence of Dr. Ray, had attained to some distinction amongst similar institutions in our country. His popularity as a gentleman and a scholar, had become associated with the Hospital, and it was with feelings of regret, that the friends of the institution heard of his resignation as superintendent. Yet your committee are satisfied that the Hospital under the direction of the present superintendent, Dr. James Bates, fully sustains the character it had acquired under the government of Dr. Ray.

Family devotions have been established in the Hospital, and

Wm. T. Johnson, Printer to the State.

many of the poor afflicted patients bow around the family altar and
offer their evening and morning devotions to the great and good
Parent who deigns to hear the supplications of his afflicted, insane
children.   Religious instruction on Sabbath evenings, is enjoyed by
the patients, and hymns of thanksgiving are heard instead of the
wailings of insanity.

The law of love and kindness appears to be the governing power
in the Hospital, and your committee can with much pleasure assure the Legislature and the citizens of this State, that they cor-
dially approve of the parental system of government adopted by
the officers of this institution, so well calculated *to gain the affec-
tions* of the patients, to soothe their sufferings and restore them to
the enjoyment of reason, the richest of heaven's blessings.

The trustees have purchased an elegant carriage for the accommodation of the patients, which is drawn by a span of fine horses
belonging to the Hospital.   And the patients are frequently seen
riding forth in pleasant weather, enjoying with a high zest, the pure
air of the morning and the rich scenery of Augusta, where the
beautiful white cottages are scattered over the landscape glittering
in the sunlight like snowdrops amidst the dark foliage of the
shrubbery.

The patients have been furnished through the kindness of friends,
with many valuable papers and periodicals during the past year,
and the library of the Hospital has been increased over one hundred and fifty volumes from the interest on a donation made by the
Hon. Bryce McLellan, late of Bloomfield.

The superintendent in his able report, has presented the public
with much valuable statistical information, showing the necessity of
sending patients to the Hospital in the early stages of the disease.
Of those patients admitted to the Hospital within three months
after being deranged, 62.9 per cent. were cured in 130 days ; over
three months and under twelve months after being deranged, 38
per cent. were cured in 164 days ; over twelve months, only
14 per cent. were cured in 280 days.   With these facts before us
founded on actual experience and observation, we think the public

must be convinced of the great importance of an early resort to the Hospital, to ensure a speedy restoration to health and to reason.

Your committee also learn that one hundred and seventy-five patients have enjoyed for a season, the advantages of this institution, during the past year, one hundred of whom were males, and seventy-five females, ninety-nine of whom have been admitted during the year. Ninety patients have been discharged, thirty-eight of whom were recovered, twenty-two improved, twenty-three unimproved, and seven of whom died.

Your committee learn from the reports of the trustees, treasurer and steward of the Hospital, that there has been an improvement in its financial concerns the past year, by an increase of funds amounting to the sum of 381·15, due from towns and from the State, for the support of State paupers.

We also learn that although providence has not smiled as heretofore, on the labors of the husbandman, yet the estimated value of the crops raised on the Hospital farm during the past year, amounts to the sum of $919·52, and that all the labor has been performed on the farm by the patients, with the exception of the service of one man at $12 per month and after deducting board, horse labor, &c., a balance remains in favor of the farm of $454.

The trustees have made a reduction in the board of patients the past year, so that the board of males, including washing and mending, in no case exceeds $2·50, and the board of females not exceeding $2·00 per week ; in common cases, $1·50 per week, for males, and $1·25 for females. The result of making the reduction has proved its utility ; the number of patients has been increased, and the blessings of the institution have been enjoyed by the poor and needy as well as by the more wealthy. The trustees request an appropriation of $602·58, to cover the expenses incurred in supporting patients directly chargeable to the State and also the sum of $600 to aid in defraying the expenses of the Hospital the present year, and your committee have included that sum in the resolve which is herewith submitted.

The governor in his message, and the trustees of the Hospital in their report, have called the attention of the Legislature to the importance of enlarging the Insane Hospital, and your committee, after having fully investigated the subject, came to the conclusion that the honor of the State and the good of the community require that an appropriation be made for building an additional wing to the Hospital. At this time there are eleven more male patients than there are rooms for their accommodation, and the number is daily increasing; and unless the Hospital is enlarged, those of our fellow citizens who may hereafter need the benefits of this institution, must of necessity be excluded for want of accommodations, and forced to seek an asylum in other States, after having contributed either by tax or donation, to the building and sustaining of the Hospital in their own State. From partial returns made in 1844, it appears that at that time there was not less than six hundred insane persons in this State, and that number has probably increased with the increase of population, and that consequently not more than one in six now enjoys the advantages of this institution, nor indeed can they unless the proposed additional wing be built for their accommodation.

At the request of your committee the trustees have furnished a plan for an additional wing to the Hospital, together with an estimate of the cost of building the same, made by Mr. Keene of Augusta.

The estimated cost of building said wing amounts to the sum of $21,400, and it will accommodate 73 patients.

It will not be necessary to expend more than eight or ten thousand dollars the present year, for the purchase of bricks, lumber, stone, &c. Your committee have therefore included in the resolve that is herewith submitted, the sum of $21,400, to be appropriated to building an additional wing to the Insane Hospital, under the superintendence and direction of the trustees of said Hospital, with authority to expend a sum not exceeding $10,000 the present year, and the balance next year.

The plan adopted by the trustees meets the approbation of your committee. The wing is to be built of granite, and to be three stories high above the basement. There is to be a kitchen and washroom in the basement story. The other three stories are to be with a gallery in each, with a tier of single bedrooms on one side and a tier of double bedrooms on the other, which are to be used for the accommodation of the sick patients who may require the constant attendance of a nurse, or for patients that may safely sleep together.

There will be a parlor, dormitory and suitable washrooms in each story; and a verandah, or room with open lattice-work, to each gallery, for a promenade for patients whose health will not permit of greater exposure. There will be 18 cells at the eastern extremity of the wing, for the use of that class of patients that from necessity must be confined.

From the governor's message we learn that an opportunity presents itself for purchasing an addition to the Hospital farm. A lot of 26 acres of good pasturage adjoining said farm can be purchased for the sum of $1,050. Your committee are of the opinion that the money would be well invested in the purchase of said lot, and that it would make a very important addition to the farm. Should the lot be purchased an addition would be made to the stock of cows belonging to the farm, and a sufficient supply of milk, butter and cheese thereby obtained to meet the wants of the patients. Milk is an important item of food; it is cheap, wholesome and nutricious, and your committee are of the opinion that the sum paid for the lot, would be saved to the State in a few years, in a reduction of the price of board. With this view of the subject your committee recommend that an appropriation be made for the purchase of said lot, and to this end they have included the sum of $1,050 in the resolve that is herewith submitted.

The governor in his message, and the trustees in their report, urged the importance of taking the census of the insane persons in this State. Your committee agree with them on this subject and consequently have reported a resolve for that purpose, which is also herewith submitted.

Your committee would remark that it is of the utmost importance that the appropriation should be made to insure the success and prosperity of this institution—an institution worthy the commendation and patronage of every friend of humanity.

Governments are instituted for the protection and happiness of their citizens. And while the legislature of Maine is fostering the great interests of the State, encouraging the development of her resources, aiding the enterprise of her citizens, and disseminating the blessings of our republican institutions among the busy multitude, let them remember the afflicted and down-trodden. Let them visit the poor prisoner in the prison-house. Let them give hearing to the deaf, eyes to the blind, and restore reason to the insane. Then shall the welcome plaudit of well done good and faithful servants, be theirs.

JOSEPH BARRETT, *Chairman.*

STATE OF MAINE.

RESOLVES in relation to taking the census of insane
persons and idiots in this State.

Resolved, That the aldermen of cities, the selectmen
2 of towns, and the assessors of the several plantations
3 in this State are hereby empowered and directed to
4 make a return to the secretary of state, on or before
5 the first day of November next, of the number, sex
6 and age of insane persons and the number and sex
7 of idiots, having their residence in their respective
8 cities, towns and plantations on the first day of Sep-
9 tember, A. D. 1846, designating the number and sex
10 of such persons in the insane hospital in this State
11 and in other States, the number and sex supported by
12 the public, and the number and sex of such insane
13 persons and idiots (if any) supported in county jails,
14 houses of correction, or almshouses.

Resolved, That the secretary of state shall prepare
2 and furnish the several cities, towns and plantations,
3 blank returns in conformity to the foregoing resolve,
4 accompanied with a copy of these resolves.

STATE OF MAINE.

RESOLVE making an appropriation for the Insane Hospital.

Resolved, That there be appropriated and paid out
2 of the State treasury for the use and benefit of the
3 insane hospital, the sum of twenty-three thousand six
4 hundred and fifty dollars, to be expended under the
5 superintendence and direction of the trustees of said
6 hospital, as follows, to wit:
7   Twenty-one thousand and four hundred dollars to be
8 expended in building an additional wing to said hospi-
9 tal, of which, a sum not exceeding ten thousand dollars,
10 to be expended the present year for the purchase of
11 materials for said building, and the balance to be paid
12 out and expended next year for finishing said building.
13   One thousand two hundred dollars of the sum here-
14 by appropriated, to be applied to the payment of the
15 expenses of supporting State paupers in said hospital
16 and for the expenses of the hospital the present year.
17   One thousand and fifty dollars of the sum appropri-
18 ated by this resolve, to be applied to the purchase of
19 twenty-six acres of land adjoining the hospital farm,
20 for the use and benefit of said hospital.

2

STATE OF MAINE.

IN SENATE, July 23, 1846.

Ordered, That 1,000 copies of the foregoing Report and accompanying Resolves be printed for the use of the Legislature.

DANIEL T. PIKE, *Secretary.*

STATE OF MAINE.

IN THE YEAR OF OUR LORD ONE THOUSAND EIGHT HUNDRED AND
FORTY-SIX.

AN ACT to incorporate the Lake Telos and Webster
Pond Dam and Sluiceway Company.

*Be it enacted by the Senate and House of Represent-
atives in Legislature assembled,* as follows:

SECTION 1.   William H. Smith, Daniel M. Howard,
2 Warren Brown and Theodore H. Dillingham and their
3 associates and assigns are hereby created a body pol-
4 itic by the name of Lake Telos and Webster Pond
5 Dam and Sluiceway Company, by which name they
6 may contract, sue and be sued, defend suits at law,
7 have and use a common seal, and change the same
8 at pleasure, make by-laws not repugnant to the laws
9 of this State for the convenient management of their
10 corporate affairs, take and hold any estate, real, per-
11 sonal or mixed, to an amount not exceeding thirty

Wm T. Johnson, Printer to the State

12 thousand dollars, and sell or convey or otherwise dis-
13 pose of the same, and have and enjoy all the rights,
14 powers and privileges necessary to carry into effect
15 the object of this corporation.

SEC. 2. The said corporation are hereby authorized
2 and empowered to make, construct and maintain a
3 sluiceway from lake Telos to Webster pond, other-
4 wise called Penobscot pond, on township number six,
5 in the eleventh range, in the county of Piscataquis,
6 sufficiently wide and deep for the passage of timber and
7 lumber of all kinds, which may be expedited to the pub-
8 lic market through that channel. And they are author-
9 ized to erect and maintain any dam or dams on said
10 sluiceway, or any stream or waters which may be con-
11 nected therewith on said township, which may be nec-
12 essary to render the transit of lumber more easy and
13 effectual, and to keep open a passage way for all logs
14 or lumber, on the waters between Chamberlin lake
15 and said sluiceway. And they are further authorized to
16 enter upon and take such land, property or material in
17 said township, as they may find it necessary to make
18 said canal or sluiceway, or upon which to locate their
19 dam or dams, and such as may be necessary along the
20 margin of their sluiceway, for the use and accommo-
21 dation of persons employed in driving lumber through

22 the same. *Provided, however,* that said corporation
23 shall pay the proprietor or proprietors of said town-
24 ship number six, for land, property or material so tak-
25 en and used for their sluiceway and dam or dams, with
26 a necessary and convenient margin, and for keeping
27 an open and free passage on the waters between said
28 Chamberlin lake and said sluiceway, such price as
29 they and said proprietor or proprietors may agree
30 upon.   And in case said parties shall not otherwise
31 agree, then said corporation shall pay such damages
32 as shall be ascertained and determined by the County
33 Commissioners for the county of Piscataquis, in the
34 same manner and under the same conditions and lim-
35 itations as are by law provided in the case of damage
36 by the laying out of public highways; with the same
37 right to either party aggrieved by the doings of said
38 Commissioners, in estimating damages, to have a jury
39 to determine that matter on their petition; unless said
40 party shall agree with the other party in interest to
41 have the same determined by a committee to be ap-
42 pointed under the direction of said Commissioners.
43 And no application shall be made to said Commission-
44 ers to estimate damages unless made within two years
45 from the time of taking said land, property and ma-
46 terials.

Sec. 3. And whereas said proprietor or proprietors
2 of said township number six, in the eleventh range,
3 have already cut a sluiceway on said township, from
4 said lake Telos to said Webster pond, which has be-
5 come to some extent available for the passage of lum-
6 ber, and the proprietor or proprietors of said town-
7 ship instead of applying for their damages as provided
8 for, in the second section of this act, may at their
9 election, at any time within two years from the taking
10 of said land, property or materials, apply to said coun-
11 ty commissioners at any regular term of said court,
12 claiming to be paid the reasonable costs and expenses
13 of making said sluiceway and dam upon said township
14 number six in the eleventh range. And thereupon
15 said court shall issue due notice to said corporation,
16 requiring them to appear before said court, and an-
17 swer to said complaint. And said corporation shall
18 pay such sum as damages, as shall be ascertained
19 and determined by said county commissioners; and
20 said commissioners shall be governed in making
21 up damages by the reservation in the deed of said
22 township to Lewis Hancock; but if damages are
23 awarded under this section of this act, no further or
24 other damages shall be allowed said proprietor or
25 proprietors. And before said corporation shall pro-

26 ceed to take any land or other property on said town-
27 ship number six in the eleventh range, the members
28 thereof shall make, execute and file with the county
29 commissioners for the county of Piscataquis, for the use
30 of the proprietor or proprietors of said land or other
31 property to be taken, a good and sufficient bond with
32 good and sufficient sureties, in the penal sum of twenty
33 thousand dollars, conditioned that such corporation shall
34 pay on demand such sum as shall be ascertained and
35 adjudged against the same under the provisions of this
36 act as the amount of damages to which said proprie-
37 tor or proprietors may be entitled to receive for said
38 land or other property: *provided* said proprietor or
39 proprietors shall on or before the first day of October
40 next file with the said county commissioners a written
41 request for said bond, with the name or names of the
42 proprietor or proprietors whose land or other property
43 is to be taken, or to whom said bond is to be given.

SEC. 4. That there may be a sufficient depth of
2 water in said sluiceway for the passage of lumber
3 therein, said corporation are hereby empowered to take
4 the dam now erected on Allegash stream, in township
5 number seven, in the thirteenth range, with the land
6 on which the same is situate. And if the parties can-
7 not agree upon the price, the owner may have the

8 same remedy for his damages on application to the
9 county commissioners for the county of Piscataquis as
10 is provided in the second section of this act, and shall
11 pay therefor the expenses and cost of its construction.
12 And said corporation are empowered to flow the con-
13 tiguous lands as far as may be necessary to accomplish
14 their object, paying the owners damage therefor; and
15 if the parties cannot agree upon the amount of dam-
16 ages, the said corporation shall not be liable to any
17 action at common law for the same; but any person
18 injured may have a remedy by a complaint for flowing,
19 in which the same proceeding shall be had, as where a
20 complaint is made under a statute of this State for
21 flowing lands occasioned by the raising of a head of
22 water necessary for the working of mills.

SEC. 5.   It shall be the duty of said corporation, to
2 keep and maintain said sluiceway and dam, so as to
3 afford at all proper seasons a safe and commodious
4 passage for all logs and other timber through the
5 same—and said sluiceway shall be open and free for
6 the use of the public generally without the payment
7 of tolls.

SEC. 6.   Any individual or individuals authorized by
2 the land agent of this State may make such improve-
3 ments and construct all necessary machinery and

4 gates on said dam and use the same for the transpor-
5 tation of logs and lumber from the lakes and streams
6 north and east of said dam into the Chamberlin lake
7 and waters south and west of said dam; subject at
8 all times to the control and regulation of the Legisla-
9 ture.

SEC. 7. Provided nevertheless, that if Rufus Dwinel
2 and associates, or others, shall be authorized and re-
3 ceive a charter during the present session of the legis-
4 lature to provide and establish an ample and sufficient
5 passage-way for the transit of lumber between said
6 lake Telos and Webster pond; and said Rufus Dwi-
7 nel and associates, or others, if authorized as afore-
8 said, shall accept their authority and charter aforesaid
9 and organize and act under the same so that said
10 company shall provide an ample passage-way for the
11 transit of lumber between said lake Telos and Web-
12 ster pond on or before the first day of October next;
13 then and in such case all the powers granted by this
14 act shall cease and terminate.

SEC. 8. The legislature reserves to itself the right
2 to alter, amend or repeal this charter at pleasure.

STATE OF MAINE.

HOUSE OF REPRESENTATIVES, }
July 29, 1846. }

Ordered, That 350 copies of the foregoing Bill, reported from the Committee on Interior Waters, be printed for the use of the Legislature.

SAMUEL BELCHER, *Clerk*.

STATE OF MAINE.

IN THE YEAR OF OUR LORD ONE THOUSAND EIGHT HUNDRED AND
FORTY-SIX.

AN ACT for the appointment of district attorneys.

*Be it enacted by the Senate and House of Represent-
atives in Legislature assembled,* as follows:

SECTION 1. Grand juries shall not be selected for
2 or required to attend the Supreme Judicial Court in
3 any county in this State; and the grand juries attend-
4 ing the district court in the several counties, in addition
5 to their present duties, shall find and return into said
6 court, indictments against all persons for all crimes and
7 offenses which now are or may hereafter be made cog-
8 nizable by the supreme judicial court.   And said dis-
9 trict court shall have the same power to issue all
10 necessary processes to compel the attendance of wit-
11 nesses and for the arrest of persons charged with
12 offenses cognizable by the supreme judicial court, as

Wm. T. Johnson, Printer to the State.

13 the supreme judicial court now has and shall have
14 power to commit or recognize persons so charged, to
15 answer at the next term of the supreme judicial court
16 to be held for the county where the indictment is
17 found, and to compel in the manner provided by law
18 in other cases, the attendance of witnesses at the next
19 term of the court having cognizance of the offense.
20 And the clerk of the district court in which such in-
21 dictment shall be found, shall return the same, togeth-
22 er with all processes issued in pursuance hereof, into
23 the supreme judicial court at the term next to be
24 holden for the county in which the indictment was
25 found and the same shall be entered and have day
26 therein.

Sec. 2. After the time when this act shall take
2 effect, all recognizances in criminal cases taken be-
3 fore justices of the peace, coroners and other magis-
4 trates, which heretofore have been returnable by law
5 to the supreme judicial court, shall be returned to the
6 district court, and all persons hereafter committed to
7 appear and answer for any offense cognizable by the
8 supreme judicial court, shall be committed to appear
9 and answer at the district court next to be holden
10 within and for the same county. And all costs in
11 cases provided for in this act, accruing before the

12 same are certified and entered in the supreme judicial
13 court, shall be taxed and allowed by the district court
14 in the same manner as they were before the passing
15 of this act, taxed and allowed by the supreme judicial
16 court.

SEC. 3.   This State is hereby divided into four dis-
2 tricts for the administration of criminal law.   The
3 counties of York, Cumberland and Oxford, shall
4 constitute the western district.   The counties of Lin-
5 coln, Kennebec and Franklin, shall constitute the
6 middle district.   The counties of Waldo, Hancock,
7 Aroostook, and Washington, shall constitute the east-
8 ern district.   The counties of Penobscot, Somerset
9 and Piscataquis, shall constitute the northern district.

SEC. 4.   The attorney general shall be ex officio,
2 district attorney in the district to which he shall be
3 assigned by commission from the governor, by and
4 with the advice and consent of the council, and in
5 each of the other districts, there shall be appointed
6 and commissioned by the governor, by and with the
7 advice and consent of the council, a district attorney,
8 who shall reside within the district for which he is
9 appointed.

SEC. 5.   The attorney general in the district as-

2 signed to him, shall appear and act for the State, in
3 all cases, civil and criminal, in which the State is a
4 party or interested, and shall within said district,
5 [discharge] all the duties which the county attorney or
6 attorney general is now by law obliged to do and
7 perform in behalf of the State. He shall also, unless
8 excused by the court, be present and conduct, in
9 whatever county the same may be, the trial of all
10 persons indicted for crimes which at the time of the
11 adoption of the constitution of this State, were pun-
12 ishable with death. He shall also, whenever request-
13 ed by the governor and council, give to them an
14 opinion in writing, upon such questions of law as
15 may be submitted to him by their direction.

SEC. 6. The district attorneys shall, within their
2 respective districts, appear and act for the State in all
3 cases, criminal and civil, except when the attorney
4 general is by this act required to appear, in which the
5 State is a party or interested; and they shall, within
6 their respective districts, perform all the duties which
7 the county attorneys and the attorney general, with
8 the exceptions herein contained, are now by law
9 obliged to do and perform in behalf of the State; and
10 in the absence of the attorney general shall attend

11 and conduct, within their respective districts, the
12 trials, which by the fifth section hereof the attorney
13 general is required to attend and conduct.

SEC. 7.   The said district attorneys may, with refer-
2 ence to their mutual accommodation, from time to
3 time interchange the duties of their offices or assist
4 each other so as best to secure the discharge of the
5 duties incumbent on them.

SEC. 8.   The several district attorneys shall annual-
2 ly, in the month of March, make to the attorney gen-
3 eral a report of the amount and kind of official busi-
4 ness done by them respectively in each county, in the
5 year preceding ; the number of persons prosecuted ;
6 the offenses for which such prosecutions were had ;
7 the results thereof, and the punishment awarded in
8 each case, with such suggestions as they may deem
9 interesting.   And the attorney general shall annually,
10 in the month of April, make and transmit to the gov-
11 ernor and council an abstract of the reports made to
12 him by the district attorneys, together with a like
13 report of his own doings as attorney general and dis-
14 trict attorney.

SEC. 9.   The several district attorneys, except the
2 attorney general, shall receive a salary of one thou-
3 sand dollars a year, to be paid to them severally out

4 of the treasury of the State in equal quarterly pay-
5 ments, in full for all services rendered by them ; and
6 the attorney general shall receive a salary of twelve
7 hundred dollars a year, to be paid to him out of the
8 treasury of the State in equal quarterly payments, in
9 full for his services both as attorney general and as
10 district attorney.

SEC. 10.   All acts and parts of acts relating to the
2 appointment, election and salaries of county attorneys,
3 and all acts and parts of acts inconsistent with the
4 provisions of this act, are hereby repealed.

SEC. 11.   This act shall take effect on the first day
2 of January next: *provided*, that the district attor-
3 neys may be appointed at any time after this act shall
4 have been approved by the governor ; such appoint-
5 ments to take effect on the first day of January next.

STATE OF MAINE.

HOUSE OF REPRESENTATIVES, }
July 31, 1846.

Ordered, That 350 copies of the foregoing Bill, reported from the Committee on the Judiciary, be printed for the use of the Legislature.

SAMUEL BELCHER, *Clerk*.

TWENTY-SIXTH LEGISLATURE.

STATE OF MAINE.

THE committee on the Judiciary, to which was referred the message of His Excellency the Governor of the third of August, 1846, transmitting certain documents relating to the Aroostook fund, so called, and also certain other documents relating to the settlement of the claims of the State of Maine against the government of the United States, ask leave to

REPORT:

That the committee recommend that three hundred and fifty copies of the Governor's message, together with " an abstract from the Comptroller's account in relation to the claims of the State of Maine against the government of the United States for expenses incurred in the prosecution of the war in defense of the northeastern boundary," from the eighth item to the close of the Comptroller's certificate following that item, be printed for the use of the legislature ; and that the other documents accompanying said message be filed in the archives of the State.

WM. C. ALLEN, *Chairman.*

IN SENATE, Aug 8, 1846.

Read and accepted.   Sent down for concurrence.

DANIEL T. PIKE, *Secretary.*

HOUSE OF REPRESENTATIVES, Aug. 8, 1846.

Read and concurred.

SAMUEL BELCHER, *Clerk.*

Wm. T Johnson, Printer to the State.

MESSAGE.

To the members of the Senate and
House of Representatives:

Since the adjournment of the last legislature, I have received from the Secretary of State of the United States, a copy of what purports to be "a detailed statement of the receipts and disbursements of the disputed territory fund", furnished to that department by the Lieut. Governor of the province of New Brunswick, and in the communication accompanying that document, notice was given me that the authorities of New Brunswick were ready to pay over to the government of the United States, the amount stated to be due from that fund, under the provisions of the fifth article of the treaty of Washington.

It will be recollected, that a statement of the balance due to the United States, belonging to the States of Maine and Massachusetts, was furnished by the government of New Brunswick in the year 1843, and transmitted to the legislature by my immediate predecessor.

The exhibit there made, was in the opinion of the Executive, entirely unsatisfactory, and in no way conformable to the provisions of the treaty; and an earnest remonstrance against its acceptance was addressed to the general government.

The account as now stated, though professing to give a full and detailed exposition of receipts and expenditures, is believed to be still imperfect, and to show a balance in favor of the fund very much below the amount, which upon a fair and just adjudication, would be found due to us.

No credit is given for receipts prior to the year 1829, though it is confidently believed, that from 1824, up to that period, considerable sums were paid into the provincial treasury from the avails of timber, cut upon the disputed territory ; the bonds remaining un-collected at the period of the ratification of the treaty, have neith-er been given up, nor cancelled ; and from the peculiar character of the lien upon the property of the obligors created by them, are regarded with uneasiness and apprehension.

A large portion of the receipts credited since the year 1829 is absorbed by expenses, alleged to have been incident to their collec-tion.   And a still larger portion by expenses, said to have been in-curred in protecting the disputed territory, erecting a boom, &c., most of which, is believed to have been improperly charged against the fund.

The whole amount stated to have been received on account of that fund is $34·800 : the amount of expenditure is charged at $19·924, leaving a balance due and payable from the provincial treasury of $14·892.

Not considering it for the interest of the State to consent to a settlement which bears upon its face such conclusive evidence of erroneous statement, I have joined with the Executive of Massa-chusetts in requesting the Secretary of State of the United States to decline the reception of the amount offered, until some measures should be adopted for obtaining a closer scrutiny, not only into the receipts which should have been credited to the fund, but into the particular items of which the large sums retained for expenses are composed.

I have been furnished by the Land Agent with a copy of a memorial addressed by the Land Agent of Massachusetts to the Secretary of State, which is also signed by the Hon. Hannibal Hamlin on the part of this State, pointing out many supposed errors in the statement of the account ; and a copy of a correspondence between the latter gentleman and the Secretary of State, from which it would appear, that all proper facilities will be afforded by the government of New Brunswick, for such an investigation as may be desired.

An agent has been appointed by the Governor of Massachusetts to make such investigation, and unless otherwise directed by the legislature, I shall join in prosecuting the enquiry, by the appointment of an agent on the part of Maine.

Copies of the account, as stated by the auditor of the province of New Brunswick, and of the correspondence connected therewith, are herewith transmitted.

I also lay before you a communication I have received from the office of the third auditor, containing "a statement of the difference arising on settlement of a portion of the account of the State of Maine, for disbursements of her militia in the year 1839, called into service by the Governor of said State, to be reimbursed under act of Congress, passed June 13, 1842."

By this statement, it appears that the sum allowed at that office is less than the amount claimed by Maine, by the sum of $49,511. Upon an examination of the very voluminous documents which accompany this statement, it appears that more than half of this sum consists of various stores belonging to the subsistence and other departments, charged to the United States, but remaining on hand at the close of the expedition, and sold for the benefit of Maine; the amount realized from these sales, was therefore very properly deducted from the aggregate claimed from the general government.

Of the balance, amounting to about $24,000, a small portion has been suspended for want of the necessary vouchers, a more considerable sum referred to other bureaus, and the residue, being about $13,000, disallowed.

The examination of these accounts having been nearly completed when the late agent of the State, Samuel L. Harris, Esq., resigned the agency, in July of last year. I did not consider it necessary to continue the agency by the appointment of another person; such assistance as was required from that time to the following September, when the settlement was finally made, was rendered by Mr. Harris, it being understood that no considerable expense would be thereby occasioned.

These sums to which I have referred, as suspended or referred to other bureaus, now constitute the whole amount of our claim against the general government, on account of expenditures growing out of the operations upon our northeastern frontier; and without a report from the agent who has had them in charge, I am at present, unable to determine whether their further prosecution will require the services of a special agent, or the probability of obtaining them, justify the expense to which it would subject the State.

Of the claims preferred against the general government, under the appropriation of $80,000, made by Congress in 1844, usually denominated the treaty claims, the settlement has been equally satisfactory and favorable to the State.

The whole amount of these claims, including the claims of individuals audited by the Governor and Council, under the resolve of March 23, 1843, was $78,593; and of this sum, there was allowed by the auditor to whom they were originally referred for adjudication, but two small items; the residue, amounting to the sum of $67,149, being, for reasons stated in the report of that officer, disallowed. From this decision of the auditor, an appeal was taken by the agent, and an argument presented to the first comptroller, clearly showing that great injustice had been done the State, in rejecting so large a portion of the expenses it had necessarily incurred in protecting its territory from foreign invasion.

Such being the condition of these claims at the close of your last session, I requested the treasurer of State, to whose care, in view of the expected termination of the special agency, they had been confided, to proceed to Washington, in the hope that his personal attention at the department there, would facilitate the settlement of the account then under consideration by the comptroller.

And as some misunderstanding had arisen as to the presentation of the individual claims included in the account, No. 3, I instructed him particularly and minutely to explain to the accounting officers of the treasury, the circumstances connected with their allowance and presentation. A written statement fully detailing their origin and character was subsequently prepared by that officer, and with copies of the official documents connected therewith, placed in the hands of the first comptroller of the treasury. Failing through the agency of the treasurer to obtain any decisive action upon the appeal taken from the decision of the auditor, the subject remained undisposed of until February of the present year. At that time, apprehending that the appropriation, being for a specific purpose, might shortly revert to the treasury of the United States, and believing that my personal attention might be useful in expediting a settlement in which the State was so largely interested, I proceeded to Washington, and in several personal conferences with the comptroller, succeeded in placing the whole matter in a train of speedy adjustment.

Upon a full and careful investigation by that officer, he came to the conclusion, that the decision of the auditor, so far as it was averse to our claims, should be reversed; and upon a re-examination of the whole account, it appeared to him, that by an equitable construction of the treaty stipulation and the act of appropriation, the amount claimed should be allowed.

In pursuance of this decision, the sum of $56,754·63 has been transmitted to the treasurer. This allowance comprehends all the items of expenditure, not allowable under former appropriations, to which the State has been subjected in prosecuting the controversy growing out of its disputed boundary. The expense of commissioners, of agencies, surveys, &c.; the preliminary expenses incurred by towns for drafting, subsisting and transporting troops; the extra pay of two and a half dollars per month allowed to the militia, and all pensions, either actually paid, or granted by the legislature and not paid, have been finally adjusted and paid to the State.

The sums due to individuals, as audited by the Governor and Council, and presented in the name of the State, under the authority of the resolve before referred to, were also allowed by the comptroller; the payment to be conditional upon the previous payment or security by the State to the persons interested, of the sums respectively allowed them.

Since receiving the statement of the comptroller, which was forwarded to me in March last, I have had no communication with the officers of the treasury; but I have been apprised, through a letter addressed to one of the claimants, that the condition has been withdrawn, and the sum allowed, ready to be paid over for their use.

Of these sums allowed to individuals, that belonging to Thomas E. Perley, amounting to $3,037, had been previously assigned to the States of Maine and Massachusetts, and a lien upon a considerable portion of that due to Edwin Plummer, is also held by this State.

The sheets containing the statement of the auditor, with the re-statement and allowance of the comptroller annexed, which were forwarded to me by the latter officer, are herewith transmitted.

A copy of the resolve of the last legislature, directing application to be made to the general government for reimbursement in money, for the value of lands, which the treaty of Washington required should be set off to the settlers upon the St. John, was duly forwarded to the President of the United States. No appropriation has yet been made by Congress to satisfy that claim; but I am advised that an effort will be made by the representatives of both States to accomplish that object before the close of the present session.

This claim, together with the small balance to which I have before referred, and the interest we have in the claim of Massachusetts, are now the only demands against the general government remaining unsatisfied.

Since the year 1843, claims upon the general government to the amount of nearly six hundred thousand dollars have been allowed and paid into the treasury of the State. They are believed to have been more expeditiously, more economically, and more fully adjudicated, than any similar claims of an equal amount heretofore allowed to any of the States.

The whole expenses attending their liquidation, have not exceeded the sum of six thousand dollars, and it is not believed, that any considerable expense will be needed to bring the small amount now remaining, to a final close.

As I shall not have another opportunity of communicating with the legislature, I have deemed it proper to make, prior to your adjournment, this detailed exposition.

H. J. ANDERSON.

Council Chamber }
August 3, 1846. }

ABSTRACT.

EIGHTH—Amount of expenses incurred by said State under said treaty, consisting of the claims of Thomas E. Perley, Shepard Cary, James Houlton, William Webster, Edwin Plummer, Isaac B. Smith, Webster & Pillsbury, and Jacob H. Smith, for injuries and losses, growing out of the operations of said State for the protection of the disputed territory in 1839—audited and allowed by the Governor and Council, per abstract marked M—but the payment of this item, to await the production of proof that said State has paid the same, $19,805 32

        Amount due State of Maine, $76,559 95

         (Signed)   R. COCHRAN.

COMPTROLLER'S OFFICE, }
    March 5, 1846.   }

[COPY.]

TREASURY DEPARTMENT, }
     Comptroller's Office.   }

I admit and certify the above corrected balance this 7th day of March, 1846, of which $56,754·63 should now be paid to James White, treasurer of said State, and the remainder, $19,805·32, be withheld until proof shall be produced that said State has paid or secured the payment of the eighth item herein specified to the parties entitled thereto.

     (Signed)   J. W. McCULLOCH, *Comptroller*.
R. H. GELLETT, Esq., *Register*.

1846·

INDEX

TO THE

DOCUMENTS OF THE HOUSE AND SENATE.

A.

Abstract of the returns of Corporations,   *mis.*
         Cashiers of Banks,   "
     proceedings of the Courts under the 36th chapter of the
   Revised Statutes,   No. 7
Adjutant General's Report,   1
Appeals from the decisions of County Commissioners,   26
Aroostook Fund, report of Committee on,   34

B.

Bank Commissioners, report of,   *mis.*
Banks, List of Stockholders of,   "
     Abstracts of returns of Cashiers of   "
     and Banking, report of Committee on,   30
Brown, Amos and others, Memorial of   10

C

Constitution, providing for the amendment of, relative to the choice of Representatives,   15
                                meeting of the
   Legislature,   29
County Commissioners, act relating to appeals from,   26
Courts, abstract of the proceedings of, under the 36th chapter of the Revised Statutes.   7
Corporations, abstract of the returns of,   *mis.*

INDEX.

D.

District Attorneys, act for the appointment of, No. 33

E.

Education, report of Committe on, 17
  Memorial of Amos Brown and others, 10
Elections, report of Committee on the case of Colburn and Hersey, 3

F.

Fugitives from justice, act in relation to, 11

G.

Georges Canal Company, to incorporate, 13

H.

Hawkers and Pedlers, relative to, 19

I.

Insane Hospital, report of trustees of, ibid.
  Committee on, 31
Intoxicating drinks, to restrict the sale of, 27
  petition of Lydia Merrill and al , 16
Inspectors of State Prison, report of, 12

K

Kennebec Log Driving Company, additional relative to, 20

'L.

Lake Telos and Webster Pond Dam and Sluiceway, to incorporate, 32
Land Agent, report of, 2
  statement of, relative to the amount expended on roads, 14

M.

Message, inaugural of Governor, ibid
  of the Governor with communication of Secretary of War, calling for Volunteers, 6
Mexico, to provide for the prosecution of the War between the United States and, 8
Mousam Navigation Company, to incorporate, 22

P.

Penobscot river, to provide for the improvement of the navigation of, 21

INDEX.

R.

Report of Treasurer of State,   *mis.*
    Bank Commissioners,   "
    Trustees of the Insane Hospital,   "
    Adjutant General,   No. 1
    Land Agent,   2
    Warden of State Prison,   9
    Inspectors of State Prison,   12
    Committee on Elections, case of Colburn and Hersey,   3
        Banks and Banking,   30
        Insane Hospital,   31
Revised Statutes, act to repeal chapter 126,   4
        amendment to,   28
    in addition to chapter 16,   5
Roads, statement of amount expended by the State on,   14
Rules and Orders of the House of Representatives,   *mis.*
    Senate,   "

S.

School Districts, authorized to borrow money, for certain purposes,   24
State Prison, Warden's report,   9
    Inspectors' report,   12
St. Croix River Canal Company, to incorporate,   23

T.

Telos Canal Company, to incorporate,   25
Treasurer of State, report of,   *mis.*

W.

War with Mexico, for the prosecution of,   8
Warden of the State Prison, report of,   9

Lightning Source UK Ltd.
Milton Keynes UK
UKHW020018201118
332599UK00016B/1790/P

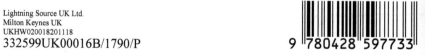